Environmental Psychology
Principles and Practice

Robert Gifford

University of Victoria

Allyn and Bacon, Inc.

Boston   London   Sydney   Toronto

To Sarah
Designer, Builder, Seeker

Series Editor: John-Paul Lenney
Production Coordinator: Sue Freese
Editorial/Production Services: Kailyard
    Associates
Text Designer: Denise Hoffman
Cover Administrator/Designer: Linda K. Dickinson

Library of Congress Cataloging-in-Publication Data

Gifford, Robert.
   Environmental psychology.

   Bibliography: p.
   Includes index.
   I. Environmental psychology.   I. Title.
BF353.G54 1987   155.9   86–26590
ISBN 0-205-10461-4

Printed in the United States of America

10 9 8 7 6 5 4 3 2 1   91 90 89 88 87

Contents

Preface

The study of environmental psychology is vital, diverse, and fascinating. Although some efforts in this field go back fifty years, intensive work began only about twenty years ago. And even though this book is based on over 1,100 studies selected from the thousands so far completed, I believe that the field is just beginning to be tapped. In fact, the first Ph.D. in environmental psychology was not granted until 1973.

Environmental psychology is a basic science and an applied science, as well as an art. Its scientific goals are to understand how and why individuals interact with their vast array of physical settings and to solve problems caused when individuals degrade environments and when environments degrade individuals. The artistic goals of environmental psychology include choosing the right issue to study, knowing how to deal with managers of settings, and knowing how to make sense of data extracted from the complex settings of everyday life.

cognition, individual appraisal and expert assessment of settings, and personality, as it relates to the physical environment.

Part Two, "Social Processes," covers personal space, territoriality, crowding, and privacy—the four interrelated processes at the interface of interpersonal behavior and the environment.

Part Three, "Societal Processes," covers broader-scale human activities as they affect and are affected by the physical environment: living in cities, neighborhoods, and individual residences, learning, working, traveling, designing settings, and managing resources.

Where possible, chapters are organized in sections that (a) describe and define the topic, (b) introduce methods for studying that topic, (c) review current knowledge in the area, (d) summarize theories that attempt to explain and integrate these findings, and (e) offer concrete examples of how knowledge in the topic area has been applied.

OUTLINE OF THE TEXT

This book defines the boundaries of environmental psychology and describes modern and classic activities in many of its neighborhoods. It is organized into three parts: "Individual Processes," "Social Processes," and "Societal Processes."

Part One, "Individual Processes," includes chapters on environmental perception and spatial

USE OF THE TEXT

An attempt has been made to cover all the major topics of environmental psychology as comprehensively as possible within the length limits necessary for a book of this type. To make the book accessible to those with little background in psychology, I have tried to explain key terms and concepts in plain English.

The book has been organized so that when time is limited or interests are particularly focused on some but not all of the five parts in each chapter (definitions, methods, review, theories, applications), the reader should be able to gain useful knowledge from reading only the selected parts. Skipping the research methods sections, for example, will obviously leave readers ignorant of the vagaries, niceties, and necessities of how to conduct a study, but they will still be able to learn what is known about the topic from the review section.

ACKNOWLEDGMENTS

A book like this is the product of the efforts of many individuals. My first acknowledgment is to my parents who gave me so much of themselves. My father's credo was "Look it up." The reader will soon be involved in one outcome of that oft-offered counsel, but I deeply regret that my father cannot be. My mother's credo is "You can do it." Without the confidence she nurtured in so many ways, this three-year odyssey would have ended as an unfulfilled dream.

My professional acknowledgments must begin with my mentor and friend, Robert Sommer. Twenty short years ago, he plucked me from the impersonal hallways of mass education and gave me a job as a research assistant that was not merely a means of support, but a personal education, an inspiration, a rescue mission, and the beginning of a friendship. Later, Lorne Kendall generously tolerated a graduate student with uncommon interests in what was then a fringe area of psychology.

The actual production of the book has been possible only because the University of Victoria has supported my work in many ways. Many assistants have devoted hundreds of hours over the last three years to the many aspects of writing that readers never directly see. They include Aileen Parkinson, Lurene Haines, Margaret Wilkinson, Wendy Ebach, Kim Stadnyk, Mark Martin, Debra McLean and Cathy Hack. My graduate students, Cheuk Fan Ng, Brian O'Connor, Julie Macdonald, and Faye Schmidt, have read draft after draft and offered many constructive suggestions. Thanks also to my undergraduate class who used

the manuscript in semi-complete form and gave me many suggestions from the reader's point of view.

The Allyn and Bacon staff—including Bill Barke, Fred Regan, Judy Shaw, and John-Paul Lenney—have been consistently helpful and supportive throughout this book's years of gestation.

It is customary to thank the typists who struggled with the author's scrawled handwriting and illegible changes in the margins. Debbie Wells, in particular, typed endless letters and other supporting documents for this book, for which I am grateful. But the times, they are a-changin', and the real workhorse on a day-to-day basis has been my trusty IBM 3178C.

Thanks to Sarah, Anna, and Jonas for your patience in waiting for an author who so often made dinner late and appeared to be lost in another world. Rumors that I am jealous because Anna and Jonas finished their first books at ages 9 and 6 before I finished mine are completely without foundation.

Thanks to all those who have adopted this book and to all of its readers. Without your interest in the field, I would not have had the opportunity to spend so many enjoyable hours cavorting in all the neighborhoods of environmental psychology. If you have comments, additions, or corrections to suggest for the next edition, I welcome them. My address may be found at the end of the Appendix.

Numerous professionals in the field read chapters of this book or the whole manuscript. Their comments have contributed immeasurably to the organization, completeness, correctness, and clarity of this work. Many of my colleagues from around the world have contributed their latest research, as well as photos, illustrations, and leads to other colleagues and information. Without them, the book would be less current and less visually pleasing. I have received valuable comments and helpful suggestions from the following reviewers:

Jack Aiello, Rutgers University

Irwin Altman, University of Utah

Frank Becker, Cornell University

David Campbell, Humboldt State University

Julian Edney, Academy of Independent Scholars

Scott Geller, Virginia Polytechnic Institute and State University

Paul Gump, University of Kansas

John Keating, University of Washington

Eric Knowles, University of Arkansas

Edward Krupat, Massachusetts College of Pharmacy and Allied Health Sciences

William Libby, University of Windsor

Steven Margulis, Grand Valley State College

Miles Patterson, University of Missouri

Paul Paulus, University of Texas

James Rotton, Florida International University

Edward Sadalla, Arizona State University

Richard Wener, Polytechnic Institute of New York

Neil Weinstein, Rutgers University

This book might never have been started if Joe Lyons had not shared his secret maxim with me.

Chapter One

The Nature and Scope of Environmental Psychology

*We shape our buildings
and afterwards our buildings shape us.*
Winston Churchill, 1943

WHAT IS ENVIRONMENTAL PSYCHOLOGY?

Environmental psychology is the study of transactions between individuals and their physical settings. In these transactions, individuals change the environment and their behavior and experience are changed by the environment. Environmental psychology includes research and practice aimed at using and improving the process by which human settings are designed.

As a field, environmental psychology is relatively new, although some social scientists have worked on the issues discussed in this book for decades. Most early psychologists concentrated heavily on processes within persons rather than person-environment processes. Yet if we consider the enormous investment society makes in the construction and maintenance of the physical environment—including buildings, parks, streets, the atmosphere, and bodies of water—the long delay before person-environment relations received adequate attention seems odd.

Fortunately, since the late 1960s thousands of studies have dealt with the twelve major topics represented by the chapters to follow. Much of this work has been stimulated by the recognition of environmental problems such as pollution, energy shortages, and unsuitable buildings. Other research is motivated by pure curiosity about how and why humans act and feel in their natural settings. Many mysteries remain about the intricacies of person-environment transactions, but we have begun to understand some of them.

In this chapter, the main issues and topics of environmental psychology are described. The dual goals of discovery and application are outlined. The origins and present status of the field are briefly discussed, along with overviews of the major theoretical approaches and a few observations on research methods. Comments on the international dimensions and future prospects of environmental psychology close the chapter.

First, the Issues

The simple definition that opens this chapter does not convey the fascinating variety of topics that environmental psychologists study. Each of the following actual headlines alludes to a problem that is discussed in this book:

"Sanctuary Now Battlefield As Neighbors Fight Fence"

"Working in an Office Is Dangerous to Your Health"

"Designers Modify the Open Office to Meet Complaints of Workers"

"Commuters Plead: Turn Off the Music"

"Don't Let Holiday Blues Get Employees Down"

"Violence: A Fact of Life in Overcrowded Jails"

"Air Pollution Threatening Pristine Alaska Wilderness"

"Quotas Slashed in Attempt to Help Troubled Herring Fishery"

"Pollution Control Edict May Force Mill Closure"

"The Noise Pollution Toll"

"Positive Ion Theory Aided by New Study"

"Crazy Summer Days Goad Child Abuse"

"The Emergence of the Cubicloids"

"Weather Stress Index Blows Ill Wind"

"Wilderness Aids Self-Healing"

"Privacy Definition Will Be Appealed"

"What's Wrong with High-Rises?"

"When Kids Crave Privacy"

"Satisfying Workers a Matter of Color?"

Don't be misled by the enthusiastic tone of these headlines; the claims implied in some are not necessarily true. What *is* real in each case is a problem. Each problem involves not just the environment but some **transaction** between individuals and settings.

The **environment,** in this book, means built settings, like houses, offices, schools, and streets, and natural settings, like national parks and wilderness areas. On the *human* side, this book refers less often to the behavior of large aggregates of people (society, humankind, or governments) than it does to the behavior of individuals and small groups (office workers, pedestrians, pupils, extraverts, shoppers, neighbors, hikers, dormitory residents, burglars, architects, commuters, and other people). (See Fig. 1–1.)

FIGURE 1–1 This uncompleted building could serve as a symbol of environmental psychology's task. It was designed 3,000 miles from its site; the architects never met most of the people who would work in it or visit it. The specific needs of its occupants could not have been adequately studied.

Most environmental psychologists recognize the need to accomplish two related goals: to understand person-environment transactions and to use this knowledge to help solve a wide variety of problems. The subtitle of this book, *Principles and Practice*, was not chosen lightly: environmental psychology distinctly includes both theory and application.

As individuals, of course, environmental psychologists are not superhuman: each one has only enough energy to work on a fraction of the topics described in the chapters to follow. Some feel more comfortable working on the *principles*, others feel more comfortable with the *practice*. The situation is similar to that in medicine, where some physicians go into family practice and others remain in the laboratory. Still, most environmental psychologists support the need for theory, research, *and* practice that may help to solve these and other problems.

Finding the Principles

To ease a real-world problem, one must have knowledge to apply. Two forms of knowledge are theory and research findings. Theory guides both research and practice by providing a coherent framework of understanding. In environmental psychology, theories do not themselves provide solutions to specific problems. Instead they provide a direction that may yield solutions.

Numerous theories are described throughout

this book. The number and variety of theories illustrates the youthful ferment and enthusiasm within the environmental psychology field. A sorting-out process among theories may eventually reduce their number, but it would be unwise to seek a single, all-inclusive theory. Even in working on a single problem, environmental psychologists find multiple viewpoints helpful in enabling them to see more of the problem's ramifications. The major theoretical approaches are briefly described later in this chapter, but most theoretical discussion occurs in the chapter where a given theory is most appropriate.

The second form of knowledge that may be applied to a problem is that gained from previous research. This book is filled with the findings of studies on dozens of topics. It may surprise you that this knowledge is also usually incapable of supplying a concrete solution to a specific current problem. Today's problem involves different individuals in a different place and time than did yesterday's problem. Differences among individuals, cultures, eras, and settings often lead to different results in studies that otherwise appear similar.

Why read about previous studies, then? First, despite what was just said, some results *do* appear time after time. Environmental psychology does not yet have a large number of established principles, but some findings have been confirmed repeatedly.

Second, previous work provides guidance for future study. Research sometimes demonstrates that a certain idea or method is a blind alley. In such cases, the main discovery may be that no one should venture in *that* direction again! More typically, however, research provokes new questions by producing unanticipated outcomes. Future studies may then be more sophisticated: researchers can avoid known pitfalls and be aware of important issues that were unknown to earlier researchers. If you plan to conduct research in environmental psychology someday, you will need this knowledge. Even if you don't, you should have a realistic picture of the field, one that accurately depicts its current width and breadth.

Third, knowledge of past research serves to reveal the amazing complexity of person-environment transactions. It explodes the simplistic notions about person-environment transactions that abound in daily conversations. The following are a few examples of current evidence: crowding bears only a weak relation to the number of other persons within an area; human territoriality is *not* primarily associated with aggression; and there is no good evidence that pink prison cells calm down violent inmates. In each of these cases, other factors are important. One of the basic messages I hope to convey is that every person-environment transaction is governed by a multiplicity of influences. Within the normal range of human experience, it is almost never true that only one influence shapes our experience or behavior.

The Principles in Practice

Though recognizing the value of theory and research, some environmental psychologists nevertheless prefer to *apply* the knowledge. Instead of working in an academic setting, they venture into private practice. After appropriate graduate training, they operate as consultants to public and private sector clients. There are not yet many practitioners, but some firms have been established for over fifteen years. The practicing environmental psychologist, like the researcher, also makes new discoveries, but these findings are primarily intended to assist a specific client in a specific place and time rather than to establish a principle for the whole discipline.

▶ **In Sum.** Environmental psychology is a young and vital discipline that genuinely requires the pursuit of both scientific principles and practical application as it seeks to ameliorate a wide variety of problems arising from person-environment transactions.

ENVIRONMENTAL PSYCHOLOGY THROUGH TIME

Roots and Edges

The field of environmental psychology may be traced far back into the history of psychology. In some ways, it seems at first to be indistinguishable from the main core of psychology; most psychologists examine the relations between environmental stimuli and human responses. Yet what sets environmental psychology apart is its commitment to research that subscribes to the following principles.

FIGURE 1-2 Environmental psychology examines transactions between individuals and their many settings. *(Lower left photo courtesy of Jonas Gifford)*

- It is ultimately capable of improving the physical environment.
- It is carried out in everyday settings (or close simulations of them).
- It considers person and setting to be a holistic entity.
- It recognizes that individuals actively cope with and shape settings, rather than passively absorb environmental forces.
- It is often performed in conjunction with other disciplines.

Its historical origins may go back to those of psychology itself, but the field of environmental psychology has always been on the edge of psychology—in two senses. First, environmental psychology still is not part of the central core of psychology. It is not taught in every college, nor can it claim as many researchers as some other areas of psychology. Second, the main concern of environmental psychology—the everyday physical environment—has rarely received serious attention in psychology. Every field within psychology implicitly refers to everyday environments, but only environmental psychology systematically investigates this *edge* within each field. To offer just one example, the study of learning ultimately relates to classrooms, yet few classic studies of learning have taken place in classrooms.

The fact that environmental psychology has deep roots within the field and is at the same time at the edge of the discipline is illustrated in the work of Egon Brunswik and Kurt Lewin, two early leaders in the field. (See Figs. 1–3 and 1–4.) Egon Brunswik (1903–1955) was born in Budapest and trained in Vienna. He emigrated to the United States in the 1930s. Brunswik originally concentrated on the process of perception (more on this topic in Chapter Two), but his ideas have been extended far beyond that. In calling for a more detailed analysis of the way that physical environment factors affect behavior, Brunswik was probably the first to use the term environmental psychology (1934). Brunswik also strongly advocated **representative design,** meaning that research should include a much wider array of environmental stimuli than psychologists of the day typically employed.

Lewin (1890–1947), the other great precursor in this field, was born in Prussia, trained in Germany, and also emigrated to the United States in the 1930s. His **field theory** (discussed in Chapter Four), was one of the first to give active consideration to the molar physical environment. Although Lewin did promote the role of the everyday physical environment as a potentially powerful force, his own research did not emphasize it. The sense in which Lewin thought of the physical environment—at least all those aspects of it of which the person is unaware—is revealed in his name for it: the **foreign hull.**

Early on, Lewin (1943) did not accept that factors outside the awareness of the individual could be a part of psychology. Nevertheless, he agreed that forces from the foreign hull do reach awareness and begin to affect psychological processes. He proposed that this field of inquiry be called **psychological ecology.**

Brunswik and others believed, however, that physical environments *could* affect us without

FIGURE 1–3 Kurt Lewin's field theory emphasized the individual's view of the environment. He advocated action research, studies that lead to social change. *(Courtesy of Miriam Lewin.)*

FIGURE 1-4 Egon Brunswik's lens model is a useful framework for describing environmental perception. He also advocated representative design for research, so that psychologists would study a broad range of environmental stimuli before drawing conclusions. *(Courtesy of the University of California, Berkeley.)*

In 1947, Roger Barker and Herbert Wright (1955) headed a Kansas research team that studied **behavior settings,** small ecological units enclosing everyday human behavior. (See Fig. 1–5.) Behavior settings include both the social rules and the physical-spatial aspects of our daily lives. The classroom, the concert hall, the restaurant, and the council meeting are examples. Barker and his colleagues worked hard to describe the social and physical characteristics of these and other identifiable behavior settings for entire towns.

Other early stirrings of environmental psychology began without any particular Lewin or Brunswik influence. In the late 1950s, Robert Sommer and Humphrey Osmond began to systematically alter the physical elements of buildings in Canada and to monitor the effects of these changes on behavior. By rearranging furniture and redesigning wards in a geriatric hospital, they found they could increase communication among the patients. At the same time, Sommer (1959) also began his studies of personal space.

our being aware of them. For example, the hum of a fluorescent light fixture might affect an office worker's satisfaction with work or productivity even though the office worker is unaware of this effect. Brunswik believed that if such factors really can affect us psychologically, they must be studied systematically. Neither Brunswik nor Lewin, however, actually carried out what today could legitimately be called environmental psychology research.

Brunswik had few students, and for many years his ideas had little influence on psychology. Lewin, however, has had a strong influence. As a dynamic person, he inspired many students who, in turn, have profoundly shaped the direction of social science. Two of these students pursued psychological ecology, later changing the term to **ecological psychology.**

FIGURE 1-5 Roger Barker developed ecological psychology and the concept of the behavior setting. *(Courtesy of Roger Barker.)*

In New York, another team, William Ittelson and Harold Proshansky, read about the Sommer and Osmond work and began to map the behavior of patients in a mental hospital ward. Proshansky and Ittelson went on to establish the first Ph.D. program in environmental psychology at the City University of New York (CUNY) in 1968. One marker of environmental psychology's youth is that the first Ph.D. in the CUNY program was earned in 1975. By contrast, the first American Ph.D. in psychology was granted in 1861, the first Ph.D. in clinical psychology just after World War I, and the first in industrial-organizational psychology (a field that is similar to environmental psychology in its dual allegiance to principles and practice) was granted in 1921.

The first conferences specifically devoted to what was then called **architectural psychology** were held at the University of Utah in 1961 and 1966. By the late sixties, the first professional journals devoted to the field were established; the most prominent of these today is *Environment and Behavior*. In 1968 the largest environment-behavior organization, the Environmental Design Research Association, was formed and has held annual meetings since 1969. (Many other organizations, journals, and graduate schools are listed in the Appendix.)

► **In Sum.** Whisperings of an environmental psychology began in the 1940s, followed by a trickle of activity in the 1950s that grew throughout the 1960s into a torrent by the beginning of the 1970s.

Environmental Psychology Today

In the early seventies, environmental psychology was borne along on the tide of environmentalism. But as a political force, environmentalism has lost some of its early naive enthusiasm and support. Those whose commitment to it was approximately as strong as their commitment to wearing beads moved on to new fads later in the 1970s. Environmental psychology suffered slightly from this defection of faddists.

Although today the growth of environmental psychology has stabilized, two conflicting forces still affect it. Psychologists and others show increasing interest, but its growth is muffled by the general funding problems that affect many sectors of society. One recent gain was the establishment of a major new international journal in 1981, the *Journal of Environmental Psychology*. Another was the publication of the *Handbook of Environmental Psychology* in early 1987.

A Topic Sampler. Environmental psychology is studied at several levels of inquiry. At the most basic level are studies of such fundamental psychological processes as perception, cognition, and personality as they filter and structure each individual's experience of the environment. Then comes the study of our social management of space: territoriality, crowding, privacy, and interpersonal distancing (or personal space). In yet wider analyses, some environmental psychologists concentrate on the complex behaviors associated with working, learning, and everyday life in cities and other communities. Finally, better design for the built environment and the psychological components of societal issues such as resource management (energy conservation, recycling, litter) are examined.

The whole enterprise of environmental psychology is difficult to comprehend in its entirety, even for professionals. This book is based on well over a thousand studies, more than 400 from the 1980s alone. Yet this represents only a fraction of all the published work in environmental psychology.

Even a thousand studies do not provide final answers to the theoretical issues and practical problems faced by environmental psychologists. Do not expect many unequivocal conclusions in the pages that follow. Instead, enjoy—if you can—the *diversity* of viewpoints and findings. These are still the pioneer days of environmental psychology, when most studies uncover previously unknown territory as much as they further our knowledge of the known terrain.

Theories and Approaches in Brief. As noted earlier, no single theory applies to all the topics in environmental psychology. Competing theories still jostle one another to explain person-environment events. If the future is like the recent past, new theories will evolve and there will be mergers, takeovers, bankruptcies, and spinoffs among the current theories. Do not be discouraged by the existence of apparently conflicting theories. Remember the ancient story about three blind sages who encounter a being unknown to them (an elephant). One sage, grasping the animal's tail, describes it as ropelike. Another, holding its trunk, claims it is like a hose. A third, arms wrapped around a stout leg, cannot believe the others are unable to realize that it resembles a tree. Similarly each of today's theories is probably an accurate but partial explanation of human behavior in physical contexts.

In this book, the major theories and approaches will be described briefly, allowing you to begin thinking about how the research findings you will soon be reading about fit together. One of the most important functions of a theory is to provide generalizations that give order and meaning to specific observations about person-environment relations.

Some theories in environmental psychology postulate a central psychological mechanism that is said to regulate the way individuals deal with settings. Many such theories have been proposed, but they fall into two broad categories. One group focuses on **stimulation** and the other focuses on **control.**

The stimulation theories (Wohlwill, 1966) conceptualize the physical environment as a source of sensory information that is crucial to our welfare. This stimulation includes relatively simple stimuli such as light, color, sound, noise, heat, and cold but also more complex stimuli such as buildings, streets, outdoor settings, and other people. Two important ways environmental stimulation can vary are in *amount* and in *meaning.* In amount, it varies in such obvious dimensions as intensity, duration, frequency, and number of sources. Meaning is provided by our psychological assessment of these environmental stimuli. Our thinking, social interaction, work performance, feelings, and even health depend on the patterning of this stimulation and our reactions to it.

One important stimulation-based theory is **adaptation-level theory** (Helson, 1964). It maintains that individuals adapt to certain levels of stimulation in certain contexts—no particular amount of stimulation is good for everyone—and that stimulation different from one's adaptation level changes one's feelings and behavior.

Arousal theories (Berlyne, 1960; Mehrabian & Russell, 1974) are based on the assumption that the form and content of a broad range of our behavior and experience are related to how phys-

iologically aroused we are. The **overload theory** (Cohen, 1978; Milgram, 1970) concentrates on the effects of too much stimulation. Much research in environmental psychology originates with problems that may be viewed from an arousal or overload perspective, such as noise, heat, cold, and crowding.

However, we also find ourselves in settings that offer too little stimulation. **Restricted environmental stimulation** (Suedfeld, 1980) causes problems for us in some circumstances, as you might expect, but in others it yields surprisingly positive results. The performance of easy cognitive tasks, for example, is improved under low stimulation conditions (Suedfeld, Landon, & Ballard, 1983).

Stress has also become an important theoretical concept in recent years. Environmental psychologists have extended the work of Hans Selye (1976) to help explain the behavioral and health effects that occur when environmental stimulation exceeds an individual's adaptive resources (Stokols, 1979). The stress concept has been applied in a wide variety of everyday contexts; suspected stressors include air pollution, hospitals, offices, extreme temperatures, traffic, noise, and disasters. Campbell (1983) has distinguished **acute stressors** (negative, intense, relatively short impacts that are in the forefront of consciousness), **ambient stressors** (negative, chronic, global environmental conditions that usually remain in the background of consciousness and seem hard to alter), and **daily hassles** (negative, nonurgent, recurrent stressors).

Two basic stress models predominate. One emphasizes physiological responses; the other emphasizes psychological responses (Evans, 1982). On the physiological side, Selye (1976) first described the **general adaptation syndrome,** a pattern of bodily reactions that remains similar even when the specific source of the stress varies. The pituitary and adrenal glands respond to stressors in a particular sequence: alarm, then resistance, then exhaustion. The psychological side of stress has long been studied by Lazarus (1966), who emphasizes the role of cognitive appraisal, that is, our efforts to assess the seriousness of the situation and to cope with the stressor. Thus, the *meaning* of the stressor becomes an important factor.

Other theorists emphasize the meaning of

stimulation even more. The bestowal of meaning—together with our selection, construction, modification, and destruction of settings—is among the ways we shape the environment during our continuous series of transactions with it. The personal meanings given to a place by a person are essential to our *experience* of the environment (Buttimer & Seamon, 1980). The meaning of the environment, in this sense, has been studied from the phenomenological perspective, a form of disciplined contemplation. The environment, as revealed by the stimulation we receive from it, forms the basis of our experience. As we become familiar with a setting, we create a meaning for it. This meaning may be positive or negative in tone, similar or different from the meanings attached to it by others, weak or strong. Places without meaning affect us differently than places with meaning; we treat places without meaning differently than we treat meaningful places.

A second set of theories in environmental psychology focuses on control rather than stimulation. We may adapt to a certain level of stimulation and sometimes be faced with too little or too much of it. But another obviously important consideration is how much control we have (or think we have) over environmental stimulation. Clearly, those who have much control over the amount and kind of stimulation that comes their way are generally better off than those who do not. We may have considerable control in some settings, such as at home, and very little in others, such as in traffic jams.

Theories of **personal control** (Barnes, 1981) have been developed to account for the effects of being able or unable to influence stimulation patterns. For example, lack of control often leads to **psychological reactance** (Brehm, 1966), an attempt to regain the freedom one has lost. Individuals who conclude that control is difficult or impossible to regain may succumb to **learned helplessness** (Seligman, 1975), the conviction that no amount of effort can succeed in overcoming an unpleasant or painful situation. In everyday social transactions, we attempt to achieve personal control through several **boundary regulation mechanisms** (Altman, 1975), such as personal space and territoriality.

A third major theoretical formulation is based on the **behavior-setting** concept mentioned earlier (Barker, 1968; Wicker, 1979), the notion that consistent, prescribed patterns of behavior, called **programs,** are found in many places. If you walk into a barber shop, a football game, or food store, you are likely to see recurrent activities, regularly carried out by persons holding specific roles. For example, every football game features two teams of players who are running, passing, and scoring; officials monitoring rule violations; and fans who cheer and boo.

Variations in the actions of individuals do occur, of course, but behavior-setting theorists pay less attention to psychological processes and individual differences among participants than do the stimulation and control theorists. They are impressed by the uniformity rather than the variability in the actions of those who occupy a given role, especially in contrast to the behavior of those occupying a different role. Consider, for example, the differences in behavior of players, officials, and fans in the football game. Behavior-setting theorists tend to explain person-environment relations primarily in terms of the social features of a setting, such as rules, customs, and typical activities, and its physical features.

One key concept in behavior-setting theory is the level of **staffing** (Wicker, 1979). For a variety of reasons, a given behavior setting may attract many or few who wish to participate in its activities. When there are too many individuals around (and the behavior setting fails to find a way to exclude extras), overstaffing results. When too few are attracted, understaffing results. You can probably recall instances of both overstaffed and understaffed behavior settings in your experience. What were the consequences for individuals in these settings?

Wicker (1987) has extended the behavior-setting concept in time. Behavior settings are not static entities; they are born, they struggle, adapt, thrive, and they die. (The sewing bee is almost extinct; make way for the suntan parlor!)

A fourth group of theoreticians have searched for a model that captures the full complexity of everyday person-environment relations. (See Figs. 1–6 and 1–7.) These approaches, which may collectively be termed **integral theories,** are attempts to capture the whole interrelated essence of person-environment relations.

Interactionism is a step ahead of older theories that attributed most or all the causes of behavior

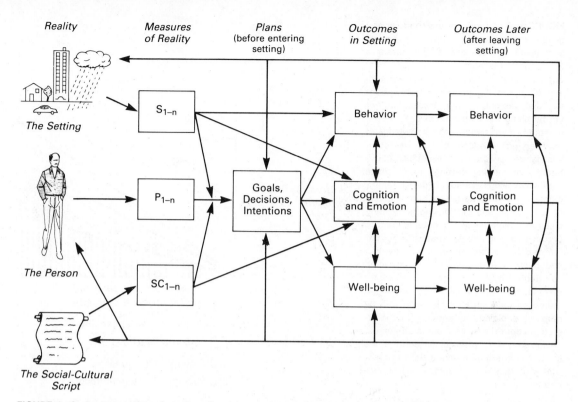

FIGURE 1-6 An integrative view of environmental psychology. In the context of political, economic, and historical forces (not shown here), a person enters a setting. The visit may be as brief as a walk through a park or as long as a lifetime spent in a neighborhood. The characteristics of the person (P_{1-n}), the form and rules of the Setting (S_{1-n}), and the social and cultural norms (SC_{1-n}) all influence a person's plans when he or she enters the setting and what occurs in it. In the setting, the person behaves (for example, perceives, interacts, performs), thinks (cognizes, recollects, calculates, develops impressions), and feels (pleasure, arousal, peacefulness, anxiety), and is healthy or unhealthy. Transactions in the setting have outcomes: the person may be better off (happier, healthier, more skilled) or worse off (overly stressed, ill, angry, less skilled). Some of these outcomes are immediate, others are delayed. Not only is the person affected, but often the setting is affected by the person, as well. The goals of environmental psychologists are to understand these transactions and to improve outcomes for individuals and settings.

either to the person *or* to the environment. Persons and environments are considered to be separate entities, but they are continually engaged in a series of interactions. **Transactionalism** (Stokols & Shumaker, 1981) emphasizes that person and environment are part of one inclusive entity. This means that neither individuals nor settings can be adequately defined without reference to the other and that activities of one necessarily influence the other (Altman & Rogoff, 1987). We influence environments and environments influence us. **Organismic theories** (Wapner, 1981) emphasize the dynamic interplay of social, societal, and individual factors in a mutual, complex system. Behavior is viewed as part of many possible developmental equilibria that have both short-term and long-term goals.

The latter two theories represent the highest and most encompassing dreams of environmental psychologists because they probably do describe "the way it is." Yet a persistent problem is a gap between their attractive themes and the reality of current research methods. Few methods have yet been developed that are capable of adequately testing transactionalist or organismic theories. Most methods are better geared to the interac-

FIGURE 1–7 A model of environment and behavior. In general, our understanding of a behavior process grows with research experience—the number of quality investigations of it. Because intensive research in environmental psychology is only about two decades old, many processes are not yet far along the horizontal axis. Fuller understanding will require more knowledge of how varying individuals (e.g., residents versus visitors, children versus adults) act differently in varying settings (e.g., single family dwellings versus high-rise apartments), and how particular combinations of individuals and settings (e.g., visiting children in high-rise apartments) *interact* to produce varying behavior patterns. For different behavior processes (e.g., crowding and play), the degree of understanding contributed by knowledge of each factor (person, setting, or interaction) may differ. That is, in some situations behavior may be primarily explained by knowing key information about the person, but in others, behavior may be better understood if we know key information about the setting or that a certain kind of person will be in a certain setting.

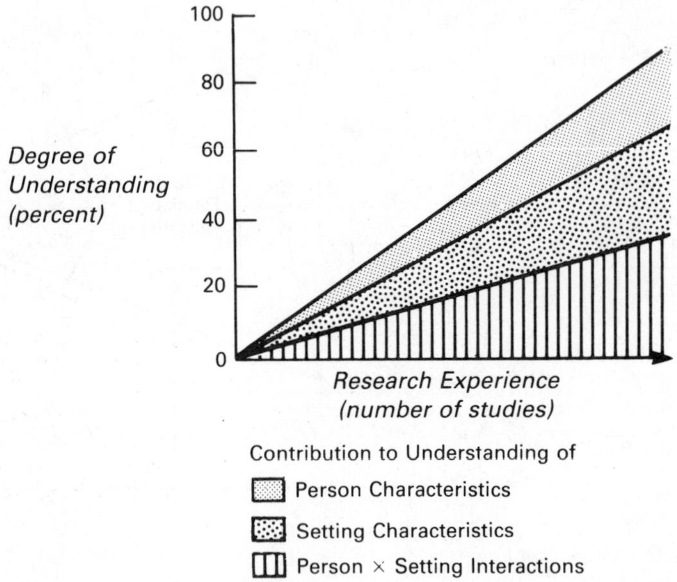

Contribution to Understanding of

▦ Person Characteristics

▨ Setting Characteristics

⫿ Person × Setting Interactions

tional variety of integral theory: Person and environment are defined separately and the influence of each in a given situation is measured.

A fifth theoretical perspective is the **operant** approach employed by some environmental psychologists (Geller, 1987). This approach is based on Skinnerian principles, and its goal is to modify the behavior of individuals whose behavior is contributing to some environmental problem. Specific problematic behaviors are identified, then appropriate positive reinforcements are delivered when individuals engage in more beneficial behavior. Two prime examples of problems that have been attacked with the operant approach are littering and residential energy wastage.

▶ **In Sum.** Theory in environmental psychology is vital, diverse, and still developing. Those emphasizing central psychological processes focus on stimulation and control. The adaptation-level approach begins with the assumption that each of us becomes accustomed to a certain level of environmental stimulation. The common occurrence of too much or too little stimulation is the focus of arousal, overload, underload, and stress theories, which predict that a wide range of behaviors and experiences will be affected.

Other theories emphasize the importance of an individual's real or perceived control over stimulation, such as personal control, reactance, learned helplessness, and boundary regulation theories. The ecological approach asserts the importance of the behavior setting, a naturally occurring small-scale social-physical unit consisting of regular patterns of person-environment behavior. Integral approaches (for example, interactionism, transactionalism, and organismic theory) attempt to describe the full interrelationship of persons and setting. Finally, the operant approach downplays abstract principles, adopting a direct problem-solving approach that employs behavior modification techniques.

Some Thoughts on Research Methods. Environmental psychologists use a wide variety of methods in their work. I believe each method is best described in the chapter covering the topic in which it is primarily used. This section, therefore, is not a detailed examination of research methods. But because research methods are important, descriptions and evaluations of them are found throughout the book. For those who are keen to learn many details of environmental research methods in one place, John Zeisel's (1981) book *Inquiry by Design* is recommended. The following four points are about research methods that are important.

First, environmental psychology is a **multiple-paradigm** field (Craik, 1977). This means that different researchers may employ not only different methods but entirely different kinds of techniques. Research methods vary not just in their procedure but in the very beliefs and values of the investigators who use them. One example is the stark contrast between the reinforcement strategies of the operant approach and the experiential strategies of the phenomenologists who study the meaning of place.

Environmental psychologists, despite occasional paradigm clashes, generally advocate the use of multiple methods to gain knowledge; they recognize that each method has strengths and weaknesses. Researchers cannot include all methods in any one study, so the findings of any single study must usually be treated as one bit of knowledge to be integrated with the findings of other studies before firm conclusions may be drawn.

Researchers must be very patient and cautious about drawing strong conclusions from single studies, which are likely to have one or more limitations. Responsible researchers search for patterns of results in a *series* of studies. Multiple methods, paradigms, and studies are necessary for understanding.

Second, some methods employed by environmental psychologists are quite standard social-science techniques, such as naturalistic observation and description, interviews, rating scales, laboratory experiments, and videotaping. Other methods—including some of the ways to study personal space, cognitive maps, and movement through buildings—are more or less unique to environmental psychology.

Third, a central concern of environmental psychology is **external validity,** the degree to which results of a study apply in contexts beyond the setting where they were obtained, such as the everyday world. This concern has led to a widespread suspicion of laboratory research, although some studies are best conducted in laboratories.

This concern with external validity naturally leads to a tendency to conduct **field studies** whenever possible. Field studies are performed in the very setting where the results are to be applied, or in one as similar as possible. Sometimes studies cannot be conducted in the setting for which the results are intended. For example, research on the performance or satisfaction of employees who will work in a proposed office complex is impossible. Yet if the research waits until the complex is built, it is too late to use the results in the design of the complex. One solution is to simulate the building before it is constructed. Sophisticated facilities have been built to simulate offices (Irvine, California), regional landscapes (Berkeley, California), and residences (Lausanne, Switzerland).

Fourth, environmental psychology accepts the idea that behavior is subject to many influences. Field studies often reveal an environment's total effect on a person but usually do not shed light on the way that particular aspects of the environment acted to produce the effect. If a researcher's goal is to isolate specific causes of behavior or to test a theory in a precise way—that is, principles of behavior rather than practice—the laboratory may be necessary.

Between the artificial but precise laboratory and the realistic but imprecise everyday setting lie various **quasi-experimental designs** as compromises. Among the requirements of true experiments are random assignment of subjects to conditions and experimenter control of the conditions or variables hypothesized to affect one's behavior or thinking. Quasi-experimental designs might, for example, include real classrooms but accept the limitation that the experimenter is unable to randomly assign pupils to the classrooms. Or, in a study of outdoor heat on aggression, rates of violent acts on hot versus normal days might be compared even though the investigator could not control the day's temperature. In sort, quasi-experimental designs *resemble* true experimental designs, yet fail to satisfy some criteria of true experiments.

▶ **In Sum.** Environmental psychologists recognize and accept that person-environment transactions are influenced by many different factors, which has led to multiple paradigms for studying them. A wide variety of research methods are employed—some standard in social science and others devised especially for environmental psychology. A strong preference for performing research in the everyday world means that field studies are common. Sometimes laboratories and simulated settings are necessary, but they are used primarily when a field study is not possible. True experiments are sometimes possible; they are desirable when a researcher seeks to isolate particular causes and effects. Quasi-experimental research designs are much more common.

International Dimensions.   From its first stirrings, environmental psychology is five to six decades old in developed countries. In Germany, Hellpach explored the concept during the 1920s (Fuhrer, 1983). The famous lighting studies at Western Electric's Hawthorne plant began in the late 1920s (Roethlisberger & Dickson, 1939) and lighting in English dwellings was studied in the 1930s (Chapman & Thomas, 1944). In Japan, Tetsuro considered environment-behavior relations throughout the 1930s (Yamamoto, 1984).

In Canada, the effects of restricted stimulation were first investigated in McGill University laboratories in the early fifties (Heron, Doane, & Scott, 1956). The first published work dealing with the social impact of room arrangements came from Saskatchewan in the late fifties (Sommer & Ross, 1958).

A strong movement has developed in Japan (Inui, 1982), beginning with an early book on architectural psychology (Kobayashi, 1961). Research illustrating activity in Japan includes studies of how the design of religious shrines affects the feelings of pilgrims (Funabashi, Shimizu, & Sekida, 1978) and investigations of behavioral responses to disasters, such as earthquakes (Abe, 1982).

Sweden has long been at the forefront of environmental psychology (Garling, 1982), placing particular emphasis on the visual perception of architecture (Garling, 1969; Hesselgren, 1967). Ecological concerns have spurred considerable research into air and noise pollution (Berglund, Berglund & Lindvall, 1976a, 1976b). Cold outdoor environments have produced much work directed towards creating quality indoor environments (Wyon, Lofberg, & Lofstedt, 1975) and understanding the very meaning of the environment (Acking & Sorte, 1973; Kuller, 1972).

Research in environmental psychology is also widespread in the Soviet Union, especially in Estonia. Soviet researchers deal with the same range of topics as other environmental psychologists, but one emphasis seems to be on the design and improvement of mass housing and neighborhoods (Niit, Kruusvall, & Heidmets, 1981). A series of national conferences in 1981, 1983, and 1985 have helped to establish environmental psychology as a discipline in the Soviet Union.

In other countries, environmental psychology has developed more slowly. Nevertheless, small devoted groups of researchers exist in the Netherlands (Kremer & Stringer, 1987), Israel (Churchman, 1984), France (Jodelet, 1987), Australia (Thorne & Hall, 1987), Turkey (Pamir, 1981), Venezuela (Sanchez, Wiesenfeld, & Cronick, 1983), Italy (Perussia, 1983), and Mexico (Diaz-Guerrero, 1984). In recent years, numerous international conferences have helped to knit the worldwide community of environmental psychology.

Environmental psychologists are also at work above and below the surface of the earth. One recent Ph.D. recipient is now researching the ability of submarine crews to orient themselves in their underwater abodes. Another directs a program concerned with the design of living and working quarters on space stations (Clearwater, 1985). (See Fig. 1–8.)

► **In Sum.** Environmental psychology studies have taken place in many countries as well as under the sea and above the earth. To some extent, the field has a unique character in each country because each country has distinct environmental problems and philosophies. In the 1980s, links among environmental psychologists have been increasing owing to more frequent international conferences and exchanges of views in prominent journals.

Future Prospects

Environmental psychology is a young and vigorous field; it will be increasingly influential as cries for a more realistic psychology are heard. Some observers see environmental psychology as a blueprint for the future of psychology as a whole (Ellis, 1980). Already, signs of the influence of the environmental psychology perspective may be

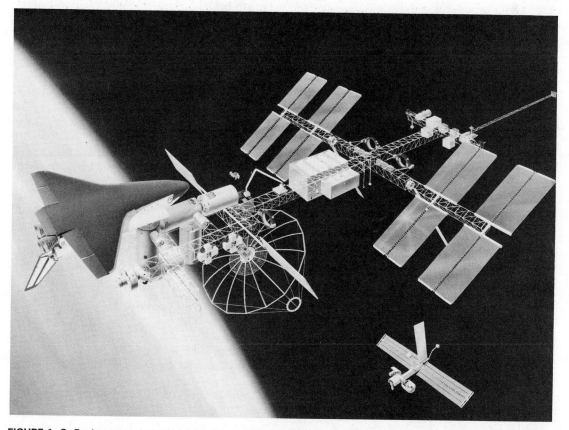

FIGURE 1-8 Environmental psychologists have studied settings to be used under the sea (Tektite III) and above the atmosphere (space station) as well as those on earth. *(Courtesy of Robert Sommer and the National Aeronautics Space Administration.)*

seen in many other areas of psychology. For instance, Altman (1981) has described environmental psychology as the leader in a revolution of relevance that is sweeping such other areas as developmental and cognitive psychology.

Despite this trend, four formidable challenges still exist. The first is the challenge of *application*. Translating research into practice has been a recognized difficulty since the beginning of the field. In this book, many successful applications are described, but the task of applying environmental psychology is rarely easy. Each new project seems to raise its own peculiar obstacles to be overcome.

The second challenge is to discover more *appropriate research methods*. Environmental psychology has come of age in its advocacy of contextualism or the integral approaches described earlier. But for the most part, research methods still haven't been developed that can do justice to the complexity of contextualism (Stokols, 1982).

The third challenge is to achieve a more *coherent core* (Canter & Craik, 1981). When fields of inquiry are mere collections of topics that are not linked together, they can be absorbed into other fields and disappear. Perspectives that show the wholeness and distinctness of environmental psychology are now appearing but more are needed. One can still hear arguments over what should be included in the field; its boundaries are still growing and changing. A chief goal of this book is to reveal the natural coherence of environmental psychology.

Fourth, theoretical diversity is stimulating and productive, but further *integration and development of theory* is necessary. More efforts like that of Willems (1974), who explored the relations between behavior-setting theory and the operant approach, are necessary. This goal is related to the third challenge; the evolution of an agreed-upon central core depends in part on the development of more comprehensive theories.

SUMMARY

Environmental psychology is a new area of psychology, but its roots go deep into the history of the discipline. It seeks understanding of person-environment transactions. Environmental psychologists aim to assist in the solution of physical setting problems, although some of them work primarily on the establishment of scientific principles while others work primarily on improving human habitats. Several complementary but distinct paradigms are used, some contemplative, some experimental, some consultative.

Around the world, the face of environmental psychology takes on somewhat different appearances, but it retains a fundamental commitment to understanding and improving human-environment relations. Environmental psychology is at the forefront of a general movement to make psychology more relevant to everyday life, but it is still challenged to find more ways to turn knowledge into practice, to devise methods that are better able to accomplish its goals, to reach greater consensus on what constitutes its central core, and to develop more comprehensive theories reflecting and embodying that core. The field is vigorous and will meet these challenges.

SUGGESTED SUPPLEMENTARY READINGS

Altman, I., & Stokols, D. (Eds.). (1987). *Handbook of environmental psychology*. New York: Wiley.

Environment and Behavior, a journal appearing since 1969.

Journal of Environmental Psychology, a journal appearing since 1981.

Russell, J. A., & Ward, L. A. (1982). Environmental psychology. *Annual Review of Psychology, 33*, 651–658.

Stokols, D. (1982). Environmental psychology: A coming of age. In A. G. Kraut (Ed.), *The G. Stanley Hall Lecture Series*, Vol. 2. Washington: American Psychological Association.

Zeisel, J. (1981). *Inquiry by design: Tools for environment-behavior research*. Monterey, CA: Brooks/Cole.

Part One

Individual Processes

No psychological process is entirely separate from the environment. However, this section explores processes that are often thought of as occurring inside the head. Chapter Two examines the way we perceive the environment and how physical space is organized in our thoughts. Chapter Three is concerned with the different ways we think and feel about places, including descriptions, personal preferences, emotional response, and expert evaluations. Chapter Four discusses the environmental aspects of personality. Behavior tendencies that bear on our interactions with the physical environment, how our plans mesh with places, and the way our very selves are linked to key settings will be explored.

Chapter Two
Environmental Perception and Spatial Cognition

ENVIRONMENTAL PERCEPTION

SPATIAL COGNITION

*We know a great deal about the perception of a
one-eyed man with his head in a clamp watching
glowing lights in a dark room, but surprisingly
little about his perceptual abilities in a
real-life situation.*

Helen Ross, 1974

It was a very promising long weekend except for the fog that clung to the valley, enveloping the town. Tom had asked Jane, whom he had recently met, to go camping in the mountains. As they made their way out of town through Friday afternoon traffic, the snail's pace made the sights along the city streets somehow more vivid. The glaring yellow motel and fast-food restaurant signs along the strip seemed larger and closer than usual.

"How far is it to the campsite?" Jane asked as they cleared town and the fog.

"Right over there," said Tom. "See that jagged peak just to the left? Guess how far it is."

"I'd say about 50 miles," said Jane. "How far is it?"

"I don't know for sure," Tom replied, "but I'd guess it's closer than that, maybe 40 miles." After they had driven for 60 miles through landscapes that gradually changed from dry golden grasses and green oaks to evergreen shrubs and slender pines, the jagged peak did look quite a bit closer, but it was still some distance away.

Entering the park finally, Tom tried to recall where that great campsite from last year was. Jane spotted a "You are here" map just inside the gates, but they couldn't orient themselves from it. They couldn't decide whether the map was too vague to be useful or if too many exams had burned out their map-reading circuits. Tom finally was able to conjure up a mental image of the park; he remembered that the roads were arranged in an unusual system of concentric circles. Now it came back: the good site was just near that giant fir on the third ring road.

As Friday evening settled into utter peace, Tom and Jane sat on a ridge watching the sun sink into a distant range of snowy peaks. A waterfall's pleasing thunder could be heard, and a deep, dark mountain lake lay before them. The meadow wild flowers around them gathered dew and began to fold their petals.

If you and I looked up and down a street, would we see the same thing? How would our thoughts about what we see differ? Environmental psychology begins with the basic psychological processes involved as we come to know our surroundings. This chapter and the next one cover several closely connected psychological processes (Ittelson, 1978) that occur as we perceive and comprehend the built and natural environments.

Environmental perception is the initial gathering of information. **Environmental cognition** includes further processing of the information: storing, organizing, and recalling it. Perception of the environment and the spatial aspects of environmental cognition are featured in this chapter; in the next chapter two other aspects of environmental cognition are discussed. **Environmental appraisal** means using environmental information to form a personal evaluation, such as whether you believe that a certain setting is good or bad, beautiful or ugly, meaningful or not, pleasant or unpleasant, etc. It includes the emotional impact of places, environmental preferences, attitudes toward the environment, and the study of the categories we use to organize our knowledge about settings. **Environmental assessment** involves combining the appraisals of group members (experts or users of particular settings) into broader-based evaluations that may be used to create relatively objective measures of the psychological qualities of environments.

The first of these, environmental perception, refers to our initial exposure to the physical settings around us. We are primarily visual beings (Gifford & Ng, 1982), but environmental perception includes the ways and means by which we collect information through all our senses. The term environmental perception is sometimes used broadly to include aspects of how we appraise and assess environments, but in this chapter it refers primarily to the initial information-gathering phase of the process.

Our experience may suggest that perception is simple and automatic, but it isn't. We are so familiar with the act of perceiving that the wondrous complexity of the process emerges only when we deliberately turn our perceptual talents back on themselves to observe what is going on as we see, hear, smell, taste, and touch the world. Perception of the everyday world is an exceedingly complicated phenomenon.

The topics in the first section include the nature and measurement of environmental perception, what influences it, theories about how it works, and some of its applications to design and planning. In the course of this discussion, we also deal with basic awareness of our immediate surroundings and perceptual adaptation.

The second section, spatial cognition, concerns the manner in which we process, store, and recall information about the locations and arrangements of places. Through experience, for example, we develop an extensive body of knowledge about the buildings, streets, and communities around us. The topics in this section include cognitive maps, spatial knowledge, memory for environments, and orientation in built and natural settings. Methods of investigating spatial cognition, as well as influences on it, theories about it, and its application to environmental design are discussed.

ENVIRONMENTAL PERCEPTION

Distinctions and Variations

Contrasts with Traditional Perception Research. When psychologists decades ago began to study perception, they quickly realized the complexity of the task facing them. Many decided that in order to learn something about the process, everyday perception would somehow have to be simplified. One way to simplify the process is to present the perceiver with a simple stimulus. Traditional perception researchers assume that understanding the perception of simple stimuli is a useful and perhaps necessary path to understanding how the much more complex stimuli of daily life are perceived. The traditional approach also favors examining the perception process in the laboratory, where maximum control over all possible extraneous influences may be exerted.

Environmental psychologists, in contrast, embrace and even celebrate the complexity of the environmental displays they present to subjects (entire buildings and landscapes, for example). William Ittelson (1970, 1973, 1978), a pioneer in this area, distinguishes between the older approach, which he calls **object perception,** and the newer **environmental perception.** (See Fig. 2–1.)

In object perception research, the emphasis is on the properties of simple stimuli, such as

FIGURE 2–1 William Ittelson helped to distinguish environmental perception and cognition from traditional psychology approaches and was a key figure in the development of the first graduate program in environmental psychology. *(Courtesy of William Ittelson.)*

brightness, color, depth, perceptual constancy, form, and apparent movement. In environmental perception research, the emphasis is on large-scale scenes, treated as whole entities. Much more research has been done in object perception than in environmental perception, as the chapter-opening quote from Helen Ross suggests.

The difference between the two approaches is not merely in the size and complexity of the stimulus presented; the role of the perceiver is another difference. In environmental perception studies, the participants often move around, in, and through the scene; they are *part* of the scene. Moving through the environmental display means that the perceiver experiences it from multiple perspectives.

A third important difference from the object perception tradition is that the perceiver often is connected to the environmental display by a clear goal or purpose. We scan a wilderness area for a clean campsite. While driving, we watch signs and lights to avoid being in an accident. We look around the restaurant for a private table.

Everyday environmental perception has many purposes, but an appropriate way to divide them is into utilitarian purposes and aesthetic purposes (McGill & Korn, 1982). Ironically, many studies of the aesthetic qualities of buildings and landscapes have been undertaken, but McGill and Korn's work shows that, at least in urban streets, typical observers actually pay much more attention to utilitarian elements of the environment (businesses, for example) than to aesthetic elements (large wall murals, for example).

An important difficulty with research in environmental perception is accounting for the myriad of personal and physical influences on the perceptual process. Despite the methodological difficulties involved, environmental psychologists prefer to investigate the perception of everyday scenes rather than the perception of greatly simplified stimulus displays in laboratories.

Awareness and Adaptation. The environment constantly offers many more pieces of information than any of us can possibly handle. We are always selecting for our attention a relatively small, manageable portion of the available information. We may focus intensely or minimally on environmental displays ranging in size from architectural details to vast panoramic landscapes that range in distance from very near to very distant. We may actively scrutinize the environment (when, for example, we evaluate an apartment as a possible place to rent) or be quite unaware of our surroundings (when we are daydreaming, reading, or deeply involved in a conversation). We may adapt or habituate to some environmental displays so that we really don't *see* them at all (for instance, a street we drive along every day), or we may be riveted to a scene by its importance or novelty (for instance, our first look at a campus where we will spend several years).

Another example of habituation is the way we adapt to seeing air pollution. Robert Sommer (1972) has suggested that we notice air pollution primarily when it is new to us—such as when we move to a smoggy place—or when there is a sudden increase in smog where we live. Basing his observations on an old principle of psychophysics called the Weber-Fechner law, Sommer points out that as the amount of air pollution increases, larger and larger increments of *new* air pollution

are needed before we notice that pollution is getting worse. The same smokestack that would have outraged a community when it had little air pollution is barely noticed after the community becomes heavily polluted.

We must not assume that our attention is always directed toward physical settings; in fact it is often directed toward other people or inward, toward ourselves. We sometimes pay very little attention to our physical surroundings even when they cause us some discomfort, a state that has been called **environmental numbness** (Gifford, 1976c). This numbness, or lack of awareness of our surroundings, often arises when more lively aspects of the world—such as the attentions of a friend or absorption in reading, problem solving, or daydreaming—command our attention. In spite of this habitual tendency, we still need to pay attention to the environment. Numb toes can become frostbitten, and numbness to the everyday environment can expose us to a variety of toxins and stressors.

On the positive side, we are capable of developing our own **cognitive sets** to enhance awareness and appreciation of the environment. Herbert Leff (1978) has provided an elaborate description of ways we might consciously direct our perceptions and cognitions to obtain richer environmental experiences. Here, very briefly, are some of Leff's exercises: rapidly switch your visual focus from one point in the scene to another while forming a vivid impression of each view; look for views in the scene that would make personally relevant photographs; imagine that you are one of the objects in the scene and what that existence would be like; see inanimate objects as if they were alive. The mental gymnastics involved in these exercises can produce very positive feelings while increasing your environmental awareness.

► **In Sum.** Environmental psychologists usually study perception of whole, everyday scenes. In doing so, they sometimes must sacrifice a degree of experimental control, but in return they obtain data on the perception of real, complex settings that the perceiver may move through and feel a connection with. Perceivers select cues from scenes, ignoring many others. Unfortunately, some cues that are ignored may be important, at least in the long run (for example, air pollution).

Some ways to enhance perception of everyday settings have been suggested.

Research Methods

How can environmental perception be measured? It is, after all, an individual's *experience*; researchers do not have direct access to their subjects' experience. Therefore, perception is usually measured indirectly. We will discuss three indirect methods (self-reports, time sampling, and inferences from behavior) and one relatively direct method (phenomenology).

First, the commonest method is simply to ask perceivers what they see (or hear, smell, touch, taste). These **self-report** methods include questionnaires, interviews, checklists, and free descriptions. An obvious shortcoming of these methods is that perceivers may produce inaccurate reports of their own perceptions. They may not pay careful attention to their own perceptions of a moment ago; they may incorrectly recall or entirely forget perceptions from the past; or they may report what they think the experimenter wishes to hear. The actual perception must be filtered through language (Lowenthal, 1972). Self-report methods are nevertheless useful as reasonably accurate, economical ways to study environmental perception.

A second way of studying what perceivers in everyday situations attend to was suggested by Brunswik (1944) and revived by Lynch and Rivkin (1959), Wagner, Baird, and Barbaresi (1981), and Feimer (1984), among others. The idea is simple: Ask observers to move through a setting and to report, at certain intervals (or afterward), exactly what they are (or were) looking at. This procedure might be used to discover whether observers pay attention more to environmental elements that are moving or stationary, large or small, near or far, straight ahead or to one side, etc. The participants in Wagner et al.'s study, for example, walked around a small college town. Most objects they looked at were within 40 meters and less than 30 degrees from straight ahead. About 40 percent of the objects perceived were moving elements, such as people or cars. Among the less common reports (5 percent or less each) were that participants were looking at animals, window displays, or nothing at all.

A third method is to infer something about perception from the perceiver's behavior. For example, the length of time museum visitors spend looking at a painting or a science exhibit has been used as an index of their interest in that display.

The fourth method involves approaching environmental perception from the phenomenological perspective. This method is similar in some ways to one of the oldest methods in psychology (introspection), but its value for environmental psychology has only recently been advocated (Seamon, 1982). Phenomenology is rooted in philosophy, but its important figures have begun to speak of concepts that are within the domain of environmental psychology. Heidegger (1971), for example, discusses *dwelling* as a process of existence through which a mere place becomes a dear home.

The phenomenological approach ultimately results in a self-report, but these self-reports differ in important ways from those discussed earlier. First, the report is made by a perceiver who is carefully trained to observe according to a certain method. Second, the emphasis is on the perceptions of an individual, or at least one individual at a time, rather than on group averages. Third, the perceiver is often (but not always) the researcher.

If the phenomenologist succeeds in observing an environment according to the precepts of the approach, valuable insights may be obtained. These precepts vary from one phenomenologist to another, but generally include an attempt to critically describe a setting as it is *in itself* after discarding all preconceptions about it (Seamon, 1982). The aims are to understand qualitatively the unique and holistic meaning of a place as revealed *by* the place, rather than to explain or predict variables *associated* with the place through the use of quantitative methods that assume causality and predictability can be established.

Because of its emphasis on the uniqueness of each setting, the phenomenology of place has produced penetrating portraits of particular locations, such as cities (Jacobs, 1961) and marketplaces (Seamon & Nordin, 1980) and particular experiences, such as topophilia (emotional attachment to places; Tuan, 1974) or existential outsideness (alienation from a place; Relph, 1976). These essays on the holistic meaning of places and experiences do not readily lend themselves to textbook condensation, but the interested reader may sample them directly in books by Buttimer and Seamon (1980), Norberg-Schulz (1980), or Relph (1981).

The phenomenological approach is not accepted by all environmental psychologists (just as the phenomenologists reject some experimental approaches). For example, phenomenology has been accused of serious inconsistencies (Livingstone & Harrison, 1983). First, it seems to advocate individualistic styles for its researchers, yet it desires agreement among those researchers. Second, it claims to be able to rid itself of preconceptions at a time when many philosophers of science believe that scientific endeavors cannot avoid presumptions. Third, it attempts to be interested in each unique setting, yet it presumes to gain knowledge about settings in general. Fourth, its advocates sometimes appear confused as to whether the object of study is human experience of a setting or the setting itself (Sixsmith, 1983). It's not surprising that advocates of phenomenology believe these critics do not understand them or the discipline of phenomenology (Seamon, 1983). It may be fair to conclude that phenomenology appeals to a different sort of researcher than experimental methods do. Even its critics do agree that phenomenology can complement the other approaches to environmental psychology in a valuable way.

Another kind of method in environmental perception research, **simulation,** is based on the necessity of presenting representations of settings rather than the settings themselves. Sometimes buildings, parks, or cities are too distant or too large to study, or are not yet built. Simulations of such settings, including models, photographs, film, video, and sketches have been used to simulate settings. A few very sophisticated laboratories have been constructed (Appleyard & Craik, 1978; McKechnie, 1977a) that allow the simulation of travel through entire regions to be carried out. (See Fig. 2–2.)

Simulations often have shortcomings, such as the exclusion of sound or the inability of the perceiver to be *in* the scene, but some simulations are surprisingly good at eliciting the same perceptual responses that the real setting does (Coeterier, 1983). Perhaps the best simulation, short of a million-dollar laboratory, is a sequence of color slides (Wood, 1972). At all times, of course, great care must be taken when using simulations to represent the setting as accurately as possible, to be aware of the limitations of each simulation, and to be cautious about generalizing the results of simulation studies to the everyday world.

► **In Sum.** Four methods of studying environmental perception have been described. Verbal reports, time-sampled reports, behavior-inference, and phenomenological methods have been used to investigate the perception of actual and simulated settings. Because each method has strengths and weaknesses, the value of employing multiple methods is stressed, here and in subsequent chapters. Multiple methods allow the researcher to more fully understand just what occurs as a person perceives a place.

Influences on Environmental Perception

Have you ever disagreed with someone about the distance to a building, the temperature in a room, or the beauty of a place? If so, you know that perceptions of the environment may differ. What accounts for these differences? Some have been attributed to variations among perceivers (their differing experiences, genders, cultures, sensory abilities, and occupations are some examples) and others have been explained by variations within or between environmental displays (city versus wilderness, visual complexity, and so on). A few studies have shown that perceptions may be explained by particular *combinations* of observer and environmental display characteristics. We should remember that no single influence, by itself, determines what an observer perceives. In this book, we are forced to discuss them one at a time, but any given perception is determined by the force of many influences, each delivering its own large or small push toward shaping the overall perception.

Personal Effects. Which characteristics of observers themselves are associated with different perceptions of the environment? Obviously, variability in perceptual ability is one factor. Impaired sight or hearing produces a restricted or fuzzy image of the surroundings. For example, veteran factory workers and rock music performers hear less well than others (Coren, Porac, & Ward, 1984).

FIGURE 2-2 The Environmental Simulation Laboratory at the University of California at Berkeley has been used to assess how different plans for the development of the region affect landscape quality in the eyes of local residents. A tiny camera at the point of the mobile apparatus at the left produces a video image on the monitor that is similar to the view a motorist driving through the region would see. *(Courtesy of Kenneth Craik.)*

One study suggests that men and women perceive distances differently (Nasar, Valencia, Omar, Chueh, & Hwang, 1985). Men judged distances to visible buildings as significantly less than distances to hidden buildings, but women did not judge the distances differently.

Another personal factor is experience with the setting. It seems that even small differences in familiarity can affect perception. For example, Edney (1972b) found that observers who had been in a room for half an hour saw it as smaller than did those who had just entered it. Nasar et al. (1985) found that buildings with which perceivers were more familiar were judged to be closer to them than were less familiar buildings.

Finally, Smith (1984) reports that individuals judge the distance to buildings they find pleasing more accurately than they judge distances to buildings they find less pleasing.

Cultural Effects. The cultural context in which individuals are raised can lead to quite different ways of seeing the world. The anthropologist Colin Turnbull (1961), for example, has described his experiences with the Bambuti pygmies of the Congo region. These people live in dense rain forest and rarely experience vistas that extend for more than 30 meters. Once Turnbull took his pygmy guide out of the forest to a broad plain where a herd of buffalo could be seen several kilometers away.

The guide asked, "What sort of insects are those?" Turnbull explained that they were plains buffalo, animals about twice as large as the rain forest buffalo with which pygmies are familiar. The guide laughed and told Turnbull not to tell such stupid stories. Turnbull drove the guide closer to the herd. As the two men approached the buffalo, the animals seemed to the pygmy to be growing in size, and he was convinced that witchcraft was at work. The pygmy's lack of experience with distance vision interfered with size constancy, the learned tendency to stabilize *perceived* size despite changes in objective distance and the size of the image on our retinas.

This is one example of what has been called the **carpentered world hypothesis,** which attributes certain differences in perception to the striking discrepancies among the perceptual environments of various societies. Urban settings, with their high frequency of rectangular objects and straight lines, produce different perceptual experiences than uncarpentered settings, simple rural places where curved, rounded lines characterize the houses and landscape (Coren, Porac, & Ward, 1984).

Within developed societies, another important cultural difference in perception occurs. When individuals receive training in a profession, they seem to acquire with it a *way of seeing* that is characteristic of the profession. Civil engineers see roads and dams where only slopes, streams, and valleys exist; architects see form, light, and color where the rest of us see walls, floors, and doors. Many studies have documented differences between the environmental appraisals of design professionals and nonprofessionals, as well as between different groups of design professionals (Hershberger, 1968; R. Kaplan, 1973a). More recent research has begun to examine the particular ways that architects' perceptions differ from those of others. Valadez (1984), for example, showed there were no differences in the perceptions of landscape architects and some other groups in the *quantitative* features of backyards (such as the number of different plants and activity areas), but the landscape architects differed significantly in their views of the *qualitative* features, such as how *defined* the landscape was. To the extent these discrepancies represent differences in the original perceptions of these professionals before the information is interpreted, and some physiological evidence suggests that it does (Payne, 1969), professional education is a key cultural difference in environmental perception.

Physical Effects. An obviously important influence on perception is the nature of the environmental display itself. For the most part, whatever our personal or cultural background, we all agree that a circle of stones containing burning embers in the center of a bare patch of ground surrounded by forest trees is a campsite rather than an apartment building; that a room with straight rows of desks, a chalkboard, and a lectern in front of the desks is a classroom rather than an office.

Nevertheless, those who study environmental perception have not always agreed on the relative importance of person-based and environment-based influences on perception. Some emphasize the considerable processing of visual information that occurs by sensory receptors and the brain, processing that involves both physiology and learning. Others point to the clear differences in the actual scenes, as noted in the examples just mentioned. Thus, one point of view is expressed in the old saying, "beauty is in the eye of the beholder," but another is expressed in the title of a presentation by a well-known environmental psychologist: "The Environment Is *Not* in the Head!" (Wohlwill, 1973). This section discusses some of the evidence that perception is largely a function of the environmental display.

Some research has been directed at how certain environmental configurations affect perception of size or distance. In a fascinating book called *Behavior and Perception in Strange Environments,* Helen Ross (1974) describes many illusions that occur in natural settings. Fog, for example, makes us believe that features of the environment are farther away and larger than they really are. The same effects occur when we view things under water, especially as the water grows murkier. The **terrestrial saucer** effect leads mountain climbers to believe that neighboring mountain peaks equal in altitude to their own are much higher than their own. It also affects the perception of roads so that, under certain conditions, slopes that are actually uphill appear to be downhill and vice versa.

Edward Sadalla and his associates have investigated similar effects in built settings. In three studies, they showed that the estimated length of a path grows as a function of the number of turns in the path (Sadalla & Magel, 1980). In further work, they showed that rectangular rooms appear larger than square rooms of equal size (Sadalla & Oxley, 1984).

Such effects in natural and built settings are not mere illusions. They could have important repercussions in the lives of those who must deal with them. The very lives of drivers and divers are at stake in the case of the fog, road, and underwater effects. The path and room size distortions may affect perceptions of crowding, status, confinement, and other psychologically important aspects of building interiors (Sadalla & Oxley, 1984).

Perceptions on city streets are also affected by physical cues. Korte and Grant (1980) found that when pedestrians are subjected to more traffic noise, their perceptual field narrows. They actually look straight ahead more, missing much information from the periphery of their paths.

▶ **In Sum.** Available evidence suggests that perceptions of qualities like length and distance are largely dependent on which physical elements are in the scene and how they are arranged. But personal factors (such as perceptual ability or finding a building pleasing), culture (such as being raised in a carpentered world), and training (for example, in architecture) also affect the very way we see the world.

Theories and Applications

Environmental perception, like the rest of environmental psychology, is too new to have fully developed theories. In fact, no theory has been developed specifically for environmental perception. Rather, certain traditional perception theories have been used as temporary guiding models in the study of environment perception. Thus, the most appropriate theoretical stance at present may be a simple model describing how personal, cultural, physical, and other factors are associated with perceptions of environments, but it is important to briefly describe some traditional theories. These traditional theories, or some combination of them, may someday yield a valuable, encompassing theory of environmental perception.

Brunswik: Probabalistic Functionalism. One influential approach to environmental perception is based on the work of Egon Brunswik (1956), whose theory may be described best by reference to his lens model. (See Fig. 2–3.) Brunswik's importance to environmental psychology derives from his view that both perceiver and environment are important:

> Both the organism and the environment will have to be seen as systems, each with properties of their own. . . . (A)s much as psychology must be concerned with the texture of the organism . . . it must also be concerned with the texture of the environment. (Brunswik, 1957, p. 5)

Brunswik maintains that the environment offers a multitude of cues; the perceiver must make sense of them to function effectively in a setting. Usually, only a small number of the cues are useful to the perceiver: Therefore, many of them are given little attention although close attention is paid to others. Some people (infants or those cast suddenly into a new setting) may be perceptually confused because they are overwhelmed with cues and have not yet learned to sort the important cues from the unimportant ones.

Ecological validity refers to the actual relations between the environment and each of the cues, weightings that would lead to effective perception of the setting if the perceiver knew them. **Cue utilization** represents the way the perceiver actually weights each cue. When perceivers weight the cues in a manner similar to the way the cues are related to the environment, the perceiver possesses an image of the setting that allows for effective perception; **achievement** will be high (that is, the perceiver's reading of the environment will closely match the actual environment).

The theory's **probabalism** refers to Brunswik's belief that no single cue is either perfectly reliable or perfectly unreliable, but rather has a certain probability of being an accurate clue about the true nature of the environment. The theory's **functionalism** comes from Brunswik's conviction that perception is an attempt to extract a *useful* image of the environment from the mass of potentially confusing cues. Brunswik views perceivers as active agents, intentionally seeking views of the environment that assist them as they make their way through the world.

After we have repeatedly sampled familiar settings as "intuitive scientists," we have few problems coping with them perceptually. Perceptual

The Setting:

The Quality to be Judged: **BEAUTY**

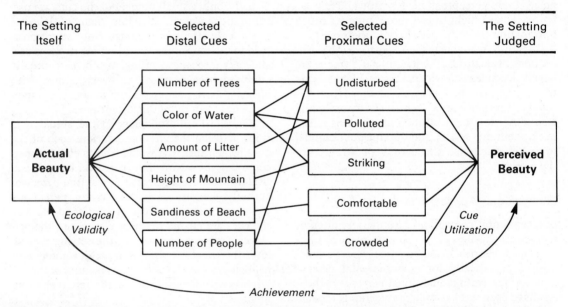

The Setting Itself	Selected Distal Cues	Selected Proximal Cues	The Setting Judged

FIGURE 2-3 Brunswik's Lens Model. Some important qualities of the setting itself, such as its beauty, are not perceived directly. Rather, Brunswik believed they are manifested in *distal cues,* objectively measureable characteristics of the setting. *Proximal cues* are the observer's subjective impressions of these distal cues. Perceived beauty is based on the observer's integration of the proximal cues. Perceived beauty will closely approximate actual beauty, (i.e., there is high *achievement*) if (a) actual beauty is really manifested in distal cues (i.e., there is high *ecological* validity), and (b) proximal cues are closely related to distal cues, and (c) proximal cues are closely related to judge beauty (i.e., observers have excellent *cue utilization*). (*Adapted from Brunswik, 1956.*)

problems primarily arise in strange settings, especially those offering patterns of cues that do not bear a resemblance to those in our familiar settings. These problems (recall Helen Ross's climbers, divers, and drivers) may lead us to draw false conclusions about the nature of the setting. These false conclusions range in seriousness from misjudging the color of a wall to misjudging a curve on the highway under foggy conditions.

The Brunswik approach guides research in environmental psychology that focuses on *which* setting cues reveal conditions that may not be directly visible. One such condition might be fear of crime in a residential neighborhood. To study the left side of the lens model (see Fig. 2–3), researchers might measure numerous observable features of a residential street to discover which of them, if any, are highly correlated with fear of crime in residents (Craik & Appleyard, 1980). In concrete terms, is the presence of a front-yard fence an indicator that the resident is afraid of crime? Brunswik would say that such a cue is neither perfectly valid (correlated 1.00 with fear of crime) nor perfectly invalid (correlated .00); it is somewhere between. The environmental psychologist's task is to discover just how strong the relation is between front-yard fences and fear of crime.

On the right side of the lens model, the Brunswik approach is to find out whether perceivers correctly or incorrectly interpret the fence cue. The perceiver can err either by overestimating or underestimating the connection between fences and residents' fear of crime. High achievement occurs when a perceiver weights a pattern of cues (right side of the lens model) the same way they are actually weighted (left side of the lens model). To be successful, for example, a burglar must accurately "read" houses: Is the resident home? Likely to have jewels? Likely to have a good alarm system?

Gibson: Affordances. James J. Gibson's approach to environmental perception (1966, 1979) differs from Brunswik's in that Gibson believed certain arrangements of cues give the perceiver *direct, immediate* perceptions of the environment. Gibson felt that the world is composed of substances (such as, clay, steel, glass) and surfaces. The arrangements of these surfaces (called layouts) provide **affordances,** or instantly detectable functions. For example, a solid horizontal surface is said to offer or *afford* support and rest. An extended solid horizontal surface affords locomotion, but a vertical solid surface affords mechanical contact and stops locomotion (Gibson, 1976).

The perception of such affordances, Gibson maintains, does not require us to interpret sensory information, construct reality, or weight cues as in Brunswik's theory. His perspective stands almost alone against a powerful tradition that assigns a much greater role to the processing of in-

formation after it is gathered. Kaplan and Kaplan (1982) maintain that some images we perceive are so similar that without cognitive processes (such as recalling past experiences or attending to neighboring contextual cues), we could not be sure what we were seeing. Nevertheless, Gibson's ideas have served to help refocus attention on the environment itself, particularly on the everyday environment, as a crucial element in perception.

The relevance of Gibson's ideas to environmental psychology and the design professions also lies in his insistence that perception is *not* composed of elemental building blocks of perception, such as color, form, and shape. Architectural education, drawing on the traditions of visual arts like painting and sculpture, emphasizes these very building blocks as the basis of design: architecture students are taught to see form and shape.

Gibson (1976) argues that this is exactly what architects should *not* be taught. Most of us, the users of architects' buildings, do not see form and shape when we see a place, we perceive affordances—what the place can *do* for us. Obviously, then, architects should be taught about the relations between surfaces and affordances. Excessive concern with form and shape occurs when architecture is seen primarily as a visual art rather than as a way to provide functional space in which people can work, live, and relax.

Berlyne: Collative Properties. Daniel Berlyne (1972, 1974) contributed important insights about environmental aesthetics. Perception and cognition are closely connected, especially so when the topic of beauty arises; Berlyne's ideas straddle the perception-cognition distinction, which is somewhat artificial anyway.

Berlyne's view is that environmental stimulation has several **collative properties,** characteristics of the stimulus that cause the perceiver to pay attention, investigate further, and compare. These collative properties include **novelty** (newness to the perceiver), **incongruity** (something out of place), **complexity** (a large variety of elements in the display), and **surprisingness** (unexpected elements).

These collative properties are presumed to influence the perceiver's aesthetic judgments and desire to explore. They do so through two psychological dimensions, **hedonic tone** (beauty or pleasure) and **uncertainty-arousal.** For simple laboratory stimuli and for two-dimensional displays such as paintings, these relations are fairly clear: images of moderate complexity, novelty, incongruity, and surprisingness are perceived as more beautiful than are images that are very high or very low on these collative properties.

The implications for environmental design *seem* clear. Several designers have suggested that buildings ought to be designed in accordance with these ideas. For example, Rapoport and Kantor (1967) argued that modern architecture should have *more* complexity because they felt most urban buildings were too simple in their lines, that is, below the optimum amount of complexity. Venturi (1966) also negatively contrasts the great regularity (low complexity) of buildings designed by the Bauhaus school of architects with the moderate incongruity and irregularity in buildings designed during the Italian Renaissance.

However, these speculations may be premature. The evidence from research in natural settings does not always support Berlyne's original ideas. That evidence does not mean the whole notion of collative properties is not valuable, but that relations between beauty and the collative properties may be different than Berlyne first thought. For example, scenes of built environments do seem to show the predicted results (moderate complexity rated highest), but landscapes do not (Wohlwill, 1976). This finding may be partly because nature scenes do not have as much complexity as do scenes of the built environment. For collative properties other than complexity, environmental perception researchers often find a straight-line relation rather than the curvilinear (inverted U-shaped) one predicted by Berlyne (Wohlwill, 1976).

Berlyne's ideas have stimulated subsequent researchers to search for properties of environmental displays that reliably lead to certain perceptions. Wohlwill (1976), for example, has suggested some revisions to the list of collative properties, changes that make Berlyne's ideas more directly suitable to environmental perception. One such idea is the notion of **fittingness,** or how well a certain element (a house) suits a certain setting (wilderness).

Berlyne's hedonic tone and uncertainty-arousal dimensions are very similar to the core concepts (pleasure and arousal) in the work of James Rus-

sell (Russell & Mehrabian, 1978; Russell & Pratt, 1980; Russell, Ward, & Pratt, 1981), whose work on the emotion-eliciting qualities of the environment is discussed in the appraisal section of the next chapter. Stephen and Rachel Kaplan's (1982) model of environmental preference also bears a resemblance to Berlyne's ideas and will be discussed in the next chapter.

► **In Sum.** The theories of Brunswik, Gibson, and Berlyne have each had major impacts on current research and applications in environmental perception. Each of them began as a traditional (nonenvironmental) theory but contained the necessary seed to be fruitful for environmental psychology: they emphasize properties of stimuli. Brunswik and Gibson in particular emphasize the importance of studying real-world stimuli. The theories have stimulated considerable pure research into the nature of environmental perception. They have also been extended into the practical domains of city planning, park planning, and architecture.

SPATIAL COGNITION

Have a little daydream. Transport yourself back to your all-time favorite place, whether it is a city, town, farm, wilderness, neighborhood, school, house, street, building, beach, or room. Conjure the place up in as much colorful detail as you can and spend a few minutes enjoying it. Can you recall how to find your way around it? What important items were there and where they were placed? The size of the setting and where it is located relative to other nearby places? This is spatial cognition—in part.

Distinctions and Definitions

Spatial cognition concerns the way we acquire, organize, store, and recall information about locations, distances, and arrangements in the physical environment. It involves spatial problem solving, navigation, trying to make sense of a chaotic street system, being lost (and found), selecting and rejecting wayfinding information that may help or mislead, and interacting with the everyday three-dimensional environment. It includes pictorial and semantic images in our heads and on signs. If you look around, evidence of cognitive mapping is in advertisements, subway maps, magazines, and in every person's memory and thinking (Downs & Stea, 1977). (See Figure 2–4.) We will also take time in this section to briefly discuss how the physical environment can affect nonspatial cognitions.

A cardinal principal of environmental cognition is that we do not process information about the environment the way cameras or computers do. Our processing, from a mechanical point of view, is full of errors. Our cognitions also differ from one person to the next. Yet, as a species, we are remarkably successful. These deviations (from objective reality and from one another), together with our success, suggest that we must entertain two ideas: first, that spatial cognition is determined in part by differences in our individual backgrounds and, second, that our imperfect im-

ages are quite useful to us. They help us to solve spatial problems, such as how to infer the way from one place to another when we have never directly traversed the route and where to find needed resources of all kinds, from the closest all-night grocery store to the best place to find truffles. They also simplify and facilitate communication. We absorb into these images the distinctive monuments, symbols, and arrangements of streets, and we can conjure them up in order to recognize and enjoy places we have known.

Understanding of the peculiar ways that humans think about their environments may be used to design better settings. The central concept in this applied area is **legibility,** or the ease with which a setting may be recognized and organized by people. The concept was established by Kevin Lynch (1960) in his classic book *The Im-*

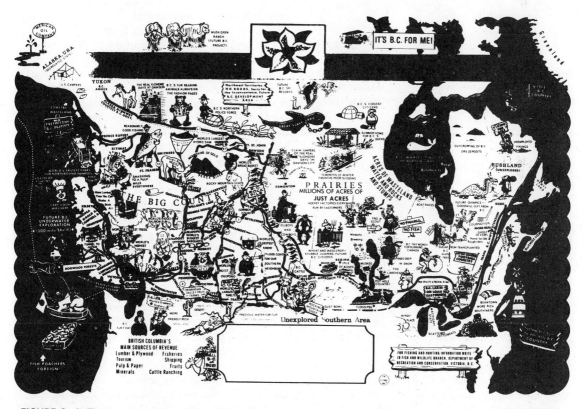

FIGURE 2–4 This humorous depiction of Canada from the point of view of a British Columbian contains a grain of truth: our cognitive maps differ from cartographic maps and tend to emphasize aspects of geography that are personally meaningful. *(Courtesy of G.H. Wood Co.)*

FIGURE 2-5 Kevin Lynch's important work on the cognitive elements of cities has been very influential both in urban planning and in research on environmental cognition. *(Courtesy of Anne Lynch.)*

age of the City. (See Fig. 2-5.) Some cities, for example, Boston, are much more legible than others, such as Jersey City or Los Angeles.

What makes a city legible? Lynch offered five elements of city images that contribute strongly to legibility (you might find it useful to think of examples of each element in your hometown):

1. **Paths.** The routes along which people travel. Typically, paths are roads, walkways, and public transit routes.
2. **Edges.** Nontraveled lines, such as cliffs or escarpments or the shores of rivers, lakes, or oceans.
3. **Districts.** Moderate-sized areas that city residents identify as having a particular character.
4. **Nodes.** Well-known points that people travel to and from, often at the junctures of important paths, such as key intersections, transit terminals, and popular plazas or squares.

5. **Landmarks.** Easily viewed elements, either on a grand scale (the tallest building in town) or on a smaller scale (a statue or unique storefront).

These five elements were suggested by Lynch speculatively, without much formal research. Their validity, however, has been confirmed by more experimental methods (Aragones & Arredondo, 1985; Magana, 1978). In these studies, the elements in maps drawn by everyday people are subjected to sophisticated statistical techniques called cluster analysis. Five distinct clusters of map elements emerge; these are very similar to the elements Lynch hypothesized. (See Fig. 2-6.)

The five elements are important components of **cognitive maps,** the stored images of the environments we know, not only at the urban scale, but up to the international scale and down to the room scale. The term cognitive map is so intuitively attractive that it is easy to oversimplify both its meaning and its role in our daily activities (Downs, 1981; Kaplan & Kaplan, 1982). It is not, after all, a folded piece of paper in the cranium; no miniature navigator sits inside our heads poring over intricacies of the maps by the light of our ideas. In fact, some cognitive psychologists who favor the information-processing approach doubt that spatial knowledge is represented at all like a map in the head (Chase & Chi, 1981). They feel that maps contain far too much information to be conjured up all at once. Instead, they believe we retrieve small subparts of the map one at a time when we draw maps or give directions.

Nevertheless, it is clear that we do possess large stores of information—partly pictorial, partly verbal—about the paths, edges, nodes, districts, and landmarks of the places we know. Spatial cognition research is concerned with memory for, orientation in, and knowledge about, physical settings. We will discuss how and why some features of the environment are remembered while others are forgotten, the processes of getting lost and getting found, and how we organize (or misorganize) the physical features of our homes, cities, countries, and even the world as a whole.

▶ **In Sum.** We do not acquire, store, and recall information about locations, distances, and arrangements mechanically. Yet our ways of doing so are effective and nonrandom. The study of cognitive maps reveals some human strategies for

FIGURE 2-6 An aerial view of the city of Boston. Can you pick out some edges, nodes, landmarks, paths, and districts?

group discussion

processing environmental information. Legible places are easier to comprehend: they have clear paths and distinct edges, districts, nodes, and landmarks.

Research Methods

Environmental cognition, like environmental perception, must be studied indirectly. The goal is to extract an accurate representation of the individual's spatial knowledge. The commonest ways of approaching this problem have been to ask individuals to sketch a map, construct a scale model, or estimate distances between pairs of places. Other methods are available (Golledge, 1976) but have not been used frequently. Perhaps the least-used method in contrast to its great potential is naturalistic observation, although this is changing (Hart, 1979).

We must remember, however, that none of these methods yields the individual's spatial knowledge itself. For example, the sketched map is not the cognitive map. It is a *version* of what is stored in the head that is limited in its accuracy by such factors as the individual's drawing ability, stage of development, memory, and problems with scale translation.

Evidence on the accuracy of these methods is mixed (Evans, 1980). Sometimes the methods are reliable (yield similar information from one occasion to the next or from one method to the next) and sometimes they aren't (Magana, Evans, & Romney, 1981). Evans believes that validity (whether the methods yield data that truly represent an individual's cognitive map) is a problem with most methods of studying spatial cognition. In one positive study, Holahan and Dobrowolny (1978) found that sketched maps did at least represent the actual movements of individuals around a setting. Thus, if maps depicting a person's activity patterns reflect a person's cognitive map, then sketched maps would seem to be reasonably accurate versions of cognitive maps. Methods that ask research participants for inter-place distance judgments, which are then analyzed with a sophisticated statistical procedure called multidimensional scaling, may be more accurate than the familiar sketch maps (Sherman, Croxton, & Giovanatto, 1979). Others (Cadwallader, 1979) believe that *any* translation from cognitive distance to physical distance will be extremely difficult.

▶ **In Sum.** Spatial cognition measurement techniques include sketch maps, model construction or manipulation, distance estimation, and naturalistic observation. Evidence for their usefulness is mixed. Once again the best solution to the problem of imperfect methods is either to employ multiple methods, so as to gain complementary perspectives on the truth, or at least to carefully select the most appropriate method for the specific investigation we wish to undertake (Downs & Siegel, 1981). The results of the hundreds of empirical studies reported so far cannot be taken as conclusive. Yet there are patterns of findings among them that are strong enough to warrant our tentative acceptance. Let's begin with a survey of factors that influence knowledge of everyday spatial contexts.

Influences on Spatial Cognition

In this section we examine some factors that seem to affect the speed of acquiring information about the environment, the accuracy of this information, and the way individuals organize the information. As Gary Moore (1979) notes, the factors may be divided into those primarily located in the person, such as age, sex, and familiarity with the setting, and those located in the physical environment, such as a town's street arrangement (e.g., like a grid or like a plate of spaghetti).

Even shared environments are not thought of in the same way by their inhabitants. Individual differences are importantly related to this variability in environmental cognition (Bryant, 1984a). The questions are *which* individual differences affect our thinking about our everyday settings, and *how* do they affect it?

The four factors to be discussed in some detail include one's stage of life, experience with the place, sex, and cognitive errors; these factors have received the most attention from researchers.

Spatial cognition may also be affected by visual or spatial abilities and personality (Bryant, 1984b), intelligence (Webley, 1981), culture (Nasar, 1984a,b), and education (Karan, Bladen, & Singh, 1980). Let's start with developmental changes.

Stage of Life. As a toddler, you were not allowed out of the house alone. A few years later, the yard or the block was the limit. Then you got a bike—and the whole neighborhood was yours. As a teen, your horizon may have been the whole community. These expansions in a child's permissible roaming are accompanied by changes in general cognitive development. Together, they mean that spatial cognition changes in important ways as children grow up (Hart & Moore, 1973).

These changes may be described in terms of Jean Piaget's influential theory of cognitive development. Spatial cognition is viewed in this theory as one aspect of the child's more general cognitive unfolding. Early on, children are **egocentric**—they believe they are the center of the world. They perceive environments in terms of how close something in it is to them, whether they can touch it or not, and whether it is part of them or not. Infants must learn, for example, that those five small pink objects flying around near them are their own toes rather than a friendly, tasty, five-headed being of independent means.

Roughly at the time of entering school, children enter a stage that allows them to adopt perspectives from viewpoints other than their own; this is sometimes called the **projective** stage. In terms of spatial cognition, children are now able to think of settings from various physical vantage points. Children at this stage are able—theoretically—to orient themselves using prominent landmarks. For example, they should be able to find their way home from school.

Later, at around eleven years of age, most children are able to think in more **abstract** terms. The reflection of this change in spatial cognition is an ability to use abstract concepts like sets of Euclidean coordinates (grid systems such as latitude and longitude) or directions such as north, south, east, and west (Hart & Moore, 1973).

In terms of what information children use to orient themselves in space and in terms of the accuracy and complexity of their spatial cognition, research generally supports the Piagetan model (Evans, 1980). However, some workers

(Spencer & Darvizeh, 1981) believe that researchers who have limited their studies to laboratory techniques have underestimated the spatial cognitive abilities of children.

For example, they cite studies showing that relatively young children can use aerial maps effectively. Six-year-olds can make spatial judgments that appear to require perspective taking or Euclidean abilities (Biel, 1982). In familiar settings, even children as young as three and a half have shown Euclidean knowledge (Conning & Byrne, 1984), an accomplishment that Piagetans might not expect for almost another decade of life! (See Fig. 2-7.) Possibly, cognitive abilities of children have been underestimated because their spatial abilities outstrip their verbal abilities: they are able to use a map or to find their way home but they are not yet able to explain how they accomplished the feat (Neisser, 1976).

What about the other end of the developmental spectrum? Some research indicates a decline in spatial ability in old age (Ohta & Kirisic, 1983; Pearce, 1981b), but other research does not (McCormack, 1982). No conclusions can yet be stated firmly, but two likely outcomes are that (1) with age, some spatial abilities decline, others do not, and some may even improve, and (2) older individuals rely on different spatial cues than younger individuals.

These changes may be due to both behavioral and physiological changes, such as reduced mobility and sensory ability. For example, Mc-

Cormack's study found no age-related performance decline in a task that required no movement through a real setting—participants were asked to recall the spatial location of typed words on cards. In contrast, Pearce's study found that after older and younger travelers drove a 340-kilometer route along the coast in Australia, the older travelers more frequently mislabeled landmarks. Other studies have shown that older people have poorer recognition for rooms in familiar buildings, but they probably had explored the buildings less thoroughly than more mobile younger people.

Older people in Pearce's study, however, remembered *more* districts and reported *more* details than did younger travelers. Research suggests that, for their memory of the environment, older people rely more on features that are more meaningful to them, such as buildings that are used more often or more easily, are historical (Evans, Smith, & Pezdek, 1982; Porteous, 1977), are unique in architectural style (Evans, Brennan, Skorpanich, & Held, 1984), or incorporate landscape elements that make them feel good (Pearce, 1981).

Familiarity or Experience. Clearly, as we spend time in a setting our spatial cognitions about it change. The most obvious change is that our knowledge about it grows. In a study of new students at a university, for example, sketch maps of the campus drawn six months apart showed sig-

FIGURE 2-7 Children gradually learn to orient themselves in their home, neighborhood, and community.

nificant increases not only in the amount of information, but in the differentiation and the integration of that information (Schouela, Steinberg, Leveton, & Wapner, 1980). (See Fig. 2–8.) Students with at least one year's experience at another campus depicted their campus with greater configurational accuracy than students with less experience (Kirisic, Allen, & Siegel, 1984). This accuracy, to be precise, may be a superiority in *relative* location of campus locations rather than a superiority in the *absolute* location of places.

When we are aware that it is important to learn the spatial layout of a place, we can do so very quickly (Garling, Book, Lindberg, & Nilsson, 1981) and more quickly than when we are not instructed to pay attention to the environment (Cohen, Weatherford, Lomenick, & Koeller, 1979).

FIGURE 2–8 Seymour Wapner has emphasized the holistic transactional nature of person-environment systems and has shown how disturbances in one part of a system cause changes in other parts of the system. *(Courtesy of Seymour Wapner.)*

In buildings (Garling, Lindberg, & Mantyla, 1983) and in the countryside (Pearce, 1981b), increased familiarity gives us better orientation, which aids us in learning new information about a place.

Several variables that represent experiential differences are also related to spatial cognition. For example, drivers may acquire different and perhaps better *organized* environmental information than their passengers even though they do not necessarily acquire *more* information (Carr & Schissler, 1969; Pearce, 1981b). Studies showing social class, urban-rural, and husband-wife differences in the form and content of spatial knowledge (Orleans, 1973; Windley & Vandeventer, 1982) presumably are demonstrating that these variables are indicators of how different individuals usually move through a place. Poorer citizens, for example, have quite different activity patterns in most cities than wealthier citizens; this leads them to know some places in the city better and other places less well (Karan, Bladen, & Singh, 1980).

One controversy in the familiarity literature arises over which features of a new environment are learned first. Some hypothesize that we learn landmarks first, before elaborating paths (Hart & Moore, 1973; Siegel & White, 1975). Others have reached the conclusion that we learn paths and districts first, then we use landmarks for orientation (Appleyard, 1976; Lynch, 1960).

The available evidence supports both positions (Evans, Marrero, & Butler, 1981; Garling et al., 1981). After a careful review, Gary Evans (1980) concluded that both may be true, depending on the physical character of the setting in question. For example, in one study, supporting the idea that paths are learned before landmarks, the authors note that participants were almost forced to learn the paths first because the distance between landmarks was so great (Garling et al., 1981). In other places, where many salient landmarks are available, they may be learned first.

Sex. Some studies find differences between the sexes in the acquisition, accuracy, or organization of spatial information, but these differences are not striking. When there is a difference, it is likely to favor men. For example, in a Swedish study, men and women either walked or were driven through an unfamiliar residential neighborhood (Garling et al., 1981). When the participants were driven, men learned about the setting slightly faster than women, but when they walked through the setting, men and women learned equally quickly. In another study, men were more accurate than women only in locating those places that were difficult to locate (Kirisic, Allen, & Siegel, 1984).

More often, men and women simply have *different* spatial cognitions. Men's sketch maps may include more territory (Windley & Vandeventer, 1982) or be more gridlike, but women's maps tend to be more home-centered (Orleans & Schmidt, 1972).

These sex differences are widely regarded as the products of different experiences that males and females are likely to have, rather than to basic differences in cognitive abilities or tendencies (Evans, 1980), and some direct evidence for this has been reported (Webley, 1981).

Cognitive Errors.
Our cognitive maps do not match cartographic maps for a variety of reasons, as we have seen. Apart from these reasons, however, we frequently err in two predictable ways, which we may call **Euclidean bias** and **superordinate scale bias.**

In the first of these biases, we think of the world as more Euclidean or gridlike than it really is. On sketch maps, many individuals draw converging streets as parallel, intersections that do not form right angles as if they did, and streets with gentle curves as straight lines (Byrne, 1979; Evans, 1980).

To illustrate the second bias, answer the following three questions for yourself. Which is farther north, Toronto or Minneapolis? Which is farther west, Athens or Warsaw? Which is farther east, Reno or San Diego? In thinking about locations that we are not sure about, we rely on superordinate scales, that is, larger categories of which the place in question is a member. Toronto is in Canada; Canada is north of the United States, where Minneapolis is located: therefore, Toronto must be north of Minneapolis. Athens is in Greece, which has been part of the Western alliance, and Warsaw, in Poland, is part of the Eastern bloc: Athens must be west of Warsaw. Reno, being a city in Nevada, which is a state east of California, where San Diego is located, must be east of San Diego. Each of these lines of reasoning, of course, is incorrect. Using larger categories

to reason about the location of places within them sometimes leads to errors in spatial cognition.

► **In Sum.** Spatial cognition—the way we acquire, process, store, and recall information about everyday settings—is affected by our stage of life, familiarity, or experience with the setting, and certain cognitive biases. The spatial cognition of children generally follows a sequence moving from egocentric to projective to abstract, although they may move through these stages faster than laboratory studies suggest. The spatial cognition of old people differs from those of young adults. Where their experience is limited by lowered mobility or sensory abilities, old people may perform less well. Their memories of the environment are more personalized and are, in some respects, better than those of young adults.

Experience in a setting gives you a fuller and better organized cognitive image of it. Both landmarks and paths facilitate the growth of place knowledge. Where one of these elements is more common than the other, examples of it will be learned first. Male-female differences in spatial cognition exist but may largely reflect the different travel experiences of men and women.

Two common cognitive biases are to envision places as more gridlike or Euclidean than they really are and to employ larger geographical entities wrongly in placing smaller ones. But spatial cognition is also affected by characteristics of the place one is cognizing about; we turn now to those factors.

Physical Effects.
It is strange that, for a real-world-oriented discipline like environmental psychology, physical features that affect spatial cognition have been somewhat neglected (Moore, 1979; Wohlwill, 1976). The situation has improved recently, but much more remains to be discovered about how the environment affects thinking about the environment (Evans, Skorpanich, Garling, Bryant, & Bresolin, 1984).

In the beginning, Kevin Lynch (1960) and Donald Appleyard (1976) hypothesized that regular, clear paths and highly visible landmarks would improve cognition of cities. Research has supported this contention (Tzamir, 1975), and extended it. Canter and Tagg (1975), for example, showed that distance judgments were more accurate in cities with more regular traffic patterns. In addition, the presence of strongly organizing features in cities such as rivers, roads, and railroads improved cognition.

We might expect that highly salient (prominent, conspicuous) features of a cityscape would further enhance our processing of information about it. Holahan and Sorenson (1985) tested this idea by comparing speed of processing and number of errors in the reading of maps that varied both in their degree of organization and in the degree of salience of certain features. They found, as Lynch and Appleyard would predict, that organization improved speed and reduced errors. But they also found that salience *without* organization significantly *harmed* spatial cognition. (See Fig. 2–9.) Apparently, salient features can enhance the cognition of settings that are clearly organized but can confuse us when their salience is not accompanied by clear organization.

So far we have focused on features of cities that affect spatial cognition. What might make a building stand out or be remembered better? Donald Appleyard (1976) pioneered this work in Ciudad Guyana, a Venezuelan city that was planned from the ground up. He assessed a variety of relatively objective characteristics of buildings in Ciudad Guayana and noted the frequency with which buildings were recalled by residents. The better-recalled buildings were tall, freestanding, distinctive in shape, easily visible, frequently used, and had much human movement around them.

Gary Evans and his colleagues found that each of these characteristics also enhanced resident recall of buildings in Orange, California (Evans, Smith, & Pezdek, 1982). (See Fig. 2–10.) A few characteristics were found to enhance recall only in Ciudad Guyana (such as singularity of the building's use) or only in Orange (such as building quality). This suggests, pending further research, that certain building characteristics make a stronger impact on individuals regardless of culture, but others make an impact in one culture but not others.

The concept **environmental cognition** may be turned around, in the sense that we may examine how the physical environment affects cognition. In an important early article, Joachim Wohlwill (1966) introduced the concept of an **optimal level of stimulation** to environmental psychology from the adaptation-level theory of Harry Helson (1964). The idea is that for any given activity, we may be either over- or understimulated, leading to a decrease in satisfaction. We are adapted to a certain level of stimulation, which may be relatively high or low depending on our circumstances. As the level of stimulation moves

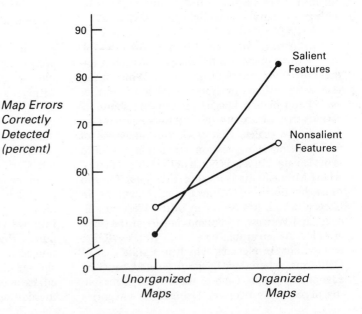

FIGURE 2–9 Accurate map reading depends on how well the map is organized and how salient, visible, or obvious features of the place are rendered on the map. *(Holahan, C. J., & Sorenson, P. F. The role of figural organization in city imageability: An information processing analysis.* Journal of Environmental Psychology, *1985, 5, 279–286. Reprinted by permission of Academic Press, Inc.)*

FIGURE 2–10 Gary Evans has been in the forefront of research in urban cognition and environmental stress. *(Courtesy of Gary Evans.)*

Same as Selye's stress model + optimal performance

slightly to moderately away from this adaptation level, pleasure increases: the change is stimulating, if you'll pardon the choice of words. But as the level of stimulation changes further in the same direction, it becomes too much or too little stimulation to enjoy.

When a setting is too novel, complex, or fast moving we find it overstimulating or stressful; not only our pleasure, but also our performance may suffer. The same outcome may occur when we find a setting understimulating: too well-known, simple, or slow moving. The cognitive outcomes of low-level stimulation have been studied experimentally by Peter Suedfeld and others. In one study, volunteers spent twenty-four hours in a dark and silent chamber (Suedfeld, Landon, & Ballard, 1983). Control group volunteers were confined to a small room, but were allowed stimulation (a phone and any activity they chose except leaving the room).

Earlier research had shown that drastic stimulus reduction can improve performance on simple cognitive tasks. Suedfeld et al. wanted to know its effects on complex and difficult tasks and selected tasks that varied on complexity and difficulty. The restricted stimulation group performed worse than the control group on complex tasks but not on difficult tasks. However, these results may depend on just what the task is. In another study, with a different kind of task, the performance of low-stimulation participants suffered with increases in both task complexity and task difficulty (Kalish, Landon, Rank, & Suedfeld, 1983). In this study, participants were asked to repeat sentences verbatim after they heard them. Difficulty was varied by increasing the number of words modifying each noun in the sentence. Complexity was varied by increasing the number of embedded clauses in the sentence to be remembered.

► **In Sum.** Environmental cognition of urban forms is improved by clear paths and visible landmarks. Some evidence suggests that visibility without organization, however, may detract from effective environmental cognition. At the architectural level, buildings that are tall, freestanding, distinctively shaped, and used often are better recalled than others. At a more personal level, thinking in general is affected by the level of stimulation we receive from the environment in comparison to the level of stimulation to which we are accustomed. But these conclusions are based on few studies; the effects of the physical environment on spatial cognition and other forms of cognition need more research.

Theories and Applications

How can all this knowledge about how we comprehend everyday settings be integrated? Clearly, information flows from the physical environment to a cognitive apparatus that must ultimately be represented in the brain. It's fortunate that the theoretical approaches to the puzzle of spatial cognition to be discussed next complement one another by originating with physical, cognitive, or physiological structures. Even better, though we have a long way to go, preliminary findings indicate the direction toward unification of these approaches.

FIGURE 2-11 One of the most legible buildings in Victoria, British Columbia.

Legibility: A Physical Perspective. The seminal work of Kevin Lynch (1959, 1960) and Donald Appleyard (1976) has been extremely influential in urban planning and environmental psychology. The concept of legibility (the ease with which a place may be cognitively organized, understood, or "read" by someone) and its relations to paths, landmarks, edges, nodes, and districts have provided the basic infrastructure for hundreds of studies. The role of information processing in the head is not ignored in this approach (as we shall see at the end of this section), but the theory does begin with and emphasize the physical arrangement of space. (See Fig. 2-11.)

The principal elements of this physical perspective have already been described. The thrust of the theory is to predict that places high in legibility are easy to comprehend and use. Lynch's ideas have been studied and applied at scales ranging from entire cities to individual buildings.

Here is a sampling of recommendations and findings.

1. *City planning.* A few of the many possible recommendations for creating more legible cityscapes based on spatial cognition research are provided by Evans, Smith, and Pezdek (1982). First, place landmarks at major decision points in the road system. Second, keep these landmarks distinctive by maximizing their visibility; this can be accomplished by making them tall, separate from neighboring buildings, unique in architectural style, and into enclosures for activities that result in much public use of the building. Third, primary roads should coincide with the functional boundaries of districts to reinforce edges. Fourth, preserve buildings that might serve as good landmarks when a district undergoes extensive redevelopment. Fifth, construct landmarks in overly homogeneous districts.

2. *You-are-here maps.* Many places, such as large buildings, campuses, and shopping centers, are difficult to find our way around in. Some of them have maps on pedestals or walls near the entrance, showing the layout of the building, complete with a little arrow and the saying "You are here." These maps are an attempt to make the building more legible. In a way, they are admissions that the building is insufficiently legible on its own.

There are good and bad you-are-here maps; some succeed in improving the building's legibility, others may be worse than no map at all. Martin Levine (1982) has summarized what it takes for such a map to be effective: structure matching and orientation. (See Fig. 2–12.) **Structure matching** means the map should usefully reflect the setting it represents. Structure matching is improved when the map contains labels that resemble actual labels in the setting, the map is placed asymmetrically along the path in which it is placed, so that its viewers can easily see the relative location of the map within the setting, and the you-are-here symbol on the map indicates both the map and an arrow pointing to exactly where the viewer is in relation to the map.

Orientation is improved when the map is aligned the same way as the setting (east is east and west is west) and has **forward-up equivalence** (the top of the map represents straight ahead in the actual setting). In laboratory and field tests, these two orientation principles have been shown to significantly improve wayfinding in buildings (Levine, Marchon, & Hanley, 1984).

3. *Color coding and numbering.* Buildings may also be made more legible through the use of color-coded paths and carefully researched num-

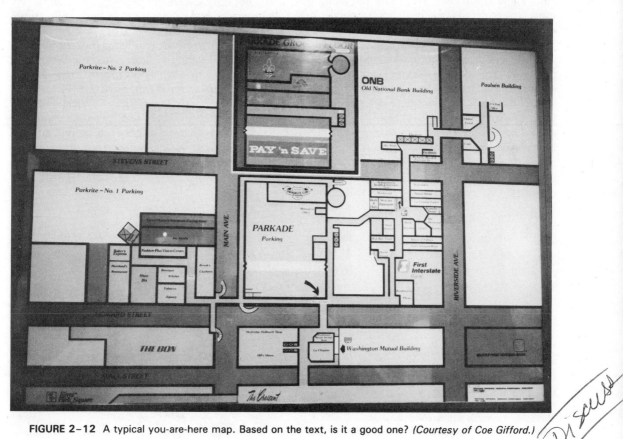

FIGURE 2–12 A typical you-are-here map. Based on the text, is it a good one? *(Courtesy of Coe Gifford.)*

bering systems. Gary Evans and his co-workers found that painting the floors of a campus building different colors reduced wayfinding errors and improved comprehension of the building by undergraduates (Evans, Fellows, Zorn, & Doty, 1980). In a hospital, researchers showed that a minor detail such as how the floors below ground are numbered can seriously affect how many patients and visitors get lost on their way to an appointment (Carpman, Grant, & Simmons, 1983–1984).

4. *Transit maps.* At the urban scale, legibility principles have been used to design bus and subway maps that improve comprehension of transit routes. The best maps do not represent transit routes cartographically, but in a simplified schematic manner that matches your experience as you move from point to point in a journey (Bartram, 1980). Maps using color coding to enhance legibility of routes give transit riders greater accuracy and confidence, but those including off-route street details result in less accuracy and more frustration (Garland, Haynes, & Grubb, 1979).

These efforts have not completely solved the problem of subway orientation. Even experienced subway riders, when asked to take a trip from A to B, chose nonoptimal routes more than half the time (Bronzaft, Dobrow, & O'Hanlon, 1976). The riders had difficulty with subway maps and signs; they often responded by selecting a *familiar* route

rather than the *optimal* route to reach their destination.

Intellectual Growth and Planning: Two Cognitive Perspectives. The legibility approach originally emphasized the role of the environment in spatial cognition; these two perspectives originally emphasized the role of cognition in environmental cognition.

The first of these perspectives speaks to the way individuals develop the capacity to comprehend space. Derived from Piagetan theory, this approach includes the egocentric, place-oriented, and abstract-coordinates stages that children are presumed to follow. This idea was described earlier in conjunction with research on children's comprehension of space.

Gary Moore (1979) has provided an extension of these ideas that serves to increase the role of the environment within this approach. (See Fig. 2–13.) He believes that in each stage the individual not only knows different things about the environment but *organizes* that knowledge differently. He also suggests there are conceptual parallels between the childhood progression from stage to stage and the short-term progression that adults move through as they learn a new setting.

As a **transactional-constructivist** (Pick, 1976), Moore asserts that we cannot understand how spatial cognition works until we understand the transactions that occur between individuals and their settings. He also believes we actively con-

FIGURE 2–13 Gary Moore has concentrated on how environmental cognitions develop and on ways to integrate psychological research with architectural design. *(Courtesy of Gary Moore.)*

struct the world from data we have gleaned about it (as opposed to those who believe the world reveals itself to us as-it-is or already constructed). Others have begun to develop formal models that simulate the process by which we make our way through, for example, a new neighborhood (Golledge, Smith, Pellegrino, Doherty, & Marshall, 1985).

What does this mean in practice? Many important consequences for the spatial cognition of both children and adults are implied. One relatively simple demonstration of constructivism in children is provided by Pick (1976). He reports studies in which children started at a certain home base *X* and were taught how to get from *X* to three other places, *A*, *B*, and *C*. The children were not taught how to get from *A* to *B*, *B* to *C*, or *A* to *C*, yet they were able to explain the spatial relations between these places. To Pick, because the children had no direct experience with these relations, they must have mentally constructed them.

Another practical application concerns getting lost. Ed Cornell has studied lost children and hunters in Canada. Describing the case of a lost three-year-old boy, Cornell shows, by reconstructing the path taken by a lost person, that their wanderings are not random (Cornell & Heth, 1984). Depending on age, experience, and the setting, the likely paths taken by people who get lost may be predicted with fair success. (See Fig. 2–14.)

The standard procedures used by police and other official searchers sometimes employ strategies, such as following a strict grid pattern, that do not take these most likely paths into account. Knowledge of a child's developmental stage and the terrain may lead to more efficient search strategies. For example, lost children under six are more often found in open spaces, but lost children in the six- to twelve-year-old range often seek enclosures or refuges when they get lost.

The second cognitive perspective involves the role of **planfulness** in environmental cognition (Garling, Book, & Lindberg, 1984; Russell & Ward, 1982). Like the constructivists, these theorists observe that we are active agents in our transactions with settings. We develop **action plans** to guide our behavior. Travel plans, one kind of action plan, partly determine what spatial information is acquired, how it is organized, and what inferences (or constructions) about settings are

drawn by a person. (See Fig. 2–15.) Even short local trips of 20 minutes require as many as fifty wayfinding decisions: travel planning and execution are considerable cognitive tasks (Passini, 1984).

Such plans are characteristic of us all, but an interesting application based on planfulness has been proposed by Smith and Patterson (1980). They describe the cognitive maps of criminals and victims and propose that law enforcement might be more efficient if cognitive mapping techniques were used to identify "fear zones" in cities. They also discuss cases of crime prevention and crime solution that involved police constructing cognitive map profiles of suspects based on their apparent plans and actual patterns of crime sites. Related studies have shown that our cognitive maps of crime locations may be distorted. For example, suburbanites may incorrectly locate high levels of crime in the downtown area of cities (Pyle, 1980).

One notable theoretical problem has not yet been mentioned. The issue is whether spatial knowledge in humans is stored as **propositions** or as **analogies.** Simply put, the propositional approach hypothesizes that our knowledge of everyday space is stored in the brain as words; the analogical approach hypothesizes that the knowledge is stored as pictorial images. The propositional approach assumes information is stored in abstract networks of meaning, or schemata (Neisser, 1976). The analogical approach assumes it is stored as a model or image of the real world (Kosslyn, 1975). As often happens in psychology, the resolution of the issue may be that both forms of information storage occur (Evans, 1980). In describing the physiologists' view of environmental cognition, this topic will arise again.

The Hippocampus: A Physiological Perspective. Rarely have connections between environmental psychology and the neurosciences been made, although presumably all behavior (including environmentally relevant behavior) is somehow represented in brain physiology. Stephen Kaplan (1976) is one environmental psychologist who has attempted to foresee the shape of relations between spatial cognition and neural networks.

But the most ambitious attempt to link spatial cognition and the brain has been that of John

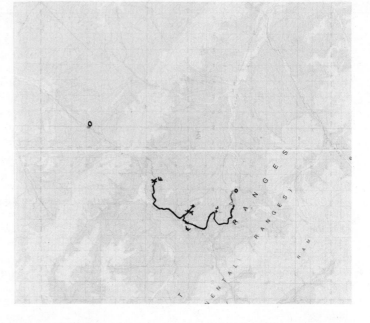

FIGURE 2–14 Two hunters who had been lost in the Rocky Mountains independently made these tracings depicting their wandering over a two-day period. Despite their different understandings of the map's scale, the two hunters seem to have cognitive maps of their experience that are very similar in shape and direction. *(Courtesy of Edward Cornell.)*

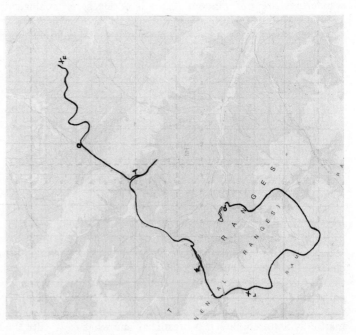

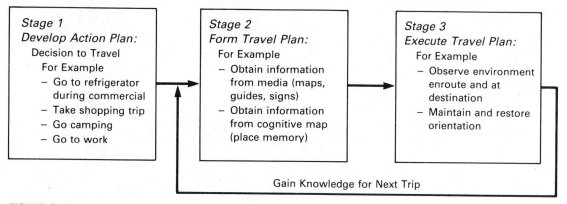

FIGURE 2–15 An information-processing model of travel and orientation. *(Based on Garling, Book, & Lindberg, 1984.)*

O'Keefe and Lynn Nadel. Working originally from studies on rats, O'Keefe and Nadel (1974, 1978) proposed that the hippocampus, a seahorse-shaped part of the limbic system in the central core of the brain, is the home of the cognitive map. (See Fig. 2–16.)

The idea that animal behavior is guided by maps was introduced to psychology long ago by Edward Tolman (1932, 1948) but not in such specific physiological detail. O'Keefe and Nadel's basic and very controversial idea is that some neurons in the hippocampus are specifically coded for place; that networks of such neurons form a framework that represents, in a three-dimensional Euclidean framework, the settings known to the individual; that in humans the portion of the hippocampus in the left hemisphere houses a semantic or word-based map and the portion in the right hemisphere houses a spatial or pictorial map.

O'Keefe and Nadel's theory also postulates the existence of two systems of spatial cognition. The **taxon** system guides the routes you take, using **guidance hypotheses** and **orientation hypotheses.** Guidance hypotheses specify objects or cues in the setting that should be approached or kept at a certain distance. Orientation hypotheses specify how this is to be accomplished behaviorally, such as "turn right 90 degrees."

The **locale system,** as its name suggests, refers to places. **Place hypotheses** are constructions by the brain that organize space knowledge important to the individual. Typical place hypotheses

might be: "this is a dangerous place" or "that place usually supplies water."

O'Keefe and Nadel's own work is primarily with freely moving rats whose brains are monitored as they explore their settings. However, their book renews evidence from human neuropsychology that appears to support their ideas. The potential applications of O'Keefe and Nadel's theory to humans are interesting. They speculate, for example, that language developed primarily as a way for us to express our place knowledge to others. They see connections between the hippocampal model of the cognitive map and the problems Korsakoff's syndrome patients experience (a pattern of cognitive deficits, including amnesia, brought on by chronic alcohol abuse).

The hippocampus is not the only brain location related to cognitive mapping. Individuals with damage to the parietal region of the cortex lose the ability to draw maps of familiar places and seem to lose their knowledge of how places they know are arranged in geographic space (De Renzi, 1982). Another brain-based (but not necessarily hippocampus-based) theory is Lieblich and Arbib's (1982) **world graph,** a representation of relations among situations encountered by the individual. Each situation is said to be encoded in a neural node, but each place may be encoded in several neural nodes. The world-graph model appears to explain certain classic findings in animal exploration research and, if extended to humans, would presumably assist in the understanding of cognitive maps.

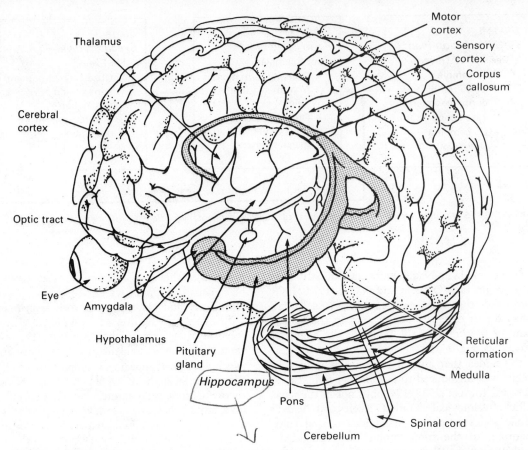

FIGURE 2–16 According to O'Keefe and Nadel, 1978, the hippocampus is the site of cognitive mapping.

SUMMARY

Environmental cognition is a human information process that does not resemble mechanical information processing but is generally effective (although certain biases do often lead to some errors). The elements of cognitive maps are studied by sketch maps, model manipulations, distance estimations, and natural observation. Cognitive maps are affected by our stage of life and experience with the setting. Legible cities and buildings are easier to comprehend. Reversing the sense of the term environmental cognition, some environ-

mental psychologists have found that different levels of stimulation affect how well we think and perform everyday tasks. Three theories of environmental cognition begin from different points of departure: the setting itself, cognitive development, and brain physiology. Obviously, these need not be competing theories, but ideas that may be integrated into a complete model of spatial cognition. Someday the physiological structures associated with spatial cognition will be fully connected with the cognitive and physical theories; the approaches we have discussed bring us closer than ever before to that eventual union of ideas.

SUGGESTED SUPPLEMENTARY READINGS

Appleyard, D. (1976). *Planning a pluralistic city.* Cambridge, MA: MIT Press.

Buttimer, A., & Seamon, D. (Eds.). (1980). *The human experience of space and place.* London: Croom Helm.

Downs, R. M., & Stea, D. (1977). *Maps in minds: Reflections on cognitive mapping.* San Francisco: Harper & Row.

Evans, G. W. (1980). Environmental cognition. *Psychological Bulletin, 88,* 259–267.

Moore, G. T., & Golledge, R. G. (Eds.). *Environmental knowing: Theories, research, and methods.* Stroudsburg, PA: Dowden, Hutchinson & Ross.

Hart, R. (1979). *Children's experience of place.* New York: Irvington.

Lynch, K. (1960). *The image of the city.* Cambridge, MA: MIT Press.

Ross, H. E. (1974). *Behavior and perception in strange environments.* London: George Allen & Unwin.

Chapter Three
Appraising and Assessing Places

ENVIRONMENTAL APPRAISALS:
PERSONAL IMPRESSIONS
OF PLACES

Descriptions: What Is It?

Evaluations: Is It Good?

Aesthetics: Is It Beautiful?

Emotions: How Does It Make You Feel?

Meanings: What Is Its Significance?

Concerns: Does It Matter?

ENVIRONMENTAL ASSESSMENT:
COLLECTIVE IMPRESSIONS
OF PLACES

Distinctions and Definitions

The Uses of Observer-Based
Environmental Assessments

Paradigms and Methodological
Considerations

Four Observer-Based Environmental
Assessments

Twenty men crossing a bridge,
Into a village,
Are twenty men crossing twenty bridges,
Into twenty villages,
Or one man
Crossing a single bridge into a village.
Wallace Stevens, 1959 from "Metaphors of a Magnifico"

Tom and Jane were sitting in the coffee shop talking to friends about their camping trip. Someone asked what the park was like.

"It's incredible," Jane quickly answered. Then she realized that statement was not very informative, so she tried to describe the steep valleys, granite mountains, and the alpine meadow with its tiny shimmering lakes. Tom broke in to relate how beautiful the deep forest was to him, but Jane looked at him with a puzzled expression.

"That place was creepy," she said. "I felt awful—almost trapped." Now it was Tom's turn to look puzzled. They didn't know each other all that well yet.

"I grew up near heavy timber like that," he said, "and we used to spend hours playing in it. It is like being enclosed, but not like being trapped—unless you feel trapped in your own natural world."

A friend asked if they knew about the new mine planned for the park. "Whaaat!" Tom and Jane exclaimed in unison.

"Don't you read the papers?" the friend asked. "Gouge Mines figures there's enough zinc in there to make a pit profitable, as long as they don't have to do too much reclamation of the land. They've offered to build a smelter near there, too, and some people are already looking forward to jobs there."

Tom and Jane looked at each other. "That's unbelievable," they said in unison.

"The government has commissioned some kind of study, though," continued the friend. "Something about assessing the impact of the mine and smelter on the scenic quality of the region. They do it by assembling a panel of observers who look at the park before development and simulations of what it would look like afterward."

"Where do I sign up?" asked Tom.

———————

Consider any place. How would you go about describing it? Is it beautiful? Good quality? How does it make you feel? What, if anything, does it mean to you? Do you care about its welfare? To what extent, do you think, is your own assessment of the place similar to one that might be made by a panel of experts or others who use the place? Do twenty individuals entering a town experience twenty "different" towns?

This chapter continues the discussion, begun in Chapter Two, of the process by which we come to know and understand the everyday physical environment. The initial gathering of information from settings, environmental perception, is followed by much cognitive manipulation of that information. We store, transform, organize, forget, and recall knowledge about settings. The spatial aspects of environment cognition were discussed in the latter part of Chapter Two. Now the focus is on two judgment processes, appraisal and assessment. The terms have been used differently by different authors (Craik & Zube, 1976), but in this book the following definitions are used.

Environmental appraisal refers to an individual's personal impressions of a setting. Both environmental appraisals and assessments involve an observer and a place, but in research on appraisals, more emphasis is placed on understanding the person than understanding the place. Many different kinds of appraisals have been studied; six kinds are discussed in this chapter.

Environmental assessment refers to the combining of ratings by several observers (experts or setting users) into a broader-based judgment of an environment. The emphasis is on investigating the environment (usually its quality or lack of quality) rather than the person.

We will discuss the different kinds of appraisals and assessments, and how they are measured. Evidence that a variety of personal and environmental characteristics—and interactions of them—combine to influence appraisals and assessments are reviewed. Personal characteristics include an individual's stage of life, culture, personality, and experience. Particularly important are the person's plans, goals, and intentions toward the setting (Canter, in press; Ward, 1977). Environmental characteristics include complexity, naturalness, architectural style, contents, state of repair, and many other relatively objective features.

An early but still useful organizing framework for the material in this chapter was provided by Kenneth Craik (1968). (See Table 3–1.) The com-

TABLE 3-1 A Process Model for the Comprehension of Environmental Displays

Observers 1	Presentation of Environmental Displays 2	Nature and Format of Judgments 3	Validational Criteria 4

Special competence
 groups:
  architects
  planners
  real estate appraisers
  stage designers
  "space" managers,
   i.e., hotel, theatre,
   resort managers,
   building superin-
   tendents, etc.
Special user-client
 groups:
  elderly persons
  migrant workers
  college students
Groups formed on the
 basis of relevant per-
 sonality measures
Everyman, general public
	Direct experience:
	 looking at
	 walking around
	  and through
	 driving around
	  and through
	 aerial views
	 living in
	Cinematic and photo-
	 graphic studies
	Sketches and drawings
	Models and replicas
	Tachistoscopic views
	Laser beam presentations
	No presentation
		Free descriptions
		Adjective checklists
		Activity and mood
		 checklists
		Q-sort descriptions
		Ratings
		Empathic interpretations:
		 "role" enactments
		 "role" improvisations
		Beliefs about human
		 consequences
		Viewing time
			Measures of objective
			 characteristics of
			 environmental displays
			Judgments by experts
			Any judgment-form in
			 Column 3 based
			 upon more extensive
			 acquaintance with the
			 environmental display

Based on Craik, 1968.

plexity of the process is evident in the many possibilities implied by Craik's framework. Many different kinds of **observers** may be shown environmental displays in many different **presentation formats** and asked to report their impressions in many different **judgment formats,** the accuracy of which may be tested by many different **validational criteria.**

Most research in this chapter involves the selection of one or two items from each column of Craik's framework, although a few investigators have systematically compared items from each of several columns within a single study to understand how they interrelate to affect perception (Feimer, 1984). Both appraisals and assessments may be studied within this framework, depending on which elements of it are selected for study and how the resulting data are analyzed. Broad or narrow judgments of either specific settings or the environment (as a global entity) may be studied.

ENVIRONMENTAL APPRAISALS: PERSONAL IMPRESSIONS OF PLACES

We like some buildings and dislike others. We develop feelings about places. We are concerned about the welfare of certain places and about the state of the environment as a whole. In general, environmental appraisal refers to at least six kinds of personal impressions: **descriptions, evaluations, judgments of beauty, emotional reactions, meanings,** and **attitudes of concern** that individuals develop for and about physical settings. Gifford (1975) pointed out that our understanding of what environments mean to individuals depends heavily on which appraisals we ask for; the questions environmental psychologists pose to their subjects are in some ways even more important than the characteristics of either the person who is asked or the setting being asked about.

The six kinds of impressions sometimes appear to be related to one another. For example, if you consider a certain city to be beautiful, you are also likely to report that it gives you good feelings to be there and that it is a good and personally significant city, one worth being concerned about. On the other hand, the different kinds of impressions do not always follow from one another. For example, a place may be significant to a person, but this meaning may derive from horrible experiences there rather than pleasant ones. Thus, different kinds of appraisals may be correlated from time to time, but they are quite distinct conceptually.

Descriptions: What Is It?

Environmental description has been left, for most of history, to poets and novelists. The centuries of practice have been fruitful. The most accurate and memorable descriptions of houses, mountains, trees, the sea, farms, towns, and prisons

have come from the best novelists and poets. If your purpose is to produce a penetrating, unforgettable portrait of a place, commission a good writer to do the job.

If, however, the purpose is to understand how everyday persons think about the settings in their daily lives, a different strategy may be necessary. In Craik's framework, it is true, one suggested method of obtaining descriptions of the environment is to ask individuals to write free descriptions of them—simply give them a blank piece of paper and a pen. (See Fig. 3–1.) This strategy can lead to some valuable insights (for example, which features of the setting are written about first; which are included and which are omitted; what themes seem to emerge naturally from the writer's narrative). But there are difficulties, too. Some people are intimidated by a blank piece of paper; some features of the setting that are important to the writer may be inadvertently overlooked; descriptions obtained from different writ-

FIGURE 3–1 A moderately complex landscape.

ers may be difficult to compare—if comparison is a goal of the study.

For these reasons, a number of environmental psychologists have tried to develop comprehensive, standardized sets of environmental descriptors. The free description technique allows the researcher to discover which dimensions observers select to describe a setting. But when the purpose of the study is to discover what observers say about certain specific aspects of a setting, standardized descriptor sets (lexicons) offer comprehensiveness and, for many observers, easier responding.

An Early System. The history of these standardized environmental descriptor sets goes back to Joyce Vielhauer Kasmar's early efforts (Kasmar, 1970; Vielhauer, 1965). She wanted to create a lexicon that could be used for the description of a wide variety of architectural settings, was meaningful and relevant in architectural contexts, and used words that are understandable by laypersons, instead of technical jargon.

Kasmar began with free descriptions. Students were asked to describe two rooms they liked and two rooms they disliked. From these descriptions and other sources, she compiled a list of over 500 bipolar adjective pairs (such as good-bad, light-dark). She then whittled down the list by asking other individuals to judge how *appropriate* these adjective pairs were for rating architecture in general and for rating specific buildings. Based on clarity of meaning as well as appropriateness, a final set of sixty-six adjective pairs was selected. Kasmar's procedure is described in some detail because it was the first of many attempts to develop a standard method of describing environments. Before her work, the only comparable way to describe settings was to borrow measures from other areas of psychology (Craik, 1968).

How Many Dimensions? An early question, raised by Kasmar herself, was whether these standardized descriptions of environments contained several distinct dimensions, themes, or factors within them. Gradually, the notion developed that environmental descriptions include a mixture of appraisals or dimensions. If so, what are these dimensions? Are some of them essential and others peripheral?

The answer, in part, is that different dimensions emerge depending on which buildings or observers are studied and which individual items are included in the lexicon. Still, perhaps because psychologists studying meaning in a broader sense (Osgood, Suci, & Tannenbaum, 1957) were successful in showing that three dimensions (potency, activity, and evaluation) seemed to pervade meaning across a wide variety of physical, cultural, and individual differences, many early environmental psychologists pushed on, attempting to find the basic dimensions of architectural meaning (Canter, 1968, 1969; Cass & Hershberger, 1973; Collins, 1969; Hershberger, 1972). (See Fig. 3–2.)

This work produced a large variety of dimensions, some of which arose frequently; others arose only in one or two studies. Apparently, simple three-dimensional systems like potency, activity, and evaluation are inadequate to characterize environments.

FIGURE 3–2 David Canter, a leading British environmental psychologist, has produced many studies of environmental evaluation and meaning. *(Courtesy of David Canter.)*

No widely accepted set of dimensions for describing the environment has emerged. Nevertheless, a sample set of central and peripheral dimensions is proposed by Cass and Hershberger (1973). (See Table 3–2.) Clearly, however, these dimensions include some that are rather broad in the sense that many features of the setting contribute to them (beauty, for example) and others that are narrow in that they primarily reflect fewer features (temperature).

▶ **In Sum.** Environments may be described along many dimensions; a good poet or novelist is probably best able to select and employ the best dimensions for describing any particular setting. Researchers, nevertheless, have tried to develop standard sets of descriptors to assist the average person's attempt to describe places. These standard sets have improved, but given the variety of settings and purposes for which settings are described, it may be both impossible and undesirable that a universal set of descriptors is developed. One benefit of the many efforts to find such a set has been to identify certain dimensions that *commonly* emerge from studies employing many diverse descriptors. The undoubted champion of these is our next dimension, evaluation.

Evaluations: Is It Good?

When asked for their impressions of a place, individuals very frequently include comments as to whether they like it or not. Evaluation includes concepts such as goodness, quality, preference, and rank order. In judgments of goodness or quality, comparisons among places are implicit; evaluators do not directly contrast one setting with another, although the standards by which they judge settings are built up from many past evaluations. However, in judgments of preference and rank order, the comparison is explicit: evaluators are specifically asked whether they like each setting better than others.

Personal Influences. Whether a personal evaluation is positive or negative depends both on the person's background and on the setting. A pioneering study by Joseph Sonnenfeld (1966) focused on personal factors. Participants were asked to express their evaluations by indicating their preference among slides depicting scenes of Alaska and Delaware. The observers' preferences were predictable from such person-based influences as age, sex, and culture. Younger individuals generally preferred the more exotic scenes. Females preferred more richly vegetated and warmer scenes. Natives of Delaware more often preferred Delaware scenes and natives of Alaska more often preferred Alaskan scenes.

More recent studies also support the idea that familiar landscapes are preferred (Lyons, 1983), but this familiarity effect does not always hold. Canter and Thorne (1972) found that Scots

TABLE 3–2 Semantic Scales to Measure the Meaning of Designed Environments: The Hershberger-Cass Base Set

Factors or Concepts	Primary and Alternate Scale	
1. General Evaluative	good-bad	pleasing-annoying
2. Utility Evaluative	useful-useless	friendly-hostile
3. Aesthetic Evaluative	unique-common	interesting-boring
4. Activity	active-passive	complex-simple
5. Space	cozy-roomy	private-public
6. Potency	rugged-delicate	rough-smooth
7. Tidiness	clean-dirty	tidy-messy
8. Organization	ordered-chaotic	formal-casual
9. Temperature	warm-cool	hot-cold
10. Lighting	light-dark	bright-dull

Secondary scales might include old-new, expensive-inexpensive, large-small, exciting-calming, clear-ambiguous, colorful-subdued, safe-dangerous, quiet-noisy, stuffy-drafty

Based on Cass & Hershberger, 1973

and Australians shown housing scenes from Scotland and Australia preferred scenes from the other country. Nasar (1984a,b) reports that Japanese and American students preferred street scenes from the other country to street scenes from their own. Kaplan (1977) and many others have shown that different personalities prefer differ settings. The main point is that individual differences *are* related to setting preferences, but the specific findings from study to study do vary.

Physical Influences. Features of the setting also matter, of course. Would *any* individual prefer a scene showing an outlet pipe discharging reddish-orange chemicals into a river already full of discarded tires and dubious floating objects to a scene depicting a sunny meadow with wild flowers? But among less dramatically attractive or unattractive scenes, the physical elements associated with visual preference are not obvious; research is necessary to identify cues that lead viewers to prefer one scene over another (Im, 1984).

Certain rather straightforward setting features reliably lead to observer liking. Kaye and Murray (1982), for example, showed that rooms with windows are more appealing than rooms without. Nasar (1981b) found that square model rooms were preferred over rectangular ones. Observers appear to prefer ceilings that are higher than the conventional height (Baird, Cassidy, & Kurr, 1978). Gifford (1980b) reports that pro-development observers prefer big, new urban buildings, and that mechanically oriented and older observers like well-lit buildings. Nasar (1983) investigated residential settings and found that observers preferred scenes depicting ornate, clean, open, and single-purpose (for example, residential use only) buildings.

Other environmental features that influence liking are more abstract. Among these less-obvious features are **congruity** and **contrast.** Wohlwill (1982) showed observers simulated landscapes into which various built structures had been placed through the wonders of model-building and photography. Landscape scenes containing buildings judged (by previous observers) to be strongly incongruous with, and in contrast to, the landscape were strongly disliked. This may not be surprising. But would observers like buildings that are very much in context and very low

on contrast, or would they prefer buildings with a moderate degree of these qualities?

Some groups in Wohlwill's study preferred the latter over the dullness of buildings that blend in almost too well; other groups showed no preference. Thus, individual differences among observers may play a role in preference of scenes that are low to medium in contrast and congruity, but few observers prefer strongly contrasting, incongruous developments in landscapes. (See Fig. 3–3.) Miller (1984) studied preferences for coastline features in British Columbia. Observers (ferry passengers) preferred natural shorelines with small built structures on them over undeveloped, plain shorelines. Miller's study seems to support the notion that moderate complexity, development, or contrast is preferred to very low levels of these qualities. The main point is that congruity is another feature of settings that is important in our evaluation of them.

Clearly, however, preferences are best explained by knowing something about the observer *and* something about the setting (Peterson & Neumann, 1969). The studies of shorelines by Miller and of urban buildings by Gifford, for example, both showed that preferences varied with observer characteristics as well as with setting characteristics.

An Integrated Approach. Another major approach to environmental preference emphasizes the contribution of observers but focuses on cognitive processes shared by all individuals rather than on personality or demographic differences between observers. Setting features are also considered in this approach. Drawing on the work of Gibson, Lynch, Berlyne, and others, Stephen and Rachel Kaplan (1982) have developed an integrative conceptualization of environmental preference. (See Fig. 3–4.)

The Kaplans believe that human preference for settings originates in the evolutionary past of our species and in the adaptive value offered by particular settings. For example, one study of landscape preference found that children prefer savannah to other landscape types (Balling & Falk, 1982). Since humans apparently originated in the African savannah, Balling and Falk suggest that the children's preference for this landscape may indicate an evolutionary basis for landscape preference, although other researchers are quick to

FIGURE 3–3 Does this modern building on the left fit into the landscape or is it incongruous? *Discuss*

point out the highly speculative nature of this suggestion. Lyons (1983), for example, believes a simpler explanation may be inferred from people's experience and familiarity with local savannahlike landscapes.

Because of the vast experience of humans (as a species) with natural landscapes, the Kaplans believe we are able to form preferences after very brief exposure to a new scene. They extend Gibson's idea that environments provide affordances—direct knowledge about the possibilities for orientation, safety, locomotion, and new information. Basically, the Kaplans believe we prefer sites that allow us to accomplish central human goals such as being safe and finding food or shelter.

In addition to these basic needs, the Kaplans postulate that humans have a strong desire to *make sense* of the environment and to *be involved* with it. One outcome of the need to make sense of places is our construction and use of cognitive maps, as discussed in the last chapter. In general, the Kaplans believe that people prefer

landscapes and interior settings that "offer promise of being involving and making sense" (Kaplan & Kaplan, 1982, p. 80).

Environments may offer promise either immediately or for the future. When involvement and making sense are combined with immediate or future promise, a 2 × 2 matrix results, yielding four elements of preference. (See Table 3–3.) In the Kaplans' preference framework, **coherence** (making sense immediately) refers to the ease with which a scene can be cognitively organized. **Complexity** (being involved immediately) refers to the scene's capacity to keep an individual busy (occupied without becoming bored or overstimulated). **Legibility** (the promise of making sense in the future) means that the environment appears to be one that could be explored without getting lost; it is arranged in a clear manner. **Mystery** (the promise of future involvement) means that the environment suggests we could learn more, interact more, or be further occupied—if we entered it.

These elements are the essence of the manner

FIGURE 3-4 Stephen and Rachel Kaplan have collaborated on an integrative theory of environmental cognition and have also shown particular interest in natural and outdoor settings. *(Courtesy of Stephen and Rachel Kaplan.)*

TABLE 3-3   The Kaplans' Preference Framework

Availability of Information	Needs	
	Making Sense	*Involve-ment*
Present or Immediate	Coherence	Complexity
Future or Promised	Legibility	Mystery

Preference for a scene is a function of the need to make sense of the scene and the need to be involved in it. Information may be immediately available to the observer or promised "around the corner." Coherent scenes allow the observer to immediately structure or organize the scene's elements. Complex scenes offer a lot of information to keep the observer occupied. Legible scenes give the impression to observers that they will not get lost or disoriented. Mysterious scenes suggest to observers that they will learn more if they venture into the scene.

in which the Kaplans have integrated person and environment considerations in conceptualizing preference. Consider coherence. Cognitive organization is a human activity, yet some scenes are easier to organize than others. Coherence, therefore, is not *in* our heads or *in* the environment; it is in the way we appraise the environment.

The Kaplans use the term **cognitive affordance** to describe their idea that these four qualities are immediately knowable but require cognition as well as information from the environment. If James Gibson (the originator of the term **affordance**) were alive, he would probably wince at the new term. He believed the environment informed us directly, without our having to process the information we receive from the environment. However, most psychologists would agree with the Kaplans that information processing plays a crucial role in our appraisals of the environment.

For the Kaplans, preference can be predicted from coherence, legibility, complexity, and mystery but not always in simple ways. Generally, preference should increase as each of these qualities increases, but there are limits. Too much legibility in a setting might necessarily reduce mystery; the setting would be clear but it would lack interest. Also, finding scenes with high levels of both coherence and complexity might be difficult. As complexity increases, the odds that the scene is well-organized would seem to drop quickly.

The Kaplans stress the role of familiarity in preference. As we succeed in making sense out of a scene, it becomes more familiar. Great familiarity sometimes leads to lowered involvement. Thus—sometimes—making sense and involvement lead us toward opposite preference tendencies for a place. When a place is new to us, our preference lies in the opportunity to make sense of it, but involvement is relatively low. Later, there may be a point where we are still making sense of the place, yet know enough about it to be quite involved in it, too. Finally we may come to know the place so well that, from a making-sense point of view, we no longer have a high preference for it.

Great familiarity, however, permits us to become very involved with the place; we now know all its possibilities to offer us whatever we originally sought in it. Some places become more and more intriguing with increasing familiarity, so that making sense is never complete and preference never wanes.

▶ In Sum. Evaluative appraisals may take the form of stated preferences, ratings of quality, or ranking of goodness. Early research showed that such personal factors as age, sex, and familiarity with the place and objective features such as room design, congruity, contrast, and complexity. The

Kaplans' newer approach integrates person and place factors into involvement, making sense and immediate versus future promise, concepts that involve person-and-environment. Preference is viewed as a complex outcome of these influences. More research is necessary, but the way is clear: preference will be investigated as a function of different levels of coherence, legibility, mystery, complexity, and familiarity.

Aesthetics: Is It Beautiful?

Four Approaches. The study of beauty has a long history of involvement with art and philosophy. When environmental psychology, with its tendencies toward activism and experimental research, collided with elements of this tradition at least four approaches to aesthetics resulted (Porteous, 1982). The activist wishes to save beautiful places now, not study them or ponder the nature of beauty. (See Fig. 3–5.) The experimentalist wants to identify the personal and setting characteristics that lead observers to appraise a scene as beautiful. The planner is an often-frustrated person trying to bridge the gap between the activists (now!) and the experimentalists (wait until you know what you're doing!). The humanist prefers to comtemplate beauty and to offer thoughtful criticisms of the other approaches and to comment on beautiful places. Porteous maintains that progress in the field of environmental aesthetics will follow when the four types fruitfully collaborate.

This section concentrates on the social sci-

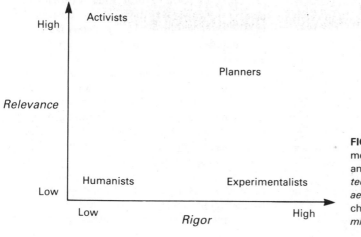

FIGURE 3–5 Four approaches to environmental aesthetics depend on how relevant and how rigorous one's concerns are. *(Porteous, J. D. Approaches to environmental aesthetics.* Journal of Environmental Psychology, *1982, 2, 53–66. Reprinted by permission of Academic Press, Inc.)*

ence approach to beauty; this is not meant to imply it is necessarily the most promising or most-deserving approach to beauty. The activist struggle against the great creeping parking lot is clear enough from the popular media that its theme need not be expanded here. One humanist approach (phenomenology) and some planning approaches (see the work of Lynch and Appleyard) were briefly described in the last chapter.

Beauty in Scenes.   Some social scientists search for beauty in the setting itself and others argue that it is in the eye of the beholder, but most environmental psychologists claim the truth lies somewhere between. If beauty is entirely a property of the environment, then every individual would agree that a certain scene is or is not beautiful. But some people think deserts are beautiful and others think rocky peaks, chaotic markets, undersea vistas, or skyscrapers are beautiful. Both viewer and scene must eventually be considered. Nevertheless, some studies concentrate on physical cues that signify beauty, and others concentrate on individual differences in the perception of beauty.

Most research on beauty from the physical perspective concerns the aesthetics of landscapes, especially natural landscapes. Most observers find the typical natural landscape more beautiful than the typical urban or suburban scene (Kaplan, Kaplan, & Wendt, 1972), and landscapes also seem to produce more positive physiological effects (Ulrich, 1981). The goal of this work has been to discover objective ways of deciding which vistas are beautiful to users of national parks. Is a wilderness scene more beautiful with water? Is a forest view more beautiful when clearings are present, or when dense tall trees create a secluded sanctuary?

Research that systematically varies landscape elements in the scene, such as the amount, type, and location (center versus periphery, and near versus far) of vegetation, water, and sky, has shown that these physical elements can explain much of the variability in judgments of aesthetics, with no allowance for individual differences among observers (Hull & Buhyoff, 1983). The power of physical cues to predict judgments of beauty varies from study to study depending on the selection of scenes and observers, but they are clearly a dominant force. In other words, this research suggests that most people will agree on the beauty of any given view. The challenge is to discover just which elements of the landscape are the most influential in defining beauty.

Two recent studies explore this challenge. Hull and Buhyoff (1983) studied judged beauty as a function of the distance to a feature in a scene. Six similar scenes were studied; each scene showed a grassy field in the foreground, a small ridge in the middle ground, and a large ridge in the background. Photographs were taken at various distances from the large back ridge in each scene. The researchers found that scenic beauty varied with the distance to the back ridge but not in a straight-line fashion. The scene was judged more beautiful when the back ridge was either relatively near or relatively far, and less beautiful at intermediate distances. In another study, the *placement* of vegetation in the scene was a significant predictor of beauty (Patsfall, Feimer, Buhyoff, & Wellman, 1984). When vegetation was depicted in the center middle ground and in the center background, beauty was greater.

▶ **In Sum.** Environmental aesthetics has been the concern of activists, planners, experimentalists, and humanists. Research shows that landscape beauty is largely a function of (a) the percentages of different landscape elements in a scene, (b) the distance to and (c) the placement of these elements in the scene.

Emotions: How Does It Make You Feel?

Presumably, settings that individuals evaluate as good and find beautiful will also make them feel pleasant. To some extent then, evaluations of quality, judgments of beauty, and positive feelings overlap. However, there are good reasons *not* to conclude that the three kinds of appraisal are redundant.

First, pleasantness is only one emotion we experience; other emotions may not neatly correspond to evaluation or beauty judgments. Second, emotion (or the term many psychologists prefer, **affect**) is conceptually distinct from evaluation and beauty. The physiological, behavioral, and cognitive aspects of emotion are quite different from those involved in merely judging goodness or beauty. Rikard Kuller (1980), a Swedish environmental psychologist, has described emotion as "a complex state of the human organism, involving not only feelings such as sadness, awe, fear, rage, surprise, joy, but also bodily changes of various kinds, as well as impulses towards all forms of behavior.''

Kuller also observes that the built environment does not usually evoke in us the strong, immediate emotions such as rage or ecstasy but rather has a persistent, cumulative influence. The environment, therefore, may have an important impact on us in the long term without receiving much notice on a day-to-day basis. Thus, for several reasons, the emotional impact of settings deserves separate attention from the description, evaluation, and aesthetics of environments.

Two leading investigators of emotion in environmental psychology have been Albert Mehrabian and James Russell. Their earlier work (1974, 1975) presented emotion as a mediator between the environment and personality on one side and behavior on the other. Their research identified three primary emotional responses: **pleasure, arousal,** and **dominance.** The three primary emotions are viewed as being independent

from each other; that is, we may experience any combination of them.

According to the Russell and Mehrabian framework, both environmental variables (for example, light, temperature, and the rate of speed that information reaches the individual) and personality variables (such as our tendency to seek arousal or not) influence the level of pleasure, arousal, and dominance one feels in a given setting. These emotions, in turn, strongly influence such key behaviors as the desire to approach or avoid a setting, work performance, and our nonverbal communication in the setting.

The framework was tested in a series of studies in which verbal descriptions of settings were presented to research participants whose personality tendencies were known and who were asked to report how they would act in the setting (Mehrabian & Russell, 1974, 1975; Russell & Mehrabian, 1977, 1978). The results can be quite complex, but a relatively simple example from the 1978 study is representative.

The curves in Figure 3–6 show a hypotheses: individuals will want to approach physical set-

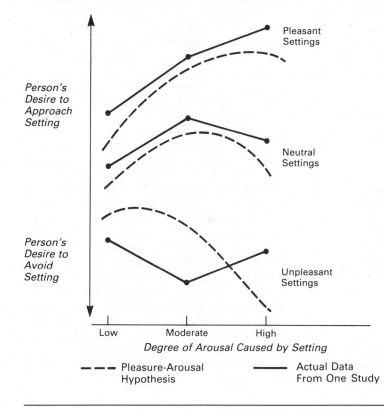

FIGURE 3–6 The pleasure-arousal hypothesis. One's desire to approach a setting varies with the setting's pleasure- and arousal-eliciting qualities. *(Russell, J. A. & Mehrabian, A. Approach-avoidance and affiliation as functions of the emotion-eliciting quality of an environment.* Environment and Behavior, *1978,* 10, *355–387. Copyright © 1978 by* Environment and Behavior. *Reprinted by permission of Sage Publications, Inc.)*

tings that are, apart from their other characteristics, moderately arousing and maximally pleasurable. Note also that as the pleasantness of a setting increases, the maximum desire to approach it is predicted to occur at higher levels of arousal. In other words, Mehrabian and Russell's **pleasure-arousal hypothesis** is that we appreciate more stimulating settings as the pleasantness of the setting increases.

The solid lines in Figure 3–6 depict the actual findings. As predicted, more pleasant settings were viewed as more approachable settings. For settings that were not particularly pleasant or unpleasant, the pleasure-arousal hypothesis was supported. Moderately arousing settings were more desirable than were low- or high-arousal settings. But, for pleasant settings, approachability did not decline for highly arousing settings, as the researchers predicted; instead, it increased. For unpleasant settings, moderately arousing settings were the *least* desirable to approach, rather than the most desirable. The results of this and other studies appear to show that the emotional impact of the physical environment is systematically related to our behavior in them, even if the theory requires some fine-tuning to account for occasional deviations from its predictions.

This research program, however, often investigated verbal descriptions of all the variables—personality, environment, emotions, and behaviors. This reliance on the self-report method has stimulated some critics (Daniel & Ittelson, 1981) to charge that the whole theory merely captures semantic associations among the variables, rather than the emotional impact of real behavior in real settings.

Russell and his co-workers defend their finding of a general structure for emotional qualities of settings by showing that the same dimensions emerge from a variety of rating methods (Russell & Ward, 1981). They also note that emotion may be studied at molar or molecular levels. Their own molar approach operates at a different level than the molecular approach advocated by Daniel and Ittelson, but the two approaches are complementary, not conflicting.

Russell has moved away from discussing the direct emotional impact of settings (Mehrabian & Russell, 1974, p. 8) toward discussing the emotional qualities of settings that individuals *attribute* to settings (Russell & Pratt, 1980, pp. 311–312), or **affective appraisal** (Russell & Lanius, 1984). Thus, to be precise, Russell now studies cognitions about place-elicited emotion rather than place-elicited emotion itself. These distinctions are drawn to point out that environmental psychology is a discipline that harbors a variety of basic paradigms or coherent systems of research methods and scientific values (Craik, 1977). Paradigms are not merely different methods; they are different *models* of the whole process of understanding phenomena. Immersion in one paradigm may blind one to the existence of, or tolerance for, other paradigms. The field is too young yet to hastily discard any paradigm that may contribute to the understanding of person-environment relations.

As for the use of simulated settings (verbal descriptions), we saw in the last chapter that at least some simulations (in particular, sequences of color slides) yield responses close to those elicited by the actual settings they represent. Some evidence goes even further, showing that responses to real and simulated settings tend to be predictable from the same observer characteristics (Gifford, 1976b). Nevertheless, many researchers would feel more comfortable about generalizing their conclusions to everyday settings if more research on emotion employed not only actual behaviors but actual settings.

Physiological measures of emotion would also broaden the base of research in environmental psychology. Neither verbal descriptions of emotion nor physiological measures of it completely capture its essence, but they can complement one another. Unfortunately, physiological studies of emotion in response to everyday settings are still uncommon except in the area of crowding.

Mehrabian continues to interpret much of environmental psychology in terms of the three primary emotions pleasure, arousal, and dominance (Mehrabian, 1976b), but Russell's research led him to conclude that dominance is a poor third as a primary emotion. Since it appeared no more important than some other minor emotions, Russell has concentrated on a model that includes only pleasure and arousal as primary emotions (Russell, Ward, & Pratt, 1981). The model asserts that combinations of the two primary emotions form a **circumplex,** or circular ordering. Russell

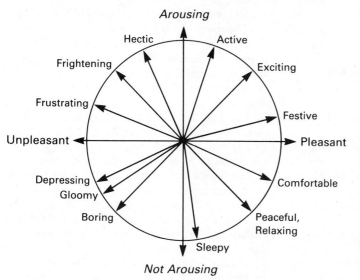

Arousing

Hectic — Active

Frightening — Exciting

Frustrating — Festive

Unpleasant — Pleasant

Depressing — Comfortable
Gloomy

Boring — Peaceful,
Relaxing

Sleepy

Not Arousing

FIGURE 3-7 Two major dimensions of emotion and their hybrids form a circumplex, or circular ordering. Which settings in your experience encourage each of these emotions in you? *(Russell, J. A., & Pratt, G. A description of the affective quality attributed to environments.* Journal of Personality and Social Psychology, *1980, 38, 311–322. Copyright 1980 by the American Psychological Association. Reprinted/adapted by permission of the author.)*

believes that appraisals of the emotional impact of settings may be located at one point or another around the circumplex. (See Fig. 3–7.)

This framework is now being used to study relations between appraised emotion and other responses to the environment. For example, Gifford and Ng (1982) found that appraisals of the pleasure elicited by city scenes depend much more on visual cues than on auditory cues, but appraisals of arousal do not depend more on visual cues than on auditory cues.

In another vein, Russell and Lanius (1984) demonstrated that affective appraisals are dependent on the level of stimulation we are adapted to. As adaptation-level theory (Helson, 1964) would predict, after individuals are exposed to a setting that elicits strong emotional appraisals (very high or low pleasure, arousal), their appraisal of a new setting will be shifted in the opposite direction, compared to the appraisal of someone who was *not* exposed to the first setting. For example, exposure to a very pleasurable place tends to push our appraisal of a subsequent place in the direction of less pleasure. To the average nine year old, the local playground probably evokes much less pleasure the day after returning from a visit to Disneyland than it did before the visit. This adaptation-level shift is clearly one reason that the same place can be appraised quite differently by different observers.

▶ **In Sum.** Emotional response to environments is usually persistent and cumulative rather than sharp and brief. Nevertheless, it is a complex mix of behavioral, cognitive, and physiological responses. Individuals report that settings evoke combinations of pleasure, arousal, and perhaps other emotions (such as dominance) in them. These reports are linked to behavior in the pleasure-arousal hypothesis, which states that we approach or like places that are more arousing when they are also pleasant. Pleasure appraisals may depend on visual cues more than on auditory cues, but arousal cues depend equally on both kinds of cues. Emotion appraisals depend on our adaptation level.

Meaning: What Is Its Significance?

Beyond the appraisals we have discussed so far is the question of meaning. Sometimes the word *meaning* is used broadly to characterize research on environmental perception, description, evaluation, or emotion, but in this chapter the term will refer to three quite different processes: (1) attachment, or the profound experience of being part of a place, (2) communication, or the way a building or place signifies some philosophical, architectural, social, or political concept to those who view it, and (3) purpose, appraisals of the building's function in relation to its form or appearance.

Attachment. In the first of these processes, places typically acquire great personal meaning only after we have long or intense experience with them. In contrast, most of the appraisals previously discussed may be made after brief exposure to a place, although altered or improved judgments of goodness, beauty, or preference might be made after a person has the benefit of longer experience with it.

The richness of meaning that a place has for a person grows with familiarity, but just what is the meaning of meaning? One dimension of it involves **place attachment** (Gold & Burgess, 1982), the process by which many individuals come to assign great personal value to their homes, communities, and other settings. A frequent theme is the *loss* of place attachment through the destruction of heritage buildings and from trends like the increase in mobility over the past several decades.

Where place attachment is allowed to grow, one outcome is that the meaning of place and the meaning of self begin to merge (Tuan, 1974). Thus, one meaning of place is that sometimes one's personal identity becomes inextricably bound up with it. Among hundreds of possible examples, Britain has its Fenmen, the United States its New Yorkers, and Canada its Maritimers. University students identify with their schools and residents of counties, states, districts, provinces, and territories identify with these jurisdictions. At smaller scales, many residents identify with their neighborhood, borough, farm, house, or even room.

Place attachment has serious implications. Its first cousin, **place identity,** is an important dimension of an individual's personality, as we shall see in the next chapter. Place attachment can even kill. In a later chapter we shall see that a major reason people do not abandon locations that are prone to natural hazards such as floods, earthquakes, and hurricanes is their deeply felt connection to a place.

Communication. The second meaning of meaning refers to the abstract concepts that a setting signifies or, despite its designer's intentions, fails to signify (Hershberger, 1970). For example, one study found that buildings constructed by Hitler's government still communicate the Nazi image intended by their architects (Espe, 1981).

Buildings are capable of reflecting the ideals and aspirations of those who construct them.

But not always, and not to everyone. For example, **modernism** was an important architectural movement whose proponents believed in purity of form. They thought the rest of us would also appreciate the simple, clear, rectangular lines of their building facades. Modernists were weary of the excessive ornamentation and detail that characterized older styles; modern for them meant clean lines. Skyscrapers with absolutely regular lines and symmetric strips of windows are typical modernist structures. The modernist architects often achieved this clarity of form and were widely admired (for a time) within their own circles, but the public has never much liked their "glass and steel boxes."

Charles Jencks (1978) thought he had a solution. He was influential in developing a reformist architectural movement. This movement, **postmodernism,** is based in part on the notion that two codes or sensibilities exist, one used by professional architects and one used by the rest of us. A code, in this sense of the word, is an understanding or implicit agreement that certain stylistic elements signify or imply—that is, mean—certain philosophies or values.

Jencks believed that modernist buildings were designed by and to a professional code that was accepted and appreciated among architects. But the public interpreted the same buildings according to a different code. Modernist buildings meant *modern* (new, clean, clear) to architects, but *alienation* (cold, hard, forbidding) to the public. Often, then, modern buildings mean different things to architects and nonarchitects. This meaning is a positive one for architects but a negative one for nonarchitects.

The new movement, postmodernism, attempts to incorporate both the professional code and the public's code, so that buildings are designed with an understanding of both codes. Theoretically, this allows both architect and nonarchitect to correctly discern the intended meaning of the building.

Postmodern buildings do not all look the same or mean the same, but some common stylistic threads among postmodern buildings include hints of traditional architectural forms, more curves, and building portions that appear almost out of place or jumbled. (See Fig. 3–8.) Postmod-

FIGURE 3-8 A modernist building (above) and a postmodernist building (below).

ernists hope their meaning shines through both the professional code and the public code. Since their intended meanings are positive, this should lead to greater popular as well as professional liking of postmodern buildings.

Linda Groat (1982) tested these ideas by showing examples of modern, transitional, and postmodern buildings to architects and nonarchitects. Her results supported Jencks' dual coding notion—the idea that architects and nonarchitects employ different processes to pick up the meaning of buildings. Unfortunately, the nonarchitects were nevertheless unable to distinguish modern from postmodern buildings. Groat concludes that some architects are now sensitive to the existence of separate codes for themselves and nonarchitects, but typically they have been unable to use that sensitivity to convey their in-

tended meanings to nonarchitects through their postmodern buildings.

Purpose. The third kind of meaning involves the way building form and function are understood by everyday observers. Much modern architecture is ambiguous; if viewers aren't given clues (like a sign over the entrance), they may not be able to decide what the purpose or function of the building is. In another account of the study just described, Linda Groat and David Canter (1979) report that one of the primary concerns of the nonarchitects when looking at the buildings was to discover the *purpose* of each building.

The reason for this concern, presumably, is that a crucial aspect of a building's meaning is bound up with the appropriateness of its form for its function. We might like the looks of a certain

---

restaurant, *as a restaurant*, but we wouldn't like to *live* in the building. For example, a study in the Netherlands found that observers judged a building differently if it was said to be, for example, a city hall, a train station, or was presented with no functional label (Prak & van Wegen, 1975). The judgments of buildings were also different from judgments of functions alone (some observers were asked what they thought of train stations but were not shown a building). Thus, the meaning of a building can vary dramatically depending on how it is being used.

A Canadian study concluded that behavior believed to occur in a place is an important component of the place's meaning (Genereux, Ward, & Russell, 1983). They showed twenty places to observers who were asked

- Why might one go here?
- What might be done here?
- What activities probably occur here?

Genereux et al. suggest that place meaning is intricately connected to an individual's plans. Some places are quite behavior-specific; only a few activities are feasible in them (such as a phone booth). Others are much less behavior-specific; many activities might occur in them (such as a beach). Less behavior-specific places therefore probably have broader meaning. If your plans are vague or include many possible variations, a behavior-specific place may have little value at the moment. But if you need to make a phone call, even a beach with its many possible pleasant associations might not be appreciated—at least until you can get back from making that phone call!

▶ **In Sum.** Environmental meaning has three sides to it: personal attachment or belonging, a setting's communication of some architectural or philosophical concept, and the communication of its purpose or function. Attachment, so far studied primarily by humanistically inclined phenomenologists, is an important process involving some of the closest person-environment bonds we ever experience. Communication, in the sense used here, occurs in some buildings but not others.

Obviously, part of the art of architecture lies in finding a nonverbal, stylistic way to get a message from the creator of a building to its users. The latest general solution, postmodernism, still works only for some buildings. The communi-

cative skill of the individual architect is still more important than any broad stylistic convention for sending messages via buildings. Meaning in the sense of a building's perceived working function, has strong effects on its appreciation. Many individuals do not like vagueness in function. Places may have broad or narrow functional meanings.

Concerns: Does It Matter?

Appraisals of concern pertain to whether individuals regard particular places or the physical environment in general as worthy of protection, understanding, and enhancement. How concerned are you about the welfare of your own room, your residence, your neighborhood, or city, a nearby wilderness area, or "spaceship earth"? An intimately related question is: If you are concerned, will you *act* to back up this concern?

Measuring Concern. Appraisals of concern have traditionally been studied as environmental attitudes. Attitudes, including attitudes toward the environment, are usually said to have three components: cognitive, affective, and conative. The **cognitive component** refers to what an individual knows or thinks about a place, including facts and opinions about it. The **affective component** refers to the emotional aspects of our attitude toward the place, a topic already discussed. The **conative component** refers to our behavioral orientation toward the place.

The primary thrust of research in this area has been to develop useful measures of environmental attitudes. Two environmental attitude measures were developed in the 1970s when ecology issues were first widely debated (Maloney & Ward, 1973; Maloney, Ward, & Braught, 1975; Weigel & Weigel, 1978). Maloney et al.'s ecological attitude scale contains four subscales: **affect, knowledge, verbal commitment,** and **actual commitment.** The latter two correspond to the conative component of attitudes; one asks respondents what they *say* they will do for conservation and the other asks them what they have actually *done*.

Both Maloney et al. and the Weigels demonstrated the validity of their measures by showing that individuals known to have pro-ecology attitudes (Sierra Club members) produced significantly higher scores on all scales than random assortments of college and noncollege individuals. Thus, when the scales are given to individuals whose environmental attitudes are not yet known, we can be reasonably certain that a high score does, in fact, indicate pro-environment attitudes.

Another avenue has been to identify the varieties of environmental concern; to think there is only one broad form of environmental concern is simplistic (Smythe & Brook, 1980; Van Liere & Dunlap, 1981). Smythe and Brook, for example, isolated separate concerns related to transportation, purchasing choices, cleanup, and public advocacy of one's convictions.

Gifford, Hay, and Boros (1982–1983) explored a variety of individual differences in environmental attitudes. The results supported the efforts of environmental education (EE) programs. Students enrolled in a university EE program were found to have significantly greater environmental knowledge, verbal commitment, and actual commitment than similar students who were not enrolled in it.

A disturbing sex difference was also found: women *said* they were more upset by antienvironmental events (affect); *said* they would do more about the problems (verbal commitment); but reported actually *doing* less (actual commitment) and *knew* less about environmental problems than men. Suggesting that these results were the outcome of social and school systems that discouraged girls from early interests in science and the environment, the authors strongly suggest that educators pay more attention to the environmental education of girls and women.

Concern Versus Action. The most important issue in environmental attitude research has been whether individuals follow up their attitudes with action. Some reviewers cite evidence that links between attitudes and behavior are quite weak (O'Riordan, 1976). Other social scientists believe that behavioral change is much more likely to occur when social environments are restructured than when educators try to change attitudes (Etzioni, 1972). For example, these social scientists would forego a lecture on the benefits of recycling in favor of tripling the deposit on cans and bottles.

Some researchers have found that pro-en-

vironmental behaviors do seem to follow from pro-environmental attitudes (Heberlein & Black, 1981). Other environmental psychologists argue that the link between attitudes and behavior has been underestimated. They complain that studies reporting weak attitude-behavior links usually focus on only one or two behaviors. Agreeing that the links between a broad attitude and any *few* behaviors might be weak, they assert that if a wider variety of behaviors are examined, the link is stronger (Fishbein & Ajzen, 1975; Gifford, 1982c).

One study shows the link is stronger with a wider variety of behaviors. Weigel and Newman (1976) investigated the correlation between attitude scores on their Environmental Concern Scale and numerous individual behaviors, such as circulating a petition, recycling, and recruiting a friend to help in an environmental action project. Correlations with *each* of these behaviors were low, suggesting support for the weak-link position. But correlations with an *index* composed of the whole group of pro-environment behaviors were much higher, supporting the idea that pro-environment attitudes really do predict pro-environmental behavior in general. Clearly, persons who care about the environment may not engage in *some* pro-environment activities but will take part in *more* activities from the whole spectrum of pro-environment activities.

▶ In Sum. Environmental concern is an appraisal, but one for which behavioral connections, if any, are of particular importance. Early research suggested there are poor links between environmental concern and action, but later work shows that when action is more broadly conceived, the links are stronger.

ENVIRONMENTAL ASSESSMENT: COLLECTIVE IMPRESSIONS OF PLACES

The lines from the Wallace Stevens poem that open this chapter suggest there may be many different impressions of a place. But it is also true to a large extent that we share similar perceptions of a place. In this section, the varieties of assessments and the differences between appraisal and assessments will be described. Contrasting paradigms for assessing environmental quality from the human point of view (in contrast to mechanical means of monitoring environmental quality) are discussed. The purposes and paradigms of observer-based environmental assessments will be described. Finally, several typical investigations are outlined, to give some flavor of current efforts to assess the quality of natural and built environments.

Distinctions and Definitions

The Varieties of Place Assessment.   Long ago (within the short history of environmental psychology), Kenneth Craik (1971) described how social scientists were beginning to use psychological assessment techniques, long used primarily to assess persons, in the assessment of places. (See Fig. 3–9.) The personality, intelligence, and other

FIGURE 3–9 Kenneth Craik has promoted the cause of environmental psychology from its earliest days. His research focuses on the assessment of environments and individual differences in environment-behavior relations.

characteristics of individuals can be measured by careful human observation, and the same general set of skills may be applied to the assessment of physical settings.

Craik described five kinds of place assessment that might be undertaken. First, physical and spatial properties of a setting may be measured. The slope of a valley, the height of a ceiling, the number of days of sunshine, and the number of rooms in a house are a few of the huge number of possible physical or spatial properties that might be assessed.

Second, the number and variety of artifacts in a place may be assessed. What kind of furniture is in a living room? What facilities in a campground? What machines in a manufacturing plant?

Third, the traits of places may be assessed. Is that landscape inviting? That office lush? That home majestic? Trait assessment must be distinguished from appraisals, which represent the viewpoint of one individual. When a group of carefully selected and trained assessors judges that a certain trait applies to a certain place, we can be more confident that the trait is truly characteristic of the place, not a reflection of the needs and experiences of any one individual making the judgment. If the term personality is used to describe the overall pattern of a person's traits, then **environmentality** may be used to describe the overall pattern of a place's traits.

Fourth, the behaviors that typically occur in a place may be assessed. As noted earlier, some places support many different human activities (for example, a park) and others support relatively few (a field of wheat). Two similar places may enclose quite different sets of behaviors (your living room compared to your neighbor's living room).

Fifth, the institutional attributes or social climate (Moos, 1973) of places may be assessed. When a hospital is described as *sterile*, the term may refer to the hygienic quality of the physical place or to the way staff interact with one another, patients, and visitors; in fact the two facets of sterility might be related, one causing the other.

In the years since Craik offered this typology, research has been unequally divided among the five kinds of assessments. The urgency of problems such as air pollution and the steady destruction of parklands and wilderness areas has led to legislation aimed at protection of the natural environment. The first step in environmental protection is to determine the location, extent, and severity of the present or potential damage (Rowe & Chestnut, 1983). Most efforts in the area of environmental assessment have consequently focused on one family of place traits, quality, and on one type of environment, the natural environment. Concern over the deterioration of ecosystems all over the globe has probably been the reason this topic has received so much attention at the expense of assessment research on other topics. The dramatic tone taken by some who express these concerns is exemplified by the words of a representative of an environmental defense organization, who was speaking about only one aspect of environmental degradation, visible air pollution: "When we lose visibility . . . an important part of our vision as a people will be lost" (Yuhnke, 1983). (See Fig. 3–10.) We should not for-

get, however, that other kinds of environmental assessments—such as those involving the great *indoors,* where we spend most of our time—are also important.

Assessments versus Appraisals. There are four differences between appraisals and assessments. First, appraisal research is *person-centered:* It focuses on the way individuals think and feel about the places around them. Assessment research is *place-centered.* It focuses on the quality of a setting from a human perspective. To understand how individuals appraise environments, their ratings of several places from their own world of experience are studied. To understand a place, ratings of several observers are obtained about one place.

Second, appraisals more often embody psychological constructs (such as emotion, meaning,

FIGURE 3–10 A plume of smoke interferes with the view in the open spaces of the Southwest United States. *(Courtesy of Erwin Zube)*

concern, preference). Assessments more often are attempts to measure physical properties, such as environmental quality, using human perceptual skills. Even similar-sounding appraisals and assessments are conceptually different. For example, Craik (1971) points out that a judgment of preference (an appraisal) and a judgment of quality (an assessment) are distinct. Observers may assess the architecture of one city as being high quality but nevertheless *prefer* the architecture of another city.

Third, assessments are more likely than appraisals to be undertaken in order to adopt or alter public policy. For example, the motive for much landscape assessment research is to help decide which vistas in parks ought to be preserved or developed.

Fourth, because assessments are place-centered, observers with specific functional relationships to the place are usually selected. The assessors are often experts either in the sense that they have professional training relevant to the setting (for example, landscape architects assessing the quality of a university's botanical gardens) or in that they have a special interest in the setting (such as tourists assessing the scenic quality of a national park).

Technical versus Observer-Based Assessments. Environmental assessment refers to the evaluation of environmental quality. These assessments may be made by **technical** or **observer-based** means. Technical Environmental Assessments (TEAs) employ mechanical monitoring equipment to produce a reading of environment quality. Observer-Based Environmental Assessments (OBEAs) employ the perceptual abilities of humans to judge the quality (or other characteristics) of settings. The OBEA is a measure of the quality of the environment as it is *experienced* (Craik & Zube, 1976b).

Both TEAs and OBEAs are useful, depending on the goal of the assessment. TEAs are valuable, for example, for assessing levels of hazardous materials in air, water, and soil that humans cannot perceive. OBEAs are more useful when the goal of the study involves assessing quality in terms of the social, aesthetic, preferential, and satisfaction aspects of environmental change. For some purposes, such as measuring the visual impact of air pollution or the aural impact of noise, TEAs and OBEAs can play complementary roles.

Some may think of TEAs as objective measures and OBEAs as subjective measures, but this is inappropriate (Zube, 1980). TEAs can be subjective in that assessors choose the times and places to sample the environment. More important, the choices of *which* dimension of the environment is examined and *when* it is examined are subjective judgments. OBEAs may be thought to be subjective on the assumption that human observers will produce a wide variety of assessments. This *may* happen, but not necessarily. In many OBEAs, the level of agreement among observers is strikingly high (Anderson, Zube, & MacConnell, 1976).

Nevertheless, no standardized OBEA yet exists. The very variety in the names given them by different research groups (Perceived Environmental Quality Indices, Visual Impact Assessment, Multiphasic Environmental Assessment Procedure, etc.) is evidence that they are still in the developmental stage.

This lack of standardization does not mean today's OBEAs are valueless. They may in fact be both impossible and undesirable to standardize, owing to the vast variety in both settings and assessment purposes. The optimal strategy may be to develop the best possible OBEA for each type of setting, just as TEAs employ many different specialized machines. Moos and his associates, for example, have spent years developing a standard instrument for the assessment of sheltered-care environments (Moos & Lemke, 1984), and Craik has spent years developing procedures for assessing landscapes (Craik, 1983a).

► **In Sum.** Place assessments may take the form of determining a setting's (a) physical and spatial properties, (b) artifacts and objects, (c) traits, (d) behavioral occurrences, or (e) social climate. Place assessment researchers have so far concentrated on one family of traits (quality) and one kind of setting (wilderness parks). Place assessments, in contrast to place appraisals, tend to be place-centered (instead of person-centered), aim to measure physical properties (instead of psychological properties), are more often policy-oriented (rather than oriented to the understanding of individuals), and more often employ observers with an expert or frequent-user relationship to the place being assessed. Place assessments may use technical or human means of observations. Each has its place; neither is necessarily more reliable or valid; each employs a variety of instruments (different machines for technical assessments, different questionnaires or rating forms for human observers).

The Uses of Observer-Based Environmental Assessments

Environmental appraisals are primarily of interest to those who wish to understand how individuals think and feel about environments. Environmental assessments have a different set of uses (Craik & Zube, 1976a). Several of these uses originate with public policy issues because concern for the deteriorating quality of the environment in the late 1960s and early 1970s culminated with laws requiring that environments be monitored. In some countries, both TEAs and OBEAs were undertaken as part of the public push to find out just how economic development was affecting parklands, air, water, and urban areas.

OBEAs have at least five purposes or uses. One of them is to allow comparisons between human and mechanical measures of environmental quality. Large gaps between TEAs and OBEAs might indicate credibility problems for TEAs. Depending on whether the TEA or the OBEA is eventually found to be more accurate, more public education or improved TEA technology might be warranted. TEAs and OBEAs do not always differ. In a TEA versus OBEA study of water pollution in France, Moser (1984) found good agreement between the two methods.

A second use of OBEAs is to assist in the development of physically based measures of environmental quality. Through an OBEA, sites that are high or low in environmental quality can be identified. Next, specific site characteristics that differentiate high from low environmental quality sites can be identified so that eventually the environmental quality of sites can be assessed directly from their physical characteristics.

For example, consider a park manager who has many potential campsites to choose from but must select only a few for development. A panel of campers could be taken on a tour of potential sites and asked to rank the quality of each as a campsite. Next, the elements common to potential sites that are assessed as high quality may be determined. Future campsite selection then could be based on knowledge of those key elements; another touring panel of campers would not have to be organized.

A third use of OBEAs is to provide knowledge of trends in environmental impact from the human point of view. OBEAs performed at regular intervals during the course of development in urban or park settings could inform policymakers of the seriousness of the impact at any given stage in a project. Similarly, the progress of environmental protection or enhancement programs could be monitored through OBEAs. For example, in England the Thames River has been subjected to an intensive clean-up program. TEAs showing drops in levels of pollution are valuable, but OBEAs demonstrating that London's residents and visitors *notice* changes in the river's color, smell, and ability to produce fish are equally valuable.

Fourth, OBEAs are useful where assessments of environmental quality that particularly relate to human interaction with the environment are needed. For example, the many types and levels of sound can be quite well measured mechanically, but sound is not the same as noise. Sound only becomes noise pollution under certain conditions, which include the preferences, goals, and activities of the *individuals* in the setting. One person's intolerable screeching is another person's jazz festival!

A fifth use of OBEAs is to educate staff in the setting (Moos & Lemke, 1984). Park managers, nursing home operators, and planners often feel certain they know all the important issues in their facilities, but they don't. I recently attended a meeting of a library board that had constructed a new branch library. It had been open for only a few months. The man who had spent over a year shepherding the project from start to finish questioned the need for an assessment of the library. "We have the best of everything there," he said. The chief librarian turned to him and said, "Bill, I hate to say this, but lighting has already been identified as a problem."

A later chapter takes up the role of social science in the planning and construction of buildings in detail, but as illustrated in this anecdote, environmental assessment is essential for architecture that is well-tailored to the needs of building users. No one person knows all the strengths and weaknesses of a large setting like a library or wilderness area. OBEAs utilize the observations of many individuals to educate those who manage settings.

▶ **In Sum.** OBEAs have at least five purposes. They (1) allow for comparisons between TEAs and OBEAs, (2) assist in the development of physical measures of environmental quality, (3) provide data on environmental quality trends from the human perspective, (4) provide assessments of quality along dimensions with particular human relevance, and (5) educate the staff of the assessed setting as to its strengths and weaknesses.

Paradigms and Methodological Considerations

Observer-based environmental assessment may be approached from at least four different paradigms (Zube, 1984; Zube, Sell, & Taylor, 1982). First, the **expert** (or professional) paradigm involves the evaluation of environmental quality by trained observers. The training may be in any of several relevant fields, such as forestry, real estate, landscape architecture, resource management, construction, or engineering. The experts usually rate a setting using principles from their own field, which may include artistic concepts like form, balance, and contrast, forestry concepts like timber age, density, and health, etc. The expert OBEA, then, is an assessment of a specific dimension of environmental quality made by persons who are skilled in a particular field. Second, the **psychophysical paradigm** involves identifying properties of settings that reliably lead to judgments of environmental quality. It is similar to approaches previously discussed, in which most of the power to predict judgments (for example, of beauty) is believed to reside in the scene rather than in the observer. The psychophysical paradigm, then, is observer-based only in its initial stages, when human observers are used to discover which properties of scenes do result in assessments of quality. Later, if the paradigm is successful, environmental assessment does not require observers, because each and every observer is presumed to respond to a given scene in more or less the same way. Knowing that a setting has certain characteristics (and does not have others) should allow for the computation of its level of quality from a prediction equation.

Third, the **cognitive paradigm** involves emphasis on the human processing of information received from the environment. Observers are presumed to combine many features of the setting into broad assessments such as satisfaction or preference (recall the research in this vein discussed in the last chapter). The psychophysical and cognitive paradigms may be joined into a single entity that Zube (1984) calls the behavioral paradigm.

The fourth paradigm may be called the **humanistic or experiential approach.** It focuses on the assessment of an active, sensitive observer who often adopts a phenomenological approach (see Chapter Two). The social and aesthetic concerns of an involved, sympathetic observer are reflected in humanistic OBEAs.

How good are these paradigms? OBEA measurement techniques must themselves be assessed to determine whether they are good enough to rely on (Daniel, 1976). The value of any assessment method or paradigm may be measured against four criteria: reliability, validity, generalizability, and utility.

A method is **reliable** if it yields consistent assessments—that is, if judgments of environmental quality for a place are similar from one occasion to another for the same observer or from one observer to another observer. However, *consistent* assessments are not necessarily *correct* judgments: observers can be consistently wrong!

The **validity** of an environmental assessment refers to how correct it is. Logically, assessments cannot be both inconsistent and correct, so they must be reliable before they can be valid. Validity, unfortunately, can be difficult to determine, because the measurement of validity requires that an investigator knows the *true* quality of an environment; the usual reason for undertaking an assessment in the first place is to *discover* something of the truth of the matter.

Generalizability refers to how widely an assessment may be applied across environments and across observers. If only one national forest is studied, the OBEA obviously should not be applied to other national forests, unless they happen to be very similar. For the same reason, an assessment made by one sample of observers (for-

statistical e.g. level of pollution

est rangers) should not be generalized to another (campers). If a group of park planners is enlisted to assess the quality of various potential campsites and the result is generalized to the average camper, mistakes may be made. The park planner's idea of a quality campsite may not be the same as that of the average camper.

The fourth criterion, **utility,** refers to the potential of the assessment to form the basis for policy or action. Environmental assessments may be valid and even widely generalizable, yet useless. For example, an OBEA that is outdated or irrelevant to the issue at hand can be virtually useless.

Employment of reliability, validity, generalizability, and utility criteria helps to ensure good OBEAs. These criteria are tough but attainable. Also, an OBEA need not be perfect to be useful. Developers of OBEAs should do the best they can to meet these criteria but not be daunted when they do not fully meet them.

▶ **In Sum.** At least four OBEA paradigms may be identified: expert, psychophysical, cognitive, and humanistic. Each has its own values and purposes, resulting in different kinds of assessments. The practitioner must always seek reliability, which is relatively easy to verify, and usually hope that validity follows, because it is usually difficult to verify. Generalizability and utility depend on wise matching of observers to the kind of assessments they are to make. OBEAs are useful if they are reliable, valid, and appropriately generalized.

Four Observer-Based Environmental Assessments

Over the last two decades, much theoretical and methodological progress has been made on OBEAs. However, some policymakers remain suspicious of a process they see as an intangible (Hamilton, 1985). OBEAs *are* needed, they *can* be useful, but they are not always *seen* to be useful by the policymakers who are in a position to fund them. Yet because OBEAs have potential value and because they are needed, many social scientists are actively working on them. Here are the stories of a few representative OBEAs.

The Scenic Quality of a Valley. The natural landscapes of many countries are being eroded quickly. Unspoiled landscape is an important

nonrenewable resource (Dearden, 1980). Economic development has its benefits, but one of its primary costs is destruction of the land as a setting suitable for native animals and plants and as a place of beauty and quiet recreation for people. Recognizing that economic development will not cease, policymakers have enacted legislation that attempts to identify the best landscapes for preservation.

A series of studies reported by Zube, Pitt, and Anderson (1975) examined common assumptions about what constitutes scenic quality. Many observers were shown slides of countryside in the northeast United States; others were taken into the field to see the vistas in person. Observers assessed the scenes using a number of different rating methods. Some of the specific issues in question were (1) which features of the landscape lead observers to assess it as scenic, (2) whether assessors from different walks of life agree on what is scenic, and (3) whether slide-simulated scenes produce the same judgments of scenic quality as field viewing of scenes. (See Fig. 3–11.)

On the first issue, Zube et al. conclude that natural landscapes are more scenic than built ones. Humans "have yet to build a landscape equal in quality to the best in nature." As for specific landscape characteristics, the authors report that scenic quality generally increases with ruggedness (for example, when much variation in vertical elevation appears in the scene), with the amount of shoreline visible in the scene, and with steepness, among other features. The image that comes to mind, then, is the classic postcard photograph of a sparkling lake set in tall mountains.

The second issue is agreement among different kinds of assessors. One cannot expect perfect agreement, but Zube et al. found quite strong tendencies for diverse groups to agree on the scenic quality of any given scene. The average correlation among groups ranging from secretaries and students to professional environmental designers was .77.

This does not mean that assessors with different roles may not have somewhat different views or should not be asked to participate in OBEAs (Craik, 1983b). In fact, despite strong agreement among assessor groups, there are *also* significant differences. Zube himself has found age and cultural variations (Zube & Pitt, 1981; Zube, Pitt, & Evans, 1983). In the scenic valley study, these dif-

FIGURE 3–11 The Connecticut River valley studied by Zube, Pitt, and Anderson. *(Courtesy of Erwin Zube)*

ferences did not appear because only one culture was studied and because the age groups that appear to have different standards for scenic quality (individuals under eleven and over sixty-five) did not participate.

The third issue is whether simulations are effective in yielding the same assessments of scenic quality produced by field visits. Of course the outcome is dependent on the quality of simulation employed. Zube et al. used color photographs and found very high correlations between assessments made after viewing the photos and after seeing the actual scenes.

Thus, one outcome of this OBEA was that local authorities found out which scenes in the districts they manage have high scenic quality. The researchers were also able to offer certain tentative conclusions about assessments of scenic quality in general. Scenic quality is highest for unspoiled, rugged terrain with shorelines visible; scenic quality is quite similar for a variety of young- to middle-aged adults of the same cul-

ture; and color photographs effectively simulate field-observed scenic quality.

The Environmental Quality of a Neighborhood. Fewer OBEAs of the built environment have been completed, but concern about the quality of housing, streets, urban parks, neighborhoods, and cities is at least as high as concern for natural settings. Most of us, after all, spend most of our time inside one building or another. Assessment of the quality of the built environment is obviously central to the slow process of creating more livable urban and suburban places.

Frances and Abraham Carp (1982b) report a large-scale OBEA involving over 2,500 residents of the San Francisco area. (See Fig. 3–12.) An extensive questionnaire yielded fifteen factors, or groups of items, each pertaining to one aspect of neighborhood physical quality (for example, air quality, outdoor noise, street maintenance, aesthetic quality).

An OBEA could stop here; it would yield an

assessment of the physical strengths and weaknesses of each neighborhood studied. Carp and Carp (1982a) decided to go beyond this step. They sought to discover relations between these assessments and objective features of the city, such as the distance to the nearest freeway, the number of different land uses within a quarter mile, and whether the block contains single-family or multiple-unit dwellings. Eventually, as noted earlier in the discussion of OBEA uses, features of the environment that are known to correlate highly with OBEAs could be used as markers. Future assessments would need only measure the objective features to know if neighborhood quality is in trouble; the time-consuming process of recruiting many assessors for an OBEA would become unnecessary.

This stage of research, however, is still far away. The Carps' research is one of the first steps in that direction. At this point, some readers might be thinking: Don't we already *know* when neighborhood quality is in trouble? Do we need fancy studies to find that out? In dramatically bad neighborhoods, OBEAs *are* probably unnecessary. But many mistakes have been made, even by professionals in the field.

Some years ago, for example, a somewhat disreputable-looking neighborhood was redeveloped in Boston; residents were rehoused in shiny new buildings. Gradually, the planners discovered that the superficial seediness of the destroyed neighborhood was not important to the residents. Many of them literally grieved for their lost homes (Fried & Gleicher, 1961). Neighborhood quality as assessed by the individuals who matter most—the residents—was not nearly as bad as the redevelopers had thought. The planners' mistake was to assume that the physical traces *they* interpreted as indicators of poor neighborhood quality would also lead residents to think the neighborhood was in trouble.

Back to the Carps' study. The long list of potential physical markers was found to contain nine factors (clusters of items) like those listed earlier. The nine marker clusters were used to predict the fifteen dimensions of quality. The more accurate these predictions, the better able planners would be to *accurately* gauge resident assessments of their own neighborhoods from physical features of the neighborhood.

The results were promising: Carp and Carp's findings included some moderately valid predic-

FIGURE 3–12 Urban neighborhoods range from cozy to murderous.

tions, but the results are certainly not ready to be used to guide planning yet. For instance, the physical markers were able to explain about half the variability in resident assessments of neighborhood aesthetic quality but only about one quarter of the variability in their assessment of noise problems.

Clearly, neighborhood OBEAs themselves can provide planners with valuable information about neighborhood quality from the resident perspective. However, connections between OBEA and physical markers of quality are only partially established—not as well established as the markers of scenic quality, for example. But the principles are the same and further research will improve knowledge of the relations between OBEAs and their physical indicators.

The Supportive Quality of Nursing Homes. OBEAs have also been used to assess the quality of smaller-scale settings, such as single institutions. Rudolf Moos and Sonne Lemke (1984) developed their Multiphasic Environmental Assessment Procedure (MEAP) as an OBEA for sheltered-care environments. The MEAP assesses both social and physical resources of these settings, in-

cluding policies, programs, residents, and staff, as well as physical and architectural features.

To focus on the physical setting, observers employ the Physical and Architectural Features Checklist, which assesses nine dimensions of sheltered-care settings (such as orientational aids, availability of space, safety features, staff lounges). Trained observers tour the facility and check off items that deal with relatively objective features. For example, raters note whether or not names are posted on the residents' doors, the hallways are decorated, the outdoor entrance is sheltered, there is a music-listening room, the floors are made of nonskid material, color-coding of floors or areas in the facility is used, and 147 other such features.

The nine dimensions are scored from these items. Together, they form a profile of the facility's physical and architectural resources. The strengths and weaknesses of a single facility may be assessed with the checklist, or several facilities may be compared. Figure 3–13 shows the profiles of two nursing homes. Consider the implications of the two profiles for daily living. Which facility would you prefer if you were ready for a nursing home?

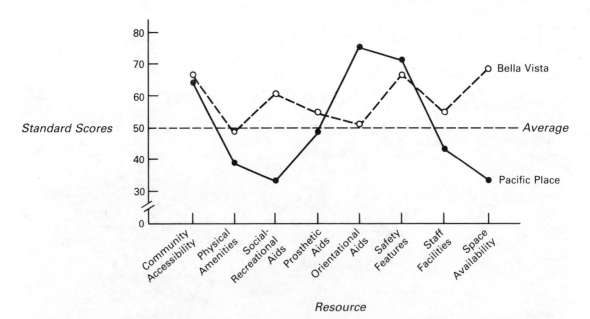

FIGURE 3–13 The physical and architectural profiles of two nursing homes, based on the Multiphasic Environmental Assessment Procedure (MEAP). *(Moos & Lemke, 1984)*

The Visual Quality of the Atmosphere. Smelters and other industrial plants produce both **plumes,** or columns of smoke, and **haze,** a general coloration of the atmosphere after plumes disperse. Many visitors to national parks find plumes and haze important sources of dissatisfaction. Visitors who come a long distance from an urban setting to "get away from it all" do not want to see another factory stack. Underlying this concern, of course, is the knowledge that air pollution in the form of acid rain has a serious effect on animals, plants, and fish in wilderness areas.

Air pollution in cities is unpleasant and harmful, too. An OBEA of air quality in Denver illustrates methods that might be applied elsewhere (Stewart, Middleton, & Ely, 1983). Six residents of the city were selected and trained to judge the visual quality of the atmosphere. Each of these residents made over 100 judgments from the five observation sites scattered around the city. The large number of judgments allowed the researchers to assess observer reliability and to obtain readings over a reasonable period (3 weeks).

The observers were found to be reliable, but were their ratings valid? The ratings were checked several ways, such as correlating them with readings from a machine called a nephelometer. This instrument measures aerosol light scattering, a key physical property of haze. The OBEA was found to be quite valid. Ratings of visual air quality by trained observers is an accurate way to assess the visual quality of the atmosphere.

Thus, the researchers were able to describe the extent and severity of air pollution in Denver, a city where air pollution stands in contrast to its image of environmental purity, and they were able to show that their method is worthy of adaptation for use elsewhere.

SUMMARY

Individuals appraise settings; selected groups assess them. In making appraisals, individuals may describe settings, make personal judgments of the setting's value, aesthetics, emotional impact, and meaning to them as well as their concern for it. Several forms of place assessments have been described, but most so far have focused on the scenic quality of natural settings. Observer-based assessments are more place- and policy-oriented than appraisals. They complement technical assessments, are particularly valuable for assessing dimensions of quality that are especially relevant to humans, and can serve as educational tools. Expert, psychophysical, cognitive, and humanistic paradigms have been used for observer-based environmental assessment. The versatility of OBEAs is demonstrated in assessments of a scenic river valley, a neighborhood, a nursing home, and urban air quality.

SUGGESTED SUPPLEMENTARY READINGS

Carp, F. M., & Carp, A. (1982). A role for technical environmental assessment in perceptions of environmental quality and well-being. *Journal of Environmental Psychology, 2,* 171–191.

Craik, K. H. (1968). The comprehension of the everyday physical environment. *Journal of the American Institute of Planners, 34,* 29–37.

———, & Zube, E. (Eds.). (1976). *Perceiving environmental quality: Research and applications.* New York: Plenum.

Gold, J. R., & Burgess, J. (Eds.). (1982). *Valued environments.* London: George Allen & Unwin.

Kaplan, S., & Kaplan, R. (1982). *Cognition and environment: Functioning in an uncertain world.* New York: Praeger.

Maloney, M. P., Ward, M. O., & Braucht, C. N. (1975). A revised scale for the measurement of ecological attitudes and knowledge. *American Psychologist, 30,* 787–790.

Zube, E. H. (1980). *Environmental evaluation: Perception and public policy.* Monterey, CA: Brooks/Cole.

Chapter Four

Personality and Environment

*The earliest mark of extraversion in a child
is his quick adaptation to the environment, and
the extraordinary attention he gives to objects,
especially to his effect upon them.*

Carl Jung, 1921

"You can't just sign up for these environmental review panels," said Tom's friend. "Usually only experts or frequent visitors to the place are invited to participate."

Tom half-heartedly remarked that he went camping in the park several times a year, then he announced that he was off to the carrels to study again. This annoyed Jane slightly.

"Why don't you come with the rest of us to study at Pat's place?" she asked. "Why are you always squirreling yourself away alone in that sensory deprivation chamber?"

Tom reflected. "I guess I've always needed to study in quiet," he said. "Even in high school, when most kids played the radio in their rooms after being locked in by their parents to do their homework, I liked quiet for studying."

Jane accepted this at face value but remained skeptical. She had always benefited from studying in a group of people. You could sweeten the work with conversational breaks, ask questions about difficult concepts, and generally feel less lonely.

"Well," she said, trying to change the subject to something less contentious, "what are you going to work on?"

"Becoming enlightened."

"What kind of an answer is that?"

"That is one of my major projects, you know," he said. "But I guess you're asking which school project I'm working on. It's an essay on the meaning of place. I'm trying to describe, from my own point of view, why that carrel has become such an important place to me. It's almost like home."

Jane counted to ten, trying not to blow up. "You and that carrel," she finally said. "What kind of person falls in love with a prison cell?"

Tom tried to be conciliatory, but he knew his own longstanding ways. "Sorry," he said, "I guess it takes all kinds."

Personality may seem a strange topic in a book about environmental psychology. It is often

thought of as something inside us; the environment is outside us. One might, therefore, wonder what connections exist, if any, between personality and the physical environment.

This view is reinforced by a glance at the definitions of personality offered by some influential personality theorists. Guilford said that personality is "a person's unique pattern of traits" (1959, p. 5). Allport defined it as "the dynamic organization within the individual of those psychophysical systems that determine his characteristic behavior and thought" (1961, p. 28). If personality is inside us and the environment is outside us, perhaps they have no connections worthy of study.

Some reasons why this conclusion is wrong lead off the next section. After that, seven systems for assessing **environmental personality,** the individual's behavioral tendencies that relate to or have consequences for the physical environment, are discussed. Next, the ways that personality variables—both traditional ones and those developed especially for environmental psychology—help us understand person-environment relations are surveyed. The chapter closes with a discussion of the uses to which personality may be put in designing environments.

APOLOGIA, BACKGROUND, AND CURRENT SITUATION

Connections between Personality and Environment

There are four reasons why personality is an integral part of environmental psychology. First, other personality theorists—from the earliest times—have seen personality as intimately related to the physical environment. Even the trait theories, when closely examined, intrinsically allow for situational factors. For example, the original definition of extraversion-introversion, a trait we think of as located inside the person, actually is based on the person's relationship to the environment. Carl Jung, who devised the concept, said the difference between the extravert and the introvert is based on the person's degree of preference for stimulation from outside.

Of course, merely asserting the existence of a connection between personality and environment does not make it exist. The second reason, however, confirms the first. Research shows that knowledge of an individual's traits helps us to understand and predict environmentally relevant behavior. John Gormly (1983) showed how knowledge of whether a person is sociable and/or energetic significantly predicts the kind of behavior setting that person is likely to select when given a choice.

Third, apart from traits or dispositions described by traditional personality theorists, such as extraversion or dominance, it has been demonstrated that individuals have dispositions that are specifically relevant to person-environment transactions. George McKechnie (1974) has identified several environmental dispositions, such as environmental trust, a measure of the individual's tendency to feel secure in potentially threatening environments.

Fourth, personal dispositions are central to one of environmental psychology's most important concepts, person-environment compatibility. One fundamental goal of designers and architects is a good fit between user and setting. To accomplish this fit, we must first be able to assess accurately both persons and environments. If these cannot be accurately assessed, we cannot be sure whether a good match between them has been achieved or not. The assessment of persons yields a pattern of personal dispositions that is an important part of the *person* in the person-environment congruence concept.

Roots of the Personality-Environment Connection

The notion that personality and environment influence one another is ancient. Within the modern era, the idea was elaborated most clearly and forcefully by Henry Murray in the 1930s and 1940s although others also discussed it (Campbell, 1934). In addition to his psychological interests, Murray, a brilliant all-around scholar, is a physician who graduated first in his class. He also has written important literary works, including a classic interpretation of Herman Melville's *Moby Dick*. Not surprisingly, given this breadth of interests, Murray's vision of personality, which he calls **personology,** recognizes and explicitly includes environmental factors (Murray, 1938). (See Fig. 4–1.)

FIGURE 4–1 Henry Murray's *personology,* with its concept of press, recognized the influential role of physical environments over fifty years ago. *(Courtesy of Jim Anderson.)*

For Murray, the basic event for personologists to study is the **proceeding,** the initiation and completion of an important behavior sequence. He distinguishes between **internal proceedings,** in which we try to represent, explain, and predict the world to ourselves (such as planning, daydreaming, solving problems) and **external proceedings,** in which we interact with other individuals or the physical environment (such as conversing, sailing, working). External proceedings have two sides to them: one corresponds to our *experience* of the external proceeding and the other corresponds to an *objective* account of the behavior sequence. When we sail, we are thinking about and feeling the weather, the water, the boat. Yet our sailing behavior, such as how long and how often we tack, could be measured objectively.

Murray views the environment itself as exerting *press,* "the power . . . to affect the well-being of the subject in one way or another" (1938, p. 1210). Press may have a positive or negative influence on us. (See Fig. 4–2.) While sailing, you may have a warm sunny day with moderate winds, or you may be capsized by a sudden squall. Press also may be social or physical in nature. Most important, press has an experiential side and an objective side, like the external proceeding. **Alpha press** is the environment considered from an unbiased, third-party point of view: what *really* confronts the individual. **Beta press** is the environment considered from the individual's own perspective.

Alpha and beta press often correspond to one another quite closely. But on some occasions, they may be strikingly discrepant. Discrepancies between alpha and beta press may be indicative of potential or actual problems. Consider a situation in which a room is at 20 degrees Celsius (71 degrees Fahrenheit) and someone complains that "it's really cold in here." If we notice this gap between alpha and beta press, we may begin to divine the reason for it. Guessing the person may be coming down with a cold, we ask, "How are you feeling?"

Murray offered several lists of press. These include aspects of both the physical and the social environment. In one list, designed to represent children's press, he included water, weather, and possessions as well as parents, praise, and friendship (Murray, 1938).

Another theorist whose ideas brought the environment into greater prominence within psychology was Kurt Lewin. His **field theory** is an attempt to represent the person and the environment in the graphic terms of topology, a branch of mathematics. The person (*P*) is viewed as existing in the psychological environment (*E*), the person's representation of the physical and social influences in the surroundings. *P* and *E* together comprise the **life space,** the totality of facts inside and outside the person. From these assertions comes Lewin's famous formula, $B = f(P, E)$. (See Fig. 4–3.)

Outside the life space, the foreign hull consists of **alien facts,** representing that which exists but has no place in the life space of an individual. The foreign hull includes portions of the physical and social environment that are not salient to the person. Of crucial importance, however, is Lewin's contention that the boundary between the life space and the foreign hull is *permeable.* Alien facts may become psychologically important

FIGURE 4–2 One form of environmental press!

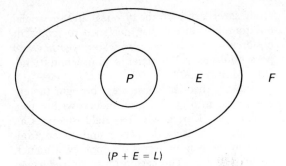

$$(P + E = L)$$

FIGURE 4-3 A simplified depiction of Kurt Lewin's view of psychology. Each person (P) exists in a psychological environment (E), which together makes up the life space (L). Outside L is the foreign hull (F), that part of the world the person has not incorporated into L through perception or awareness.

facts. That is why Lewin (1951) believed that the study of alien facts themselves—an enterprise he termed psychological ecology—is worthwhile.

One implication of this permeability, then, is that aspects of the physical environment that never before affected an individual in any psychologically important way may begin to do so. Madame Curie was not particularly concerned about the consequences to her health of experimenting with radium. By now, however, we know all too much about the carcinogenic properties of radioactive materials. Concern about them is an important part of living near a nuclear power plant.

A second, and perhaps even more important implication of permeability, is that permeability is bidirectional. That is, psychological facts may also influence alien facts. This feature of Lewin's theory is early formal recognition of an important current perspective of environmental psychologists: that persons should be viewed as active agents of environmental change. Often we are able to choose which setting we wish to use for a given purpose, to alter that setting if need be, and, on a larger scale, to influence decisions made on environmental issues by governments, business firms, and other oganizations.

As we become aware of more and more elements of the physical environment that affect us, we incorporate more of the foreign hull into our life spaces. This increased awareness does not mean that all of us become environmentally ac-

tive, but that most of us become more active at least in our own territories, that many of us become more active on a larger scale, and that nearly all of us could be more active agents of environmental improvement.

Another interesting implication of the permeability idea is that we sometimes affect the foreign hull unintentionally, without realizing either that we have had an effect or the magnitude of that effect. On the societal level, that's what happened with the widespread use of DDT; for years we did not realize that it was working its way up the food chain and endangering predatory birds by weakening the walls of their eggs. On a personal level, one's decision to recycle glass and paper affects individuals, organizations, and the physical environment far beyond our own life space.

Lewin's theory seems very simple, but it is conceptually powerful and has had enormous impact in psychology. In environmental psychology, it is the direct basis of several current theories, including ecological psychology and social ecology. The theory has been criticized, however, as unclear about the difference between E, the psychological environment, and P, the physical environment (Allport, 1955; Brunswik, 1943). These critics maintain that Lewin confuses the objective environment and the person's psychological representation of the environment.

This confusion has probably made the theory more influential rather than less so. Social psychologists have fruitfully taken E as the person's cognitive representation of the social and physical world. Some environmental psychologists have fruitfully used E as the objective physical world. Both groups have found the theory a useful guiding framework for research.

Much applied and nonapplied research has been based—sometimes directly, sometimes loosely—on Lewin's ideas. The applied work often employs Lewin's own concept, **action research** (Sommer & Amick, 1984), which aims to change social and physical conditions.

Murray and Lewin are the most influential predecessors of today's environmental psychologists who include personality concepts in their work. However, other theorists have also contributed valuable ideas. One of these is Andras Angyal (1941), whose ideas about the relationship between person and environment are summed up in his concept of the **biosphere,** a holistic notion of person and environment in which both are "aspects of a single reality which can be separated only by abstraction" (1941, p. 100). Biospheric occurrences are to be studied not by investigating the relations between two components of the world but by studying the system containing both phenomena. Angyal believes a given phenomenon has been properly studied when we locate the context in which the phenomenon belongs and determine its position in this context. This early version of the systems approach, in which position in a context is important, was a harbinger of many approaches that employ the systems framework today.

One distinction in Angyal's theory that is particularly applicable to environmental psychology is that between **autonomy** and **homonomy.** Autonomy, or a person's tendency to satisfy desires by using, mastering, or altering the environment, may be contrasted with homonomy, the tendency to find happiness by submerging yourself in the environment. The environment here includes both the social and physical environments. Autonomy might be exemplified in environmental psychology by the gardener who roots out every weed and stone and plants carefully selected varieties in neat rows (See Fig. 4–4.) Homonomy, by contrast, is exhibited by the stalker of edible wild plants who, rather than manipulate the earth to produce a garden, enjoys a walk through undisturbed woods in search of mushrooms, truffles, teas, and greens.

Angyal's seminal work, *Foundations for a Science of Personality* (1941), contains many other contributions that foreshadow the development of enviornmental psychology. Little attention has been paid, however, to Angyal's book compared to the works of Lewin and Murray. The idea of a holistic unity of person and environment is attractive, but some view it as too "cosmic" to

FIGURE 4–4 Some like them neat.

serve as a realistic basis for research. Theories that cannot be tested are not very scientifically valuable, although they can be very satisfying personally.

The importance of Angyal's work, besides its specific proposals such as the autonomy-homonomy distinction, is to remind us that person and environment are part of a unified system. When we separate them temporarily to measure and study them, we should put them together again when we think about the big picture (Murphy, 1956).

Current Concerns

The ideas of Murray, Lewin, and Angyal are *grand*, by which I mean that they cover much ground and describe many of the essential features of the personality-environment connection. Their elegantly stated frameworks and philosophies still make enlightening reading over 40 years after they were devised. Current theorists have much more data from which to draw their models and the advantage of having had access to the grand theories from the beginning of their careers. The time has come to build integrations of the grand theories, devise theories that reflect our appreciation of the enormous complexity of personality-environment interaction more completely, and test these newer models. Unfortunately, for reasons to be discussed, progress has been delayed.

Murray (1938) preferred the term **personology** over "the psychology of personality" because he aimed to understand the whole of a person, including the general course of the person's life as well as all the various aspects of psychology we call emotion, behavior, cognition, and physiology. Personology may be seen as the "queen of psychology," the approach that would integrate understanding of the manifold processes and attributes of the human being. This integration is a formidable goal. Personologists have made some progress, as we shall see, but they are not yet able to "construct a scheme of concepts for portraying the entire course of human development, and thus provide a framework into which any single episode—natural or experimental—may be fitted" (Murray, 1938, p. 4).

This has not been for lack of effort on the part of personologists. It is problematic because "persons are extraordinarily complex and multidi-mensional entities" (Craik, 1976, p. 60), and it is inherently difficult to understand an organism that is equally complex as oneself (how far would jellyfish get in studying jellyfish?). In addition, personology has been sidetracked in controversy of late.

The controversies have included debates on whether psychological testing is useful or ethical, whether individuals exhibit consistency in their behavior, and even whether the field of personality ought to exist. Some valuable lessons may be learned from examining these controversies (Pervin, 1978). But whether those lessons have been worth the enormous amount of effort and debate—much of it acrimonious and repetitive—is unclear. Certainly the controversies have consumed much energy and time that might have been devoted to pursuit of the ambitious goals of early personality theorists.

In the next section we review some of the attempts to characterize individuals as they interact with the physical environment. Most of them begin with the assumption that each of us has "fairly enduring styles of relating to the everyday physical environment" (Craik, 1976) that vary from individual to individual. We can identify four broad approaches to characterizing these individual differences.

First, and most plentiful, are those who recognize **dispositions** or tendencies to behave in a certain pattern in most situations. Disposition-oriented theorists usually assume that every individual may be located along each of a certain number of dimensions.

The second approach is to begin with individuals instead of dispositions and to find the **personal constructs** that each individual employs in manifesting a relatively enduring pattern of behavior. It follows that each individual in this approach may have different numbers of different constructs that guide action and thought.

A third approach is to develop concepts that refer directly to the manner in which individuals **process environmental stimulation** (Wohlwill, 1976). In this approach, individuals differ in the amount, kind, and duration of stimulation they prefer and are able to work with effectively.

A fourth approach is to investigate individual differences in **demography,** such characteristics as sex, occupation, age, educational level, and marital status. The personologist who wishes to consider the whole person certainly must take these demographic features of the person into account.

Each of these approaches, except the demographic, are represented in the next section. References to demographic variables as they affect environment-behavior transactions are scattered throughout the rest of this book.

► **In Sum.** Personality is a part of environmental psychology because (a) the trait concept does not merely refer to persons but includes consideration of how persons interact with their environments, (b) traits help predict the behavior of individuals in the environment, (c) traits exist that specifically characterize our environmental tendencies, and (d) traits form an important part of the *person* half of person-environment compatibility.

The important early formulations of Henry Murray, Kurt Lewin, and Andras Angyal are reviewed because some of their ideas are still influential, others are being revived, and some deserve more attention. Henry Murray's personology introduced the concepts of alpha and beta press (the actual and perceived power of the environment to affect our welfare), and internal and external proceedings (subjective and objective accounts of the initiation and completion of a behavior sequence). Lewin's field theory, which conceptualized persons as actively interacting with their environments in their life spaces, produced the famous formula $B = f(P, E)$. Our representation of the physical environment and some elements of the unrepresented physical environment (the foreign hull) affect our behavior and experience. Lewin's action research concept, in which theory and application are fused, guides many environmental psychologists today. Angyal's holistic, systems-oriented approach has not been widely acknowledged yet represents an early version of a theoretical position that is widely held today.

An illustrative concept from this organismic-contextual theory is autonomy-homonomy, in which individuals are viewed as ranging from those who wish to blend into the environment to those who wish to remake the environment into their own image. Controversy over the whole notion of personality has occupied researchers and slowed progress in this area. Four kinds of individual differences are dispositions, personal constructs, styles of processing environmental stimulation, and demographic differences.

ENVIRONMENTAL PERSONALITY ASSESSMENT

The basis for the personality theorist's models are ideas about the ways that one individual may differ from another. If these concepts are to be useful, they must be measured. Personality assessment, whether employing traditional concepts or the newer ones that relate to environmental activities, is an attempt to accurately summarize a person's primary behavioral tendencies.

In the **idiographic** approach to personality assessment, the psychologist's main goal is to understand the behavioral tendencies of one person at a time. This approach is used when the focus is on a single individual, such as in some varieties of psychotherapy or in designing an environment for one specific person. In the **nomothetic** approach, the main goal is to discover how individuals of a certain psychological *type*—extraverts, for example—interact with their social and physical environments. Psychologists may use either approach, depending on the purpose of their study.

This section is a review of personality assessment concepts and measures employed by psychologists who are particularly interested in person-environment relations. Since the 1960s, numerous environmental-personality concepts and associated measures have been suggested. The earliest ones concentrated on one or two hypothesized dimensions, rather than attempting to comprehensively measure all aspects of personality that might be related to the physical environment.

Person-Thing Orientation

One of the earliest such concepts posits simply that some individuals are primarily attuned to objects and environment and others are more attuned to people (Cottle, 1950; Thurstone, 1946). The modern developer of this concept, Brian Little (1968, 1972, 1976), proposes that each of us tends toward one of four possible orientations. Some of us are **person-specialists,** and others are **thing-specialists,** as already noted. Some of us are **generalists;** we show a marked interest in both people and things. Some of us are **nonspecialists,** not very interested in either people or things.

Knowing which of these types best characterizes an individual should enable us to predict some of that person's behavior. Which type would most likely take an environmental psychology course? Which type would prefer a social psychology course?

The person-specialist, according to Little, is likely to have a smaller personal space zone, to use first names in conversations more, and to send more letters. The thing-specialist, when not working on a computer or tinkering with the car, probably prefers solitary nature walks or gardening and reads magazines that focus on hobbies, electronics, or collecting. (See Fig. 4–5.) The generalist cares about both people and things but may have a problem with information overload. The generalist may be frustrated when attempts to involve an acquaintance who is a computer addict (thing-specialist) in the Computer User Club prove futile, and when it is nearly impossible to involve a friend who is majoring in social work (person-specialist) to even look at a computer.

If the nonspecialist cares little for people or environment, what *is* important? The usual answer—perhaps not always evident at first—is *me*! Little suggests that a better name for this type might be *self-specialist*. These individuals spend much time attempting to understand and predict their own behavior, severely limiting the amount of time they have to devote to others or to the environment.

Little's measures of these concepts, called the Person-Thing Orientation Scales, are in questionnaire format. Friedman (1974) developed a different measure of the same basic concept, which he called **thing cognitive complexity.** Adapting a technique from the personality theorist George Kelly (1955) called the **repertory grid,** Friedman attempted to assess the complexity of the individual's conceptualization of things. Individuals who are very thing-cognitively complex have many different ways of distinguishing or grouping objects or environments.

Environmental Personality Inventory

A second early typology was constructed by Joseph Sonnenfeld (1969). It includes four concepts. The first of these, **environmental sensitivity,** is reminiscent of Little's thing-specialist concept in that it measures the amount and complexity of the environment's impact on the individual. When asked to indicate whether numerous features of their home environments have positive, negative, or neutral connotations to them, environmentally sensitive individuals report that many features do have connotations of one sort or another.

The second dimension in Sonnenfeld's inventory is **environmental mobility.** By asking individuals to rank how much they would like to visit certain places around the world and how risky and exotic they believe each place to be, Sonnenfeld derives a measure of the individual's mobility. In general, highly mobile individuals are those who

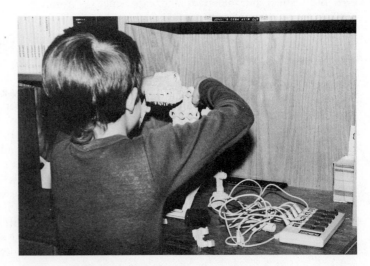

FIGURE 4–5 A young thing-specialist.

would very much like to visit the same places that they believe are risky and exotic.

Sonnenfeld's third dimension is **environmental control,** a measure of how much individuals believe the environment controls them, or vice versa. In the case of flooding, individuals differing on this dimension might prefer to avoid flood plains, work to control flooding, learn to live with floods or even appreciate the excitement and challenge that floods provide.

Sonnenfeld's last dimension is **environmental risk-taking,** a measure of one's propensity to take risks and to evaluate various activities as being risky or not. We all know individuals who climb icy slopes, raft down whitewater rivers, or race cars, and others who would never engage in these activities. But Sonnenfeld's concept also includes the individual's beliefs about whether these (and other more common activities) are or are not risky. Thus, one individual may believe mountain climbing is very risky, yet climb rock cliffs every weekend, but another person climbs frequently but does not believe climbing is very risky. Yet other individuals may believe climbing is risky and avoid it or believe that it is not risky but never care to go.

Environmental Response Inventory

The most ambitious effort to measure environmentally related personality is George McKechnie's Environmental Response Inventory (ERI), which contains scales to measure eight concepts. McKechnie (1974) calls the ERI a **broadband assessment instrument,** meaning that for the first time an attempt is made to measure most or all personal dispositions relevant to our everyday interaction with the physical environment.

This raises the question: How many such dispositions are there? Craik (1970) has observed that so far personality researchers who specialize in environmentally relevant behavior have no overall guiding theory to supply an answer to this question. Therefore, the ERI includes more concepts than any other assessment method to date, but it cannot be regarded as comprehensive. Still it is definitely the most complete environmental personality assessment system we have. It is also probably the best-developed and most-researched system.

The ERI was developed in a complex, multi-stage test construction sequence (McKechnie, 1974). After much creation, exploration, evaluation, shortening, and testing of the scales, the following concepts were considered to be adequately measured by scales that are each about twenty questions long:

Pastoralism. The tendency to oppose land development, preserve open space, accept natural forces as influences, and prefer self-sufficiency.

Urbanism. The tendency to enjoy high-density living and appreciate the varied interpersonal and cultural stimulation found in city life.

Environmental Adaptation. The tendency to favor the alteration of the environment to suit human needs and desires, oppose development controls, and prefer highly refined settings and objects.

Stimulus Seeking. The tendency to be interested in travel and exploration, enjoy complex or intense physical sensations, and have very broad interests.

Environmental Trust. The tendency to be secure in the environment, be competent in finding your way around, and be unafraid of new places or of being alone.

Antiquarianism. The tendency to enjoy historical places and things, prefer traditional designs, collect more treasured possessions than most other individuals, and appreciate the products of earlier eras.

Need for Privacy. The tendency to need isolation, not appreciate neighbors, avoid distraction, and seek solitude.

Mechanical Orientation. The tendency to enjoy technological and mechanical processes, enjoy working with your hands, and care about how things work.

We see in these dimensions certain similarities to previously developed systems. Stimulus seeking is not unlike Sonnenfeld's environmental mobility. Mechanical orientation is similar to Little's *thing-specialist* concept. Need for privacy is similar to Nancy Marshall's (1972) privacy concepts, although McKechnie views privacy tendencies as more deep-seated and long-lasting than Marshall, who sees privacy as a more changeable set of attitudes (Taylor, 1983; also see the privacy chapter in this book for more on Marshall's ideas).

Nevertheless, McKechnie's system includes some new dimensions and provides us with a set of concepts that can all be measured at the same time with the same basic instructions and materials. More important, it allows for the beginning of research into the question of how many dimensions of interest to environmental psychologists exist and how they are interrelated. From McKechnie's own work, we know that antiquarianism and pastoralism are strongly correlated (but not so alike that they are redundant), but environmental trust and environmental adaptation are completely uncorrelated. Ultimately, one goal is to know all the important dimensions and how they fit together.

Thus far we have focused on the *dimensions* of personality. McKechnie's broad-band approach opens another possibility: assessing an individual's *pattern* of personal dispositions. For certain applications, such as designing a home or workspace that is primarily for one individual, knowing that person's configuration of environmental tendencies can be of considerable value.

With eight or more tendencies to consider, this could be a complex decision, but let's consider a relatively simple case. Mark Zowie scores very high on stimulus seeking and antiquarianism, and Ezekiel Oldham scores very high on antiquarianism and very low on stimulus seeking. To keep matters simple, assume both men have average scores on the other scales. How would you design an office for each man?

I see Mark in an office covered with photos of himself on safari and on top of mountains. On his desk are some pieces-of-eight he found while diving in the Caribbean. There is a set of genuine armor in the corner. His antique map collection fills an entire wall.

I see Ezekiel in an office that also reveals the collector tendency. Oldham, however, is into stamps and coins; display cases figure prominently in one corner of the office. In contrast to the electric blue carpet and orange walls of Zowie's office, Oldham has brown carpet and weathered barn-board on one wall. Subdued lighting, Victorian leather furnishings, and bookshelves full of first editions complete the scene in Ezekiel's office.

The ERI's value has been increased by an adaptation of it for use with children. Trudi Bunting and Larry Cousins (1983) changed many items to reflect the activities and interests of children as young as nine. The *Children's Environmental Response Inventory* (CERI) should allow researchers to discover the tendencies of individual children, understand why they like and dislike certain settings, and assist in planning children's settings.

Another elaboration of an ERI theme was undertaken by Taylor and Konrad (1980), who set out to develop more differentiated measures of the individual's disposition toward the past. In a study of historic and prehistoric sites in Toronto, four "subspecies" of the ERI's Antiquarianism were uncovered. (See Fig. 4–6.) **Conservation** is the tendency to support (or not) the preservation of historic buildings and archeological sites. *Heritage* is the tendency to appreciate (or not) the past as a cultural entity that has value in the present as a source of national identity or of lessons that could usefully guide today's decisions. *Experience* is the tendency to desire (or not) direct experience with historic or prehistoric places, such as wanting to visit reconstructed pioneer villages or living in a nice old house. **Interest** is the tendency to think often (or not) about or reflect on past events and places.

All four scales are highly correlated with antiquarianism, but Taylor and Konrad offer them as tools for use when the researcher is specifically interested in the different aspects of dispositions toward the past and its artifacts.

Environmental Preference Questionnaire

Rachel and Stephen Kaplan spent several years developing a shorter, more direct measure of individual tendencies in the environment. The EPQ (Kaplan, 1977) assesses preferences in seven areas. The **nature scale** taps the tendency to enjoy wilderness, woodlands, campfires, and other outdoor activities in relatively undeveloped places. The **romantic escape scale** also measures one's tendency to get out into natural settings, but instead of heading to the woods, the romantic escapist is fleeing from the urban-suburban life.

The **modern development scale** is reminiscent of the ERI's environmental adaptation scale. It assesses the individual's preference for modern housing and relative disregard for the degradation

FIGURE 4–6 Some like them Victorian.

of the physical environment. The **suburbs scale** measures the tendency to espouse such archetypal suburban values as owning property, engaging in routine activities, watching sports, and considering law and order to be an important issue. The **social scale** is similar to traditional measures of affiliative tendency, the desire to be with and enjoy the company of people. The **passive reaction to stress scale,** which indicates a tendency to respond to pressure by engaging in low-energy behaviors such as going to a movie, going to sleep, or eating. The **city scale,** like the ERI's urbanism scale, measures one's liking for the varied and extensive stimulation provided by urban settings.

Stimulus Screening and Noise Sensitivity Scales

These two measures, developed separately, both deal with how the individual processes incoming stimulation. The **stimulus screening** concept (Mehrabian, 1976a) includes individual responses (such as "slow to be aroused" or "quick to adapt") to different kinds of stimuli (sound, texture, odor, and heat) that arrive in different patterns (novel, complex, or sudden). Mehrabian's goal is to assess the individual's *automatic* screening of irrelevant stimuli. Screeners are those who are able to overcome the distraction that irrelevant stimuli cause nonscreeners. (See Fig. 4–7.) In general, Mehrabian posits that screeners are less "arousable" than nonscreeners.

The Noise Sensitivity Scale, developed by Neil Weinstein (1978), focuses on one's emotional response to noise in the immediate area. Weinstein constructed it under the assumptions that we differ in our initial response to noise and in our abilities to adjust to noise that continues. Noise sensitivity appears to be related to a more general tendency of individuals to be critical or uncritical

FIGURE 4-7 Some can screen out unwanted stimuli and study in public places. *(Courtesy of John Driscoll.)*

of their physical surroundings (Weinstein, 1980). (See Fig. 4–8.)

Personal Projects Analysis

Some investigators have taken a quite different path in the search for units of analysis in personality-environmental research. This path rejects the assumption, common to all the systems discussed so far (except Freidman's variant of person-thing orientation), that every personality construct in the system applies, to a greater or lesser degree, to every individual. Stated more positively, the personal constructs approach assumes that different constructs are important to different individuals.

The basis for the personal construct approach is the theory of George Kelly (1955). He developed a method (the Repertory Grid Test) by which individuals could, with a little guidance, produce for themselves the constructs that are important to their own experience. In Kelly's own work, these constructs tended to be cognitive in nature, such as good-bad or fast-slow. Perhaps the first to recognize the application of Kelly's ideas to environmental concerns were John Harrison and Philip Sarre (1971, 1975). They proposed that individuals' responses to environmental images and

FIGURE 4-8 Neil Weinstein's long interest in noise has included studies of traffic, office, and classroom noise as well as individual differences in noise sensitivity. *(Courtesy of Neil Weinstein.)*

their mental models of the environment could be studied profitably with Kelly's methods.

Brian Little (1972, 1976, 1983) has taken the personal constructs idea much further, introducing the concept of **personal project,** "an interrelated sequence of actions intended to achieve some personal goal." Little's system retains the Kellian idea that each individual has a unique set of constructs but shifts the focus from cognitive constructs to concrete projects. In so doing, the idea reflects not only Kelly's approach but Henry Murray's concepts of episodes and serials and the idea of the individual as an active planner (Russell & Ward, 1982; Stokols, 1982).

A personal project is literally something that you are working on. It might be a long-term project, such as getting your degree or retiring by age forty, or a short-term one, such as doing well on the exam for which you are cramming or giving a successful party this weekend. Projects may be shared (keeping a relationship healthy or building a canoe with a friend) or solitary (writing a paper or bench-pressing 100 kilograms). They may be concrete (pouring a concrete patio) or abstract (discovering the secret of the universe).

Little (1983) reports that when asked to generate a list of personal projects, the average person reports about fifteen, although some individuals have reported many more. (See Fig. 4–9.) Little believes that understanding an individual's personal projects tell us much about both their personality and their relationship to the physical settings in their lives.

So far the relevance of personal projects to the physical environment has not been mentioned. Little (1983) describes three links. First, the Personal Projects Matrix (the equivalent of Kelly's Repertory Grid Test) asks not only for a list of projects but for the respondent to describe certain characteristics of each project. One of these is *where* the project is undertaken. When the location of a person's projects is known, together with all the other characteristics of projects, a variety of conclusions might be drawn. We might discover that every personal project in one physical setting is difficult or contentious. The family home seems to be that kind of setting for some adolescents. Or we might observe that an individual has many or few settings in which to undertake projects. Having relatively few potential settings probably hinders the very possibility of undertaking some projects.

A second link between personal projects and environment involves health, stress, and quality of life. Certain projects must occur in specific kinds of settings; if such settings are health hazards, then undertaking that project is likely to endanger your health. Consider the rock musician whose major project is to make a living from music. Unless the musician is one of those rare few who hit the big time very early and suddenly, many hours will be spent playing loud music in smoky bars late at night. The physical and social environment required for such a project almost necessarily places the musician in danger. Similarly, many industrial employees work in dangerous settings, and sales managers risk alcoholism because of customary boozy business luncheons.

The third area of overlap between personal projects analysis and environmental psychology resides in discovering which kinds of settings tend to support which kinds of individuals' project systems. Consider, for example, elderly people who live in one kind of institution or another. Are the kind of personal projects typically enjoyed by these residents well-supported by the institution? Are some institutions easier to adapt to? Are there physical features that ought to be present in every institution to ensure that residents' personal projects are supported by the physical setting?

Place Identity.   One more approach to personality and environment is concerned with **place identity.** This approach, primarily developed by Harold Proshansky (1978) and his colleagues (Proshansky, Fabian, & Kaminoff, 1983), focuses on the individual's incorporation of place into the larger concept of self. (See Fig. 4–10.) That is, some places become important parts of ourselves. Place-identity researchers want to understand this process.

Home, of course, is the place many of us feel is the most essential part of ourselves. But other places are important too: our office, the school, the tennis court, our town. What happens when one or more of these settings is left behind (for example, when we go away to college) or taken away (the old neighborhood gets redeveloped, the family home sold)? Place-identity research is con-

Personal Projects Matrix

List of Projects	1 Importance	2 Enjoyment	3 Difficulty	4 Visibility	5 Control	6 Initiation	7 Stress	8 Time Adequacy	9 Outcome (likelihood of success)	10 Self Identity (How typical of you?)	11 Others' View (of importance)	12 Value Congruency (Consistency with your values)	13 Positive Impact	14 Negative Impact	15 Progress	16 Challenge	17 Absorption	18 With whom?	19 Where?
1 Search for Summer Job	9	9	8	10	1	10	5	8	10	8	10	8	10	3	8	10	8	Shell.	Field
2 Complete School	10	8	4	9	10	10	6	10	8	10	10	10	8	8	9	8	8	Richm. Stev L.	C.V.
3 Staying in Shape	8	8	1	7	10	10	1	7	9	9	9	10	7	4	8	4	6	Dark	Phys. Ed.
4 Choosing Career	9	9	3	8	10	10	5	7	6	9	8	8	8	8	3	7	9		
5 Meaningful relationship	7	8	6	8	8	9	8	4	8	8	8	9	6	7	8	8	8	Cathey S.	Anywhere
6 Budget money better	8	9	6	8	10	10	6	6	7	9	8	8	8	6	6	8	4		
7 Keep house clean	5	3	10	4	3	3	0	2	4	7	6	7	3	3	3	10	2	Deural. Tim R.	home
8 Improve Dart Game	0	10	2	4	10	10	0	0	8	3	3	7	0	0	0	3	4		
9 Better Use of Study Time	8	7	3	8	10	10	6	1	8	7	8	8	8	8	8	8	7		work library
	7.1	9	4.6	9	8	9.1	4.1	5.6	6.7	7.5	7.7	6.3	6.4	4.6	6.2	7.3	6.6		

FIGURE 4-9 A completed Personal Projects Matrix.

FIGURE 4–10 Harold Proshansky was instrumental in the development of the first graduate program in environmental psychology and has investigated the concept of place identity. *(Courtesy of Harold Proshansky.)*

cerned with the acquisition, interaction, and loss of relationships with places that are important to the individual sense of self.

▶ **In Sum.** Seven systems for conceptualizing our differences in relating to the environment have been described. Idiographic analyses focus on the personality pattern of one individual at a time; nomothetic analyses focus on the lawful relations between personality and behavior across many individuals. The inventories developed by Little, Sonnenfeld, McKechnie, Taylor and Konrad, Mehrabian, and Weinstein assess over twenty dimensions of personality as it relates to the environment. Little's Personal Projects Analysis uncovers a "custom" set of dimensions for each individual. Proshansky's place identity concept deals with the ways that places become part of ourselves.

TRADITIONAL PERSONALITY DIMENSIONS AND BEHAVIOR-ENVIRONMENT RELATIONS

When environmental psychology was new, no one had yet developed the measures of personality just discussed. Those who believed that the study of personal dispositions might help us understand behavior in the environment were forced to employ existing measures of personality. These measures were not, for the most part, designed to predict environmentally relevant behaviors. However, certain constructs measured by traditional methods appeared to be relevant. Environmental psychologists therefore attempted to use them to help elucidate environment-behavior relations.

For example, the frequency of engaging in six outdoor recreation activities was correlated in one study with scores on a general purpose personality test (Driver & Knopf, 1977). The results demonstrated that personality is modestly related to one's choice of outdoor activities. In a second example, Eddy and Sinnett (1973) assessed the personality of special-needs residents at a university. They found that extraverted individuals spent more time in the lobby and in bars, where more social interaction occurs. Of course, personality is not a perfect predictor of such activities, but even these traditional measures perform fairly well as predictors. Given that the measures usually were not designed for environmental psychology, they have been quite successful. Let us survey some of these results.

Outgoing versus Reserved Individuals

One fundamental dimension in traditional personality theory is tapped by constructs such as extraversion-introversion, sociable-unsociable, and warm-cold. These constructs are not identical, but in general they all differentiate individuals who enjoy being with others from those who do not.

Sociability is predictive of many environmentally relevant behaviors, particularly the individual's use of space. Specifically, this includes preferred interpersonal distance, reactions to high-density situations, furniture arrangement preferences, evaluation of landscapes, and even, it seems, sense of direction.

Most but not all studies show that outgoing individuals prefer closer interpersonal distances than do reserved individuals (Altman, 1975, p. 73). The mixed results may be because personality has a more complex relation to interpersonal distance than first thought. Interpersonal distance preference may be a function of an individual's *pattern*

---

of dispositions, above and beyond the effect of any single disposition.

In a study that examined this idea, participants were asked to draw chairs in a diagram of a room, placing the chairs where they would feel comfortable talking to another person in eighteen different social situations (Gifford, 1982a). In general, warm individuals placed their chairs closer to the other person than did cold individuals; this is a straightforward relation of the type already discussed. But a more complex pattern was also evident. Those who were cold *and* ambitious chose significantly larger distances than those who were cold but *not* ambitious. But among warm individuals, ambitious and nonambitious individuals did not choose different distances. Thus, if we combine knowledge of at least two of a person's dispositions, we can make better predictions about that person's preferred interpersonal distance.

A similar complexity is evident in the way outgoing and reserved individuals react to lack of space. Both outgoing and reserved individuals prefer lower densities, but they differ in how much stress they experience, according to a study of dormitory residents (Miller, Rossbach, & Munson, 1981). Outgoing students who lived in high-density dorms reported less stress than reserved students who lived in high-density dorms, but the two groups experienced about the same amount of stress in low-density dorms. Apparently, outgoing individuals find the high-density setting compatible with their preferences and social skills, but reserved individuals find high-density difficult to cope with. Miller et al. report several other interactions between density level and degree of personal reserve that, together, confirm that personality and environment are often related in complex ways.

Reserved individuals—at least reserved professors—seem to arrange their office furniture differently from more outgoing professors (McElroy, Morrow, & Ackerman, 1983). Faculty offices may be characterized as open (when the desk is placed against a far wall, so it does not constitute a barrier between professor and visitor) or closed (when the desk intervenes between professor and visitor). McElroy et al. found that outgoing professors more often used the open furniture arrangement. Both personality and social factors (such as the number of visitors to the office) probably influ-

ence furniture arrangement (Hensley, 1982), but the McElroy study demonstrates how an outgoing personality may be reflected in such commonplace behaviors as how one arranges furniture.

Some evidence suggests that outgoing individuals evaluate landscapes differently than do reserved individuals (Craik, 1975; Feimer, 1981). In Craik's study, individuals who reported needing the support of others found landscapes near San Francisco more serene, beautiful, and cultivated than those who reported needing less support from others. Feimer's study of the same area found that outgoing individuals perceived the landscapes as more active and busy than did reserved individuals. These studies demonstrate that personality is connected to environmentally relevant behavior in some nonobvious ways.

As another example of a nonobvious personality-environment relation, consider Kendall Bryant's (1982) finding that the tendency to be outgoing or reserved is related to one's sense of direction. More sociable individuals, it seems, are better able to point out correct geographical directions than less sociable individuals. As further evidence that such relations are really not obvious, Bryant asked participants how good their sense of direction was and found no differences between outgoing and reserved individuals. Thus, even those who use their sense of direction more effectively seem to be unaware that they are more skilled than others.

Internal-External Locus of Control

Some of us feel that we can exert a reasonable amount of control over our destinies; others believe our lives are strongly influenced by powerful others or by fate. This belief that control is primarily inside or outside ourselves (internal versus external locus of control) has been examined in relation to environmentally relevant behaviors because of its seemingly obvious connection to person-environment relations. In fact, most locus of control measures refer more to a belief that our lives are controlled by the *social* environment or fate rather than the physical environment. Nevertheless, locus of control does play a significant role in some person-environment transactions. Among these are use of space, response to natural hazards and smog, responsible environmentalism (recycling, antipollution activities), and preferences for architectural style.

The spatial activities related to locus of control include interpersonal distance and reaction to high density. Individuals who believe their life is controlled by external forces seem to prefer larger interpersonal distances from strangers than those who believe they primarily control the course of their own lives (Duke & Nowicki, 1972; Heckel & Hiers, 1977). Perhaps those who believe that others, especially strangers, exert considerable influence over them feel safer and more secure if they are literally out of reach.

Several studies report that internals tolerate high densities better than externals (Sundstrom, 1978; Verbrugge & Taylor, 1980). One explanation is that internals have learned more and better coping strategies. Those who believe life is reasonably controllable naturally seek to fulfill that belief by developing methods of handling difficult situations.

This principle is illustrated in the manner in which internals and externals respond to environmental threats. Sims and Baumann (1972) examined how individuals differing in locus of control responded to the threat of tornados. As expected, internals believed that luck had less to do with the damage resulting from tornados than did externals. More significantly, internals actually took more recommended precautions than externals did.

Personality has been related to responsible environmentalism. Arbuthnot (1977) compared regular recyclers with nonrecyclers and found that recyclers had significantly more internal locus of control tendencies. Internals recycled more even though they also had higher scores on a scale measuring environmental cynicism; they were less optimistic than nonrecyclers that their efforts would solve environmental problems. Perhaps they recycled more because, in addition, they scored higher on an environmental responsibility scale. They more strongly believed that environmental problems were their personal responsibility. Nonrecyclers and recyclers held equally pro-ecology attitudes. Recyclers are not more committed in terms of attitude, and they are more pessimistic about their efforts. But because they believe that they can influence their own destiny in general and that environmental problems are their own, they recycle.

These locus of control studies described so far seem to indicate patterns of behavior far less complex than those we observed in the outgoing-reserved studies. A complicating factor was found, however, in a study of individuals' response to smog (Evans, Jacobs, & Frager, 1982a). From the research just described we might expect that internals would cope with smog by engaging in more preventative behaviors than externals would. Unfortunately, both groups seem to adapt to smog. Evans et al. found that new residents of Los Angeles who were internals took more anti-smog steps than long-term residents who were internals. Internal long-term residents took as few preventative measures as external long-term residents. (See Fig. 4–11.) Adaptation, sadly, seems a stronger influence on antismog behavior than locus of control.

Similar interactions among variables also have been found in the relations between locus of control and antipollution behavior (Trigg, Perlman, Perry, & Janisse, 1976). Internals engaged in five pro-ecology activities, such as joining an environmental group or writing to the government on ecological issues, more than externals. But Trigg et al. also measured the optimism of their participants and found that optimistic internals engaged in more activities than did pessimistic internals. This interaction between locus of control and optimism contrasts with Arbuthnot's study of recyclers, in which pessimists recycled more. Trigg et al. offer several possible explanations for the discrepancy, but only further research can clarify the situation. One repeatedly confirmed conclusion, however, is that those who believe they have some control over their lives do engage in more responsible environmental activities.

Locus of control may be related to preferences for architectural style. Juhasz and Paxson (1978) showed slides depicting classical building styles (renaissance and 1950s international) versus romantic building styles (baroque and 1950s naturalism). Individuals with a tendency to external locus of control preferred buildings within the romantic style; those tending to internality preferred buildings in the classical tradition. Juhasz and Paxson speculate that internality implies the exercise of control, and this preference for control carries over into a preference for more controlled environments. Classical building styles, most architects would agree, include more straight lines

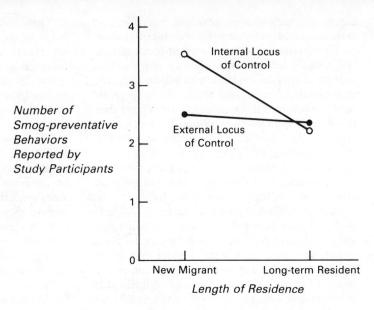

Number of Smog-preventative Behaviors Reported by Study Participants

FIGURE 4–11 Whether or not one copes with smog by engaging in behaviors that reduce its impact is a function of both personality and length of residence. "Internals" who move to Los Angeles initially cope more than newly-arrived "externals," but as time passes their coping behavior sags to the level of "externals." *(Adapted from Evans, Jacobs, & Frager, 1982a.)*

and are more severe than the more flowing, rolling romantic styles.

Other Traditional Dimensions

Outgoing-reserved and internal-external locus of control have received the most research attention among traditional personality measures, but a variety of other dimensions have also been examined. One of these might be termed psychological health, measured as ego strength, adjustment, self-confidence, or lack of neuroticism. Individuals in good psychological health seem to withstand better the stresses of poor housing (Salling & Harvey, 1981), to choose more beneficial settings (Eddy & Sinnett, 1973), and even to have a better sense of direction (Bryant, 1982).

Conventionality and traditionalism have also been examined. Hensley (1982) found that professors with traditional orientations to education reflected this through closed office arrangements, although this was mediated by a social factor: the number of students the professor advised. As you would expect, unconventional individuals choose unconventional places to be (Eddy & Sinnett, 1973) and less conservative individuals recycle more (Arbuthnot, 1977).

As we saw earlier, personality and the physical

setting can interact to influence behavior. One study hypothesized that participation in conversations depended both on personality and on the physical arrangement (Gifford & Gallagher, 1985). Neither personality (defensive versus trusting) nor seating arrangement (row versus half circle) was independently related to participation. However, participation was significantly higher for defensive individuals when the chairs were arranged in a row and for trusting individuals when the chairs were arranged in a half circle. Apparently, when seating arrangements face participants toward one another, allowing for more visual surveillance than a straight row would, the wariness of defensive individuals is increased and they "clam up." Trusting individuals, it seems, feel uncomfortable holding a conversation in a row arrangement and participate less than they would in a half circle.

▶ **In Sum.** Some traditional personality measures assist in the understanding of behavior that has environmental significance. Outgoing individuals generally prefer smaller interpersonal distances and may experience less stress in higher density situations. They arrange furniture in a more open manner, perceive landscapes differently, and have a better sense of direction than reserved individuals. Those with an internal locus of control also prefer smaller interpersonal distances and tolerate high density better than those with an external locus of control. Internals often engage in more pro-environment activities, such as recycling, although other factors can alter this. They also may prefer more "controlled" architecture. Psychological health and conventionality have also been linked to environmentally relevant behavior; such behaviors have been shown to be influenced by the joint effects of personality and the physical setting.

ENVIRONMENTAL PSYCHOLOGY'S PERSONALITY DIMENSIONS AND BEHAVIOR-ENVIRONMENT RELATIONS

Because they are newer than the traditional measures, published research on the measures designed specially for environmental psychology is not plentiful. Most research concerns the manner in which the measures relate to, or are independent of, the traditional personality measures. Also, much of it is aimed at assessing the reliability and validity of the new measures. Nevertheless, enough research is available to give some flavor of the potential uses of the new measures.

Person-Thing Orientation

How might our disposition to specialize in persons or things (or both, or neither) relate to our transactions with the environment? Little (1976) reports that person specialists have more constructs with which to differentiate other individuals; they are more knowledgeable about the myriad types of individuals that exist. Thing specialists use more physicalistic constructs when assessing places, compared to those with low thing scores. In another study, Little asked residents of Berkeley to generate constructs that would distinguish among three local shopping areas. Generalists produced the largest number, but person specialists again produced more people-oriented constructs and thing specialists produced more physical constructs.

The foregoing results show that the person-thing orientation scale has validity; individuals behave as their score leads us to expect they would. Another study, by Kazu Murata (reported in Little, 1976), reports a less obvious finding. Residents of Vancouver, British Columbia, were asked to estimate urban distances (on the order of 6 kilometers). All four types of specialists overestimated distance, but there were large differences among them in the amount of error. Generalists only overestimated by 8 percent, followed by thing specialists at 15 percent, person specialists at 33 percent, and nonspecialists at 45 percent. Can you explain these nonobvious results based on the person-thing orientation concept?

Environmental Response Inventory

McKechnie (1974) proposed the ERI as a broadband assessment tool useful in any research setting where it is desirable to obtain information about how individuals think about and relate to the everyday physical environment.

Gifford (1980b) used the ERI to predict how students and residents of towns would judge ten everyday buildings on a university campus and in the small town surrounding it. Participants were shown color slide sequences of the buildings and asked to rate them on several dimensions. Many significant relations were established between the eight ERI dimensions and how much participants liked the buildings, but most of these first level results would be of interest only to residents of the town studied.

To achieve greater generality, the buildings were divided into several objective categories: newer versus older, larger versus smaller, brightly lit versus dimly lit, and buildings photographed with people versus slides of buildings without people. At this second level of generality, significant relations have a greater chance of applicability to other buildings and towns. The study found that pastoralists, antiquarians and mechanically oriented participants preferred pictures of buildings in which people were not visible over those in which people were present. Recall that these three personality types share strong interests in activities that do not emphasize people. Those high on environmental adaptation liked larger and newer buildings more than older and smaller ones, but antiquarians, as you might expect, preferred older buildings to newer ones.

At a third level of generality, the study revealed how participants judged the buildings as a whole—that is, an approximation of what they thought of everyday architecture in general. Those high on environmental adaptation liked the buildings; pastoralists and antiquarians disliked them. The study concluded that the ERI is indeed a promising tool for understanding which sorts of individuals are likely to prefer which sorts of buildings.

A current problem in medical training is that graduates gravitate more often to urban than to rural areas, resulting in unequal medical services to the population. Kegel-Flom (1976) used the ERI to identify differences among optometrists who chose to practice in inner city, urban, suburban, and rural locations. The research showed that those who located in more urban areas scored higher on the urbanism scale. This has two implications. First, it shows that the ERI has some degree of validity (those who score high on an urbanism scale really do elect to live in cities). Second, it suggests that the ERI might be used to identify applicants for medical school who are likely to prefer practicing in rural areas, should a medical school be prepared to rectify the imbalance in medical services to rural areas.

Finally, McKechnie (1977b) describes how the ERI may be used to illustrate graphically the differences between conservation group members, government officials, and members of a fishing and hunting club, for example, or the differences within a profession, such as student planners versus practicing planners.

Environmental Preference Questionnaire

Rachel Kaplan (1977) has shown how the EPQ distinguishes among our environmental inclinations. In using the EPQ, she finds that individuals with different EPQ scores not only vary in their activities but vary in their reasons for their choice of activities. Those high on the nature scale, for example, engage in their favorite activities to gain peace and quiet, to be involved in the process that characterizes the activity, and to be outdoors in natural settings.

In contrast, the person high on the suburbs scale engages in preferred activities because they offer a physical workout and a chance for accomplishment. Kaplan (1973) has also used the EPQ to determine who tends to benefit from gardening and in what ways.

Stimulus Screening and Noise Sensitivity

The scales meant to measure individual ways and means of dealing with extraneous sensory input have been shown to predict several behavioral tendencies. We all have our favored and less-favored places, but work by Mehrabian (1978) suggests that screeners and nonscreeners differ in how they respond to these settings. Nonscreeners seem to resist entering disliked settings more than screeners do; once there, they may socialize with others less and work less than screeners do. This research was based on the self-reports of university students in response to photographic slides rather than behavioral measures in actual settings, so the findings must be regarded as tentative. Nevertheless, if confirmed, these findings would have important implications for both environmental designers and personnel managers.

Another study of screeners' behavior examined the responses of residents to dormitories of different designs (Baum, Calesnick, Davis, & Gatchel, 1982). In general, long-corridor designs are seen as more crowded and are associated with more behavioral helplessness. However, screeners in the Baum et al. study who lived in long-corridor dormitories adapted to the situation more successfully than did nonscreeners.

Neil Weinstein's research with the noise sensitivity dimension shows that these tendencies affect noise-related attitudes and behavior. In one investigation of noise sensitive university students, Weinstein (1978) found that they were not only more bothered by dormitory noise at the beginning of the school year, but they became more disturbed by it by the end of the year. Students who were less noise sensitive were less disturbed initially and did not become more disturbed as the school year wore on. Noise-sensitive students also had a history of lower academic performance.

Weinstein (1980) also examined noise sensitivity and the tendency to be critical among residents of a neighborhood that experienced the introduction of a new highway through its midst. The more critical and noise-sensitive residents were more annoyed with noise from the new highway, and they reported more effects of its noise. This unsurprising finding nevertheless shows that individuals who are likely to have negative experiences with planned noise sources can be identified months ahead (Weinstein's personality assessment occurred 7 months before his noise-annoyance and -effects survey). The more critical residents might be regarded by some as chronic complainers, but Weinstein's study showed this to be untrue. The more critical residents gave more differentiated (i.e., less uniform) judgments than did the less critical residents.

Place Identity

Place identity is more akin to the personal-constructs approach than to the dispositions approach in that it emphasizes the manner in which we *personally construct* our notions of place. Humanistic researchers have long argued that individuals develop rootedness (Tuan, 1980) or a sense of place (Buttimer, 1980; Relph, 1976).

Research into place identity has often been phenomenological, based on the perceptions of the world-as-it-is to sophisticated observers, such as professional geographers or philosophers. Were it not for this approach, major place-identity concepts such as belongingness and placelessness would be far less understood.

Some place-identity researchers have employed the commoner strategies of surveying and observing the behavior of others. The classic work may be Fried and Gleicher's (1961) study of what happens to residents whose neighborhood undergoes redevelopment. Before this work, planners generally assumed that residents of older neighborhoods would be pleased to move to newer, cleaner housing. Yet Fried and Gleicher discovered that many relocated residents sat in their new apartments grieving for their lost home. The old neighborhood may have been physically rundown, but it was the foundation for a complete way of life. When the neighborhood was bulldozed, so was the way of life that permeated it. Our homes are an integral part of our self-identity; self-identity in turn is an essential part of our personality.

Though relatively underresearched so far, place identity is important throughout our lives. Boys and girls seem to have different senses of the areas surrounding their homes (Saegart & Hart, 1978). The well-being of children (van Vliet—, 1983) and adolescents (McMillan & Hiltonsmith, 1982) is crucially related to the form and content of their homes. Leaving home to take a job or go to college can be disastrous or fulfilling. Residential mobility for families is stressful for most individuals (Stokols, Shumaker, & Martinez, 1983). At some point, through divorce, conviction of a crime, mental disability, or pure exhaustion in old age, most of us eventually lose our homes. In general, place identity is revealed most clearly when the settings we hold most dear are threatened. (See Fig. 4–12.) Home and work settings are especially close to our sense of self; they are also subject to many threats.

▶ **In Sum.** Research involving personality dimensions designed for environmental psychology has so far largely examined the validity of the dimensions. The results have been positive: for example, thing-specialists have more constructs for objects and settings, those with high scores on Environmental Adaption like large, new buildings, and screeners adapt to the high-density dormitory better than do nonscreeners. Place identity, too, has been shown to be an important everyday experience that becomes particularly salient when we are threatened with separation from a cherished place.

THE USES OF PERSONALITY IN ENVIRONMENTAL DESIGN

We have described in some detail the different approaches to assessing those aspects of personality most relevant to environmental psychology, the instruments that have been developed to support those approaches, and some of the research linking those instruments to environmentally relevant cognitions and behaviors. We may still ask just how such knowledge might be used.

Of course, one such use is to increase our knowledge of how human beings respond to the physical environment. This pure knowledge is interesting to some researchers in and of itself or because it allows for the confirmation or refutation of theory, which should lead to a better psychology.

Others, however, want knowledge that may guide immediate practice. Can the results of personality studies help architects, designers, and planners, for example? Personality is essentially the study of how individuals differ; if so, how can any one design make all the individuals in it satisfied or productive?

FIGURE 4-12 Threats to home include new development. *(Courtesy of Coe Gifford.)*

Kenneth Craik (1976) has described three categories of uses to which personality assessments may be put.

Description

Description, of course, may be accomplished by the judicious use of the measures described above, whether they are based on dispositional, personal construct, information processing, or phenomenological approaches. Whether the description is of a single person or of the typical member of a certain group, environmental designers cannot take the person into account until the person's qualities are known.

In addition, the question may be turned around: who are the designers, the managers of water resources, those who allocate space in organizations? Knowing their personalities helps us undestand how they will tend to design and manage the environment.

Comparison

Comparison, the second use, allows planners (designers, user group advocates, budget managers) to become aware of the differences between individuals or between groups. For example, knowledge of the differences in personality of snowmobilers and cross-country skiers should help park planners to design better new recreation areas and to develop effective policies for existing ones.

Many other possible group comparisons might be made as part of the design process. Is the typical student different from the typical professor in terms of environmental tendencies? Are nurses different from physicians? Patients from both? In every behavior setting there are several user groups. If their typical personalities are different, how so? Clarifying these specific differences should help designers create settings that better fit the needs of each group.

Prediction

The third use of personality knowledge is prediction. The assessment of individual differences frequently allows a forecast of satisfaction or productivity in a given design. McKechnie's ERI has been used to predict which medical students will migrate. Stokols et al. (1983) discovered that some individuals (those who have a tendency to explore environments) can handle high residential mobility better than others (those who tend not to explore environments). The other uses of prediction from personality virtually parallel the chapters of this book. It may be used to understand how individuals think about their surroundings, use the space around them, and manage their resources.

SUMMARY

This chapter describes the seemingly unlikely connections between personality and environment. Reasons why environmental psychologists should consider personality are offered. The classic theories of Murray, Lewin, and Angyal are described. The controversial present status of personality is briefly reviewed. Seven systems for assessing environmental personality are described. The ways that traditional personality variables (such as outgoing-reserved and internal-external locus of control) help explain behavior of interest to environmental psychology are noted. Personality dimensions devised especially for environmental psychology appear to be useful, but research employing them has been limited. The uses of personality assessment in environmental design include description, comparison, and prediction. Knowing the behavioral tendencies of those who are to use or control a setting may help designers produce a more compatible fit between occupant and habitat. Knowing how individuals and groups *differ* on key personality dimensions can help the designer become more aware of how settings for different people should reflect their distinct psychological makeups. Knowing the environmental personality of individuals allows better prediction of their satisfaction with and performance in different physical settings.

SUGGESTED SUPPLEMENTARY READINGS

Craik, K. H. (1976). The personality research paradigm in environmental psychology. In S. Wapner, S. B. Cohen, & B. Kaplan (Eds.), *Experiencing the environment.* New York: Plenum.

Little, B. R. (1983). Personal projects: A rationale and method for investigation. *Environment and Behavior, 15*, 273–309.

McKechnie, G. E. (1977). The environmental response inventory in application. *Environment and Behavior, 9*, 255–276.

Proshansky, H. M., Fabian, A. K., & Kaminoff, R. (1983). Place-identity: Physical world socialization of the self. *Journal of Environmental Psychology, 3*, 57–83.

Taylor, R. B. (1983). Conjoining environmental psychology with social and personality psychology: Natural marriage or shot-gun wedding? In N. R. Feimer & E. S. Geller (Eds.), *Environmental psychology: Directions and perspectives.* New York: Praeger.

Part Two

Social Processes

In this section, we move from the basic processes of environmental perception, cognition, and personality to interpersonal behavior. The social aspects of environmental psychology are broadly concerned with how we share and divide space. Chapter Five focuses on the small domain, personal space, that armslength (or so) distance extending around our bodies wherever we are. Chapter Six covers human territoriality, the tendency to set aside larger spaces to be used only by selected individuals for specified activities. Chapter Seven deals with instances when space is, or seems to be, in short supply: high density or crowding. Chapter Eight discusses the search for privacy or the management of physical settings to optimize our social needs.

Chapter Five
Personal Space

Some thirty inches from my nose
The frontier of my Person goes
And all the untilled air between
Is private pagus or demesne.
Stranger, unless with bedroom eyes
I beckon you to fraternize,
Beware of rudely crossing it:
I have no gun but I can spit.

W. H. Auden
From ''Prologue: The Birth of Architecture,''
About the House

FIGURE 5-1 Robert Sommer pioneered research in personal space and consistently engages in environmental design research aimed at improving settings for inhabitants and users. *(Courtesy of Robert Sommer.)*

After studying for hours in his carrel, Tom felt like taking a break and decided to go to a movie. At the theater, he found himself in a lineup. Someone behind him stood so close that he felt uncomfortable and tense.

Across town, Jane was introduced by a friend to a foreign student. He seemed pleasant enough, but for some reason he stood so close to her that she felt overwhelmed and wanted to get away from him. She backed away, but he seemed pushy, and she spent half an hour feeling cornered in a conversation.

After the movie, Tom happened to meet an acquaintance of Jane's while walking home. She insisted that he come to a postgame celebration. He wasn't interested in her romantically, but he thought the party might be interesting. As they walked, she suddenly took Tom's arm and the two of them were shoulder to shoulder. Tom hoped none of his friends would see him this way.

The best way to explain personal space may be to ask you to place yourself in these scenarios, situations in which your personal space is abused. Most of the time, when our personal space is not abused, violated, or mishandled, we aren't even

aware of its existence. In this chapter we will concentrate on one of the most widely studied areas of environmental psychology. Over 1,000 studies on personal space have been reported (Hayduk, 1985). It has been described as hidden, silent, and invisible, yet everyone possesses and uses personal space every day. If you never considered personal space before, this chapter may fundamentally change the way you think about yourself and others.

After defining it and describing the major ways of measuring it, the factors that affect the size of personal space are surveyed. Next, the ways personal space is connected to a variety of other behaviors is described. Then its functional values to us are discussed and some integrative theories presented. Finally, the role of personal space in environmental design is illustrated with several examples.

WHAT IS PERSONAL SPACE?

A Basic Definition

A simple definition was offered by Robert Sommer years ago: "Personal space refers to an area with invisible boundaries surrounding a person's body into which intruders may not come" (Sommer, 1969, p. 26). (See Fig. 5–1.) But almost nothing in environmental psychology is simple. The "bubble" image of personal space has been challenged (Patterson, 1975). First, it implies personal space is stable, when in fact it stretches and shrinks with circumstances. Second, it is not really personal but interpersonal. Personal space only exists when we interact with others. Third, it emphasizes distance to the exclusion of strongly related aspects of social interaction such as angle of orientation and eye contact. Fourth, it suggests personal space is an either-or phenomenon (we are either intruding or not), when it is more like a gradient than a boundary (Knowles, 1980a).

Personal space, therefore, may be defined as the distance component of interpersonal relations. It is both an indicator of, and an integral part of, the growth, maintenance, and decline of interpersonal relationships.

Elaborations

This concise definition contains within it numerous important implications that are developed in this chapter. Three aspects of personal space are described to illustrate some of these implications.

A Personal, Portable Territory. Territories are places where entry is controlled; some outsiders are allowed in, others are not. Personal space differs from other territories in that it is portable. Wherever you stand or sit, you are surrounded on all sides by personal space. Yet the borders of this territory are not sharp like property lines but gradual. (See Fig. 5–2.) Unauthorized intrusion is usually either an accident (someone bumps into you in a store because they were not watching where they were walking) or not (you get mugged). Authorized intrusion is possible, too (your mother gives you a hug).

A Spacing Mechanism. Observers of birds (Howard, 1920) and animals (Hediger, 1950) have long known that certain species maintain characteristic distances between individuals of that species. These distances have biological value; they regulate fundamental processes like food-gathering and mating. Some species, such as sea lions during breeding, at some times have almost zero personal space, but other species, like wolves living in the tundra, have very large ones. (See Fig. 5–3.)

Environmental psychologists who consider personal space a spacing mechanism tend to refer to personal space as **interpersonal distance** (Becker & Mayo, 1971). Some studies of interpersonal distance examine not only the distance between individuals, but also the angle of orientation between them (such as side by side, face to face).

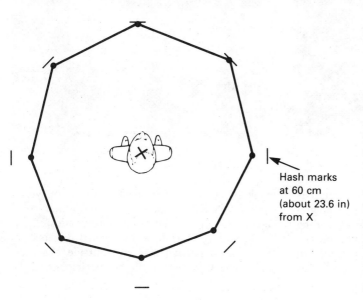

Hash marks
at 60 cm
(about 23.6 in)
from X

FIGURE 5–2 The shape of personal space. The dots represent average distances around the bodies of students when approached by a young male researcher until they told him they felt uncomfortable about his closeness. *(From Hayduk, L. A. The shape of personal space: An empirical investigation. Canadian Journal of Behavioral Science, 1981, 13, 87–93. Copyright © 1981. The Canadian Psychological Association. Reprinted by permission.)*

FIGURE 5–3 The study of personal space originated with observations of animal spacing, but as we see from the picture below, humans also use quite consistent spacing.

A Communication Channel. Edward Hall is the primary example of a social scientist who prefers to think of personal space as a way of sending messages. The title of his earliest book on the subject, *The Silent Language* (1959), provides an indication of his viewpoint. One chapter in his book is called "Space Speaks." Over the years, Hall developed an approach to the human management of space that he calls **proxemics.**

According to Hall, interpersonal distance informs both participants and outside observers about the very nature of the participants' relationship. You have probably seen couples strolling along, arm in arm. In our culture, the inevitable message is that this couple is in love.

Hall (1966) described eight gradations of interpersonal distance. Each one provides participants with a slightly different set of sensory information; each one indicates a slightly different relationship between the participants. The eight distances are composed of the near and far phases of four main distances.

Intimate Distance. The near phase of intimate distance (0–6 in. or 0–15 cm) is for comforting, protecting, lovemaking, wrestling, and other full-contact activities. People who interact at this distance are on intimate terms, or they are behaving within a strict set of rules (such as wrestling), or there are probably strong negative emotions and activities occurring (a temperamental baseball manager heatedly disputing an umpire's interpretation of the rules).

The far phase of intimate distance (6–18 in. or 15–45 cm) is used by individuals who are on very close terms. (Note, incidentally, how the English language contains many words reflecting interpersonal distance, such as *close, in touch, distant,* etc.) A typical behavior at this distance is whispering. Generally, the participants in an interaction at this distance are very good friends.

Personal Distance. The near phase (18–30 in. or 45–75 cm) is the zone for those who are familiar with one another and on good terms. Good friends or a happy couple will use this distance to talk. Hall says that if your spouse enters this zone, acquaintances will hardly notice, but if someone else of your spouse's sex comes this close to you, that is "an entirely different story" (Hall, 1966, p. 113).

The far phase of personal distance (2.5–4 ft. or 75–120 cm) is used for social interactions between friends and acquaintances. If you observe two classmates who are acquainted but are not special friends talking in a hallway, chances are they will be standing in the far phase of personal distance.

Social Distance. Despite the name, this zone is used more for interaction between unac-

quainted individuals or those transacting business. Perhaps Hall should have called it business distance. The near phase (4–7 ft. or 1.2–2 m) is the distance someone might select while being introduced to a roommate's mother, or while buying a stereo.

The far phase of social distance (7–12 ft. or 2–3.5 m) is used in more formal business. Here there is little sense of friendship or even of trying to be friendly. The interaction is best described as the meeting of two organizations' representatives. For example, if the company owned by your roommate's mother is about to buy out the stereo store, she and the stereo salesman's boss might interact at this distance.

Public Distance. This zone is used less often by two interacting individuals than by speakers and their audiences. The near phase of public distance (12–25 ft. or 3.5–7 m) would be used by a lecturer whose class has grown just large enough that speaking from a seated position no longer feels comfortable. When someone is speaking to a group of thirty or forty, the average distance between speaker and listener is likely to be in this range.

The far phase of public distance (over 25 ft. or 7 m) is used when ordinary mortals meet important public figures. If you met a head of state, you would probably halt your approach at about this distance. Because it isn't easy to hold a normal conversation at this distance, the important public figure must beckon you closer if communication any more personal than a salute is to pass between you.

The three conceptions of personal space as territory, spacing mechanism, and communication channel are complementary. Even a basic definition must include all three aspects. Later in this chapter when we examine theories of personal space, we will see that most of them are based on these three fundamental elements.

Awareness and Choice

Did you already know about personal space before you read about it here? Certainly you use Hall's distances; your spacing from other individuals is not random. But were you aware, until you read the first part of this chapter, of these behavioral choices you have been making? Most of us know the rules of personal space but have never consciously considered them. As an old sage once said, you don't have to know the laws of physics to shoot a basketball accurately. Similarly, most of us use personal space every day according to certain rules, yet we have a low level of awareness about the whole process.

Personal space is culturally acquired. In each culture, children gradually learn the rules. Eventually they learn the rules so well that they no longer need to clog their moment-to-moment cognitive processing with them.

When personal space rules are broken, however, lack of awareness of them can have negative consequences. By definition, of course, when someone else is too close to you or too far away, you are uncomfortable; that is one negative consequence. Anecdotal evidence (Hall, 1959) and some experimental evidence (Patterson, 1968) suggests that another negative consequence comes when others approach us too closely; we tend to attribute unfavorable traits to them. We do not attend to the personal space rules per se; instead we conclude that the other person is pushy, rude, cold, or aggressive. Now it is true that for some people these attributions are correct. There are other situations, however, in which too-close interpersonal distances are inappropriately interpreted to develop an unfavorable impression of others. As we shall see, one such situation can occur when the other person comes from a different culture.

Awareness of personal space has another dimension to it. Notice that all the foregoing descriptions of it refer to objective distances. Environmental psychologists measure these distances from a third-party vantage point. But when personal space is actually used on the street, in the halls or in the office, we operate on the basis of *perceived*, not objective, interpersonal distance. Ultimately, personal space is a phenomenological experience.

For years, influential reviews of the personal space literature (Evans & Howard, 1973; Hayduk, 1978) have been calling for research into the cognitive aspects of personal space. Yet of the hundreds of experiments on personal space, only a handful have investigated the experience of personal space.

Gifford and Price (1979) suggested there are two kinds of personal space. **Alpha personal space** is the objective, externally measurable distance between interacting individuals. It might be called the psychologist's personal space. **Beta personal space** is the subjective experience of the distancing process. Like all experiences, it must be measured indirectly. Beta personal space is the individual's sense of distance in social encounters.

One way to investigate beta personal space is to ask individuals at normal interpersonal distances to estimate the distance from themselves to the other person. When Gifford (1983) performed this simple experiment, he discovered that beta personal space, measured as the perceived distance between self and other, was 24 percent larger than alpha personal space, the actual interpersonal distance. In normal social interaction, we seem to believe that we are farther away from the other person than we really are. As we move from definitions into a discussion of how personal space is measured, this alpha-beta distinction may be useful to bear in mind.

► **In Sum.** Personal space refers to the interpersonal distance chosen during social interaction. It involves elements of territoriality, spacing, and communication. It varies with and reflects the rise, current status, and decline of relationships. Alpha personal space is the objective distance between interacting individuals, but beta personal space refers to the experience of that distance.

MEASURING PERSONAL SPACE

There are three general ways to measure personal space. Each method to be described has its advantages and disadvantages in ease of performing the measurement, effectiveness in tapping the key dimensions of personal space as viewed by the different theories, and reliability and validity of the measurement.

From the most-used to the least-used, but also from the worst to the best, the three main ways of measuring personal space are the simulation, the stop-distance, and the naturalistic observation methods.

Simulation Methods

Numerous simulation methods, sometimes called *projective methods*, have been used. But their general defining characteristic is that subjects report what their own personal space would be in a given situation, rather than actually engaging in a social encounter. The subject is asked to reconstruct the distance between the self and another person from memory. Usually, the reconstruction is performed with small figures cut out of paper or felt or by asking the subject to draw figures on a piece of paper.

Simulation methodology was first used by James Kuethe (1962). He asked his subjects to place felt cutouts representing the self and others on a felt board. Kuethe discovered that his subjects did not place the figures randomly. Placements showed considerable consistency and organization. Kuethe interpreted an individual's arrangements as indications of **social schema,** psychological representations of the closeness of the individuals represented by the figures. For example, child-sized figures were usually placed closer to a figure representing a woman than to a figure representing a man.

Kuethe himself did not refer to his technique as a measure of personal space. Soon, however, researchers who were interested in personal space noticed Kuethe's work and seized on it as one way to measure personal space. A large flurry of simulation techniques and studies soon appeared.

One such simulation technique was the **Comfortable Interpersonal Distance Scale** (CID), devised by Duke and Nowicki (1972). This variant on the simulation theme asks individuals to mark on a prepared form where they would place themselves in relation to others. (See Fig. 5–4.) The self is shown in the center and eight lines radiate from the self. The subject is asked to imagine someone approaching from each direction and to mark on the form the distance at which the other person's approach would begin to produce discomfort.

The large number of simulation studies lent credence to the idea that personal space really was being measured. The most important question concerning the simulation measures is whether or not they are valid. Are they accurate indications of alpha personal space?

There are three reasons why one would expect the simulation measures not to be valid. First, they require the subject to recall a social encounter; your memory of the last time you stood talking to a particular friend, for example, may be fallible. Second, they require the subject to transpose

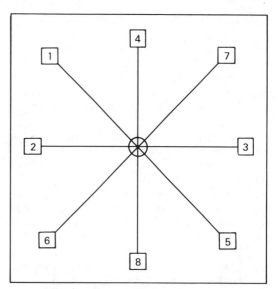

FIGURE 5–4 The Comfortable Interpersonal Distance (CID) scale is a projective method of studying personal space. Respondents are instructed to imagine they are in the center of a room and someone is approaching them from one of the eight directions. They are to mark the line at the point they would begin to feel uncomfortable. Then the procedure is repeated for the other several directions. Compare this figure with Figure 5–2. *(From Duke, M. P., & Nowicki, S., Jr. A new measure and social learning model for interpersonal distance.* Journal of Experimental Research in Personality, *1972, 6, 119–132. Reprinted with permission from Academic Press and the author.)*

an actual distance to a scale-model distance. The subject may innocently err in this scaling process. Third, the simulation techniques render the personal space process a conscious one, but everyday distancing occurs at a low level of consciousness. Once the process is brought into full awareness, many distortions may occur. The subject may place or draw a figure where it ought to be, or where the subject thinks the experimenter wants it to be.

Thus, the simulation techniques lack **face validity,** that is, they do not give even the appearance of measuring real or alpha personal space. But do these techniques have **construct validity?** How do the simulation measures actually correlate with alpha personal space? Love and Aiello (1980) measured alpha personal space. They then asked the same subjects, just a few minutes later, to do their best to replicate their own real personal space using three simulation measures. Love and Aiello actually found a negative correlation between the subjects' live, unplanned personal space and their replicated personal space, suggesting that alpha and simulated personal space are not only unrelated, they may be inversely related.

Apparently, as suggested by the reasons listed earlier, simulation measures do not match actual distances very well. Other researchers have reached similar conclusions (Greenberg, Strube, & Myers, 1980; Knowles, 1980b). Some have concluded that simulation measures probably should not be used to measure personal space (Hayduk, 1978, 1983).

The simulation techniques, however, may be useful for a different purpose. Recall that Kuethe (1962) did not describe his technique as a measure of personal space; he cannot be guilty of inventing an invalid measure of it. Instead, Kuethe said he was measuring social schemas that resemble the concept of beta personal space more than they resemble alpha personal space. The simulation measures may be reasonable indications of how we experience our spatial relation to others, which is not the same thing as how we act in relation to others. When a researcher's goal is to understand the experience of personal space or beta personal space, the simulation methods may be useful.

The Stop-distance Method

Researchers who desire a more realistic measure of alpha personal space have often used the **stop-distance technique.** In this method, participants are usually studied in a laboratory situation, but in a live encounter. The participant is asked to stand some distance away and then to walk slowly toward the experimenter. The participant is asked to stop at the point of discomfort. The resulting interpersonal distance is taken as a measure of personal space.

Sometimes the experimenter approaches the participant, who asks the experimenter to stop when the participant feels uncomfortable. Occasionally this procedure is repeated for different angles of approach, but most often the two participants face one another during the measurement. The stop-distance method is very reliable (Hayduk, 1985). What about its validity?

Two of the disadvantages of the simulation methods (as measures of alpha personal space) are overcome in the stop-distance method. The subject need not rely on memory and is not asked to scale down personal space distances. However, one disadvantage is carried over; the participant is very aware of the distancing process. Therefore, distances chosen under stop-distance conditions may not correspond very well to those chosen in everyday meetings in which awareness of the distancing process is low.

If the researcher's goal is to measure alpha personal space without the subject's awareness of the distancing process, then the stop-distance technique may not be advisable either. This conclusion appears straightforward, but at least one environmental psychologist is ready to question it. Eric Knowles has argued that what he calls the **undisguised methods** (simulation and stop-distance) should not be dismissed out of hand. Knowles notes that the undisguised methods may be subject to fewer extraneous influences than the **disguised methods** (such as naturalistic observation) and therefore may be better measures of our general interpersonal distance tendencies (Knowles & Johnsen, 1974).

Furthermore, in another study Knowles (1980b) reported that even though the undisguised measures correlate poorly with the disguised ones, the effects on both (for example, gender differences or level of acquaintances) are about the same. This seems paradoxical, but even though different methods of measuring personal space yield different estimates of the size of alpha personal space, Knowles found they all reveal the same effects of various influences (such as degree of acquaintance) on personal space. One reviewer, Hayduk (1983), agrees that Knowles' argument may hold for degree of acquaintance, but argues that it does not hold for other variables affecting personal space.

Perhaps Knowles' claim that undisguised methods work as well as disguised methods is true only for the very strongest influences on personal space. Consider an astronomical analogy. If you were trying to observe a comet that is passing close to earth, you might begin by looking up with your naked eye. The brightest comet is visible with the least sophisticated instruments. However, if you couldn't see the comet with your unaided vision, you might try putting on your glasses. If that doesn't work, you could drag out your binoculars. Finally, you could rush out and buy a telescope. The point is that if the influences on personal space are strong enough, you can see it using even the simplest, crudest technique. But if a certain influence on personal space is weak, only a very good personal space measure will detect it.

Naturalistic Observation

So, I can almost hear you asking, why not do the equivalent of running right out to buy a telescope? Study personal space by measuring the unplanned interpersonal distances of individuals in natural settings. This disguised method would dispose of the last disadvantage, the awareness of the individuals involved.

There are three reasons why naturalistic observation is not used. First, some environmental psychologists believe it is unethical to measure the behavior of people without their prior informed consent.

Second, and probably more crucial, measurements made under natural conditions are subject to many uncontrolled variables. For example, if you went out to measure personal space in a park, the pairs you observe would probably include many levels of friendship, topics being discussed, roles, and combinations of personality. Without knowing the status of each person on these variables, it would be hard to explain why some pairs stood at large interpersonal distances but others stood at small ones. The problem with measuring personal space naturalistically is not so much in determining the size of personal space, but in determining the reasons for differences in size—and the latter is usually the purpose of the study.

Third, the measurement itself can be tricky. Would you simply estimate the interpersonal distance of each pair from a distance? Not very accurate. Would you casually stroll up to them and ask them to freeze so you could stretch a tape between their chests? Even if you are bold enough to do this, your quarry will probably shift position by turning to look at you. They may even move back a step or two or run away from this

obviously deranged intruder! You could try to photograph pairs, but there are considerable technical difficulties in translating photographic distances to life-size distances, particularly if the angle of the camera shot is not exactly perpendicular to the conversing couple.

These difficulties can and have been overcome, but not often and not easily. Telescopes are expensive, and naturalistic observation can be too. That is why simulation and stop-distance techniques are used more often than naturalistic methods. However, there are reasonable compromise methods. One way to obtain a relatively naturalistic measure is the following laboratory technique, which may be performed with either seated or standing subjects.

In the seating variant, subjects are brought to a setting (often the lab, but anywhere will do) on some pretext other than personal space. The experimenter apologizes for not providing enough chairs and points to a stack of chairs against the wall. "If you'll just help yourself to a chair there, we'll get started," says the crafty experimenter. When the unsuspecting subject returns with a chair, places it near the experimenter, and sits down, the seated interpersonal distance of the subject can be measured.

A second version of this laboratory method measures standing personal space. The subject enters the lab and is asked to "come over here and we'll get started." Personal space is determined as the point where the subject stops. Either version could also be adapted so that the experimenter is not personally involved. Two subjects are asked to get chairs for themselves or to move to a place where the study can get started.

▶ **In Sum.** Personal space has been measured using simulation, stop-distance, and naturalistic observation methods. The simulation techniques may produce the same results as the others, but are perhaps better suited to studying beta personal space than alpha personal space. The stop-distance technique, if done without the subject's awareness, is probably the best method. Naturalistic observation can be technically difficult and often does not allow the investigator to distinguish among different possible reasons for variations in personal space. The researcher must be aware of both the advantages and disadvantages of each method, the theoretical implications of selecting a method, and the pitfalls involved in actually making the measurement. Let us turn now to a survey of the major influences on the size of personal space.

INFLUENCES ON PERSONAL SPACE

What size is personal space? This simple question has been the focus of many investigations since 1959. As you might expect, the overall conclusion about the size of personal space is this: It depends. What it depends on are influences that fall into three categories: personal factors, situational factors, and cultural-ethnic factors.

Personal Influences

Personal space is a function, in part, of an individual's own characteristics that are carried from situation to situation, such as personality, gender, mental health, and age. It should be remembered that each of these characteristics has an important role in personal space, but in practice they cannot operate on their own. The personal characteristics of the other person and the situation will also have an effect. For this reason, it is difficult to tease out the precise role of a given personal characteristic. By studying personal characteristics across a variety of contexts, however, the environmental psychologist can begin to sort out the effect of a single personal characteristic (gender, for example) from the effects of all the other influences.

Your personal characteristics presumably remain constant across situations, yet if situation X involves talking to a gruff old professor about why you failed an exam and situation Y involves discussing with your best friend where you're going out Friday night, your interpersonal distance is likely to be different. You therefore appear to be inconsistent in your use of personal space. Your distances, however, in the two situations may both be greater than those chosen by someone with different personal characteristics. Thus an individual's characteristics do affect personal space even while other influences are at work. Let's tour the main individual influences on personal space.

Gender. Generally, the male-male pair keeps the largest distances (Gifford, 1982b; Lott & Som-

mer, 1967; Pellegrini & Empey, 1970) followed by the female-female pair and the male-female pair (Kuethe, 1962; Kuethe & Weingartner, 1964).

However, many varying results concerning gender can be found (Altman, 1975, p. 75). One possible reason is that sex differences in personal space probably reflect differences in the socialization of males and females rather than biological differences. Depending on their upbringing and other social influences, men may even interact more closely than women.

Another reason was suggested by a study that focused on sex, race, and age simultaneously (Severy, Forsyth, & Wagner, 1979) and found that sex influenced personal space only in interaction (i.e., combined influence) with race, age, and the other person's sex, not by itself. Sex is simply not as powerful a determinant of personal space, on its own, as are other variables. At a given age boys and girls may differ in personal space, but over the span of childhood, age is a much stronger predictor of personal space than sex is. (See Fig. 5–5.)

Age. Personal space increases with age (Hayduk, 1983). Infant personal space is hard to measure because infants have little independent mobility. Developmental psychologists do, however, refer to infants who like to be hugged and others who resist contact. Perhaps these young resisters would have larger personal space zones than the huggers if someone could find a way to measure them. By the age of eighteen months, however, children do choose different interpersonal distances depending on the person and the situation (Castell, 1970). By about age twelve, children use personal space approximately the way adults do (Evans & Howard, 1973).

Once again, it is important to recall that in any given social situation other factors may influence this generalization. Gender is one such factor. Tennis and Dabbs (1975) hypothesized that personal space varies with both age and gender. The personal space of boys and girls from five to eighteen was measured. As usual, older children displayed larger interpersonal distances than younger children. But the age by gender interaction was also significant. Rather than boys or girls having larger personal space in general, older boys chose larger distances than older girls, but among the younger children there was no difference between boys and girls.

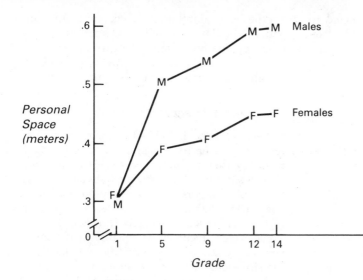

FIGURE 5-5 Personal space increases with grade in school, with males showing larger increases than females. *(Based on Tennis and Dabbs, 1975.)*

Culture is another factor that modifies the age trend in personal space. Aiello and Pagan (1982) found that children in Puerto Rico increase their interpersonal distance at a later age than Puerto Rican children living in New York.

Incidentally, surprisingly little is known about personal space after early adulthood. As we become more aware of important developmental changes in middle and late adulthood, we realize that personal space may change during these phases of life too. But so far, no one has investigated this possibility.

Personality. An important review conceptualizes personality as the frequency with which an individual engages in behaviors within certain categories (Buss & Craik, 1983). These categories, such as dominance, warmth, or aloofness, may be grouped into one of several supercategories or domains (Wiggins, 1979). Some of these domains are interpersonal behavior, temperament, character, and analytical style.

This minilesson in personality is offered because it may help to clarify what sometimes seems to be a muddy picture. Some reviewers have concluded there is no consistent relation between personality and personal space (Hayduk, 1978). This may be because the relevant research has not always been well-planned (Altman, 1975). Some failures to find connections probably were reported because researchers investigated per-

sonal space in relation to personality domains where there was no good reason to expect a relation.

In which personality domain might significant relations be expected? Probably the one most relevant to personal space is interpersonal behavior, including such dispositions as dominance-submissiveness, warmth-coldness, and extraversion-introversion. Variables within the interpersonal domain are combinations of these two dimensions (Wiggins, 1979). For example, extraversion is viewed in this theory as a combination of warmth and dominance; aloofness is seen as a combination of submissiveness and coldness.

Indeed, when the relation between personal space and personality variables within the interpersonal domain are examined, some clear trends appear. Most studies of extraversion or affiliativeness or interpersonal warmth have shown that individuals with these tendencies have smaller personal space zones (Cook, 1970; Mehrabian & Diamond, 1971; Patterson & Holmes, 1966). One study investigated the whole interpersonal behavior domain (Gifford, 1982b). The strongest correlations involved extraverted and gregarious persons (smaller personal space) and with cold and quarrelsome persons (larger personal space).

Another domain where personal space appears relevant is temperament. One temperament variable, *trait* anxiety (as opposed to short-term or *state* anxiety) has consistently been linked to larger personal space zones (Karabenick & Meisels, 1972; Luft, 1966; Patterson, 1973; Weinstein, 1968).

Psychological Disturbance. Individuals who have some form of emotional problem often have unusual personal space zones. Because most psychological disturbances involve anxiety and difficulties in communication, interpersonal relationships, and perceptual processes, this is not surprising.

The very first empirical study of human personal space (Sommer, 1959) examined the interpersonal distances chosen by schizophrenics. Sommer found that, compared to hospital employees and nonschizophrenic patients, schizophrenics sometimes chose much greater seating distances and sometimes chose much smaller ones. Horowitz, Duff, and Stratton (1964) also reported that the personal space zones of schizophrenics are more variable. Later studies have reported that other psychological disturbances result in larger or smaller interpersonal distances. The obvious conclusion is that emotional problems are associated with inappropriate distancing, which may mean too close or too distant spacing depending on the nature of the individual's psychological problem and other factors.

Horowitz (1968) performed an interesting study that illustrates the relation between degree of disturbance and personal space inappropriateness. He measured the personal space of newly admitted schizophrenics, who were presumably quite disturbed, and found that they had very large personal space zones. Horowitz then measured the personal space of the schizophrenics every three weeks during their hospital stay. As the schizophrenics improved (by independent judgment), their personal space moved much closer to that of nonpatients.

▶ **In Sum.** Personal space may be predicted in part from knowing an individual's characteristics. Males typically use larger distances than females. Young adults typically use more personal space than children. Interpersonally warm and nonanxious individuals probably have smaller personal spaces than others, but other relations between personality and personal space are inconsistent. Psychological disturbance often leads to more variable or inappropriate personal space.

Yet the personal influences affect one another importantly; to know an individual's personal space tendency one must know the person's age, sex, race, culture, and personality. We know some but not all of the combined effects of these factors.

Situational Influences

Collectively, the individual characteristics just reviewed add up to a generalized personal space tendency that an individual carries from situation to situation. But once the individual enters any situation, personal space is influenced by a new range of factors. These situational factors are of two types, social and physical. Social situational factors focus on the quality of the interpersonal relationship between the individuals in the situation. The physical situation, or setting, includes all the nonhuman portions of the situation.

The Social Situation. The social qualities of a situation may be broadly grouped under the headings of attraction, cooperation-competition, and status. We will consider in turn the effects on personal space that each of these qualities exerts.

Attraction, acquaintance, and friendship all refer to the degree of positive or negative attitude one person holds toward the other. One of the strongest generalizations we can make in personal space research is that attraction draws us physically closer. In a classic study, Little (1965) found that drawings of individuals described as good friends were placed closer together than were drawings of strangers. Little's results have been confirmed in naturalistic observations (Willis, 1966), for other cultures (Edwards, 1972), and for children (Aiello & Cooper, 1972).

Some researchers have examined similarity between individuals or pleasantness of manner. These are closely related to attraction and the same results are found; as similarity and pleasantness of manner increase, personal space decreases (King, 1966; Rosenfeld, 1965; Smith, 1954).

A few studies have investigated the negative side of interpersonal relations. In one study, college men were scolded for being late for the experiment. The experimenter told the participants, none of whom was actually late, "It said right on the sign-up sheet to be on time—what's the matter, can't you read?" After a few similar insults, personal space was measured with the stop-distance technique. It's not surprising that the participants who were insulted showed larger personal space zones than did participants who were not insulted (O'Neal, Brunault, Carifio, Troutwine, & Epstein, 1980). The researchers showed that the larger zone was specific to the insulter; participants did not show larger zones when another person measured their personal space. Criticism and insults lead to dislike, which leads to increased interpersonal distance (Guardo & Meisels, 1971).

A special case of negative attraction is stigma. Handicaps often unfairly lead to a form of negative attraction. Participants choose greater distances when the other is a mental patient, an amputee (Kleck, Buck, Goller, London, Pfeiffer, & Vukcevic, 1968), a drug user, a facially disfigured person (Rumsey, Bull, & Gahagan, 1982), a homosexual, or a fat person (Wolfgang & Wolfgang, 1971). Stigmatized persons are sensitive to the increase in distance. They realize that although other persons may still be helpful, such as in giving directions when asked (Worthington, 1974), their choice of greater interpersonal distance is a telltale sign of their true, unfavorable attitude.

A second quality of the social situation concerns the competitive or cooperative nature of the interaction. Sommer (1969) performed a series of simulation studies on this topic. Individuals indicated they would select closer seats when they were cooperating, as you might expect. Moreover, these studies suggested that angle of orientation is important. In competitive situations, subjects said they would choose more direct orientations (face to face), but in more cooperative situations they would choose less direct orientations (side by side).

Cook (1970) discovered, in trying to replicate Sommer's work in naturalistic settings, that the customs and physical layouts of particular places will alter these tendencies. (See Fig. 5–6.) If you went to a fancy, dimly lit restaurant with your dearly beloved, presumably a situation that is more cooperative than competitive, you would probably select seats facing one another. Two men sitting in a singles bar waiting for the right woman to appear, presumably a more competitive than cooperative enterprise, are more likely to sit side by side against the wall.

The competitive or cooperative quality of a social situation may even affect personal space in subsequent situations. Tedesco and Fromme's (1974) subjects played a game with a confederate of the experimenter. The confederates were instructed to use either a very cooperative or very competitive strategy in the game. The interpersonal distance of the subjects was observed in another room during a second phase of the experi-

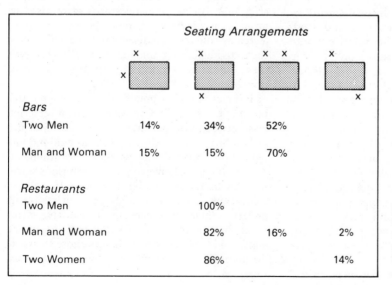

Seating Arrangements			
Bars			
Two Men	14%	34%	52%
Man and Woman	15%	15%	70%
Restaurants			
Two Men		100%	
Man and Woman		82%	16%	2%
Two Women		86%		14%

FIGURE 5–6 Seating choices observed in three bars and a restaurant. Both the setting (bar vs. restaurant) and the sex of the pair (MM, FF, MF) affect seating choices. *(From Cook, 1970.)*

ment. Those who had played with a cooperative confederate selected smaller distances than those who had played with a competitive confederate.

A third quality of a social situation pertains to the status, power, or dominance of the participants. Personal space is related more to differences in status than to the amount of status (Mehrabian, 1969); the greater the difference, the greater the interpersonal distance (Gifford, 1982b). Lott and Sommer (1967) found that students sat closer to fellow students and farther from both higher-status others (professors) and lower-status others (a student said to be failing).

The Physical Setting. Relatively few studies have examined the effect of the physical situation, as opposed to the social situation, on personal space. The results of these studies are more suggestive than conclusive. Smaller distances seem to be preferred in wide or narrow rooms, compared to very large or very small rooms (Daves & Swaffer, 1971). Individuals appear to use more space in corners of rooms than in the center (Tennis & Dabbs, 1975). Little's (1965) subjects, who were told to pretend they were theater directors, placed actresses farther apart in office waiting rooms than in lobbies or on street corners. Males seem to need more space when the ceiling is lower (Savinar, 1975). From these and other studies, a general conclusion appears to be that we prefer more space between us when the overall supply of space is low.

Another dimension of the physical setting is simply how many other people are around. Paul Sacilotto (1983) hypothesized that if office workers toiled in relative isolation, they would have a greater need for social contact. He predicted that this greater need would be reflected in smaller personal space zones. Sacilotto compared the personal space of women who spent their working day entering data on video display terminals with that of women in the same building whose jobs offered much more social interaction. He was surprised to find that the isolates preferred significantly *more* personal space. Instead of producing a greater need for social contact, it may be that working in isolation either attracts individuals who already prefer more space or that isolates adapt to the isolation and feel less comfortable with others.

In review, we know that gender, personality, psychological disturbance, age, attraction, competition, status, and certain physical environment variables such as the abundance of nearby space affect personal space. In any everyday situation, all these variables are probably at work simultaneously, some adding to interpersonal distance while others subtract from it. Two natural questions are: Which of these variables have the strongest influences? How do they combine to produce a particular interpersonal distance on a particular occasion?

Evans and Howard (1973) wondered the same thing over a decade ago. They could find very few studies that had examined several variables in the same study in order to answer this question. There is still a shortage of such studies, and more are needed. **Multivariate** studies not only allow us simultaneously to compare the effects of several influences, they also permit examination of interaction effects: measures of the joint effect of two or more variables, i.e., their effect on personal space separate from and in addition to the main effects of the variables considered by themselves.

In one multivariate study, the effects of personality, gender, and social situation (degree of attraction, status differences, and cooperative versus competitive activity) were examined (Gifford, 1982b). Overall, attraction was the strongest single effect, followed by competition-cooperation. Smaller distances were chosen when the subject liked the other and when the task was a cooperative one. Personality and status were also significant, as predicted. Larger distances were selected by cold individuals and in situations where the individuals were unequal in status. However, these effects were not as powerful as the situational ones.

Interactions also predicted interpersonal distance. (See Fig. 5–7.) One significant interaction was between two personality variables, warmth and ambitiousness. More ambitious cold individuals chose larger distances than less ambitious cold individuals. However, more ambitious warm individuals chose smaller distances. In another significant interaction, high-status participants preferred larger distances in competitive situations than in cooperative situations, but equal-status and low-status participants chose the same distance in competitive and cooperative situations.

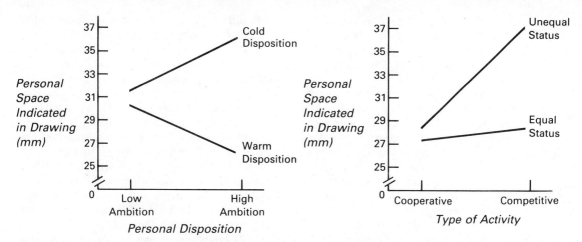

FIGURE 5-7 Personal space varies with one's **pattern** of personality dispositions (left) and with different *combinations* of status and activity (right). *(Based on Gifford, 1982b.)*

Multivariate studies can become complicated; sometimes one wishes for a simpler set of results. Unfortunately, personal space (like other behavior processes) really is multidetermined. Progress in understanding it demands further systematic multivariate research.

▶ **In Sum.** Social and physical features of the situation alter interpersonal distance. Attraction, cooperation, and equal status are associated with smaller personal space; stigma and unequal status lead to larger personal space. Orientation, as opposed to distance, is less well understood. We seem to prefer more space when the physical environment offers less room. Again, these factors combine to produce interpersonal distances that are different from what would be expected from consideration of each influence by itself; multivariate research is helping to untangle these complex effects.

Cultural and Ethnic Variations

Nearly all the research discussed so far was performed in North America. Yet Hall's original point (1959) was that space utilization varies across cultures. Based on his own observations of Arabs, French, South Americans, Japanese, and English, Hall believed that his four zones retained their order but not their size. Let Hall tell his own story.

I had the good fortune to be visited by a very distinguished and learned man who had been for many years a top-ranking diplomat representing a foreign country. . . . Dr. X was interested in some of the work several of us were doing at the time and asked permission to attend one of my lectures. He came to the front of the class at the end of the lecture to talk over a number of points made in the preceding hour. While talking he became quite involved in the implications of the lecture as well as what he was saying. We started out facing each other and as he talked I became dimly aware that he was standing a little too close and that I was beginning to back up. Fortunately I was able to suppress my first impulse and remain stationary because there was nothing to communicate aggression in his behavior except the conversational distance. . . . Someone who had been so successful in the old school of diplomacy could not possibly let himself communicate something offensive to the other person except outside of his highly trained awareness.

By experimenting I was able to observe that as I moved away slightly, there was an associated pattern of interaction. He had more trouble expressing himself. If I shifted to where I felt comfortable (about twenty-one inches), he looked somewhat puzzled and hurt, almost as though he were saying: "Why is he acting that way? Here I am doing every-thing I can to talk to him in a friendly manner and he suddenly withdraws. Have I done any-thing wrong!" (Hall, 1959, pp. 161–162)

Such an interaction with a less-sensitive ob-server than Hall (who eventually rooted himself at the close distance to facilitate the discussion) could have had undesirable repercussions. Re-member, we begin to attribute negative charac-teristics to those who interact with us at inap-propriate distances. This can, and indeed has, contributed to negative cultural stereotypes.

In an early experiment, Watson and Graves (1966) studied cultural differences in some detail. They simply asked groups of four male students to come into the laboratory. The students were told they would be observed, but they were given no other instructions. Half the groups were com-posed of Arabs, half of Americans. The average interpersonal distance chosen by Arabs was about the length of an extended arm, but the average interpersonal distance of the Americans was noticeably further. The Arabs touched one an-other much more often and their orientation was much more direct. Generally, the Arabs were much more immediate (Mehrabian, 1966) than the Americans. Such findings have led to some overly simplistic generalizations of stereotypes even among researchers.

Following Hall, Watson (1970) asserted that cultures may be described as either *contact* or *noncontact*. Yet two studies (Forston & Larson, 1968; Mazur, 1977) found that students from al-legedly contact cultures (Latin America, Spain, and Morocco) sit farther apart from one another than do students from a noncontact culture (Americans). Shuter (1976) further illustrated the dangers of generalizing by showing that not all Latin Americans use the same amount of space. Costa Ricans, for example, choose smaller inter-personal distances than do Panamanians or Co-lumbians.

Inconsistent subcultural differences have been reported, too. Several studies have shown that blacks use more space than whites, but others have shown the reverse or no differences. Scherer (1974) suggests that, like other black-white dif-ferences, the reason may be socioeconomic rather than cultural. A study by Jones and Aiello (1973) supports this conclusion. It showed that black-white differences in personal space decreased as amount of school experience increased.

This is not to deny that some cultural differ-ences do exist, as the Watson and Graves study suggests. But, as usual, distancing is a complex process. Sussman and Rosenfeld (1982) found that Japanese subjects used more distance in conver-sations than did American subjects, who used more than Venezuelan subjects. But when the Japanese and Venezuelans spoke in English in-stead of their native tongue, their conversational distance moved toward that of the Americans. Language, an important part of culture, can mod-ify one's cultural tendencies to use more or less interpersonal distance. (See Fig. 5–8.)

Hall's original goal was to find some reasons for antagonism between cultures; he suggested that the differential use of space was one key fac-tor. This idea was tested by Collett (1971) who taught English students how to act more like Ar-abs in their nonverbal behavior. Arabs interacting with the trained students liked them more than students who had not received training. Consider the implications for diplomats and for ordinary tourists.

▶ **In Sum.** Culture is a major modifier of inter-personal distance. There is some evidence for a continuum that ranges from the closeness of Ar-abs and Latin Americans to the distance of Eng-lish and Germans. But differences within these groups, occasional results that do not fit this neat pattern, and other factors such as the language we speak during a particular interaction all may af-fect personal space.

PERSONAL SPACE AND HUMAN BEHAVIOR

In this section we will survey what happens when individuals deliberately invade others' space or innocently choose inappropriate interpersonal distances. The notion of appropriate distance is central to personal space. In each situation, only a small range of distances is acceptable. In his story, for example, Hall first considers the possi-bility that the diplomat is aggressive. On the too-close side, inappropriate distance will be per-ceived as invasion of personal space; on the too-far side it will be perceived as a lack of involve-ment or coldness. Furthermore, recall that Hall's

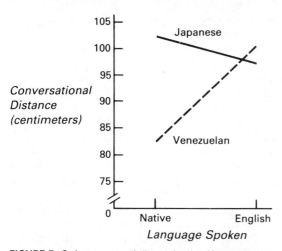

FIGURE 5-8 Interpersonal distancing is affected by the language spoken by conversation partners. *(From Sussman, N. M., & Rosenfeld, H. M. Influences of culture, language, and sex on conversational distance.* Journal of Personality and Social Psychology, *1982, 42, 66–74. Copyright 1982 by the American Psychological Association. Reprinted by permission of the authors.)*

diplomatic admirer actually began to have communication difficulties when Hall moved too far away from him.

Attraction

Intuitively, we might hypothesize that appropriate use of space leads to attraction—or at least does not harm personal relations—but inappropriate use of space leads to dislike. Research does support this conclusion, but a problematic word in this simple statement is *appropriate.* The very same distance may be appropriate for one person but not for another.

Fisher and Byrne (1975) studied the preferences of male and female university students. The experimenter went to the campus library and looked for a student sitting alone. The confederate then selected a seat next to, one seat away from, or directly across from the student. The confederate pretended to read for a short while and then left.

Enter, stage left, a second confederate, who asked a few questions about the subject's opinion of the first confederate. Both male and female students liked the female who sat very close to

them more than they liked the male who sat very close to them. Thus, appropriateness of distance partly depends on the gender of the person who invades your personal space. Fisher and Byrne also report that female students expressed greater attraction for confederates who sat across from them, but male students preferred confederates who sat next to them.

Cook (1970) observed where males and females sit in natural settings. He found that 82 percent of male-female pairs sat across from one another in restaurants, but in bars 70 percent of male-female pairs sat next to one another. This may be due both to different seating arrangements in bars and restaurants and to the preferences of couples. Either way, it seems that early in the evening at a restaurant couples usually choose to sit in a pattern which, according to Fisher and Byrne's results, facilitates her attraction, but later in the evening at the bar, they choose to sit in a pattern that facilitates his attraction.

Another outcome of attraction is the formation of shared or group personal space. Pairs or larger groups walking along a hallway, for example, seem to form a cohesive whole. The idea that individuals who like one another coalesce into an invasion-resistant entity has received some support (Knowles, 1972; Knowles & Brickner, 1981).

Arousal. Inappropriately close interpersonal distance is often viewed as an invasion. We feel uncomfortable; on the physiological level arousal occurs. This arousal was demonstrated in an unusual and widely discussed study by Middlemist, Knowles, and Matter (1976). The researchers hypothesized that arousal due to spatial invasion would manifest itself in altered patterns of urination. In a lavatory, a hidden camera measured how long it took men to begin urinating and how long they urinated when they were alone, when another man stood one urinal away, and when another man stood at the adjacent urinal. As predicted, urination took longer to begin and lasted less time when someone stood closer. Arousal due to closeness seems to have literally tensed up the subjects.

Social Influence. Can you influence someone merely by adjusting your interpersonal distance? In attempting to answer this question, Mehrabian and Williams (1969) showed participants films of discussions. Actors who used smaller interpersonal distances and less direct orientations in the film (more side by side than face to face) were judged by the film observers to be more persuasive.

Notice that Mehrabian and Williams' data do not show that individuals who stand close are actually more persuasive, merely that outside observers perceive them to be more persuasive. Albert and Dabbs (1970) assessed the actual change in listeners' attitudes when a speaker voiced an opinion at close, medium, and far distances. They found that the far speaker had the most influence, contrary to Mehrabian and Williams' conclusions. Albert and Dabbs suggest that far speakers may be more persuasive because the listener is less guarded when the persuader is beyond normal interpersonal distance. The two studies illustrate, however, that perceptions do not always match behavior.

Flight and Affect

If you have ever had your personal space invaded, you probably felt at least a short burst of emotion. Even when the invasion is excusable, as for example in a crowded elevator, some negative emotion usually surfaces. We might then hypothesize that appropriate distance in a given situation is associated with positive or neutral affect, but too-close and too-far arrangements lead to bad feeling.

Surprisingly few studies have directly tested this idea. However, if aversive behaviors such as leaving the scene are considered to be the result of negative emotions, there is abundant evidence in favor of this simple hypothesis. The classic evidence comes again from the work of Robert Sommer (1969). He began by simply sitting down quite close to (6 in or 20 cm) other men who were sitting alone. The men happened to be mental patients at the hospital where Sommer worked, but as we shall see, the results are similar for other groups of people.

After 1 minute, 30 percent of Sommer's participants had moved from their place. After 10 minutes, 55 percent had moved away. Each man whose space was invaded was matched with another seated man whose space was not invaded. After 1 and 10 minutes, 0 percent and 25 percent of these controls had moved. Inference: When

someone sits down within your personal space, there is a good chance you'll find a reason to leave sooner than you would have otherwise.

Later, Sommer's student Nancy Felipe Russo invaded the personal space of women studying alone in a university library. The closer she sat, the faster they left (Sommer, 1969). Incidentally, less than 2 percent of all the individuals in these studies responded verbally by asking Sommer or Russo to move or leave.

Barash (1973) extended the Sommer-Russo studies by adding status as a new aspect of the invader. When the invader was dressed as a faculty member, students fled more quickly than when the invader was dressed as a student.

In these studies, negative affect is implied but not directly studied. Baker and Shaw (1980) examined the feelings of individuals who were asked to stand too close, about normal, or too far from another individual. Participants reported feeling most negative about the far distance. They felt no worse about the close distance (12 in. or 30 cm) than about the normal distance (24 in. or 60 cm). This was true for pairs who were strangers as well as for pairs who were friends.

Baker and Shaw's finding that very close distances do not lead to negative emotions is surprising. Emotion was measured by self-report in their study; it is possible that the subjects simply did not report their true feelings. Other studies, investigating physiological measures of emotion, have reported that invasion does indeed affect actual behavior (Middlemist, Knowles, & Matter, 1976).

Attribution and Impression Formation

Consider the following film scene. You see a man sitting at his desk in an office, sorting through a card index. Another man knocks at the door and enters. In one version of the film, the second man begins to speak to the first man from just inside the door. In the second version, he walks over to the desk, produces some papers, and then begins to speak. Observers of this film judge the visiting man to be a subordinate if he stays just inside the door, but more equal in status to the other man if he walks over to the desk (Burns, 1964).

In a study by Patterson and Sechrest (1970), subjects engaged in a discussion with someone who happened to be a confederate. The confederate sat at four different distances but gave the same answers in response to the subject's questions. When asked to judge the personality of the confederate, subjects evaluated the confederate more negatively at larger distances. In another study, when a confederate selected a larger-than-normal distance, participants evaluated the confederate as more rejecting and aggressive (Aiello & Thompson, 1980b).

What if the impression comes first—that is, you enter a social situation where you expect to meet someone with a given set of characteristics? Kleck (1969) told participants in his study they were about to meet someone who was warm and friendly or unfriendly. The participants chose smaller interpersonal distances for the warm and friendly confederate. Similarly, observers will attribute intimacy to pairs of individuals they note are physically close together (Goldring, 1967; Haase & Pepper, 1972).

An important point about these attributions is that they may or may not match individuals' behavior, as we saw earlier in the case of persuasive attempts. The man who stops just inside the office door to talk may simply be a very polite boss rather than a subordinate. People who choose large interpersonal distances may not have unpleasant personalities and couples who walk very close to each other may not be lovers. But these studies indicate that observers will form such impressions, accurate or not. What impressions are your interpersonal distance choices creating in the minds of others?

Helping Others

Interpersonal distance seems to affect the desire to help others, but again the relations are not simple. In one study, the personal space of pedestrians was invaded, then the invader dropped something. Even when the dropped object was an important one, moving pedestrians whose space was invaded helped (by picking up the object) less often than did moving pedestrians whose space was not invaded. This makes sense. We would not expect a person who has just been dealt with rudely to be generous (Konecni, Libuser, Morton, & Ebbesen, 1975).

Yet in a subsequent study (Baron & Bell, 1976), requests for help were more successful under invasion conditions. Baron and Bell suggest that the conflicting results may be due to different attributions by the invaded individuals in the two studies. In the Konecni study, the invader may have been seen as personally unpleasant, but in the Baron and Bell study the request's importance was salient; the invasion was not perceived as intentional.

Baron (1978) tried to clear up the confusion with a study that explicitly examined the need of the invader. When the invader pleaded great need for help on a course project and stood very close, pedestrians offered the most help. When the invader stood near but didn't stress that the course project was essential, they were offered the least assistance. At a relatively far distance, this situation was reversed. Low need received more offers of assistance than high need.

This study is not only valuable for the way it reveals how personal space and helping behavior are linked, but for once again showing how variables interact to produce results that are not clearly predictable from either variable alone. The earlier studies reached conflicting results because they each emphasized one variable but did not adopt a multivariate approach.

Working in Small Groups

Imagine working on a project with a small group of others. Will the pattern of distances and orientations among you influence productivity or the way the members interact? Sommer's (1969) research showed that individuals very often say (on questionnaires) that they would select face-to-face arrangements for competition. However, another study indicates that face-to-face seating seems to lead to cooperation, not competition (Gardin, Kaplan, Firestone, & Cowan, 1973). Male subjects were asked to play a game in which either a cooperative strategy or a competitive strategy could be used to win. The subjects were asked to sit next to each other or across from each other; in both arrangements the subjects either could see one another or not (a visual barrier was used to accomplish this). Cooperation was greatest in the face-to-face, visual-access condition. So although such an arrangement is often viewed as competitive, it actually seems to elicit cooperation.

This may happen because the face-to-face arrangement makes the other person very salient.

When the other person has so much visual presence we may be loath to compete, fearing that competition will produce conflict and negative emotion. Gardin and his colleagues suggest that individuals responding to a questionnaire underestimate the emotional power of a face-to-face arrangement; that's why they report that they would sit face to face for competitive activities (the stereotypical arrangement), but actually cooperate more when placed in a real face-to-face situation.

In another study, groups of four men and women were asked to cooperate with each other or to compete as individuals while at small or large distances (Seta, Paulus, & Schkade, 1976). Their task was to solve a complex maze. When the instructions called for subjects to compete with each other, performance was better at the larger distance (5 ft. or 150 cm) than at the smaller one (2 ft. or 60 cm). When the subjects were asked to cooperate, however, the smaller distance led to better performance.

In the Gardin study, then, placing a group member in a more visually immediate position, even though it was farther away, led to more cooperation. In the Seta study, bringing individuals closer (without a change in orientation) led to better performance when they were asked to cooperate, but the more distant arrangement facilitated performance when the subjects were instructed to compete.

Cooperation, it seems, occurs more and leads to better performance when group members are made very aware of each other either because they are face to face or because they are very close. Competition occurs more and is associated with higher productivity when the competitors are less directly oriented or are simply farther apart. These conclusions must be tentative and limited, but the questions they deal with are very important. Millions of employees work in settings where the seating arrangements are based on custom, fashions in office decor, or no rationale at all. These studies suggest that cooperation and productivity may be enhanced by moving the furniture.

► **In Sum.** Personal space is intimately intertwined with numerous facets of human behavior. Changing our interpersonal distance may allow one individual to exert social control over another (Edinger & Patterson, 1983). Moving close in a positive relationship may lead to greater attraction, but doing so when the other person is a stranger leads to flight. Impressions are often formed on the basis of interpersonal distances we observe in others, but these attributions are not always valid. Help may be forthcoming when individuals approach close to others *and* impress their need on the other. Cooperation occurs more when and leads to better performance when individuals are *immediate* (closer and facing one another). When they are less immediate, performance is better in competitive conditions. Human behavior *is* complex! Let's examine some ideas that offer clarifying principles.

THEORIES OF PERSONAL SPACE

So far we have defined personal space, described how it may be measured, discussed many influences on it, and surveyed some of its effects on other human behaviors. It is time to attempt a drawing together of these strands of a complex process. Just how does personal space work?

Acquiring Personal Space

Most environmental psychologists believe personal space is culturally acquired. However, we should not forget that although many differences exist between cultures and even subcultures (Baxter, 1970), personal space is something that all humans seem to have. In that sense, personal space is not culturally acquired, but acquired as part of our genetic inheritance as human beings. Not every species is as socially inclined as ours. Therefore, in phylogenetic terms, personal space is genetically acquired, but once we restrict our study to humans, the differences in personal space are personal, situational, and cultural.

The only theory concerning the acquisition of personal space borrows from an approach prominent in other areas of psychology: **social learning theory.** Duke and Nowicki (1972) assert that personal space is a gradually learned behavior resulting from an individual's history of reinforcement. Parents and others often deliver verbal reinforcements to children about the appropriateness of their interpersonal distance: "Don't go near strangers." "Give your Auntie Maud a big kiss, now." "Stay close to your brother on the way to school."

Children apparently do learn the rules early. One study found that by the age of three, children already have learned to stay further from boys than from girls, a pattern that generally holds throughout life (Lomranz, Shapira, Choresh, & Gilat, 1975). Gifford and Price (1979) found that by the age of four, children already follow at least four personal space rules. These early patterns are: (1) boys keep greater distances from boys than girls do from girls; (2) children stay closer to acquaintances than to strangers; (3) children stay closer together in a formal setting (such as the teacher's office) than in an informal setting (such as their own playroom); and (4) if the other child is a stranger and the setting is formal, children keep a larger distance than they would from the same stranger in an informal setting, but if the other child is a friend and the setting is formal, they keep a smaller distance than they would even in an informal setting. (See Fig. 5–9.) If we learn this much by age four, consider the number of personal space rules we must know by adulthood.

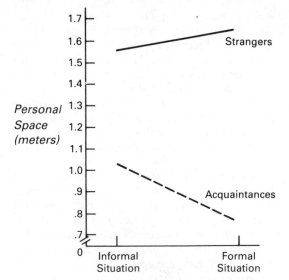

FIGURE 5–9 Even by age four, we choose different interpersonal distances depending on the situation (e.g., acquaintance vs. stranger). *(Based on Gifford & Price, 1979.)*

The Functions of Personal Space

Theorizing about the purpose or function of personal space has been much richer. Most formulations about the functions of personal space are arranged around the familiar notion of appropriate distance. In various formulations, inappropriate spacing is said to cause discomfort, a lack of protection, arousal, stress, stimulus overload, anxiety, misattribution, disequilibrium, poor communication, and constraints on our freedom. Obviously, inappropriate interpersonal distancing usually has one or more negative outcomes, but appropriate spacing usually has positive outcomes. As you read about these seven functions, consider how they overlap as well as how they are distinct from one another.

Comfort.   When Sommer first began researching personal space, the simple notion he used to guide his work was that we seek the appropriate distance to preserve our comfort. "It seems obvious that people feel uncomfortable when they talk to others who either stand too close or too far away" (Sommer, 1959, p. 247). This is self-evident in the case of someone standing too close,

but does it hold for the case of someone standing too far away?

In one of his anecdotes, Hall (1959) describes the effect that army regulations can have. A private, according to Hall, is supposed to stand three paces from an officer unless given an "at ease" order. When the private must hold a conversation with an officer, Hall says three paces is just too far for comfort. Research does show that inappropriately far interpersonal distances do cause discomfort. However, one problem with the comfort notion is that "comfort" is poorly defined. Later theories take up this issue.

Protection.   One of the more venerable models conceives of personal space as a protection device (Dosey & Meisels, 1969). The concept of threat is central to this model. Dosey and Meisels assert that as the threat to one's body or self-esteem grows, so does personal space.

This idea is not easy to test ethically. Most psychologists do not wish to threaten their subjects. We can, however, study individuals who are already threatened. Violent prisoners have personal space zones up to four times larger than prisoners with no history of violence (Hildreth, Derogatis, & McCuster, 1971; Kinzel, 1970; Roger

& Schalekamp, 1976). These authors infer that violent prisoners not only threaten others but very likely feel threatened themselves. Their fear of retribution may lead to larger **body buffer zones** (as personal space has occasionally been called) that serve as increased protection.

Another study indirectly tested the threat hypothesis. Gifford and Price (1979) found that children in a mildly threatening setting (the teacher's office) moved closer together if they were acquainted but further apart if they were strangers. This suggests that the protection model should be amended to include interpersonal distancing among individuals who are positively inclined toward one another. Instead of increasing their body buffer zones as protection from one another, individuals who like one another move together to create a common pool of protected space against external threats.

Communication. The communication approach, as we have seen, originated with Hall. The basis of communication lies in the sensation and perception of the other person's face, body, odors, vocal tone, and other channels. If you are inappropriately close (imagine yourself in full-body contact with a stranger during a conversation), you experience an avalanche of unwanted information. Sights, sounds, smells, and touches spill over, interrupting or eliminating the content of the conversation.

Several invasion studies have supported this model by finding that in inappropriate spacings, we get hung up on such things as the facial features of the other person and cannot easily carry on a conversation. Notice, however, that if the other person is indeed on intimate terms with you, a full-body contact conversation constitutes very appropriate spacing and can be among life's high points.

The basic communication model has been expanded in several directions by subsequent writers. Pederson and Shears (1973) have considered the communications aspect of personal space within a **general systems framework.** They view personal space as a mechanism for the communication of facts, feelings, and attitudes between individuals. The general systems approach assumes that an individual seeks information "needed to maintain a steady state which is his body" (Pederson & Shears, 1973, p. 367). Personal space is a primary vehicle for the information transfer process used to service this need.

In another extension, Kaplan (1977) adapted a traditional social psychological model of communication (Smith, Lasswell, & Casey, 1946), emphasizing nine components of messages. The model was originally conceived for studying verbal messages, but Kaplan's point is that the same components apply to the study of messages sent and received through personal space, a nonverbal communication channel. Kaplan's model maintains that at a given moment in an interaction, a *source* communicates a certain *message* to a specific *recipient* through one or more *channels* (in personal space, these are distance and orientation) for some *reason,* in a particular *place* and *time* and in a given *manner,* all of which achieves or fails to achieve an *effect* on the recipient.

In the next moment, of course, the recipient replies! Conversations are incredibly complicated patterns of sent and received messages. The true complexity of the nonverbal components of conversations, including personal space, are only recently being discovered through videotape analysis. My colleague Janet Beavin Bavelas has remarked that the advent of good quality slow-motion technology and methodology is to the social scientist exactly what the microscope was to the biologist. A whole world, previously unnoticed, is waiting to be discovered.

Stress. At first glance, the stress approach to personal space appears quite similar to the comfort approach. What else is stress except discomfort? However, the work of Gary Evans and his coworkers on the stress model has contributed two extensions that are not included in the comfort model (Evans, 1974; Evans & Eichelman, 1976; Evans & Howard, 1973).

First, Evans notes that inappropriately close spacing in animals often leads to aggression. Scientific evidence in this area with human subjects is difficult to obtain, but Evans cautiously theorizes that personal space may function as an antiaggression mechanism. Many acts of aggression in prisons, ranging from isolated attacks on one prisoner by another to full-scale riots, have been attributed to insufficient space. Most of us, most of the time, are fortunate enough to have sufficient interpersonal space even if we live in small quarters. Evans would hypothesize that being confined to small quarters with strangers might lead to aggression.

Second, Evans has asserted that the mere presence of a **stressor** does not necessarily lead to **strain.** (Stressors are external stimuli; strain is the effect on a person.) This is because, according to Evans, an important mediator of strain for humans is our ability to think about the stressor. If you enter a crowded elevator and it gets stuck between the thirtieth and thirty-first floors, you probably will not immediately respond to the stress by striking out at your fellow sufferers. You'll interpret the situation as temporary and unavoidable. You will decide that the intentions of others are not hostile. These cognitive processes play an important role in personal space in Evans' stress model.

Optimal Stimulation.   Another approach to personal space claims that its function is to regulate the amount of stimulation we receive from others. Nesbitt and Steven (1974) tested this idea in an amusement park. They dressed confederates in bright clothes and cologne and observed the interpersonal distances that visitors to the park chose for these confederates compared to more moderately attired confederates. As expected, the confederate who emitted high levels of stimulation elicited greater distances.

Nesbitt and Steven's model might also be interpreted to predict that especially low levels of stimulation should lead to the selection of smaller interpersonal distances. Individuals should be seeking more stimulation as compensation. Paul Sacilotto's (1983) study, mentioned earlier, tested this idea (although social stimulation was investigated instead of visual and olfactory stimulation). Contrary to a prediction based on Nesbitt and Steven's optimal stimulation theory, the socially deprived employees chose significantly larger interpersonal distances.

Sacilotto's findings may mean that individuals who are understimulated for long periods of time adapt to their low levels of stimulation. When they do meet someone new, their need for stimulation is not higher, but lower; they stay farther away from others. It is possible that new employees who hold socially deprived positions would operate according to optimal stimulation theory. The experienced employees simply have a new, lower optimal level of stimulation.

Affiliative Equilibrium.   The most fertile theory about the function of personal space was originally formulated by Michael Argyle and Janet Dean (1965). The affiliative-conflict theory maintains that, like cold porcupines, we have conflicting social motives: a desire to draw closer to others and, at the same time, a desire to move away from others. These conflicting tendencies arise because we are simultaneously attracted to others or want information from them but also wish to retain our individuality and freedom or may not want to reveal information about ourselves to others. In several nonverbal channels—not only interpersonal distance but others such as amount of eye contact, smiling, and intimacy of the discussion topic—individuals are presumed to seek an equilibrium between their approach and avoidance tendencies. In stable interpersonal relationships, the various channels add up to a total level of intimacy, the equilibrium point.

If, for some reason, one of the individuals in the relationship alters the equilibrium, then the other individual will, according to the theory, compensate by adjusting one channel or another so as to reestablish the previous level of intimacy. As an illustration, imagine that you and an acquaintance are strolling along to the cafeteria together, chatting about one of your classes. Arriving at the cafeteria, you discover that the lineups are long. You squeeze into line anyway because you are both quite hungry. Now you are inappropriately close to your acquaintance; neither of you can avoid it under the circumstances. Argyle and Dean's theory predicts that the resulting disequilibrium in the interpersonal distance channel will be compensated for in other channels. You might reduce eye contact or smiling or shift the conversation to less intimate topics. The affiliative-conflict theory has been tested many times; most but not all studies support its basic tenets (Patterson, 1973).

Integrative Theories of Personal Space

More recent theories recognize the complementarity of the personal space functions just described. Four recent models represent refinements and extensions of affiliative-conflict theory.

Social Penetration.   A major shortcoming of affiliative-conflict theory is its failure to account for changes in relationships. When we fall in love, an increase in the nonverbal intimacy of one partner often will be reciprocated by the other, not compensated for. Instead of moving away when you move close, the other person maintains the shorter distance or even moves closer to you. In general, when relationships are growing, changing, or dying, affiliative-conflict theory may fail to predict individual responses to disequilibrium.

Altman and Taylor (1973) and Sundstrom and Altman (1976) have proposed a form of affiliative-conflict theory that deals with these changes. Their dialectical approach posits that compensatory and reciprocal behaviors occur as individuals gradually adjust to changes in their desired level of interaction with others.

Limits of Compensation. Jack Aiello and his colleagues have shown that compensation processes do not work well outside a certain range of distances (Aiello, 1977; Aiello, Thompson, & Baum, 1981). (See Fig. 5–10.) This is partly due to growing discomfort as interpersonal distance becomes more inappropriate.

In one study, observers were shown videotapes of pairs interacting at different distances. The observers judged the degree of comfort that individuals in the film would feel at the different distances. Maximum comfort was thought to be at the moderate distance; at shorter and longer distances the comfort ratings declined (Thompson, Aiello, & Epstein, 1979). Aiello postulates that outside a **critical discomfort** region the usual channels cannot easily be used to restore equilibrium.

In several studies Aiello and his colleagues (Aiello, 1972; 1977; Aiello & Thompson, 1980b) have also found sex differences in the distances at which the critical discomfort region is reached. Males show more discomfort as the distance grows inappropriately close, but females show more discomfort as the distance grows inappropriately far. In one study (Aiello & Thompson, 1980b), women who were too far away from the other person had greater difficulty in using any of the other channels to reestablish equilibrium.

Arousal-Cognition. An important consideration in all versions of equilibrium theory is that compensation and reciprocation occur at low levels of cognitive awareness, but not all theories about the functions of personal space discount the role of cognitive processes. If you move too close

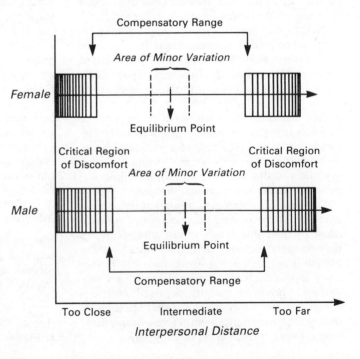

FIGURE 5–10 Some environmental psychologists view personal space as a continuum rather than as a fixed distance. When interpersonal distance is a little too small or a little too large (but within the compensatory range), minor discomfort can be reduced by averting eye contact, changing the topic of conversation, or other behaviors that help overcome the uncomfortable discrepancy between actual and optimal interpersonal distances. But when the discrepancy is *too* large (in the critical region of discomfort), these behaviors can no longer compensate for the strong discomfort caused by very inappropriate interpersonal distance. *(From Aiello & Thompson, 1980b.)*

to someone, you become aroused. There is nothing surprising about this arousal; the only mystery might be whether the arousal is negatively toned (annoyance-anger) or positively toned (pleasure-sexual).

Miles Patterson, the chief spokesman for the arousal approach, believes that changes in arousal have a cognitive component. He asserts that we are aware of changes in our arousal, and we tend to label that change positively or negatively. Patterson predicts that arousal shifts accompanied by positive affect will lead to reciprocation. Only negatively labeled arousal-shifts, according to Patterson, lead to the compensatory behaviors described by Argyle and Dean (1965) in their affiliative-conflict theory.

Approach-Avoidance. Argyle and Dean's original formulation of affiliative-conflict theory suggested that we use interpersonal distance (and other nonverbal behaviors) to balance conflicting desires to approach and to avoid the other person. Eric Knowles (1980a) has examined this assumption more closely and postulates three clarifications of the approach-avoidance assumption. (See Fig. 5–11.) These clarifications, by the way, also represent a more articulate definition of the comfort concept used by early theorists.

First, nearly every interpersonal situation involves avoidance tendencies. Even in rewarding relationships, we wish to avoid getting too close, involved, or committed. Second, some interpersonal situations result in approach tendencies. Thus, we only want to become involved with some individuals, but there is a limit to how involved we want to become with every individual. Third, discomfort in interpersonal situations results from a discrepancy between approach and avoidance tendencies.

These clarifications, based on much previous work including that by Lewin and Sundstrom and Altman, are reflected in Figure 5–12. In interpersonal situations, individuals may be interacting or not (external forces may have put them in proximity, such as in a crowded elevator, bus, or room). The shaded areas in diagrams A and C represent the discrepancy between approach and avoidance tendencies at close and far distances. Diagrams B and D depict the resultant discomfort experienced by a person at these distances.

FIGURE 5–11 Eric Knowles has contributed important insights into individual and group management of interpersonal distance, including the notion of *social physics*. *(Courtesy of Eric Knowles.)*

▶ **In Sum.** The individual's acquisition of the rules concerning interpersonal distance are probably well characterized by social learning theory. The functions of personal space are characterized by numerous minimodels (comfort, protection, communication, stress, optimal stimulation, and affiliative equilibrium).

More encompassing theoretical integrations have begun to appear. The social penetration model emphasizes the role of personal space in the rise and fall of relationships. The limits-of-compensation model highlights the outer limits of interpersonal distance, showing that as discomfort grows interaction becomes more difficult. The approach-avoidance model hypothesizes differences between the desire to get close to someone and the desire to keep one's distance. Discomfort is seen as the discrepancy between the two desires.

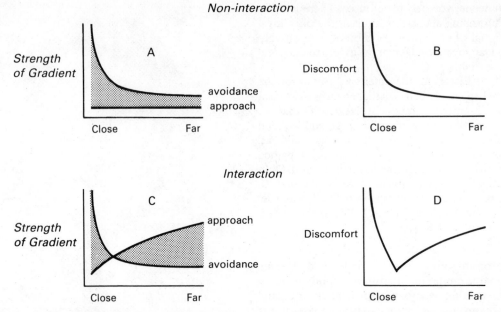

FIGURE 5–12 Discomfort associated with interpersonal distance depends on whether we are involved in an interaction with the other person or not and on the strength of our approach and avoidance tendencies toward the other person. When we are not involved (diagrams A and B), we have no approach tendency (A) so discomfort decreases as distance increases (B). When we are involved (diagrams C and D), we have both approach and avoidance tendencies (C) so discomfort is lowest at an optimal middle distance (D). *(Reprinted with permission from Eric Knowles, 1981.)*

PERSONAL SPACE AND ENVIRONMENTAL DESIGN

In the early days of personal space research, there was hope that personal space would be an essential part of planning and architecture. Robert Sommer (1969) subtitled his classic book on personal space, *The Behavioral Basis of Design*. Only five years later, however, Sommer had adopted quite a different view:

> When I did this research originally, I believed that it would be of use to architects. Since architects were concerned with designing spaces and this research was concerned with space, there must be something useful in it for architects. Looking back I think this assumption was, if not unwarranted, at least overoptimistic. I do not believe that the personal space bubble is a logical unit in architectural design. (Sommer, 1974, pp. 205–207)

Personal space research has slowed recently, but not everyone shares Sommer's opinion. It is true that personal space will never be the cornerstone of architecture. For one thing, there are simply too many other considerations. Local regulations, siting, other social factors, budgets, materials, and aesthetics are also important.

Personal space may not be the essence of environmental design, but it is one important consideration among other important considerations. Edward Hall has remarked that research on interpersonal distance cannot tell an architect how to design a building, but it certainly can provide the architect with information that can be worked into a design. Designers have become very much more sensitive to the spatial needs of their clients over the last fifteen years.

A number of researchers have specifically examined the role of personal space in the built environment. Most of these studies have concentrated on personal space as reflected in seating arrangements. When you think about it, architects have little to say about conversational behavior between standing individuals. Most research, then, has been concerned with optimal furniture arrangements, and it has been conducted in such public spaces as libraries, airports, schools, offices, and restaurants. Most research has centered on the effect of furniture arrangements on social interaction. Some arrangements seem to foster social interaction and others seem to hinder it.

Sociopetal and Sociofugal Arrangements

An insightful psychiatrist, Humphrey Osmond, coined these terms to refer to settings that facilitate (*sociopetal*) or discourage (*sociofugal*) social interaction (Osmond, 1957). Osmond himself did not restrict the terms to seating arrangements. He describes, for example, hallways as sociofugal and circular medical wards as sociopetal. Most subsequent research, however, has emphasized the sociopetal or sociofugal qualities of seating arrangements.

A typical sociopetal arrangement is the dining table in most homes, where family members sit around the table facing one another. A typical sociofugal arrangement, often found in airport waiting areas, is a trio of chairs bolted so that chair occupants face outward, away from one another, in three directions. Most seating arrangements are neither sociopetal nor sociofugal but fall along a continuum from one extreme to another. (See Fig. 5–13.)

Initially, we may conclude that sociopetal arrangements are good and sociofugal arrangements are bad. After all, don't we wish to foster social interaction everywhere possible? Not necessarily. There are situations in which a minimum of social interaction is the best pattern.

In the reading room of a library most of us expect others to work quietly. In some community libraries, however, and in certain parts of large university libraries, librarians may wish to encourage users to discuss issues, ask questions, and generally interact. This, in fact, is the very heart of the matter. Few designs (sociopetal, sociofugal, or otherwise) are inherently good or bad. The question is, what behavior pattern is valued in this particular setting, and which arrangement will encourage this valued pattern?

Seating arrangements that orient individuals toward one another do not always facilitate conversation (Gifford, 1981). This may be because other factors, like personality, also affect socia-

bility. Defensive individuals seem to be more sociable in sociofugal arrangements, but less defensive individuals are more sociable in sociopetal arrangements (Gifford & Gallagher, 1985). Let's turn now to a study of personal space and seating arrangements in a library.

Libraries

Eastman and Harper (1971) began their study by simply noting how the patrons of a reading room in the Carnegie-Mellon University library used the space. The goal, however, was not to understand how the space was managed by its users, but to develop an approach that might predict how patrons in any roughly similar setting would use the available spatial arrangements.

Eastman and Harper recorded which seats were taken, in what order, for how long, and by what sort of user. Their initial model assumed that within the near phase of Hall's social distance (a radius of 6 ft. or about 2 m), once a seat was taken, other seats in the zone would be avoided. This was confirmed, but Eastman and Harper 'also found a strong tendency for users to select unoccupied tables if they were available. Individuals avoided choosing side-by-side arrangements, but when they did sit side by side, conversation almost always ensued.

Eastman and Harper propose that data such as their own could be utilized by a mathematical model to assist in designing or renovating library reading rooms. If the model is provided with basic facts such as the number of seats available and the physical arrangements of the seats, then information on user preferences or informal rules such as that provided by their own study may be used to build up a predicted pattern of usage for alternate designs for a reading room. Some of the usage rules that emerged from Eastman and Harper's study are

1. The most desirable seats are those at vacant tables.
2. If a table is occupied, the next most desirable seat is the one furthest from the other person.
3. Seats allowing a back-to-back arrangement are preferred over side-by-side arrangements.
4. When the room is over 60 percent full, users will go elsewhere.

Some universities already use models like the one Eastman and Harper discuss to predict the

FIGURE 5-13 Examples of sociopetal seating and sociofugal seating. *(Top photo courtesy of Robert Sommer.)*

flow of students from dormitory to cafeteria to classroom to study spaces.

Restaurants and Bars

Establishments selling food and drink for on-site consumption vary tremendously in design. Certain aspects of design are controlled by local laws; every state and province seems to have its own bizarre rules about the serving of liquor. But many others are controlled by the proprietor's own vi-

sion of the clientele's tastes or whether the proprietor's goal is to turn over the clientele quickly or slowly.

Mark Cook's (1970) work, discussed earlier, bears on the personal space implications of both restaurants and drinking places. Several of his findings are relevant here. First, questionnaires about seating preferences do not match actual behavioral choices very well. Second, actual seating choices vary considerably depending on whether the diners are of the same sex or not. Third, actual seating patterns in restaurants differ from those in bars. Observations like these provide valuable information for architects who are commissioned to build or renovate a restaurant or bar. As noted earlier, these personal space factors are certainly not the architect's only considerations, but they may well be the difference between a space in which customers feel comfortable and one in which they do not.

Sherri Cavan obtained her Ph.D. by hanging around bars in San Francisco. Of course, she wasn't merely hanging around, she was engaged in participant observation of the behavior patterns of the customers (Sommer, 1969). She observed the social isolation and interaction patterns at the bar itself and at the tables. As in both the Eastman and Harper and the Cook studies, there is a definite pattern to the interplay between an individual's goals and the layout of the space.

If you wish to drink alone, Cavan found, you should select a distant bar stool or table, hunch over, and stare into your drink. Even this behavior may not keep others away; bars are widely perceived as settings that are expressly created for social interaction. However, the bar itself usually has a more sociofugal arrangement than the tables, so the lone drinker has a greater chance of avoiding social contact.

Cavan found that patrons rarely initiated a conversation over a span greater than two bar stools. If two men begin to talk over a single empty stool, they are unlikely to move to the empty stool. But if a man and woman begin talking over any number of empty stools, the gap will rather quickly be erased.

A basic principle of design is illustrated by the bars studied by Cavan. Proprietors of such establishments discovered long ago that some customers like sociopetal arrangements and others prefer more sociofugal ones. The solution is to give the customers their choice. Studies like Cook's and Cavan's can assist in the design process by suggesting the proper mix of seating for a given clientele, location, and size.

Airports

Osmond (1957) said that one of the most sociofugal places was the railway waiting room. Their modern equivalent, the arrival and departure lounges of airports, are often equally sociofugal. Sommer (1974) graphically describes the long rows of chairs in many airports, bolted together and facing in the same direction. Sometimes the chairs are fixed together in groups of three, back to back, like sociofugal Siamese triplets. The overall atmosphere of these huge rooms is certainly antisocial.

Yet it must not be forgotten that such arrangements probably suit some portions of the airport's clientele. The businessman who travels frequently and alone presumably does not wish to be forced into a chatty little conversation by a tight little circle of seats. On the other hand, such sociofugal arrangements are quite unsuitable for other travelers. Families waiting for a cherished member's arrival or departure would probably prefer that cozy circle of seats while they anticipate the reunion or the temporary separation of the family.

Children, Sommer notes, may explore the waiting area regardless of how hostile it is. But why don't more airports have facilities designed especially for children? Sommer observed children adapting to back-to-back chairs by kneeling on them to talk across the joined backs of the chairs.

Why not just move the chairs to a more suitable arrangement? First, many rows of chairs interlock or are bolted together. It is often difficult or impossible to move them. Second, when Sommer and his wife began unhooking a row of interlocking chairs, other passengers looked at them as if they were crazy. Awareness of the possibility of altering public furniture is amazingly low (Gifford, 1976c; Sommer, 1972).

Aren't airports interested in pleasing their customers? Why aren't airport designers as sensitive to customers' needs as bar designers? First, airports tend to have little local competition, whereas bars have much local competition. Second, recall that sociofugal seating may please a large portion of the flying public (the lone businessman), even though many others' needs are not met. Third, what might be called the "Conrad Hilton effect" applies. Sommer (1969) says that Hilton noticed in his hotels that many individuals sat around in the comfortable lounges without spending much money. So, in his new hotels and in renovations, Hilton shrunk his lobbies and made the seating less inviting but increased the amount of space in his bars and restaurants. The new spaces were very comfortable and sociopetal. The effect is to drive people into places where they cannot help spending money.

Some airport managers may not strive to make their public waiting areas especially comfortable for the same reasons. On top of this motive, Sommer (1974) notes that airports usually have special VIP lounges that are nice; they are subsidized partly by the price of a first class ticket, but mostly by the economy class ticket holders who are barred from it.

Counseling Settings

A basic component of many counseling clients' problems is difficulty in communication. Schizophrenics typically do not communicate much or well. Neurotics may communicate too much but not well. Even family problems are often based in communication difficulties. Seating arrangements during psychotherapy may be important mediators of success in this delicate situation.

Winick and Holt (1961) observed that chairs themselves can be psychologically significant. They suggest that if a person feels ready to crumble emotionally, the therapist could do much better than to offer a folding chair. Winick and Holt describe the spontaneous arrangements of chairs that occur in group psychotherapy as clients experience anxiety, withdrawal, or a strong need for companionship.

Paul Goodman (1964) offers an interesting analysis of the chair arrangements recommended by the leaders of four prominent schools of psychotherapy. Freud's approach is very sociofugal; the patient lies on a couch with the analyst sitting at the head of the couch, entirely out of sight. This psychologically distant arrangement is congruent with Freud's belief that such an arrangement facilitates the free expression of repressed ideas.

Harry Stack Sullivan, the father of a more interpersonally oriented school of psychotherapy, recommended an arrangement in which the client and therapist face one another directly, across a desk. Sullivan, who specialized in helping schizophrenics, believed this direct orientation promoted better communication with the small part of the schizophrenic's personality that still wants to communicate.

Wilhelm Reich, representing a third, more body-oriented form of psychotherapy, asked his patients to lie on a couch with the therapist sitting beside the couch, facing the patient. This arrangement was rooted in Reich's belief that character defenses in individuals with psychological problems are reflected in rigid muscles and other bodily manifestations. His furniture arrangement was designed to allow the therapist to touch and massage the patient frequently during therapy.

The fourth school, usually attributed to Fritz Perls, is gestalt therapy. Perls believed there should be no fixed arrangement of chairs. In fact, he would often direct clients in group therapy to move themselves or the furniture around for different activities, such as role-playing or recounting dreams. Perls sometimes ordered clients to abandon the furniture entirely in favor of the floor.

Meeting Rooms

The average midlevel manager is said to spend over a third of the working day in meetings. The furniture arrangements for such meetings can be quite rigid. Often, by choice or custom, the chairperson sits at the head of a long, narrow table (Strodbeck & Hook, 1961). Is this the best arrangement?

That depends on the goals of the organization. The arrangement just described is congruent with an organization that desires a strong vertical hierarchy. Individuals who sit along the sides of a long, narrow table do not have good visual access to anyone except the person directly across from them and the boss at the head of the table. The boss, however, has good visual access to most or all the others. Baker (1983) has shown how various arrangements offer different and unequal visibility to different positions; visibility, in turn, is related to power. (See Fig. 5–14.)

On the other hand, an organization with a flatter hierarchy and more democratic ideals is best served by equalizing visibility, which is best achieved by selecting a round table. The sociopetal qualities of the round table leave a subtle impression that all participants are equal partners in the organization.

Charles Green (1975) studied the connections between social and spatial variables in the policy meetings of a large mental hospital. He found that

FIGURE 5-14 Long narrow meeting tables affect conversation differently than do round tables.

as committee members participated more, they moved—over the course of several meetings—closer and closer to the chairperson. Further analyses suggested that moving closer led to more effective communication, which led to a greater capacity to influence the meeting, which led to even greater participation. This cyclical pattern can be interrupted by other factors (the day's agenda may not include items of interest to a member, or seats close to the chairperson may already be filled), but it illustrates how personal space and social interaction can be intertwined in everyday meetings.

SUMMARY

Personal space is the distance component of interpersonal relations. It has objective (alpha) and experiential (beta) aspects. The best way to mea-

sure it for most purposes is probably the disguised stop-distance technique. Naturalistic observation is realistic but often difficult and usually does not allow for measurement of extraneous influences. Simulation methods are poor at measuring alpha personal space but may be useful for measuring beta personal space. Interpersonal space generally grows with age and personal coldness. Males have larger personal spaces and psychologically disturbed individuals have more variable personal space. These influences interact, so caution must be exercised in predicting interpersonal distance in everyday social transactions. Similar caution is necessary in the case of situational influences. Attraction and cooperation generally lead to smaller interpersonal distance, but stigma and unequal status lead to larger interpersonal distances. When the physical setting is less spacious, we seem to want more interpersonal distance. Cultural differences in interpersonal distance exist, but again other factors often operate to alter the simple stereotype of contact and noncontact cultures. Interpersonal distance may be used to influence others. Inferences about others are drawn on the basis of the interpersonal distance they choose. Close distances may lead to reciprocation or to flight, depending on the quality of the relationship. They may also evoke helping in others, if a person's need is clearly expressed. Closeness in cooperative circumstances and distance in competitive circumstances lead to better performance. Integrative models of personal space incorporate its functions as a communication medium that protects us from stress by allowing control of stimulation from others in interpersonal encounters. They emphasize the dynamic nature of relationships, the role of cognitive appraisal (beta personal space), and the management of approach-avoidance conflicts. Personal space is an important, though not the only, behavioral basis for designing buildings. As the costs of construction rise and more of us are crammed closer and closer together, increasing attention should be paid to the arrangement of space. Personal space transactions are omnipresent and crucial to social interaction yet often go unnoticed and unplanned for. At the very least, we can conclude that designers should offer either a variety of seating arrangements or flexible arrangements so that individuals can find comfortable spaces for interaction.

SUGGESTED SUPPLEMENTARY READINGS

Aiello, J. R., Thompson, D. E., & Baum, A. (1981). The symbiotic relationship between social psychology and environmental psychology: Implications from crowding, personal space, and intimacy regulation research. In J. H. Harvey (Ed.), *Cognition, social behavior, and the environment.* Hillsdale, NJ: Erlbaum.

Edinger, J. A., & Patterson, M. L. (1983). Nonverbal involvement and social control. *Psychological Bulletin, 93,* 30–56.

Gifford, R. (1982). Projected interpersonal distance and orientation choices: Personality, sex, and social situation. *Social Psychology Quarterly, 45,* 145–152.

Hayduk, L. A. (1983). Personal space: Where we now stand. *Psychological Bulletin, 94,* 293–335.

Knowles, E. S. (1980a). An affiliative conflict theory of personal and group spatial behavior. In P. B. Paulus (Ed.), *Psychology of group influence.* Hillsdale, NJ: Erlbaum.

Sommer, R. (1969). *Personal space: The behavioral basis of design.* Englewood Cliffs, NJ: Prentice-Hall.

Sundstrom, E., & Altman, I. (1976). Interpersonal relationships and personal space: Research review and theoretical model. *Human Ecology, 4,* 47–67.

Chapter Six
Territoriality

*Territory . . . is valued for the way it facilitates
making sense, for the opportunity for choice and
control it provides, as well as for the many
positive associations it comes to have.*

Stephen and Rachel Kaplan, 1978

Jane wanted a raise. To improve her chances of talking the boss into it, she prepared a mental list of her accomplishments since her last raise, thought about the order in which to present them, and even planned how she would enter the office, where to sit, and how much eye contact to make with the boss. Precisely at the appointed hour, she knocked on Mrs. Black's door. As she did so, she felt but then suppressed the notion that Mrs. Black's office would be very nice to have someday. It had that solid door, that brass nameplate, those leather chairs, and those little conference tables scattered around.

Summoned inside, Jane realized that somehow she hadn't entered the room with all the panache and presence she had hoped to. Mrs. Black leaned back in her chair with her back to a huge sunny window. Jane could hardly make out the expression on Mrs. Black's face because of the light streaming from behind. At the same time, Jane suddenly thought, her own face was so exposed to the bright light that she was squinting. She tried to express her reasons for seeking a raise, but somehow the whole idea now seemed rather lifeless. She stammered out her list, confusing her order, and even forgetting some reasons. Finally, although Mrs. Black was pleasant enough, she ceased the painful recital knowing that it had not been very convincing.

Mrs. Black said she would think the matter over. Jane returned to her own "home sweet home," a small work space partitioned off in the middle of many other small spaces. She felt comfortable there, at least, but not at all optimistic about her raise.

Territoriality is an extremely widespread phenomenon. It is operative in our largest-scale endeavors, war and global trade, as well as in many of our smallest, such as claiming our seats at the dinner table. Once you recognize them, indicators of human territoriality are everywhere: books spread out on a library table to save a place, nameplates, fences, locks, no trespassing signs, even copyright notices. (See Fig. 6–1.)

Territoriality is associated with some of the ugliest scenes we ever witness, but some environmental psychologists view it as a mechanism that helps us *avoid* considerable conflict.

Despite its pervasiveness, territoriality has not received the amount of study it deserves. There are difficulties in precisely defining it, in actually doing research on it, and even in reaching agreement that humans truly exhibit territoriality.

In this chapter, we will explore the meaning of territoriality, describe how it has been measured, survey the factors that influence and are influenced by it, discuss several theories of territori-

FIGURE 6–1 Territoriality in the form of steel. *(Courtesy of Coe Gifford.)*

ality, and show how it may be used to design better human environments.

WHAT IS TERRITORIALITY?

Perhaps it is best to preface a formal definition of territoriality with an impressionistic one, so you get a feel for the kinds of concepts involved. Julian Edney (1974) observes that it involves physical space, possession, defense, exclusiveness of use, markers, personalization, and identity. (See Fig. 6–2.) To this list, one could add dominance, control, conflict, security, claim staking, arousal, and vigilance.

More than a dozen formal definitions have been proposed, each including one or more of these elements. Most psychological definitions stress that territoriality involves behavior related to a place, although some authors believe that

FIGURE 6–2 Julian Edney's research and theoretical writings have advanced our knowledge of territoriality and the management of scarce natural resources. (See also Chapter 13.) *(Courtesy of Julian Edney.)*

territoriality includes relevant attitudes, too (Sebba & Churchman, 1983). The lack of agreement on definitions is a matter of emphasis, that is, which elements from the list above are emphasized by a researcher. One difficulty is that some elements are never actually manifested by the territory holder, although the potential for them to be manifested is clear. For example, a key element in many definitions is *defense* of a territory. Yet some territories are never challenged, so that the individual in control of the territory is never actually forced to defend it.

Territories may be controlled by individuals or by groups; they may be large or small; they are usually physical (but some theorists have considered ideas as territories, as in the notion of patents); and they consist of space (but some have considered objects that individuals possess and defend to be territories). A simple formal definition, therefore, is not easy to offer, but the following will serve as our operating definition: **Territoriality** is a pattern of behavior and attitudes held by an individual or group that is based on perceived, attempted, or actual control of a definable physical space, object, or idea and may involve habitual occupation, defense, personalization, and marking of it.

Types: Primary, Secondary, Public, and More

There are thousands of territories in the world; some are large, others small, some are nested within others, and some are shared. To understand how territoriality works, it is useful to find a system for classifying territories. If a good system is discovered, we can then study selected territories of a given type and reasonably assume that our findings apply to other territories of the same type.

The best-known system of classifying territories has been developed by Irwin Altman (Altman & Chemers, 1980). A key element in Altman's typology is the degree of privacy, affiliation, or accessibility allowed by each type. The first type is the **primary territory.** (See Fig. 6–3.) Paralleling the notion of primary groups (that is, groups composed of individuals who are central to one another's lives), primary territories are owned by individuals or primary groups, are controlled on a relatively permanent basis by them, and are cen-

FIGURE 6-3 One person's primary, secondary, and public territories.

tral to their daily lives. Examples include houses, bedrooms, company offices, and nations. Note that although the size and number of occupants are not uniform, the psychological importance of a primary territory to its occupants is always high.

Secondary territories are less important to us than primary territories, but they do possess moderate significance to their occupants. Your desk at work, favorite restaurant, locker in the gym, and home playing field are examples. Control of these territories is less essential to the current occupant and is more likely to change, rotate, or be shared with strangers.

Public territories are areas open to anyone in good standing with the community. Beaches, sidewalks, hotel lobbies, trains, stores, and ski slopes are public territories. Occasionally, through discrimination or unacceptable behavior, public territories are closed to individuals. Bars and taverns, for example, are public territories except that they discriminate against underage individuals. Those of age who cause trouble may be banned from the bar; bouncers are agents of territoriality. Notice, however, that instead of being closed to outsiders until specifically opened (as primary territories usually are), public territories are open to all outsiders who are not specifically excluded.

A typology by Lyman and Scott (1967) overlaps to some extent with Altman's but proposes two types of territory that are not directly comparable to his. The first of these is **interactional territories,** which are areas temporarily controlled by a group of interacting individuals. Examples include a classroom, a family's picnic area, and a football game in the park. Little overt marking of these territories may occur, yet entry into them is perceived as interference, rudeness, or "crashing."

Another Lyman and Scott idea is to regard one's physical self as a **body** territory. This is not the same as personal space, because the boundary is at one's skin rather than some distance away from it. Bodies may be entered with permission (as in surgery) or without permission (as in a knife attack), but individuals certainly act to personalize, defend, and control their bodies.

Two other types exist, although they are not universally considered territories (Altman, 1975). **Objects** meet some of the criteria for territories—we mark, personalize, defend, and control our books, coats, bicycles, and calculators.

Ideas are also, in some ways, territories. We defend them through patents and copyrights. We have rules against plagiarism. Most software authors try to protect their programs by "locking" them with codes.

Must territories be places? This is certainly implied in the everyday meaning of the word. But the notion of territoriality came to environmental psychology from those who study animal territoriality. Animals exhibit little territoriality toward objects and ideas. Perhaps our reluctance to consider objects and ideas as territories stems from our familiarity with the word territoriality as it is used in animal research, where it primarily refers to space. Objects and ideas may be considered the most human of all territories, in the sense that they are based in cognitive processes that are more developed in humans than in any other species. Nevertheless, it must be said that very little research has yet examined objects or ideas as territories.

Types of Infringement

Research and experience indicates there are several ways that a territory may be infringed upon (Lyman & Scott, 1967). The most obvious form is **invasion,** in which an outsider physically enters the territory, usually with the intention of taking control of it from its current owner. This can occur at any scale from one nation invading another to a spouse taking over a sewing room to install the family's new computer.

The second form of infringement is **violation,** a more temporary incursion into someone's territory. Usually the goal is not ownership but annoyance or harm. Vandalism, hit-and-run attacks, and burglary fall into this category. Sometimes a violation occurs out of ignorance, as when a boy who cannot yet read stumbles into a women's washroom. Sometimes the violation is deliberate. Computer pranksters have wormed their way into the programs of large companies. There are even reports of uncontrollable worms—prankster programs that know how to worm their way from computer to computer beyond the direct control of the pranksters. Violation may occur without the infringer personally entering the territory. Jamming radio waves and playing loud music are examples of territorial violation.

The third form of infringement is **contamination,** in which the infringer fouls someone else's territory by leaving something awful behind. A large chemical company left a poisonous stew in the ground under New York's Love Canal for subsequent homeowners. The former occupant of your apartment left the cupboards filthy. You loaned you tennis racquet out, and it came back scratched.

Types of Defense

Just as there are a variety of ways to infringe on territories, there are different ways to defend them. However, we should remember that territories are not always infringed and that when they are infringed they are not always defended. Mark Knapp (1978) lists six factors that affect whether, and how much, territory holders respond to infringement.

First, who is the infringer? Friends and peers, for example, are more often welcome—we may not even think of their entrance as an infringement—than strangers and individuals who are different from ourselves in some important way. One study even shows that infringement by the right person can have positive consequences. Women on beaches were asked how often their territory was invaded by men (Jason, Reichler, & Rucker, 1981). On average, the women reported about one invasion per visit. Many intrusions were unwanted (over half the women said they wanted to dissuade men from approaching), yet quite a number of intrusions resulted in dates and 10 percent of the women were currently going out with someone who had encroached on their beach territory!

Second, why did the intruder infringe? Some infringements are accidental and some are made by individuals who honestly did not know their mistake, but others are perceived as intentional. Obviously, we will react more strongly in the latter instance.

Third, what type of territory was invaded? Primary territories and body territories, for example, are likely to elicit stronger defensive reactions to intrusion than are secondary and public territories.

Fourth, how was the infringement accomplished? Knapp suggests, quite reasonably, that a touch applied to a body territory will be defended against more strenuously than a stroll across someone's grass. Of course, as noted earlier, whose touch it is and the apparent reason for the touch are also relevant.

Fifth, how long was the infringement? Presumably, defensive reactions to seemingly short infringements are weaker than those to seemingly long infringements.

Sixth, where did the infringement occur? Did it occur in a place where alternative territories may be found? In general, infringements of territories where there is plenty of space (so that the territory holder may simply move to another spot) will not result in defensive actions as vigorous as those in response to infringements of irreplaceable territories. Consider the difference, for example, in your reaction to someone taking your seat in a theater when the house is sold out compared to when the theater is half empty.

Knapp divides defenses into two general types: **prevention** and **reaction.** Such markers as coats, towels, signs, and fences are preventative defenses. One anticipates infringement and acts to stop it before it occurs. Reactions, on the other hand, are responses to an infringement after it actually happens. Examples of reaction-type defenses range from slamming doors and physically striking out at the infringer to court actions for patent or copyright violations.

A third type of defense is the **social boundary** (Cashdan, 1983). (See Fig. 6–4.) Used at the edge of interactional territories, the social-boundary defense consists of a ritual engaged in by hosts and visitors. For example, you needed a password to get into the speakeasies of the 1920s. Bushmen groups in Africa meeting at a border exchange certain greetings before allowing outsiders into their territories. The equivalent in the developed world is the customs office at the border. Social boundary defenses serve to separate wanted visitors from unwanted ones through social interaction.

▶ **In Sum.** We recognize seven types of territory: primary, secondary, public, interactional, body, object, and idea. This list is gathered from the work of several researchers, so the different types probably overlap to some extent. No one as yet has refined a category system that has a place for every type and every type in its place. The seven types of territory may be infringed upon in at least three ways: invasion, violation, and contamination. In turn, territory holders may utilize preventative, reaction, or social boundary defenses.

MEASURING TERRITORIALITY

Territoriality, by its very nature, is nearly impossible to study in a laboratory. Territoriality takes time to develop, and subjects in laboratory studies usually spend an hour or less in the lab. Ownership and control are central to territoriality, and subjects have very little opportunity to experience these in the experimenter's laboratory. This inability to study territoriality in the lab has two unfortunate consequences. First, laboratories offer considerable experimental control; without it, conclusions about the causes and effects of territoriality are difficult to draw. Second, because of the many difficulties of field research, few studies of human territoriality (compared to personal space and crowding, for example) are available.

The primary methods for studying human territoriality are field studies and field experiments, surveys and interviews, and the naturalistic observation of territorial behavior. Let us consider some examples of each approach.

FIGURE 6–4 A social boundary in the developed world.

Field Studies and Field Experiments

Field experiments are attempts to exercise experimental control: to randomly assign participants to the various experimenter-controlled conditions in a real-world setting. **Field studies** are also performed in real-world settings, but the focus is on naturally occurring associations or correlations between variables, with no explicit attempt to assign subjects randomly to conditions or to exercise control over the variables.

Field experiments require unusual creativity and perseverance to design and carry out. A rare example is a study of territoriality and decision making by Ralph Taylor and Joseph Lanni (1981). The purpose of their experiment was to discover whether being in one's own territory gives a person greater influence than a visitor on the outcome of a mutual decision. In addition, Taylor and

Lanni wanted to find out whether dominance (as a personality trait) influenced the process. The researchers asked groups of three students to meet in a room in which one student was resident and the other two were visitors. The group was asked to discuss a budget problem and reach a consensus.

Both random assignment and control over the variables were used, so that Taylor and Lanni's conclusions could, with some justification, be said to represent causal links (rather than mere associations) among territoriality, dominance, and decision making. The random assignment involved choosing on a chance basis which subjects participated in their own territory and which of them were asked to be visitors. Control of the dominance variable was achieved by assigning one low-, one medium-, and one high-dominance participant to each group of three decision makers.

Taylor and Lanni found that dominance did not affect decision making much. Instead the final consensus reflected the territory owner's point of view in the debate much more than it reflected the visitors' point of view. The results suggest that if you want decisions to go your way, you should try to get others to discuss the decision at your place. This strategy, it appears, works whether or not you have a dominating personality.

In a typical field study, several variables are measured but not controlled experimentally, and there is no random assignment to the experimental conditions or settings. For example, Smith (1981) studied territoriality on beaches. Sunbathers tend to mark off territories using radios, towels, and umbrellas. Smith found that females claim smaller territories than males, and that mixed-sex groups and larger groups claim less space (per person) than do same-sex groups and smaller groups.

However, because participants were not assigned randomly to the different types of groups, we cannot be sure that group size, for example, causes differences in size of territoriality. Some third factor may both cause certain individuals to go to the beach in larger groups *and* cause these individuals to space themselves rather closely, so that the group as a whole claims a relatively small space on the beach.

Surveys and Interviews

Another way to study territoriality is to ask individuals about their behavior and experiences. Self-report methods such as surveys and interviews have the disadvantage that respondents may not be able or willing to report their behavior accurately. However, these methods usually have two advantages: the researcher's resources can be stretched to include a much larger number of individuals in the study, and the opinions, beliefs, feelings, and other cognitions of respondents can be studied.

A good example of the interview approach is a study of 185 residents of high-rise buildings in Israel (Sebba & Churchman, 1983). Every member of forty-five families, including children over five, were asked about their actual behavior relevant to territoriality and about their territoriality-relevant cognitions. For example, residents were asked where in the apartment they chose to engage in specific activities (a behavior question), and who, in their opinion, owned various places within the apartment (a cognition question).

Not every self-report technique involves the traditional question-and-answer format. In a study examining how different arrangements of fences, plantings, curbs, and ornaments affected resident perceptions of the property's security, participants were shown line drawings (Brower, Dockett, & Taylor, 1983). (See Fig. 6–5.) In the drawings, the different arrangements were systematically varied to find out how each of them affected the resident's perception of the likelihood that passersby might cut across the property, steal a bike parked on the property, etc. Surveys and interviews may involve many variants on the general theme of showing the territory to individuals and asking how they would behave or feel in such a territory. Territories may be displayed "live" or in a simulation (model, picture, drawing).

Naturalistic Observation and Unobtrusive Measures

A third strategy is to observe ongoing territoriality behavior in a careful, structured way. The researcher may watch how children occupy and defend certain areas of a school playground. When unobtrusive measures are employed, the researcher may count the number and location of items that individuals deploy to control a space. For example, my university's cafeteria is so heavily used that experienced students going to lunch first locate a vacant seat, where they deposit their books on the table and their coat on the back of the chair, *then* go to the food lines.

The two commonest unobtrusive measures of territoriality are marking and personalization. **Marking** involves the use of an object, usually one that is recognized as someone's personal property, to inform others of our territorial ambitions. Coats, books, and beach towels have been discussed as examples. **Personalization** involves altering the territory to indicate ownership or control. For example, Greenbaum and Greenbaum (1981) wished to discover whether some ethnic groups expressed territoriality through personal-

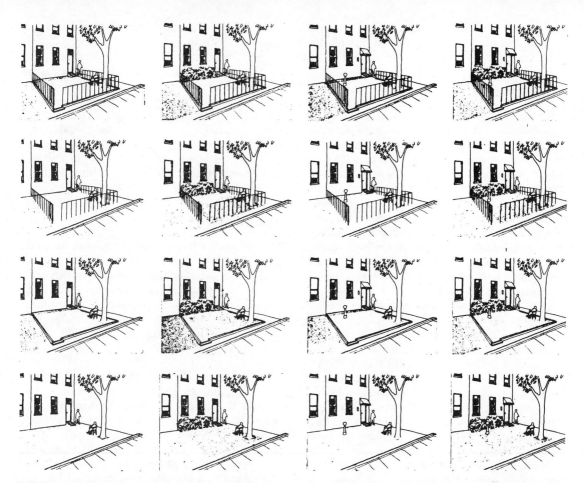

FIGURE 6–5 The diagrams presented to participants in the Brower, Dockett, and Taylor study. *(From Brower, S., Dockett, K., & Taylor, R. B. Resident's perceptions of territorial features and perceived local threat.* Environment and Behavior, *1983,* 15, *3–30. Copyright © 1983 by* Environment and Behavior. *Reprinted by permission of Sage Publications, Inc.)*

ization of their front yards more than other ethnic groups. They found that inner-city Slavic Americans did personalize more than their non-Slavic neighbors. They landscaped their yards more, maintained their houses better, and placed more potted plants in view.

▶ **In Sum.** Territoriality is nearly always investigated in the field. Researchers occasionally perform true experiments but more often examine correlations between territoriality and other behaviors or attitudes, ask for the participant's self-report of territoriality activities, or observe how individuals mark or personalize territories. Because each method has both strengths and weak-

nesses, researchers should, if possible, employ several methods. If only one method can be used, care must be taken to select the method best suited to the particular research question. For example, if the hypothesis concerns territorial actions, naturalistic observation of the actions is preferable to a questionnaire about the actions.

INFLUENCES ON TERRITORIALITY

Who is territorial? Under what conditions does territoriality emerge out of the complexities of human behavior as a distinct pattern? In this section, we will see that territoriality is a function of individual differences, situational differences, and culture.

Personal Factors

Territoriality varies with personal characteristics such as sex, age, and personality. Perhaps the most consistent finding is that males have larger territories than females. This is true in the beach studies discussed earlier, in a study of territoriality in dormitories (Mercer & Benjamin, 1980), and in some earlier studies. In the Mercer and Benjamin study, residents were asked to draw on a map of their double-occupancy room which areas the participants considered their own, which parts belonged to the roommate, and which were shared territories. Males drew larger "own" territories than did females.

Men, of course, still hold high-status occupations more often than women, and thereby claim larger spaces at work more often. The Mercer and Benjamin study suggests that men are more territorial even before they formally acquire higher status—that is, when both men and women are still in the student phase of their lives. But what of territories in the home? Is a man's home his castle, or does the woman make up for her lack of territory in a work setting by claiming more space at home?

Sebba and Churchman's study of Israeli families provides some intriguing answers. First, both parents agreed that the kitchen belongs to the woman. In apparent contradiction, however, over 30 percent of the fathers said the *entire* home was theirs. On the other hand, more fathers (48 percent) than mothers (27 percent) said they had no place at home. Generally, then, mothers were quite consistent in believing that the home as a whole was a shared territory, but that their own territory was the kitchen.

Men delivered a more confused image, more often saying the entire home was theirs, yet granting the kitchen to their wife and also frequently reporting that they actually had no territory at home. Depending on the beliefs in any given home, the mix of territoriality beliefs could lead to considerable disagreement about who is allowed to do what in which areas of the home.

What about other individual differences? Are some personality types more likely to claim and

defend territories than others? In Mercer and Benjamin's (1980) investigation of territoriality in shared dormitory rooms, more intelligent residents of both sexes marked off larger areas for themselves, residents of both sexes who came from larger homes marked off more space for themselves, and males who were more apprehensive marked off larger territories. Females who were more self-assured but *less* dominant marked off larger territories. These results suggest that gender and personality play an intertwined role in territoriality.

The Situation

Is territoriality fostered by the kind of situation one is in? Would any given individual express more, less, or different kinds of territoriality merely because of changes in circumstance? The answer appears to be yes; this section examines some of the evidence. We consider two aspects of the situation: its physical characteristics and its social characteristics.

The Physical Setting.   How might the physical setting influence someone to be more or less territorial? Most evidence bearing on this question has emerged from investigations of Oscar Newman's theory of **defensible space** (1972, 1980). The theory deals with residential crime and fear of crime, two phenomena related to territorial invasion. It proposes that certain design features, such as real or symbolic barriers to separate public territory from private territory and opportunities for territory owners to observe suspicious activity in their spaces (surveillance), will increase residents' sense of security and decrease crime in the territory.

Quite a number of field studies have tested Newman's theory, and most of them provide at least mild support for it (Taylor, 1982). Definite conclusions are not possible, however, because these studies usually are unable to take into account the many other (nondesign) influences on crime and security. Most research has investigated whether defensible space design features increase residents' sense of control and the amount of surveillance they engage in. Frequently it does. But a key question, of course, is whether criminals themselves respect properties with defensible space features more than those without these features. Unfortunately, research on the offender's perspective is so far sketchy and incomplete. A few studies (Brown & Altman, 1983) and careful observations of offender activity do suggest that defensible space features do reduce criminal activity.

In one, the territorial features of areas in which stripped cars were found were examined (Ley & Cybriwsky, 1974a). The areas lacked design features that would indicate someone exercised control or vigilance over them. In another, antisocial behavior in city parks after dark was a problem except in one park. When researchers went to discover why, they discovered that one resident whose house bordered on the park was in the habit of training a powerful spotlight on late-evening park users (Brower, 1981). This is the epitome of Newman's idea of surveillance.

The barriers and surveillance opportunities we have been discussing are not purely environmental solutions. That would smack of architectural determinism. A more appropriate perspective assumes that the design features affect both residents and offenders, and these effects in turn are the true causes of crime reduction. Two ways that residents may be affected are that their feelings of territoriality are increased and their behavior changes so as to facilitate surveillance. Let's take a look at each of these.

The process must begin with residents feeling more territorial. In one study, residents of Baltimore were shown line drawings of houses that varied in such design features as curbs, fences, and plantings. Some drawings also depicted a person in the yard; others did not. Some participants lived in high-problem areas, others in low-problem areas. When the pictures depicted fences and plantings, residents believed that trespassing was less likely, that theft was less likely, and that the house was safer. (See Fig. 6–5.)

The researchers also discovered that when a person was depicted in the drawing, residents of high-problem areas viewed this as a sign of potential trouble, but residents of low-problem neighborhoods viewed the person as a factor that would *deter* crime. Recall that individuals in the pictures were mere line drawings. It appears that residents of high-problem areas tended to see these persons as outsiders who might be planning a crime, but residents of low-problem areas saw them as neighbors who were working or relaxing

outside their own homes. If the person in the line drawings had been labeled *neighbor* or *unknown passerby*, the resident of high- and low-problem areas might have agreed on whether the person was a threat or a hindrance to crime. Nevertheless, it is interesting (and unfortunate) that a vaguely defined person is seen as a threat in some areas. Living with crime seems to make us generally suspicious of people. Design changes will not make all residents feel more secure.

If we consider residents' behavior rather than their feelings, some research suggests that design changes alter their actual behavior in a way that in turn reduces crime; residents' actions become more territorial. Oscar Newman (1980) provides some observational data on this change. Certain streets in St. Louis have defensible space features, including gatewaylike entrances, alterations that restrict traffic flow, and signs that discourage traffic. (See Fig. 6–6.) Residents who live on these streets are often seen outside their homes, walking and working in their yards. Such behaviors may not be overtly territorial; residents may not think of themselves as guarding the neighborhood, yet they seem to have the effect of discouraging antisocial activity. Presumably, intruders are discouraged by this naturally occurring surveillance. However, these are naturalistic observations; they cannot lead to causal statements. Nevertheless, it appears that restricting traffic flow may direct some potential trouble away from the neighborhood and make outdoor activities more pleasant for residents which discourages those few potential intruders who pass through the neighborhood from criminal activity.

Different street forms may facilitate behaviors that are more positive than merely driving burglars away. In comparison to through streets, cul-de-sacs seem to promote greater neighborhood attachment among residents (Brown & Werner, 1985). Closer neighborhood ties were found in this study to be reflected in greater concentrations of holiday decorations on cul-de-sacs.

The Social Situation.   Do some social circumstances give rise to increased or decreased territoriality? This question has not received much attention. One social factor in territoriality, however, is legal ownership. Both renters and homeowners control residential territory in the sense we have defined territoriality, but legal owner-

FIGURE 6–6 A residential show of territoriality.

ship appears to increase the homeowner's territorial behavior (Greenbaum & Greenbaum, 1981). Specifically, homeowners engage in more personalization than renters. This is not surprising, given the greater commitment of resources made by homeowners.

The social climate of a neighborhood also appears to influence territoriality. In a study of twelve Baltimore districts, Taylor, Gottfredson, and Brower (1981) found that congenial social climates were associated with improved territorial functioning. In more congenial neighborhoods, residents were better able to distinguish neighbors from intruders, experienced fewer problems of territorial control, and felt more responsibility for neighborhood space.

A third social factor is competition for resources. You might expect more territorial behavior when individuals must struggle with others

for resources. Everyday experience suggests that when cafeteria chairs, space in the library, or any other resource is in short supply, individuals begin to mark, personalize, claim, and defend territories to preserve their share of the resource.

On the other hand, some cost-benefit theories of animal territoriality predict that territoriality is greatest when resources are abundant, because that is when the benefits of territoriality are worth the effort of defending them (Cashdan, 1983). When resources are scattered and scarce, these theories say, territories must be larger to provide enough food; the effort of defending such a large space outweighs the meager living the animal can obtain from it. Thus, animals living in conditions where resources are difficult to find abandon territoriality in favor of a catch-as-catch-can approach.

Considerable evidence from animal field studies does support this cost-benefit model, but does it apply to humans? Among a variety of "primitive" peoples, the model seems to apply in some cases and not in others. Cashdan has supplied some reasoning and evidence, from her study of African Bushmen, that help explain this.

In her view, territoriality occurs when there is competition for resources. However, different forms of defense are used when the resources are abundant than when they are scarce. When resources are abundant, territories tend to be small (because groups need not search far to obtain all they need) and defense takes the form of perimeter displays and skirmishes. That is, the boundary itself is the focus of territoriality activity.

When resources are scarce, perimeter defense is no longer practicable, and animals might give up territoriality entirely. But humans, Cashdan says, control their territories through social boundary defense in which the focus is on reciprocal access to territories by members of competing groups. The boundary itself is no longer so important; instead, visitors to a territory must go through various permission rituals to enter an owner's territory. Once they "pay their dues," they are welcome to share in the resources of the territory.

Cashdan found that the Bushmen, contrary to cost-benefit theory, are more territorial when resources are scarce than when they are plentiful. That is, Bushmen more often deny outsiders access to the resources they control when resources are limited. If this holds for our culture, too, it would confirm that territoriality operates differently in humans and animals. Speaking of cultures, let us turn to the cultural aspects of territoriality.

Culture

Are some cultural and ethnic groups more territorial than others? Do different cultures express their territoriality differently? The first question has not yet been clearly answered. A reasonable speculation would be that all human cultures are equally territorial, at least after differences in living conditions are taken into account. A related proposition would be that territoriality is merely expressed differently in different cultures.

A good example of a study bearing on these points is Smith's (1981) investigation of territoriality on French and German beaches. The study was closely patterned on an earlier American study (Edney & Jordan-Edney, 1974), so that the beach territoriality of Germans, French, and Americans could be contrasted. Smith found that the three cultures were similar in *some* respects. For example, in all three cultures larger groups claimed smaller per-person spaces, groups composed of males and females claimed smaller per-person spaces, and females claimed less space than males.

Yet in other respects, the cultures differ. The French seemed less territorial. They had some difficulty with the very concept of territoriality, often saying that "the beach is for everyone." The Germans engaged in much more marking. They frequently erected sand castle barriers, signs declaring that "their" area of the beach was "reserved" between two particular dates, and signs indicating that certain areas were reserved for certain groups (families with children here, nudists there, etc.). Finally, territorial *sizes* were quite different among the three cultures, but the *shapes* of the territories were quite similar. The Germans more often claimed very large territories, but in all three cultures individuals marked out more eliptical territories and groups marked out more circular territories.

A study of how two cultures (Greek and American) respond to litter demonstrates again how territoriality is similar yet different across cultures (Worchel & Lollis, 1982). The experimenters deposited a bag of litter in one of three places: in the front yard, on the sidewalk in front of the house, or on the street curb in front of the house. Bags of litter in the front yards were removed equally quickly in both cultures, but the Americans removed litter placed on the sidewalk or curb faster than Greeks did.

Are Americans therefore more territorial than Greeks? Worchel and Lollis say no; the difference lies in the way the two cultures think of territory around their homes. Americans think of the sidewalk and curb as semipublic—or one might say semiprivate—so they clean up the litter in "their" territory faster than Greeks. Greeks, according to Worchel and Lollis, think of the sidewalk and curb as public territory; therefore litter on it is not of great concern to them.

Even the study of home personalization comparing Slavic-Americans to their non-Slavic neighbors (Greenbaum & Greenbaum, 1981), which found certain differences (discussed earlier), found *no* differences in other comparisons. For example, Slavic and non-Slavic neighbors personalized their front door with initials at the same rate. Thus, territoriality varies across cultures in some ways but is similar in other ways.

Territoriality is often quite evident in a culture's youth gangs, who must face other gangs on what is nominally public territory. Campbell, Munce, and Galea (1982) compared British and American gangs and found the American ones express much more territoriality.

Does this mean American youths are more territorial than British youths? Not necessarily. Campbell et al. restrain themselves from this simplistic conclusion, reminding us that British and American youths have quite different living conditions. The British gang tends to be a working class reaction to middle class values. Because working- and middle-class Britons do not live in the same areas, the gangs need not establish competing territories in their own neighborhoods. They aren't fighting one another so much as they are fighting the middle class. American gangs, however, tend to be composed of different racial and ethnic groups who do share the same general neighborhood. Territories are carved out and defended because the gangs *are* competing against one another.

▶ **In Sum.** Personal factors, physical and social aspects of situations, and culture can lead to territoriality. Males appear, in general, to manifest more territoriality than females. Dominance (as a personality trait) is inconsistently related to territoriality. As for physical setting sources of territoriality, Newman's theory argues that physical arrangements increase territoriality feelings and behavior and that this increase leads to a decline in territorial invasions. The physical arrangements may be at the block or neighborhood level (altering traffic flow) or at the house level (fences and plantings). Research generally favors the theory, but the evidence is not conclusive and defensible space features certainly do not guarantee that intrusions will not occur.

Although research is skimpy, territoriality appears to increase with three social factors: ownership compared to renting, positive social climate, and greater competition for resources.

Cultures do differ in their *expression* of territoriality, although the question of whether some cultures are *more* territorial than others has not been clearly answered. These personal, situational, and cultural factors are associated with individual expression of territoriality. Next we explore behavior patterns that are linked with territoriality.

TERRITORIALITY AND HUMAN BEHAVIOR

Territoriality functions as a central process in personalization, aggression, dominance, winning, cooperation, and control.

Personalization and Marking

If other individuals are to know that you have claimed a territory, you must inform them. This may be done verbally. Sister tells brother, "This is my room, please get out." Often, however, we provide clues for the wanderer—signs, fences, and personal objects placed in strategic locations. The terms personalization and marking are both applied to this practice. The two terms overlap in meaning, but **personalization** is more likely to refer to decoration of one's primary or secondary territories on a relatively permanent basis (such as placing a poster on your door or a sign carved with the family name on it outside your house), but **marking** usually refers to defense of your claim to part of a public territory, like your seat on a plane or your campsite. (See Fig. 6–7.)

Personalization and marking occur in a wide variety of settings, including some you might not expect. For example, restaurant diners were found in one study to mark their plates by touching them about three times more often when the plate was served by another person than when they served themselves (Truscott, Parmelee, & Werner, 1977). Because diners probably do not consciously mark the plate as their own in this manner, it appears that some of our marking behavior occurs out of our awareness. A similar pattern was found by Werner, Brown, and Damron (1981) in a video-game arcade. Naturalistic observation of players suggested that players touch the machines to establish territory and touch them longer when others intrude on them. When a con-

FIGURE 6-7 Personalization in a workspace.

federate of the investigators touched the machines, other players were discouraged from using them.

Personalization and marking are also quite deliberate at times. When we erect signs reading "No Hunting" or "No Trespassing" or "No Agents, Vendors, Solicitors, or Salesmen," we do so with a clear and conscious purpose. Urban gangs mark their turf boundaries with spray-painted signs on the walls of buildings (Ley & Cybriwsky, 1974b). We must be careful, however, not to assume that every sign or piece of graffiti is a territorial marker. Graffiti may be mere vandalism, and someone may put a coat on the back of a chair because there is nowhere else to hang it.

Personalization and marking serve notice of our claim; but if they are ignored, we often do not follow through with stronger defenses of the territory. Especially when the territory is a public one, such as space at a library table, when an intruder disregards an occupant's territorial markers, the occupant often abandons the space rather than actively defends it (Becker, 1973).

Personalization has positive side effects. When residents of a psychiatric ward were allowed to personalize their territories, the social atmosphere of the ward improved (Holahan, 1976). Unfortunately, many organizations discourage personalization. One Canadian university, however, encourages it by holding an annual door-painting contest in its dormitories. Personalization of dormitory rooms has also been linked to staying in school (as opposed to dropping out), although many other factors influence such a decision (Vinsel, Brown, Altman, & Foss, 1980).

Aggression and Territorial Defense

In the popular mind, perhaps spurred by accounts of violent disputes over territory in some animal species, territoriality and aggression go hand in hand. At the national level, too, the tragedy of territorial war is all too common. However, aggression receives more attention than peaceful coexistence. Research in environmental psychology suggests that aggression over human territories is actually not very common (Edney, 1976). This, in part, is because humans have developed so many nonviolent ways of settling disputes—language to negotiate with, customs to guide behavior, and a legal system to settle most disputes.

This is not to say individuals do not defend their territories. All the nonviolent means just listed, and more (yelling and dirty looks, for example) *may* be used as territorial defenses. Defense of territory through marking, personalization, and other means is common, but violent defenses are uncommon. One such nonviolent defense is vigilance. In an early field study, Julian Edney (1972a) found that residents of houses with defense displays (like signs reading "Private Property, Keep Out") responded to a knock at the door significantly faster than residents without defense displays.

Unfortunately, aggression does occur under some circumstances. The more that the territory is valued, for example, the more likely it will be actively defended (Taylor & Brooks, 1980). Many societies even condone violence in the defense of a primary territory. For example, individuals have been acquitted when they shot burglars in their own homes.

Aggression may also occur when territorial boundaries are vague. When the boundaries between the turf belonging to urban gangs is not clearly agreed upon, more violence occurs than when boundaries are clearly agreed upon (Ley & Cybriwsky, 1974b).

Finally, we may speculate that violence is used as a territoriality defense when all other means have been exhausted, an individual is unaware of alternatives, or an individual is denied other means—such as when some groups, through poverty or discrimination, are denied equal access to the justice system.

Dominance and Control

These two terms do not quite mean the same thing. As Edney (1975) points out, territoriality has most often been associated with **dominance,** a social behavior that implies winning. As noted earlier, sometimes dominance or rank in a hierarchy is closely associated with the amount and quality of territory an individual holds, and sometimes it is not. Edney suggests that human territoriality may be more closely tied to control, a broader concept than dominance. **Control** refers not only to influence over other individuals but influence over space, ideas, and other resources in the territory. He observes that control may be *active,* as when control is exercised offensively and is initiated by the territory holder, or *passive,* when the territory holder acts defensively, responding to or resisting a challenge by outsiders. Edney believes that we should think more in terms of control, particularly passive control,

when considering human territoriality. He thinks individuals rarely engage in direct attempts to assert dominance but often may be seen engaging in nonviolent behavior that promotes their control over territories. For example, in a dispute concerning a boundary between two properties, individuals are much more likely to engage in a courtroom battle of words than in fisticuffs.

Let's look first at dominance. In early studies of territoriality and dominance in mental hospital patients, Esser and his co-workers found that the middle and bottom thirds of the dominance hierarchy among both adult and child patients possessed territories on the ward in keeping with their position in the hierarchy: the middle third of the patients had large central territories and the bottom third had small remote territories (Esser, 1968; Esser, Chamberlain, Chapple, & Kline, 1965). The top third of the hierarchy, though, had no particular territory—they wandered freely throughout the setting. In one sense they had no territory; in another sense the entire setting was their territory.

Another study linking personal dominance with territoriality was conducted in a residence for profoundly retarded women (Paslawskyj & Ivinskis, 1980). The researchers first constructed a dominance hierarchy, based on the women's actual behavior (how often they initiated and participated in social interaction). Paslawskyj and Ivinskis found that the more dominant women had larger territories. It is interesting that the women who were next to each other in the dominance hierarchy (for example, numbers 3 and 4) tended to have territories that were far apart. This practice may serve to minimize aggression; if women adjacent in dominance also had adjacent territories, they might engage in more active competition for territory.

Sundstrom and Altman (1974) studied dominance and territoriality in a school for young male offenders. They found that territoriality was correlated with dominance as long as membership in the group remained unchanged. However, when two very dominant individuals left the group, conflict increased and the correlation between dominance and territorial behavior decreased. Later, as group membership grew stable again, the links between territoriality and dominance strengthened among the middle and bottom thirds of the hierarchy. The most dominant individuals, however, were still struggling and had not yet established clear territories. Sundstrom and Altman conclude that with more time, the group's original strong ties between territorial behavior and dominance might reemerge.

Of course, the Esser research just described suggests another possible outcome. The most dominant residents might have established "territories" that allowed them to move freely throughout the setting. The important point, however, is that the strength of dominance-territoriality relations varies with the situation; shake-ups in the composition of a group as well as other social factors can strengthen or weaken them.

Altman (1975) reports other studies indicating that dominance and territoriality are not always related neatly in humans. He suggests the relation also depends on who the individuals are (such as mental patients versus corporate executives), how dominance is measured (as a personality variable, as popularity, or as number of interactions one initiates, for example), social dynamics (such as how the organization is run), and the value of

the territories involved (sometimes space, as in a mental hospital ward, may not be worth fighting for).

Does the possession of a territory help humans to dominate activities in it, to win? We have already seen that decisions made on our own turf reflect our own position on the issue more than they reflect others' positions (Taylor & Lanni, 1981). The courtroom is one place where victories and defeats occur. In an intriguing assessment of environmental psychology in a North Carolina courtroom, Austin (1982) suggests that objectivity and equality between the prosecution and defense are not always reflected in the physical arrangements of the courtroom. Austin concluded after observing the locations of the judge, jury, prosecution, and defense of the courtroom that the prosecution had a significant advantage over the defense. For example, the prosecution was located nearer the jury, allowing prosecutors to subtly convince jurors that they were literally on the same side in the case.

Territorial dominance also appears to affect the outcome of sports events, a phenomenon known as the **home court advantage.** In every league,

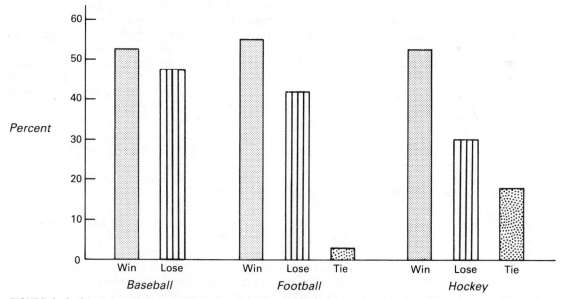

FIGURE 6–8 Outcomes of home games in three professional sports. Differences in winning percentages are not large, but with ties as possible outcomes to their games, hockey teams lose much less often at home than do baseball teams. *(Based on Schwartz & Barsky, 1977.)*

teams bemoan road trips. They mean travel, which becomes wearisome, and they mean the odds of winning are lower. Or do they? Is the home court advantage myth or reality?

Schwartz and Barsky (1977) examined the home and away records of teams in hockey, basketball, baseball, and football. They found that the home advantage exists but is greater in some sports than others. In the baseball season they examined, home teams won 53 percent. This advantage is small, considering the legends in the game about grounds keepers "doctoring" the playing field to suit the home team or to foil visiting base stealers and bunters.

Professional and college football teams won 55 and 59 percent at home, respectively. Professional hockey teams won or tied 70 percent at home, and college basketball teams in one league won at approximately the same rate.

Schwartz and Barsky considered numerous reasons for their findings but concluded that the main reason was fan support, magnified by the form of the physical environment. (See Fig. 6–8.) Hockey and basketball fans cheer their teams in closed buildings; this intensifies their vocal support for the team, compared to the effect fans can have in baseball and football, where cheers partially dissipate into open skies. Indoor venues also decrease the distance from fan to player, which increases fan input even more. A study of booing at basketball games (Greer, 1983) revealed that home team performance increased slightly just after booing by its fans and that visiting teams committed more fouls and generally performed worse just after the booing. The home advantage is stronger, then, for indoor sports than for outdoor sports.

The home-field advantage can backfire when the pressure to succeed becomes extreme. In baseball's World Series, home teams win over 60 percent of first and second games but less than 40 percent of seventh games when the whole series is decided in one game (Baumeister, 1985). Yet during the regular season, the home advantage is stronger for better teams. James (1984) sorted baseball teams by overall winning percentage and found that those winning 55 to 65 percent of their games averaged 12 percent more wins at home than on the road, but teams winning 33 to 43 percent averaged only 7 percent more wins at home. This finding underscores the connection between dominance and territoriality. Even mediocre teams benefit from the home-field advantage, but the strength of generally strong teams is magnified at home. (See Fig. 6–9.)

What about control, as opposed to dominance? In everyday life, we notice that visitors and hosts enact rituals; the visitor is usually expected to act in a restrained, cautious manner, and the host usually encourages the visitor to feel *at home.* The implicit assumption on both sides is that the host is in control. The guest's role is to acknowledge this; the host's role is to graciously surrender it.

Nevertheless, the visitor's maxim is "when in Rome, do as the Romans do." Sometimes visitors are so loath to alter their host's arrangements that they subject themselves to a variety of minor tortures. This pattern is not restricted to homes. In a study of environmental awareness, I found that students working on a lab assignment for a psychology class went to great lengths not to disturb a furniture arrangement that caused them considerable difficulty in moving around the lab (Gifford, 1976c). Their behavior was partly due to their lack of awareness of the physical environment, but some students later pointed out that "one does not move furniture around except in one's own home." In the lab, there were no prohibitions against moving furniture around, especially if it was interfering with progress in the lab. Yet the students felt that *someone,* such as the lab instructor or the janitor, must have wanted the furniture that way. The students felt such a lack of control that they didn't even raise the issue of restructuring the furniture arrangements, let alone actively lobby for a change.

An important consideration in the relation between territory and control, therefore, is whether the territory is primary, secondary, or public. The students in the lab, for example, clearly viewed the lab as a secondary or public territory rather than a primary one. We should have most control in primary territories. Taylor and Stough (1978) investigated whether individuals at least *believed* they exerted more control in primary territories than in the other kinds. Their subjects did report feeling more in control when they occupied such primary territories as bedrooms with the doors closed and bathrooms than they did in secondary territories such as their backyard, the sidewalk in front of their house, or in such public

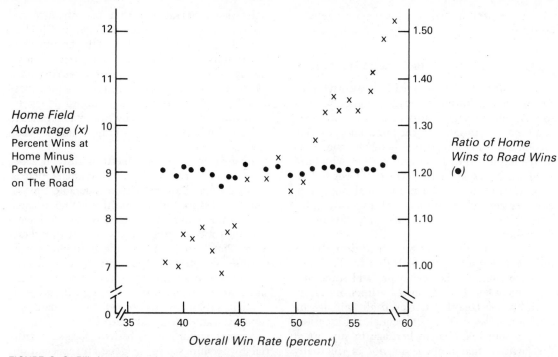

FIGURE 6–9 Bill James' puzzle. In baseball, home teams win more than visiting teams. But teams with overall winning records have a *larger* home field advantage (percent wins at home minus percent wins on the road) than would be predicted from their record. Teams winning 58 percent of all their games win 64 percent of their home games, not 58 percent. Teams with overall losing records have *smaller* home field advantages than would be predicted from their overall victory rates. The puzzle is this: Why do winners have an *extra* home field advantage? I cannot answer the puzzle, but I have determined that the extra home field advantage (ratio of extra home wins to road wins) is a constant. Regardless of overall winning percentage, baseball teams win about 1.20 times more at home than on the road. *(From James, 1984.)*

territories as streets, supermarkets, or recreation areas.

► **In Sum.** We have seen that territoriality is associated with a variety of behaviors: personalization, aggression, dominance, and control. Personalization and marking (a) are very common (but territoriality is not the basis of every public display), (b) may occur with or without awareness, (c) signal ownership but do not always lead to active defense, and (d) seem to offer psychological benefits to the territory holder beyond merely informing the world of a territorial claim.

Popular writers have exaggerated the relation between overt aggression and territoriality in humans; some are too willing to generalize from animal behavior. This doesn't mean humans never defend territory violently (witness the hundreds of wars and assaults that occur at the national and individual levels), but many more everyday disputes are settled nonviolently.

Territoriality does seem to help us control and dominate our territories, but this end is usually accomplished through passive means that do not involve direct bullying of others. In the home advantage in sports, for example, fan support or perhaps "doctoring" the field is used in attempts to control the outcome of the game.

THEORIES OF TERRITORIALITY

What governs territoriality? The ancient debate in psychology between inheritance and learning as determinants of behavior is more relevant to territoriality than to any other topic in this book.

Are our territorial tendencies part of our genetic heritage?

Territoriality: Part of Our Genetic Heritage?

Many animal species are clearly territorial with a heavy genetic influence, leading some theorists to treat human territoriality as a direct extension of animal territoriality. In the forefront of this approach are many European ethologists and some North American writers (Ardrey, 1966) who have been quick to suggest an instinctual basis for human territoriality. The ethological approach, whether applied to animals or humans, emphasizes the aggression and defense elements of territoriality.

There is no proof that human territoriality is inherited, despite the parallels that can be drawn between some human behaviors and some animal behaviors. Indeed, some writers appear to overlook the fact that not even all animals are territorial; we could, with equal justification, point to our mammalian heritage in support of the position that humans are *not* instinctually territorial. For example, some of the great apes, our closest relatives, exhibit very little territoriality. Until or unless geneticists discover a specific gene for territoriality in humans, most environmental psychologists prefer to construct theories that explain territorial behavior as it occurs rather than to speculate on its origins. Instead of concentrating on aggression and defense, environmental psychologists tend to focus on habitual occupation of space and how it affects the social behavior and cognition of occupants and visitors.

Territories as Organizers

Recall that human territoriality simply is not often characterized by attempts to dominate visitors (Edney, 1976). Rather, human territoriality serves to *organize* human behavior so that violence, aggression, and overt domination are unnecessary. When an individual or group controls a setting, many aspects of behavior become ordered, including choice of activities, access to resources, and behavioral customs. Many individuals who have been employed by others dream of owning a business themselves, partly for finan-

cial reasons, but also so they can organize and control the policies of their workplace. Children want their own room so that their activities and decorations do not have to be negotiated with a sibling. Thus, one motivation for seeking territory is to have the opportunity to obtain these organizing prerogatives. According to Edney, organization and order are provided by territories to (1) communities, (2) small groups, and (3) individuals.

First, communities benefit mainly because territories geographically fix individuals, that is, because each of us spends considerable time in specific territories. If community members spent time in many different places, we would have a difficult time locating those we want to interact with. Thus territories provide individuals with reliable access to the contacts they need. The community as a whole is better off because time and effort spent in communicating with others is much less than if we had to look everywhere each time we wanted to speak with someone.

Second, small groups benefit because territorial ownership seems to generate expectations about how visitors and hosts will behave. Clubs and drinking establishments, for example, often have written or unwritten rules of conduct. I once saw a sign erected by the proud owner of a new backyard swimming pool: "We don't swim in your toilet, please don't pee in our pool!" These conventions (particularly those more serious than the pool owner's sign) increase order and security by providing a mutually acceptable set of ground rules on which social behavior can be transacted. As noted earlier, these conventions generally assign control to the host, but the host uses this control to be considerate of the visitor's needs. For example, the host offers the visitor a choice of drinks, serves the visitor first, and suggests where the visitor should sit.

Third, Edney believes that individuals benefit from the organizing function of territories. Because they control social and resource management aspects of the territory's operation, territory holders are better able to plan and anticipate future events. Familiarity with the territory also gives individuals a sense of competence that would be impossible if they moved randomly from place to place. Individuals gain a sense of identity by simply being spatially separate from others. Also, individuals typically enact long chains of related behaviors. When these occur in a single place, they are better organized and ordered because of the individual's familiarity with the territory. An everyday example is cooking a meal. The process is much easier in our own kitchen than in someone else's because we know where the ingredients and implements are stored.

Territoriality and Behavior-setting Theory

Ecological psychologists view territorial behavior from a behavior-setting perspective. Willems and Campbell (1976), for example, point out that the organizing function of territoriality is quite similar to concepts from the work of Roger Barker (1968), the father of ecological psychology. For example, in ecological psychology a **program** is "a prescribed sequence of interactions between people and objects in the setting" (Wicker, 1979). Other concepts from ecological psychology explicitly incorporate the notion of control. For example, **sensing mechanisms** and **executive mechanisms** (usually a person in control, but sometimes a servomechanism such as a thermostat) examine the setting for incorrect conditions and correct them. In general, the ecological psychology approach of the behavior setting (Wicker, 1979) overlaps considerably with Edney's ideas about organization and control.

Territoriality and the Brain

A quite different perspective comes from Aristide Esser (1976), who speculates that territoriality is related to the structure of our brain. Esser suggests that territoriality originates in the oldest part of the mammalian central nervous system, the brainstem. These ancient impulses, however, are transformed in the newer parts of the brain (the neocortex) and are subject to the complexities in spatial behavior that we observe in humans. He speculates that hemispheric specialization (the localization in our brain of some key functions on the left side of the brain and others on the right) is responsible for the complexity of human spatial behavior. Esser does not deny, however, that learning and culture are also important determinants of human territoriality. His main point is to remind us that we have a long

evolutionary past, and that many of our cousins in the animal kingdom are very territorial, suggesting that territoriality must have some representation in the brain.

In a similar vein, Evans and Eichelman (1976) suggest that neocortical brain functions like cognitive mapping and the ability to allocate energy render the old functions of territoriality characteristic of animals unnecessary. Humans do not need specific, fixed areas to assure themselves of resources because we can store extremely detailed maps of resource locations in our heads.

These ideas are largely untested, but they point toward a time when neuroscientists and environmental psychologists may begin a meaningful exchange. Few of us would deny that most behavior and thought is somehow located in brain functioning, but neuropsychologists still know very little about how and where thought and behavior processes occur in the brain.

Territoriality and Large-scale Conflict

Territoriality operates at many levels. In this book, we have concentrated on the interpersonal level, but larger entities (such as nations) engage in territorial behavior, too. At the larger scale, the stereotypic link between territoriality and aggression seems much more viable. Hundreds of wars and border skirmishes have occurred even in the brief period of history since World War II.

Philip Schrodt (1981) offers a detailed model of conflict as a prime determinant of territoriality. The model is based on computer simulations of conflicts between individual nations, although Schrodt believes his model may apply to smaller groups. Although the model is specified in specific mathematical equations, Schrodt says his model may informally be thought of as the "street gang theory."

It begins with a collection of individuals who are not organized into territorial groups. Potential conflict occurs when one individual, for whatever reason, feels like getting into a fight. If the individual is surrounded by individuals who are *like* him in religious, ethnic, or political ways—that is, in the same gang—actual conflict may not occur. But if someone *different* is around, a fight does begin.

The winner will usually be the combatant who

can summon the most bystanders who are like him, such as members of his gang. The winner acquires the territory on which the fight took place. Gradually, through many conflicts, territories develop even though the individuals had no specific territorial goals. (See Fig. 6–10.)

Schrodt's model applies not only to violent conflict but to nonviolent ones. For example, linguistic, religious, political, or economic territories may be formed through conflict processes that aren't necessarily violent. For example, if an individual family emigrates to a place where most people speak a different language, the usual outcome of the strife between family members and members of their adopted society is that the family, at least by the second generation, learns the new language.

Schrodt's model concludes that spatial and other kinds of territories must result from conflict. The only assumption he makes is that different types of individuals exist in the beginning of the process.

► **In Sum.** Theories of territoriality remain diverse, speculative, and largely untested. Ethology, organization, behavior settings, brain structure, and conflict are quite disparate concepts around which to construct a theory of territoriality. If we assume that each of them is partially correct, a future theory that synthesizes them coherently will surely picture human territoriality as an extremely complex process.

Despite the shortcomings in theory, environmental psychologists know enough about territoriality to use it in their contributions to better

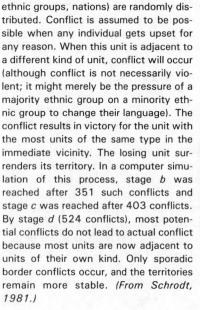

FIGURE 6–10 Schrodt's street-gang theory of territory development. In *a* the original units (e.g., individuals, families, ethnic groups, nations) are randomly distributed. Conflict is assumed to be possible when any individual gets upset for any reason. When this unit is adjacent to a different kind of unit, conflict will occur (although conflict is not necessarily violent; it might merely be the pressure of a majority ethnic group on a minority ethnic group to change their language). The conflict results in victory for the unit with the most units of the same type in the immediate vicinity. The losing unit surrenders its territory. In a computer simulation of this process, stage *b* was reached after 351 such conflicts and stage *c* was reached after 403 conflicts. By stage *d* (524 conflicts), most potential conflicts do not lead to actual conflict because most units are now adjacent to units of their own kind. Only sporadic border conflicts occur, and the territories remain more stable. *(From Schrodt, 1981.)*

a. Initial Distribution

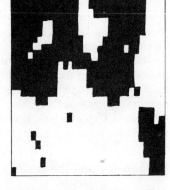

b. After 351 Actual Conflicts

c. After 403 Actual Conflicts

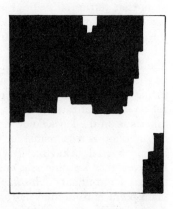

d. After 524 Actual Conflicts

environmental design. We turn now to that enterprise.

TERRITORIALITY AND ENVIRONMENTAL DESIGN

When applied to particular design situations, territoriality should be facilitated in the plans wherever it appears to serve the needs of clients. That is, recalling our list of human behavior patterns that are linked to territoriality, designs for territoriality should reduce aggression, increase control, and promote a sense of order and security. A rather bold conclusion, supported by some research and refuted by none so far reported, is this: The more a design can provide primary territories for every person at home, school, and work, the better.

Of course, an important restriction on the supply of primary territories is money; space costs can be high. A second restriction is the policies of some organizations, which require that employees be under the direct surveillance of a supervisor. A third restriction is that some jobs, by their very nature, require that other employees or the general public have access to the individual holding the job. The only refuges of front-line employees are the staff room and the coffee break.

On many jobs, groups must work together in close communication most of the day. Individuals in such jobs may not perform best if each one is located in a separate primary territory. However, territories may be occupied by groups. Such work groups should have their own collective primary territory.

In many home, work, and institutional settings more could be done to provide primary or secondary territories for individuals and groups. Very often, no one has seriously considered how the lives of affected individuals would be improved by access to an owned space.

In this section, we will examine some suggestions for territorializing neighborhoods, homes, schools, and hospitals. The design recommendations were developed for these specific settings, but with a little imagination, we can conceive of designs for other settings using the principles involved. Changes in the design of larger settings (such as neighborhoods) are more difficult to implement than changes in small settings (like our own home). Nevertheless, whole neighborhoods *have* been territorialized to varying degrees.

Neighborhoods

A recent political issue in Vancouver, British Columbia, involved a proposal to place barriers at strategic intersections to restrict traffic flow through the neighborhood. Residents believed that too much traffic flowed through their streets. Commuters, of course, believed the streets were there to help them get to and from work efficiently. Concern for children's safety and about traffic noise are the neighborhood's explicit reasons for the barriers, but the move to territorialize the neighborhood may have less obvious benefits.

Blocking off streets, which has occurred in many other cities too, serves to give residents a sense of control and identity. The cars that now move through the streets are neither so numerous nor so foreign; they are owned by neighbors. Because there are fewer cars, residents have a better chance of recognizing strange ones. This may serve to reduce crime, because "different" cars are noticed by residents. Burglars who have several neighborhoods to choose from would be better off selecting a more anonymous neighborhood. Oscar Newman's defensible space theory would support neighborhood design changes that increase the resident's sense of ownership, eliminate space about which no one in particular feels vigilant, and increase space that is easily watched by residents.

Changing whole neighborhoods, unfortunately, is politically difficult. Traffic barriers, for example, are opposed not only by commuters who are inconvenienced, but by residents of neighborhoods that will experience increased traffic as a result of the new barriers. Smaller-scale changes—to individual houses, for example—are much easier politically, but some of them cost that individual homeowner more.

Brown and Altman (1983) compared houses in the same neighborhood that had been burglarized with those that had not been burglarized. Houses that were personalized (for example, displayed signs with the owners' names on them) and had markers at the property line (such as hedges and low barriers) were burglarized less often. Note that these mere symbols appear to deter burglars.

As might be expected, houses with more substantial (and costly) barriers, such as fences, also were burglarized less often than those without. Houses where residents displayed their territoriality, consciously or not, by leaving signs of occupancy (such as parked cars and operating sprinklers) were also burglarized less. (See Fig. 6–11.) Finally, as predicted by defensible space theory, houses that afforded better visual surveillance (i.e., were more visible from other houses) were less often burglarized.

The design changes implied by these findings obviously do not burglar-proof a house. Skilled burglars are capable of entering nearly any house.

Defensible space design changes make the house less desirable from the burglar's point of view; unless you possess something especially desirable, the burglar might as well strike elsewhere. Another spinoff from personalizing and marking your house apparently is that you feel safer (Pollack & Patterson, 1980).

Hospitals

No one likes to be hospitalized. Besides the obvious reason (hospitals mean being ill or injured) another reason we may not enjoy our stay is the way space is managed in hospitals. Unavoidably,

FIGURE 6–11 Based on the text, which house is more likely to be burglarized? Why? (*Top photo courtesy of Julie Macdonald.*)

we go to a setting where we have no preestablished territory. Immediately, this affects our sense of control and security. Even if we are given a private room or our own bed, we are compelled to perform behaviors (such as sleeping, grooming, and discussing private matters) in a secondary territory that we are used to performing in our own primary territories (Shumaker & Reizenstein, 1982). If we have no lockable cupboard, for example, our feeling that we can control our possessions is compromised.

Shumaker and Reizenstein believe the answer is to allow patients personalization and control wherever possible. Lockable cupboards, viewable bulletin boards, and more table space to display our pictures, books, and other meaningful possessions are some suggested design changes. An even simpler rule may be to ask staff to respect the way patients arrange small objects within their reach. Some evidence that the creation of primary territories does have a beneficial effect comes from a study in a nursing home (Nelson & Paluck, 1980). In double-occupancy rooms, visible markers that divided the room into two separate spaces increased residents' self-esteem and sense of adequacy.

As in most institutions, however, there are strong pressures against some of these design changes. Staff complain that tables are cumbersome, cupboards take up valuable space and bulletin boards are expensive. Staff often object to the inefficiency caused by idiosyncratic arrangements of furniture and personal possessions. As Robert Sommer (1969) pointed out long ago, the issue is whether institutions are primarily for the welfare of clients or staff. Surprisingly often, judging by the arrangements of hospitals and other institutions, the answer is that staff needs come first.

Staff needs are legitimate, of course. However, too often client needs are underserviced because they are in no position to voice their needs in an effective way, because they are ill, injured, and often very temporary occupants of the hospital. The best solutions to the staff versus client design dilemma will be reached when designers carefully examine both groups' needs and base architectural changes on the costs and benefits to both groups. According to Shumaker and Reizenstein, more changes favoring patient privacy and territoriality over staff efficiency are needed because, to this point, staff needs have usually prevailed.

Institutional Residences

A number of environmental psychologists have investigated territoriality in dormitories and similar group living settings. Craig Zimring and his colleagues studied the effects of changes in the design of a school for the developmentally disabled (Zimring, Weitzer, & Knight, 1982). Before its renovation, the school had large open sleeping wards and other typically institutional features. The renovation provided three alternative designs: suite style (where two, three, or four residents occupied rooms that surrounded a lounge), corridor style (where one or two residents shared rooms along a corridor), and modular arrangements (where, as in open-plan offices, partitions were used to separate residents in the existing large wards). In the areas changed to suite and corridor arrangements, residents interacted with others more, were more alert, and used their own space more than they did before the renovation.

Some architects thought the corridor design was too institutional in appearance, but it produced the most positive changes in resident behavior. Apparently, the basis for the success of the corridor design was that it allowed residents more control over their immediate physical environment, such as lighting and temperature, and their social life. They were better able to control when, whether, and with whom they interacted. In addition, the new design provided symbolic barriers that enhanced residents' sense of ownership of a specific space.

Some research (Taylor & Lanni, 1981) suggests that clients may be more influential in group decision making when they have a space than if they have no space of their own. However, the power and benefits accruing from territorial ownership are recognized by some who hold key positions in organizations; this is exactly why they sometimes do not wish to grant territories to others.

Often there are legitimate space problems that preclude granting everyone a primary territory. If we assume, however, that some individuals have better territories than others, the question becomes: What ranking rules are used in this priority system that allow person A to have a large primary territory while person B is stuck with a public territory?

Another thorny problem is sorting out the justifiable claims of some individuals (staff) that others (clients) should not have primary territories because the efficiency of staff would be seriously impaired. Such claims, on the other hand, are sometimes made when a careful analysis reveals that staff motives are based more on their own convenience or need for power than potential work inefficiency.

In the end, the premise of this chapter is that many spatial arrangements, despite these problems, could be considerably improved so that everyone in the building is better off. Environmental designs that creatively include territoriality can significantly improve quality of life.

SUMMARY

Territoriality in humans is a pattern of behavior and experience related to the control (usually by nonviolent means such as occupation, law, custom, and personalization) of physical space, objects, and ideas. Seven forms of territory are identified; several infringement and defense strategies are employed in jostling for territory. Field experiments and studies are best for studying territorial behavior, but territorial cognitions are best studied by interviews and questionnaires. Males are often more territorial than females. Certain arrangements of dwelling exteriors and street plans may enhance residents' territoriality and reduce crime. Ownership, positive social climate, and resource competition are three social factors that seem to increase territoriality. Behavior related to territoriality is usually passive but oriented toward controlling space. Personalizing, marking, and status are used more often than physical aggression. Theories of territoriality are not well developed but focus on its organizing function, a presumed neural basis that derives from the ethological perspective, and behavior setting theory. Designers may incorporate knowledge so far gained about territoriality to build better homes, offices, and institutions. The overall goal is to provide individuals with territories that allow them as much control as they are capable of exercising responsibly and as the organizational context allows. When this can be accomplished in a design, territory holders will benefit from a greater sense of self-determination, identity, and perhaps even safety.

SUGGESTED SUPPLEMENTARY READINGS

Brower, S., Dockett, K., & Taylor, R. B. (1983). Residents' perceptions of territorial features and perceived local threat. *Environment and Behavior, 15,* 419–437.

Brown, B. B., & Altman, I. (1983). Territoriality, defensible space, and residential burglary. *Journal of Environmental Psychology, 3,* 203–220.

Edney, J. J. (1974). Human territoriality. *Psychological Bulletin, 81,* 959–975.

Newman, O. (1972). *Defensible space.* New York: Macmillan.

———. (1980) *Community of interest.* New York: Anchor Press/Doubleday.

Taylor, R. B., Gottfredson, S. D., & Brower, S. (1981). Territorial cognitions and social climate in urban neighborhoods. *Basic and Applied Social Psychology, 2,* 289–303.

Chapter Seven
Crowding

Rather than attempting to provide spacious gardens or solitude in search of some impossible pastoral existence, building design should encourage healthy, lively contact among neighbors.

Jonathan Freedman, 1975

The best band to hit town in months was playing the Zanzibar Club. The recent slump in the supply of good music guaranteed that lots of people would be there Saturday night, but Tom couldn't believe the place. Lineups stretched around the block. He and Jane just got in as the manager started mumbling something about fire regulations. Tom was already a little grumpy after the long search for a parking spot, the "special" cover charge, and the seats behind a column that blocked their view of the bandstand. Somehow Jane had managed to stay cheerful through all this—a bit too cheerful for Tom. She asked him again if he wanted to dance.

"Are you kidding? Not one more person could fit on that dance floor." Jane tried to improve his mood, pointing out friends in the crowd, telling him about the good grade she got on her chemistry exam, remarking that the band was playing Tom's favorite piece. She seemed not to notice the noise, heat, sweat, and smoke. Tom couldn't seem to rise above the sea of awful sensations to appreciate Jane, the music, or the boisterous atmosphere.

To Tom, the place seemed unbearably full of generally unspeakable folks. To make matters worse, an old friend of Jane's sat down at their table and the two of them engaged in a marvelous series of recollections of the old days. Tom struggled to overcome his hostile mood, realizing it was endangering the whole evening, but he just couldn't escape a sense that it was all too much to take and that he couldn't do much about the situation. He decided to leave before things got worse. Interrupting Jane and her friend, he announced that he was going home. Jane looked up at him and . . .

The world is increasingly crowded. Most of us have experienced the frustration of crowded roads, living space, working space, or leisure space. Traffic jams, tripled dormitory rooms, squeezed employees, and campgrounds with waiting lists are some of the many situations that produce crowding stress.

Crowding at the personal level, as in the above examples, makes an immediate impact on us, but it occurs against the backdrop of an absolutely staggering population increase at the global level. Despite many efforts at population control, the world's population curve is nearly vertical; it currently requires only three or four decades to double.

It is true that much of this increase seems far away to those who live in developed countries where zero or near-zero population growth has been achieved. Nevertheless, in one way or another, the population explosion is bound to touch your life, if it hasn't already. At the very least, scenes of famine on television will upset us and motivate some to offer food or financial aid. At the most, economic and political upheaval in countries where the populace has become desperate will serve to disrupt lines of supply to, and the quality of life in, countries that have no population problem themselves.

Environmental psychologists who study crowding and high density hope to understand the causes of crowding stress and the effects of high density so that, in concert with political and economic researchers, they can offer knowledge that eases the stress of crowding. Most of the work discussed in this chapter focuses on crowding within the built environment. The emphasis is on how individuals come to experience a situation as crowded, the psychological processes associated with crowding, and the consequences of high density and crowding. No matter what Tom thinks, you should know that this chapter is not all gloom; sometimes high density can be quite pleasant—just ask Jane. The concluding section describes some of the architectural innovations that have succeeded in alleviating crowding stress.

WHAT IS CROWDING?

Crowding has an everyday meaning and several technical meanings. In some ways these meanings overlap and in other ways they do not. In everyday conversation it doesn't much matter exactly how we use the word, but environmental psychologists have learned the hard way that it is important to make certain distinctions clear if understanding of crowding is to progress. One reason for this is that we behave quite differently when we are subjected to the different forms of density. Early studies of crowding reached confusing and contradictory findings because researchers had not yet learned the importance of distinguishing among the varieties of crowding. We are still learning some of these distinctions. Let's tour the standard distinctions and some newer proposals.

Some Distinctions

Crowds versus Crowding.   To early social scientists, crowding meant the formation of large, temporary groups of emotional individuals. These could include swarms of peaceful concertgoers or fair patrons but more often meant lynch mobs, rioters, or panic-stricken disaster victims. LeBon (1903) believed such crowds were explicable in terms of local history, culture, and politics. The formation of crowds was generally traced to irrational motives or a desire to be immersed in a feeling of universality (Allport, 1924). Although

it might seem that joining such a crowd would increase arousal, many writers saw crowd-joining as a form of tension release (LaPiere & Farnsworth, 1942). (See Fig. 7-1.)

Many studies of evangelical meetings, mutinies, theater fires, bar fights, and mass desertions during battle were conducted in the first four decades of the century. Then, somehow, the topic lost favor. Although the old studies still make fascinating reading, the research often was not of the highest quality by today's standards, sometimes lacking objectivity and attention to the interpersonal processes involved in crowding. Much of it was almost purely descriptive. One concept from these crowding studies that has been recently revived is **contagion,** the idea that a dominant emotion or behavior originates with a given person and spreads quickly through the crowd (McDougall, 1920; Sidis, 1895).

Crowds and crowding differ and research reflects their differences. Modern crowding re-

FIGURE 7-1 Research on crowds has dwindled compared to research on crowding.

search focuses on the individual's experience, although recent theorists have tried to emphasize that crowding is, after all, a group phenomenon (Epstein, 1982).

Crowd researchers naturally focused on the formation of crowds (James, 1951), their shape and structure (Milgram & Toch, 1969), and their movement (Bruce, 1965). These facets of behavior are not particularly relevant to the crowding researcher.

The older crowd research usually adopted a sociological perspective, considering broader social, political, and economic influences. This approach was strengthened by reports of strong connections between indicators of economic activity and mob violence. Hovland and Sears (1940) found that cotton-price decreases in the southern United States between 1882 and 1930 were strongly correlated (.63) with increases in mob lynchings in those years.

Finally, as noted earlier, crowd research has declined and crowding research has increased dramatically. We are tempted to explain this by saying that the subject of crowd research (the highly charged, temporary aggregation of people) is less common now; we don't have many lynchings today. True, but crowds still exist. Remember the panic-stricken residents of Bhopal fleeing poison gas? Mobs destroying football fields after big victories? Street gang clashes? Schoolyard brawls with rings of onlookers? Before Christmas shopping? After Christmas clearance sales? Perhaps crowd research needs a revival.

FIGURE 7–2 Daniel Stokols. *(Courtesy of Daniel Stokols.)*

Crowding versus Density versus Perceived Density.

The terms crowding and density were used more or less interchangeably until Daniel Stokols (1972) made a distinction that is now generally accepted. (See Fig. 7–2.)

Density is a measure of the number of individuals per unit area. It may be calculated for any area from the whole earth (there are, by the way, about thirty inhabitants per square kilometer, or eighty per square mile, of land in the world as a whole), to nations (Japan has about 300 people per square kilometer, compared to 325 for England, 28 for the United States, 3 for Canada, and 2.5 for Australia), to cities (from 40,000 inhabitants per square kilometer in the urban portions of Hong Kong to 7000 in Toronto, 11,000 for London, 34,000 in Manhattan, 8,500 in New York City as

a whole, and only 125 for Metropolitan Los Angeles, which includes considerable open space spread over five counties), to neighborhoods, to buildings and homes, and even rooms. In smaller places it is likely to be measured in people per square meter rather than per square kilometer, but the same principle holds: density is an objective measure of individuals per unit of area.

Density is objective but not unvarying; it differs with geographic scale. The distribution of population is such that you may live in a densely populated city that is situated in a large, nearly uninhabited area (this is how most Canadians live, for example) or in a densely populated rural region. In Java, as a contrast to Canada, the population density is about 1,000 people per square kilometer, even though Java is largely rural. Density is a variable gradient: the room, building, neighborhood, city, region, and nation in which the individual is located may all have different densities. One issue in crowding research has been, which of these densities best helps us understand human behavior? Later we will discuss some of the research bearing on this question.

Crowding, on the other hand, refers to our *experience* of the number of other people around. Instead of a physical ratio, it is a personally defined, subjective feeling that too many others are around. Crowding may correspond to high density, but it does not necessarily correspond to density. I have felt crowded by one other person in a large room and not crowded when I was with thousands of other people at a concert. Crowding is a function of many factors, including characteristics of the individual and the social situation.

The relatively small relation between the two is illustrated by the results of a very large-scale study of household density in Chicago (Gove & Hughes, 1983). Density, measured as persons per room, was correlated with two measures of crowding: the residents' perception that too many demands were placed on them and their perception of privacy loss. Both correlations were about .30, meaning that less than 10 percent of the variation in the experience of crowding was explained by density. In a study of Australian workers, crowding and density were even less related to each other; crowding and density were significantly correlated with entirely different aspects of job satisfaction (O'Brien & Pembroke, 1982).

Perceived density is a related but distinct concept. It refers to an individual's *estimate* of the density in a place, accurate or not, rather than the actual ratio of individuals per unit area (Rapoport, 1975). This distinction is based on the hypothesis that behavior is sometimes influenced more by one's perception of density than it is by density itself. West (1982) interviewed campers in a national forest about crowding and density in their vicinity. Campers had relatively inaccurate estimates of the actual density of others in the nearby forest. Correlations between actual density and perceived density were very low. West found, as he expected, that the behavior of campers was more related to perceived density than to actual density.

Social Density versus Spatial Density. Although density is the ratio of individuals to area,

it may vary in two ways. Consider a classroom with thirty students. We could double the density either by adding another thirty students to the room or by slicing the classroom in half and putting all thirty students in one half. Mathematically, these two procedures lead to the same density, which is twice the previous density. Psychologically, however, the two procedures lead to different outcomes (McGrew, 1970). When crowding is studied by varying the number of individuals in a fixed space, we are investigating **social density**. When crowding is studied by varying the amount of space available to a fixed number of individuals, we are investigating **spatial density**.

Inside Density versus Outside Density. Some researchers study crowding at the room or building level of analysis, while others focus on crowding at the block, neighborhood, community, or even national scale. Densities inside and outside a single building can vary dramatically. If one lives in Hong Kong or Manhattan, density measured as the number of people per block is very high. Yet one person may have a four bedroom apartment while, in the same city, a one-room apartment is shared by a whole family.

Indoor density is the ratio of individuals to space inside buildings, whereas **outdoor density** is the ratio of individuals to space outside buildings. The contrast in density from indoors to outdoors in these two cases may be related to quite different experiences and outcomes (Schmitt, 1957; Zlutnick & Altman, 1972). (See Fig. 7–3.)

Density versus Proximity. The inside versus outside density distinction is viewed by some environmental psychologists as a preliminary attempt to measure more central factors: how many others are present and how close they are. Eric Knowles (1979) asserts that indoor versus outdoor density is merely an approximation of a more basic and powerful influence, the actual proximity of others.

All density measures implicitly assume that individuals are more or less evenly distributed across the area. But, of course, in most settings individuals are clustered in groups. Knowles believes that crowding is better defined by the number and nearness of others in such clusters than by area-based measures. It follows, he believes,

FIGURE 7-3 This high-rise apartment building has been called an eyesore and a variety of behavior problems have been associated with it.

that proximity-based measures of crowding will clear up certain confusions in previous research and provide better predictions of behavior.

Knowles (1983) tested his ideas in a study that related crowding to proximity. The proximity concept is modeled on the law of gravitation and is part of a larger approach to the psychology of social influence called social-gravity theory or social-physics theory. In a manner analogous to the gravitional effects of planets and stars in space, effects on an individual are posited to be a function of mass (number of others present) and their distance.

As Knowles predicted, judgments of crowding closely paralleled a **proximity index** composed of these variables. From the results, Knowles proposed a more general law of social interaction. The effects of others on an individual will *increase* with the square root of their number and *decrease* with the square root of their distance. (See Fig. 7–4.)

The Components of Crowding

Internal-External Focus. Crowding is a multidimensional experience. It may refer to ourself or to the setting. The difference was revealed when patrons of a college bookstore, during the rush at the beginning of a term, were asked to describe the situation (Kalb & Keating, 1981).

FIGURE 7-4 Five graduate students share this 8 × 12 foot office. Two of them often don't even try working on campus.

Analysis of their descriptions showed that one kind of crowding refers to their own negative *feelings* (internal focus) and the other refers to their estimate of how crowded the *setting* is (external focus).

Situational, Emotional, and Behavioral Aspects.   Many studies have shown that crowding (the internally focused variety) has at least three aspects (Stokols, 1978; Sundstrom, 1978). First, it is based on some situational antecedent: too many people (or even one person) approach too close, our goal is blocked by a glut of people ahead, space is reduced by the arrival of a visitor or new roommate, or needed resources are swamped by congestion (Aiello & Thompson, 1980a). Second, it implies affect, usually negative affect. Third, crowding will produce some kind of behavioral response, ranging from overt aggression (rarely) to subtler responses such as leaving the scene, avoiding eye contact, or withdrawing from social interaction.

Each of these three dimensions might be represented by many specific examples. One study tried to discover the main situational, affective, and behavioral aspects of crowding (Montano & Adamopoulos, 1984). Through a complex series of steps involving (a) selection of a variety of different crowding situations, (b) ratings by individuals as to how they would act and feel in each one, and (c) analyses by a sophisticated statistical technique called three-mode factor analysis, Montano and Adamopoulos were able to conclude that there are four major situation modes, three major affective modes, and five major behavior modes in the crowding experience.

The **situation modes** include experiences in which we feel that our behavior is constrained, we are being interfered with physically, the mere presence of others causes us discomfort, or our expectations have not been met.

The **affective modes** of crowding include negative reactions to others, negative reactions to the situation, or positive feelings. The latter may be surprising. Although some theorists (Freedman, 1975) have maintained that high density is sometimes positive, most believe that crowding—as a subjective experience—is, by definition, negative. Montano and Adamopoulos discovered that positive emotion is associated with crowding only when individuals feel they have successfully coped with it. Therefore, positive emotion seems to be a part of crowding only when we believe we have overcome it.

Montano and Adamopoulos uncovered five primary **behavior modes** in response to crowding, including assertiveness (protesting, expressing an opinion, changing the environment), activity completion ("let's finish this up and get out of here!"), psychological withdrawal (staying, but trying to tune out the crowding), immediate physical withdrawal ("let's *not* finish this up; I'm leaving *now!*"), and adaptation (making the best of the situation by interacting with others, watching the fun, or making the physical setting more comfortable).

This three-mode definition portrays crowding as an experience consisting of antecedents, affect, and behavior. By multiplying out the factors (3 × 4 × 5), we see that sixty kinds of crowding experience are described by the Montano and Adamopoulos model. Although further research may refine the model, it is the kind of specific, multidimensional approach needed to adequately characterize the complexity of crowding.

▶ **In Sum.** The phenomenon of crowds—although intriguing—has declined as a research topic. Crowding is an unpleasant experience of spatial restriction, whereas density is a physical ratio of persons per unit area. Perceived density is the individual's estimate of this ratio. Crowding, density, and perceived density are not always correlated with one another. The notions of social versus spatial density, indoor versus outdoor density, and proximity have been advanced as ways to refine the density ratio into a variable with more predictive power. Crowding has scores of situational, emotional, and behavioral aspects.

How Crowding Is Studied

If you wanted to do a study of crowding, what methods or approaches could you take? Three major methods are used, although many variations are employed in the hundreds of studies so far reported. These are what I will call the aggregate, field, and laboratory methods.

The **aggregate approach** usually examines the relation between some measure of density and some pathological consequence. Typical aggregate measures include the density of a city, census tract, block, or building. In general, research following this approach has shifted toward smaller and smaller scales. Large-scale aggregate studies now often focus on persons per room (Gove & Hughes, 1983), because research at the smaller scales has generally been more productive.

Aggregate studies attempt to find connections between density and such outcomes as social breakdown and disease. Any links found must be treated cautiously, because the studies do not use experimental techniques that allow the researcher to draw causal conclusions. Aggregate studies also usually ignore the immediate interpersonal and experiential aspects of crowding. They are better considered as investigations of the broad, cumulative effects of living in high density.

Field studies take place in natural settings, but they usually attempt to satisfy some of the demands of experimental rigor by studying natural variations of density in otherwise comparable settings. One setting that often has been studied this way is the university dormitory, where fate and financial problems sometimes require universities to put three or more students in a room meant for two. Field studies combine the advantages of quasiexperimental design and a certain degree of external validity (applicability to everyday settings). The field study as an interview often examines crowding as an experience, as well as the effects of social and spatial density.

The **laboratory study** offers the greatest opportunity for drawing causal conclusions, because the experimenter has more control over the variables and can assign subjects to conditions randomly. Laboratory studies have focused on all aspects of crowding, including antecedents (such as high density), the subjective experience, and many different consequences.

Two drawbacks to laboratory studies are brevity of exposure (usually an hour or even less) and possible lack of external validity. Yet laboratory studies offer the best chance to carefully observe crowding-related processes, such as physiological changes, interpersonal transactions, nonverbal behavior, and other fleeting and difficult-to-measure behaviors.

▶ **In Sum.** Aggregate studies offer the best avenue for examining the gross effects of density on entire populations. Laboratory experiments offer the greatest opportunity to draw causal conclusions. The field experiment represents a compromise that is capable of investigating effects on individuals (a drawback of aggregate studies) and of claiming some relevance to everyday life (a drawback of the laboratory experiment).

INFLUENCES ON CROWDING

Under what conditions do we feel crowded? We might laugh at such a seemingly naive question. Don't we feel crowded when too many people are around? Of course, in extremely dense settings nearly all of us would report being crowded. When we are alone in a cozy room with a good book, almost none of us would feel crowded. Yet environmental psychologists find that many situations lead some individuals to feel crowded and others to feel uncrowded. That is, certain personal characteristics are associated with a lower tolerance for proximity to others. In addition, for any given individual, certain situations lead to the experience of crowding while others do not.

A major task of researchers is to identify the personal and situational variables that lead individuals to label an experience *crowded*. In general, my position is that personal and situational

factors *interact* to produce the crowding experience. However, some personal or situational influences may be so strong that they produce the crowding experience regardless of other influences.

Personal Influences

Personality, Preferences, and Expectations. What sort of individual is likely to feel crowded when, under similar circumstances, others do not? The most-researched variable of this type is **locus of control,** the tendency of individuals to believe (or disbelieve) that they exercise considerable influence over their own lives. Individuals with this belief (**internals**), might be expected to be able to handle the stress of crowding better than those without it (**externals**). If the beliefs of internals are at all grounded in reality, they have learned how to overcome a variety of difficulties in life. Indeed, most research supports the idea that internal locus of control eases crowding stress (McCallum, Rusbalt, Hong, Walden, & Schopler, 1979), although not every study does (Walden, Nelson, & Smith, 1981).

One exception was a study of dormitories where some students had to live three to a room while others lived two to a room. Internals were found to experience *more* stress than externals (Aiello, Vautier, & Bernstein, 1983). This unexpected finding may occur when, under some levels or types of density, externals resign the struggle while internals continue fighting for a successful coping strategy, thereby incurring more stress.

Personal control is an important component of crowding (Schmidt & Keating, 1979), but the generalized tendencies represented by personality measures may not predict your reaction to a specific situation as well as measures that assess your sense of control in that situation or *actual* degree of control in the situation.

Another personality variable relevant to the crowding experience is affiliative tendency or **sociability.** Individuals who generally like to be with others seem to have a higher tolerance for dense situations than individuals who are not very affiliative. In two studies, Stuart Miller and his colleagues have shown that this tendency does mediate the crowding experience. In one (Miller &

Nardini, 1977), participants with higher affiliation scores placed more stick figures in a model room before they thought of the room as crowded. In the other (Miller, Rossbach, & Munson, 1981), residents in a dormitory who were more affiliative experienced more stress when they were assigned to a low-density dorm than when they were assigned to a high-density dorm. (See Fig. 7–5.) Apparently, high affiliators find it easier to deal with a social overload (higher density) than a situation requiring them to be independent (lower density).

In another study of high-density dormitories, the crowdedness of students who varied in **stimulus screening** was compared (Baum, Calesnick, Davis, & Gatchel, 1982). Stimulus screening (Mehrabian, 1976a) is the tendency to be able to focus on desired stimuli while successfully tuning out unwanted stimuli. The researchers hypothesized and found that screeners could indeed cope with the social overload inherent in high density situations better than nonscreeners could.

Finally, most crowding studies have focused on college dormitories, prisons, and other indoor settings, but some have examined crowding outdoors. National parks are heavily used at times.

Peter Womble and Stacy Studebaker (1981) investigated the role of personal factors in determining when an Alaskan park was experienced as crowded. They found that the preferences and expectations of campers about density influenced their perceptions of crowding. Those who *preferred* higher densities felt less crowded; those who *expected* higher densities than they found felt less crowded. Incidentally, both these variables were better able to predict crowding than could an objective measure of density.

The finding that anticipation of high density leads to negative outcomes confirms earlier laboratory findings (Baum & Greenberg, 1975). When subjects expected ten others to join them in a room, they reported feeling more crowded than subjects who expected only four others to join them, even though the same number of others (only two) arrived in both conditions. Womble and Studebaker's park findings suggest that these subjects would have reported less crowding after they discovered that fewer others actually arrived than they had been led to expect.

Culture, Experience, and Sex. Past experience with high density can modify crowding ex-

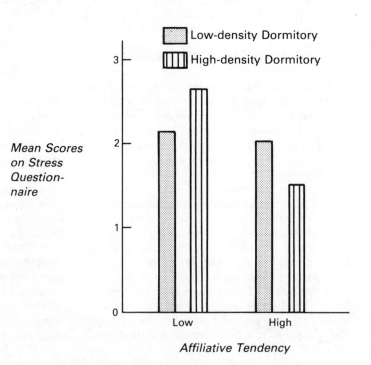

FIGURE 7–5 Stress varies with both personality and density. In low-density dormitories, stress levels are similar for affiliative and non-affiliative residents, but at high density stress is greater for non-affiliators and less for affiliators. *(Adapted from Miller, Rossbach, & Munson, 1981).*

perience in the present. This past experience may include a lifelong immersion in the culture or a short-term experience such as living in a dormitory or sharing a house. Gender is included in this section because sex differences in response to crowding are likely to be the result of differential socialization.

The interplay between high density and culture has received considerable attention, and will be discussed in a later section. Far fewer studies comparing the crowding experiences of different cultures are available. Even in an international symposium focusing exclusively on crowding, not a single paper was devoted to comparing the ways that members of different cultures experience crowding (Gurkaynak & LeCompte, 1979).

One recent study did compare the crowding of Asians and Mediterraneans who resided in the same dormitory in North America (Nasar & Min, 1984). Based on earlier observations by Edward Hall (1966), Nasar and Min expected that when space is in short supply, Asians would prefer social barriers but that Mediterraneans would prefer physical barriers. Thus, Nasar and Min predicted, that Mediterraneans would report more crowding than Asians when placed in the relatively constricted physical space of a single dormitory room. This was confirmed.

It is interesting that American students living in the same dormitory reported less crowding than either of the other groups. This seems odd because Americans likely came from the largest family homes and presumably had to make the largest space adjustment of the three groups. Future research may find that living in your own culture accounts for this finding, or that students able to come to the United States for an education were wealthy enough to have come from very spacious family homes.

If one thinks of rural, suburban, and urban regions as reflecting different subcultures, then these backgrounds may be another cultural factor in crowding. In a Florida study, dormitory residents from suburban homes reported more crowding than residents from urban or rural backgrounds (Walden, Nelson, & Smith, 1981). A large study of residential crowding in Chicago, however, found that individuals raised in the country were more reactive to crowding than individuals raised in the city (Gove & Hughes, 1983). The inconsistency in these results suggests that other

factors, such as amount of space in the childhood home (regardless of whether it was rural, suburban, or urban) might be more influential.

Personal experience with high-density situations or familiarity with a behavior setting where crowding occurs may affect the degree of distress that is experienced. Several studies support an adaptation effect, that is, persons with a history of exposure to high density tolerate it better in new settings (Sundstrom, 1978).

This does not always hold, however. William Rohe (1982) interviewed downtown residents of a college town. He found that residents with more high-density living experience reported having more arguments with other residents than did residents whose past residential experience was with lower-density housing. Because these are correlational findings, causal conclusions are not possible, but Rohe suggests that a history of high-density living does not seem to give residents of higher-density housing the kind of interpersonal lessons that allow for harmonious house-sharing.

On the other hand, Baum, Fisher, and Solomon (1981) investigated the responses of bookstore patrons who were either experienced with the store or not, at the beginning of the school term when the bookstore was very busy. As might be expected, those who were experienced with the store were able to use the store to find information more effectively than those who were less familiar with the store. That is, experience with high density helped rather than harmed these bookstore patrons.

To reconcile the differences in findings between these last two studies, a distinction suggested by Stokols (1978) between primary and secondary environments is useful. **Primary environments** are those in which one spends much time, usually with personally significant other people, doing personally significant things. The home and office are two obvious examples. **Secondary environments** are those involving interactions with strangers which are usually brief and relatively unimportant. Some examples include our visits to retail stores, public swimming pools, and government offices. Note that Rohe studied a primary setting (home), whereas Baum et al. investigated a secondary setting (bookstore). It may be that familiarity can help us cope with high density in secondary settings, but cannot overcome the effects of high density in primary settings. In other studies, crowding has been shown to be more aversive in primary environments than in secondary environments.

Experience in high-density settings may allow one to successfully adapt physiologically, if not interpersonally. In a large-scale Toronto study, Booth (1976) found that men who grew up in high-density households were less likely than men who grew up in low-density households to have stress-related diseases when they lived in high density as adults.

Gender, probably through differential socialization of the sexes, also predisposes men and women to react differently to high density. Research performed in laboratory settings usually finds that men respond to high density more negatively than women; their mood, attitudes toward others, and social behavior are more hostile. Women seem, in these situations from which there is no easy escape, to handle the stress better

FIGURE 7-6 John Aiello is one of the most prolific researchers in crowding and related topics. *(Courtesy of John Aiello.)*

(Aiello, Thompson, & Brodzinsky, 1983). (See Fig. 7–6.)

This may be because women more often define the situation as one that calls for sharing the distress; men are less able to share distress, perhaps because they are discouraged from showing emotion (Epstein & Karlin, 1975). Alternatively, men may handle high density less well because they prefer greater interpersonal distances (Aiello, Epstein, & Karlin, 1975). Whatever the reason, the sexes exhibit this pattern as early as nine years of age (Aiello, Nicosia, & Thompson, 1979).

In field studies, these sex differences are often reversed. Studies of dormitory residents living two to a room versus those living three to a room usually (Aiello, Baum, & Gormley, 1981), but not always (Walden, Nelson, & Smith, 1981), find that women report more crowding than men. A key reason for this reversal appears to be the amount of time men and women actually spend in their rooms. Men more often cope with the high density by leaving their rooms, something they are less free to do in laboratory studies. Women, perhaps more involved with their roommates, spend more time in their rooms, thereby incurring more stress and health problems (Aiello, Thompson, & Baum, 1981a).

Thus, the tendency of women to share crowding distress may benefit them in short-term, low-control situations but harm them in longer-term, high-control situations. Women in dormitories are also more sensitive to the room's physical advantages and disadvantages, perhaps because they spend more time there, and even think of crowding in more architectural terms than do men (Mandel, Baron, & Fisher, 1980).

Social Influences

The preceding section surveyed characteristics that individuals acquire before they enter any particular situation. In this section, we examine social influences on crowding. Individuals are predisposed to experience more or less crowding in any given setting owing to characteristics they bring to it, but the influence of others in that setting can either worsen or ameliorate crowding stress. Some of these social factors include

1. The mere presence and the behavior of nearby others

2. Coalitions that tend to form in small groups
3. The quality or type of relationship among the individuals
4. The kind of information that crowded individuals receive.

The Presence and Behavior of Others. High density means many others around you, but crowding may be intensified by it or not, depending on what those others are doing. For example, if they are watching you do something, your performance is likely to improve or deteriorate, depending on whether you are good at the task, what rewards you expect, and whether your attention is on yourself or the audience. (See Fig. 7–7.)

Eric Knowles (1983) found that the performance of simple learning and memory tasks declined as the number of onlookers rose from two to eight, even though their physical closeness (in the range of 1 to 7 meters away) did not affect performance. In a field setting, Schiffenbauer (1979) reports that dormitory residents felt crowded in proportion to the number of visitors they had. Residents who received more visits were also more dissatisfied with their rooms, roommates, and studying.

If others are touching you, crowding is worse than if they aren't, even though density is unchanged. In a laboratory study (Nicosia, Hyman, Karlin, Epstein, & Aiello, 1979), subjects' physiological responses, mood, performance, and tolerance for frustration were measured during a 30-minute exposure to extremely high density (four individuals in about 1 square meter) or low density (four individuals in about 15 square meters). In the high-density condition, some individuals were separated by barriers (meter-high Plexiglas partitions between bodies) to prevent physical contact, which was unavoidable when others were not separated by barriers.

FIGURE 7–7 Performance can depend on the number and distance of onlookers.

Physiological arousal increased significantly over the 30 minutes for all subjects, and men's arousal was higher than women's. The arousal of men who were forced to touch increased faster than that of men who did not touch, but this did not happen for women. Men reported being in worse moods than women after being in the situation where touching was unavoidable, but women reported worse moods when there were barriers. Subjects in the crowded-touch situation showed lower toleration for frustration on certain tasks than did subjects in the crowded-nontouch situation. The researchers conclude that touching while in high density is more stressful for men than nontouching in high density, but women seem less stressed by touching.

A field study throws some light on how the behavior of nearby others affects crowding in natural settings. Womble and Studebaker (1981) queried campers in an Alaskan park about crowding. They discovered that the number of others in the campground was not a major reason for campers to feel crowded. Instead, campers felt crowded when others engaged in activities they disliked: "My crowded feelings were directly related to the neighboring campers. If they were noisy, inconsiderate, or loud, I wanted to flee to the backcountry." Another camper felt crowded because he happened to pick a site that other campers frequently walked through. In contrast, others did not feel crowded even when forced to share a campsite (after discovering that every empty site was taken) because they discovered they liked the people with whom they shared their site.

According to Stokols (1978), an important aspect of social behavior pertains to whether the interference with our activities is intentional or not. Stokols calls interference that we believe is directed at us **personal thwarting,** and interference we believe is not directed at us personally **neutral thwarting.** Personal thwarting, according to Stokols, produces more stressful crowding than neutral thwarting. Your assessment of *why* someone touches you or barges through your campsite is an important determinant of how intense your crowding experience is.

Coalition Formation.

In residential settings, many studies support the idea that increasing social density increases crowding (Aiello & Baum, 1979). Most of these studies have examined the consequences of adding a third roommate to a university dormitory room and found them to be negative (Aiello, Epstein, & Karlin, 1975; Aiello, Vautier, & Bernstein, 1983; Baron, Mandel, Adams, & Griffin, 1976; Walden, Nelson, & Smith, 1981). When social density increases, privacy is lowered, the same number of resources must be spread thinner, more physical interference is encountered, and our sense of control is reduced.

One consequence of increased social density is that triads sometimes degenerate, interpersonally, into a pair (or coalition) and one isolated roommate. Isolated residents experience the most stress, tension, bad feelings, loss of control, and even poorer grades (Aiello, Baum, & Gormley, 1981; Aiello, Vautier, & Bernstein, 1983; Gormley & Aiello, 1982; Reddy, Baum, Fleming, & Aiello, 1981).

Residents who form part of a coalition experience less stress; in fact, they may experience no more stress than residents of double rooms (Baum, Shapiro, Murray, & Wideman, 1979). In further support of the notion that stress is primarily suffered by isolates, one study found that residents of four-person rooms reported no more stress than residents of three-person rooms (Reddy, Baum, Fleming, & Aiello, 1981). Presumably, two pairs form and no one is isolated. Thus, the stress of crowding is apparently mediated by group formation.

The Quality of Relationships.

A related social factor that also mediates crowding is the quality of the relationships among those who must share space. In a laboratory study of short-term crowding, Schaeffer and Patterson (1980) found that when participants were led to believe that another participant held very similar views to their own—that is, they could expect interpersonal compatibility—they reported less crowding than when they were led to believe the other participant held dissimilar views. Crowding was most intense when the incompatible other person gazed at the participant more. These findings were the same in rooms that differed in size by a factor of three. Thus, crowding in Schaeffer and Patterson's study was significantly affected by how well participants expected to get along with another person and how much that person gazed at the participant, but not by changes in spatial density.

The Provision of Information. Crowding is also affected by the amount and type of information one is given before and during a high-density experience. Jeffrey Fisher and Andrew Baum (1980) led participants in a laboratory study to think that they were the first of ten subjects to arrive at a fairly small room. The participants reported feeling more or less comfortable depending on what kind of information they were given about the imminent high-density situation. Those who received no information at all or received messages concerning their likely *emotional* reactions ("you may be uncomfortable because others will be close to you") reported feeling more discomfort than those who received *situational* messages ("others will be close to you").

In a follow-up field study, Baum, Fisher, and Solomon (1981) gave different kinds of advance warning to patrons of a busy (high-density) bookstore. In addition to situational and emotional information, some patrons were given sensory information (the physiological sensations they were likely to experience) and others were given positive information (that the large numbers of other patrons might make them feel comfortable and more productive). Situational messages produced the least discomfort of all, significantly less than giving patrons no information or positive information. Emotional and sensory information reduced discomfort for patrons who were familiar with the bookstore, but not for those who were unfamiliar with it.

If we wished to put this knowledge into practice, we probably would not be able to distinguish patrons who are familiar with the store from those who are not. If, however, we gave all patrons situational information, it should significantly reduce crowding in a busy store. Baum, Fisher, and Solomon suggest that accurate, objective information about impending high density serves to validate one's experiences, thereby making it less aversive.

Information may be provided verbally, as it was in the above studies, but a more practical alternative may be to present the appropriate information on a sign. Richard Wener and Robert Kaminoff (1983) investigated whether signs offering simple directions and information (such as Pick Up Visitor Forms Below) would alleviate crowding in the lobby of a prison administration building that is often densely populated. (See Fig. 7–8.) Visitors felt significantly less crowded, confused, and angered after the signs were introduced, compared to visitors interviewed before the signs were introduced. The time required to complete the registration process was shorter and visitors made fewer navigational errors in the lobby.

FIGURE 7–8 The sign that reduced crowding in the Wener and Kaminoff study (1983). (*Wener, R. E., and Kaminoff, R. D. Improving environmental information: Effects of signs on perceived crowding and behavior.* Environment and Behavior, 1983, *15,* 3–20. Copyright © 1983 by Environment and Behavior, Reprinted by permission of Sage Publications, Inc.)

Physical Influences

Individuals import their predispositions to be crowded to the situation. In the situation, various social factors further influence whether or not they will feel crowded. Finally, the physical setting can increase or decrease crowding stress. High density itself is the most obvious such factor but, as we have seen, it does not always lead to crowding. Other physical factors associated with crowding include what scale is under investigation (room, building, neighborhood, city) and architectural variations (ceiling height, furniture arrangement, window placement, partitions, and barriers, etc.).

Scale. How might scale affect crowding? Answer the following questions for yourself: Is your city or town too crowded for you? Is your neighborhood too crowded for you? Is your residence too crowded for you? If you are like respondents in a study by Schmidt, Goldman, and Feimer (1979), yor answers to these three questions are not necessarily the same.

If crowding is indeed a function of which scale we consider, what leads a person to feel crowded (or not) at each level? To answer this, Schmidt et al. measured several physical indices (densities, distances to commercial-industrial areas, freeways, and parks) and several psychological indices (attitudes about urban development, privacy, this city compared to other cities, traffic, etc.).

Schmidt et al. found that crowding at the smallest scale (residence) was equally well predicted by physical and psychological factors, but crowding at the larger scales was much better predicted by the psychological scales. It is possible that these results were due in part to the researcher's particular selection of measures chosen to represent the physical and psychological domains. But the relation between crowding and objective measures at the smaller scales has been confirmed by other studies (Loo & Ong, 1984). Therefore, crowding apparently depends on which geographical scale is being considered and the different factors at each scale that lead individuals to conclude that they are crowded.

Finally, we should observe that, congruent with the general model of environment-behavior relations adopted in this book, crowding at the residence and neighborhood scales in the Schmidt et al. study was best predicted by combinations of physical and personal (or psychological) scales.

Architectural Variations. Crowding is affected by the arrangement of space in rooms and buildings. In this section, we consider studies of preexisting variations in architecture and changes made by building users. In a later section we survey the results of active architectural interventions by environmental psychologists, designers, and other outsiders.

Studies of high-rise dormitories clearly show that when the design involves long corridors, as opposed to clusters of suites or short corridors, residents experience more crowding and stress (Baum, Aiello, & Calesnick, 1978; Baum, Davis, & Valins, 1979; Baum & Valins, 1977). The long-corridor designs are also accompanied by greater competitiveness and social withdrawal and by reduced cooperativeness and lower feelings of personal control. (See Fig. 7–9.)

Living in a high-rise building (compared to a low-rise building) may lead to greater feelings of crowdedness and other negatively toned attitudes such as less perceived control, safety, privacy, building satisfaction, and lower quality of relationships with other residents (McCarthy & Saegert, 1979). This pattern of results may be modified, however, by how high one lives in the high rise. Schiffenbauer (1979) found that residents of higher floors felt less crowded than did residents of lower floors. This may be because fewer strangers venture to the upper reaches of a building or because views out the windows of upper-level apartments provide more visual expanse (Schiffenbauer, 1979) or visual escape (Sundstrom, 1978) than do lower-level windows. Upper-level rooms have been rated as lighter and less crowded (Nasar & Min, 1984). Unfortunately, another study (Mandel, Baron, & Fisher, 1980) found that crowding was not related to floor height or to view, so more research on these architectural variables is needed.

Rooms receiving more sunlight are perceived as less crowded by women (Shiffenbauer, 1977; Mandel, Baron, & Fisher, 1980) and perhaps by men (Nasar & Min, 1984). Sunlight cannot easily be made to enter north-facing windows, but Shif-

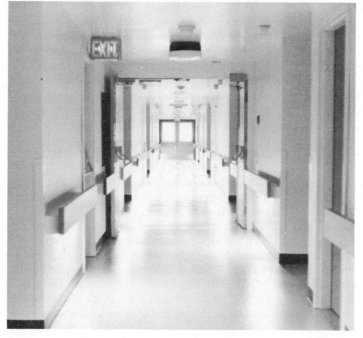

FIGURE 7-9 Long residential corridors may increase crowding.

fenbauer suggests that crowding may be reduced by brightening a room with light colors or graphic designs.

Another architectural feature, ceiling height, affects crowding; higher ceilings, as you might expect, are associated with less crowding (Savinar, 1975).

Ceilings are difficult to rearrange, but some dormitory residents arrange furniture in curious ways. When I was in my first year of university, my dormitory contained rooms with bunked beds (that were not designed to be bunked) and even, in the never-ending search for thrills and more space, bunked *desks*.

In another furniture arrangement study, Wener (1977) found that when seats are arranged sociofugally so that individuals tend to face away from one another, the room is rated as more crowded than when seats are arranged sociopetally with individuals facing one another. Wener suggests that when individuals face each other, the overload approach would predict more crowding, which did not occur. He speculates that sociopetal seating does not lead to more crowding when social relationships in the group are reasonably good.

► **In Sum.** This section reviews the influences that lead us to feel crowded. At the personal level, personality, expectation, and preference influence whether an individual experiences a given situation as crowded or not. We may conclude that internal locus of control, high affiliative tendency, a tendency to screen unwanted stimuli, a preference for high density, and an expectation for low density *predispose* us to experience less crowding when density is high.

Researchers have not yet clarified how different cultures respond to crowding (as an experience). Personal experience with high density may reduce crowding stress in secondary but not in primary environments. In confined settings, women usually manage high density better, but men seem to cope better when escape is possible. Social influences can worsen crowding or ease it. Sheer numbers of others will sometimes, but not always, produce more crowding. If others are watching you or touching you (particularly if you are male), or if you are engaged in activities you dislike, crowding may be worse even when density is equivalent. Being left out produces more crowding stress than sharing space with another person who is compatible with you. Objective, accurate information about high density settings reduces crowding. Crowding is likely to be worse when density is higher, the building is higher, the corridors are longer, the ceiling is lower, sunlight rarely finds its way in, and, perhaps, if you live or work on the lower floors of a tall building and arrange the furniture in certain ways.

HIGH DENSITY AND HUMAN BEHAVIOR

We have seen that certain personal, social, and physical influences may cause an individual to feel crowded. High density is just one such influence, and it does not always lead one to feel crowded. In this section, we begin with the individual in a densely populated setting and survey the effects that density has. Some environmental psychologists' interests are primarily in the antecedents of crowding (the last section), but others believe that you are not really studying crowding unless you begin with high density and focus on its effects (this section).

The effects of high density on animals have been extensively studied, sometimes with animal responses as the terminal purpose (Wynne-Edwards, 1965), sometimes with animal responses viewed as generalizable to human responses (Calhoun, 1971; Wynne-Edwards, 1971). Although animal research may be valuable in its own right (for example, as a basis for planning nature reserves, national parks, or zoos), we must be very cautious in generalizing findings from animal studies to humans. Animal responses to high density are more stereotyped because they have less cognitive capacity; their behavior is more directly a result of biological programming. Some animals naturally live in much higher or lower densities than humans. Their preferred densities sometimes vary with the season. Humans often have more opportunity to leave a high-density situation or more ability to cope in a larger variety of ways.

Nevertheless, animal research has stimulated much crowding research because its findings have provided challenging hypotheses for research with humans. The most influential such work was done by John Calhoun (1962, 1966, 1971). His studies of Norway rats enclosed in four adjacent pens with adequate supplies of food, drink, and other necessities of life are landmarks in the study of crowding. He found that female rats distributed themselves about equally in the four pens, which were connected, but that a few dominant males controlled each of two end pens. All other males had to live in middle pens; density in these pens was very high and all manner of horrible consequences occurred in these **behavioral sinks:** aggression, impaired maternal behavior (up to 96 percent of the young born in this area died before weaning), hyperactivity, cannibalism, and bizarre sexual activity.

However provocative Calhoun's research has been, its validity even for animals has been questioned. Norway rats are not usually penned in this manner. Rodents in natural settings faced with high density simply emigrate (Archer, 1970). Calhoun's housing design was set up so that behavioral sinks almost had to develop. If one wants to know just how awful life can be under a worst-case scenario, the research has value. As an attempt to discover how humans or even rats behave in natural settings, the research is less valuable. Depending on our moral views on animal research, we might even question the ethical wisdom of Calhoun's work. I focus on the human response to high density in this chapter but acknowledge that much of it is based on studies that were stimulated by Calhoun's research.

In this book, high density and crowding are viewed as part of an integrated and complex process. A variety of factors, including high density, lead to crowding (as a subjective state). High density (sometimes without any sense of being crowded) has a variety of effects, even including some positive outcomes. One major task of environmental psychology is to discover the conditions under which high density will have negative effects and those under which it will have positive effects (Freedman, 1979a). We next survey the effect of high density on physiology and health, performance, social interaction, emotion, and sense of control.

Physiology and Health

Many investigations of human response to high density have shown that it leads, both in short-term laboratory studies and in long-term field studies, to stress and arousal (Epstein, 1982). Specifically, high density affects blood pressure and other cardiac functions (D'Atri, 1975; Epstein, Woolfolk, & Lehrer, 1981; Evans, 1979a) as well as skin conductance and sweating (Aiello, Nicosia, & Thompson, 1979; Cox, Paulus, McCain, & Schkade, 1979; Nicosia, Hyman, Karlin, Epstein, & Aiello, 1979).

Given that high density has these physiological effects, does it actually lead to health problems? We should remember that arousal isn't necessarily bad; some awfully good times are accompanied by high-arousal levels. Unfortunately, joyful high-density occasions have rarely been researched. On the negative side, very high density can precipitate illness merely due to the ease with which disease organisms can move from person to person (Cox et al., 1984). Moderate to high residential density, such as is found in prisons, is correlated with an increase in health complaints (McCain, Cox, & Paulus, 1976). Health is affected by high inside density, but not by high outside density (Freedman, 1975; Levy & Herzog, 1974; Marsella, Escudero, & Gordon, 1970).

Personal factors may worsen crowding, as we have seen. Individuals with preferences for larger interpersonal distances experience more physiological stress in high-density situations than do individuals who prefer smaller interpersonal distances (Aiello, DeRisi, Epstein, & Karlin, 1977). (See Fig. 7–10.)

Performance

The effect of high density on individual performance depends largely on the kind of task. Early studies found that moderately high densities did not affect the performance of relatively simple tasks in which individuals sat in one place for an hour or so and worked without interacting with others.

Later studies found that performance is affected if some of these conditions are different. Gary Evans (1979a) varied spatial density by a factor of six (about 1 versus 6 square meters per person) and asked individuals, participating in groups of ten, to perform several tasks requiring basic information processing and decision making. Simple and complex versions of each task were presented. On most of the tasks, performance of the complex version was worse in the high-density condition, but performance of the simple task did not vary with density. That is, high density may affect the performance of complex but not simple tasks.

Eric Knowles (1983) investigated performance when density varied and everyone present watched one person learn to trace a maze. He

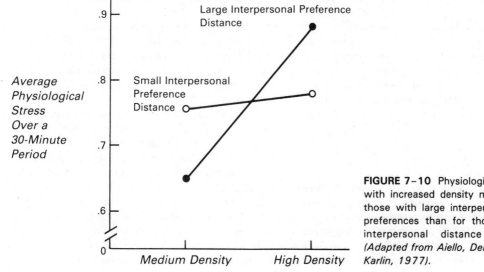

FIGURE 7–10 Physiological stress rises with increased density much faster for those with large interpersonal distance preferences than for those with small interpersonal distance preferences. *(Adapted from Aiello, DeRisi, Epstein, & Karlin, 1977).*

found that learning *rate* declined as audience size (and social density) increased. However, during rest periods, participants in the high-density conditions forgot less of what they had learned than did participants in low-density, low-audience conditions. Performance, therefore, was both worse (slower learning) and better (less forgetting) as density and audience size increased.

In many high-density settings, performance depends on the physical interaction of individuals, either through direct communication or because they must move around the setting to acquire, process, and deliver materials. Offices, retail stores, and laboratories are everyday places where this occurs. In a study of this possibility, Heller, Groff, and Solomon (1977) asked participants to perform a simple office task (collating paper) under two conditions: when pages of the manuscript were placed in an orderly sequence and when the pages were placed around the room in no particular sequence. In the first condition, participants were not forced to interact physically as they performed, but in the second they were. Performance was not different in high- and low-density conditions when the task did not require physical interaction, but was significantly worse in high-density, high-interaction conditions compared to high-density, low-interaction conditions.

Expectations about the situation also affect performance. Individuals who are subjected to high density and believe they will not do well on the task perform poorly (Schkade, 1977). Expectancies about density itself also affect performance. Students who were led to expect a high- or low-density situation but then encountered the reverse situation performed more poorly than students who found what they expected (Klein & Harris, 1979). This is reminiscent of work we discussed earlier in which accurate forewarning of high density to bookstore patrons helped them feel less crowded.

Social Interaction

What are the effects of high density on social relations? The answer depends on several considerations, of which the two most important are scale (room density to community density) and type of social relations. High density has now been shown to affect eight aspects of social behavior: attraction, aggression, cooperation, withdrawal, nonverbal behavior, spatial behavior, and even humor.

Particularly when high density is undesirable (it wasn't your choice or it occurs in an unpleasant place), social outcomes are generally negative—others in the situation seem less attractive, and there is more aggression, less cooperation, and more social withdrawal. Consider for yourself the difference between spending an hour packed into a tiny room for a laboratory experiment, which you agreed to participate in only to gain points in a class, and spending an hour packed into a tiny room that contains a rollicking party with good friends, good food, and good music.

When negative feelings develop they can do so quickly. Baum and Greenberg (1975) showed that the mere *anticipation* of high density led to less liking of others. If high density usually creates negative attitudes toward others, one must predict that antisocial or asocial behavior will follow. For the most part, that is exactly what happens. Nine- to seventeen-year-olds exposed to extremely high spatial density (about one-quarter square meter per person) for little more than half an hour displayed more competitive strategies in a game played afterwards than others who were not exposed to high density (Aiello, Nicosia, & Thompson, 1979). University students showed the same effect even though they had about four times the amount of space per person, which still amounts to very high density (Evans, 1979a).

Individuals subjected to high density often respond by withdrawing from social interaction. A classic example is the commuter who is engrossed in reading a newspaper on a busy train as much to avoid social contact as to learn what is in the news. Even well-acquainted individuals speak less and more quietly when they enter a crowded elevator. They may be respecting the right of others to a relatively quiet ride, or they may wish to avoid being overheard. Social withdrawal is manifested in various ways: leaving the scene, choosing less personal topics to talk about (Sundstrom, 1975), making remarks about leaving, adopting a defensive posture (Evans, 1979a), turning away, avoiding eye contact, or increasing interpersonal distance (Baum & Greenberg, 1975).

In an interesting variant of this theme, Richard Reichner (1979) investigated whether residents of corridor-design or suite-design dormitories react more negatively to being ignored. Because corridor designs usually require residents to share bathrooms and lounges more than do suite designs, they have higher social densities in public areas. Reichner reasoned that the greater, perhaps excessive, social stimulation received by residents of corridor-design dorms would allow them to be less adversely affected by the experience of being ignored. In the extreme, being ignored can be a welcome relief from too much social interaction. In his study, Reichner found that no one who was ignored in a discussion liked the experience, but corridor-design residents who were ignored reported the *least* discomfort and suite-design residents who were ignored reported the *most* discomfort, as predicted.

High density usually leads to less helpfulness. In one study, stamped and addressed envelopes were "accidentally" dropped by experimenters in high, medium, and low-density dorms (Bickman, Teger, Gabriele, Berger, & Sunaday, 1973). Residents of high-density dorms more often left the letters on the floor; residents of low-density dorms more often picked them up and mailed them. In another study, cafeteria patrons respected a sign requesting them to return their trays from their tables to the dishwashing area less often when the cafeteria was more densely populated (Jorgenson & Dukes, 1976). (See Fig. 7–11.)

High density, especially for males and especially over a long-term exposure, increases aggression. In short-term laboratory studies, high-spatial density is likely to produce such mild forms of aggression as taking the central chair in a room (Baum & Koman, 1976) or, in a hypothetical court case, sentencing a convict to a longer sentence. Nancy Thalhofer (1980), investigating a mild form of aggression in a field setting, observed the frequency with which passersby violated the personal space of a person standing near a fountain. Under high-social density, but not high-spatial density, her space was invaded more often than under low-density conditions.

Male adults may feel more aggressive in short-term exposure to high density, but they are socialized not to express it directly. Men in longer-term, high-density situations, such as convicts, are more likely to act aggressively. Cox, Paulus, & McCain (1984) report astonishingly high correlations between density and violence in south-

FIGURE 7–11 High density in eating areas may reduce responsiveness to pleas like this one.

ern United States prisons. One prison in Mississippi experienced a 30 percent reduction in population over a period of a few months. The rate of inmate assaults on other inmates dropped during that period by about 60 percent. Later the prison experienced a 19 percent increase in population; a 36 percent increase in assaults followed. Of course, these are correlational data and other nondensity factors may have been at work. However, Cox, Paulus, and McCain report similar patterns of aggression in many prisons, despite having made substantial efforts to take other possible factors into account.

Children are less socialized than adults; do they behave more aggressively in high-density conditions? Chalsa Loo has extensively investigated this question. She finds that higher social density (about 1.5 square meters per child) pro-

---

duces more aggression (Loo & Kennelly, 1979). Higher spatial density, on the other hand, leads to a slight (nonsignificant) decrease in aggression (Loo, 1972). Once again, a sex difference was found; boys were more likely to aggress than girls.

Increased social density often means fewer resources per person; increased spatial density often means no decrease in resources (except space itself). If this is true, increased aggression in higher social density may be due to increased competition for desirable resources, whether they are toys among preschoolers or good seats in the lounge for adult prisoners. Indeed, when resources were made scarcer on a playground, aggression among preschool children did increase (Smith & Connolly, 1977).

Overall, it seems that males have a more difficult time handling lack of space. They can manage to avoid aggression if the high density situation doesn't last very long. If thrown together with other men for long periods, they are more likely to act aggressively in proportion to increases in density and, perhaps, in proportion to decreases in resources.

The effects of density on social interaction discussed so far are pretty grim. There does appear to be one bright spot—high density may enhance humor. In one study, groups were shown humorous films (Freedman, Birsky, & Cavoukian, 1980). At the end, one person began clapping to indicate appreciation of the film. When this occurred in high density, more others joined the clapping than when it occurred in low density. In another study, participants listened to some comedy records (Aiello, Thompson, & Brodzinsky, 1983). Those in high spatial density conditions thought the comedians were funnier than did those in lower spatial density.

Humor appreciation may be enhanced in high density either by a contagion effect (according to Freedman et al.) or by tension release (according to Aiello et al.). The contagion explanation is related to Freedman's density-intensity hypothesis (high density tends to magnify existing feelings). If one person defines a film as very funny by going to the trouble of applauding it, applause may spread contagiously in high-density situations. The other explanation assumes that high density creates more tension; when an opportunity to dispel some of it arrives (a joke is heard), more laughter and appreciation of the joke follows. Unfor-

tunately, there is even a somber note in the humor research. Some studies show that high density may reduce appreciation of humor and diminish the power of humor to produce good feelings (Prerost, 1982; Prerost & Brewer, 1980). As this varies with age and sex; more research is necessary to clarify the effects of density on humor.

Moving to the community scale, very early studies reported positive correlations between population density and various forms of social pathology such as crime, divorce, suicide, and mental illnesses. Studies showed that long-term exposure to high community density was associated with social withdrawal, at least among males (Sundstrom, 1978). This led to the widespread belief that cities, by their very nature as densely populated areas, were bad places to live.

Later, researchers found that when poverty is taken into account, density's relation to social pathology shrinks considerably. Other studies began to show that scale is important. In general, density measured at smaller scales (such as room density) correlates more highly with the existence of social pathology than does density measured at larger scales. These two discoveries are related, because poor people live in high indoor densities, whereas middle class or upper class people may live in low indoor densities in the midst of a high-density community. The message becomes either don't be poor and live in the city or don't live densely indoors. In large cities, these two pieces of advice are usually synonymous.

Affect

Does high density produce negative emotion? Your immediate response might be, "Of course—isn't high density always unpleasant?" However, recall that Freedman (1975) would assert the possibility that high density can magnify preexisting feelings, including positive feelings. In fact, he and his colleagues conducted two laboratory studies in which participants were praised or criticized on the quality of speeches they made, in order to create positive or negative feelings. As predicted, the most positive feelings were reported by those in higher spatial density rooms (Freedman, 1975). However, several other investigations showed no such intensification effect (Sundstrom, 1978).

In contrast, many studies show that higher

density does lead to negative affect. This has been demonstrated in both lab studies (Epstein, Woolfolk & Lehrer, 1981; Evans, 1979a) and in field studies (Aiello, Baum, & Gormley, 1981). High density typically produces tension, annoyance, physical discomfort, and hostility. Children in high spatial density conditions also report these feelings (Aiello, Nicosia, & Thompson, 1979).

Control and Coping

Another consequence of high density may be the perception that one has little control (Aiello, Baum, & Gormley, 1981; Baron, Mandel, Adams, & Griffen, 1976). Earlier research assumed that high density itself produced these feelings. However, later studies of dormitory residents (Gormley & Aiello, 1982; Reddy, Baum, Fleming, & Aiello, 1981) have found that control problems are felt most acutely by tripled residents who are excluded from a coalition. High density itself probably does lower our sense of control, if only because we must share resources and decision making with more people as density increases. But poor interpersonal relationships appear to further reduce our sense of control.

When crowding occurs, coping strategies appear. If no physical escape is possible, then nonverbal behavior is used; individuals look away, talk less, and generally signal unwillingness to socialize. If escape is possible, it obviously will be used as a way of coping. We can make friends away from the high-density residence or workplace, find little-known cubbyholes to hide in, or spend more time on the streets. Where they are possible, such coping mechanisms can reduce crowding in a densely populated setting. Presumably, some individuals are better at discovering and using coping strategies than are others. (See Fig. 7–12.)

Culture as a Mediator

The consequences of high density depend in part on our cultural background. Earlier we discussed cultural differences in the experience of crowding. Now we take up the issue of high density's effects on different cultures. We will see that culture acts as a buffer or mediator to high density, sometimes providing its member with a kind of shield against it and sometimes failing to equip them with effective means of coping with high density.

Perhaps the most important conclusion we can draw from this worldwide research is that high density does not necessarily cause personal or social pathology. The density of Hong Kong is about four times that of downtown Toronto, yet its crime rate is about one-fourth that of Toronto, and Toronto has a much lower crime rate than many other large cities in North America (Gifford & Peacock, 1979). The same study did show, interestingly, that *fear of crime* appears to be more related to high density than to actual crime rate. Although high density at the community scale may be related to more social pathology in some North American places (Galle & Gove, 1979), it is not in other places, such as the Netherlands (Levy & Herzog, 1974) and parts of Africa (Draper, 1973).

A relevant factor appears to be the age of the culture. Crowding is often associated with social breakdown in cultures that are relatively young. A clear possibility emerges in young cultures that have not had time to evolve ways of coping with high density. More aggression, mental and physical illness, and crime are often found in them. As centuries pass, customs that regulate high-density social interaction develop so that potential trouble is avoided.

Waves of immigration have benefited the United States in many ways, but also have produced continuing unrest in high density areas as recent immigrants experience clashes between the values and customs of their old and new countries. Black people, who have been most closely associated with social breakdown in some studies (Galle & Gove, 1979), have gone through this process twice. First, over a two-century period, they were imported as slaves; second, over the last century, they were given nominal and, gradually, genuine freedom into a largely unwelcoming culture.

In their large-scale study of Chicago, Gove and Hughes (1983) found important differences in the responses of blacks, Hispanics, and others (mostly whites) to high density. Even after controlling for education, poverty, sex, age, and other possibly influential variables, Gove and Hughes found that blacks are most reactive to crowding, particularly as it impinges on their privacy. Hispanics are least responsive to crowding, perhaps because of cul-

FIGURE 7-12 One strategy for coping with crowding at the library or the dormitory, if the weather suits. *(Courtesy of John Driscoll.)*

tural norms favoring close proximity. But because Hispanics live under relatively high densities, their cultural predisposition for closeness is sometimes not enough to prevent negative outcomes of high density. Thus, although in terms of density, blacks are intermediate between whites and Hispanics, the cultural preference of Hispanics for closeness means that high density has the greatest impact on blacks.

A century or two seems a long time to North Americans, but when compared with the thirty or forty centuries of experience that some cultures have, it isn't. What are some of the strategies used by experienced cultures to make high density bearable or enjoyable? The !Kung of Southwest Africa live in camps that place thin-walled dwelling places within arm's length of each other, but they have few problems with density and even seem to prefer it. But the !Kung have a valuable mechanism to peacefully regulate their social interaction (Draper, 1973). Members may leave the group they live with and move to another, or even begin their own group, without incurring the opposition that such moves often evoke in other societies.

The Chinese have also dealt with high density so well that they often choose high density even when offered a low-density alternative (Aiello & Thompson, 1980a). Robert Sommer (1969) recounts a story about housing construction in

Hong Kong, where low-cost apartments were designed to offer about 3.5 square meters per person. A construction supervisor, when asked why more space per person was not considered, replied that if the apartments were designed to offer 6 square meters per person, the tenants would sublet part of their space.

In many Chinese households, there are firm rules about access to one another's space, and children may be punished for even looking into another family's space (Anderson, 1972). Interaction between specific groups, such as men and women, high- and low-status individuals, and adults and children, is circumscribed by definite rules. Household sounds that might be labeled noise in other cultures are viewed instead as a sign of action and life. Adults may discipline the children of other adults without being perceived as interfering. Finally, a relatively low level of emotional involvement is expected. Aiello and Thompson (1980a) speculate that one reason many recent communal living experiments in North America failed was an unrealistic expectation that high-density living can be successfully combined with high levels of emotional involvement.

Because the Chinese have successfully adapted to high density, it is tempting to conclude that most Chinese like crowding. Chalsa Loo and Paul Ong (1984) believe this is a myth. In a survey of San Francisco's Chinatown, they found that nearly all Chinese residents believe that crowding is undesirable and harmful. (See Fig. 7–13.) Unfortunately, Loo and Ong did not ask residents whether they actually felt crowded but if they thought crowding is good or bad. Like most environmental psychologists, the residents seem to agree that crowding is bad by definition. The questions remain: Do the Chinese experience high density as negatively as do other cultures? Do they merely think the setting is crowded (external focus), or that they are crowded (internal focus)?

If it is incorrect to conclude that the Chinese like crowding, at what level of high density do they or most members of any culture begin to feel crowding stress? Some cultures may adapt to and even prefer higher densities than do others. At

FIGURE 7–13 Are residents of Chinese districts really crowded?

least two circumstances of the high density situation must be considered, however: first, whether a person chooses high density or was forced into it and, second, with whom the person shares space.

On the first consideration, some Chinese may choose to sublet some household space as a way to supplement income, which is seen as an important way of assisting the family. Knowing they are helping in this way, they may not experience the resultant high density as crowding. On the second, many Chinese may find high density preferable when the dwelling is filled with family but not if it is filled with outsiders.

These speculations remain to be tested. Early studies showing adaptation to high density did not study the experience of crowding, and the Loo and Ong study merely asked Chinese if they thought crowding was good or bad. Will someone please ask the Chinese if they actually *feel* crowded? A study is needed that resembles Gove and Hughes' (1983) comparison of black, Hispanic, and white crowding and density in the household.

In East Africa, three cultures that live in densities varying by a 1:3:6 ratio were compared (Munroe & Munroe, 1972). The culture that lives in the highest density (the Logali) have the strongest norms against close personal contact, both physical and emotional. In nearby cultures friends may often be seen holding hands, but this is discouraged among the Logali. Once again, low emotional involvement emerges as a mechanism by which high density is managed.

Other high-density societies have developed architectural and behavioral preferences that are compatible with high-density living. Both the Japanese and Dutch cultures have developed special affection for objects that take up very little space, such as jewel boxes, bonsai, and miniature paintings. In the Japanese home, the same room is used for more than one purpose; elaborate rules govern the use and transformation of space from one function to another. In both Japan and the Netherlands, citizens create minicommunities within high-density areas (Canter & Canter, 1971; Rapoport, 1977). In Tokyo, many such districts each provide easily accessible places for individuals to meet and interact, so that each person's small home need not absorb any further popula-

tion pressure. Dutch towns tend to be very compact and separate, with accessible green space between them, allowing an uncrowded feeling in a very densely populated land.

▶ **In Sum.** High inside density usually leads to physiological and psychological stress, at least for those who prefer larger interpersonal distances or are socially isolated. Performance may be harmed under high density when the task is complex, when others are watching, and when performers must physically interact to accomplish the task. When a person's expectancies about density are unfulfilled, performance may suffer. Performance may even be worse in *low* density if the performer expected high density. Some aspects of performance may even improve when density or audience size is increased. High density often has negative effects, but under some conditions—perhaps when we perform activities in which we are already competent—it may improve performance.

Inescapable high inside density harms a wide range of social behaviors, particularly for men. Except in prison, those effects take more passive forms (lack of helpfulness) than active forms (aggression). High density may enhance humor. Although perhaps the magnification effect has not been studied enough to draw firm conclusions, most research supports the conclusion that high density almost always creates negative emotion. High density reduces our sense of control; in turn, a variety of coping mechanisms are used.

Centuries of experience may be necessary before a culture can live successfully with high density. If newer cultures wanted to learn from older cultures, they might consider

- Encouraging more psychological distance between individuals
- Allowing times and places for escape
- Developing stricter norms about what may be said to whom
- Restricting who may go where within the home and how each space within the home is to be used
- Discouraging social interaction with acquaintances inside the home but encouraging it in public places
- Learning to appreciate higher levels of social stimulation

THEORIES OF CROWDING

Now that we have reviewed a considerable body of knowledge about what leads an individual to feel crowded and the effects of high density, the time has come to attempt an integration of the research findings. Fortunately, a rich panorama of integrative formulations has already been proposed. Half a dozen major theories of crowding have been advanced, as well as many smaller proposals, distinctions, and refinements.

This profusion of theory does have a negative side; the reader can come away from it all quite confused because the theories differ not merely in the explanatory mechanisms they propose, but in other ways. For example, theories vary in what they focus on. Some emphasize features of the physical environment that *lead* an individual to label a situation as crowded. Others center on the psychological process that takes place *during* the crowding experience. Finally, some primarily focus on the *outcomes* of crowding. Theories of crowding also differ in complexity, level of analysis, underlying assumptions, and testability (Edney, 1977).

At an international symposium on crowding in 1977 these problems were very obvious. For the first day or two of the symposium, some of the formal and informal discussions about crowding were so unsuccessful that a few participants wondered if they had mistakenly arrived at the wrong conference. Until basic definitions were fully discussed, the symposium was threatened by fundamental differences among participants about the nature of crowding and the appropriate methods and goals of research into crowding. Since that symposium, fortunately, theoretical perspectives on crowding have been significantly clarified.

Building on subsequent attempts to organize thinking about crowding, this section presents an overall framework that has a place for each of the major theories. (See Fig. 7–14.) The framework is a temporal-sequential description of the antecedents, processes, and consequences involved in crowding (Sundstrom, 1978). The framework begins with an assumption that a variety of influences (physical, social, and personal) leads, via perceptual-cognitive and physiological mechanisms, to a stressful state labeled *"crowding."* This stress is more specifically defined by psy-

chological processes such as perceived lack of control, stimulus overload, and behavioral constraint. These crowding processes, in turn, lead to a variety of consequences—coping, helplessness, behavioral deficits (and occasional benefits), and physiological after effects.

The framework also recognizes that high density may lead directly to some kinds of outcomes, without the individual's awareness of being crowded. That is, the processes characteristic of the crowding state may not always be evoked; high density may directly lead to some outcomes without the individual labeling the experience as crowded (Cox, Paulus, & McCain, 1984). Let's take a closer look at the components of this model. Each of the major theories will be covered as part of the component that it primarily deals with.

Antecedents

Personal. Most crowding theories acknowledge that individual differences play a role in crowding, but none of them *primarily* concerned with personal factors. Researchers seem content at present to amass lists of personal factors that consistently, at least consistently under specific sets of circumstances, lead to crowding. This is a subarea of crowding that requires a theoretical integration of its own. However, a tentative list of such factors might be: being male, coming from a relatively new culture, being unfamiliar with the setting in question, being a nonscreener, tending to external locus of control, preferring low density in general (or having a large personal space zone), and anticipating a different level of density than is actually experienced.

Physical. While research exists that documents links between architectural variables and crowding (see the next section of this chapter as well as the earlier section on this topic), no theory primarily concerns itself with them. Crowding may be reduced by the judicious use of partitions in large open residential or work spaces and perhaps by such factors as which floor we live on, what color and temperature the room is, the height of the ceiling, and whether the room receives much sunlight. Geographically, crowding perceptions depend on what scale is considered,

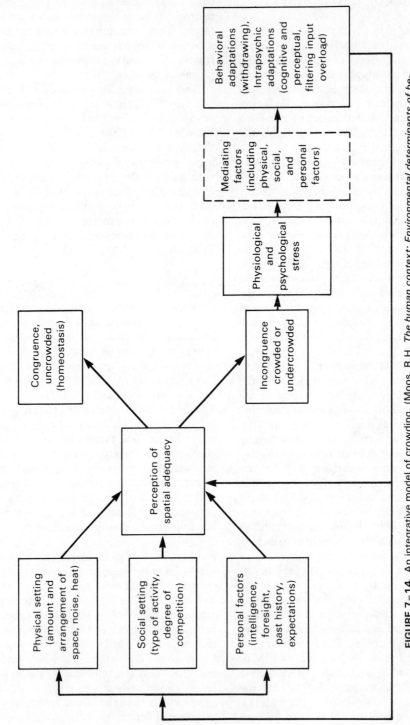

FIGURE 7–14 An integrative model of crowding. (Moos, R.H. *The human context: Environmental determinants of behavior.* New York: Wiley 1976. Reprinted by permission of John Wiley & Sons, Inc.)

room, neighborhood, or community. But all these influences are seen by crowding theorists as examples or instances that illustrate tenets of theories yet to be discussed; none are the central focus of a theory.

One theory does include physical objects as central. This is the ecological approach of Roger Barker (1968) and Allan Wicker (1979). While relying on a different terminology than do most crowding theorists (**overstaffing** being the nearest equivalent term), ecological theorists emphasize resource shortages as a key element of crowding. Physical resources can mean crayons in a preschool, tools in a shop, word processors in an office, or books in a classroom. To control crowding, access to the few available resources must be restricted, leading to lineups, priority rankings, waiting lists, and restriction of entry to the setting. Space itself might be in short supply, in which case overstaffing is similar to high density. But the point is, shortages of space are just one kind of resource shortage that may cause crowding (Fischer, 1976).

The flip side of a resource shortage is, of course, an excess of people. Whether resource shortages or an excess of people is the focus of attention depends on which of the two is more easily altered. If public schools are overcrowded, we do not look for ways to eliminate children, but if a national park is overcrowded, we consider ways of restricting access to it through booking or quota systems. When we view the problem as an excess of people, the distinction between physical and social antecedents of crowding blurs. (Is a crush of people a physical entity or a social entity?) Let's consider it a social factor.

Social. To put it mildly, a leading cause of crowding is too many others around. Two theories focus on *number of people* in the immediate vicinity as a central concept in crowding.

The first is Jonathan Freedman's (1975) density-intensity theory, mentioned briefly earlier. In this approach density is paramount, crowding almost incidental. Listen to Freedman (and bear in mind that his second and third uses of the word crowding in this passage refer to what this chapter calls density—the physical measure):

Some authors have assumed that crowding means stress and have defined it accordingly.

. . . This obviously takes as conclusion what is at issue—how crowding affects people. We are not asking whether crowding is stressful, helpful, or anything else, so we must not assume that it is any of these. Stokols did make the important distinction between physical and psychological crowding, the former referring to the amount of space and the latter to the internal feeling. But he then seems to emphasize the latter, whereas it is mainly the former that must be studied. (Freedman, 1975, p. 155)

With this emphasis on density, Freedman proceeds to assert that density itself is not harmful. It merely *magnifies* whatever else is going on; if that is negative, then density will worsen the situation. High density in prisons has adverse effects not because of the high density itself, but because prison is basically an awful setting. Inmates are there involuntarily; the prison population includes some fundamentally unpleasant people; the architecture and decor are not exactly uplifting.

If, on the other hand, the atmosphere is positive, then density will intensify that instead. Freedman, a champion of urban life, has implied that for the average urban person, density more often magnifies pleasant reactions than unpleasant ones. He even claims that animals are not adversely affected by high density (Freedman, 1979a). But, in the end, his position is that density is *neutral* and the task of social scientists is to specify the conditions under which high density leads to happy or unhappy outcomes. (See Fig. 7–15.)

A second number-of-people approach is that of Eric Knowles (1983), who observes that all density measures ignore the fact that individuals are rarely distributed evenly across a room, neighborhood, or city. The key elements in this **social physics** model are the distances from others to an individual and whether the others form an audience, are merely present, or happen to be a few meters away but on the other side of a wall.

Knowles (1983) and others (Freimark, Wener, Phillips, & Korber, 1984) have presented evidence that a social physics approach does predict observers' rating of settings as crowded or uncrowded. Perceived crowding in these studies is more closely approximated by a logarithmic or

FIGURE 7–15 City life is certainly not all crowding and stress.

other exponential function of density than it is by density itself. These functions, resembling laws developed in another area of psychology called psychophysics, reflect the basic idea that social influence depends on the number and distance of others from the individual (Latane, 1981).

Psychological Processes

The personal, social, and physical antecedents of crowding give rise to stress. At least six stress processes have been described, although considerable similarity among them is apparent. We will organize most of these within two broad processes, **personal control** and **overload.**

Personal Control.   Perhaps the most inclusive of the two processes is personal control. When individuals are crowded, an essential feature of the

experience is that they have lost much of their ability to control what happens to them. The world either becomes unpredictable or predictably undesirable. Traffic jams are a perfect example. You want to get home or to work, but the traffic takes away your ability to control the rate at which you drive. You don't know how long it will take, but you are quite sure it will take longer than you wish. (See Fig. 7–16.)

In their integration of crowding and personal control, Donald Schmidt and John Keating (1979) distinguish between three forms of personal control: cognitive, behavioral, and decisional. They believe that even under high-density conditions, if we are able to attain one or more of these forms of control, crowding stress will be reduced.

We showed earlier how accurate signs and information reduce crowding; this strategy may be successful because it imparts a sense of **cognitive control** to individuals in densely populated areas.

Behavioral control refers to the ability (or lack of it) to act toward a goal. The studies showing that crowding is worse when physical interaction hampers efforts to accomplish a task may be seen as examples of crowding due to lack of behavioral control. When you are enjoying a great game in a packed stadium, you aren't especially crowded. But when the game is over and you move toward your car, the crush of fellow fans greatly reduces your behavioral control.

Decisional control refers to the amount of choice available in a setting. When individuals perceive strong limitations in their options, they are apt to feel crowded. If you enter a theater to see a film and discover that the only remaining seats are behind people wearing large hats, your decisional control is reduced to nil.

Control-based theory may be seen as including or superceding some of the other theories. The **behavioral constraint** (Stokols, 1972) and **behavior interference** (Schopler & Stockdale, 1977) theories developed out of research demonstrating that crowding results when actions are restricted or goals are blocked. However, both formulations are very similar to the behavioral control notion. Another early theory within the control perspective was that crowding represented a loss of freedom of choice (Proshansky, Ittelson, & Rivlin, 1976) and an increase in frustration. Control theory would view this as an example of reduction in decisional control.

Overload. A second major theory of crowding as a psychological process involves the notions of social and informational overload (Cohen, 1978; Milgram, 1970). The idea that densely populated cities are likely to stimulate residents beyond their capacity to process the information may be traced back to Wirth (1938) and Simmel (1957). It

FIGURE 7–16 Sometimes getting to or from the city can be stressful.

is possible to view the overload approach as a branch of the control approach; an overloaded person's behavioral, cognitive, and decisional control is probably impaired (Schmidt & Keating, 1979). However, the overload approach is sufficiently different that it deserves separate treatment. It focuses on the relation between the amount of incoming information as compared to the individual's preferred level of stimulation and current ability to absorb it.

Current ability and preferred level refer to the adaptation-level theory (Helson, 1947) idea that individuals, at different times, adapt to different levels of incoming social and informational stimulation. When that level is exceeded, crowding due to overload is experienced. In general, by concentrating on the match (or mismatch) between actual incoming stimulation and preferred level of stimulation, overload approaches emphasize the cognitive aspects of the crowding process.

Consequences

Once individuals are crowded, perceiving a loss of personal control or a serious overload of information, they respond physiologically, behaviorally, and cognitively. Some of these responses may help to reduce stress, but others are manifestations of the stress. Some responses are more or less immediate, others are delayed. If we can find a way to successfully cope with crowding stress, then some of its negative consequences can be avoided.

Physiological.   We have seen that inescapable high density, such as that experienced in an overpopulated prison, can lead to heightened blood pressure, illness, and other biochemical changes (Cox, Paulus, & McCain, 1984). Cox et al. report that even the ultimate physiological consequence, death, is strongly correlated with population density in a psychiatric facility. If high density has any positive physiological effects, as Freedman's density-intensity theory predicts, they have not yet been demonstrated.

Behavioral.   A wide spectrum of behavioral consequences have been reported. Heightened physiological activity means that even in everyday settings, we walk faster when density is higher (Bowerman, 1973). Overload theory predicts that individuals will try to cope by escaping the setting. Indeed, we have discussed studies showing that residents of densely populated dormitories, especially male residents, simply spend little time in their dormitory.

Another response, less desirable, is the development of **learned helplessness.** The personal control approach in particular predicts that a persistent lack of control teaches individuals that attempting to cope is fruitless. Children who spend much time in overpopulated classrooms may eventually give up attempting to learn (Baron & Rodin, 1978).

Antisocial behavior, ranging from withdrawal to overt aggression, is another possible consequence of crowding. These responses may be primarily associated with deficits in perceived personal control. When our goals are frustrated, constrained, blocked, or interfered with, reactance (Brehm, 1966) is likely to develop. **Reactance** is the tendency to maintain or restore freedom of choice when it is threatened. How reactance is expressed probably depends on our personal history. Prisoners too often find violence a convenient vehicle. Some who are chronically faced with high density merely become stonelike, shutting others out. Others develop devious ways to strike back at whoever or whatever they perceive to be the source of their stress.

Cognitive.   Crowding can be dealt with by changing the way you think about or perceive the world. The overload approach postulates that crowded individuals simply filter out some aspects of life around them. Milgram (1970) suggested that the reason city dwellers sometimes walk past persons who are collapsed on the street is not because they are less kind, but because they are forced to rank-order their social priorities to manage the extremely heavy amount of stimulation they face each day. Unfortunately, there are many needy individuals on the streets of large cities; most individuals could not manage a normal life if they attended to the needs of every needy person they encountered.

▶ **In Sum.** Certain personal, physical, and social antecedents lead to the experience of crowding. Among these are resource shortages (behavior-setting theory) and the number of other people nearby (density-intensity and social-physics theories). Sensory overload and a lack of personal control are psychological processes central to the experience of crowding. The consequences of crowding include physiological, behavioral, and cognitive effects, including learned helplessness and reactance.

CROWDING AND ENVIRONMENTAL DESIGN

Earlier, I described some architectural features that seem to promote or reduce crowding. That discussion was limited to studies of buildings that already possessed certain design features or where building users altered their own space. Deliberate alterations of existing buildings to ease crowding through architectural design were not covered. This section is specifically devoted to interventions by architects or environmental psychologists, including residences, public areas, wilderness parks, and prisons.

When crowding is the problem, the obvious design solution is to provide more space. But there are two problems with this commonsense solution. First, economic considerations do not always favor creating more space. Second, as we have seen, crowding is not always the result of high density. We shall see that certain *arrangements* of space can also be effective antidotes to crowding. In some cases, optimal arrangements may even be *better* solutions to crowding than simply providing more space.

Residences

High density in any primary environment is likely to be a problem. We spend much time in primary environments, engage in some of our most important activities in them, and interact in them with those who are most important to us. Home is our most important primary environment. I am aware of no study that reports positive effects of high density in the home. Can anything be done when in-home density is unavoidably high?

Most studies of residential crowding as an experience or as an interpersonal process have been conducted in dormitories. A few of these examine the effect of actually changing some aspect of the dormitory to see if crowding is ameliorated. In one such attempt, Andrew Baum and Glenn Davis (1980) followed up on a suggestion (Freedman, 1979b) that where corridors are long, crowding might be reduced by shortening them. Baum and Davis' architectural intervention was quite simple. They arranged for a wall and double doors to be installed in the middle of a long dormitory corridor. After several weeks, residents on the divided-corridor floor felt significantly less crowded than did residents of a similar floor that remained undivided. Even though the double doors were not locked, the division of the floor into two halves seems to have reduced overload, encouraged separate use of public facilities (such as bathrooms) by the two groups of residents, and assisted in friendship formation.

Others have offered a variety of possible interventions. Gary Evans (1979b) suggests that crowding could be lessened if, even in a four-bare-walls setting, residents were given some way to divide up the space. Even partitions or light movable walls, though not soundproof, at least restrict visual surveillance among individuals who are forced to share a room. They may, therefore, reduce sensory overload and improve their sense of control. Sometimes full control over a small space is preferable to shared control over a larger space. Second, Evans says, the freedom to personalize primary space can impart a sense of control that, in turn, can reduce the amount of crowding individuals experience.

Amos Rapoport (1975), following his notion of perceived density, suggests that some designs (stark high-rise apartment blocks) look as if they are chock-full of people when alternative designs could give the appearance of lower density. Low rises of equal density (measured at ground level) would cover more ground, but if they were intermixed with such nonresidential settings as shops, libraries, or neighborhood pubs, they would *seem* to have lower density.

Public Areas

Crowding in secondary areas has also been alleviated by design interventions. We already discussed how the mere addition of signs to a prison-visitor waiting room lessened crowding. In the same study, behavioral changes were also observed. Visitors completed forms faster and made fewer navigational errors in the lobby (Wener & Kaminoff, 1983). Other studies have examined whether low partitions or other people-separating devices might reduce crowding in public areas.

In an early study of scale-model rooms (Desor, 1972), partitions did seem to reduce crowding. But does this apply in the real world? In a densely populated waiting area of a government motor vehicle office, partitions actually increased crowding by a slight amount (Stokols, Smith, & Proster, 1975). This unexpected result may have occurred because those waiting in line felt as if they were being herded.

If the overload approach is correct, public areas that are highly complex should elicit more crowding than simple ones. One explicit test of this hypothesis, using model rooms, supports it (Baum & Davis, 1976) at least in the case of waiting rooms, particularly waiting rooms that are both visually complex and relatively dark. However, the effects of both partitions and complexity on crowding in everday settings need more research before definite conclusions may be drawn.

Wilderness Parks

Many wilderness areas have become popular spots for camping and other outdoor activities. This has become so prevalent in parks that combine great beauty with proximity to large cities that parts of them have essentially been converted into full-scale towns. Crowding may occur in the urbanized entry areas of parks and in the areas reserved for camping and related activities.

Allan Wicker (1979) describes attempts made by himself and his colleagues to deal with crowding and other problems at bus stops in the urbanized part of Yosemite National Park in California. The bus was set up by park managers to reduce traffic in the rest of the park. It transports passengers to campgrounds, trail heads, stores, motels, and other places in the park.

Youthful zest seemed to encourage not only frequent use of the free service but also some undesirable ways of using the bus, such as running on board and pushing (the patrons also entered through windows, shouted, drank, and hung out the windows). To curb some of the disorderly activity, a post-and-chain queuing device was installed at the bus stop. It wasn't pretty, but behavioral observations demonstrated that it did reduce running and pushing and increase the orderliness of boarding. Unfortunately, this change

was not perceived by bus drivers; in fact they believed no change had occurred. Passengers, at least initially, didn't like it. Before the results of the behavioral observations could even be tabulated, park authorities decided the queuing device was inappropriate for a national park, and they tore it out.

In the back areas of parks, there are also problems with too many campers. The standard approach of park managers to high density in campgrounds is to restrict entry. However, the number of campers may not be as important as their activities (West, 1982). Campers have a variety of different purposes: some hope for a pure wilderness experience, some for a chance to be with their children in an outdoor setting, and others see an opportunity for a great party. Crowding in campgrounds may be due more to the unfortunate proximity of campers with incompatible goals than an overall shortage of space. West proposes **behavioral zoning** in parks so that campers with similar values and activities will find themselves in compatible company. The national park equivalent of smoking and nonsmoking zones might include party zones, family zones, and wilderness-isolation zones. Overall park density would be about the same, but crowding might well be less.

Prisons

Prisons are unpleasant; densely populated prisons are worse in every way that anyone has so far studied, including more suicide, aggression, death, illness, and rule violation (Cox, Paulus, & McCain, 1984). Increasing space in prisons can be extremely expensive. When more individuals are convicted and sentencing is tougher, prison populations increase at the same time that public interest in providing more space is at a low ebb. (See Fig. 7–17.)

Nevertheless, a few environmental psychologists have examined the effects of spatial arrangements in prisons, trying to find those with the least negative impact. Verne Cox, Paul Paulus, and Garvin McCain have compared the responses of inmates to quite a range of spatial densities and found few ill-effects. Whether an inmate has 5 or 10 square meters to himself seems to matter little.

On the other hand, varying social density is

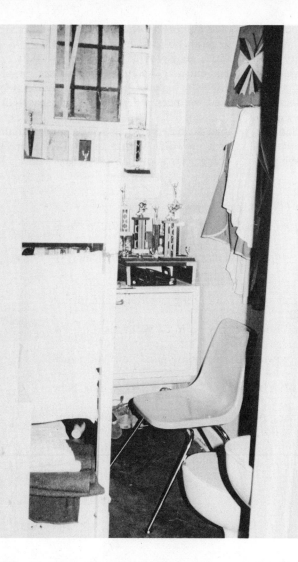

FIGURE 7-17 Perhaps the worst high-density living in North America occurs in prisons. *(Courtesy of Paul Paulus).*

quite different. When the number of inmates per cell rises, so does crowding and the incidence of illness complaints. Double-inmate cells are associated with more rule violations than single-inmate cells. Larger, open dormitories seem to produce psychological disturbances more often than do single-inmate cells.

Cox et al. conclude that the best alternative for high-density prisons is to provide single-inmate cells (even if they contain only 5 square meters) rather than house prisoners together in groups. They report studies indicating that simple cubicles placed in otherwise open dormitory space are beneficial to prisoners. Mere cubicles may not be as desirable as completely separate cells, but they seem to provide enough personal control among inmates to be superior to open dormitories.

SUMMARY

Crowding is an experience that is only mildly related to high density, a physical index. Aggregate and laboratory approaches to its investigation have their places as research methods, but field studies may be the best overall method. The experience of crowding is accentuated by personal factors (personality, expectations, sex), social factors (number and actions of others, quality of relationships), and physical factors (architectural arrangements). Prolonged high indoor density often impairs health, performance, and social interaction. Individuals and cultures attempt to cope with it, but sensory overload and lack of personal control lead to many negative outcomes. Short-term high density indoors may have positive outcomes when social and physical conditions are positive; high outdoor density, as in large cities, may provide an enjoyable variety of social and cultural experiences. To reduce the negative effects of high density through environmental design, we need not provide more space (although that can help). Rather, careful environmental design (such as partitions and behavioral zoning) can ease crowding within the limited space that is characteristic of many settings.

SUGGESTED SUPPLEMENTARY READINGS

Aiello, J. R., & Baum, A. (Eds.). (1979). *Residential crowding and design.* New York: Plenum.

Baum, A., & Epstein, Y. M. (Eds.). (1978). *Human response to crowding.* Hillsdale, NJ: Erlbaum.

Cox, V. C., Paulus, P. B., & McCain, G. (1984). Prison crowding research: The relevance of prison housing standards and a general approach regarding crowding phenomena. *American Psychologist, 39,* 1148–1160.

Epstein, Y. M. (1982). Crowding stress and human behavior. In G. W. Evans (Ed.), *Environmental stress.* New York: Cambridge University Press.

Gove, W. R., & Hughes, M. (1983). *Overcrowding in the household.* New York: Academic Press.

Gurkaynak, M. R., & LeCompte, W. A. (1979). *Human consequences of crowding.* New York: Plenum.

Knowles, E. (1979). The proximity of others: A critique of crowding research and integration with the social sciences. *Journal of Population, 1979, 2,* 3–17.

Schmidt, D. E., & Keating, J. P. (1979). Human crowding and personal control: An integration of the research. *Psychological Bulletin, 86,* 680–700.

Chapter Eight
Privacy

*. . . each individual must . . . make a continuous
adjustment between his needs for solitude
and companionship. . . .*
Alan F. Westin, 1967

There was a knock at the door. After scrutinizing her visitor through the peephole and deciding that the plump matronly woman was not threatening, Jane answered the door. She found that her friendly neighborhood census taker wanted to ask her a few questions. "Well, I guess that would be OK," Jane said hesitantly. After a few standard questions, the census taker started asking strange things, like how many bathrooms were in the house and what Jane's income was. The questions became increasingly personal, Jane thought, and finally she refused to answer. The census taker smiled, said that answering the questions was mandatory, and left, saying that her supervisor would return later to obtain the answers.

Just as Jane closed the door, the phone rang. It was that nerd from her Biology class, bugging her again about going out. He didn't seem to get the message when she politely refused, so she bluntly told him never to call again. The phone rang again immediately. "Phones!" Jane fumed to herself. "I wish you could tell who's calling." Gingerly picking up the receiver, certain it was the nerd again, she said, "Hello?"

When she heard Tom's familiar voice asking her if she'd like to try the new Japanese restaurant, she was relieved. "I'm really sorry about the Zanzibar Club, Jane," he said. "Sometimes I just can't take all that noise. Over dinner, I'd like to talk about some of the apartments I've been looking at for us," he said. "Seems like we have to choose between enough space to stretch out in and going to school next year. I don't see how we can afford both." Jane felt apprehensive again. "I guess we've never really taken a look at how much space we need or, in this case, how little space our relationship can survive," she said.

Seated on the mats in their little room in the Japanese restaurant, Tom and Jane tried to talk about it, but there were two problems. For one thing, there seemed to be many more interesting and easy things to talk about. For another, that Biology nerd had somehow landed not only in the same restaurant but in the next room. They were able to prevent his leering looks by closing the curtains, but he was laughing and talking so loudly with his friends that Tom and Jane could hardly carry on a conversation.

Privacy, like personal space, is a process that is at once an extremely important dimension of our daily lives, yet one we often manage at a low level of awareness. To accomplish our privacy goals, we must be skilled at balancing our own desires, those of others, and the physical environment.

To many people, privacy means one of two things. One of these is being apart from other people. The other is being sure that other individuals or organizations do not have access to certain information about them. These two everyday meanings represent only part of the meaning of privacy. For example, one prominent view of privacy in environmental psychology is that privacy processes sometimes lead individuals to seek *more* social interaction.

Privacy is addressed not only by psychologists but also by political scientists, sociologists, anthropologists, and lawyers, reflecting its social, cultural, and legal aspects. Privacy is manifested in our behavior, beliefs, values, and expectations. It is facilitated and eroded by the physical design of our homes, workplaces, schools, public places, and institutions. Invasions of privacy occur when someone physically intrudes on us or when someone collects information about us that we do not want them to have.

Some of us need more privacy than others; some of us need different *kinds* of privacy; all of us need more privacy at certain times and less at others. Privacy is closely tied to territoriality, crowding, and personal space. It is even related to how we speak, to our nonverbal behavior, and to our developmental processes. It is intimately involved with other important psychological processes, including emotion, identity, and our sense of control.

All of these facets of privacy are interesting in their own right, but understanding privacy serves a larger purpose: assisting in the design of better built environments. We cannot accomplish this goal without knowing how to measure privacy, what personal and situational factors influence it, and how privacy is related to other behavior processes. We must also have useful models of privacy's workings. After surveying what is known about these facets of privacy, this chapter concludes with a section on the most important privacy issue: how to optimize it through environmental design.

WHAT IS PRIVACY?

We have seen that privacy means many things to many people. Any attempt to define it precisely risks excluding some important aspects of privacy; overly broad definitions risk meaninglessness. Probably the best definition of privacy yet developed is one by Irwin Altman. Privacy, he says, is "selective control of access to the self or to one's group" (1975, p. 18). (See Fig. 8–1.)

FIGURE 8–2 Being alone is just one form of privacy. *(Courtesy of Coe Gifford.)*

FIGURE 8–1 Irwin Altman is one of the pioneers of environmental psychology and his ideas on privacy as a central organizing function for social behavior are central to the environmental psychology of social behavior. *(Courtesy of Irwin Altman.)*

Altman's definition captures the essence of privacy—the twin themes of **management of information** about oneself and the **management of social interaction.** That is, "access to self" may refer either to information about oneself or to social interaction with oneself.

Altman's definition also has room for other dimensions of privacy. One involves the number of individuals encompassed. We normally think of *individuals* seeking privacy, but as Westin (1967) has pointed out, we sometimes seek to be alone with one or more selected others. Everyone dreams of being alone in a favorite spot with that special someone; the *two* of you are seeking privacy at that point. At other times, classmates, businesspeople, or football players huddle together in groups, excluding others. That is why Altman's definition includes one's group. (See Fig. 8–2.)

The words "access to self" also cloak a range of sensory avenues. For example, a head of state may stand on a prominent balcony so that citizens have visual access, yet no individual citizen may be granted an audience. You may seek privacy by going into your room to study but be bothered by music or conversation produced by others. Many others grant us both visual and acoustic access to them (as in a conversation) yet not allow us to touch them. Office employees in open-plan offices often have visual privacy but complain that their acoustic privacy is poor.

On the other hand, as Altman (1975) points out, even a stripper who is past her last G-string on stage may yet have considerable privacy. Her body has absolutely none, it is true. But if she successfully adopts a blank, closed expression, she manages to control access to a more important part of herself. She is denying the customers access to her thoughts, her interests, and any shred of social involvement. This is an extreme example, but it illustrates one complexity of privacy. Some channels of communication may be open while others are not.

The notion of open and closed channels leads us to a final observation on Altman's definition. "Selective control" implies that access may be *granted* as well as denied; privacy is not merely shutting out others. It often includes enjoying social interaction and gladly sharing information about yourself with others. The key word is *control*. A person who is fully enriched with privacy is not necessarily a hermit or recluse, but one who is able to find either companionship or solitude more or less at will (social interaction management); a person who, similarly, is able to either share or halt the flow of self-related information (information management).

MEASURING PRIVACY

Those who would measure privacy well must carefully consider its complex definition. To be comprehensive, the measure should include both the social and the informational themes, acknowledge that pairs and larger groups may seek privacy as well as individuals, note that privacy may vary across the various communication channels as well as over time, and recognize that privacy-seeking may actually lead an individual to search for a party to attend. (See Fig. 8–3.)

Privacy may be measured as a behavior, as a belief, as a value, as a preference, and as an expectation. Carol Weinstein (1982b) erected some

FIGURE 8–3 Sharing important events with others, such as birthday parties, is part of the privacy process, too.

"privacy booths" in an elementary school classroom and observed the children's actual use of and behavior in the booths. Others have examined individuals' privacy *preferences*. In one study, the privacy preferences of dormitory residents were affected by crowded living conditions (Walden, Nelson, & Smith, 1981). The privacy *values* in question are often those of others toward our privacy. Gary Melton (1983) claims that many adults do not believe adolescents are sufficiently developed as persons to warrant privacy; that is, adults often do not value adolescents' privacy. Finally, independent of our privacy preferences, behaviors, and values, we may have high or low *expectations* for privacy. Prisoners, for example, have very little privacy. When they move to new facilities, though, even prisoners may expect an increase in privacy (Smith, 1982).

No comprehensive measure of privacy has yet been developed. Most privacy investigations have actually studied *perceived* privacy, using surveys, questionnaires, or interviews. After all, in order to study privacy behavior by field observation, the investigator is almost forced to violate the subject's privacy! The few naturalistic observations of privacy focus on schools, other institutions, or offices, where either age or location of the subjects decrease the likelihood that sensitive areas of behavior will be under surveillance. Subjects' self-reports of their privacy behaviors, values, preferences, and expectations form the foundation of psychological research into privacy.

Questionnaire measures of privacy are often based on the pioneering typology of Alan Westin (1967). Westin reasoned that privacy has four faces: solitude, intimacy, anonymity, and reserve. **Solitude** is the popular but limited notion of privacy: being alone. **Intimacy** refers to group privacy, as when a pair of lovers wish to be alone together. **Anonymity** suggests the times when individuals wish to be among others and to interact as one person among many but do not want to be personally identified or held accountable in their own names. For example, kings and presidents occasionally desire to walk among their people, as just another person, to see what normal life is like. Ordinary individuals, too, sometimes desire anonymity. Do you ever go to a shopping center to absorb and be a part of the bustling atmosphere without wanting to interact on personal basis with anyone?

The last form of privacy in Westin's typology is **reserve,** the creation of a psychological barrier against intrusion. In public or in private, reserve means that you wish to limit communication about yourself to others. The form and extent of this reserve varies, of course, but it is facilitated when the others around you respect your limits.

The first large-scale attempt to create an instrument for measuring privacy was made by Nancy Marshall (1972). In analyzing a pool of eighty-six privacy items, she found six groups of them, or factors, that are strongly reminiscent of Westin's typology: anonymity, reserve, solitude, intimacy, seclusion, and "not neighboring." Only the last two factors are different from Westin's, and the differences are more like embellishments than new kinds of privacy. **Seclusion** refers to living out of sight and sound of traffic and others. **Not neighboring** means disliking neighbors who casually drop in and generally not desiring much contact with neighbors.

Another privacy measuring instrument, developed independently and more recently, also confirms Westin's basic typology (Pedersen, 1979, 1982). Besides the original four factors, Pedersen's results suggest adding another (isolation) and splitting intimacy into two kinds: intimacy with family and intimacy with friends. **Isolation** is similar to solitude in that you wish to be alone. However, Pedersen's work indicates that isolation implies aloneness *far away* from others (such as living in the woods), whereas solitude implies aloneness in the midst of others (such as being alone in your room while others are around the house).

► **In Sum.** Empirically derived questionnaire measures support Westin's speculations about the varieties of privacy and add several others. Privacy may be considered as a preference, expectation, value, and behavior. Measurement of privacy through naturalistic observation of behavior is rare. Privacy measurement is well-developed in the area of questionnaires, but few methods are available for studying privacy as it actually unfolds.

INFLUENCES ON PRIVACY

Differences in privacy behavior, beliefs, values, preferences, and expectations originate with differences in personal characteristics and differences in situations. Some of us, because of our culture, personality, or other characteristics, require more privacy or express our privacy needs differently from others. Some situations, regardless of who is in them, engender greater or lesser privacy needs. First we will examine personal factors.

Personal Influences

Demography. Differences in a person's background are related to privacy needs. Marshall (1972) found that individuals who grew up in homes they felt were crowded prefer more anonymity and reserve as adults. Those who had spent more time in cities preferred more anonymity and intimacy. Wanderers (those who are farther from the place where they grew up) prefer less intimacy, as you might predict of individuals who found a reason to leave their families and friends behind.

There are also sex differences in privacy. In a study of dormitory residents (Walden, Nelson, & Smith, 1981), men and women responded differently to two-person and three-person room arrangements. Men assigned to two-person rooms increased their preferences for all forms of privacy (compared to their preferences before they moved into the dorms), but men assigned to three-person rooms actually decreased their preference for solitude (their preferences for other forms of privacy were unchanged). Why would men assigned to two-person rooms begin to prefer more privacy if those assigned to three-person rooms do not? The researchers discovered that men in three-person rooms stayed away from their residences more. Apparently, men in three-person rooms coped with the higher density by deciding they really didn't want to be alone so much after all (thus bringing preferences into closer agreement with reality) and by avoiding their rooms more. (See Fig. 8–4.)

Women, on the other hand, did not show changes in preference for privacy when they were assigned to two-person or to three-person rooms. They also spent as much or more time in the three-person rooms as in the two-person rooms. This suggests that women respond to high-density living arrangements more favorably than men—a finding that crowding researchers have confirmed. We need not conclude that women do value privacy less than men. Women may enjoy the company of others more and, when asked to live in higher-density situations, may have more privacy-regulating mechanisms *within* the social context. In contrast, men seem to cope by adjusting the value they place on privacy and by escaping the social context if they can.

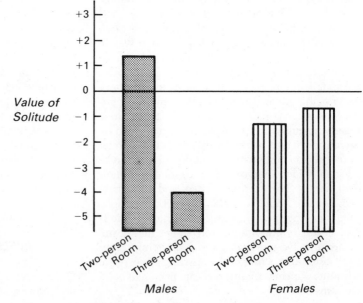

FIGURE 8–4 In higher social density dormitory rooms, male students placed *less* value on solitude. See text for a possible reason for this finding. *(Adapted from Walden, Nelson, & Smith, 1981.)*

SOCIAL PROCESSES

Another study of dormitory living supports this idea (Rubin & Shenker, 1978). This study focused on informational privacy. Women told roommates more about interpersonal matters than men did, and friendship among women is more closely tied to intimate disclosure than it is among men. As Rubin and Shenker put it, their results are consistent with the image of women as "social-emotional specialists."

A study of nursing home residents found that women had a greater preference than men for environments that allowed for controlled disclosure; that is, being able to speak confidentially (Firestone, Lichtman, & Evans, 1980). This finding could be interpreted as further support for the social-emotional image (women prefer to "target" their disclosures, but men spray them indiscriminately) or against it (by old age, women seek to disclose less than men). This issue is not yet resolved, but these studies give a flavor of the differences between the sexes in privacy preferences and behaviors.

Personality. Psychologists who have investigated the relations between privacy and behavioral dispositions have generally emphasized the social "closing-off" side of privacy, rather than its "opening-up" side. George McKechnie (1974) investigated the relation between need for privacy and personality. Those with higher needs for privacy had a lower sense of well-being, less ego strength, and experienced more anxiety. Marshall (1972) reports that individuals who felt they did not have enough privacy were more "distractable."

A decade later, Darhl Pedersen (1982) took a closer look, examining the relations between personality and the various dimensions of privacy. The results confirm the general picture painted by McKechnie, but are more specific. Those who are more reserved and those who seek more solitude and anonymity tend to have lower self-esteem. Illustrating the usefulness of the distinctions between types of privacy, Pedersen found that introspective individuals are *more* likely to be reserved but *less* likely to seek intimacy with their family.

Situational Influences

Personal characteristics influence privacy, but so does each situation we find ourselves in. If you have just returned home from a night on the town with your beloved, you will probably want more privacy than if you are going to discuss this weekend's big game with some friends. If you are discussing your finances with a bank manager, you probably want more privacy than if you were responding to a questionnaire on your attitudes

FIGURE 8-5 Privacy in traditional (walled) and unconventional open-plan (partitioned) offices. Employees of a large corporation who were moved to new offices rated their privacy before and after relocation. *Level 1* employees shared space at both locations. *Level 2* employees moved from a traditional office shared with one person to an individual enclosure with 60-inch high partitions. *Level 3* and *4* employees moved from traditional offices with doors to doorless individual enclosures with 60-inch and 78-inch high partitions, respectively. *(Sundstrom, E., Herbert, R.K., & Brown, D. W. (1982). Privacy and communication in an open-plan office: A case study.* Environment and Behavior, *14, 379–392. Copyright © 1982 by* Environment and Behavior. *Reprinted by permission of Sage Publications, Inc.)*

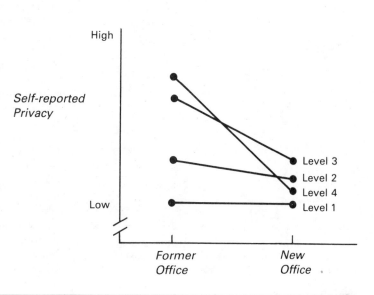

toward campus architecture. In general, our preferences for and satisfactions with privacy vary with the situation (Foddy & Finighan, 1980), that is, the physical setting or the social atmosphere.

The Physical Setting. What about the environment itself might lead an individual to have greater privacy preferences or lower satisfaction with privacy?

Eric Sundstrom and his associates have found that *satisfaction* with privacy at work is related to the degree of physical enclosure you are allowed. In their study of office workers who changed offices, they found that employees who left walled offices for open-plan offices reported a significant decline in privacy (Sundstrom, Herbert, & Brown, 1982). (See Figs. 8–5 and 8–6.) In another study of office workers, the best predictor of satisfaction with privacy was simply the number of partitions around the employee's workstation (Sundstrom, Town, Brown, Forman, &

FIGURE 8-6 Eric Sundstrom's conceptual and empirical work has enriched the study of human spatial behavior. *(Courtesy of Eric Sundstrom.)*

McGee, 1982). In general, these studies suggest that satisfaction with privacy is, as might be expected, a function of how much the environment allows us to be alone.

Nancy Marshall (1972) examined the relation between privacy preferences and the environment. In her study of single-family dwelling residents, she found evidence that sharing a residence with more people was correlated with a preference for less privacy. Marshall speculates that her subjects, who were college students and their parents, had adapted to relatively high density, so that they preferred less privacy than did residents of less dense households. However, Marshall's subjects were upper middle class individuals; few of them were very crowded.

Marshall also found that residents of houses with open plans (where more rooms are visually open to one another) preferred less privacy. At work, then, open spaces are associated with dissatisfaction with privacy, but at home open spaces are associated with preferences for less privacy. It is not clear whether these apparent discrepancies are due to locale (work versus home) or to satisfaction with privacy versus preference for privacy. At work, we might prefer more closed spaces because co-workers are not always our favorite companions, but at home open spaces shared with family or friends are more welcome. On the other hand, privacy preferences and privacy satisfaction are different. One aspect is concerned with how *much* social interaction an individual desires (whether or not that desire is met); the other is concerned with how well the individual's desires are met (regardless of how much privacy is desired). These issues remain to be sorted out, but as a whole this research suggests that physical setting (and who shares that setting with you) are important influences on privacy.

Other environmental factors are related to privacy in the home setting. For example, as you might expect, persons whose home insulates quiet activities from noisy ones are more likely to be satisfied with their privacy than those whose home fails to separate noisy activities from quiet ones. In addition, someone who is far from neighbors and cannot see very many other houses from the windows is more likely to be satisfied with privacy (Marshall, 1972).

Some research focuses on the different dimensions of privacy (intimacy, solitude, etc.) rather than treating privacy as a global, unified process. Marshall's work itself demonstrates how the environment affects some privacy dimensions differently from others. She found that those who live in less spacious surroundings generally prefer less privacy, but this finding did not always hold. When many houses were visible from their windows (suggesting a high-density neighborhood), Marshall's subjects tended to prefer less seclusion—a result that is consistent with her general findings. However, they also tended to prefer *more* of another privacy dimension, reserve. Clearly, privacy should not be considered a unitary phenomenon.

Each kind of privacy, then, may be influenced differently by the environment. Sometimes, however, settings are so discrepant in their opportunities for privacy that their inhabitants' views are different for all types of privacy. This is illustrated by a study of privacy in a nursing home (Firestone, Lichtman, & Evans, 1980), in which the preferences of residents who lived in open wards was compared with those of residents who lived in private rooms. Private room residents desired more privacy of all three kinds studied (more isolation, less solidarity, and less disclosure) than ward residents did. As in Marshall's study of single-family dwellings, it seems that individuals adapt to their surroundings.

An important and unresolved design question is implicit here. Assuming individuals *can* adapt to settings with apparently low levels of privacy, such as wards, is this a healthy adaptation or an unhealthy one? If it is healthy, or at least not particularly harmful, designers could save space by designing more nonprivate areas. But if residents in the Firestone et al. study expressed satisfaction out of a sense of fatalism, and if privacy is important for resident welfare, then more private spaces should be built.

The mention of fatalism brings us to another aspect of privacy. So far we have been concerned, for the most part, with *satisfaction*, the difference between how much privacy an individual believes is available in the present setting and how much privacy the individual prefers. An aspect of privacy mentioned earlier, however, is the individual's *expectation* of privacy (Walden, Nelson, & Smith, 1981). In some settings, we may desire more privacy and expect that we can somehow obtain it. Those of us who do not reside in institutions often are able to select from a range of settings to suit our current privacy needs. In other settings, individuals may desire more solitude or anonymity but be forced to recognize that no more is forthcoming and become fatalistic.

Prisoners, for example, are often subjected to low levels of privacy. Dale Smith (1982) studied both the privacy preferences and the privacy expectations of prisoners who were moved from an old facility to a new one. The old jail housed four inmates in each 6-square-meter (64-square-foot) cell. The new jail offered a 6-square-meter cell to each inmate. Smith found that privacy preferences changed little after the move, but that expectancies for some types of privacy (solitude and intimacy) rose significantly.

Because the prisoners had preferred more solitude and intimacy than they expected in the old jail and expected about as much as they preferred in the new jail, we can guess that they were more satisfied with their new jail. It is hardly astonishing, of course, that people are happier when space quadruples from 1.5 square meters per person to 6 square meters per person, but the study demonstrates that expectancy is an important component of the privacy process.

Another study reveals that expectancy does not always operate as it did in the prison study. Investigating the response of dormitory residents to different room densities (two per room versus three per room), Walden, Nelson, & Smith (1981) found that expectancy was the same for both densities. Of course, there are important differences between the lives of college students and prisoners. Chief among these are the freedom to satisfy our privacy or social interaction needs in many more settings, and the amount of space per person. Expectancies may have changed in the prison but not in the dormitory because students have many more opportunities to achieve privacy than do prisoners.

The Social Situation. The emphasis of research discussed so far has been on privacy's social theme—how physical settings affect the individual's management of interpersonal contact. In principle, both the physical setting and the social situation may influence both social privacy and informational privacy. However, most research on the social theme has investigated the effect of the physical setting and most research on the information theme has investigated the social situation. Therefore, we turn now to the informational theme of privacy—how the individual's management of information relevant to self is affected by the social situation.

What is meant here by "social situation"? Some considerations are: which person or organization is asking for private information, what will be done with the information, what kind of personal information is sought, and what social consequences will follow should the information become widely known.

Eugene Stone and his associates interviewed individuals about their experiences, intentions, beliefs, and values concerning informational privacy (Stone, Gueutal, Gardner, & McClure, 1983). The participants' responses depended on the kind of organization seeking information from them—their employer, a lending institution, a law enforcement agency, credit grantors, insurance companies, or a taxation agency. For example, which organizations (if any) *should* be allowed to collect, store, use, and disseminate information about you? According to the Stone study, many believe lenders should be allowed to do so more than law enforcement agencies. Which organizations actually *do* collect, store, use, and disseminate information about us? Employers, participants in the study believed, do so much more than credit-granting agencies. (See Fig. 8–7.)

When is informational privacy invaded and when isn't it? Over 2000 employees in several corporations were presented with a hypothetical situation in which an employee was applying for

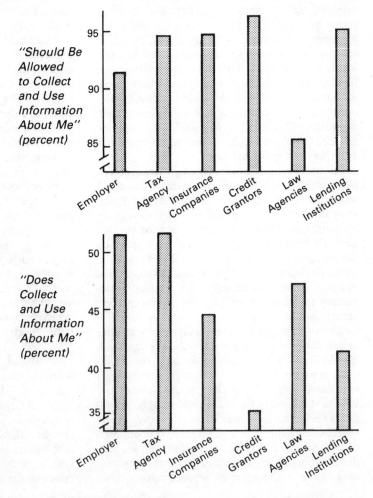

FIGURE 8–7 Values ("Who should . . . ") and beliefs ("Who does . . . ") about informational privacy. Note the discrepancies between values and beliefs for different types of organizations. (Adapted from Stone, Gueutal, Gardner, & McClure, 1983.)

SOCIAL PROCESSES

promotion and queried more broadly about informational privacy at work (Tolchinsky et al., 1981; Woodman et al., 1982). The employees felt their privacy was compromised more if the information

Concerned their personality rather than their performance
Was obtained without their permission rather than with their permission
Was disclosed to outsiders instead of insiders
Had negative rather than positive consequences for them
Seemed irrelevant for the purpose it was requested.

A consistent undercurrent in these studies is the individual's concern with *control* of information about self. Consider, for example, the Tolchinsky et al. study in which privacy is believed to be compromised more when information is obtained about personality (over which we have little control) than when it is obtained about performance (over which we have more control), when we don't give permission for it to be collected, and when it is given to outsiders (who may speed the spread of the information beyond our control). This concern with control was confirmed by Fusilier and Hoyer (1980), whose subjects also read an employment application scenario. As in the Tolchinsky et al. study, a key factor in whether the subjects believed their privacy was invaded was whether they granted permission for the information to be collected.

Only a few studies have investigated physical setting influences on informational privacy. The emphasis in these information-oriented studies is on self-disclosure, how much self-related information one person chooses to tell another. For example, "soft" rooms, furnished with cushioned chairs, rugs, wall decorations, and incandescent lighting, have been found to elicit more intimate self-disclosure than "hard" rooms with bare floors and walls, hard chairs, and fluorescent lighting (Chaikin, Derlega, & Miller, 1976).

Of course, the social and informational sides of privacy are linked. This link is demonstrated in Rubin and Shenker's (1978) study of dormitory roommates. Students who had lived in a residence hall for 4 months together were asked how much they had disclosed to others who lived on their floor. Roommates disclosed more about themselves to each other than did students who merely lived on the same floor. Assuming that roommates share space more than hallmates, the study indicates that less privacy in the shared-space sense leads to less privacy in the sense of information sharing.

Cultural Influences

Do individuals from different cultures require the same amount of privacy, or do some cultures desire more than others? First, there is no doubt that different societies appear to vary widely in the amount of privacy that members actually have. In some Arab societies, families want to live in houses with high solid walls around them. Elsewhere, housing patterns can be quite different. I lived for a short while in a fishing village in southern India where all the families had grass huts very close to each other, so that very little privacy was available. The villagers did not seem to desire more separation from their neighbors.

A number of studies have shown, however, that superficial appearances are deceiving. Both desired privacy and achieved privacy may be as high in the Indian society as in the Arab society.

This is illustrated in a study of privacy among the Iban society of Sarawak, in Borneo (Patterson & Chiswick, 1981). The Iban live in longhouses with very little privacy in the First World sense of the term—opportunity for solitude or intimacy behind closed doors. (See Fig. 8–8.) Are the Iban desperate for privacy, or do they not desire as much privacy as individuals in developed countries? Patterson and Chiswick found that the Iban seem to need about as much privacy as we do, but they achieve it through different mechanisms. These mechanisms are largely *social* conventions instead of the physical means we rely on. For example, the Iban have special maneuvers for changing clothes in public that preserve their modesty; there are rules against criticizing others' children, which helps to keep disputes among adults to a minimum; the longhouse is closed to outsiders on many occasions; and beginning at puberty the sexes use separate sleeping areas.

The highly mobile Gypsy society is also short of physical means for privacy and has developed the following rule, among others, to allow members privacy (Yoors, 1967). On rising each morn-

FIGURE 8-8 Privacy mechanisms in other cultures, such as this Borneo longhouse, are different from those in Western countries. *(Courtesy of Arthur Patterson.)*

ing from sleeping around the campsite, Gypsies decide when to wash their faces. If you feel grumpy, need some time to think, or just want to be alone, you simply do not wash your face. Others would not be so rude as to interrupt this self-imposed social isolation until those seeking privacy had washed their faces.

Jan Yoors, who lived with Gypsies for 10 years, found they had a different view of privacy from the Gaje (the non-Gypsy). Gypsies recognize privacy as a two-way concept. You do not pry by watching others change their clothes or perform the "functions of nature," as Yoors calls them. Also, however, an onus is on the person seeking privacy to avoid places and times where others could not possibly avoid observing these private activities.

A wise old Gypsy woman declared that privacy is a state of mind. To the Rom (the name Gypsies have for themselves), the Gaje's practice of building walls and doors is both an insult to others, suggesting they would not respect your privacy by looking away or never mentioning an accidental breach of privacy, and at the same time an enticement or challenge to pry, spy, or peep on someone so distrusting that they hide behind closed doors. Privacy, therefore, is a state of mind

because it involves courtesy, tactfulness, restraint, and respect in managing an unwalled life.

These findings and others support Altman's (1975) view that cultures are not different in the amount of privacy they desire, but they vary considerably in how they achieve that privacy.

► **In Sum.** Privacy preferences, expectations, and satisfaction are influenced by personal characteristics, by physical setting and social situation characteristics, and by culture. City-raised individuals prefer more anonymity and intimacy. Women seem to manage privacy in close groups by discussing more interpersonal and intimate matters and men often achieve privacy by removing themselves from the setting and talking less about delicate matters. Personality studies suggest that individuals who have greater-than-average privacy needs are less sure of themselves and more anxious.

The physical setting has important effects on privacy preferences, expectations, and satisfaction. For example, open space at work often breeds dissatisfaction while at home it is preferred. These influences are both close, like the doors and partitions surrounding us, and less immediate, like the distance between houses and the number of neighbors visible from one's house. Researchers have not yet sorted out the differences in preference for, satisfaction with, or expectation of privacy among home, work, and institutional settings, but they do know that privacy attitudes and behaviors vary from setting to setting.

Informational privacy is primarily affected by who wants the information from us, what information they want, and how they attempt to obtain it. Perceived informational privacy sometimes differs from actual informational privacy. Some privacy fears could be reduced if employees gave informed consent to the gathering of information about them. Members of different cultures are believed to have similar privacy needs but, depending on how the environment supports those needs, may use different means of achieving privacy. Next we explore how privacy is connected to other important psychological processes.

PRIVACY AND HUMAN BEHAVIOR

We have seen that privacy is influenced by personal and situational factors. In the course of human activity, it is also inextricably linked with other important behavior processes. Once again we are indebted to Westin (1967) for describing most of these essential functions. First, privacy is clearly related to **communication.** Both the informational and social themes of privacy are deeply involved with communication. Second, privacy is intimately connected to our sense of **control,** or autonomy. Being able to choose solitude or the company of others endows us with a sense of self-determination; not having that choice makes us feel helpless. Third, privacy is important to our sense of **identity.** Solitude and intimacy, in particular, can be used to evaluate our progress in life, who we really are, what our relationship to others is and what it ought to be. Fourth, privacy allows for **emotional release.** In private we can weep, make faces at ourselves in the mirror, sing loud crazy songs, and talk to ourselves.

Westin's four functions of privacy provide a good framework for research on the relation between privacy and other human behaviors. Privacy is connected to more than these four functions, however. We cannot overlook the relation

between privacy and territoriality, crowding, and personal space. The four processes are all part of the way we manage social space. They overlap in important ways, yet remain distinct in others. How we adapt to space is an important privacy-related issue, as is the link between privacy and developmental factors. We will first survey the research substantiating Westin's four functions of privacy then discuss the links between privacy and other behavior processes.

Communication

One reason we seek privacy is for protected communication (Westin, 1967). When we wish to talk to a friend, lawyer, teacher, counselor, or co-worker about something personal or important, we try to find a private place. Many things never get said because we cannot find a private place to say them in.

Privacy and communication at work have been the subject of several investigations. In a study mentioned earlier, Sundstrom, Herbert, and Brown (1982) found that employees who moved from walled offices to open-plan offices were dissatisfied with privacy. More specifically, the employees were unhappy about communication; they felt that the confidentiality of their conversations had suffered.

As another example, I recently received a call from an acquaintance in another city. It was basically a business call, but the caller waited until after 5 P.M. local time so the call could be made after hours, when other employees were away. This is merely one of many instances in which we seek privacy for the purpose of protected communication.

Control

Westin describes how privacy can facilitate an individual's sense of control or autonomy. Beginning on the bleak side, those who have little solitude of their own choosing—institutionalized individuals, for example—have little control over their physical or social environment. Having little control leads an individual to feel a lack of autonomy or independence. On the fortunate side of life, wealthy individuals are able to control their access to others and others' access to them nearly all the time, using an endless succession of private rooms, private offices, private clubs, private transportation, and private elevators.

There are more studies of individuals who greatly lack privacy than of individuals who have it in abundance. This in itself is a comment on privacy and research. Those with privacy often also have more power; they can more easily refuse to be studied or find an excuse not to be part of a study. Smith's (1982) study of prisoners, for example, also looked into prisoners' sense of control in relation to their privacy. In their former (cramped) quarters, the more prisoners preferred solitude and reserve, the less control over their lives they felt. One outcome of moving to their new, more spacious quarters was a significant change in this relation between privacy and control. In their new quarters, the more that prisoners valued solitude and reserve, the greater their sense of control. Clearly, the physical setting acts as a mediator between privacy and control. In this case, the prisoners' actual preferences for solitude and reserve did not change with the move to new quarters, but presumably their sense of control increased significantly. Those who particularly valued solitude and reserve were able, in their new more private surroundings, to feel they had greater control over their lives.

In the Stone et al. (1983) study, discussed earlier, individual perceptions of informational privacy in various organizations were examined. The participants were asked how much control over information about themselves they had in each type of organization. Participants believed they could control the information-handling practices of their employers the most; those of credit agencies the least. Thus perceived control over information depends on which organization holds the information.

In a study of wilderness solitude, Hammitt (1982) found that a very desirable feature of wilderness is that compared to the pressing demands of everyday urban life, it allows us to control what we pay attention to and which activities we engage in. Hammitt suggests that we do not go to the wilderness primarily to be isolated but to be able to experience the "cognitive freedom" involved in controlling our experiences. "Getting away from it all" to the wilderness means escaping from a place where you are subjected to many controls to a setting where *you* can decide what to do.

Control over information may even be related to your physical health. Several studies indicate that when hospital patients have better control over information pertinent to their health (such as diagnostic and treatment information), they cooperate more and experience less stress (Shumaker & Reizenstein, 1982). Control over information and control over access to others are central to the concept of privacy and are closely related to one's general sense of self-determination in life.

Identity

Privacy is an important part of the individual's sense of self or identity. This may seem a strange declaration; what does either informational or interpersonal privacy have to do with self-definition? Westin (1967) demonstrates how privacy is essential to enable us to integrate all the information from daily exchanges with others. It isn't easy to make sense of all the things that happen to us while we are still on the public stage. Privacy allows the time and space to reflect on the meaning of events, to fit them into our understanding of the world, and to formulate a response to them that is consistent with our views of ourselves.

For example, if you have ever felt swept away by love in a new relationship, you can understand this function of privacy. Certainly the first rush of love is a pleasant experience, but a common feeling accompanying it is that you are losing yourself while gaining a relationship. Even when, in the first stages of such a relationship, part of you very much desires intimacy, another part desires solitude or reserve. We need to take a step back even from a very pleasant experience to evaluate whether this is "the real me" or whether entering the wonderful relationship might not harm our very identity.

This notion of privacy as a facilitator of identification is taken seriously enough by some theorists (Foddy & Finighan, 1980) to be considered the central idea in their privacy framework. Unfortunately, identity is not an easy concept to investigate empirically. Foddy and Finighan's support for the centrality of identity comes largely from sociological analyses of novels and plays. This does not detract from the value of identity for privacy; it merely means that empirical support for the idea is difficult to obtain.

Emotion

The fourth function of privacy, in Westin's approach, is to allow for emotional release. Society discourages us from public emotional displays except under exceptional circumstances such as weddings and funerals. We often feel more emotion than we are able to display, so privacy serves as a vehicle for emotional release. A person may feel very bad, for example, and head for the nearest secluded place to cry.

But less obvious situations arise, too. Have you ever been to a concert so good that on the way home in the car you sang and yelled, riding the excitement? If you stopped to eat on the way home, you may have walked into a restaurant full of people who did not share your exhilaration; you contained your excitement so they didn't think you were crazy and felt frustrated at the restraint imposed on you.

Another example of emotional release, closer to the informational theme of privacy, is the tradition of "off the record" comments made by politicians to reporters. Politicians must present only part of themselves to the public if they wish to survive; they know and feel much more than they can afford to tell the public. The pressure that inevitably builds up—especially on a long road trip where a spouse or trusted aide is not available—leads to candid conversation between politicians and reporters who can be trusted to honor the off-the-record tradition. In these private conversations, politicians often criticize their own party or admit to fearing that a recent public statement was ill-advised. The reporter must honor the unwritten code against publishing remarks like these in order to maintain a trustworthy status not only with that politician but all others. If the confidential information is publicized, word will quickly spread that the reporter cannot be trusted to keep off-the-record comments off the record.

Relation to Crowding, Personal Space, and Territoriality

What are the relations among the four space management processes to which chapters in this book

have been devoted? Some writers have perceived one or another of them to be primary, with the other processes serving the individual's interests in the primary process. For example, Altman views privacy as the central concept among the processes. Personal space and territoriality are, in his model, mechanisms by which a person regulates privacy. Crowding is the failure to obtain privacy. (See Fig. 8–9.) Others have adopted different views—for example, that privacy is a process meant to serve our territorial interests (Pastalan, 1970).

Taylor and Ferguson (1980) have pointed out that theoretical advancement in this area obviously depends on straightening out the relations among these concepts. To that end, they asked students to describe places they choose for solitude and for intimacy. Different kinds of territories were selected for the two kinds of privacy. For example, individuals seeking solitude more often chose *public* territories (spaces where no one has control over who has access), but individuals seeking intimacy more often chose *primary* territories (spaces where the individual has considerable control over who has access).

Taylor and Ferguson conclude that neither privacy nor territoriality is more fundamental. Rather, they are linked on an equal basis as follows. Desiring privacy, an individual seeks a particular kind of territory. Once established in that territory, however, not only privacy needs but other needs are also served by the individual's possession of the territory. That is, privacy is foremost at some stages in the sequences of social behavior and territoriality is foremost at others.

Edney and Buda (1976) chose to study the differences between privacy and territoriality by asking individuals where they preferred to engage in a variety of everyday activities. They offered four alternative types of space: (1) home territory with privacy (isolation), (2) home territory but without privacy, (3) privacy in someone else's territory, and (4) no privacy in someone else's territory. The participants made strong distinctions about where they would like to do various things, indicating that privacy and territoriality are clearly distinct concepts to the participants.

In a second study, Edney and Buda found further differences between privacy and territory. Participants who were given no privacy tended to attribute their behavior to the influence of others;

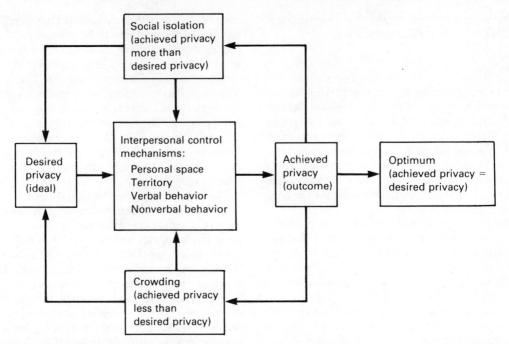

FIGURE 8–9 Altman's perspective on privacy as the central process among our space-regulation behavior processes. *(From* The Environment and Social Behavior *by I. Altman. Copyright © 1975 by Wadsworth Publishing Co., Inc. Reprinted with permission of Brooks/Cole Co., Monterey, California.)*

those who were given a place to territorialize tended to attribute their behavior to their own personality. The authors conclude that privacy and territoriality must be distinct if they produce these different influences on cognitive activity.

A Japanese study helps to distinguish privacy and territoriality as they relate to another of the space management processes, crowding (Iwata, 1980). Participants were queried as to how they would feel in a variety of social situations.

Across situations, when participants' need for privacy and need for territoriality rose, the tendency to experience crowding also rose. Because privacy and territoriality are both associated with a tendency to feel crowded, we might conclude they are the same thing. However, privacy orientation and territoriality orientation were *not* correlated. This suggests that although they both lead a person to feel more crowded, they do so for different reasons.

Iwata's research does not inform us what those different reasons are. One possibility, however, is that privacy primarily refers to social and infor-

mational access and territoriality primarily refers to spatial access. The two kinds of access may be sometimes desired at the same time, or one kind of access may facilitate the other kind of access, but there are many occasions when the two kinds of access have nothing to do with each other. For example, someone may want a territory for its economic value or for its personal significance; social-informational access (privacy) is irrelevant. Or, a politician on a campaign visit may wish to maximize social access to voters; while the politician concentrates on that activity, territoriality is minimally at issue.

Growing Up

The privacy needs of infants are unknown, but it is probably safe to assume that infants have little need for privacy, especially solitude, reserve, and anonymity. But as the child develops, privacy needs grow. Informational privacy becomes an issue when the preadolescent is first given a diary (and the parent wrestles with the temptation to read it). Signs reading Keep Out begin appearing on the adolescent's door. Too few studies have examined the process by which infants with no privacy needs develop into adults with important and diverse privacy needs. This may be, as Melton (1983) notes, because we often forget that children value and deserve privacy. Nevertheless, a few key pieces of research have begun to explore the development of privacy.

Maxine Wolfe (1978) has extensively studied the development in children of the *meaning* of privacy (See Fig. 8–10.) She began by simply asking children what they meant by the word "privacy." Their answers were coded according to whether they contained certain themes—being alone, managing information, controlling access to specific places, autonomy, quiet, being undisturbed.

Being alone is the theme most mentioned by children of all ages, followed by information management. The youngest children (aged four to seven) mention aloneness less often than the older children (aged eight to seventeen) in their definitions of privacy. Information management themes are expressed more by the older children (thirteen to seventeen) than by the younger ones (four to twelve). It is interesting that control of access to a place peaks as a definitional theme in the middle age group (eight to twelve).

If we think of the definitions not only as expressions of the meaning of privacy, but also of a child's present need for privacy, this peak at eight to twelve years of age may represent a dilemma of preadolescence. At that age, the need for solitude is growing but the child still has a restricted range of places to go outside the home. The only way for the child to obtain privacy is to go into the bedroom and close the door. Many

FIGURE 8–10 Privacy needs change during childhood and adolescence. *(Courtesy of Coe Gifford.)*

struggles between parents and children in this age group develop over access to the child's bedroom. The parents have not yet fully recognized the child's growing privacy needs and still feel they have a right to enter at will; the child wants the opportunity to be alone.

However, the battle over access to a place is often over by adolescence because the parent has finally adjusted or adapted to the child's need for privacy and because the adolescent now has a larger range of destinations outside the home and can find privacy in many more places than the bedroom. At that point, the theme of "a place of my own" fades from the child's definition of privacy because the place issue has subsided.

The autonomy theme—being able to do what you choose—is the least common one in Wolfe's study. However, it is the only theme that significantly rises from early to middle to late childhood, appearing in about 6 percent of the four- to seven-year old's definitions and about 23 percent of the thirteen- to seventeen-year-old's definitions.

Parke and Sawin (1979) investigated the privacy-related *behavior* of children rather than the meaning of privacy to them. A common expression of privacy needs is the closing of bedroom and bathroom doors. The researchers asked children of different ages when and how often they closed their doors and found that door closing is a function of both age and the size of the child's house. Children who live in houses with more bedrooms and bathrooms close the doors more often. By the adolescent stage, however, the number of bathrooms doesn't matter—even when there was only one bathroom, 100 percent of the ten- to seventeen-year-olds said they closed the door.

Adaptation and Regulation

A final area of privacy and behavior includes the mechanisms by which we regulate privacy. When we have less privacy than we desire, we may adapt so that we no longer believe we need as much as before. In the short term, we may avoid others or seek them out to obtain the amount of social contact we desire. In the long term, some evidence suggests that if we continue to face more or less privacy than we desire, we adapt by changing our social goals to fit reality. Let's take a look at the evidence.

First-year university students who live in dormitories are especially sensitive to the privacy process. Uprooted from their family homes, they need social contact. Thrown together with many others in a residential building, they also sometimes need to get away from others. As everyone who has experienced dormitory life knows, the first year is full of ups and downs related to overexposure and underexposure to other people. What mechanisms do dormitory residents use to open themselves to others and to close themselves to others? What are the long-term effects of employing these mechanisms?

Vinsel, Brown, Altman, and Foss (1980) asked students how they handled contact with others. The most popular means of seeking others out were, as you might expect, phoning others, visiting others' rooms, leaving one's own door open, and inviting others to one's room. To avoid contact, students close their doors and find quiet places, tune out noise, and go for walks alone.

Not all students, however, use the same number or kinds of mechanisms. Hypothesizing a connection between the use of privacy mechanisms and success in school, the researchers compared the number of privacy mechanisms used by students who were still in school about one year later versus those who had dropped out of school. The "stay-ins" were found to have reported using both more contact-seeking mechanisms *and* more contact-avoidance mechanisms than the dropouts.

The implication, although other factors could have played a role, is that students who know how to regulate their privacy better will do better in school. This does not mean that better students always avoid others; notice that they also used more contact-seeking mechanisms. The few mechanisms that were used more by the dropouts are revealing: they went to the dorm lounge more (to seek contact) and they turned up their stereos loud (to avoid contact). The latter mechanism, in particular, may be seen as maladaptive; if you play loud music to drive others away, you probably cannot study very well either.

Sometimes, it seems, individuals stop trying to achieve privacy. In a study of nursing home residents mentioned earlier (Firestone, Lichtman, &

Evans, 1980), those who lived in wards recognized they had less privacy than those who lived in private rooms but were not less satisfied. Firestone et al. conclude that the residents had adapted to more social contact; they no longer desired to reduce the amount of time spent with others. The authors suggest that the residents "come to take the realities of their living circumstance as unchangeable facts." This acceptance grew with the length of time the resident had been institutionalized.

▶ **In Sum.** A major goal of our social behavior is to regulate the amount of contact we have with others. Those who know how to use the environment to accomplish this may be more successful in areas of life beyond the social realm. Some individuals adapt to or accept situations that would seem to offer too much or too little social contact. Others faced with a shortage of traditional mechanisms of regulating social interaction (recall the Gypsies) develop creative solutions to the problem.

As a key process in our dealings with others, privacy is inextricably linked to communication, autonomy, identity, emotional release, and growing up. The four space management processes (personal space, territoriality, crowding, and privacy) overlap in some ways. For example, in one way or another they all pertain to an individual's control of access to self. At the same time, they each have unique functional value to the individual and are useful in understanding separate areas of person-environment transactions.

It is neither useful to attempt to force them into a single superprocess, nor to ignore their shared purposes. Researchers have correctly begun the task of specifying when and how the processes are similar as well as when and how they are distinct. Use of many privacy regulation mechanisms may be one hallmark of success; satisfaction with little privacy a sign of growing institutionalization.

THEORIES OF PRIVACY

We shall see that one theory dominates thinking about privacy, although there are alternative models. Some of these models interpret privacy primarily as a reflection or mechanism supporting some other process. As noted earlier, Foddy and Finighan (1980) see privacy as a vehicle by which individuals define and maintain their identity. Others have taken pains to demonstrate how privacy is interwoven with many aspects of our lives. We will survey some of the narrower and some of the broader approaches to privacy. The dominant theory, proposed by Irwin Altman, is described first, and then some attention is paid to the alternative ideas.

Selective Control of Access to Self

Altman (1975, 1977) conceptualizes privacy as a three-dimensional process. First, privacy is a **boundary control process:** individuals do not merely attempt to exclude others; they also find themselves seeking out others. The gate to the self swings both ways. Second, privacy is an **optimization process.** The individual is not seeking more and more solitude, reserve, or anonymity; often intimacy or being together is the goal of social activity. According to Altman, the ultimate in privacy is not necessarily being alone most of the time, but in being alone when you want to *and* being with others when you want to.

Presumably, some individuals want to be alone more than others. Therefore, some individuals might rarely see others yet still not have much privacy because they never want to see anyone. Others might be with friends most of the time and still have much privacy. Their optimum level of socializing is high. Privacy is having the *right* amount of social contact, whether that is a large or small amount.

In addition, each individual's privacy desires are assumed to vary. Thus, if I desire solitude, even one other person's presence may ruin my privacy, but when I want to be with many friends, having only two around may be too much privacy for me. For Altman, too much privacy is isolation, or loneliness. Too little privacy is crowding. Yet loneliness and crowding do not depend merely on how many others surround me; they depend on how many others are around *in relation to* how many others I would like around me.

Third, in Altman's model individuals and cultures employ a variety of means to optimize their privacy; that is, privacy is a **multimechanism process.** As we have seen earlier, there is some empirical support for the idea that privacy is a cultural universal. Even societies without walls find ways to allow members ways to achieve privacy. Most people tend to think of privacy in terms of doors and walls, but privacy may be regulated by other mechanisms.

Nonverbal behavior is one. A person who desires solitude may convey that desire to another person who comes near with a look that clearly says, "Leave me alone." Verbal behavior is another. Have you ever delivered an invitation to "drop by sometime" knowing that you would probably never specify exactly *which* time, mainly because you do not really want that particular person close to you? The situation can arise when you feel compelled by social pressure to make the invitation, but you don't really want to. Your parents keep asking you to invite their friends' son over for dinner. You think he's a jerk; the feeling may be mutual. Now, having made the invitation as above, you can claim that you invited him over, but he just doesn't seem too enthusiastic. Clothing can be another privacy mechanism—consider the use of the veil in traditional Moslem society and the use of sunglasses, even on cloudy days, by some members of our society.

Altman's descriptive framework of privacy is probably the most comprehensive in environmental psychology. In reviewing it and others, Margulis (1977) concludes Altman's is the best in many ways, but that it does have some shortcomings. Since Altman employed concepts that have multiple definitions, such as self, boundaries, and optimum level of privacy, Margulis fears that confusion may result when the framework is used. In the following sections, other problems and points of view are raised in the search for a better theory of privacy.

Life Cycle, Culture, and Time

Maxine Wolfe, Robert Laufer, and Harold Proshansky have tried to expand our conception of privacy to include a clear role for developmental, cultural, and temporal factors. In addition, they agree with other theorists that control and choice are key elements in privacy. Wolfe and her colleagues show how the management of social interaction and the management of information take on fresh meaning when the individual's life cycle is considered. As we have seen, young children have little sense of privacy. By adulthood, most individuals have strong privacy preferences.

Laufer and Wolfe's (1977) work begins to demonstrate which kinds of privacy are understood and desired at which of life's stages, including adulthood. Consider, for example, the mother of several young children who often has little privacy, in comparison with the same mother twenty years later who may suffer from an oversupply of privacy (the empty-nest syndrome) when her children have all left home.

Wolfe and her colleagues point out that the development of the self is based on a gradual realization that self and nonself are distinct; this distinction is closely related to the individual's understanding of privacy and the availability of privacy. In addition, they point out that the great cultural differences in privacy behavior are acquired as a person develops *within* a culture.

Finally, Wolfe reminds us that privacy always has a time dimension to it. This is obvious in that the life cycle is a temporal dimension, but another interesting aspect of privacy and time is that individuals at one life stage may not be able to understand and appreciate the privacy needs of individuals at another life stage. Children may not understand the needs of their parents because they have not yet experienced adult situations. Also, as Melton (1983) points out, adults seem to forget their own adolescence when they underestimate the desire for privacy as well as the competency for privacy of their own adolescents.

Don't Forget the Environment

Our review of research showed that the physical setting affects privacy. Although the environment often supports or denies privacy, it has not been clearly included in privacy theories. John Archea (1977) believes this is odd, especially for environmental psychologists. Archea argues that privacy theories must include the environment as a full partner in the model, not as a fuzzy backdrop.

Archea reminds us that we vary privacy largely by changing and selecting sites for our behaviors. Because he views privacy primarily as an **information distribution process,** Archea believes that the physical environment regulates the flow of privacy. The arrangement of settings can concentrate, diffuse, segregate, or localize information. Archea would have us analyze physical settings to determine how each one affects the flow of information in these four ways.

As a simple example, consider the difference between solid walls and partitions in a psychotherapy clinic. The difference between these two kinds of room dividers will probably have a large effect on the flow of spoken information between client and counsellor, as well as between that client-counsellor pair and another client-counsellor pair in the next room. (See Fig. 8–11.)

Archea also points out that in different physical settings individuals may be *visually* conspicuous to others or not. Think, for example, of the surroundings you would select for solitude versus those you would select for intimacy versus those you would select for anonymity. Compare the differences in the three settings that would hinder or promote your visibility in each one. Walls,

doors, and line-of-sight to others are some features that affect visibility. In general, Archea argues that we could understand privacy much better if we specifically considered the properties of physical settings in studies of privacy more often.

A Hierarchy of Needs

In the course of studying privacy in offices, Eric Sundstrom and his associates have raised the possibility that privacy needs are organized in hierarchical fashion. That is, at lower job levels certain aspects of privacy are more salient and at higher job levels other aspects are more salient. The general outlines of the theory are reminiscent of Abraham Maslow's theory of motivation, in which individuals are said to have needs that must be satisfied in a specific hierarchical order.

Employees at the lowest level in many organizations are also the most visually conspicuous,

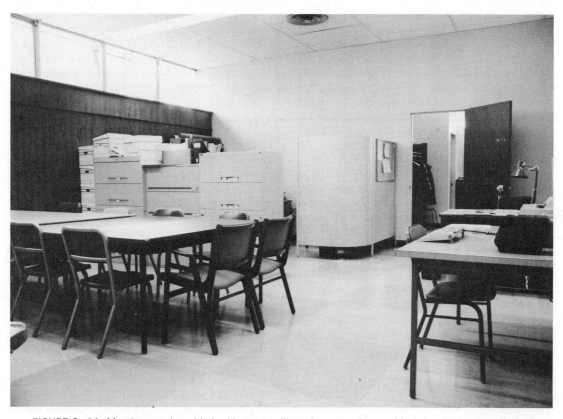

FIGURE 8–11 Meetings at the table in this room will not be very private, either visually or acoustically.

to borrow Archea's phrase. Working in the view of many others, their greatest privacy need, according to Sundstrom et al., is for social control—in particular, keeping others out.

At the middle level in many organizations, employees have walled offices; keeping others away is no longer as big a problem. However, because their work often requires more concentration than that of lower-level employees, their main privacy need is for a setting that allows freedom from distractions, such as noise floating down a hallway.

Nearer the top of the organization, neither social control nor distractions are the main problem. Walls and secretaries protect the executive from unwanted intrusions. Yet the executive still has a need for privacy, but of a different sort. Executives desire privacy in the sense of having few direct checks of their work by superiors. Their greatest concern is that they be "allowed to run my own ship" without much interference from headquarters.

Notice that as we rise up the privacy hierarchy, the employee's privacy needs are less immediate and pressing. Nevertheless, as we noted in the discussion of Wolfe and Laufer's theory, we must experience a situation before we really know the privacy needs of an individual in that situation. In one sense, the executive has more privacy than the secretary, reflecting the difference in their power. Yet it may be that their different privacy needs are experienced equally strongly.

Sundstrom's theory, at first glance, seems to apply only to the work setting. Yet its basic premises may well apply much more widely, wherever there are power or status differences that are reflected in the privacy-facilitating qualities of individual territories, in schools, homes, and institutions as well as workplaces.

▶ **In Sum.** As we reflect on these theories of privacy, an overriding impression is that we do not yet have a theory with a claim to completeness. Altman's model dominates the area, but other theorists remind us that one aspect or another of privacy has not received due consideration. Privacy may be an optimizing boundary-control process, but there are some problems with the definition of (and therefore with the measurement of) key terms in this approach. Central to the issue is whether privacy is fundamentally a self-defined concept or an objectively definable one.

When privacy is considered a subjective and dynamic phenomenon, it can be difficult to measure, and scientific tests of theories holding this position may be difficult. Archea, for example, observes that privacy has a strong environmental component, although he recognizes the psychological aspects of privacy (we select our settings wherever possible). Laufer and her colleagues note that privacy preferences, expectations, and satisfaction vary over the life cycle and Sundstrom observes that at any one point in the life cycle, our privacy needs vary as a function of our status.

PRIVACY AND ENVIRONMENTAL DESIGN

The goal of the designer must be to give everyone as much privacy as possible. This does *not* mean constructing houses, offices, schools, institutions, and outdoor spaces so that each person has a separate compartment! All the theorists agree that privacy means openness to others as much as it means being closed to others. The important thing is to live and work in settings that allow an individual to *choose* openness or not.

A Hierarchy of Spaces

Craig Zimring (1982) is the latest in a series of design-oriented environmental psychologists to suggest that space may be categorized into a hierarchy ranging from very public to very private. **Public spaces,** exemplified by shopping malls and sidewalks are, in cities, more often sites for interactions between strangers than between friends. In smaller settings, of course, an individual may encounter a greater proportion of acquaintances and friends. Most interactions in public spaces, large and small, are unplanned and ritualistic.

Designing for privacy in public spaces is largely a matter of arranging space so that ritualistic encounters between strangers are peaceful and efficient. In terms of peacefulness, privacy at this level chiefly means control over the unwanted attentions of muggers, panhandlers, rapists, and pamphleteers. In terms of efficiency, it means arranging space so that pedestrians do not bump into one another and so that business transactions occur smoothly. It also means designing spaces that allow for positive interactions between those strangers or acquaintances who choose to interact—for example, by having lunch together in a downtown plaza (Whyte, 1980).

Slightly more private than public spaces are **semipublic spaces,** such as apartment hallways, community rooms, unfenced yards shared by neighbors, classrooms, and lobbies. Designing for privacy in semipublic spaces is largely a matter of creating arrangements that facilitate social interaction or discourage it. In a library reading room, for example, designing for privacy often means installing carrels to shield patrons from one another visually and acoustically. (Carrels do not always succeed acoustically. The latest complaint I've heard concerns the noise created by someone punching away madly at calculator buttons in the next carrel.) In housing developments, designing for privacy may mean arranging units to increase the probability that residents will meet one another, so that the chances of building a friendly and cohesive community are enhanced.

Semiprivate spaces include places like open-plan offices, teachers' staffrooms, VIP lounges, living rooms, and other settings where most outsiders are excluded, yet a heterogeneous group of individuals are welcome. A primary design objective at this level is to create effective boundaries between activities that might otherwise cause conflict (Zimring, 1982). Boundaries are hardly noticed where they work well to promote privacy, but when visual or acoustic barriers are absent, or where they are inadequate, there are problems.

In one city hall, a whole planning department is housed in one large room on the assumption that employees will frequently need to communicate and pass drawings among themselves. Yet the employees complain bitterly because they also need to engage in less public activities such as talking on the phone, writing reports, or holding two-person conversations. Semiprivate spaces are difficult to design well, unless they include private spaces—in which case the semiprivate space may be underutilized because everyone flees to private space.

The nineteenth-century utopian community of Oneida, New York, which survived successfully for over 30 years, solved this problem by making the community hall much more spacious and comfortable than the private rooms (Moos & Brownstein, 1977). Oneida chose this arrangement precisely because the community wanted to encourage social interaction to maximize solidarity and control behavior by subjecting it to more public scrutiny.

Private spaces are normally open to one or a few individuals, at least at any one time. Bedrooms, bathrooms, executive elevators, private offices, and cars are private spaces. Zimring (1982) believes that, contrary to the assumptions that prevailed at Oneida, when individuals have private spaces they are *more* sociable, rather than less sociable. By giving an individual private space, we also give them a sense of control; they are less likely to skirmish with others over public space, thereby disrupting the social life of a place. Studies of institutions, dormitories, and prisons all suggest that private space is not only highly desirable but produces less stress than no-private-space designs. We turn now to specific design examples in housing, offices, and institutions.

Housing

A residence is already a relatively private space. In the developed world, the walls and doors provided by our houses are probably the commonest mechanisms we actually use to manage privacy, even though some surveys report that many individuals associate residential privacy with exterior factors, such as lot size and distance from neighbors (Harman & Betak, 1974; Marshall, 1972). Within the house, different levels of privacy are needed for different family members. Of course, if a house is very large, privacy is not a problem unless it is so large that family members become isolated and alienated from one another. More often, unfortunately, the problem is insufficient space or poor arrangement of the available space (Finighan, 1980).

Outside the residence itself, privacy may vary as a function of design in multiunit housing projects. McCarthy and Saegert (1979) studied privacy in the lobbies, elevators, and other public areas within low-rise and high-rise buildings. Naturally, such areas offer less privacy than a person's own apartment, but McCarthy and Saegert found that public areas in the low-rise design were judged by residents to offer more privacy than public areas in the high-rise design. In concurrence with the notion that having much privacy does not mean being isolated, the low-rise tenants were more socially active and belonged to more voluntary organizations than did the high-rise tenants.

In a study comparing dormitories with long-corridor designs and those with short-corridor designs, residents of long-corridor dormitories reported more difficulty in maintaining adequate privacy than did residents of short-corridor dormitories (Baum, Aiello, & Calesnick, 1979). In both studies, lack of privacy may result when residents must pass more strangers in the public areas of their building.

Christopher Alexander is an architect who has thought about privacy in housing for many years. Zeisel (1975) describes one solution devised by Alexander when indoor space is limited, the **privacy gradient.** Based on careful consideration of cultural practices and interviews, Alexander arranged space in low-cost Peruvian homes from the most public, near the entrance, to the most private, located farthest from the entrance. (See Fig. 8–12.)

Clearly, there is no universal design for residential privacy. Each family or client's needs must be carefully considered if the designer is to provide a cost-efficient yet private dwelling. However, some groups of clients are sufficiently similar that some design considerations may apply to most buildings serving them. We turn next, then, to privacy in institutions.

Institutions

For those who live in public institutions such as convalescent hospitals, residences for older people, ships, or penal institutions, privacy can be an acute problem. Usually not enough money is available to provide each individual with enough space to permit much solitude; other forms of privacy are often in short supply, too. Opportunities for intimacy with friends and family are sadly lacking in many institutions, for example.

Let us consider just one type of institution, the residence for older people. Sandra Howell (1980) studied privacy and resident patterns of behavior in relation to building design in fifty-three homes for the aged. After talking to hundreds of residents and viewing both the spatial arrangements supplied to the residents and the adjustments and adaptations to those arrangements made by the residents, Howell suggests a number of design guidelines that would help optimize privacy. Some of these pertain to space inside the units. A sample: "Avoid direct views from the entry of the more private areas in the unit like the bedroom, bathroom, and kitchen sink." Another: "Guests should not have to pass through the sleeping and dressing area to reach the bathroom."

Others pertain to the semipublic areas of the housing complex. For example: "An area should be provided where residents can observe coming and going activities but opportunities for offensive surveillance should be minimized." These

FIGURE 8–12 Christopher Alexander's plan for a low-income housing project in South America. The wavy lines at top show how most guests' entry into the house may be comfortably restricted to the entry way and sala areas. Closer friends and relatives may be invited further into the house. Privacy is facilitated because strangers do not proceed far into the more intimate zones of the house. *(Alexander, C., et al., 1969. Houses Reprinted by permission of the au- Center for Environmental Structures. Reprinted by permission for the author.)*

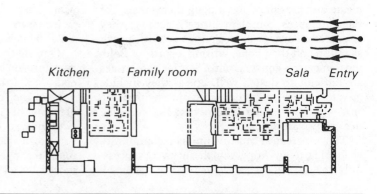

Kitchen   Family room   Sala   Entry

guidelines emphasize the optimization of visual privacy, but others are directed at acoustical privacy and informational privacy. Some of the guidelines sound obvious, but unfortunately the reason Howell presents them is because many residences for older people that she studied were designed without these considerations.

Privacy in Offices

Privacy at work is a growing issue. Recent studies of the visual, acoustical, social, and informational privacy in offices suggest that many arrangements are far from satisfactory (Wineman, 1982). In an important book devoted to office design, Frank Becker (1981) observes that arrangements are all too often made on such crude considerations as the number of employees per square foot, when they should be made on the basis of work efficiency. Yet employees consider privacy very important. One study of faculty offices found that privacy was considered more important than amount of space, temperature and ventilation, furniture, lighting, view, and general aesthetics (Farrenkopf & Roth, 1980).

As with houses, the preferred office is usually one that is large and solidly enclosed enough to ensure "control of access to one's self." But not everyone has such an office, owing in part to the pervasive system of allocating office space on the basis of rank and seniority. Ideally, should offices be designed for isolation? The answer depends on the type of work, personal preferences, and social norms.

First, not every job would be performed best in a totally private office; therefore the type of work being done is one important consideration. Some work (writing) requires solitude, and other work is better suited to open office plans (brainstorming or interdepartmental communication). Second, not every person wishes to work in a totally private office; personal tendencies are another important consideration. Some writers work best as a team; some brainstormers produce more alone than as part of a group. Third, social interaction norms must be taken into account (Justa & Golan, 1977). The kind of social interaction you engage in (such as informal banter versus financial decision making) is often linked to certain locations within offices. For example, informal conversation typically occurs in hallways and around the water cooler, but financial decisions are usually made by an individual or group in a physically isolated setting. Office arrangements should reflect these norms.

Office design then, should never be haphazard or based simply on tradition, but should be tuned to rank, type of work, personal preferences, and norms. Very little empirical research on work spaces has yet managed to consider all these factors.

Field research may take all these factors into account but lack experimental control; consequently some researchers have approached the office design problem by investigating one or two carefully controlled factors at a time. One study adopting an experimental approach (Ng & Gifford, 1984) focused on a work activity that comes before all other types of work—applying for the job. To obtain the kinds of experimental control only available in a laboratory, we decided to simulate the job interview situation. Individuals who responded to a newspaper ad came to the laboratory, which had been furnished and decorated very much like a typical personnel office. They applied for one of four positions that students might really seek (community project officer, management trainee, research assistant, and clerk) and role-played the application and interview procedure.

To vary privacy during the interview, we arranged for half the applicants to hear someone typing intermittently on the other side of a partition (low privacy); the other half heard no one else in the office except the interviewer (high privacy). Applicants in the low privacy condition expressed significantly less satisfaction with the job interview. In particular, applicants interviewed in the low privacy condition reported feeling significantly more inhibited in their answers than applicants in the high privacy condition. (See Fig. 8–13.)

Interviewing for a job is the first work situation in which most individuals prefer protected communication. After you get the job, there are many more occasions when you will desire privacy. Informational privacy is a frequent issue where confidential information is involved, and every organization deals with confidential information of one sort or another. Social privacy on the job is also a problem as we have seen. Unfortunately, privacy at work has been an issue for

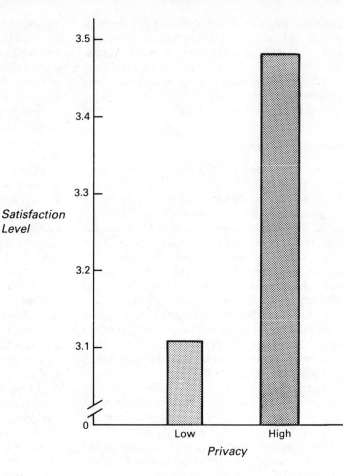

FIGURE 8-13 When job applicants believe that a third party can overhear their interview for a new job (low privacy), they are less satisfied than if they think no one can overhear the interview (high privacy). *(Adapted from Ng & Gifford, 1984.)*

years but relatively few studies are available to the practicing environmental psychologist.

SUMMARY

Privacy is a process in which we attempt to regulate interaction with others, including social interaction and information about the self that may be kept on file. It has largely been studied through questionnaires and interviews. Preferences, expectations, values, and behaviors of individuals vary from person to person and from occasion to occasion as individuals attempt to manage their desires for solitude, reserve, anonymity, intimacy, and other forms of privacy. Privacy is intimately linked to other psychological processes, such as the other space management mechanisms and control, communication, identity, emotion, adaptation, and growing up. The physical environment plays a key role in facilitating privacy regulation, either making the task easy or forcing those with few architectural resources to become creative in the search for privacy. Some who have little ability to regulate privacy seem to adapt to these circumstances; whether that has harmful effects or represents successful coping is unclear. Sensitive designers can arrange architectural space in public places and institutions to maximize the individual's ability to regulate interaction with others.

SUGGESTED SUPPLEMENTARY READINGS

Altman, I. (1975). *The environment and social behavior.* Monterey, CA: Brooks/Cole.

Archea, J. (1977). The place of architectural factors in behavioral theories of privacy. *Journal of Social Issues, 33*(3), 116–137.

Laufer, R. S., & Wolfe, M. (1977). Privacy as a concept and a social issue: A multidimensional development theory. *Journal of Social Issues, 33*(3), 22–42.

Margulis, S. T. (1977). Conceptions of privacy: Current status and next steps. *The Journal of Social Issues, 33*(3), 5–21.

Patterson, A. H. & Chiswick, N. R. (1981). The role of the social and physical environment in privacy maintenance among the Iban of Borneo. *Journal of Environmental Psychology, 1,* 131–139.

Stone, E. F., Gueutal, H. G., Gardner, D. G., & McClure, S. (1983). A field experiment comparing information-privacy values, beliefs, and attitudes across several types of organizations. *Journal of Applied Psychology, 68,* 459–468.

Sundstrom, E., Herbert, R. K., & Brown, D. W. (1982). Privacy and communication in an open-plan office. *Environment and Behavior, 14,* 379–392.

———, Town, J. P., Brown, D. W., Forman, A., & McGee, C. (1982). Physical enclosure, type of job, and privacy in the office. *Environment and Behavior, 14,* 543–559.

Taylor, R. B., & Ferguson, G. (1980). Solitude and intimacy: Linking territoriality and privacy experiences. *Journal of Nonverbal Behavior, 4,* 227–239.

Part Three

Societal Processes

This part of the book is concerned with basic processes in our lives that are usually identified with key settings in society. Chapter Nine discusses living at home where home includes our residence, neighborhood, and city, and living includes activities such as moving, shopping, avoiding muggers, waiting for the bus or subway, deciding who really owns the kitchen, relaxing, and being prepared for potential disasters. Chapter Ten centers on learning and related activities in relation to the physical environment. Classrooms are the focus of the chapter, but learning in other settings is also discussed. Chapter Eleven covers the process of working. Performance and satisfaction in offices, factories, and other workspaces are related to physical features of the workplace. Chapter Twelve describes how settings are (or ought to be) designed, constructed, and evaluated. Architecture increasingly includes social science input about the activities, preferences, and needs of those who will live and work in its creations. Chapter Thirteen discusses the management of natural resources by individuals and small groups. Basic resources such as trees, oil, and fish are being exploited much faster than they regenerate. Psychological factors that encourage or discourage activities such as energy conservation, recycling, and littering are reviewed.

Chapter Nine

Thriving and Surviving at Home and in the City

We must restore to the city the maternal,
life-nurturing functions, the autonomous
activities, the symbiotic associations
that have long been neglected or suppressed.
For the city should be an organ of love.
Lewis Mumford, 1961

Tom wandered aimlessly through his grandfather's big old house. He had spent so many childhood hours happily lost in its nooks, playing on the wonderfully smooth, worn, mahogany stairs and gazing at the titles of the heavy books on the shelves. His grandfather, weakening but still of sound mind, had just told Tom the house was to be his after his grandfather's death.

Tom loved its walls, the rooms, the pictures, the steep roof. Unfortunately, its formerly tranquil semirural neighborhood had been overtaken by the city. The house, which properly belonged on a small farm, was stuck only a few meters from a busy six-lane road. The ills of the modern city lay just outside the door to the house that belonged in another, more peaceful century. The windows had been broken and his grandfather had been the victim of three recent break-ins and one mugging.

Tom longed to show the house to Jane, but at the same time he was uncertain whether she would like it. For one thing, his grandfather's house had been flooded several times in its lifetime; each time, Tom's grandparents had lost heavily. As he was about to abandon the dream of living with Jane in the old place, he remembered a few good points. It was right on the bus line, close to downtown shopping and a great old park, and taxes were low. And then there were the spacious rooms, the beautiful woodwork his grandfather had spent years carving, and the high ceilings that made you feel you were in a real house instead of one of those modern crackerboxes. Full of these thoughts, Tom set off to tell Jane of his coming inheritance, his new old home.

Home is the most important place in our lives. This characteristic gives it great potential for helping us to thrive—or for threatening our very survival. In this chapter, the focus is on environmental psychology in the residence, neighborhood, community, and city street. "Home" is a word that can refer to small places, such as our room, house, or apartment, or to broader areas, such as the immediate neighborhood, the district, the town, or even the nation.

Home remains an important refuge from the stresses of work, school, and the street life. Unfortunately, many people live in residences that cannot provide protection and rejuvenation. When this primary territory does not serve these basic needs, it can become more hellish than the secondary and public territories you left for the peace of home. Four main concerns in this environmental psychology of home are emphasized.

In the first section, environment-behavior issues concerning residences are surveyed. What determines whether individuals are satisfied with their present residences? Why do individuals prefer different types of residences? Inside our homes many environment-related activities occur: we manage space for work and relaxation; we may develop a special sense of place. What are the positive and negative consequences of living in different residences?

The second section moves to a larger scale, recognizing that our residences are embedded in neighborhoods and communities. The community may be urban, suburban, or rural; it may be divided by major roads or crisscrossed by gently curving cul-de-sacs; it may be heavily industrialized or parklike. What are the satisfactions, stresses, and social effects of living in different communities? Traffic, noise, heat, pollution, and crime are some important factors in urban environmental psychology. They are related to prosocial, antisocial, and *non*social behaviors.

The third section deals with the threat of natural and technological hazards. Many residences and communities are subject to floods, earthquakes, nuclear disaster, volcanoes, or violent storms. How do individuals respond, and fail to respond, when these hazards are mere threats—and when the threats become real disasters?

Finally, four examples of the application of environmental psychology to the design of homes and communities are offered.

ENVIRONMENTAL PSYCHOLOGY IN THE RESIDENCE

What Is a Home?

To describe a residence, we might consider who lives there, what kinds of activities occur there, and what its typical design is. But probably no definition based on these criteria could include all the physical structures that residents call home, especially if we adapt an international perspective (Rapoport, 1969). Inhabitants of residences are not always connected by kinship ties. A wide variety of work and relaxation behaviors occur in the residence. Housing comes in many different designs, sizes, and functional arrangements. (See Fig. 9–1.)

Perhaps "home" is ultimately more a symbol than a place (Cooper, 1976). It has received eloquent attention in the work of some philosophers (Bachelard, 1969). The meaning of the attic and cellar as parts of home have been explored (Korosec-Serfaty, 1984). The very word "home" carries a much broader, more personal, and richer meaning than the words "house" or "residence."

Adopting a descriptive approach, Irwin Altman and his colleagues (Altman & Chemers, 1980; Altman & Gauvain, 1981) have characterized residences along five dimensions: (1) permanent/temporary, (2) differentiated/homogeneous, (3) communal/noncommunal, (4) identity/communality, and (5) openness/closedness.

First, in industrialized countries, residents usually have permanent dwellings, although apparently this situation is not entirely satisfactory because many householders also maintain temporary homes such as cabins, cottages, and recreational vehicles. In some less industrialized countries, residents move frequently and often construct temporary homes in new places.

The second of Altman and Chemers' dimensions (differentiated/homogeneous) refers to the separation, or lack of it, in the functions of rooms. A highly differentiated residence has many rooms, each of which houses a specific activity; in a homogeneous residence nearly any activity may occur in nearly any room. Differentiation, of course, is partly a function of wealth; it isn't easy to be poor and have a highly differentiated home. Little research on the effects of differentiation is available, although it is obviously an important environmental influence on our daily behavior. For example, privacy and territoriality must be strongly affected by the degree of differentiation in our home.

Third, residences vary in communality, or the degree to which nuclear families live together or in different homes. In many Eastern cultures, several generations of a family live in one household.

In some African and Native American cultures, numerous unrelated families live in one home.

Altman and Gauvain (1982) suggest further dimensions. Fourth, dwellings vary in identity/communality, where the term "communality" has a different meaning. Residences often reflect the personal touches of their occupants. Identity is the extent to which a residence depicts the unique interests and needs of its residents. Communality is the extent to which a residence meets the common stereotype of a home in that culture. A tipi on a suburban lot in North America might be high on identity, but it would be low on communality. The same tipi, if it had few personal embellishments, would be low on identity and high on communality at a pow-wow on the open plains of the central United States. Typical homes in every culture contain elements of both identity and communality.

Fifth, residences vary in their openness to outsiders. This varies both within cultures and between cultures. In some places, houses typically are surrounded by walls or hedges; in others they are not. Dwellings signal their residents' willingness to interact with neighbors.

Rapoport (1969, 1984) and Altman and Gauvain (1982) present a fascinating panorama of residential variation across cultures. Variation also occurs within any single culture, such as our own. Yet the psychological effects of these variations are still largely unknown. We cannot experiment by placing residents randomly in different kinds of homes, so we may never fully understand the effects of different home types. We can and should, however, study what happens when individuals move from one type of home to another, such as from the family home to a dormitory or nursing home. In this culture, where the ideal probably is a permanent, differentiated, noncommunal home, many reside in homes that are temporary (dormitories, apartments, rented houses), homogeneous (because we cannot afford a place that has space for the separation of dining from cooking, or hobbies from entertaining, or laundering from automobile storage), and communal (roommates are necessary to pay the rent).

Residential Satisfaction

Are you happy with the place where you live? Where would you like to live? What would your

FIGURE 9–1 Residences take many forms and influence many of our behaviors. *(Photo at top left courtesy of Robert Sommer.)*

SOCIETAL PROCESSES

dream dwelling look like? The match between your preferences and the physical qualities of your residence is naturally linked to satisfaction. If you are already living in your ideal residential environment—or something close to it—you are probably quite satisfied. Many individuals, unfortunately, live in dwellings that are far from ideal and their dissatisfaction is strong.

An Organizing Model.   To understand residential satisfaction, it must be adequately measured. But measuring it is not as simple as asking, "Do you like your apartment?" For example, satisfaction may vary depending on whether individuals are asked to compare their residences (for example, to their previous residence or to their ideal residence) or not (Craik & Zube, 1976). Satisfaction may be different for different sections of the residence, different qualities of it (such as spaciousness, beauty, or lighting), and the relation between these qualities and their use by the resident (such as lighting for a party versus lighting for washing the dishes), etc. (Canter, 1983).

Several research groups have systematically investigated dwelling satisfaction (Galster & Hesser, 1981; Michelson, 1977; Weidemann, Anderson, Butterfield, & O'Donnell, 1982). Figure 9–2 is presented as an organizing framework for this and other research. The framework is loosely patterned after Brunswik's **lens model** (see Chapter Two) and Craik's model of environment comprehension (see Chapter Three).

Beginning at the left of the framework, note that residences consist of many physical cues. Researchers select certain of these cues for study and present them to observers via different media; the cues are differentially filtered and interpreted by these observers who vary in many ways; this varied interpretation leads to satisfaction (or dissatisfaction), home-based behaviors of many sorts, and well-being (or not).

The physical and personal influences on satisfaction are discussed first. As Galster and Hesser (1981) point out, there are some residences that would make *anyone* dissatisfied. They are so run-down, poorly maintained, or poorly located that almost no one would want to live there. Also, there are individuals who will not be satisfied by any residence; they are so fussy, cranky, neurotic, or perfectionistic that they would find fault with nearly every residence. Between these extremes,

however, are most homes and most residents. Different homes satisfy different residents.

Each home has thousands of characteristics, some unimportant and some important. To help in the understanding of residential satisfaction, the researcher must *select* for study some objective characteristics (**distal cues**) of the dwelling that will actually have some impact on satisfaction. Some of these objective characteristics are the type of housing (single-family dwelling, apartment, condominium, etc.), its size (number of bedrooms, bathrooms, etc.), age, location, market value, lot size, and architectural style.

Many (but not all) of these distal cues are perceived by the resident. But how is the residence displayed? The resident may experience a dwelling over the span of a few minutes (as a prospective buyer who tours a house) or many years (in the case of long-term residents). The perception is usually "live," but if the residence happens to be still in its planning stages, it may have to be simulated. The observer's experience with the residence may be thorough, including an inspection of every corner, or cursory, merely viewing the place while driving by.

The next element in the model is the observer. Who is this person? What culture, personality, gender, age, occupation? How much experience with different homes does this observer have? In evaluating a residence, will the observer compare it to an ideal residence, to past residences, or to standards of residential quality acquired from friends or from the media? Is the observer a resident of the dwelling in question, or a passerby, real estate agent, neighbor, or tax assessor?

So far, then, selected distal cues are perceived through two filters: the mode of presentation and the observer's personal characteristics. These interact and, presto, impressions, or **proximal cues,** emerge. "Aha," says the observer, "this house is cozy (or grimy, or gloomy, or functional)."

These impressions are not, in themselves, conclusions about the ultimate value of the residence. For example, an observer may decide that a house is "traditional," but that does not automatically indicate approval or disapproval of the house; some of us like traditional houses and others don't. That is why the model includes the observer a second time, between proximal cues and outcomes.

As noted earlier, residential satisfaction is only

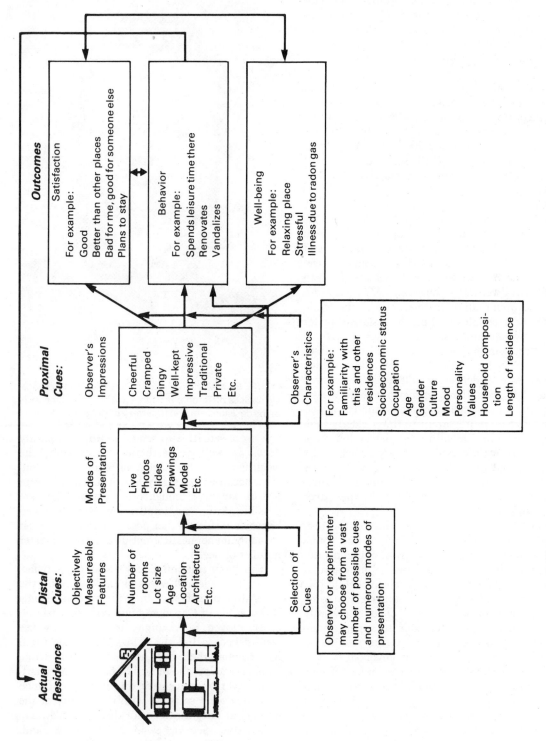

FIGURE 9–2 A research model of residential satisfaction, behavior, and well-being.

one outcome; the model also includes behavior and health of residents or observers. But first we consider some resident and some physical characteristics that have been linked to satisfaction with individual dwellings.

Personal Influences.   Apart from the physical qualities of the residence, satisfaction and preference obviously depend on who the resident is. The characteristics of individuals influencing satisfaction include demography, cognition, and personality. Let's begin with some examples of demographic indicators of satisfaction. (See Fig. 9–3.)

First, differences in residential happiness are associated with age or **stage in the life cycle.** Age-linked differences in satisfaction are presumably due to the changes in our needs, purposes, and position in society that usually accompany age. Over 85 percent of residents of all ages wish to own their dwelling (Michelson, 1977), but families with young children prefer the suburbs, while some older couples and single residents prefer downtown apartments.

In an examination of dwelling style, Nasar (1981, 1983) found that younger adults valued more ornate residences, and older adults preferred more plain ones. Plainness may not sound attractive, but it does imply simplicity and clarity, attributes that are important to those elderly individuals who find mobility and perception more difficult than they used to. The younger adults liked a residence with mystery, but the older adults didn't; they may prefer to find their mystery in a novel, where it won't make their lives more difficult.

Not much evidence is available on the residential satisfaction of individuals at the young end of the age range. One study of children's satisfaction reports that their views are quite similar to those of their parents (Michelson, 1977).

Second, residential satisfaction is related to **socioeconomic status.** In general, of course, wealthier individuals are better able to supply themselves with homes that meet their standards, resulting in greater satisfaction. Beyond this level, however, wealthier and poorer members of society may be attuned to *different* features of their homes. Salling and Harvey (1981) found that wealthier individuals were sensitive to the aesthetic qualities of their home, but poorer individ-

FIGURE 9–3 William Michelson's research on the housing choices of Toronto residents revealed the complexity of the decision to move. (*Courtesy of William Michelson.*)

uals were sensitive to safety, health, and family needs as well as aesthetics. Presumably, the wealthier were less sensitive to the other concerns because their safety, health, and family were not in danger, although other explanations are possible. Still, one implication of Salling and Harvey's results is that poorer individuals must spend their energies attempting to satisfy a greater number of needs.

Third, our **role** influences residential satisfaction. Husbands and wives often disagree on the suitability of a home. In William Michelson's (1977) study of Canadian households that had recently moved, for example, husbands and wives were asked to list the things that made them happy about their new homes and apartments. Among couples who moved to a downtown apartment, over 40 percent of the wives mentioned that they were satisfied with the quality of the home, but only 5 percent of the husbands mentioned this. (See Fig. 9–4.) On the other hand, among couples that moved to suburban apartments over 50 percent of the husbands mentioned quality of the home as a source of their satisfaction, but only 5 percent of the wives did.

Fourth, the **time** dimension is important in residential satisfaction (Michelson, 1980). Satisfaction with our present dwelling depends in part on whether or not we dream of different and better housing in the future. However, those who do not yet live in their dream house are not necessarily dissatisfied with their present dwelling. They seem able to tolerate its limitations as long as their aspirations seem possible. If, for some reason, the dream becomes impossible, however, dissatisfaction may grow.

David Canter (1983) has described two further cognitive processes related to residential satisfaction. He believes that our evaluation of a residence's satisfactoriness is necessarily **purposive.** Purposive evaluations have several facets to them, the level, referent, and focus facets.

First, satisfaction may vary in its specificity or **level.** Residents may be asked to evaluate a single part of the residence (like the kitchen), or a larger portion of it (like the bedrooms as a whole). Second, residents may be asked to assess different qualities of the residence (its beauty, lighting, or spaciousness). These qualities are called **referents;** each one suggests a certain purpose the residence serves well or poorly. The lighting referent, for example, is important when the resident considers tasks such as reading or sewing that require good lighting. Third, questions may take focus into account. The meaning of **focus** depends on the referent, but one way to think of it is to ask how broadly we are asking the resident to evaluate something. With reference to lighting, is it the ability of this particular lamp to light a study desk, or is it broader—lighting in the home as a whole? The role of purpose emerges when we ask what is the resident's relationship *to* the home. Some residents feel as if they will live in the house forever, but others intend to move soon, or are renting. Thus, in general, a resident's purpose in doing an evaluation is itself a crucial factor in satisfaction.

The other cognitive factor of interest is **comparison.** Whether we explicitly ask observers to

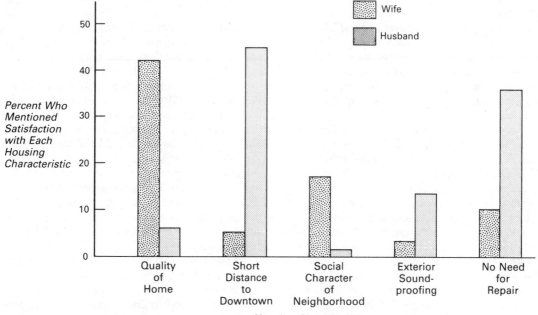

FIGURE 9–4 Husbands and wives moving to a downtown apartment in Toronto report some different sources of satisfaction with their new dwelling. *(From* Environmental Choice, Human Behavior, and Residential Satisfaction *by William Michelson, Copyright © 1977 by Oxford University Press, Inc. Reprinted by permission.)*

compare a specific residence against a series of others or merely ask for a rating of the present one (without explicitly pointing out others), evaluators cannot help at least implicitly comparing the residence in question with others in their experience.

When an observer compares residences, a discrepancy between residences will appear. Some approaches to residential satisfaction focus on this discrepancy between present and past residences, or between present and ideal residences. Perceived physical qualities of a residence (such as its appearance and provision for privacy) are important predictors of satisfaction (Weidemann, Anderson, Butterfield, & O'Donnell, 1982), and so are preferred physical qualities. However, the *difference* between perceived and preferred qualities is a separate but important predictor of housing satisfaction (Handal, Barling, Morrissy, 1981; Morrissy & Handal, 1981).

A few significant relations between personality and residential satisfaction have been reported. Wiggins (1975) studied satisfaction with army housing as a function of soldier personality. He found that aggressive soldiers were generally dissatisfied with their housing. Soldiers with a desire for structure in their lives particularly appreciated the physical features of their living environment, as did those with nurturant personalities. Soldiers whose personalities lead them to seek considerable social support expressed greater preferences for design features that would assist this need, such as more private visiting areas and more telephones.

Some environmental psychologists are skeptical about the value of learning how person-based variables relate to residential satisfaction. Individuals are all so different, they would say, that an architect or planner cannot possibly satisfy everyone in the residence. Designers should just concentrate on the environmental attributes of housing, searching for arrangements and styles that please as many individuals as possible.

However, a key element in the design process is assessment of the needs of the clients who will occupy the building. Yet a major hurdle to such assessments is that designers and architects often do not understand their clients. One of the commonest research findings is that architects and their clients evaluate buildings differently (Hershberger, 1970, 1974). Knowledge of how res-

ident characteristics are related to residential satisfaction is especially needed when architects think differently from their clients. Thus, other environmental psychologists believe that designers do need to know as much about their residents as possible.

Environmental Influences. Many physical factors affect our satisfaction with a residence. In this section, three are discussed: type of housing, room arrangement, and household density.

William Michelson (1977) was able to investigate housing type when he undertook a large-scale study of Toronto residents who moved. Over 50 percent of those who moved to a single-family dwelling said they were "definitely satisfied" but less than 25 perent of those who moved to an apartment said they were "definitely satisfied." This preference for the single-family dwelling has persisted in North America for many years (Marans, 1976). Sometimes condominiums or apartments are said to be growing in popularity, but often these reports are because high cost forces the purchaser to rule out single-family dwellings.

Inside the residence, everyday experience suggests that the arrangement of rooms can be an important factor in a purchaser's decision. It is unfortunate that what little empirical data there is on this question is mixed. Cunningham (1977) reported that American university students preferred floor plans that showed the living room in the upper right corner of the drawing. However, Weisenthal and Tubiana (1981) repeated the study with Israeli students and found less support for the right-hand preference idea. Weisenthal and Tubiana tried to assess the effect of other relevant variables, such as which room arrangement their subjects actually lived in but were unable to clarify the differences between their results and those obtained by Cunningham. Much more study is required before we can reach any firm conclusions about which individuals prefer which room arrangements.

Another physical variable that affects satisfaction is household population density. As we saw in Chapter Seven, high indoor densities have often been linked to stress and social problems. William Rohe (1982) confirmed this linkage in a study of off-campus residents in a small college town: Reported stress increased as the number of individuals per room rose. Rohe hypothesized, however, that density-related dissatisfaction is not quite as simple as it sounds.

Rohe's study is a good example of research that delves beyond the obvious to discover the kind of subtleties that are typical of our complex interactions with the environment. He tested the idea that dissatisfaction is mediated by such factors as the closeness of the relationships among the household's residents (such as family versus unrelated roommates) and residents' previous experience with high-density living. For example, is dissatisfaction less if residents are all from the same family or if they have lived through high-density residential situations before?

Surprisingly, those residents who had closer relationships and those who had lived in high densities before were *more* dissatisfied with high-density living. Instead of having learned to live with it, residents who were more experienced in high-density living seemed to possess lower tolerance for it. Residents with closer social ties (those who lived with family), instead of being able to overcome the pressures of high density, were more strongly affected by it. The study yielded some unexpected results that need further study. How would *you* explain Rohe's results?

Stress and Mobility: Outcomes of Residential Dissatisfaction

In the model of residential satisfaction described earlier, outcomes of people's experience with a dwelling were said to include not only dissatisfaction but also behavioral and health consequences. One such outcome is mobility. Dissatisfaction with housing contributes to the decision to move, and moving is very common. In any given 5-year period, about 45 percent of North Americans, 36 percent of Britains and Japanese, and 48 percent of Australians move, according to Dan Stokols and his colleagues.

Not all decisions to move are the result of dissatisfaction with previous housing, but mobility is nevertheless associated with a number of adverse outcomes. Those who move more often report more illness-related symptoms than those who move less often (Stokols, Shumaker, & Martinez, 1983). This stress is mediated by personal characteristics. Among individuals in the Stokols et al. study who were highly mobile, those who

were generally less inclined to explore the environment reported more illness than those who were more inclined to explore the environment. This suggests that mobility is more damaging to those who move often but simply don't enjoy seeking out new places.

In another examination of the effects of mobility, Sandra Newman and Michael Owen (1982) note that mobility may be chosen or forced. The poor and the elderly, whose mobility is often forced, typically become more crowded after a move, and displaced residents often pay more for their new housing than they did for their old housing. Stokols et al. (1983) found more reported illness among residents who moved *less* often but were unhappy with their present residence and felt they had little choice of residence. Thus, *lack of mobility* can also be damaging when our options for moving are restricted.

One group with restricted options is the family headed by a female single parent, which now comprises over one-quarter of all households in the United States. They are more mobile than other households (Masnick & Bane, 1980); and owing to landlord discrimination, higher rent costs (in relation to income), and relative lack of transportation, they face a more stressful housing search (Ahrentzen, in press). Even among a group that presumably does have some choice in leaving home—students leaving home for university—60 percent report being homesick (Fisher, Murray, & Frazer, 1985).

Environment and Behavior in the Home

It is much easier to study satisfaction *with* a home than it is to study behavior *in* the home. Satisfaction may be surveyed from any convenient public place where respondents may be found, but many of our beliefs and customs work against allowing researchers to monitor our behavior in the sanctity of our homes. For that reason, this section is much shorter than the "Residential Satisfaction" section. Nevertheless, researchers have begun to provide knowledge about behavior in the home in at least three categories: space management, the effects of home design, and home-based leisure. Considerable research on another home behavior, energy conservation, appears in Chapter Thirteen. Let's look at space management first.

Space Management. As we interact, work, and play at home, we must work out how to use the available space. The self-other boundary regulation processes (Altman, 1975) described in Chapters Five to Eight can become particularly complex when the confines of a residence are combined with the closeness of household ties. Space management varies with the family or resident group and with the physical arrangement of the dwelling.

For example, differentiated and homogeneous homes (recall Altman's five dimensions for describing residences) encourage different patterns of space use.

In a highly differentiated home with many special-purpose rooms, privacy may be obtained through the use of walls and closed doors. In less differentiated homes, privacy must be obtained through a set of social customs, such as modulating the voice to avoid being overheard and looking away when others are dressing.

Parke and Sawin (1979) describe the complex process of home privacy with special reference to children. As they grow up, children are taught which rooms are open to them at which times; later they make privacy demands of their own. Privacy conflicts may occur depending on which activity a person is engaged in, which parent or child desires access, the size of the home, and the accepted child-rearing practices in the home. Frank Becker (1974) has described three family strategies for dealing with space conflicts. **Time territory** strategies involve rotating a particular space (like the TV setting) among family members. **Space territory** strategies attempt to place conflicting activities in different parts of the home. **Cooperation-capitulation** arrangements occur when a dominant family member determines that everyone will engage in one activity, together, at the same time.

The traditional kibbutz in Israel took the radical step of separating parents and children. To discourage "privatism" and individualism in the socialist atmosphere of the traditional kibbutz, children lived in communal houses; parents visited the children's house for a few hours each day. Recently, as political and social values have changed, some kibbutzim have altered this pattern so that children sleep in their parents' house. The differences between families using the two types of arrangement were compared (Raviv & Palgi, 1985). Those using family-based sleeping arrangements said that they helped, supported, and were more committed to one another than families using the communal arrangement. They also said they encouraged family members to act and speak more openly. Those whose children slept communally said they participated in more social and recreational activities and placed more importance on the planning and organization of family activities and responsibilities. These differences are traced in part by the authors to the different sleeping arrangements but also to differences in values between families that have chosen one system or the other.

Perhaps because of the difficulty of conducting research inside homes, most residential crowding research has been conducted in dormitories, prisons, and a variety of unusual temporary homes such as submarines and oil drilling platforms (Aiello & Baum, 1979). High densities in these settings leads to dissatisfaction with the physical environment and social support (Holahan & Wilcox, 1979) as well as more behavioral and health problems (Stokols, Ohlig, & Resnick, 1979). Stokol et al. suggest that crowding in homes, where more important social interaction occurs, has more serious consequences than crowding in public environments.

High density in the home has, in fact, been strongly linked with various social pathologies, including juvenile delinquency, mental hospital admissions, and high fertility and mortality rates (Galle & Gove, 1979). Galle and Gove used a statistical method for controlling for poverty to find out whether density had any effect *apart* from the effect of poverty. They found that mental hospital admission rate was predicted reasonably well by density alone, and that juvenile delinquency and fertility were also related to density alone, although not as strongly. They conclude that high density is hard to separate from poverty, but it does seem to have a moderate negative effect on its own. In another study, data from sixty-five countries showed that higher residential densities (persons per room) were correlated with higher murder rates (Booth & Welch, 1973).

A number of studies focus on the effects of high-density living on parent-child relations. When the household is crowded, children may receive less attention of a constructive nature yet may be struck more often by their parents (Booth

& Edwards, 1976). Thus children from high-density homes may be forced outdoors more often, leading more of them into trouble on the street—delinquency—and in school—behavior problems—(Booth & Johnson, 1975; Saegert, 1980).

Judith Rodin (1976) found that children who lived with many other individuals exercised less control when they *were* given the power to make choices than did children from low-density homes. It seems high-density children may not learn to persist in tasks or to make active choices when given the chance. Perhaps children in high-density homes are less often given such opportunities to learn about or exercise choice and control than are children in lower-density homes.

In another series of studies, high density in homes was linked to school performance (Bradley & Caldwell, 1984a, b). The homes of twelve-month-old children were surveyed; those with higher indoor densities were found to have poorer physical organization and fewer play materials (even after various statistical controls were applied). Reading performance 5 years later was lower for children who had fewer play materials at home as one-year-olds, even after their intelligence test scores were controlled for. Other studies (Heft, 1985; Wachs, 1979) reveal that the noise often accompanying high density impairs the perceptual-cognitive development of young children. Saegert (1980) also found lower school performance in children from high-density homes.

These results suggest that physical characteristics of homes have long-term effects on the development of important skills in children and that parent-child relations are disrupted by high indoor density. The importance of these effects has been debated (Booth, Johnson, & Edwards, 1980; Gove & Hughes, 1980). The negative effects of residential high density may appear smaller than they really are because families can, with effort, muffle the strain of high-density living through various coping strategies.

Architecture and Home Behavior.   Amazingly little is known about the effect of architecture on behavior in the home, apart from the space-management research covered above. Again, this lack is largely due to our discomfort about allowing researchers inside our homes to conduct research. Thus, most research reaches "inside" homes by interviewing residents or giving them questionnaires, rather than monitoring actual behavior in the home.

A major architectural distinction is between single-family dwellings and multiple-unit dwellings. Van Vliet—(1983) reviewed the research on the effects of apartments. He cites many studies that paint apartments as poor places for children to grow up and for adults to thrive. He lists studies showing that apartment living is associated with numerous childhood afflictions, including retarded movement skills, more respiratory diseases, more aggression, insomnia, more nervous disorders, reduced social skills, and disrupted play. If all this is true, we may wonder how any child can survive in an apartment. However, van Vliet— is quick to note that many of these studies are lacking in experimental rigor; their results must be questioned. His point is that housing trends indicate that more of us will be living in apartments and we had better do more and better research on the effects of apartment living on children.

One form of apartments, the high rise, does seem to have negative effects, particularly on nuclear families. For example, Dennis McCarthy and Susan Saegert (1978) compared the effects on adults of living in high-rise and low-rise multiple-unit residences. High-rise and low-rise tenants of the buildings, part of a low-income project in New York, were of similar age, education, and other demographic indicators. However, residents of the high rises felt more socially overloaded, more anonymous, less safe, less satisfied with their building and had more difficulty establishing supportive relationships with their neighbors. They also felt more powerless to change building policies and believed they had less privacy. When families with young children live in high rises, parents find it difficult to allow children outside to play. When play is thereby confined largely to the apartment, tension and conflict in the family rises (Becker, 1974).

At the other end of the housing spectrum, Weisner and Weibel (1981) investigated what influences lead California single-family dwelling homeowners to adopt different kinds of home environments. The researchers began by describing a wide variety of homes on thirty-eight different dimensions (such as cleanliness, number of books, need for repair). These factors were grouped into four factors using statistical procedures: disorder/functional complexity (the physical state and maintenance of the home), decorative complexity (material richness), warm/child-oriented (number of child-centered items), and books (number and variety of books). Next, Weisner and Weibel examined the connection between home type (based on the four factors) and several antecedent factors, such as family type (traditional nuclear family, unmarried parents, communal household, single mother), income, and lifestyle. The goal was to find which of these antecedent factors may have led homeowners to arrange their houses as they did.

Weiser and Weibel found that the homes of un-married parents had the highest scores on disorder/functional complexity: their lawns were more overgrown and their houses more "funky" than those of traditional-marriage parents. The communal homes had more books than the traditional-marriage homes. Higher-income homes had lower scores on disorder/functional complexity. It is surprising that as women's income rose, number and variety of books in the home dropped. Parents with natural/organic lifestyles had homes with higher scores on disorder/functional complexity. (See Fig. 9–5.)

Leisure. A primary purpose of the home is to provide a place for relaxation and entertainment.

FIGURE 9–5 Funky and trim dwellings reflect different lifestyles.

Over half our recreational time is spent inside the home (Glyptis & Chambers, 1982), so it is important to understand the role of the physical environment in residential leisure behaviors such as playing games, watching TV, gardening, crafts, reading, and just lounging.

Home-based leisure is strongly affected by the size and differentiation of the home. Those who live in bachelor apartments may feel driven outside to find suitable recreation, but denizens of mansions wander from pool room to indoor pool to computer room to the bar. In relatively homogeneous homes, leisure is apt to conflict with other activities; in households where necessity or values favor work, leisure time and quality are likely to suffer. We may regard home-based leisure as too commonplace and unimportant for serious attention, yet its value in relieving stress and serving as an important vehicle for social bonds within the home seems clear.

This assertion is consistent with the results from a study of the home-based leisure activities of adolescents and their families (McMillan & Hiltonsmith, 1982). A strong positive relation was found between the amount of time the adolescents spent with their parents in recreational activities at home and their general sense of well-being. Of course, all leisure activities are not equally valuable. Adolescents in the study who watched more television were found to be less oriented to intellectual and cultural activities. It is unfortunate that these hints from studies that home-based leisure can have important positive and negative effects on us remain to be verified, expanded, and refined by future researchers.

▶ **In Sum.** "Home" is a rich personal experience that may develop in a residence. Residences may be described in many ways, but five dimensions are: permanent versus temporary, differentiated versus homogeneous, communal versus noncommunal, identity versus communality, and open versus closed. Residential satisfaction is a function of person and residence characteristics. The more congruent the residence is with our stage in the life cycle and role in the family, the more satisfied we are likely to be. Rated satisfaction also depends on the purpose of making the evaluation, the dwelling's purpose to the resident, and which other residences are compared to our own in judging satisfaction. As for physical characteristics, the single-family dwelling is by far the preferred residence form. Single and elderly individuals, however, often prefer apartments.

High indoor density is a key dissatisfier. Moving is one outcome of dissatisfaction; it is a source of stress in itself. Individuals who have little residential choice or don't enjoy new settings experience even more mobility stress. Behavior *in* the home (such as space management, the effects of architectural style on behavior, and home-based leisure) is rarely studied except through interviews, primarily because of the difficulties involved in conducting research inside the home.

Privacy and crowding are the biggest problems, primarily as they harm child development. High rises, in particular, seem inappropriate for children. Factors other than the height of the building play a role, but most such factors do operate in the typical high rise.

Resident lifestyle is reflected in the physical organization of the home (as in the California study). Home is an important place for experiencing the growth and relaxation that leisure can provide.

ENVIRONMENTAL PSYCHOLOGY IN THE COMMUNITY

In this section, we move from the dwelling itself into the streets. We will explore person-environment relations in public places: the neighborhood, the community, and on city streets. Some of the questions to be addressed are: What constitutes a satisfying neighborhood? Under what environmental conditions will individuals in public places tend to help or hurt one another? What is the nature of social interaction in public places? How does the physical environment influence shopping? We begin with the sources of satisfaction in neighborhoods.

Sources of Neighborhood Satisfaction

Physical and Personal Factors. Once you are outside, on the streets near your home, are you satisfied with what you see and hear? Does your neighborhood make you feel proud or ashamed? Do you feel as if you'd like to escape as soon as possible, or that you'd like to spend your whole life in such a great place?

The answer depends partly on the physical

characteristics of the neighborhood itself. Is it noisy, expensive, downtown, split by major transportation routes, smoggy? Taylor (1982) concludes from his survey of research that physical deterioration and lack of nearby green space are strongly related to dissatisfaction with the neighborhood. Widgery (1982) also confirms the commonsense notion that satisfaction with a neighborhood depends in large part on the aesthetic quality of the neighborhood.

Cities reflect the culture and times in which they are embedded (Rapoport, 1985). Within any single culture or era, we tend to overlook the ways in which neighborhood forms mirror our values in the same way that fish are said to be the last to discover water. Consider different eras within one culture, for example. Rapoport (1985) describes how a city on the U.S. East Coast has been remade several times. First it had an "organic" irregular street pattern. This pattern was replaced by a strict grid system that represented a modern point of view at one time. Now the streets have become curves with many culs-de-sac, not unlike their original layout! Satisfaction with this and many other features of cities that vary with time and culture presumably is a function of congruence between residents' culture and the era with which they identify (Gifford, 1984–1985) and the physical form of the community.

Cross-cultural diversity may characterize some features of communities, but other features seem to have a near-universal meaning (Rapoport, 1982). For example, religious buildings from the cathedral at Chartres to temples in India to basilicas in Milwaukee to sacred buildings in Papua, New Guinea all use height to express holiness. The idea of reaching toward the heavens with buildings seems to have occurred to most of the world's designers of religious buildings, reflecting a similar idea that is part of many cultures. Other features of communities also show widespread similarity across cultures. Satisfaction with community presumably is a function of whether these near-universal features are present in the buildings and form of our own community.

Cities are sometimes viewed as unrelenting sources of noise, crime, ugliness, and crowding. The overload approach suggests that urban stimulation is so great that individuals are *forced* to become apathetic and rude. Stanley Milgram's (1970) classic article on the topic was meant to defend urbanites by showing they had little choice in the face of an avalanche of stimulation. They must select for their attention and care only the most important stimuli, which means ignoring other stimuli that might seem important to outsiders. Overload was seen to "deform" the daily life of urbanites.

This perspective may have improved the image of city dwellers by arguing that they couldn't help being rude and unhelpful; but city dwellers aren't always like that anyway, and it made *cities* look bad as well as city dwellers. On the first issue, it may be true that city dwellers are less friendly to neighbors and strangers than are rural residents, but they are just as involved with family and relatives (Franck, 1980; Korte, 1980).

On the second issue, the specter of overload in the city is not true for everyone. After an initial period of actively coping with the admittedly higher levels of stimulation found in the city, most new residents are able to find a social and physical niche that protects them from undesirable levels of stimulation. Of course, this protection depends in part on your resources; it is often said that New York is a great place to live if you have money. Still, it is obvious that millions of urbanites lead satisfying lives that are sheltered from excessive stimulation.

Daniel Geller (1980) has invoked the concept of optimal level of stimulation to develop a more balanced view of city life. The large amount of stimulation found in cities may be too much (an overload) for some individuals, such as some new arrivals, but just right for others. He suggests that an adaptation-level approach helps us understand who likes cities and who doesn't. Those who are adapted to quite low levels of stimulation—perhaps a villager—might find the sudden drastic increase in stimulation unpleasant. Similarly, city dwellers used to lots of action may find villages painfully boring. Helson (1964) suggested that *moderate* discrepancies from our adaptation level are pleasing. In the case of communities, this could mean that a villager would be pleased by a town but not a city, and that city dwellers would rather vacation in a small town than in a village or out in the wilderness.

An individual's community satisfaction also depends on other personal factors, such as whether you own or rent and your stage of life (Michelson, 1977). Frances and Abraham Carp's

(1982a) study of the impact of San Francisco's Bay Area Rapid Transit system (BART) on neighborhood satisfaction, discussed in Chapter Three, illustrated the idea that *both* person and environment factors are important. But what exactly are these person-environment sources of satisfaction?

William Michelson's (1977) study of Toronto families who had recently moved reveals that satisfaction with physical aspects of the community is strongly influenced by availability of public transportation and parking facilities, appearance of the neighborhood, and distance to green spaces. However, satisfaction is mediated by other factors, such as whether the resident lives downtown or in the suburbs and whether the residence is an apartment or a house. For example, distance to green spaces is a greater source of dissatisfaction for downtown residents than it is for suburban residents. Lack of public transportation is a bigger source of unhappiness for suburban apartment dwellers than it is for downtown residents.

Michelson reports one source of dissatisfaction that is surprising. Noise is one of the most dissatisfying features of many communities (Llewellyn, 1981). Because we think of urban areas as noisy, we might expect downtown residents to be most upset about noise. However, Michelson found that two or three times as many residents of suburban houses were dissatisfied with noise from the environment as were residents of downtown houses. This suggests that (a) downtown neighborhoods are actually quieter than suburban neighborhoods, or (b) downtown residents have adapted to higher noise levels and no longer notice the noise, or (c) suburbanites expect their homes to be even quieter than they are.

This raises the question of adaptation to community noise. Can we get used to noise, so that it doesn't bother us anymore? Neil Weinstein (1982), after reviewing the research in this area, concludes that the evidence does *not* support the idea that people can get used to anything. In a study of his own, the same residents were interviewed 4 months and 16 months after a major new highway opened in their community. The new highway raised sound levels 16 to 20 decibels above that in similar neighborhoods with no highway. The residents' annoyance with the increased sound did not decrease in the 12 months interval between surveys. Weinstein reports that residents became more pessimistic about their ability to adapt. This is one sample of individuals who do not believe that you can get used to anything!

Nevertheless, some individuals may be able to adapt to noise. Mehrabian (1977) proposes that some of us are capable of screening out unwanted stimulation. Another mediating variable may be anxiety level. A study of over 100 individuals' responses to traffic noise found that low-anxiety respondents appeared able to adapt to the noise, but high-anxiety respondents did not (Jonah, Bradley, & Dawson, 1981).

In many neighborhoods, another source of dissatisfaction is noise from aircraft. Near a busy Southern California airport where air traffic alone created an average 65 decibel of sound all day, 84 percent of residents said aircraft noise was a problem (Jue, Shumaker, & Evans, 1984). Once again, annoyance was mediated by a personal factor: residents with low perceived control over the noise were more annoyed than residents who believed they could have some control over it.

Individuals may, however, adapt to other community stressors, such as air pollution. Gary Evans and his co-workers found that long-time Los Angeles residents were just as *capable* of perceiving smog as newer residents, but they were significantly less likely to actually report a given day as smoggy (Evans, Jacobs, & Frager, 1982b). It seems they could *see* smog, but at lower levels they no longer realized that what they saw was indeed smog. Presumably then, long-term residents' satisfaction with their community would not be adversely affected by low levels of smog. It may, however, adversely affect their social behavior and their health, as we shall see.

Among other features of the environment that influence residential satisfaction, one of the most important is the visual quality of the immediately surrounding area—the streets of the neighborhood. Jack Nasar (1983) showed sixty residential scenes to design professionals and to adult laypersons. These groups preferred scenes that showed well-kept yards, ornate rather than plain buildings, scenes depicting single-use buildings (such as all residences as opposed to residential-commercial mixtures), and scenes that appeared open. (See Fig. 9–6.) These characteristics are typical of more expensive housing, which we would

FIGURE 9–6 Mixed residential-commercial development is common in cities but may be less preferable to some residents than purely residential districts.

expect to be satisfying to many individuals. However, the value of research like Nasar's is that we begin to learn which specific aspects of expensive housing are preferred. Certainly houses have been constructed that are very expensive yet do not satisfy their residents; mere expensiveness does not guarantee satisfaction.

This is illustrated by another study by the same researcher, indicating that not everyone prefers housing with these expensive qualities. Nasar (1981) found that elderly observers also preferred residential scenes that were open and well-kept, but they did not prefer scenes with single-use buildings over scenes depicting mixed-building types, and some of them preferred plain buildings to ornate ones. In addition, the older judges preferred more uniform scenes over more diverse ones, more organized scenes over more disorganized ones, and scenes with little mystery over others with more mystery.

Social Factors.   What about the social environment of a community? Doesn't our satisfaction with a neighborhood depend on the quality of its social life? Surprisingly, social networks may be important sources of satisfaction only in a few communities. Marc Fried, who coauthored a classic study indicating the crucial role of social ties for residential satisfaction (Fried & Gleicher, 1961), now feels that most residential satisfaction is largely due to the *physical* quality of the neighborhood (Fried, 1982). Interviews of 2,500 individuals in over forty municipalities suggested that social ties are an important source of neighborhood satisfaction only to those who strongly value social ties. The implication is that many of us simply no longer value the neighborhood as a source of friends—we look to work, school, and other nonneighborhood places for our social needs. Another study (Handal, Barling, & Morrissy, 1981) directly compared physical and social aspects of neighborhoods, and found that the physical aspects predicted resident satisfaction better than the social aspects did.

Nevertheless, there are still some groups who see the neighborhood as crucial to residential and life satisfaction. Rivlin (1982) describes, for example, a religious group that explicitly works toward building close physical ties (by buying or renting in one neighborhood) to facilitate close social ties. This is a pattern many ethnic groups follow, especially among members who remain more oriented to the language and customs of the old country than to the dominant culture. But as Loo and Mar (1982) show, many ethnic group members begin to seek housing outside the traditional ethnic enclave as soon as they have enough money and feel comfortable in the dominant culture. This seems to reinforce Fried's position that social ties are less important for most residents than the physical qualities of the community.

Freedom from Crime. Fear of crime is another important factor in neighborhood satisfaction. It isn't easy to feel good about a community if every time you go outside, you half expect to get mugged or raped. It is interesting that fear of crime does not heavily depend on the actual crime rate. It may be inflated by flashy media portrayals. In a study of Hong Kong and Toronto, fear of crime was more closely associated with population density than with actual crime rates (Gifford & Peacock, 1979). This is an unresolved issue, however, because others have concluded that density is more associated with crime than it is with our fear of crime (Taylor, 1982).

Oscar Newman's (1980) theory of defensible space, discussed in Chapter Six, argues that certain arrangements of streets and other public territories create settings where space is easily given surveillance and clearly defined as to ownership. Whether such designs really lower crimes is not proved (many other factors may play a role), but the designs do seem to make residents *feel* safer. For example, lighting designed to facilitate sur-

veillance of public areas reduced the fears of individuals even though crime may not have been reduced (Tien, O'Donnell, Barnett, & Mirchandani, 1979).

Prosocial and Antisocial Behavior in Urban Settings

What environmental conditions in the streets of our communities influence individuals to help or hurt others? Temperature, noise, crowding, and air pollution have all been linked to altruism and aggression. Elements of the environment have been linked to social problems (in studies, for example, relating high outdoor temperatures to rioting) and social problems have been linked to behaviors that affect the environment (in studies relating poverty to vandalism).

Vandalism. Beginning with the latter, vandalism is a widespread destructive behavior. Not every alteration of public territory is vandalism, of course. Robert Sommer (1972) distinguishes between vandalism and people's art. Part of the distinction involves motive: the artist's goal is to beautify an ugly environment. Vandals are destructive or egocentric; instead of painting a mural that reflects a social concern, they break off a young tree or scrawl their own name on a subway wall. In contrast, public artists usually seek anonymity yet creatively enhance a bleak place.

The vandal's motive may often be revenge. An equity-theory model views the vandal as a person who feels unfairly dealt with (Baron & Fisher, 1984). Vandalism may be particularly likely when this perceived unfairness is combined with a perceived lack of control, a feeling that the injustice cannot be rectified through normal channels, although very low perceived control may lead vandals to become passive. Whether or not potential vandals have a role model—someone who engages in vandalism—may also be important (Baron, 1984).

Weather. Perhaps the best-known of these variables is temperature. A popular idea is that high temperatures or, more precisely, heat discomfort (Harries & Stadler, 1983) causes riots and other social aggression. Police have subscribed to this notion for a long time (Bell & Greene, 1982), but public awareness of the hypothesis was heightened by a report from the U.S. Riot Commission (1968). The commission's figures indicated that all 1967 riots except one began when the temperature was at least 27°C (80°F). The Commission did not intend this as proof that heat causes aggression. However, as sometimes happens when informal studies confirm an intuitively attractive idea, many readers accepted the data as proof that high temperatures cause riots. What is the empirical evidence?

Baron and Ransberger (1978) studied riot and temperature records over a 4-year period and concluded that riots *did* increase with temperature—to about 28°C (83°F). However, at higher temperatures, they seemed to decrease. Baron and Ransberger hypothesized that over this peak, the temperature may be *too* high to promote riots.

The following year, Carlsmith and Anderson (1979) reexamined the temperature and riot records and pointed out that riots decreased on days over the peak temperature mainly because there simply weren't that many days over the peak! They suggested that when this **base-rate problem** was corrected for, antisocial behavior does, after all, rise steadily with temperature. (See Fig. 9–7.)

Other field studies (Anderson & Anderson, 1984; Cotton, 1982) also show that, within the normal range of temperatures (up to about 35°C or 95°F), the hotter it is the more aggressive acts occur. Field research thus supports the linear hypothesis (more heat equals more aggression) rather than the curvilinear hypothesis (aggression peaks at moderately hot temperatures and declines in very hot temperatures).

However, Baron and Ransberger's basic contention—that antisocial behavior declines at very high temperatures—almost certainly is true at sufficiently high temperatures. My own experience with 45°C (113°F) temperatures is that no one any longer wishes even to *move,* let alone run amok in a riot. However, the temperature at which aggression begins to decline because potential aggressors are too hot to hit is so high that for all practical purposes, aggression does increase with temperature.

On the positive side of social behavior, Cunningham (1979) asked individuals to help him with a questionnaire under different climatic conditions. He found that temperature affected how much subjects were willing to help, but the effect was not the same in the summer as it was in the winter. In summer, they helped more on cooler days, but in winter they helped more on warm days. It seems we help more when the weather is "nice" (warm winter days and cool summer days). Assuming that most of us think of sunshine as pleasant, Cunningham's work supports the following nice-weather hypothesis: In both summer and winter, we are more willing to help when it is sunny.

These results appear tidy until we examine a study by Frank Schneider and his colleagues. They carefully studied four different helping behaviors, both outdoors and indoors, and found that temperature made no difference (Schneider, Lesko, & Garrett, 1980). Schneider is continuing his research, trying to solve the mystery of these conflicting results.

Noise. Does loud noise reduce helping or increase aggression? Again, if noise is loud enough,

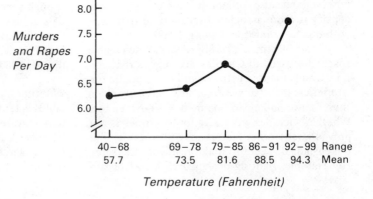

FIGURE 9–7 The number of murders and rapes per day in Houston, Texas, as a function of the maximum temperature on the day of the crime. *(Anderson, C. A., & Anderson, D. C. (1984) Ambient temperature and violent crime: Tests of the linear and curvilinear hypotheses.* Journal of Personality and Social Psychology, 46, 91–97. *Copyright 1984 by the American Psychological Association. Reprinted by permission of the author.)*

many of us try to escape it, rather than help someone in need. Loud noise may reduce helping because in attempting to escape, our attention is narrowed. We walk faster and gaze straight ahead more (Korte & Grant, 1980). Of course, another factor is the seriousness of the other person's predicament. If someone's life is in danger, we will probably risk noise loud enough to hurt our ears in order to render assistance. But if, as in some studies, the other person's only problem is a dropped book, we may not help. For example, Page (1977) found that construction noise (92 decibels as opposed to 72 decibels away from the construction) hindered individuals from giving a quarter to a person who asked for one. Panhandlers are advised to avoid noisy corners.

The "seriousness" factor was supported in a study by Mathews and Canon (1975), who observed how many passersby helped a person who dropped an armload of books. They arranged for a nearby lawn mower with no muffler to be running during the incident (87 decibels) or not (about 50 decibels). In addition, the person who dropped the books either was wearing a cast or not. Without a cast, the book dropper was helped by 20 percent of passersby under low noise and 10 percent of them under high noise. A much larger difference occurred when a cast was worn. Under low noise 80 percent helped, but only 15 percent under high noise.

Schneider, Lesko, and Garrett (1980) also included a needy case in their study—someone using crutches—but found no temperature differences; over 95 percent of passersby helped in hot, cold, and comfortable temperatures. Apparently, then, there is a big difference between helping in extreme temperatures and helping in noisy conditions. Why should this be?

One possibility is that we can usually anticipate and dress for cold or hot temperatures, thereby reducing the adverse effects of temperature. But when we encounter noise in public places we cannot counter the annoyance easily, except by leaving. When the noise is localized (as with a lawn mower), we realize that a little fast walking, which incidentally carries us past the person who needs help, will carry us beyond the awful din.

Noise in the streets may even affect how we think about others. Siegel and Steele (1980) asked their subjects to form impressions of others under low- and high-noise conditions. In the noisier conditions, these interpersonal judgments were more *extreme*. It seems that noise, perhaps because it acts as a general arousal agent, influences us to reach stronger conclusions about others than we might make under normal conditions.

Air Pollution.   Following several earlier studies suggesting that bad odors negatively affect mood and attraction to others, James Rotton searched for links between air pollution and social pathology in a community setting. Rotton and Frey (1985a, b) discovered that higher levels of photochemical oxidants in the air were correlated with more domestic disputes and more instances of psychiatric disturbance. Correlation does not imply causation, but Rotton and Frey were able to eliminate several alternative explanations for their findings. Rotton (1983) found that students exposed to a bad-smelling pollutant judged peers (shown in photographs) lower on a scale of well-being.

Of course, the intermediate stages of the phenomenon remain to be discovered. What does smog do to us that, in turn, influences some individuals to engage in antisocial behavior? If Rotton and Frey's work is confirmed by subsequent research, the implications are very important for two reasons. First, we may expect that high temperatures and loud noise harm social relations, but we don't usually think of air pollution as an antisocial agent. Smog may be a hidden cause of aggression. Second, those committed to fighting smog could reasonably argue that it erodes more than paint, vegetation, and the pH balance of lakes. It erodes human relations.

Number of People.   Finally, the number of bystanders is related to helping. This idea was strengthened by the many studies stimulated by a 1964 episode in which a young woman, Kitty Genovese, was killed on a New York street while over thirty neighbors watched without helping her (Latane & Darley, 1970). Subsequent research has found that, under most conditions, the more individuals who witness someone having a problem, the smaller the odds that any one of them will help.

In one field study, the experimenter appeared to lose her contact lens. Helping behavior was defined as the length of time that the subject helped her look for it. When the shopping mall where the study occurred was moderately full, subjects helped less than when it was moderately empty (Cohen & Spacapan, 1978). In another field study (Kammann, Thomson, & Irwin, 1979), density in the immediate vicinity of the person needing help was more closely related to helping (high density was associated with less helpfulness) than was density at the communitywide level.

Urbanites do, of course, help those in need under some conditions. Once again, mediating variables such as a heavy workload (Cohen & Spacapan, 1978), where we are raised, and cognitive complexity (Weiner, 1976) play an important and sometimes counterintuitive role. For example, in Weiner's study, those who were raised in the *city* helped more than those who were raised in the country. Thus high immediate densities may cause unhelpful behavior, but who the potential helper is and the circumstances other than high density surrounding the event also affect helping behavior.

People As Part of the Urban Environment

When we see a film in which the camera wanders through a city with not one person to be seen, we feel something is terribly wrong. The presence of other people as we walk through the streets is a necessary component of normal reality. Yet, at least in towns and cities, we usually do not know most of the individuals we deal with. Although it may sound inhuman, people in the background of the urban panorama may be considered part of the environment. How do we interact with this part of the environment?

For the most part, even though we would feel very strange if we were the only ones on the street, we try to avoid contact with most individuals in public. For example, commuters are less willing to make eye contact with a stranger in the city than they are with the same stranger in the suburbs (McCauley, Coleman, & De Fusco, 1978).

Lyn Lofland (1973) says that urbanites operate according to a **mini-max principle:** Minimize involvement with others, maximize social order. A good example of this principle is provided by research on pedestrian behavior (Wolff, 1973). Films of urban pedestrians were analyzed, and Wolff found they consistently followed certain rules. As predicted by Lofland, these rules promoted non-

contact and cooperation. When pedestrians are headed on a collision course with one another, one of them will move aside when the distance between them is about 2.1 m (7 feet) when the sidewalk density is low, and at about 1.5 m (5 feet) when the sidewalk density is high. Wolff found half-a-dozen other common patterns that pedestrians use as they make their way along a sidewalk full of strangers, including the "step-and-slide" pattern, the "head-over-the-shoulder" pattern, and the "spread effect."

Sometimes strangers become familiar. In an interesting study, Stanley Milgram (1977) describes how some members of the anonymous mass confronting us become known quantities, even though we never talk to them. Do you see the same bag lady or jogger or oddly dressed person frequently? Even in a large city, certain individuals, both normal and odd, regularly cross our paths. Milgram calls such individuals our **familiar strangers.**

In one study, his students photographed groups of commuters waiting for the subway or bus. The photographs were then showed to some of the commuters in the picture, who were asked about the other individuals in the picture. About 90 percent of them recognized at least one person; the average person pointed out four others that they recognized but had never spoken to. Many commuters said they often think about these familiar strangers, noticing when they get a new coat or trying to figure out what kind of life they lead. One of Milgram's respondents said she once helped a woman who had collapsed on the street. Why? The woman had been one of her familiar strangers for years. (See Fig. 9–8.)

Sometimes the meanness and anonymity of city streets is overemphasized. There is crime and fear of crime, but Wolff's and Milgram's studies show that we definitely take each other into account, sometimes in a positive or helpful way.

The Environmental Psychology of Shopping

Shopping is an essential human activity. It has always had social and recreational aspects as well as the utilitarian function of obtaining the basic necessities of life. Many forces shape our shopping habits; among these are physical setting influences such as location of the store, decor, light-

FIGURE 9–8 Some familiar strangers wait for a bus.

ing, weather, sounds, crowding, smells, and displays.

Many unresearched or poorly researched claims about shopping environments have been made, but recently more and better studies are being done. Retailers have become conscious of environmental psychology (Donovan & Rossiter, 1982). The most researched variable has been store location.

Location.   An old adage in the retail trade is that the three most important keys to retail success are location, location, and location. Research tends to substantiate this claim, although of course location isn't quite the entire story. When other factors are equal, shoppers choose the closest store that stocks what they want to buy. Also, in general, shoppers will select the largest store. These two physical variables, size and location, explain much variance in consumer choice of stores (Hawkins, Best, & Coney, 1983).

Another key variable in this **gravitation model** is the attractiveness of the product. For especially attractive products (usually the more expensive ones), the gravitational effect due to size and lo-

cation is weakened and shoppers will travel farther. For example, in one study of **outshopping** (the practice of leaving our community to buy goods) researchers found that 34 percent of furniture and 33 percent of cars were purchased away from a small city, but only 4 percent of food and groceries were (Williams, 1981).

Layout.   Large stores may draw more shoppers, but not every shopper is happy with the usually impersonal environment in these retail settings. Robert Sommer and his colleagues compared the social and physical qualities of supermarkets with those of farmer's markets. In farmer's markets, shoppers more often arrive in groups and spend more time interacting with the sellers and with other shoppers (Sommer, Herrick, & Sommer, 1981).

The researchers observed that the spatial layout of supermarkets (block shape, aisle orientation, linear checkout arrangements) is a key factor in their sacrifice of friendliness in favor of traffic efficiency.

The length of aisles may affect buying behavior. One study found that when aisles were shorter, shoppers often just looked down the aisle rather than walked down it (May, 1969). Long aisles cannot be so easily surveyed, so shoppers walk down them and often fall victim to the impulse to buy an item they are attracted to but did not intend to buy before entering the store.

As more of us register our dissatisfaction with settings that encourage alienation, shopping environment design will become more sensitive to the social needs of shoppers.

Display. Purchasing is affected by how goods are displayed. Most research has been done in grocery stores. Shelf height, end-aisle placement, and location within the store all may affect normal buying as well as impulse buying (Cohen, 1981). For example, items placed on the end of an aisle will sometimes stimulate sales of that item. However, because shoppers searching for that product no longer need to travel down those long aisles where the item normally is located, overall stores sales may suffer. If the shopper does make the journey down the aisle, the height of an item affects its sales. One survey reports that sales of the same jars of applesauce increased fivefold when they were moved from waist level to eye level (Leed & German, 1973). Basics like dairy products are usually placed at the back of the store so the shopper is drawn past nonessentials; impulse purchases of these nonessentials often occur. Another key layout variable is store cleanliness; clean stores attract more customers (Patricios, 1979).

Density. Crowding in the shopping environment is another physical setting influence on consumer behavior. Objective density affects the shopper's perceptions and cognitions about the store (Harrell, Hutt, & Anderson, 1980). Feelings of crowding often ensue, which lead to adaptive strategies such as leaving the store earlier than planned. The shopper's attitudes toward the store may then take a negative turn.

▶ **In Sum.** Neighborhood satisfaction is related to such physical factors as the availability of nearby green space, general upkeep, and noise. Yet these factors interact to some extent with personal characteristics (screening tendency, perception of control, and residence type). Cities are stimulating, but their impact does not constitute an overload for everyone. We seem to adapt to some stressors (air pollution) more than others (noise). Neighborhood social ties may be less important than they used to be, except for a few determined groups. Vandalism and street art are different in motive and expression. Vandals destroy settings out of a sense of revenge; artists enhance settings while expressing social concerns. Crime and fear of crime are important neighborhood problems that may be eased in part through defensible space-design principles.

Climate is an especially complex variable, but aggression probably does increase with air pollution and with temperature. Yet sunshine combined with moderate temperatures seems to increase helping. Noise in the community reduces helping unless the victim's need is serious.

Interaction among strangers on the street generally follows a mini-max principle. Frequent exposure to the same strangers, however, leads to a kind of distant affection. Environmental factors in shopping include store location and layout, the display of goods, and shopper density. Research in the retail environment has been slow to begin, but has a bright future.

NATURAL AND TECHNOLOGICAL HAZARDS TO THE HOME

A primary human goal is to forestall the possibility of violent death and destruction from fire, storm, flood, explosion, avalanche, earthquake, and other major hazards. Despite these efforts, the annual death toll from such hazards is increasing. Each year about 250,000 individuals are killed by extreme events of nature (Burton, Kates, & White, 1978). Naturally, then, we need to learn more about human response to the threat and the reality of environmental hazards. This section covers human preparation and response to these environmental disasters. Unfortunately, it also must cover human failure to prepare for and respond to them.

Efforts to classify hazards, as a preliminary step to organizing knowledge about them, are still preliminary (Cvetkovitch & Earle, 1985). Environmental hazards may be easier to characterize by listing common types than by attempting a formal definition, but the following one is reasonably accurate and comprehensive. **Environmental hazards** are events of unusually large magnitude, often unpredictable and allowing little or no preparation, that cause death or injury to many people, destroy much property, and disrupt many social and economic activities. Sometimes they are nonevents like droughts. Sometimes, as with spring floods, they are somewhat predictable and greater preparedness is possible.

Nearly everyone's home is threatened by one or more possible disasters. Some of these are **natural hazards:** flood, fire, storm, earthquake, heat or cold wave, volcano, drought, tsunami, avalanche. **Technological hazards,** in contrast, result from human works: nuclear plant accidents, radioactive or chemical spills and seepages, nuclear bombs, falling space debris, large explosions, floods due to broken dams.

Apart from their natural or human origins, these two kinds of environmental hazards differ in other ways. Technological catastrophes are more likely than natural ones to have direct long-term effects, to have effects far beyond the original place of impact, and to threaten us differently than natural hazards do (Baum, Fleming, & Davidson, 1983). For example, the 1986 nuclear accident at Chernobyl, U.S.S.R. is likely to have physical and psychological effects that spread farther and last longer than those from a tropical storm. Both technological and natural hazards may have important *indirect* long-term effects. The eruption of Santorini ruined the Minoan civilization and stimulated the rise of Greek culture—the basis of our own civilization. Most large disasters spark legislation, which governs building codes and zoning for many subsequent years (Foster, 1980).

Natural hazards usually occur rather suddenly, but technological hazards sometimes act slowly. A problem in the poorer areas of many urban areas, for example, is lead contamination. Lead occurs in some paints, in soil and air near smelters, printing factories, foundries and other industrial plants, and in traffic fumes. It has been associated with mental retardation, hyperactivity, and a variety of illnesses (Spreen, Tupper, Risser, Tuokko, & Edgell, 1984).

The study of environmental hazards harks back to 1917, when a Red Cross supply ship collided with another ship loaded with 3,000 tons of TNT and other explosive materials in the harbor at Halifax, Nova Scotia. The resulting explosion was the largest ever recorded until the first atomic bombs were dropped. It killed about 2,000 people, injured about 8,000, and flattened many homes in Halifax and the neighboring town of Dartmouth. You can still see pieces of the ships embedded in the walls of surviving buildings. The social-psychological responses of the victims were studied, and recommendations were made for methods to avoid future disasters and to improve community relief efforts if they did reoccur (O'Riordan, 1984).

Since then, a large and well-coordinated international research effort has evolved. The principal figures in this work have been Ian Burton, Robert Kates, and Gilbert White, who have summed up many of these efforts in *The Environment as Hazard* (1978). These studies have sought to:

1. Assess the extent of human occupancy of hazard zones
2. Identify the full range of possible human adjustment to the hazard
3. Study how individuals perceive and estimate the occurrence of the hazard
4. Describe how damage-reducing strategies are adopted
5. Estimate the optimal set of adjustments, taking social and cultural consequences into account.

Preparation and response to environmental hazards may be divided into three phases. *Before* the calamity, individuals who differ in age, education, and attachment to the community have more or less knowledge about hazards, including estimates of the likelihood that a given hazard will actually occur, more or less experience with previous hazards, and more or less education about hazards. *During* a calamity, individuals obviously experience a great deal of stress. They may be killed, injured, extremely frightened, lose friends or relatives, and see their property destroyed. *After* the calamity, victims must somehow adjust or adapt to the experience. They seek a variety of solutions to future occurrences as well as compensation for their losses. Let us begin at the beginning—before calamity strikes.

Before the Calamity

Before disaster strikes, most of us are engaged in our normal routines. We are aware that disaster may strike, disaster plans may be in place, but unless someone refreshes our memory, we pay little attention to the possibility. After all, environmental hazards are relatively rare, most of us have never experienced one, and many other causes of death kill people more frequently. However, only one eruption, tornado, hurricane, bomb, quake, flood, or fire can easily end your life. Take a moment to consider which disasters might strike the place where *you* live.

Research on the precalamity phase suggests that the disaster preparations of individuals (if any!) are influenced by our past experience with disasters, associated with certain personal characteristics, and, perhaps most interesting, based on our cognitions about disaster—such as our estimate of the disaster's likelihood.

One factor that *ought* to be facilitating our preparations for environmental hazards, but is *not* doing that very well, is education. Sorenson (1983) reports that educational programs about disaster are fragmented and, as a consequence, so is individual knowledge of local potential disasters. Publicity about disaster plans can be surprisingly poor at raising community awareness (Nasar & Greenberg, 1984).

Where disasters have not occurred recently, preparations for them are rare. Where they are frequent, preparations are more often incorporated into daily living. Thus education in the absence of any recent disaster may be ineffective, but frequent or recent experience is a great teacher. Those who live in the Ganges delta of Bangladesh suffer from frequent storms and floods. They are poor, yet they still invest much effort in small levees, elevated platforms for themselves and their livestock, and special anchoring devices. Of course, the larger cyclonic storms overcome these preparations, killing many people, and destroying agricultural lands.

The lack of preparation for uncommon disasters means that the most dangerous environmental hazards are the rare but large ones. Most of us are aware that cataclysmic events may occur, but this awareness does not often lead to action (Sims & Baumann, 1983). For effective action on the part of potential victims, Sims and Baumann note that vague warnings will not suffice. Where warnings are possible, they must (a) be clear, containing specific directions, (b) come from a credible source, (c) be reinforced socially at the local level, and (d) use an appropriate medium of communication. Sims and Baumann warn of a pervasive myth that may be expressed as follows: If we educate, that will change attitudes, which in turn will change behavior. Research to date indicates that this sequence simply does not occur in most environmental hazard situations.

Awareness of a hazard threat may lead to better preparation if that awareness is grounded in experience. Twenty-two years after a tornado ripped through Flint, Michigan, residents who lived near the path of the tornado were interviewed (Hanson, Vitek, & Hanson, 1979). The investigators discovered that residents who were aware of the 1953 tornado were more likely to make preparations such as taking shelter upon hearing a tornado warning and having tornado insurance. Awareness of the tornado hazard was an even better predictor of preparedness than was personal experience of a tornado. These findings are encouraging in the sense that they suggest better preparedness need not result only from bitter experience; if individuals can be made aware of the specific hazard possibilities, they may be better prepared for disaster. Disasters, simulations, and field exercises clearly improve preparedness (Foster, 1980).

Unfortunately, another force is at work that tends to reduce preparedness. This force is in our heads—it concerns our tendency to think unclearly about the hazard. The term for this curious thought process is **bounded rationality** (Slovic, Kunreuther, & White, 1974). (See Fig. 9–9). Three varieties of bounded rationality are described by Slovic et al. First, we tend to perceive and adopt a narrower than necessary range of **adjustments** to the possibility of a disaster. Often, of course, *no* adjustments are made; we simply wait for disaster to strike. Even when we do make adjustments, such as taking out insurance, we tend to make fewer of them than we are aware of. We also tend to be aware of fewer adjustments than are actually available.

Second, we seem to prefer **crisis response,** that is, to wait until disaster strikes before doing anything about disaster. Third, and most interesting, we routinely *misperceive risks* from environmental hazards (Jackson, 1981). Some of us erroneously believe that hazards occur in cycles and "it isn't time yet," some of us place too much faith in such protective devices as dams, and some of us deny that the hazard exists at all. One flood

FIGURE 9-9 Paul Slovic is a central figure in the study of environmental risk. (*Courtesy of Paul Slovic.*)

200 billion (Logsdon, 1983). Kushnir found that misperceptions were related to several personal characteristics. Younger individuals, women, less-educated individuals, and more anxious individuals overestimated their chances of being struck by Skylab.

Such overestimates, as opposed to underestimates of other hazards, are clearly influenced by heavy media coverage. To borrow terminology from cognitive psychology, the **heuristic** (inferential rule) used to estimate the probability of being struck was, in the case of Skylab, unduly influenced by the availability of **fallible indicators,** such as the high degree of "memorability" and "imaginability" (Slovic, Fischhoff, & Lichtenstein, 1979) of the event due to extensive media coverage.

An unfortunate but prominent finding in risk perception research is that laypersons and experts disagree strongly. Compare, in Table 9-1, the risk rankings (out of thirty presented) of some technological hazards by League of Voters members, college students, and experts (Slovic, Fischhoff, & Lichtenstein, in press). Such disagreements reflect the serious policy, planning, and expenditure conflicts among environmental activists, middle class citizens, and experts. They also create an ominous potential for chaos in the event of large-scale disaster since the biggest difference is between experts and laypersons (students and women voters).

Fischhoff, Slovic, and Lichtenstein (1983) suggest several reasons for these disagreements. One is that experts and the rest of us speak different languages when it comes to hazard risks. To experts, for example, the very word *risk* tends to mean average fatalities per year. To nonexperts, however, risk often means fatality rate plus other factors, such as the evenness with which the risk is spread through the community. Second, experts and nonexperts may be trying to solve different problems. When faced with a particular risk, the two groups may perceive different sets of possible solutions and different sets of potential consequences of the risk. They may think they are struggling with the same threat, but their differing conceptions of that threat mean that they often are not really on the same track.

Third, experts and laypersons often disagree about which solutions are feasible. In considering what to do about a risk, experts are often aware

victim, when asked why he had not prepared, answered that he didn't prepare because floods didn't happen in his town—"only high water."

Many of us incorrectly estimate the odds of particular environmental hazards. For example, in one study individuals were asked the odds of a lightning strike in comparison to another hazard, botulism (Slovic, 1978). The average response was that botulism was 3.33 times more likely; actually, lightning is 52 times more likely!

Another example of risk misperception is provided in a study of a technological hazard, the falling of Skylab in July, 1979 (Kushnir, 1982). On the day before the expected crash, Kushnir asked Israelis what their chances of being injured by falling debris were, on a scale of 0 to 100 percent. Over half the respondents gave an answer over 1 percent, which itself is a very large overestimate. One expert calculates that the odds of Skylab striking any specific person were about 1 in

TABLE 9–1 Selected Risk Ratings by Experts and Laypersons

	League of Women Voters	College Students	Experts
Nuclear power	1	1	20
Pesticides	9	4	8
Motor vehicles	2	5	1
Hunting	13	18	23
Skiing	21	25	30
Mountain climbing	15	12	29
Electric power	18	19	9

Raters judged the risk of 30 hazards (low ranking signifies high risk). (Data from Slovic, Fischoff, & Lichtenstein, 1979.)

of a greater variety of possible technological solutions but also feel constrained to limit their actions to a certain policy mandate or budget. Concerned citizens, on the other hand, tend to see political action as a solution—that is, changing the policy or budget rather than being constrained by it. Fourth, experts and others may actually see the facts differently. This difference in perception may arise because experts withhold some key information, because nonexperts fail to do their homework, because the mass media distort facts, or because the two groups gained their facts from different sources.

The following procedures should, therefore, help bring experts and laypersons together in combatting hazards. Terminology must be agreed upon. Alternative solutions and possible consequences must be clarified. The feasibility of technical and political strategies for nullifying hazards must be discussed. All pertinent facts, including the sources of the facts, must be disclosed and recognized. The general risk problem is so important that the *Journal of Environmental Psychology* devoted an entire issue to it (March, 1985), the first time the journal gave a whole issue to one topic.

During the Calamity

For obvious reasons, not very much research exists on human behavior during environmental catastrophes. It is clear, however, that individuals do not always panic during disaster. There are many well-documented cases of victims acting as calmly, rationally, and effectively as possible un-

der the circumstances (Quarantelli, 1976). Others, of course, collapse completely or act in ways that endanger their own and others' lives. (See Fig. 9–10.)

The goals of research in this area are to discover who panics under what specific circumstances and to find ways to reduce panic in future situations. For example, in one study investigating the calmness of flood victims, Hansson, Noules, and Bellovich (1982) found that the calmer individuals were those who knew more about the flood hazard in their area.

After the Calamity

The most compelling reason for postdisaster research is that the postdisaster phase also happens to be the period preceding the next disaster. Surviving victims, of course, suffer considerable stress from the losses they suffer and the shock of experiencing an overwhelming event. Foster (1980) has offered a system for estimating the stress resulting from different environmental hazards. (See Table 9–2.) Adams and Adams (1984) analyzed the stress reactions of residents living near Mount Saint Helens after the eruption of 1980. Comparing the rates of various social and personal pathological behavior before and after the event, Adams and Adams documented increases in alcohol abuse, family stress, illness, and violence. One ray of positive light emerged when the researchers discovered a 90 percent decrease in child abuse; unfortunately, other domestic violence rose by almost 50 percent. After some disasters, mental health professionals have banded

FIGURE 9–10 Disaster strikes. Understandably, not much is known about human response during disasters. (*Courtesy of the National Geophysical Data Center.*)

together to provide relief for the survivor's typical feelings of grief, guilt, isolation, anger, depression, and anxiety (McLeod, 1984).

In a more experimental study, residents living near Three Mile Island at the time of the nuclear reactor accident there were examined for stress and sense of control (Davidson, Baum, & Collins, 1982). Three Mile Island residents reported feeling less control over their lives and performed more poorly on tasks measuring persistence. Those reporting more loss of their sense of control also had more symptoms of stress. Nearby residents, particularly men, showed elevated levels of biochemicals associated with stress for at least 17 months after the accident (Schaeffer & Baum, 1984).

Faced with possible loss of life, property losses,

and strong increases in stress, what can individuals do? One might think victims would take a great number of actions to prevent reoccurrence of their losses. However, the loss of a sense of control over our destiny suggested by the Three Mile Island study casts doubt on the victim's ability to act vigorously against future loss.

However, some forms of coping may reduce stress more than others (Collins, Baum, & Singer, 1983). Emotionally focused coping by residents ("I let my feelings out") resulted in lower stress levels than problem-focused coping ("I make plans of action and follow them"). Although problem-focused coping may be more effective in dealing with manageable situations, the Three Mile Island accident was beyond the control of individuals. Residents who normally reduce stress by

TABLE 9-2 An Attempt to Quantify Human Stress from Disasters

Infrastructural Stress Values

Event Intensity	Designation	Characteristics	Stress Value
I	Very minor	Instrumental.	0
II	Minor	Noticed only by sensitive people.	2
III	Significant	Noticed by most people including those indoors.	5
IV	Moderate	Everyone fully aware of event. Some inconvenience experienced, including transportation delays.	10
V	Rather pronounced	Widespread sorrow. Everyone greatly inconvenienced; normal routines disrupted. Minor damage to fittings and unstable objects. Some crop damage.	17
VI	Pronounced	Many people disturbed and some frightened. Minor damage to old or poorly constructed buildings. Transportation halted completely. Extensive crop damage.	25
VII	Very pronounced	Everyone disturbed; many frightened. Event remembered clearly for many years. Considerable damage to poorly built structures. Crops destroyed. High livestock losses. Most people suffer financial losses.	65
VIII	Destructive	Many injured. Some panic. Numerous normal buildings severely damaged. Heavy loss of livestock.	80
IX	Very destructive	Widespread initial disorganization. Area evacuated or left by refugees. Fatalities common. Routeways blocked. Agriculture adversely affected for many years.	100
X	Disastrous	Many fatalities. Masonry and frame structures collapse. Hazard-proofed buildings suffer considerable damage. Massive rebuilding necessary.	145
XI	Very disastrous	Major international media coverage. Worldwide appeals for aid. Majority of population killed or injured. Wide range of buildings destroyed. Agriculture may never be reestablished.	180
XII	Catastrophic	Future textbook example. All facilities completely destroyed; often little sign of wreckage. Surface elevation may be altered. Site often abandoned. Rare survivors become life-long curiosities.	200

Continued

squarely facing problems experienced greater stress by squarely facing a problem they couldn't solve as individuals.

Most investigations have examined individuals' **adjustments** (short-term responses) to hazards, rather than their **adaptations** (long-term responses) to them. Adaptations include more basic changes throughout the social fabric or even the biology of the species and are perhaps best studied by anthropologists or biologists. Adjustments include purchasing insurance, devising warning systems, constructing dams and levees (for floods) or shock-resistant buildings (for earthquakes, storms, and bombs), or simply bearing the cost of the disaster. These adjustments group naturally

into three types: reducing one's vulnerability to the hazard, accepting losses by bearing them (alone or by sharing), and leaving a hazardous location.

The latter adjustment, moving away, may seem the most logical, but it is rare. Why don't individuals, especially those who are repeatedly subjected to hazards, simply move away? A few do; I know a psychology professor who left the Los Angeles area as soon as he could after the disastrous San Fernando Valley earthquake of 1971. But most do not move. A study of Los Angeles residents confirmed that neither objective earthquake hazard (such as living near a fault), nor perceived hazards (such as fear of quakes) was related

Examples of Event Magnitude

Event	Location	Date	Magnitude
Plague (Black Death)	Europe/Asia	14th century	10.9
Spanish Armada	British coastal waters	July 21–29, 1588	7.2
Black Hole of Calcutta	Bengal, India	1756	5.0
Eruption of Mt. Pelée	Martinique	May 8, 1902	7.3
Landslide	Frank, Alberta, Canada	April 29, 1903	5.1
Titanic sunk by iceberg	South of Newfoundland Grand Banks	April 14–15, 1912	6.1
World War I	Europe	1914–1918	10.5
Munitions ship explosion	Halifax, Nova Scotia, Canada	1917	7.1
Train derailment in tunnel	Modane, France	Dec. 12, 1917	5.2
Great Purge	USSR	1936–1938	10.2
World War II	World	1939–1945	11.1
Atomic Bomb	Hiroshima, Japan	Aug. 6, 1945	8.2
Tsunami	Hawaiian Islands	April 1, 1946	5.8
USS Thresher lost	Off Cape Cod, Mass.	April 10, 1963	4.7
Glacier avalanche	Yungay, Peru	May 31, 1970	8.1
Mass poisoning from fungicide-treated grain	Iraq	1971	7.4
Flood	Rapid City, S. D.	June, 1972	6.6
Earthquake	Managua, Nicaragua	Dec. 23, 1972	7.9
Tornado	Xenia, Ohio	April 3, 1974	6.4
Cyclone (Tracy)	Darwin, Australia	Dec. 25, 1974	6.6
Bus skidded into lake	Japanese Alps	Jan. 1, 1975	4.1

Foster developed a formula to estimate total community stress (Magnitude, above) from the number of casualties, damage to the infrastructure (Stress Value, opposite page), total population affected, and whether the disaster occurred in a developing or developed nation. (*Reprinted with permission from Harold D. Foster. From* The Professional Geographer, *"Assessing Disaster Magnitude: A Social Science Approach," Vol. 22, pp. 244–245, Table 2 and 3, Association of American Geographers, Washington D.C., 1976.*)

to residents' intentions to move away (Kiecolt & Nigg, 1982). (See Fig. 9–11.)

Instead, moving was related to a group of variables we may call **attachment to community.** Older individuals, those with children, those who own a home, and those who were satisfied with their community did not intend to move, but those who were less attached to the community did intend to move. The earthquake hazard is just too remote and ambiguous to be a factor; in fact, the researchers discovered that, if anything, residents who were more afraid of earthquakes were *less* likely to move! In an area of Hamilton, Ontario, that is subject to multiple hazards, residents do not move primarily because of community attachment and the relatively low housing costs there (Preston, Taylor, & Hodge, 1983).

After the Three Mile Island incident, 15 percent of those who moved gave the incident as a reason for moving, suggesting that, after all, haz-

ards do cause some residents to move. Yet after appropriate comparisons between the movers and others who stayed in the area were made, it became clear that the movers did not have different attitudes to the incident (Goldhaber, Houts, & DiSabella, 1983). It appears that movers were not more upset than others, but because they were moving anyway they began to *believe* that their decision was due to the nuclear accident. Further support for this conclusion is based on the overall rates of moving before and after the incident. No more residents moved away after the incident than had moved before the incident.

If residents won't move, what do they propose? A number of studies suggest that catastrophe victims in developed countries generally favor tehnological and engineering solutions to environmental hazards (Ives & Furuseth, 1983). Interviews of flood plain residents in Australia showed that they are very aware of the flood haz-

FIGURE 9–11 The potential of a natural hazard does not usually provoke residents to move. *(Courtesy of Robert Sommer.)*

ard, yet most residents make few adjustments, favoring the construction of dams, levees, and other public works to solve the problem (Payne & Pigram, 1981).

In general, individual response to environmental hazards is not very impressive. Despite occasional heroics during a calamity, the larger scenario is one in which many of us fail to prepare for disaster, deny, or underestimate the probability of being victimized (except when the hazard is highly publicized, in which case we often ridiculously overestimate our chances). Further, we fail to move away from hazardous locations yet expect to be protected from the hazard by engineers paid for largely by other taxpayers, and we hope to be compensated by the government when disaster strikes! (Incidentally, the latter is not a good bet; in major disasters, aid rarely covers more than a third of actual losses).

Can you construct a defense against this unflattering portrait? That is, are there any justifiable reasons for the apparent lack of self-protective behavior? By the way, what preparations have *you* made for those hazards that might strike your area?

▶ **In Sum.** Most homes are subject to one or more serious environmental hazards, some natural and others technological. In the precalamity phase, governments attempt to reduce risk through engineering and education, but when

neither of these are effective, many lives are lost. Specific warnings and awareness-raising simulations can help, but effective personal action is often blunted by our tendency to bounded rationality: underpreparation, crisis response, and risk misperception. During disaster, losses may be high, but individuals generally act in relatively rational ways. The outcome of disaster is stress in many forms. Some forms of coping reduce stress better than others. Community attachment and economic factors often prevent residents from vacating high-risk areas; they would rather see governments engage in massive public works to protect their homes.

HOME, COMMUNITY, AND ENVIRONMENTAL DESIGN

Environmental psychologists have made many efforts to improve homes. Home may include a room in an institution, single-family or multiple-unit dwellings, public spaces such as streets and plazas, the community as a whole, or an entire region. The examples to follow fall into the middle range of this scale: the dwelling itself, outdoor spaces near the dwelling, public plazas, and disaster shelters. The last example may seem remote, but it is possible that someday you will require emergency housing.

A New Apartment

A current movement among designers that emphasizes involvement of building occupants in design is called **social architecture** (Hatch, 1984). Many actual projects from all over the world are described in Hatch's book; they demonstrate the advantages (and occasional disadvantages) of user participation.

One intriguing project is a housing complex built at Les Marelles, near Paris, by a team of architects and social design researchers. Three buildings, three and four storys in height and allowing for between 70 and 104 apartments, were envisioned. Most of the usual constraints were in place—financial limits, building codes, legal considerations, and technical constraints. For these reasons, the overall site plans and building plans were made by the architects.

The future residents, with the advice of the architects, were able to exercise their choice in four very important areas: (1) total floor area of their apartment, (2) exterior colors, (3) interior floor plan, and (4) finished material and cabinetwork for the interiors.

To allow for this freedom, the overall building consists of hollow square concrete tubes, assembled as the horizontal and vertical supports of a large, empty frame. The tubes carry basics such as water, electricity, and heating. The complex was then sold to new residents at a certain price per square meter—residents could buy as much or little of the empty shell as they desired or could afford.

The architects supplied advice, instruction, design models, user handbooks, and extensive catalogs of furnishings and equipment to the residents. Each residence was then constructed literally from the floor up, including the walls and everything else normally found in a home. (See Fig. 9–12.) Those who chose to take part in this process were pleased that they did not have to adapt to some distant architect's whim. The residents were able to create dwellings that had a deep personal meaning to them even before they moved in.

They did find that the design opportunity was double-edged. The freedom to design also meant that they had to directly confront the nature of family relationships in order to express them in the layout of their new dwelling. No longer could they passively complain about some impersonal "they" who designed the apartment.

The project also experienced problems. Not many future residents *wanted* to spend the time and effort required to participate. The production schedule was disrupted by the diversity of apartment designs. Financial constraints were greater than anticipated, restricting the number of participants and the range of diversity in the apartments.

Nevertheless, the architects and social scientists feel the project proved their point. Residents *can* design their own spaces and architects are only required as technical advisers. The final plans created by the residents were not extremely innovative, but they were sufficiently personal that the architects felt certain many of them would not be found in standard housing projects. Developers would likely resist constructing them for fear they were too different to sell. In general, design constraints were not erased at Les Marelles, but many of them were at least under the control of its residents.

Defensible Space in Row Housing

Oscar Newman's ideas about defensible space have been controversial for years. Many psychologists feel they have some validity, yet the research supporting the concept, like any field research, has been problematic. In this space, we take a closer look at an actual project of Newman's, renovations of a low-income housing project adjacent to the South Bronx, in New York. Clason Point consists of rowhouse clusters housing from twelve to forty families per cluster.

One of the goals of the renovations was to increase defensible space, thereby reducing both fear of crime and actual crime. Following defensible-space principles, the renovations (a) assigned as much public space to the control of specific families, using both substantial and symbolic fencing, (b) reduced the number of pedestrian routes through the project and improved lighting along the paths, and (c) improved the project's image and encouraged a sense of personal ownership by resurfacing the dwellings, giving different colors to individual dwellings.

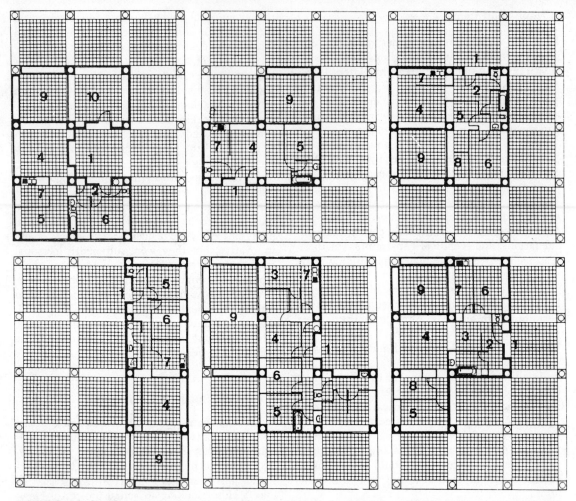

FIGURE 9-12 Six floorplans developed by Les Marelles residents for themselves. Which would you rather inhabit? For all plans, the numbers indicate rooms as follows: 1 = entry, 2 = foyer, 3 = dining room, 4 = living room, 5 = master bedroom, 6 = bedroom, 7 = kitchen, 8 = study, 9 = terrace, and 10 = office or studio. *(From* The Scope of Social Architecture *by C. R. Hatch, 1984. Copyright Van Nostrand Reinhold. Reprinted by permission of author and publisher. Georges Maurios, architect, Paris)*

Newman reports that residents took new pride in their dwellings, planting grass, adding their own new modifications, and even sweeping the public sidewalks. According to Newman, maintenance costs and crime both were reduced significantly. Serious crimes like burglary, assault, and robbery were said to drop by 61.5 percent. The number of residents who said they felt they had the right to question strangers in the project doubled. The results were not entirely positive (Kohn, Franck, & Fox, 1975), but the renovations appear to have had a generally beneficial effect on Clason Point.

Plazas as Social Space

William Whyte (1974) has documented an increasing amount of positive social interaction (as opposed to carefully managed avoidance) in cities. Some theorists, such as Newman, concentrate on urban designs that minimize crime and insecurity, but Whyte (1980) emphasizes the pursuit of design features that promote positive social interaction in public places. In particular, he has extensively studied urban plazas, searching for characteristics that distinguish beneficial plazas from useless spaces.

Over several years Whyte and his co-workers observed and filmed eighteen plazas in New York City. They counted how many individuals used each plaza on pleasant days and began to relate usage to various features of the plazas.

In general, plazas become more useful as the number of amenities rise. For example, many unused plazas simply have no place for people to sit. Some features of successful plazas besides "sittable space" include water (fountains and pools), food stands, trees, accessible food outlets, and activities to watch (jugglers, mimes, etc.). The siting of plazas is also important. Successful plazas have a sunny orientation, provide shelter from wind, and are located on busy streets rather than hidden away. (See Fig. 9–13.)

In 1961, New York City offered developers a deal. For every square foot of plaza they included in a new project, their new building could exceed normal zoning restrictions by 10 square feet. This deal certainly increased New York's supply of open space downtown. However, the new plazas tended to be vast empty spaces devoid of most features just described.

In 1975 and 1977, a new deal was offered. Perhaps as a result of Whyte's work, New York would only give extra square footage away if developers offered plazas that include many of the amenities identified by Whyte. New plazas are markedly improved social spaces that increase the city's pleasantness.

Housing Disaster Victims

Emergency housing is needed at many sites around the world each year. The art and science of providing shelter for disaster survivors is rel-

FIGURE 9–13 How many elements of a good plaza are evident in this view of Toronto's Nathan Phillips Square?

atively new and is developing rapidly. Probably no donations of emergency shelter by outside countries occurred before World War II, yet within 10 days of a large 1976 quake in Turkey over 6,500 tents had been delivered (Davis, 1978).

Many technologically advanced solutions to postdisaster housing have been devised, including parachutes that turn into free-standing tents ready for immediate occupancy on landing, polyurethane igloos, and instant floating marinalike shelters for flood victims. The UN and other agencies have sponsored competitions for emergency housing designs that are very low in cost, very lightweight, collapsible, easy to erect, and sturdy.

Yet, surprisingly, this may not be at all what is required. Ian Davis (1978), who has extensive experience with international agencies that provide disaster shelter, has listed seven unsupported beliefs about emergency housing. First, "after disasters there is a need for many new shelters." Actually, most families only go to official shelters when all else has failed. Second, "survivors show no clear patterns of housing preference after a disaster." Actually, a clear order of preferences usually emerges: go to (1) the homes of friends and family, (2) locally improvised shelters, (3) converted buildings such as school gymnasiums, and finally (4) officially provided shelter.

Third, "compulsory evacuation is an effective policy." In fact, attachment to community is so strong that no such evacuation in the last 40 years has been successful. Fourth, "tents make an effective shelter." Actually, despite stockpiles of up to 10,000 tents in various places around the world, tents tend to be late in arriving and underused once they arrive. Fifth, "emergency shelter is a matter of life and death." Actually, it usually is not; local coping mechanisms take care of most serious threats. Sixth, "in disastrous circumstances people will be prepared to live in unusual housing." In fact, novel housing is often rejected as culturally alien (remember, the need for *any* official housing is lower than we often think). Seventh, "in a disaster, people are willing to live communally." In fact, people usually become more conservative, clutching to their family unit where possible.

Four more myths pertain to the reconstruction phase. First, "temporary housing is needed prior to reconstruction." Actually reconstruction of regular dwellings starts—at least in the Third World—immediately; people ignore temporary housing. Second, "an important priority is clearing rubble." In fact, except for clearing access roads, the rubble is often best left in place, to be recycled into new homes. Third, "crash programs by agencies and governments are an effective way of solving postdisaster housing needs." In fact, local people respond faster and better in rebuilding. Fourth, "community relocation is ideal." So far, most attempts to relocate entire communities have been unsatisfactory.

Given all this negativity, what does Davis suggest? One prime goal of those who would like to help in some way should be to train local people how to rebuild their own houses with safer materials and, if possible, in a safe site in the same area. (See Fig. 9–14.) The safer design should, of course, respect local cultural traditions (Rapoport, 1969).

These efforts should be at the grassroots level; efforts to persuade governments to institute new building codes often have no practical influence on house construction. Meetings in villages and comic-book depictions of safe construction techniques are more likely to change the house construction techniques that are passed down the generations.

Second, *some* technological advances in housing technology may be useful. However, they should be compatible with the cultural form of existing housing, amenable to local means of construction (should not require heavy equipment) and ready to go *before* the disaster, to minimize delays. Victims will be reconstructing their houses out of local rubble a day or two after the disaster.

SUMMARY

Residence and community are physical settings that are crucial to human well-being. Besides meeting minimal standards of space and maintenance, residential satisfaction is largely a matter of fit between stage in the life cycle and residence characteristics. Moving is a stressful experience that is increasing in frequency. Residential crowding is still a problem in many households. Other household problems may exist but have not yet been researched. Neighborhood satisfaction is related to the absence of noise, air

FIGURE 9–14 Recommended house reconstruction practices for Guatemala's earthquake-prone districts. *(Courtesy of N. Norton/OXFAM.)*

pollution, and ugliness, although some people seem able to adapt to some of these stressors. Except for certain groups, it is less related to neighboring than it used to be.

Climate influences pro- and antisocial behavior mildly. High temperatures and bad air increase aggression, "nice" days increase helping, and noise depresses helping. Out in the community, people try to maximize order and minimize social interaction although repeated exposure to strangers often leads to a certain degree of attraction.

The environmental psychology of the retail world is just beginning, but physical variables clearly influence shopping behavior.

Most communities are subject to natural and technological hazards. Many individuals behave rationally and admirably during calamitous events, but planning for the event by individuals and by governments is often inadequate. Risks are misperceived and residents exhibit attachment to high-risk homes. Environmental design of homes spans the range from room design to regional planning; examples of the design of apartments, outdoor space in row housing, urban plazas, and emergency housing are offered.

SUGGESTED SUPPLEMENTARY READINGS

Adams, P. R., & Adams, G. R. (1984). Mount Saint Helens's ashfall: Evidence for a disaster stress reaction. *American Psychologist, 39,* 252–260.

Aiello, J. R., & Baum, A. (Eds.). (1979). *Residential crowding and design.* New York: Plenum.

Altman, I., & Werner, C. M. (Eds.). (1985). *Home environments.* New York: Plenum.

Anderson, C. A., & Anderson, D. C. (1984). Ambient temperature and violent crime: Tests of the linear and curvilinear hypotheses. *Journal of Personality and Social Psychology, 46,* 91–97.

Evans, G. W., Jacobs, S. V., & Frager, N. B. (1982). Adaptation to air pollution. *Journal of Environmental Psychology, 2,* 99–108.

Fried, M. (1982). Residential attachment: Sources of residential and community satisfaction. *Journal of Social Issues, 38*(3), 107–119.

Korosec-Serfaty, P. (1984). The home from attic to cellar. *Journal of Environmental Psychology, 4,* 303–321.

Krupat, E. (1985). *People in cities.* New York: Cambridge University Press.

Patricios, N. N. (1979). Human aspects of planning shopping centers. *Environment and Behavior, 11,* 511–538.

Rapoport, A. (1982). *The meaning of the built environment: A nonverbal communication approach.* Beverly Hills, CA: Sage.

Rivlin, L. G. (1982). Group membership and place meanings in an urban neighborhood. *Journal of Social Issues, 38*(3), 75–93.

Rotton, J., & Frey, J. (1985). Air pollution, weather, and violent crimes: Concomitant times-series analysis of archival data. *Journal of Personality and Social Psychology, 49,* 1207–1220.

Slovic, P., Fischhoff, B., & Lichtenstein, S. (1986). Regulation of risk: A psychological perspective. In R. Noll (Ed.), *Social science and regulatory policy.* Berkeley, CA: University of California Press.

Stokols, D., Shumaker, S. A., & Martinez, J. (1983). Residential mobility and personal well-being. *Journal of Environmental Psychology, 3,* 5–9.

Taylor, R. B. (1982). Neighborhood physical environment and stress. In G. W. Evans (Ed.), *Environmental stress.* New York: Cambridge University Press.

Weinstein, N. D. (1982). Community noise problems: Evidence against adaptation. *Journal of Environmental Psychology, 2,* 99–108.

Whyte, W. H. (1980). *The social life of small urban spaces.* New York: The Conservation Foundation.

Chapter Ten
Learning and the Physical Environment

*Nowhere else are large groups of individuals packed
so closely together for so many hours, yet expected
to perform at peak efficiency on difficult learning
tasks and to interact harmoniously.*
Carol Weinstein, 1979

Walking through the woods to the university's field station where they had a lab for their forestry class, Tom and Jane started reminiscing about the schools they had attended. Jane's city-center childhood had put her through some huge two- and three-story schools that resembled Monopoly hotels come to life. They usually sat in the middle of an expanse of asphalt, surrounded by wire fences. "The windows were tall and narrow and the globe lamps hung down on long wires. In those ancient rooms with tall ceilings I felt small and out of place," Jane recalled. "I can still see those big, old oak desks with generations of initials carved on initials."

"Sounds like doom itself to me," said Tom. He had grown up in a rural district that was being swallowed by suburbia. "My elementary school was certainly different. It was almost new, only one-story and surrounded by grassy fields." He thought for a minute. "There was something else quite different from yours. It was one of those open-plan schools, you know, with big spaces where the teachers could merge their classes or divide them up by subject instead of by age. I remember some of the teachers just couldn't handle it. They would try to fence out the rest of the school with filing cabinets and bulletin boards."

"Sounds like chaos itself to me," said Jane, gently mocking him.

"You're right, actually. The noise level would steadily rise all day until you could hardly hear the bell at the end of the last period."

"That's strange. Your whole school experience must have been so different from mine. Those old rooms were like caverns, huge and quiet. Your voice would sort of disappear into space." Jane actually shuddered as the sounds and smells came back to her. "Maybe the place seemed like that because our high school only had 1100 students left and the place was built for 2000."

Tom was surprised. "Really? My schools were always too full. My high school was crowded the day it opened and by the time I graduated, it had 900 students—and it was built for 600." Lost in these musings, they suddenly found

themselves in front of the field station. "Well, back to forest ecology," said Jane. "Uh, Jane," said Tom, "There's this house downtown that I would like to show you sometime. . . ."

Learning is a central part of everyone's life. It often occurs even when we don't think of ourselves as learning, such as when we take a stroll through the woods or when we talk over the events of the day with friends. We often associate learning with school, but of course much learning also occurs before we reach school age, outside school hours, and after we have completed school. It occurs in places where learning is the designated purpose of the setting (school, seminars, practice fields, libraries, conservatories, museums, training grounds) and in places where learning is incidental to the primary purpose of the setting (playgrounds, street corners, parks, dinner tables, family rooms, offices, hallways).

This chapter is concerned with the role of the physical environment in learning, including such influences as architecture, noise, light, temperature, crowding, furniture arrangement, and room design. Most research focuses on the school setting, but some examines learning outside schools. In addition, we will discuss the nature of learning about the environment, the process of developing **environmental competence.** (See Figs. 10–1 and 10–2.)

From the very large amount of attention psychology pays to *nonphysical* factors in learning, we might conclude that physical factors are not very important. Indeed, some studies do report that one physical factor or another does not significantly alter learning or learning-related behavior. However, we do not expect every aspect of the physical environment to affect every learning-related behavior. Yet many studies are now being conducted (Weinstein, 1982a) and some of them do report dramatic changes in behavior. (See Fig. 10–2.)

For example, Dorothy Wollin and Mary Montagne (1981) changed a typical sterile Introductory Psychology classroom into one with softer lighting, plants, posters, cushions, and rugs. Student exam scores after five weeks in the room were significantly higher than those of students who spent five weeks in a similar room that had

FIGURE 10-1 We spend years in schools; their physical environments have strong effects on our learning and other behaviors.

FIGURE 10-2 Learning also occurs outdoors and on nonacademic topics. *(Courtesy of Toby Talbot.)*

not been modified. Physical factors *can* make a significant difference.

We spend vast sums to educate individuals of all ages. Environmental psychologists believe that educational settings can and should make education both more efficient and more enjoyable. The physical setting may not make or break education on its own—to believe that would be a naive form of architectural determinism—but it can interact with nonenvironmental factors either to promote or to hinder the learning process.

As Figure 10–3 illustrates, our overall model asserts that the personal characteristics of students (past school experience, attitudes toward learning, age, gender, personality) interact with physical features of the learning setting (its size, noise level, climate, population density, and design) and the social-organizational climate (rules, curriculum, teaching style, progressive or traditional orientation, etc.) to produce learning-related attitudes (satisfaction with school, dissatisfaction with classroom, commitment to learning, etc.) and behaviors (class participation, attention to learning materials, questioning, appropriate or inappropriate activity, persistence, creativity, and, of course, learning and performance).

Most researchers cannot consider all these factors in a single study, but most would agree that interactions among them should be considered where possible. An example of a study that included both personal and environmental factors and found important interactions is one by Traub and Weiss (1974). They sought to discover whether open-space school designs were equally beneficial to students from urban and suburban neighborhoods. Traub and Weiss found that suburban students achieved about as much in open and traditional schools, but that urban students achieved more in traditional schools than in open schools. One cannot simply conclude that open schools are either better or worse. The interactions of personal and environmental variables suggests the more accurate conclusion that open schools are better than traditional schools for certain students but not better for other students.

Weinstein (1981) has summarized four assumptions made by researchers in learning and the physical environment.

1. Although the setting usually does not teach directly, it can either facilitate or hinder learning, both directly and symbolically. Loud noise may directly interfere with the transmission of information from teacher to learner. In addition, a drab untidy classroom may symbolize to learners that the school and teacher care little about their progress.

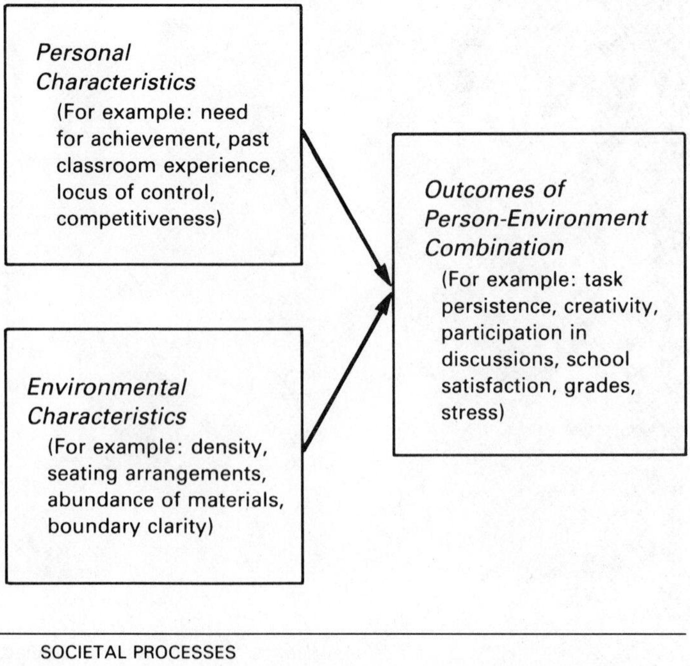

FIGURE 10–3 A framework for conceptualizing person-environment relations in learning settings. A poor fit between learner and setting will result in lower performance, lower satisfaction, and higher stress. *(From Ahrentzen, S., Jue, G. M., Skorpanich, M., & Evans, G. W. In G. W. Evans (Ed.),* Environmental Stress. *New York: Cambridge University Press, 1982, pp. 29–36. Reprinted by permission from Cambridge University Press.)*

Personal Characteristics (For example: need for achievement, past classroom experience, locus of control, competitiveness)

Environmental Characteristics (For example: density, seating arrangements, abundance of materials, boundary clarity)

Outcomes of Person-Environment Combination (For example: task persistence, creativity, participation in discussions, school satisfaction, grades, stress)

2. The effects of the physical setting on learning are not universal but are mediated by the social and instructional context. For example, open schools, or "schools without walls," work poorly when educators merely import their teaching methods from schools with separate classrooms but often work better when teaching methods suited to open space are used.

3. There is no single best learning setting. The best physical settings are those congruent with the type of material being learned, the goals of the class, and the characteristics of the learners. The very same setting, therefore, may produce wonderful results in one case and terrible results in another. This becomes dramatically obvious if we consider how well children could learn to play football in a hockey rink.

4. Learning is maximized when the physical setting is considered as carefully as are other aspects of the learning situation, such as the curriculum, the teacher's verbal ability, and other teaching aids. Unfortunately, most educational programs still pay little attention to the physical setting (Weinstein, 1981). (See Fig. 10–4.)

The task of environmental psychologists who study learning is to identify conditions under which physical and nonphysical elements of the setting combine to result in improved learning. But what *is* learning? It is usually defined as a relatively permanent change in behavior that occurs as a result of experience. This relatively narrow technical definition of learning excludes important parts of the complex pattern of teacher and learner behavior that is part of the learning process.

In this chapter, we will examine the effects of the physical environment on four dimensions of learning although the last of these has only very scantily been researched: learning itself, feelings about learning, social behavior related to learning, and the health and stress aspects of learning. Beginning with a look at how settings as a whole affect these dimensions of learning, the chapter will continue by examining the effects of more specific physical variables, including noise, light, color, temperature, crowding, and room arrangements.

FIGURE 10–4 Carol Weinstein has worked to promote and extend our understanding of learning and the physical environments of schools. *(Courtesy of Carol Weinstein.)*

THE SETTING AS A WHOLE

Knowing the Place

Many years ago McGeoch (1942) postulated that learning occurs "in a complex context of environing conditions not specific to it" (p. 501). That is, learning is partially dependent on the background context where it occurs. If this is true, our performance of the learned material might be better in the place where we learned something than in a different, novel place. Indeed, a number of studies, beginning with Abernathy (1940), have shown that college students perform better on exams when they are tested in the room where they learned the material than when they are tested in an unfamiliar room. In a dramatic field example of this, Godden and Baddeley (1975) showed that when divers are given a list of words to memorize either on dry land or underwater and then asked to recall them either on dry land or underwater, they do best when recalling the words in the same setting in which they learned them.

Apparently, placing the learner in the physical setting where the learning originally occurred produces optimal performance. Not every study of this *familiar-context effect* has confirmed Abernathy's original conclusion, and not every task seems to follow this principle. For example, distance estimation, a skill we all learn to some extent (although rarely in a formal learning setting) seems to be more accurate in novel environments than in familiar ones (Cohen, Weatherford, Lomenick, & Koeller, 1979).

The reason for the inconsistency in the familiar-context findings is probably that the experimenters are unable to specify *which* aspects of the environment promote or hinder performance. Something about the general learning context has an effect, but in these early studies, no effort was made to identify which aspect of the environment affects learning.

One might argue that the key factor is familiarity with the setting. Unfortunately, this explanation begs the question: What is it about familiarity that helps us perform better? Perhaps we are less anxious in the familiar setting; our greater anxiety in the unfamiliar setting interferes with performance. This seems plausible when we consider taking a final exam in a room we've never entered as opposed to the regular lecture room. But what about the divers in Godden and Baddeley's study? They may be more anxious underwater (or the fanatic diver may feel more anxious out of water), but they performed better wherever they happened to learn, not wherever they were least anxious.

A second explanation is that somehow the learning is *associated* with the general environmental context, even though that context had no direct role in the teaching-learning process. An interesting study by Steven Smith (1979) supports this idea. He asked subjects to recall memorized words in a novel setting and in a familiar setting. When the subjects in the novel setting had their associations to the original learning setting strengthened (the experimenter asked them to vividly recall it, or showed them slides of it), their performance was about as good as that of subjects who learned and recalled words in the same setting.

We therefore seem to perform better in settings where we learned the material, and the reason for this is that our learning is somehow associated with the physical characteristics of that whole place. An intriguing but still-unanswered question is this: Just what is the nature of these associations? Once again, a general term is used when the specific mechanism is unknown. In attempting to understand the role of the physical environment in learning, most environmental psychologists have studied specific features of the setting, such as its size.

Size

Is there a relation between learning and the sheer size of a school? Operating from an ecological psychology perspective, Paul Gump and Wallace Friesen (1964a) studied five high schools ranging in size from 35 to 2,300 students. They found that size does affect some aspects of learning. First, larger schools offer a wider variety of instruction to their students. Variety does not, however, increase as fast as size. A school that is much larger than another offers its students only slightly greater choice of classes.

Second, Gump and Friesen found that participation in activities outside regular class hours was about the same for large and small schools. The important difference is that students in smaller schools participated in more kinds of extracurricular activities, and that they much more often participated in central or responsible positions.

Third, in line with the last finding, students in large schools reported that their satisfactions were more often derived from vicarious experience (being from the school that won a championship). Students in smaller schools reported that their satisfactions came more from direct participation (being part of the newspaper staff).

Gump and Friesen (1964b) found that students from small schools more often believed their participation helped them to learn skills, be challenged, engage in important activities, be valued by others, and be involved in an active group. On the other hand, students from large schools more often believed their participation helped them enjoy being part of the organization, learn about school activities, and gain credit for classes.

Because Gump and Friesen's research included only five schools, others have studied school size to determine whether their findings would be confirmed. Leonard Baird (1969) investigated the school activities of about 21,000 college-bound high school students. He discovered that students from small schools reported more achievements (defined as public recognition of their efforts, such as getting a poem published or winning an election) than did students from large schools in writing, music, drama, and leadership.

In another study, Allan Wicker (1968) found further support for Gump and Friesen's conclusion that students in small schools feel more involved and challenged than students in large schools. His research also demonstrated that these conclusions are not universally true. A key factor underlying most of the school-size findings we have discussed is that activities in small schools are chronically **understaffed** (some ecological psychologists prefer the term "undermanned"). Students in small schools are almost forced to accept a more active, central, and challenging role because there is often no one else to do the job.

But what about activities in small schools that happen to be overstaffed and activities in large schools that happen to be understaffed? Wicker found that when the staffing of activities was about equal in large and small schools, typical experiences (involvement, challenge, skill development, and being valued) were about equal too. Apparently, the degree of over- or understaffing of a particular activity is the critical variable. Still, many more activities are understaffed in small schools than in large ones.

Elizabeth Prescott (1970) considered the effects of size in daycare centers. She concluded that larger daycare centers are more economical to the sponsoring agency, but problems arise when the number of students exceeds sixty or so. The necessary increase in programming leads to less freedom of choice in the child's activities and to fewer teacher-child interactions.

Plan and Age

Two other characteristics of the setting as a whole that affect learning are the overall design of the school and its age or condition. A basic architectural distinction may be drawn between schools that are decentralized, with numerous smaller separate buildings, and schools that are centralized, with one or two large buildings. Myrick and Marx (reported in Moos, 1976) interviewed hundreds of students in three high schools that varied in centralization. Students in the decentralized campus needed more time to move from class to class. Apparently, time spent in transit restricts between-class student-teacher conversation; students and teachers interacted 20 percent less in decentralized school classrooms. This suggests that learning itself is adversely affected in decentralized schools, although the researchers do not report evidence on this question.

Does the physical condition of a school affect learning? The question is not easy to answer because the quality of a school's physical plant is usually tied to other relevant factors such as neighborhood quality and the socioeconomic status of its students. Nevertheless, it is reasonable to hypothesize that a dilapidated learning setting will harm the attitudes of both students and teachers, resulting in less learning. David Canter and Peter Stringer (1975) report a British study that investigated this question by interviewing teachers in both older and newer schools.

As might be expected, teachers in newer schools were generally more satisfied. However, teachers in older schools were not always dissatisfied with their buildings; teacher satisfaction was a function of the number of changes and improvements to the physical plant. Alterations and improvements to an older building do lead to greater teacher satisfaction. The study investigated teacher satisfaction rather than student learning, but if satisfied teachers are better teachers, the results suggest that learning suffers in older buildings if they are not renovated or improved as they age.

▶ **In Sum.** Certain features of the learning setting as a whole affect pupil performance. Students often perform better in the place where they learned the material. Many learning experiences are affected by school size, which is often linked to nonoptimal staffing. Students in large schools have a slight edge in the variety of things they can learn about. Yet partly because time at school is limited, students in large schools do not actually participate in more activities than students in small schools. Students in large schools more often learn and enjoy as spectators; students in small schools more often learn and enjoy as participants. In most areas of learning, students in small schools achieve more as a result of developing competence through direct involvement in activities. However, when activities in large schools are understaffed and activities in small schools are overstaffed, these outcomes may be reversed. Decentralizing school buildings may decrease student-teacher interaction. If satisfied teachers are better teachers, then construction or renovations should be undertaken when necessary.

NOISE

Is learning impaired in a noisy setting? Common sense certainly suggests that it is. Teachers spend much time combating noise in the classroom, suggesting that they believe it does. Behavioral psychologists have investigated methods of controlling noise, such as installing voice-activated relays. In one home economics class, the teacher allowed students to listen to their favorite radio station as long as the sound level stayed below a certain level (Wilson & Hopkins, 1973). When the sound exceeded this level, the relay automatically turned off the radio.

In another class, if the chosen noise level was not exceeded for 10 minutes, students were given 2 extra minutes of gym and a 2-minute break from study period (Schmidt & Ulrich, 1969). In an elementary school version of this antinoise strategy, quiet periods in the classroom lit up one light after another on a smiling clown figure, but loud noise extinguished the lights (Strang & George, 1975). These efforts to quench noise are based on the premise that noise harms classroom performance. Yet the scientific evidence on the question is far from conclusive. Under many conditions noise does not affect performance and under certain conditions it may even enhance it (Hockey & Hamilton, 1970).

The relation between noise and learning is complex because it depends on (a) the physical properties of the sound (loudness, pitch, continuity, meaningfulness), (b) the characteristics of the learner (motivation, personality, intelligence, feelings of control) and (c) the type and complex-

ity of the task (reading, memorizing, problem solving, listening). In addition, most research so far has been correlational rather than experimental. Many of our conclusions about the effects of noise remain to be confirmed by methods that can establish causal rather than associative links between variables. With these cautionary notes in mind, let's examine the available evidence concerning noise in the learning setting.

Performance

Researchers try to identify specific conditions in which they hypothesize that noise affects performance. For example, is it a hindrance during the period we are learning new material or later when we try to demonstrate that we have already learned it (as on a test) or both? One relatively well-controlled study confirms the conclusion that noise during learning reduces later performance more than does noise at the time of recalling the learned material (Bell et al., 1984).

Students are, of course, often exposed to noise both during learning and during performance of what they have learned. Arline Bronzaft (1981) measured the reading ability of children in a New York school. On one side of the building trains passed frequently; the other side was relatively quiet. Bronzaft found that the reading scores of children on the noisy side of the school were significantly lower. The local government then installed rubber sound-reducing materials on the train tracks. Bronzaft measured the children's reading one year later and found that the differences in scores had disappeared.

Other schools are plagued by the noise of aircraft takeoffs and landings. The mathematics and reading achievement of third graders in an area of Los Angeles that experiences an overflight every 2½ minutes of the school day was measured (Cohen, Evans, Krantz, Stokols, & Kelly, 1981). Their scores were compared with those of students who worked in classrooms that had sound insulation (16 decibels quieter) and with those of children who went to schools out of the air corridor (22 decibels quieter). The reading scores of children in sound-insulated classrooms were significantly higher than those in noisy classrooms. Oddly, the scores of children in the sound-insulated classrooms were even higher than those of children in the schools away from the air corridor. The schools away from the air corridor may have been different in other ways (such as poorer quality teaching), or perhaps the children in the sound-insulated classrooms were so glad to come into a relatively quiet classroom from the thunderous outdoors that they were happy to work on their schoolwork!

The size of the effect reported in the Los Angeles airport study is small. That is, noise had a significant effect statistically, but did not explain the achievement scores very well by itself. In that sense, the results are typical of other noise studies that appear to show noise has little effect on learning (Slater, 1968). Two conclusions are possible. Perhaps noise affects no one's learning very much. Perhaps it only affects the learning of some individuals strongly. If the second conclusion is true, important negative effects on certain learners may be overlooked in studies that examine the average scores of entire classes. Several studies offer relevant findings.

Daniel Christie and Carl Glickman (1980) hypothesized that boys and girls perform differently in noisy conditions. First- to fifth-grade children worked at visual puzzles in noisy (70 decibels) or quiet (40 decibels) classrooms. In the noisy conditions, boys solved more puzzles than girls, but in the quiet conditions, girls solved more puzzles than boys. It is important to note that if the performances of boys and girls in Christie and Glickman's study are lumped together (as they are in most noise studies), the data show no difference between noisy and quiet conditions.

A subsequent study of college students (Hykin, 1984) confirmed these results, which is important because statistical interactions (that is, the pattern of results indicating that girls are better and boys worse in quiet conditions, but boys are better and girls worse in noisy conditions) are often not replicated in follow-up studies. (See Fig. 10–5.) These investigations support the conclusion that noise affects the performance of different learners differently; if researchers do not examine the scores of groups (such as boys and girls) separately, the effects of noise may be overlooked.

Another example of the importance of individual differences is provided by Sidney Zentall (1983). Reviewing the evidence on noise and learning among exceptional children, Zentall concludes that moderate noise actually helps hyperactive children learn, but not autistic children. Apparently, rock music encourages hyperactive children to be less disruptive and less

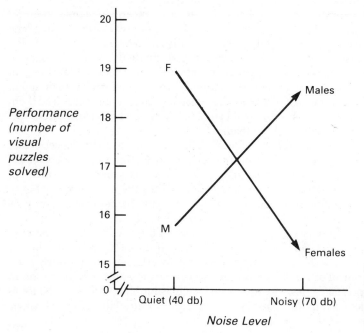

FIGURE 10–5 Performance of a moderately difficult task varies with noise and sex. Females as a group perform better when it is quiet, males when it is noisy. *(Adapted from Hykin, 1984.)*

verbally aggressive, but autistic children often respond to noise by becoming even more passive and repetitive than usual in their actions.

The role of the material to be learned has not yet been mentioned. Zentall's (1983) review concludes that for difficult tasks, individual differences fade. That is, both normal and exceptional children perform difficult tasks less well in noisy conditions than in quiet conditions (Zentall, 1983).

A few investigators have tried to determine whether noise affects learning after the noise has ceased. The Los Angeles air-corridor study, for example, discovered learning decrements even when students are away from the noise they normally experience. The evidence is mixed (Cohen & Weinstein, 1982), but the majority of studies support the conclusion that the effects of noise outlast the noise itself. In the best-known examination of this issue, third to fifth graders who lived in apartments built over a busy road were tested on their reading ability (Cohen, Glass, & Singer, 1973). All children were tested in quiet conditions, but those who lived in noisier apartments scored lower than those who lived in quieter apartments. Heft (1979) also found that children from homes their parents described as noisy performed more poorly in quiet conditions than children from homes described as quiet.

How can noise harm a learner's performance after it is no longer present? There are at least four possible reasons (Cohen & Weinstein, 1982). First, noise during the learning process may interfere with moment-to-moment communication between student and teacher. The student may miss key instructions, or the teacher may be forced to repeat instructions often so that less material can be covered in a class period. A cumulative deficiency may then develop over the course of the school year that affects learning even in quiet situations.

Second, noise may interfere with the development of children's strategies for processing information. Learning is subsequently impaired even in quiet surroundings because the child uses inadequate strategies for thinking about the material to be learned.

Third, when noise is beyond the control of students—as it often is—their sense of personal control may be damaged. When the student attempts to master a new concept later, even in quiet, that sense of personal control, so important to learning, may not be there.

Fourth, noise raises the learner's blood pressure semipermanently. This chronic increase in physiological arousal may interfere with learning even in quiet periods. We have focused in this section on the effects of noise on performance, but this is evidence that noise affects the health of children, too.

Feelings

By definition, noise is unwanted sound. In classrooms, then, noise is nearly always unwelcome. Perhaps the most common single statement in the public school is "Quiet down, now, class." Nevertheless, there are some distinctions about attitudes toward noise to be drawn.

Brunetti (1972) found that students in general (in both elementary and high school, and in both traditional and open-plan schools) report they are more distracted by social conversations than by schoolwork-related conversations. Brunetti also found that even when objective sound levels are the same, noise was reported to be more distracting in nonlaboratory settings than in laboratory settings and noise is more bothersome when classroom density is higher.

Teachers are as concerned about *potential* noise as they are about existing noise. Some teachers, especially in open-plan schools, modify their instructional methods to avoid creating noise. Some effective methods of teaching, of course, naturally produce relatively high sound levels. Thus, teachers' fear of noise may lead them to avoid good teaching methods (Ahrentzen, Jue, Skorpanich, & Evans, 1982).

► **In Sum.** The evidence strongly suggests that noise interferes with learning both while it occurs and, if the learner is subjected to noise for long periods, even after the noise is gone. Noisy classrooms may impair the performance of girls more than boys, that of autistic children more than hyperactive children, and that of most children when the task is difficult. Noise may hinder performance by interfering with information processing, lowering the student's perception of control, and increasing blood pressure. Noise is more bothersome in nonlaboratory settings, higher density settings, and when it concerns social rather than schoolwork topics. To combat noise, instructors have changed their methods—sometimes sacrificing a good method for a quiet one—and have successfully employed behavior modification techniques such as sound-activated electrical relays that control reinforcers such as radio music and extra recess time.

LIGHT AND COLOR

The human eye is remarkably able to adapt to various levels of light intensity. Stein (1975) asserts that after a few minutes to adjust, students can read just as fast at 3 footcandles (very dim light) as they can at 53 footcandles (standard classroom lighting). This is fortunate, because in surveying public classrooms, Stein found that the light intensity at desktop in actual classrooms varied from 8 footcandles to 1,000 footcandles (the latter is found when direct sunlight streams through a window onto a desk).

Many people believe that lighting and color affect human behavior in general and learning in particular. The popular press frequently carries stories connecting certain kinds of light with psychological and physiological disturbances. The focus of most research has been fluorescent lighting. Because it is undeniably more energy-efficient and economical than traditional incandescent lighting, fluorescent lighting has gradually become standard in schools and most other public building interiors. Yet few people find it aesthetically pleasing; many consider it a necessary evil rather than welcome progress (Taylor, 1980).

Several improved kinds of fluorescent lamps have been developed in response to this aesthetic criticism. One of the most popular alternatives is the daylight lamp, which radiates a spectrum of light closer to that of sunlight than does the older cool-white lamp. A lamp that perfectly mimics sunlight is nearly impossible to invent, because the intensity and spectrum of sunlight itself changes through the day and across the seasons; also, fluorescent bulbs cannot avoid having spikes in certain wavelength bands that sunlight does not have (Fletcher, 1983). Given that a truly natural indoor light does not exist, does fluorescent lighting affect learning or health?

Performance

In one comparison of lighting types, ninety-eight first graders in four classrooms were filmed during regular school activities (Mayron, Ott, Nations, & Mayron, 1974). All classrooms were windowless, to control for effects of sunlight. Two classrooms contained cool-white fluorescent lamps and two contained daylight or full-spectrum fluorescent lamps. The study found that children in the daylight condition paid more attention to the teacher and were less fidgety. On reading and other tests, one daylight class scored better than both cool-white classes, but the other daylight class scored worse than both cool-white classes. It would seem that, on the whole, some learning and learning-related behaviors were affected by the difference in type of light; however, the study's methodology has been criticized (Fletcher, 1983). It is worthwhile listing the criticisms because they apply to many studies, not only of lighting but of other environmental variables.

First, the children apparently were not randomly assigned to classrooms. Thus the differences in behavior may have preceded the lighting experiment and had nothing to do with light. Second, the total amount of light was apparently not carefully controlled; the classrooms may have had not only different bulbs, but different intensities of light. Third, teachers may have influenced the results through their teaching methods (they do not seem to have been randomly assigned either) or through their knowledge and expectations of the two kinds of lighting. Fourth, the experimenters did not explain exactly how they observed and scored the children's behavior. This makes it impossible for subsequent researchers to replicate the study. Fifth, the observers may have been aware of which lighting condition they were observing (we do not know because the experimenters do not inform us). If they were, their own expectations about the outcome of the study may have influenced the results. Sixth, the experimenters report no estimate of the observers' reliability. We cannot be sure the behaviors were measured consistently between observers or consistently over time for the same observer. Seventh, it is not clear whether the observations were done at the same time in the four classrooms. If they were not, differences could be due to natural fluctuations in classroom activity, such as increased restlessness just before lunch and recess breaks.

These criticisms are not meant to disparage the Mayron et al. study in particular; they are meant primarily as a partial list of concerns that every experimenter should have. Lighting and other effects that are delicate and elusive require especially careful experimental procedures. An analogy to chemistry or physics might be drawn. If a chemist is searching for a rare but important compound, the failure to use perfectly clean equipment may contaminate a solution and lead to the false conclusion that the compound does not exist. A physicist searching for a new subatomic particle must use great care with the photographic records of nuclear collisions; careless observation or poor-quality film development could cause a particle that actually exists to be overlooked.

There are lighting studies that have carefully controlled most sources of error. In one of these, college women performed learning-related tasks under cool-white and daylight lamps (Dalezman, Jones, Bevlig, Polf, & Keeny, reported in Fletcher, 1983). The experimenters even controlled for **veiling reflection,** a source of error not on our list above. Veiling reflection results when a light source bounces off a work surface into an individual's eyes. It becomes a factor in the outcome of lighting studies when the various lamps to be compared are installed in different kinds of fixtures—some that throw light directly onto a work surface and some that do not. If veiling reflection is not controlled for, a difference in results might be attributed to the difference between lighting types when the real cause is a difference in fixture design. The conclusion of this well-controlled study: Basic information processing related to decision making was better under daylight lamps than under cool-white lamps.

Another well-controlled study (Munson & Ferguson, 1985) found that some effects of lighting require weeks of exposure before they appear. Several tests and observations of elementary school children's behavior were made over 20 weeks under cool-white and daylight (full-spectrum) bulbs. After 2 weeks, no significant differences were found. However, after 7 to 8 weeks, children exposed to daylight bulbs had a significant *decrease* in the strength of their grip and in the number of gross motor movements, and an *increase* in hand steadiness. (See Fig. 10-6.) These findings are consistent with the hypothesis that cool-white bulbs are more physiologically arousing than daylight bulbs.

The effects of color on learning have received little attention from researchers. Contemporary aesthetic standards seem to favor bright colors for learning settings. Whether this preference merely reflects today's fashions or actually helps children learn is not clear. One study reported in the popular press ("Blue is Beautiful," 1973) claimed that IQ scores measured in bright rooms (blue, orange, yellow) were 26 points higher than those in drab rooms (white, brown, black). A 53 percent increase in friendly behaviors in orange rooms was also reported. Many of the problems with experimental control listed earlier were also present in this study, so these dramatic results must be classified as suggestive rather than conclusive.

Health and Stress

Complaints are sometimes heard about fluorescent and sodium-vapor lighting systems. Do these complaints merely reflect a nostalgic preference for the old familiar forms of light or are they really a menace to our well-being?

First, as is true for every aspect of the physical environment, the preferences of individuals who work or live in a building should be respected; in principle, it should not be necessary to demonstrate that something in the environment fries our brains or causes insanity before it is replaced. On the other hand, if one option costs significantly more than another, the space manager (the school board, in this case) may be forced to consider whether the cheaper alternative (fluorescent lighting) actually harms students and teachers or merely displeases them.

As in the lighting-performance relation, it is important to determine whether any health problem we discover is due to lighting type itself or perhaps to some ancillary factor (such as the design of the lighting fixture). Teachers in a school where sodium vapor lamps had been installed complained of eyestrain, nausea, and headaches (Ponte, 1981). Lighting experts who examined the installation reported that the lighting had been improperly installed; it was producing far too

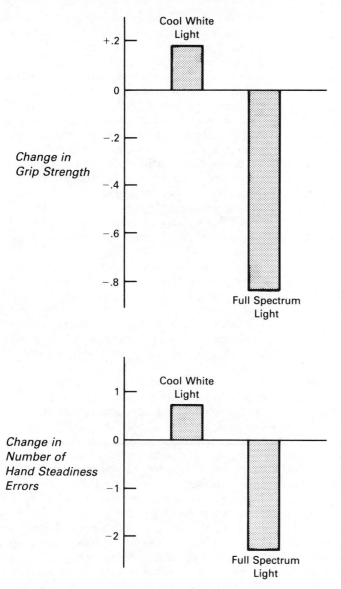

FIGURE 10-6 Lighting and elementary pupil performance. In a carefully designed study, children working for several weeks at school in full spectrum fluorescent lighting made fewer errors on a hand steadiness task than when they worked under cool white fluorescent lighting. However, cool white fluorescent lighting produced greater grip strength than the full spectrum fluorescent lighting did. *(Adapted from Munson & Ferguson, 1985.)*

much glare (Fletcher, 1983). According to them, the problem was glare rather than the type of light. Unfortunately, the experts were from a large lighting manufacturer. They did not perform a properly controlled study; their conclusions may well have been influenced by their unwillingness to believe that the lamps themselves could be harmful.

Fluorescent lighting has demonstrated no dramatic, negative health effects. Two relatively well-controlled studies, however, show that cool-white fluorescent lamps increase the hyperactive behavior of children who are already prone to autism and other emotional disturbances (Colman, Frankel, Ritvo, & Freeman, 1976; Painter, 1976–1977). In the Colman et al. study, most autistic children engaged in more repetitive behaviors under fluorescent lamps than under incandescent lamps. It is interesting that the increase ranged from zero to a doubling of repetitive behavior, suggesting again that the effects of lighting vary across individuals (Fletcher, 1983).

Some strange outcomes of exposure to fluorescent lighting have been reported. First graders who spent 5 months under daylight fluorescent lamps have been reported to have fewer cavities than others who spent 5 months under cool-white bulbs (Mayron, Ott, Amontree, & Nations, 1975)! This surprising result has not been substantiated, and it is difficult to imagine the mechanism by which cool-white lamps would cause cavities.

More plausible outcomes have also been reported. Fletcher (1983) cites several Soviet studies that indicate a variety of health benefits result when ultraviolet light is added to fluorescent light. Because sunlight contains ultraviolet light and fluorescent lighting normally does not, the addition of ultraviolet light makes the spectrum of indoor light more natural. One of these studies found that children in the supplemented light increased their height and weight more rapidly than children in the plain fluorescent light. Again, however, some controls may have been absent in these investigations.

▶ **In Sum.** Incandescent lighting is preferred by many, but it is more expensive than fluorescent lighting. Fluorescent lighting has not been shown to have dramatic negative effects on the performance or health of most students, although some odd claims have been made.

Despite inadequate methodology in some studies and the lack of significant differences in others, light does affect some kinds of performance, such as basic cognitive and motor activities. Short exposures to the different kinds of light in many studies may have led to incorrect conclusions that light has no effects. As with noise, the important effects may be on specific subgroups of individuals; when studies of whole classes or schools are done, large effects on a few learners may be obscured by an absence of effects on most learners.

CLIMATE

Performance

Indoor climate, temperature and humidity, certainly affects learning. Climate is not an issue, however, in many schools where temperature and humidity are well-controlled. Where climate does vary noticeably, learning is affected in complex and unexpected ways.

As an example, you might suppose that the most comfortable climate would produce the best performance. Several studies, however, refute this commonsense notion. Auliciems (1969) examined arithmetic and intelligence test scores in British classrooms. The best performance was found when the temperature was slightly *below* the optimal comfort level. Performance was also better when humidity was low and air circulated moderately. Auliciems' study was correlational and not well-controlled, so the findings must be considered tentative. Nevertheless, similar findings are reported in work settings (see Chapter Eleven, Working and Traveling).

A few studies report relatively simple relations between climate and performance. In the gymnasium, rising temperatures are correlated with poorer fitness and performance (Flatt, 1975). In a Swedish study, performance of language tasks by elementary school children was worse in warm than in moderate temperatures (Ryd & Wyon, 1970).

But these straightforward relations are the exception rather than the rule. Pepler (1971, 1972) studied climate and performance in suburban Portland, Oregon schools. Air-conditioned and non-air-conditioned schools, matched geographically and in the socioeconomic status of the students, were selected. Comparisons of performance in subjects ranging from spelling to languages to mathematics were made. When the temperature was high, the performance of students in the non-air-conditioned schools was more *variable* than it was on more comfortable days. In the air-conditioned schools, performance on hot days remained less variable; presumably the air conditioning prevented the heat from disrupting performance.

Note that performance in Pepler's studies was not *better* in air-conditioned schools, but it was more consistent. The increased variability of performance in non-air-conditioned schools on hot days appears to indicate that the performance of some students is lowered by heat but the performance of others is enhanced. Once again it seems that the environment (in this case, climate) affects individuals differently. The task of future research is to discover which kinds of students are negatively affected by heat and which are positively affected by it.

Wyon (1970) studied children's reading performance in controlled temperatures ranging from 20 to 30°C (68 to 86°F). Reading scores declined as the temperature rose, but at the highest temperature they rose again slightly! We might intuitively expect that performance changes steadily in one direction or the other as temperature changes, but the relation may not be linear after all. (Recall the temperature and aggression debate in Chapter Nine.)

Feelings

Both teachers and learners want the atmosphere to be pleasant, of course, but there is no single set of conditions that is pleasant for everyone. Engineers have sought the elusive **thermal comfort envelope,** or set of temperature and humidity standards, for many years. Such standards have been published, but they are envelopes (ranges of temperature and humidity levels rather than precise numbers) indicating that individuals vary in their preferences for indoor climates. For example, males and females were once thought to differ significantly in their climate preferences, based on office surveys. However, men often wear more clothing than women; when they wear the same amount of clothing, these sex differences disappear (McNall, Ryan, & Jaax, 1968). Of course, the conclusion still holds that climate preferences vary with amount of clothing that one wears.

Type of activity also affects climate preferences. Clearly, students who are physically active in the gym will have different preferences than students who are reading at a desk. Another factor is the length of time spent in the classroom. Students, more than teachers, change classes or go outside for recesses. Teachers and students may develop preferences for different climates because they have different patterns of physical activity, and students change temperature and humidity levels more often as they move in and out of the classroom (Moos & Sommers, 1976).

▶ **In Sum.** We may conclude that there are few simple, direct relations between climate and educational behavior; some combination of person and setting variables may "mediate, transmit, modify, or resist" the variations of climate (Moos & Sommers, 1976). Research is difficult because climate is composed of many possible patterns of temperature, humidity, and air movement. Perhaps the best-supported conclusion is that performance is best in slightly cool but not humid classrooms (Ahrentzen, Jue, Skorpanich & Evans, 1982). Even when care is taken in the control of indoor climates, they must inevitably be a compromise that considers individual differences in amount of clothing, type of activity, and indoor-outdoor movement. There may also be preferred temperature levels based on adaptation to home climate or cultural background.

SPACE

An aspect of the physical environment of learning settings that has been researched considerably more involves the amount of space available and how that space is arranged.

The amount of available space is obviously related to how many individuals are trying to use it. **Density,** you may recall from Chapter Seven, is the ratio of users to area. Density may vary either by changing the number of users in the same amount of space (social density) or by changing the amount of space for the same number of users (spatial density). This distinction is made because the two kinds of density appear to have different effects on behavior (McGrew, 1970). Crowding, by contrast, is the individual's perception that density is too high (Stokols, 1972).

The arrangement of space also affects learning. By arrangement, we most often mean seating arrangements (traditional rows versus clusters or circles) and the presence or absence of walls (open versus traditional classrooms).

Performance

Density. High density harms learning under certain conditions, but not others. Density may cut into performance when the task requires mobility or physical interaction among individuals (Heller, Groff, & Solomon, 1977). In a classroom, reading performance on a given afternoon is not necessarily affected simply because there are many students in the room. However, performance in a laboratory where students must move about from a supply counter to a workspace to instruments might well be damaged by high density.

Similarly, one might expect that learning in a pure lecture format would not be affected by increasing density—as long as enough air to breathe and space to write are available. But learning that relies on discussion in groups might be harmed by increases in density. This is precisely what a study by Loewy (Weinstein, 1979) found.

Crowding may occur when a learner feels that the space available does not allow for appropriate distance between people (Epstein & Karlin, 1975), when a learner perceives a shortage of resources, such as the lack of needed equipment and materials, or when a learner's individual history leads to a definition of a certain combination of density, task, and other individuals present as crowded. Consistent with the latter idea is a study reporting that only those students whose performance in a high-density room was below average found the room crowded (Gochman & Keating, in Weinstein, 1979).

Sometimes it is unclear whether behavior is affected by density or by crowding. In a study of kindergartners (Krantz & Risley, 1977), attentiveness to the teacher was measured under two conditions: when the children crowded round to listen to a story versus when they sat in separate, dispersed spaces. Attentiveness was clearly greater when the children were not close together. This might have occurred, however, because: (a) each child was able to see and hear better; (b) in the dispersed condition each child experienced less interference from other children; (c) fewer children defined the dispersed condition as crowded; or (d) separate, dispersed space clarified activities and reduced conflicts among children.

To sort out such explanations, researchers systematically vary density and other relevant variables. In one study both density and the amount of materials available to children were carefully varied (Rohe & Patterson, 1974). When density increased and materials were in short supply, behavior that was inconsistent with learning increased. As density and the amount of learning materials increased, so did learning-related behavior. The most learning-related behavior occurred when density was high and amount of materials was high; the least learning-related behavior occurred when density was high and amount of materials was low. (See Fig. 10–7.) This clearly shows that density should not be considered in isolation. We must also pay attention to how many resources are available to the learner.

Gary Evans (1978) has also pointed out that learning complex concepts may be more difficult in high-density conditions than learning simple concepts. He believes the reason some early studies of high density found no learning decrements is that very simple tasks were used.

In a recent study, performance on concepts that are relatively complex for ten-year-olds (arithmetic) was examined as a function of density and territoriality (Haines, 1985). Four classrooms of the same size that naturally varied in social den-

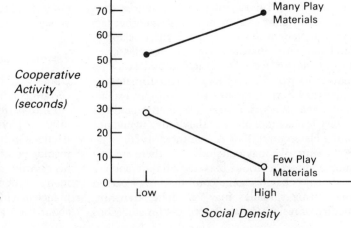

FIGURE 10–7 Cooperation among preschool children depends partly on social density and availability of play materials. More cooperation occurs when more play materials are available. As social density increases, children with more materials cooperate even more, but the cooperation of those with half as many play materials declines almost to zero. (Adapted from Rohe & Patterson, 1974.)

sity (thirty-two students versus twenty-two students) were selected. In one high- and one low-density classroom, territoriality was encouraged; students were assured they would keep the same desk and they were given name tags to affix to their desks. In the other class, the normal policy of periodic desk switching was in force and students were discouraged from personalizing their desks. Pre- and posttest scores on arithmetic tests over a 6-week period were administered. Students in low-density classes scored significantly better than students in high-density classes. In addition, there was a density-territoriality interaction. In high-density classes, students whose territoriality was encouraged learned more than students whose territoriality was not encouraged, but in low-density classes, students whose territoriality was encouraged learned less. Thus, low density is better for learning, but if a class is stuck with high density, encouraging students to feel that they have a secure place of their own helps.

An extensive investigation of preschoolers concluded that the chief effect of varying spatial density in the range of 25 to 75 square feet per child was to influence the amount and kind of activities they engaged in (Smith & Connolly, 1980). When given more space, the children engaged in more running and chasing and vigorously used their play equipment. When given less space, there were more physical contacts among them and more use of equipment for climbing and sliding.

Teachers, of course, also spend much time in classrooms. Several studies report that they respond to high density differently than do students. In denser elementary school classrooms, teachers (but not students) said they experienced more restricted movement and crowding (Ahrentzen, 1980). When we recall that in many classrooms, students sit while teachers circulate, this finding makes sense. Similarly, Ahrentzen (1981) found that in classrooms with cluster seating, larger clusters made students feel more distracted and crowded than teachers, but small clusters made teachers feel more distracted and crowded than students. This contrast in crowding is also presumably due to the different ways that students and teachers use classroom space.

Spatial Arrangements.   Can learning be facilitated by certain furniture arrangements or by improved decor? What are the effects of open classrooms? Do windowless classrooms harm performance? Can performance be improved by selecting certain seat positions in the learning setting? (See Fig. 10–8.) Little evidence is available about the effects of chair arrangements on learning itself, but their effects on learning-related behaviors such as attentiveness, participation, use of learning materials, and grades have been studied.

Some comparisons of traditional rows versus the newer cluster-style seating have found that rows produce more educationally-oriented student activity (Axelrod, Hall, & Tams, 1979; Wheldall, Morris, Vaughan, & Ng, 1981). However, one study found that cluster and single large-circle arrangements produced more on-task learning activity than rows (Rosenfield, Lambert, & Black, 1985). Table arrangements may produce more interaction among students (Gill, 1977).

Will changing the overall design of the learning setting, rather than just the seating arrangement, affect learning-related activities? Wollin and Montagne's amiable classroom, mentioned earlier, resulted in significantly better grades on Introductory Psychology tests. Wollin and Montagne spent $450, but estimated that the alterations directly responsible for the improvements cost only about $75 to $100. The classroom was not vandalized, either, although some schools might be more vulnerable to this threat than others.

In a comparison of two third-grade classrooms that were similar in most respects, Zifferblatt (1972) noticed that students in one class had longer attention spans, were more involved in their schoolwork, and were less noisy. The comparison was not a proper experiment with random assignment and control of outside factors, but Zifferblatt concluded that the differences in learning-related behavior were probably due to spatial arrangements. In the better class, the teacher's desk was in a corner. She could not easily direct activities from it and therefore was forced to move throughout the room, resulting in closer supervision of students. In the other class, the teacher's desk was in the middle of the room; she tended to sit there rather than move through the class to supervise students more personally.

Second, desks in the better class were arranged so that a maximum of two or three students could

FIGURE 10–8 Examples of a traditional classroom above and an open-plan classroom below. *(Bottom photo courtesy of Robert Sommer.)*

work together, but in the other class up to twelve desks were placed in each cluster. Third, different activities in the better class were separated by barriers (bookcases, etc.). In the other class, incompatible activities (one producing noise and one requiring concentration) were not very well separated.

Carol Weinstein (1977) attempted a more experimental approach to design changes (although because it does not meet all the criteria for a proper experiment, the study is more accurately called a quasiexperiment). The changes were made to meet the teacher's specific goals: to increase use of certain classroom areas that students were not using much, to make each classroom area more versatile, so that a variety of activities could occur in each one, and to increase the students' use of learning materials that they could manipulate and rearrange themselves. Weinstein attempted to meet these goals by rearranging furniture and by adding tables, shelves, and individual study carrels.

Weinstein carefully measured the children's behavior before the changes were made and allowed some time to pass after the changes were made so that behavioral changes could not be ascribed to the mere novelty of the design alterations. Then she measured the children's behavior again and found that the design changes had indeed resulted in improvements in the learning-related behaviors desired by the teacher.

In one daycare center, children were having difficulty staying involved in activities. Since one of the main ways that preschoolers learn is through involvement, Perkins (in Weinstein, 1981) analyzed the spatial arrangements of the daycare and recommended certain design changes. Clear boundaries were established between different activity areas, traffic paths were rearranged so that children were not forced to cut through the playhouse to get to the blocks, and learning materials were placed in easy-to-reach, clearly organized arrangements. Again, comparing previous behavior with postdesign changes in learning-related behavior showed that children spent more time involved in learning activities and in more constructive play.

In a major Canadian study involving over 1,000 preschoolers in thirty-eight classrooms observed over three years, Nash (1981) compared randomly arranged classrooms with deliberately arranged classrooms. In this case, deliberate meant that five groups of educational activities were placed in specific locations within the classroom. The program (time schedules, equipment, teacher-student communication) was similar in random and deliberate classrooms. Nash found that children in deliberate classrooms had significantly better scores on creative productivity and creative skills, generalization of number concepts, language use, and utilization of prereading materials. Carefully planned locations for different kinds of educational activities appears to be an important, and often overlooked, factor in preschool development.

Lesley Mandel Morrow has been concerned with the relation between classroom design and elementary school children's use of literature. In one study, she surveyed over 130 classrooms and found that few had special areas of the classroom for reading (library corners), but where library corners existed, students engaged in more literature activities (Morrow, 1982).

Sean Neill (1982b) investigated the effect of carpeting and thin screens that provided visual but not auditory privacy on the educational involvement of students and teachers in a nursery school. Carpeting increased the amount of time the staff spent in direct, close, educational activities with the children. The screens led teachers to engage in more administrative, noneducational activities. Neill found that carpeted rooms with no visual screens produce the highest teacher-student involvement in the nursery school. He suggests that carpeting allows more direct interaction because noise is lower and that the absence of screens discourages teachers from going off to do paperwork because they are more visible by others.

Changes to the decor of the learning settings may even facilitate learning. Many educators today believe that classrooms should be decorated with many pictures, posters, and other visual images. Carol Porteous (1972) investigated the educational effects of visual complexity (number of colorful pictures and posters on the wall). It is surprising that she found that eight- and ten-year-old children learned best in the plainest learning setting. The more background visual stimulation provided by the room's decor, the less children learned. We must be cautious about generalizing Porteous' results to actual classrooms, because the study took place in a trailer, the only persons present were the experimenter and one child, and the time span of the study was short. Nevertheless, her study suggests that plentiful visual stimulation may interfere with learning.

In another study of decor, Santrock (1976) investigated the persistence of children in rooms decorated with happy, neutral, and sad pictures. Children in the happy settings persisted longest on their work. Perhaps few teachers would display sad pictures anyway, but the study underscores the idea that learning-related behavior can be affected by room decor.

Do windows in classrooms make any difference? **Windowless classrooms** have been built under the assumptions that costs will decline as the school offers fewer glass targets to vandals, fewer windows means lower heating and cooling costs, and windows distract students from classwork. Most studies, however, show that windowless environments have little positive or negative impact on the achievement of students (Ahrentzen, Jue, Skorpanich, & Evans, 1982). This does not mean, however, that students like windowless classrooms, as we shall see later.

Is there a best place to sit in the traditional classroom? This is a delicate question, as we shall see, but the answer appears to be yes. The seats in the front and center of the classroom have been called the **action zone.** Students who sit in the action zone get higher grades than other students (Becker, Sommer, Bee, & Oxley, 1973). Students in the action zone participate more (Sommer, 1967). They are more attentive and they spend more time in learning-related activities (Schwebel & Cherlin, 1972). So, in that class you're having trouble with, all you have to do is move into the action zone, right?

Not necessarily. Perhaps students who sit in the action zone are those who already have considerable interest and talent in that subject; their success may not be due to their choice of seats, it may simply reflect their penchant for that subject. We do know, for example, that students who choose action-zone seating are zealous or even overzealous (Walberg, 1969) and have higher self-esteem (Dykman & Reis, 1979) or at least higher self-esteem regarding schoolwork (Morrison & Thomas, 1975). MacPherson (1984) has clearly shown that students are very aware of the implications of seating location for their social lives,

their control over classmates and teachers, and their academic accomplishments.

On the other hand, it could be that by choosing seats in the action zone, students are able to see and hear better, become more involved in the course, begin to receive more attention from the teacher, and consequently feel better about themselves and school. In real classrooms, the first of these assertions is probably true. Students who like a subject and have a knack for it gravitate to the action zone, and from that vantage point they see, hear, and are treated better than students outside the action zone. But the question remains, can you benefit academically by moving into the action zone when you otherwise might have sat in a back corner?

Researchers have tried to answer this by randomly assigning some students to the action zone and others outside it. Stires (1980) did this and also allowed students in an equivalent class to choose their own seats. He found that regardless of whether students were assigned seats or given their choice, those who sat in the action zone got better grades, liked the course more, and liked the instructor more than did students outside the action zone. Unfortunately, other studies have reached a variety of conclusions. Wulf (1977) found that participation was higher in the action zone but only when students selected their own seats; grades were not higher either when students chose seats or when they did not. Millard and Stimpson (1980) found no relation between grades and seating position. Finally, another study found higher grades in the action zone when students selected their seats but, contrary to Wulf's results, no differences in participation (Levine, O'Neal, Garwood, & McDonald, 1980).

Perhaps the conflicting results of other studies may be explained by taking the characteristics of individual students into account. Koneya (1976) examined the role of individual differences by randomly assigning students previously known to be vocal or quiet to the action zone and outside it. (See Fig. 10–9.) Vocal students who were assigned to the action zone participated much more than vocal students who were assigned to sit outside the action zone. But students known to be quiet did not participate more after being assigned to the action zone. Once again, the environment affects some individuals more than it affects others. Carol Weinstein (1979) has reviewed

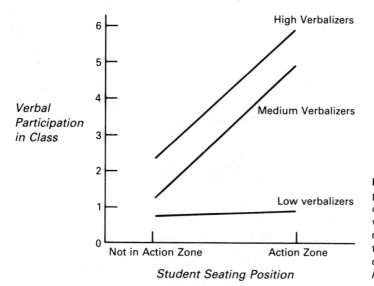

FIGURE 10-9 Participation in class depends on the students' pre-existing tendency to contribute to discussions and where they sit in the room. High and medium verbalizers contribute more if they sit in the central "action zone," but quiet students do not. *(Adapted from Koneya, 1976.)*

other studies on this question and concludes that most students could indeed increase their achievement by moving into the action zone. Of course, some kinds of students (such as those who are very shy) may not benefit from the move.

Besides furniture arrangement, wall decoration, and seat selection, one other major space factor may affect learning. This is the **open classroom,** in which large spaces are shared by more than one class. Many schools over the last three decades have been built "without walls," and many studies have examined their effectiveness.

The open-plan classroom has lost favor recently. There has been a perception that student performance is affected by higher noise levels. Neill and Denham (1982) found, for example, that more open preschools in Scotland sometimes reached 98 decibels and students received significantly less instruction in educationally valuable activities than did students in more traditional preschools with more separated spaces. However, not every study of open space finds these decrements. Weinstein and Weinstein (1979) compared the reading performance of elementary students in open classrooms when the noise levels were naturally high and low. No differences in accuracy or speed were found for either good or poor readers.

Probably the biggest single problem with open classrooms is that teachers have not been ade-

quately trained in their use; they try to apply teaching methods suited to traditional walled classrooms to open classrooms with very unsatisfactory results. Gump and Ross (1977) examined twenty-one open-space schools and found that two-thirds of them did not have programs suitable for open space. From a behavior-setting theory perspective, open space without an appropriate program is a violation of **synomorphy,** the principle that physical and social aspects of the setting should fit together well.

Teachers who use traditional methods in open-space schools often try to create walls with whatever materials are at hand—bookcases, dividers, file cabinets, or easels (Ross, 1980). They are upset at noise distraction, which probably hinders their effectiveness as teachers. They may avoid useful but relatively loud activities in their own space in order to avoid bothering neighboring classes (Gump, 1978). Open-space environments, then, have decidedly negative implications for learning when the educational program is geared to the traditional, walled classroom.

Open-space classrooms matched with open-space teaching methods, which include team teaching and less frequent but more intimate contact with students, do produce certain learning-related behavior changes (Gump, 1978). On the positive side, children seem to develop more initiative and autonomy. Since more activities occur simultaneously, children may learn to cope with distraction better than children in quiet, focused, traditional classrooms. If so, open-space children should be able to concentrate better, which should allow them to work more persistently. One study specifically tested this idea by giving puzzles to children from the two kinds of classroom; those from open-space classrooms worked more persistently on the puzzles than children from the traditional classroom (Reiss & Dyhaldo, 1975).

On the negative side, children in open-space classrooms (even with appropriate programs) may spend more time in transition between activities and on off-task activities (Cotterell, 1984) and spend less time than children in traditional classrooms actually engaged in educational activity (Gump, 1978). (See Fig. 10–10.)

FIGURE 10–10 Paul Gump pioneered the study of school size as an influence on school activities. *(Courtesy of Paul Gump.)*

Overall, neither open-space nor traditional classrooms produce clearly superior student achievement in general (Ahrentzen, Jue, Skorpanich, & Evans, 1982), but we should note that the advocates of open-space education never really claimed it would produce higher achievement levels. Instead, open space is promoted as a more suitable arrangement by those who think of the learner as active, curious, and responsible. When students are not motivated and responsible, open space may not be appropriate. Several studies report that children with socioeconomic, intellectual, or developmental problems perform worse in open-space classrooms (Bell, Switzer, & Zipursky, 1974; Grapko, in Weinstein, 1979; Traub, Weiss, Fisher, & Mesulla, 1974). The average student may score higher on standard achievement tests in a traditional setting (Bell, Switzer, & Zipursky, 1974; Wright, 1975), but the good student may score higher in open space (Gron, Bertil, & Engquist, cited in King & Marans, 1979). The parents of creative children may prefer open-space classrooms because they have educational goals other than scoring high on achievement tests, such as developing their child's social or artistic skills.

Nevertheless, school administrators believe there are problems; as the open-plan classroom declines in favor, many schools are faced with the problem of reshaping large, open spaces to fit today's teaching styles. Environmental psychologists have been involved in remodeling them. The addition and careful placement of sound-absorbent partitions can turn a poorly functioning classroom into one in which more relevant questions are asked of the teacher, traffic flows are separated from work areas, and privacy is increased (Evans & Lovell, 1979).

As we stress throughout the book, behavior is a product of the interaction of personal attributes, sociocultural context, and the physical environment. One study of open-space classrooms should be singled out because it paid particular attention to these interactions. Solomon and Kendall (1976) used both the student's degree of motivation and the type of classroom to predict achievement and other learning-related behavior. They found that students who are self-directed but not academically inclined had more discipline problems in traditional classes than in open classrooms. The same students, however, had higher achievement scores in traditional classrooms than in open-space classrooms. (See Fig. 10–11.)

Paul Gump (1978) reminds us that the design of the physical setting must not be considered separately from what ecological psychologists call the program. In the case of the learning setting, the program is the social environment, including curriculum and teaching style. In fact, as we have noted before, a given physical setting might be very beneficial for one educational program but not for another. This means that much research examining the value of particular physical arrangements in particular educational programs remains to be done, which might seem a formidable, even insurmountable, task. On the bright side, there are many similarities among educational programs that purport to be "different," "advanced," or "new and improved." Thus, more research is needed to clarify the role of physical arrangements in different programs, but the task is not impossible.

▶ **In Sum.** The amount and arrangement of space in educational settings is very important for classroom performance and behavior. High density may affect learning when the activity involves physical movement around the classroom, when learning is dependent on some classroom resource that is not increasing as fast as the number of learners, when a particular situation *seems* crowded to a particular learner, and when the concept to be learned is complex.

Among preschoolers, high density alters the child's choice of activities. Numerous classroom arrangement features have been linked to educational performance.

Benefits appear to accrue in classrooms that have the teacher's desk in a corner, that have different kinds of activities carefully arranged and separated, possess library corners, and are carpeted. Action-zone seating benefits some students. Open-space classrooms have positive outcomes *when* teachers use techniques suited to open-space classrooms and students have fewer behavioral or other problems. They can be noisy but can foster student autonomy. All these findings depend in part on grade level and teaching style.

Feelings

Our survey to this point has focused on behavior in the classroom. How do the physical features of

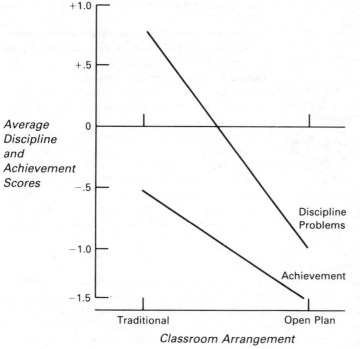

FIGURE 10–11 Classroom arrangements can produce mixed outcomes. Self-directed but nonacademically inclined students, for example, seem to have fewer discipline problems in open-plan arrangements compared to those in traditional arrangements, but they also demonstrate lower achievement in open-plan arrangements. *(Adapted from Solomon & Kendall, 1976.)*

learning settings affect the *feelings* of students and teachers?

Density. We have seen that increasing the number of individuals per unit of space (density) does not necessarily lead to increased discomfort (crowding). Nevertheless, high density in classrooms often does, in fact, lead to feelings of being crowded. Sommer and Becker (1971) examined over thirty classes that met in the same college classroom. As the number of students in the class rose from five to twenty-two, the number of complaints about room size and ventilation approximately doubled.

High density usually increases discomfort, but performance may not be affected if the task doesn't last very long. If all your classes are overenrolled, however, crowding discomfort may well lead to performance decrements. Elementary school pupils often must sit in the same class all day, yet the effect of high density in elementary school settings has received almost no study (Weinstein, 1979).

Spatial Arrangements. Many students' feelings about the layout of schools may be expressed by a student interviewed by Robert Coles (1969):

> I'd like comfortable chairs ... ones that have cushions so your back doesn't hurt and your bottom either. I'd like us sitting around ... looking at each other, not in a line. ... I'd like a sink, where you could get water to drink, and you wouldn't have to ask the teacher to go down the hall. ... We could have our books in a bookcase, and we wouldn't have to sit in the same place all the time. ... {most of all a skylight, so I could} just look up and see the sky and the clouds and the sun ... and you'd like it better, being in school. (pp. 49–51)

Many educators have wondered why we persist in making classrooms hard and linear when many students would prefer softer, rounded ones. Several reasons may be advanced: the burden of advocating and executing changes usually falls on an overworked teacher who often ends up accepting the traditional classroom rather than pursuing change in addition to normal duties, custodians often complain that such changes upset their work routines, administrators resist offering financial support, and some educators, parents,

and even students believe the hard, linear classroom is best for learning. Whether or not any of these beliefs are valid, they usually triumph. Most classrooms remain relatively hard and linear.

Some researchers have explored the roots of these preferences for the traditional classroom. Some teachers' support for it appears to be related, in part, to their need for control. In one study, teachers were asked to choose among a variety of classroom layouts. Those with a high need for control selected traditional formations in which the teacher was in a clear position of control, but those with a low need for control preferred formations where the teacher was not so obviously in a controlling position (Feitler, Weiner, & Blumberg, 1970).

Satisfaction with the classroom is also, in part, a function of its physical characteristics. Ahrentzen and Evans (1984) found that when a room has fewer solid walls, teachers believe there are more visual and aural distractions. When a room has lower ceilings, they reported more visual and movement distractions. Another study reminds us that satisfaction is a function of the congruence between program and setting. Teachers who use open-space methods and operate in open-space environments are more satisfied than teachers in traditional classrooms (Traub, Weiss, & Fisher, 1977).

Students also differ in their spatial preferences. Krovetz (1977) offers two concrete examples, citing research showing that (1) deviant adolescents prefer larger interpersonal distances than nondeviant adolescents and (2) students prefer larger interpersonal distances in the morning than in the afternoon.

Open-plan classrooms seem to cause greater anxiety about schoolwork among students than traditional classrooms do (Cottrell, 1984). On the other hand, the same study found that traditional classrooms appear to produce more organizational problems for the student, such as not knowing what to do, being unsure of the rules, or getting into trouble.

These results suggest that no single classroom design is likely to be best for everyone. Is it possible, then, to build a school that makes most of its users happy? Martin Krovetz (1977) argues for **pluralistic schools,** designs that overcome differences in school-form preference by providing several kinds of space within a single school. When schools are built or remodeled, uniform designs might be avoided in favor of a variety of classroom plans that satisfy the needs of different users.

Consider the varying personal space needs of students, noted earlier. Class size and density in a pluralistic school might be arranged so that problem students are given a little more elbow room and so that students engage in more individual work in the morning and more interactive work, such as discussions and labs, in the afternoon.

Another feeling that many students express is a desire for more time alone, away from the harried life in the classroom. Open-space classrooms, in particular, can be noisy and overstimulating (Neill & Denham, 1982). Most of us need to get away from it all at least briefly during the day, but public school children are given few opportunities to be alone. Of course, schools have the responsibility to preserve the health and welfare of their students, which seems to mean constant surveillance. Yet a few experimenters have offered students getaway spaces within classrooms; these efforts to meet privacy desires will be discussed in the social behavior section below.

Windows have little impact on actual performance, but studies of student feelings about windows have reached mixed conclusions. An early investigation found generally positive feelings about windowless classrooms (Chambers, 1963). Later surveys found the more expected ambivalence or dislike of windowless classrooms (Weinstein, 1979). Collins (1975) notes that a perference for windowless classrooms at one school turned into dislike after one year.

The belief that students in windowless classrooms are deprived of something important received support in a study that asked children in both kinds of classrooms to draw pictures of schools (Karmel, 1965). Students in the windowless school included significantly more windows in their drawings than did students in schools with windows. A tentative conclusion may be drawn from this study. When students are deprived of windows, they are forced to compensate by creating mental images of a school that includes what their real school lacks.

We have not yet considered the feelings or perceptions of those who are neither students nor teachers: third-party observers such as principals,

office staff and visiting parents. Little, indeed, is known about these observers' impressions of classrooms. Carol Weinstein and Anita Woolfolk (1981) have, however, made a beginning in this area. Outsiders were shown slides of vacant classrooms that were either open-plan or traditional, and were either neat or messy.

The observers judged that teachers in neat classrooms were probably more kindly, inventive, and organized than teachers in messy classrooms. They also felt that open-plan teachers were probably more kindly and inventive than were teachers in traditional classrooms. Another general impression was that students in neat classrooms were probably happier and better behaved than students in messy classrooms. Classroom arrangements send messages to outside observers; the messages may or may not be valid, but they are certainly sent and received.

► **In Sum.** Space in classrooms affects student and teacher feelings. Most students and teachers prefer lower-density classrooms, because lower densities usually feel less crowded. Providing satisfying physical arrangements within schools is best accomplished by furnishing a variety of layouts. Softer, more homelike classrooms will not become common until attitudes change. School authorities must be willing to spend a bit more, janitors must be willing to deal with rooms that are probably harder to clean, and parents must be willing to believe that a real education is possible in a nontraditional classroom. Students like the one whose wistful comments were quoted by Robert Coles probably wouldn't have to change their attitudes very much at all.

Social Behavior

Density. What are the effects of high or low densities on social behavior in the classroom? In many places, fiscal restraint has meant even greater classroom densities than in the recent past. (See Fig. 10–12.)

Early research on classroom aggression produced seemingly mixed results. Aggression among students was sometimes found to increase with density and sometimes to decrease with density. Gradually, several important realizations emerged that allow us to make sense of the findings. The first was based on McGrew's (1970) finding that social and spatial density have dif-

FIGURE 10–12 High-density classrooms can harm academic performance and create dissatisfaction. *(Courtesy of John Thompson, Times Colonist.)*

ferent effects on children's behavior. On reviewing the relation between density and aggression in children, Weinstein (1979) noted a pattern in the results of the early studies. Increases in social density were associated with increases in aggression, but increases in spatial density were not. Why might this be?

Changes in density are usually accompanied by changes in the amount of resources (access to the teacher, toys, lab equipment) available to each student. When more children are added to the same room (an increase in social density), the result may be greater competition for resources that have not been increased. However, when a class of children is moved from a larger classroom to a smaller one (an increase in spatial density), it is likely that they have access to about the same amount of resources. There is still one teacher for the same number of students and often the new classroom has as many books, toys, and equipment as the old one.

This idea has been supported by research. Children in high-density plus high-resource situations were less aggressive than children in high-density plus low-resource situations (Rohe & Patterson, 1974). However, if spatial density is increased not by shifting to a smaller classroom but by slicing an existing classroom in half, aggression does increase (Rohe & Nuffer, 1977). In the latter case, many resources were also divided when the room was halved.

The second important realization was that the

effects of density are modified by the classroom's program. Rohe and Nuffer observed that high-density situations seemed to discourage students from selecting activities requiring much concentration. Teachers who are faced with large classes may modify their lesson plans to avoid confrontations among students (Fagot, 1977).

A third recognition was that architectural features such as ceiling height and perimeter space may modify the effects of density (Ahrentzen, Jue, Skorpanich, & Evans, 1982). Imagine the difference in perceived crowding between a windowless basement room with one tiny door and a low ceiling and another one with the same floor size except that it is a second floor room with a panoramic view, high ceilings, and double sliding glass doors. When perceived spaciousness is increased by these architectural features, aggression and other antisocial behaviors may decrease.

To quote Paul Gump: "Clearly, the number of persons present is only a starting datum for studies on (classroom) size or density. . . . " (1978, p. 141). The type of density, the availability of key resources, the program, and architectural features other than floor size are also important. Confusion in the findings of early studies on density and aggression is largely resolved when these factors are considered. Still, if classroom density is sufficiently high, aggression may occur in some populations. Smith and Connolly (1980) found aggression increased in preschoolers when density reached one child per 15 square feet.

Aggression is not the only social behavior affected by classroom density. Several studies have reported that students tend to withdraw and behave randomly, deviantly, or as spectators (rather than as participants) in high-density classrooms (Weinstein, 1979). One study (Shapiro, 1975) found low involvement both at very high and at very low densities; another (Smith & Connolly, 1980) reports less social interaction when density rises to one student for every 15 square feet. This implies that classroom involvement is greatest at moderate density; based on Shapiro's work, this would be about 3 to 4 square meters (about 30 to 40 square feet) per student.

Unfortunately, little research on the relation between positive social behaviors and density has been reported. Rohe and Nuffer, who reported increased aggression when they sliced a classroom in half, did find that installing partitions to separate various activities increased cooperation.

Spatial Arrangements. Classroom layout affects the social interaction of both teachers and students. Research in the area has examined the effects of special booths that can provide privacy for students and the differences in social interaction between open-plan and traditional classrooms.

Carol Weinstein (1982b) explored the idea of offering elementary school children privacy booths, places where they could be alone during regular school hours. The booths were very popular—for awhile. For the first 10 days that the booths were installed about 70 percent of the students visited the booths each day. Over the next 2 weeks, however, usage averaged about 15 percent and by 25 days less than 5 percent of the students used the booths each day. The privacy booth experiment appears to be a surprising failure; the students seemed not to value the booths except as a novelty. However, the children in this study had abundant opportunities for privacy at home. Children without so much privacy at home might use privacy booths more. The study also found that some children consistently used the booth more than others. Boys rated by their teachers as more distractible, more aggressive, and less sociable used the booths more; girls who sought more privacy at home used the classroom booths more.

Unexpected findings also emerged from another study of student privacy (Ahrentzen & Evans, 1984). Students in elementary school classrooms that allowed for privacy (separate rather than shared desks and secluded study areas within the classroom) reported that they had less privacy than did students in classrooms *without* amenities for privacy. This may have occurred because students were not allowed free access to the secluded study areas. When you can see but not enter a desirable place, you may feel less privacy than if the desirable option was not available at all. The design lesson may be this: If expectations are raised by providing something desirable, but use of the new facility is restricted, discontent may be greater than if the desirable feature had never been built.

Social interaction is different in open-plan and

traditional classrooms. Since classes in open-plan classrooms are often combined, teachers interact with one another more, students meet with teachers more, and students move around more than in traditional classrooms (Weinstein, 1979). This increased interaction may, of course, create more noise and disruption than is found in traditional classrooms (Stebbins, 1973). Open classroom space may be associated with more aggression, at least at the preschool stage (Neill, 1982a; Neill & Denham, 1982). Despite this image of barely controlled chaos, more students report being able to find an adequate place to study by themselves in open-plan classrooms than in traditional classrooms (Brunetti, 1972).

In this section we have reviewed several major environmental influences on the learning process. Is there a way to integrate this knowledge within a single framework? If we could do so, such a framework might provide an overall set of guidelines for the design of learning settings.

One proposed framework is the **optimal stimulation** approach (Wohlwill, 1966; Zentall, 1983). Sidney Zentall, in focusing on optimal stimulation in the learning setting, suggests that all the influences we have discussed—noise, light, space, resources, and climate—may be characterized as presenting the learner with too little, too much, or optimal stimulation. Regardless of which modality the stimulation arrives in, the assumption is that teachers and learners perform better, feel better, and interact better when the total amount of stimulation is optimal. But what is optimal and how much stimulation is optimal?

Optimal stimulation is the amount required to produce an arousal level in the individual that in turn produces the best work, the best feelings, and the best social interaction of which the individual is capable. But the question remains: How much stimulation is needed to produce the ideal amount of arousal?

In general terms, Zentall says that it is a function of three factors. The first is individual differences in the need for stimulation. Hyperactive children need more stimulation than typical children who in turn need more stimulation than autistic children. The second factor is type of activity. We all perform better or feel better when engaged in certain activities (studying for an examination) when relatively little physical stimulation comes our way, but perform or feel better in other activities (dancing) when relatively much stimulation is present. The third factor is length of time. From the time a situation is new to us until it begins to fatigue or bore us, the optimal level of stimulation changes. Normally, the longer we are in the same setting, the more we adapt to the stimulation it offers, so that the optimal level of it rises with time. Theoretically, we could identify quantities of stimulation that would be optimal when an individual's personal qualities, the nature of the activity, and the length of exposure to the activity are known.

▶ **In Sum.** Increased social density leads to increased aggression and withdrawal when other resources, architectural features, and teaching style do not counteract it. Attempts to provide more privacy for students in the classroom have so far not been very successful. Open-plan classrooms increase social interaction. Classroom arrangements should provide optimal stimulation. The proper amount in any given situation cannot yet be specified, but the student's need for stimulation, the type of activity, and the length of time spent in the activity must be considered.

ENVIRONMENTAL COMPETENCE

As noted at the outset of this chapter, not all learning occurs in classrooms. In this section, we focus on learning about the environment, the development of **environmental competence,** defined by Fritz Steele (1980) as "people's ability to deal with their immediate surroundings in an effective and stimulating manner" (p. 225). This form of competence includes many of our relations with the environment, such as wayfinding, sense of direction, knowledge of the best and worst parts of a city, knowledge of and appreciation for different architectural styles, knowing the power structure of an organization so that design modifications might be lobbied for instead of merely commented upon, skill in navigation or wilderness hiking, outdoor skills, and the ability to personalize quickly.

We begin to develop environmental competence at birth and we may seek to increase it throughout our lives by traveling or paying special attention to local settings. Yet, as Steele points out, we give little formal attention to the individual's development of environmental competence after early childhood. In youth and adulthood, we are usually left to develop environmental competence on our own. (See Fig. 10–13.) Paralleling this neglect, researchers have not yet investigated most forms of environmental competence very much. Nevertheless, enough work has been completed and the topic is important enough to devote this space to it. After discussing the nature of environmental competence, we will turn to methods for developing it further.

The Varieties of Environmental Competence

Steele has proposed three kinds of environmental competence. The first kind includes personal style, attitudes, and awareness. One of these personal forms of environmental competence is **awareness** of your own environmentally relevant skills, abilities, needs, and values. Do you know where you stand on environmental issues? Have you ever actively assessed your own needs for

FIGURE 10–13 We learn—or try to—on the streets, too. *(Courtesy of Coe Gifford.)*

space? Do you believe you could find your way out of a forest if you lost your way? In addition, skill in perceiving the environment without too much distortion or too many blind spots is part of this personal dimension of environmental competence. Do you know anyone who consistently misjudges physical distances? Anyone who seems to be completely out of reach with the physical surroundings? Curiosity about the environment—the desire to explore new settings and learn more about familiar ones—is also very important. Someone who is not curious about the environment is unlikely to develop much competence!

A second kind of environmental competence concerns the individuals **knowledge** about the surroundings. This includes scientific knowledge relevant to environmental issues, knowing how to get around in a particular building or city or wilderness area as well as knowing how to find out how to get around. Some students have acquired knowledge of how to get around that labyrinthine campus building; others have not, but at least they know who to ask or where to ask, and they feel comfortable about asking. But some get lost in it even after months of trying and are too embarrassed to inquire.

Some psychologists have formally studied the process of learning routes. Edward Cornell has been studying this problem with a view to better understanding how individuals get lost and what strategies they employ as they struggle to find their way back. He has investigated the behavior of hunters lost in the mountains and which medium (slides, videotapes, or walking) helps young children learn a route best (Cornell & Hay, 1984). Walking helps most, it seems.

Steele says that technical knowledge of our surroundings—for example, the difference between fluorescent and incandescent lighting—is an important component of environmental competence because it provides us with design possibilities to draw upon if we are faced with awful offices, classrooms, or airports. These design possibilities may then be offered to those charged with the maintenance and modification of the building. We don't always care enough to bother offering, pushing, petitioning, or politicking over design changes, but without some knowledge of design possibilities, we would probably never bother.

Knowledge about people in relation to settings is another valuable aspect of knowledge about our surroundings. From those who know little or nothing about any part of the environment to those who take their Ph.D. in a specialized area, the range of environmental knowledge is immense. In a study that explored individual differences in knowledge about environmental issues, we found that natural science majors know more than social science or nonscience majors and that environmental studies students know more than nonenvironmental studies students (Gifford, Hay, & Boros, 1982–83). We were dismayed, however, to discover that men knew more than women (even when field of study was taken into account). It seems that the differential socialization of men and women includes educating males better than females in the realm of environmental issues.

Knowledge about how our social system deals with the physical setting is a final aspect of environmental knowledge. What are the rules of the game governing remodeling? Who decides whether to move or who gets which office? When are the meetings about this? What are the general norms in the organization concerning space, furniture, and other physical design features? Very often, space and design decisions are made by powerful managers who fail to consult with those who will be directly affected by the changes. The environmentally competent individual will, however, discover at least some of the answers to the questions above, and perhaps try to exert some influence. The environmentally incompetent individual is likely to shrug and give up the quest almost before it begins.

The third kind of environmental competence described by Steele involves **practical skills** related to the environment. These practical skills include being able to scout a setting, match oneself with appropriate settings for different activities, personalize a setting, and creative custodianship.

Scouting is the ability to get the feel of a place and to systematically canvass it through focused searching. As an example, I once hosted an eminent and much-traveled environmental psychologist. Lunch time arrived and I couldn't think of a restaurant suited to the occasion. We began cruising and within minutes, under the direction of my guest, who had no experience in my city but has great scouting ability, we found a very suitable restaurant.

Matching is the ability to find the right place for the right activity at the right time. Have you actively considered just where you work best? The difference between successful and unsuccessful students is often that successful ones discover the physical and temporal conditions in which they work well. Socially, some individuals seem to have a knack for selecting places for getting together that make the event worthwhile; others rarely think of the place to meet, focusing exclusively on the social aspects of the meeting.

On the negative side, some kinds of vandalism are activities that are "out of sync" with the setting. The same energy and talent required to spray paint a slogan or mural often could, with slight redirection, become widely admired art. In fact, the line between vandalism and art is a fine one; some unauthorized murals are artistic and community treasures, but unimaginative slogans or the graffitist's own name spray-painted on a wall constitute vandalism.

The ability to personalize a setting well and quickly is another useful dimension of environmental competence. College students, for example, move relatively often. Some seem to be able to transform a barren room into a glowing reflection of themselves. But others manifest no interest or ability in personalizing, sometimes preferring to complain about the plainness of the building.

At the public school level, one enlightened architect (van der Ryn) developed a service to provide inexpensive materials for teachers and students to personalize their classrooms (Sommer, 1972). It is amazing that some organizations still restrict or prohibit employees from personalizing their workspaces. Steele (1980) aserts that some organizations actively block the development of environmental competence in their employees. They seem to believe that environmental competence may lead to agitation for more democratic decision making on design questions. They are probably correct!

Finally, **creative custodianship** is Steele's term for the skill involved in using a setting without unduly upsetting its essential character in the process. Some campers go to great lengths to leave no trace of their temporary habitation. Some vandals, on the other hand, go to great lengths to en-

sure their presence does leave an ugly and preferably permanent mark on the environment. The reasons for vandalism in wilderness areas may involve revenge or perceived injustice (see Chapter Nine). Unfortunately, research on environmental incompetence is even rarer than programs devoted to increasing environmental competence. Perhaps that is why we presently see more vandalism than low-impact camping. However, there are some interesting programs devoted exclusively to the development of one variety or another of environmental competence.

Developing Environmental Competence

Formal Education. Of course, many forms of environmental competence are taught in postsecondary schools, including architecture, landscape architecture, town planning, environmental studies, and geography as well as environmental psychology. These are useful, but they are primarily directed at environmental competence in a technical or professional sense. Steele notes that the most extensive training in environmental competence often occurs in the military. He believes that high schools and colleges ought to teach courses in environmental competence in the broad sense of creating a citizenry interested in and knowledgeable about local everyday physical settings. This teaching creates ordinary citizens who are capable of responsible criticism of those settings, when criticism is needed.

In the rush of environmental activism that opened the 1970s, many traditional elementary school classes in biology and geography were suddenly transformed into environmental education classes. The emphasis shifted from mere description of ecology to stress on the fragility and limitedness of "spaceship earth." New curricula were quickly developed, such as a series of "environmental encounters" that William Stapp (1971) proposed for the whole public school age range, from kindergarten to the end of high school. (See Fig. 10–14.) Stapp suggested that the program would develop awareness and knowledge of such concepts as

1. *A closed system.* Except for solar energy, we live in a closed and limited system.
2. *An ecosystem.* Humans, other living organisms, and the nonliving environment are in-

FIGURE 10-14 In this environment education class, students played representatives of a mining company and an environmental activist group to experience some of the dialogue that occurs between developers and conservationists.

separably interrelated and vulnerable to sudden changes.

3. *A land ethic.* Humans must develop an ecological conscience; we are not conquerors of the environmental community, we are citizens of it.

4. *Population.* The whole system is threatened by the growth of human numbers; the problem is not so much a lack of space, but too many people for the available resources.

5. *Environmental quality.* Too many people leads to contamination; we must develop concern for both the physical and psychological effects of pollution.

6. *Environmental decisions.* We must rethink individual and collective behavior patterns; new policies and ethics must emerge and lead to decisions that are based on long-term environmental benefits.

These principles, so familiar to us now, were fresh ideas when Stapp sieved them from the ferment of late 1960s environmental activism. At that time, we were so impatient to learn more about the problems that we spontaneously attended environmental teach-ins (Lingwood, 1971). Since then, some of the urgency has gone from the environmental movement, but environmental education has developed steadily. Evidence of its continuing vitality is the continuing stream of curriculum guides and manuals that fulfill the objectives set forth by Stapp and others (Robinson & Wolfson, 1982).

Some research has been concerned with the effectiveness of programs aimed at developing environmental competence in schools. The field trip, that hallowed and beloved institution, has been examined for its pedagogical value. Martin, Falk, and Balling (1981) taught ten- to thirteen-year-old summer students two principles of plant ecology in their home schoolyard and in a natural setting (on a field trip). Learning was significantly better in the home schoolyard. The novelty of a day out of school is pleasant, but it may interfere with the learning of concepts. On the other hand, students on a field trip may learn something important other than the intended concepts. Educators must decide just what they hope to gain from a field trip.

Schwab (1982–1983) assessed the effectiveness of methods of teaching environmental competence. Schwab's survey indicated that teachers believe active-involvement instructional methods (such as debates, simulation games, field trips) are the most effective, but that most teachers actually use passive-involvement methods (such as lectures and readings). Apparently the effective teaching of environmental competence within the formal school system is hindered by a reluctance to relinquish the traditional forms of knowledge transmission, ones developed to teach classical disciplines such as philosophy and history.

Some active-involvement alternatives do exist within formal educational settings. Over thirty-five university-based science programs that provide symbiotic links with the National Park Service in the U.S. have been established in the last decade or so (Agee, Field, & Starkey, 1982–1983). Some students are being taught how to design settings, including their own classrooms. Students as young as eight have been taught enough architecture in hour-long, once-a-week sessions to produce good quality designs for classrooms and other settings (van Wagenberg, Krasner, & Krasner, 1981).

Programs Outside Schools. A wide variety of programs promote environmental awareness in community settings. Robert Sommer (1972) has described many of them in his book *Design Awareness*. One school gave four-year-olds the task of designing their own classroom. Another, developed by Meyer Spivack, taught children about personal space and crowding by drawing circles on the floor and asking the students to squeeze into its circumference. Sommer himself has conducted workshops in schools and hospitals that serve to sensitize staff to the environment as it is experienced by their clients. Many physicians, for example, have never rolled down a hospital corridor on a gurney. When teachers are asked to sit at a student's desk for an hour without leaving it, they better understand why some children are fidgety and restless. The environmental competence developed in these workshops can help to create settings that reflect new respect for the needs of those who usually have little input into design decisions: students, patients, clients.

Outdoor environmental competence, such as that gained through outdoor challenge programs and interpretation trails, has also received attention. Rachel Kaplan (1974) provided one of the earliest empirical studies of the effects of taking part in an outdoor challenge program. Adolescent boys spent 2 weeks in a primitive 17,000-acre forest working on survival skills. By their own account, the boys felt that the experience significantly improved a variety of skills, including their knowledge of the woods, map reading, compass use, food finding, and ecological knowledge. Although their self-esteem was not significantly improved—those boys who chose to go on the challenge already had relatively high self-esteem—they did find the experience challenging, educational, and enjoyable.

The interpretation trail is an increasingly common feature of our parks. Guides take individuals or small groups on short hikes, pointing out forest delights that might otherwise be overlooked. In one study (Brockmeyer, Bowman, & Mullins, 1982–1983), the merits of interpretations emphasizing a sensory approach (including many opportunities and exhortations to listen, touch, smell, and even taste the forest) were compared to a nonsensory approach (in which the emphasis was more on verbal information). The sensory approach led to more expressions of enjoyment from the hiker, but the nonsensory approach led hikers to ask more questions and to engage in more social interaction. These investigations will help to fine-tune the process of developing environmental competence.

▶ In Sum. Environmental competence involves learning *about* the environment. Three kinds include (1) personal style, attitudes, and awareness of physical settings, (2) knowledge of physical settings, including technical knowledge, how to unearth new information, knowledge about how social systems control space, knowledge of person-environment relations, and (3) practical environmental skills such as scouting, matching, personalization, and creative custodianship. Programs in and out of school teach many different facets of environmental competence, from basic environmental ethics to campfire starting to architectural design. While many subareas of environmental competence have received considerable attention, the concept as a whole so far has not received much attention.

LEARNING AND ENVIRONMENTAL DESIGN

Environmental psychologists have been involved in the design of many educational settings. Unfortunately, many educational designs have also been undertaken without any social science input either in the planning stages or in research evaluating the effects of the design on the behavior or feelings of students and instructors. In this section, three examples of educational design research by environmental psychologists are presented. The examples span the age range: kindergarten and college classrooms and a technique for enhancing the environmental competence of the elderly.

Kindergarten Classrooms

The reader may recall Leslie Morrow's finding that few classrooms have library corners, but where they exist students use them frequently. That study was correlational; the use of library corners may have been due to other factors—such as teachers who stressed reading—as much as it was due to the library corners themselves.

To test the idea that having a library corner directly leads to increased literature activities when students have a choice of activities, Morrow and Carol Weinstein (1982) attempted a more experimental study of thirteen kindergarten classrooms. None of the classrooms already possessed special library corners or much preexisting literature activity. Each classroom was randomly assigned to one of four conditions: control (no changes), new library corner, library program, or both library corner and program.

Morrow and Weinstein allowed some time for the novelty of the changes to wear off, then measured how often children used literature during their free-play periods. The number of children who used library materials during free play rose about twentyfold in the new library corner condition (from .28 users per free-play period to 5.75 users per free-play period). Introducing a new library program also raised the number of users (to 5.54 from 1.21). The combination of library corner plus program also produced more reading, but not more than a new library corner alone or a new library program alone. In the control classrooms, usage remained significantly lower than in all three experimental conditions. Thus, the mere existence of a library corner in a kindergarten classroom would seem to increase children's literature activity.

The results were mediated by individual differences; girls used literature more than boys in all three experimental conditions. The challenge for future research in this area: design a library corner that will attract boys!

College Classrooms

All of us have sat through classes in plain, boring, hard rooms. We can cope with such rooms; they probably don't cause brain damage or cocaine addiction. Nevertheless, they are not pleasant. If they could be made at least slightly more tolerable, would they help in any measurable way?

Robert Sommer and Helge Olsen (1980) redesigned a plain, thirty-seat college classroom at the Davis campus of the University of California. With a very small budget, they changed it into a soft classroom with semicircular, cushion-covered bench seating, adjustable lighting, a small carpet, and some mobiles. (See Fig. 10–15.)

Sommer and Olsen found that, compared to traditional classrooms of similar size, student participation increased markedly in the soft classroom. The number of statements per student tripled and the percent of students who spoke in class approximately doubled.

The soft classroom, contrary to the expectations of some, was not damaged or vandalized even though some of its components were vulnerable to vandals. Besides the dramatic increase in participation, students using the room wrote many glowing comments about it in a logbook

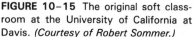
FIGURE 10-15 The original soft classroom at the University of California at Davis. *(Courtesy of Robert Sommer.)*

placed in the soft classroom. This research, together with Wollin and Montagne's work (described earlier) showing that soft classrooms for introductory psychology improved performance, suggests a tentative conclusion: college classrooms need not be plain and hard. In fact, the early evidence suggests that inexpensive changes to make them more pleasant have very tangible benefits.

The Environmental Competence of the Elderly

We all have to move from time to time. Moving is a stressful activity. Learning "the ropes" in a new residence, school, or workplace can take considerable effort and time.

If our ability to get around isn't what it used to be, this transition to a new setting is even more stressful. Michael Hunt (1984) studied ways of easing this problem for the elderly. When older individuals move to a strange building, their well-being may be related to their confidence and ability in finding their way around the building. To build their environmental competence, Hunt explored the potential for teaching older people about a new building through simulations of it (models and slides). If simulation techniques can

help individuals learn enough about a new setting to get around in it competently, the effort of doing so in person is saved.

Hunt compared the gain in way-finding ability and confidence attained through the simulation technique with that attained in an actual visit to the new building. He found that the simulation was actually *superior* to the site visit in bestowing way-finding confidence and ability upon older people. The potential of the simulation techniques for teaching children about their new school, college students about their new university, and employees about their new workplace appears promising.

SUMMARY

Educational activities—including learning, participation, classroom social interaction, and feelings about school settings—are affected in important ways by the physical setting in conjunction with other factors such as teaching style and age of the learner. The size, plan, and condition of the setting as a whole is one set of influences. Noise has a larger effect than light and climate, but this may be because in the typical school the latter two are usually provided at reasonably acceptable levels, but noise often varies widely from classroom to classroom.

Budget crunches have created space crunches. The resulting larger class sizes (increased social density) are linked with numerous difficulties in the learning process. Open-plan classrooms can work well when teachers are appropriately trained and students are able to handle the flexibility they provide. Aggression and withdrawal accompany greatly increased social density.

Environmental competence refers to learning about environments ranging from a classroom to the great outdoors. It involves a personal dimen- sion (your orientation toward learning more about the environment), technical and social knowl- edge of specific settings, and practical skills. All forms of environmental competence may be de- veloped through programs in and out of schools. Examples include lessons in resource conserva- tion, field trips, and workshops for adults.

These design research interventions are de- scribed in which the use of books was increased in kindergarten, participation in college classes was increased, and the way-finding ability of el- derly individuals was improved by using a build- ing simulation technique.

SUGGESTED SUPPLEMENTARY READINGS

Ahrentzen, S., Jue, G. M., Skorpanich, M., & Evans, G. W. (1982). School environments and stress. In G. W. Evans (Ed.), *Environmental stress.* New York: Cambridge Uni- versity Press.

Bronzaft, A. L. (1981). The effect of a noise abatement program on reading ability. *Jour- nal of Environmental Psychology, 1,* 215–222.

Fletcher, D. (1983). Effects of classroom lighting on the behavior of exceptional chil- dren. *EEQ: Exceptional Education Quarterly, 4,* 75–89.

Gump, P. V. (1978). School environments. In I. Altman and J. F. Wohlwill (Eds.), *Chil- dren and the environment.* New York: Plenum.

Krovetz, M. L. (1977). Who needs what when: Design of pluralistic learning environ- ments. In D. Stokols (Ed.), *Perspectives on environment and behavior: Theory, re- search and applications.* New York: Plenum.

Nash, B. C. (1981). The effects of classroom spatial organization on four- and five-year- old children's learning. *British Journal of Educational Psychology, 51,* 144–155.

Rivlin, L. G., & Weinstein, C. S. (1984). Educational issues, school settings, and envi- ronmental psychology. *Journal of Environmental Psychology, 4,* 347–364.

Steele, F. (1980). Defining and developing environmental competence. In C. P. Alderfer & C. L. Cooper (Eds.), *Advances in experimental social processes, 2,* 225–244.

Weinstein, C. (1979). The physical environment of school: A review of the research. *Review of Educational Research, 49,* 577–610.

Wollin, D. D., & Montagne, M. (1981). College classroom environment: Effects of ste- rility versus amiability on student and teacher performance. *Environment and Be- havior, 13,* 707–716.

Chapter Eleven
Working and Traveling

. . . facilities planning tends to be delegated to accountants or office management people whose training and experience are almost exclusively in dealing with figures. It is therefore not surprising that the quantifiable costs—construction costs per square foot, cleaning costs per week—are weighted heavily and that the less quantifiable factors—decreases in stimulating contacts, lack of identification with the system—tend to be ignored when decisions are made.

Fred Steele, 1973

Tom struggled into consciousness as the clock radio dribbled out the dreary 7 A.M. news. After dragging himself through the bathroom and kitchen, he went outside—to discover that his car had a flat. "What do I do now?" he moaned to himself. If he wanted to make it to work on time, the only choice was to take the bus. The bus schedule was in a drawer somewhere, but of course he couldn't find it. Tom stood in drizzling rain for 20 minutes before the bus pulled up. The driver tossed out a cheery, "Morning, there! Wet today, isn't it!" All this for a part-time job!

At work, Tom passed the shop on the way to his office. Even if he were in a good mood, he muttered to himself, he wouldn't understand how those people could stand all that noise of machinery and yelling. He sat down at his desk, wishing he could just quietly let his clothes dry and his emotional health improve. Unfortunately, the open plan of his office made him the center of attention and he felt compelled to pretend the whole situation was humorous. This did not improve his emotional health.

Throughout the day he waited for a minute when his co-workers were all away from their desks so he could call Jane for a little sympathy, but there was not one moment when he was left alone. However, some of them didn't seem to mind calling to place bets at the track, to arrange for parties, or to reach their friends.

Between his own desire for a moment's solitude and the steady stream of distracting conversations that he couldn't help overhearing, Tom was a wreck by the end of the day. He was determined to ride off into the sunset, even on a bus. Then he remembered that his place was east of the office.

Working can provide some of the best and some of the worst experiences in life. For Sigmund Freud, it was one of the two major paths to fulfillment (the other one was love). Many factors determine our productivity and satisfaction at work, but for decades psychologists have realized that the physical environment is an im-

portant mediator of employee productivity and satisfaction. (See Fig. 11–1.)

It all began with the famous Hawthorne studies (Roethlisberger & Dickson, 1939), in which psychologists learned to avoid simple environmental determinism in favor of the notion of mediation. The Hawthorne studies included years of work on the effects of the environment on the productivity and satisfaction of assembly-line workers at the Hawthorne plant of the Western Electric Company, near Chicago. Many separate studies were completed, and the meaning of the voluminous results are still debated, almost half a century later.

However, certain basic conclusions from the Hawthorne studies are widely accepted. For example, in some early studies at Hawthorne it was hypothesized that changing the level of lighting on an assembly line would affect productivity. This is a straightforward hypothesis that anyone new to environmental psychology might reasonably propose. If workers can see better, they probably will be able to assemble more items, and production will rise. However, the researchers were surprised to discover, in several separate studies, that production did *not* vary with lighting level. The amount of light was even reduced by 70 percent without a loss of productivity. They became convinced that something very odd was happening when they replaced a set of lights with bulbs *of the same intensity* and found that the employees expressed satisfaction with the "increased illumination."

Some observers took these results as evidence that the physical environment was not important. Because the Hawthorne studies were one of the first large-scale investigations of environment and behavior, this conclusion may have set back the development of environmental psychology by as much as three decades. Unfortunately, the conclusion was wrong.

Three important findings of the Hawthorne study were overlooked by those drawing this inappropriate conclusion. First, the findings refute an assumption that is itself faulty. The simplistic notion that lighting directly affects work output is a form of naive environmental determinism. Environmental psychologists believe that physical setting influences are mediated by employee perceptions, beliefs, preferences, experience, and personality. For example, the behavior of employ-

FIGURE 11–1 Adults spend much of their lives in offices and factories. The effect of these settings on people's behavior deserves study. *(Bottom photo courtesy of Coe Gifford.)*

ees in the Hawthorne studies was clearly affected by their *perception* of the work environment. In the bulb-changing study, employees probably assumed that a bulb someone took the trouble to replace was deficient; a new bulb must be an improvement.

Second, as Steele (1973) points out, the conclusion focuses on one environmental variable when a *different* environmental variable, more subtle but perhaps more important for that very reason, was operative. Employees in some of the Hawthorne studies were moved to a different room, away from most employees. This room made the employees feel special and its physical and social characteristics may have affected performance more than the environmental variables being examined by the researchers. For example, the experimental employees were further away from the watchful eyes of supervisors.

Third, the layout of the room facilitated social contact among employees. This probably encouraged the employees to form and maintain informal norms about how much to produce in a given day.

In general, the Hawthorne studies discomfirm naive determinism but confirm that physical settings have definite influences on work behavior, but these are more complex than previously thought because they involve broader, more subtle aspects of the setting which in turn are mediated by employee characteristics. (See Fig. 11–2.)

In this chapter, we consider research on the relations between the physical environment and (a) getting to work, (b) performance, feelings, social behavior, health, and stress at work, and (c) trying to enjoy life *after* work (in particular, by traveling). Throughout, we must resist the tempting but simplistic notion that changes in the physical setting will directly determine employee behavior.

GETTING THERE

It could be because we are wrapped up in our thoughts about people and problems we will encounter once we arrive. It could be because the experience is so often unpleasant. It could be because the experience is literally transitory. Whatever the reason, it is easy to forget that transpor-

tation settings are part of the environment. Cars, buses, roads, and rail lines are important settings both to the traveler and to those whose neighborhood the traveler passes through.

Transportation, of course, plays a very large role in our lives. In economic terms, many of the largest corporations either manufacture vehicles or produce goods for vehicles. The cultural and social life of most developed nations is interwoven with the myths and realities of cars, trucks, trains, and planes.

Environmental psychologists are investigating many transportation-related behaviors, attitudes, impacts, and choices (Altman, Wohlwill, & Everett, 1981). They are providing answers to questions such as these: How do commuters choose their mode of transport, and how can those choices be changed? What is the impact of each transportation mode on the commuter? What is the impact of the traffic created by commuters on neighborhood residents? How do commuters view the places they pass through on the way to work? What role can transportation choices play in energy conservation? Can we design urban transit systems that meet the needs of both commuters and the residents of neighborhoods through which they move?

Some of these issues are dealt with in other chapters. In particular, the impact of transportation systems on residents is considered in the last chapter, and some of the design issues are saved for the next chapter. Here the focus is on the commuter's choice of transportation mode and the consequence of that choice for the commuter's well-being.

Choosing a Way to Get to Work

In some North American cities, as many as 85 percent of employees drive a car to work (Stokols & Novaco, 1981). In a few cities, up to 95 percent of commuters use rail or bus transit systems (Taylor & Pocock, 1972). There are always some who bicycle or walk. And then there are the nonconformists—a friend of mine used to *row* to work every day!

The Car: Wasteful or Adaptive? Most research has concentrated on cars versus urban transit as alternatives, because commuting by car is both popular and very expensive. Over half the

FIGURE 11–2 At this University of California at Irvine simulation laboratory, a variety of office conditions can be investigated. *(Courtesy of Dan Stokols.)*

petroleum used in the United States goes for transportation. About 85 percent of all trips are made in cars, and three out of four cars on their way to work contain only one person. Only 4 percent of all trips are on public transportation (Zerega, 1981). Thus, most people in the United States use the most expensive form of travel. There is a real energy conservation problem in transportation.

For these reasons, some observers see the automobile as a very dysfunctional part of society. It requires enormous expenditures by individuals (and by governments, as they are responsible for providing and maintaining the road system). Because we continue to choose cars over urban transit, even when we know they are very expensive, Joseph Reser (1980) raises the question: Are we actually *addicted* to automobiles?

Reser suggests that the car does serve several important needs besides mere transportation, including a sense of freedom, a way to express ourselves, privacy and security, and an opportunity to exert control over a powerful machine. Reser concludes that for many of us, the use of cars is an adaptive response to a stressful macroenvironment. If we wish to kick the car habit, Reser believes that we will have to alter many of those negative aspects of the environment that cars help us to cope with. To help with the problem, environmental psychologists have scrutinized not only transportation alternatives (for example, offering suggestions on how to design urban transit vehicles) but also commuters themselves.

Who Uses Cars?   To begin the empirical study of why commuters prefer cars, researchers have investigated what sort of individuals, with what sort of attitudes, choose which form of transit. Individuals who have cars and higher incomes use public transit less (Hartgen, 1974). Those who believe public transit is easy to use, reliable, safe, and uncrowded tend to use urban transit more (Tischer & Phillips, 1979). Those who have bad memories of transit, hate to be tied to fixed schedules, and believe that only the poor use transit systems tend to use urban transit less (Gilbert & Foerster, 1977).

Why Do Commuters Choose Cars?   Some environmental psychologists have investigated the transportation choices of commuters by

trying to discover what information commuters themselves use in deciding how to get to work. For example, Levin and Louviere (1981) describe how concepts from economics (consumer theory) and psychology (decision theory) may be blended to produce a model of the commuter's choice process. The blend includes objective facts, such as the cost of urban transit, and subjective impressions, such as the commuter's attitudes toward urban transit. Even when a commuter's subjective impressions are incorrect, they play a major role in transit choices (remember Hawthorne!). For example, Levin and Louviere found that commuters who choose to drive cars markedly underestimate the overall cost of operating their cars.

Levin and Louviere's **behavioral choice modeling** approach proposes two general solutions to the transportation energy problem. First, we could provide more objective information setting out the true costs and benefits of alternative forms of transit. Often, but not always, this information suggests that, both individually and as a society, we should build and use better urban transit systems. Second, we could examine commuter preferences and alter existing transit systems, or provide new ones that better fit these preferences. For example, Eliahu Stern (1982) examined Israeli bus riders' perceptions of their transit system with the goal of altering the bus service to fit these preferences. The notion of evaluating transport services from the user's point of view seems obvious, but it has not been done often enough.

Can Commuters Be Pried from Their Cars? Environmental psychologists who are primarily oriented toward problem solving treat these demographic, attitudinal, and cognitive findings as mere first steps. To them, the important research involves finding a way to use these and other findings to *change* commuter choices. Given the energy conservation problem, this usually means finding ways to encourage commuters who drive to work alone to use urban transit facilities or at least to form and use car-pooling or ride-sharing opportunities. In one study, bus fares were reduced to zero in nonrush hours (Studenmund & Connor, 1982). Ridership increased, but because such a large proportion of people drive cars, even free fares did not significantly reduce auto traffic in the city. (See Fig. 11–3.)

FIGURE 11-3 Some transit authorities have tried to encourage increased ridership by offering fare cuts.

Reducing fares may increase ridership, but obviously this approach may cost more than the transit authority can afford. Other solutions must be considered. One such solution might be positive information about alternate forms of transit. Bonsall, Spencer, and Tang (1983) organized several car-sharing programs in England. They began each program with publicity ranging from an article in the company paper to posters, newspaper stories, and television notices. Only a small percentage (less than 2 percent) of the target populations joined the programs and survived the critical first few days of trying them out. About 10 percent of the participants dropped out every 6 months, so that 4 years later about half the car-sharing arrangements had disappeared. These car-sharing programs did not change the transit patterns of about 98 percent of the individuals they were aimed at. On the other hand, they did change the lives of those who joined by saving them money and by enriching their social lives.

Another low-cost solution might be asking drivers to commit themselves to a certain amount of bus riding. Bachman and Katzev (1982) found that getting commuters who normally drove to work to commit themselves to taking the bus twice a week was just as effective as giving away free tickets in increasing bus use.

Environmental psychologists are now at-tempting to understand why some programs are more effective than others. Dallas Owens (1981), for example, interviewed commuters who stayed in a ride-sharing program and those who dropped out, seeking variables that might distinguish between the groups. Once such variables are identified, programs might be retooled so they respond better to the needs of commuters. Owens found that what distinguished successful groups from unsuccessful groups was whether the group could find a mutually acceptable pickup and drop-off route, the quality of agreements made in the group, the degree of similarity among the group members, and (here comes Hawthorne again!) degree of *perceived* equity (fairness of costs and benefits). All these were related to satisfaction with the group, which in turn contributed significantly to the success or failure of the ride-sharing group.

Consequences of Transit Mode Choices

Some researchers have emphasized the importance of investigating the behavioral and emotional consequences of driving or riding to work. One important consequence is stress. All forms of commuting have their sources of stress. First, no matter how you get to work, there is a chance of an accident. Besides such well-known causes of accidents as poorly planned roads and careless driving, a study in Britain by Timothy Monk (1980) suggests that drivers must even be wary of time changes. Monk examined the incidence of traffic accidents in the week following the annual switch to daylight saving time and found that accidents increased. Monk hypothesizes that "desynchronosis" (a syndrome resulting from shifts in our regular schedule) is one cause of accidents.

Second, whether we drive or ride, we must deal with people who impede our progress or comfort—other drivers or other transit passengers. In one survey of automobile drivers (Turner, Layton, & Simons, 1975), 12 percent of the men and 18 percent of the women said that at times they could gladly kill another driver! It is not surprising that one behavioral effect of driving is an increase in adverse physiological reactions, such as chest pain (Aronow, Harris, Isbell, Rokaw, & Imparato, 1972), and other forms of stress.

In some places there are so many transit passengers that people are literally pushed onto the trains. Here is the account of a Canadian student who went to study and work in Japan:

> Although the crowding in Kyoto is extreme at certain times and in certain places, it fades in comparison to the normal state of affairs in Osaka. I have taken the Osaka subway at all different hours of the day, including times when I was squeezed in so tightly that I could not turn around or even raise my arms. One time, at the tail end of the morning rush hour, I saw passengers pushing each other into a train in the same way that Canadians push a snowbound car. Just before the door closed, the pushers turned backwards, grabbed the doorframe over their heads, and literally "butted" their way into the train. (G. Brockelbank, personal communication, July 11, 1983)

Personal and Route Causes of Commuting Stress. Dan Stokols and Ray Novaco (1981) present evidence that adverse reactions to commuting are linked to personal characteristics and to the number of hindrances we face on the journey (measured as the time and distance from home to work). Commuters who drive longer distances have higher blood pressure. The more interchanges commuters must negotiate on their way to work, the more days they are ill enough to be hospitalized. These are important but not very surprising findings.

Stokols and Novaco also report a less obvious result. In their study a commuter is Type A (a coronary-prone individual who struggles to control the environment and is more upset in situations where little control is possible) or Type B (the opposite qualities). The type, A or B, *interacts* with the number of hindrances on the journey to predict the amount of stress commuters experience. We might expect that the interaction would take the following form: Commuters who are Type A *and* must overcome many hindrances experience the most stress. However, Stokols and Novaco were surprised to find a different significant interaction, one that is not easy to explain. Type B's who dealt with many hindrances experienced more stress (high blood pressure level) than did Type A's who dealt with many hindrances. They suggest that commuting stress will not be fully understood until we look at another side of stress: how well individuals have learned various coping strategies. In addition, commuting cannot be studied separately from the rest of our life; the quality of life at home influences and is influenced by the amount of commuting stress we experience. (See Fig. 11–4.)

▶ **In Sum.** Most research on getting to work has been broadly concerned with encouraging commuters to help save energy. Environmental psychologists and others have created demographic profiles of car and urban transit riders, devised models of commuter preference, provided positive information about urban transit, evaluated existing transit systems, and offered reduced fares. This research has not yet had very large effects on our automobile addiction, but the more promising approaches are being sorted out from the less promising ones. Stokols and Novaco's results indicate that the impact of commuting on the commuter is real, but that we need to learn more about how commuting stress works and who will experience the most stress.

ENVIRONMENTAL PSYCHOLOGY ON THE JOB

Once you have decided how to get there (and have suffered appropriately for that choice!), you arrive

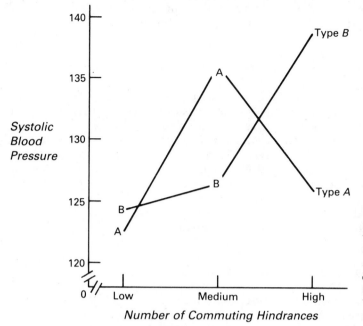

FIGURE 11-4 Comuting, stress, and personality. After shorter commuting trips, hard-driving Type *A* personalities and mellow Type *B* personalities have similar blood pressures. As the number of commuting hindrances increases, the blood pressure of Type *B* rises but that of Type *A* rises and then falls. *(Adapted from Stokols & Novaco, 1981.)*

at work. The physical environment at work is crucial to employees' performance and satisfaction. Over a 40-year life cycle of an office building, perhaps 2 to 3 percent of all funds are spent on the initial costs of the physical environment and about 90 percent is spent on salaries and benefits (Wineman, 1985). If the 2 to 3 percent is well-spent, very large savings on the later personnel costs might be achieved. Good workplace design begins with knowledge of behavior in workplaces. What is known about the relations between the physical environment and work behavior?

First, we must remind ourselves of the tremendous variety of job activities. Psychologists have long sought a simple classification system to make the huge number of things that go on at work more manageable. We will rely on a taxonomy adapted from earlier ones proposed by Steele (1973) and by Parsons (1976). Most behavior at work falls into one of four major categories: performance (actual productivity, activities, and attendance), feelings (evaluations, attitudes, emotions, and perceptions), stress (physiological changes and health), and social behavior (space, interaction, privacy, status).

What affects these four kinds of work activity?

Five major aspects of the physical setting that can affect employees include: sound (noise, music), temperature (heat, cold), air (pollution, freshness), light (sunlight, incandescent, fluorescent, windows, views), and space (amount of it, arrangement of work stations). These aspects of the environment are, of course, related to behavior in many nonwork parts of life, too. This chapter emphasizes research concerned with work settings.

Let us stroll through the known relations between the five major environmental aspects of workspaces and the four major categories of work behavior. Not every cell in this 4 × 5 matrix has been well-researched. If you notice a missing cell, such as the effects of air quality on social behavior, it doesn't necessarily mean there are no effects; it may simply mean little or no research has yet been done in that area. We will proceed by covering the effects of each environmental aspect, beginning with sound, on all the work behavior categories.

Sound

On the job, sound may come from jackhammers, typewriters, background music, co-workers talking, and many other sources. Some of these sounds may be expected, natural, or even desirable—silence isn't always pleasant—but others may be unwanted and annoying. Fancy formulas exist for specifying the conditions under which sound is likely to be labeled noise (Dunn, 1979) but the most straightforward way to define it is: **noise** is unwanted sound. Desirable, beautiful sound, on the other hand, is called **euphony.**

Whether a particular sound is heard as noise or as euphony depends on the individual and the situation. One person's euphony may be another person's noise. A whisper at 2 meters (30 decibels) may be euphonic but a moon rocket lifting off at 300 meters (200 decibels) may be noise. Yet to those who labored long to enable the rocket to lift off, even 200 decibels may be euphonious. (See Fig. 11–5.)

Performance. Early noise research focused on hearing damage from industrial sounds that were too loud. Even today, many industrial workers are exposed to sound levels that can cause either temporary or permanent hearing damage. Usually, individuals do not go deaf suddenly; instead, the lowest level of sound that one can detect at a given frequency gradually rises. **Temporary threshold shift,** or TTS, is defined as a threshold shift that reverses itself within 16 hours (about the length of time between leaving the noise source at work and returning to it the next day).

If a threshold shift is repeatedly allowed to last into the next workday, it may become a **permanent threshold shift** (PTS). This process may easily go unnoticed and the victim may gradually lose considerable hearing ability. TTS can occur after only 10 minutes of 100-decibel sound (Dunn, 1979), a sound level that may be found in very noisy factories and in many concerts and night-clubs. TTS can also occur after 90 minutes of 90 decibels, a sound level found in many factories; it is about the loudness of noisier kitchen waste disposers and electric lawn mowers at a distance of 1 meter (Reif & Vermeulen, 1979).

Sound levels in offices rarely reach levels that endanger hearing, but that does not mean sound is unimportant in offices. The sound level in most offices ranges from about 45 to 65 decibels, but other factors such as the source, meaning, controllability, and predictability of the sound may be more important than sound level. As the source of the sound becomes more relevant to an employee, as its meaning grows, and as its controllability and predictability decrease, sound is more likely to be perceived as noise and negatively affect work behavior.

Whether noise affects actual productivity at realistic sound levels in actual offices is not yet clear (Broadbent, 1979). (See Fig. 11–6.) Many employees and researchers believe that noise interferes with performance, but the evidence itself is contradictory. In fact, noise has occasionally even been shown to improve performance (Miller, 1974). Noise-performance relations remain unclear partly because of inadequate research funding. Government funding on the topic in the late 1970s was less than one-twentieth of the amount spent on noise-induced hearing loss (Goldstein & Dejoy, 1980). This is unfortunate because sound itself and research on sound effects on behavior are both extremely complex.

A good example of the complex relations between noise and productivity is provided by Neil Weinstein (1974). He asked subjects to proofread in a room that was either quiet or received intermittent bursts of teletype sound at 70 decibels. The subjects could detect just as many spelling errors and they could recall the passages they had proofread just as well in the noisy condition as they could in the quiet condition. First conclusion: performance is not affected by noise.

However, Weinstein also found that subjects could not detect as many grammatical errors when it was noisy. Second conclusion: performance *is* affected by noise. When the room was noisy, subjects started working more slowly and they worked less steadily. Once more, performance is found to be affected by noise. Yet in the noisy room, subjects worked *more* accurately. Third conclusion: performance is affected, but in the opposite-from-expected direction!

Don't throw up your hands in exasperation yet. The Weinstein study illustrates some common trends in noise research and these trends lead us to some tentative conclusions that clarify these apparently conflicting results.

First, the *type* of work matters. One leading researcher, Donald Broadbent (1979), has reviewed numerous similar studies and concludes that when an employee (a) performs a routine task, (b) merely needs to react to signals at certain definite times, (c) is informed when to be ready, and (d) is given clear visual signals, performance

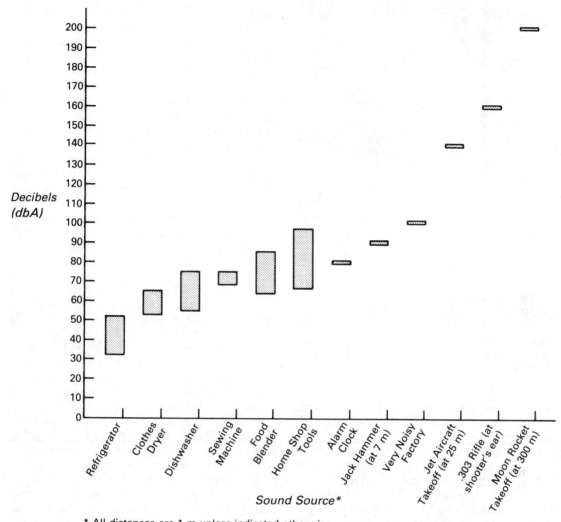

Decibels (dbA)

Sound Source*

* All distances are 1 m unless indicated otherwise.

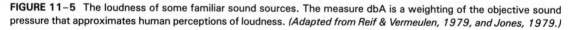

FIGURE 11–5 The loudness of some familiar sound sources. The measure dbA is a weighting of the objective sound pressure that approximates human perceptions of loudness. *(Adapted from Reif & Vermeulen, 1979, and Jones, 1979.)*

will not be affected by continuous loud noise. Examples of work fitting this description include servicing a machine we know well or writing a routine letter.

Tasks that are often affected by noise include those that ask the employee (a) to pay attention to multiple sources of information or (b) to perform more than one task at a time (Cohen & Weinstein, 1982). If an employee must monitor several other employees or machines, or think

carefully while performing, performance is more likely to be affected.

The effects of noise on performance differ for simple versus complex tasks. When one of several tasks is more important, noise tends to increase the effort extended on less important tasks (Broadbent, 1979). Consider, for example, the difference between finding spelling errors and finding grammatical errors in Weinstein's study. For most of us, spelling errors almost leap off the

FIGURE 11-6 Donald Broadbent's research and theory are central to our understanding of the effects of noise on behavior. *(Courtesy of Donald Broadbent.)*

page, so performance on this almost automatic task may not be affected. On the other hand, the detection of grammatical errors requires more thought, and performance is more likely to suffer.

Second, *who* the employee is matters. Some individuals appear to be able to screen out unwanted stimuli better than others (Mehrabian, 1977). Possibly, these "screeners" can tune out noise because they have developed coping strategies that the "nonscreener" doesn't have. Also, employees who have control over sound probably are less affected by it than are employees who do not have control over the type of sound or whether it is on or off. Employees who can turn on the radio when they believe it will not affect their present task and turn it off when it bothers them will probably accomplish more than employees who don't have any choice in the matter.

Third, characteristics of the sound itself are important. Sound may be loud or soft, high or low, continuous or intermittent, familiar or novel, meaningful or not, musical or mechanical, or natural or human. One of the clearest research find-

ings is that *novel* sounds reduce performance (Broadbent, 1979). Of course, novelty wears off; the same sound may not affect performance shortly after its introduction.

Broadbent (1979) suggests that intermittent noise often causes temporary setbacks in performance during the noise, but that some employees can compensate with increased efficiency during quiet periods, so that overall performance is similar to that under uniformly quiet conditions. When noise is unpredictable, coping strategies are more difficult to implement and performance may suffer more than when the noise is intermittent but at predictable intervals. Some of the complexity is resolved by assuming, as Broadbent does, that noise is a general arouser. Arousal benefits the performance of some individuals in some circumstances, but impairs performance on other occasions. A safe general conclusion is that performance is *variable* in noisy conditions.

What about the effects of music on performance? A widespread impression is that music can speed up production or slow it down. This is an idea that suppliers of planned indoor music systems would like us to believe. As usual, the effects of music are not that simple. They depend on the kind of music, the type of work, and the characteristics of the individual employee.

A fair number of studies support the idea that music improves productivity (Fox, 1983), but there are three problems with this research. First, most research on music was performed decades ago. It often supported the basic notion that music improves productivity, but research methods often left much to be desired. For example, control groups were not often used. Second, music on the job was a novelty and, in historical context, a rare privilege. Positive effects might have been due to these factors, rather than to the music itself. Third, most researchers examined the effect of music on simple, repetitive tasks, leaving open the question of its effects on cognitively demanding work. In general, early research of questionable quality did show that productivity could be enhanced by music, at least for simple tasks, although novelty and gratitude for the granting of a privilege may have played a crucial role.

Fox (1983), who has reviewed this research, nevertheless concludes that light music will help even in modern workplaces with their greater cognitive demands. But as he points out, a great variety of results have been found, including studies showing that music harms performance. When you consider the vast variety of tasks we undertake at work, combined with the vast variety of musical styles, tempos, and volumes, the only reasonable summation is that no general conclusion is possible. Presumably, music *may* increase (or decrease) productivity, but the conditions that lead to one outcome or the other still have not been clearly identified.

Employee *feelings* about noise and music are clearer than are performance effects, as we see next.

Feelings. Noise is, by definition, unwanted sound. If you ask industrial or office workers their opinion about noise, they quite naturally tell you they don't like it and wish it would go away. Noise adversely affects their own productivity. In a typical survey (Harris and Associates, 1978), over 1000 office workers rated the "opportunity to concentrate without noise and other distractions" as the single most desirable office characteristic (out of seventeen choices). In rating their own workspace, all but two of the seventeen office characteristics were rated *more* satisfactory than "the opportunity to concentrate without noise."

In another survey of employees at fifty-eight sites, job satisfaction declined as noise from people talking and telephones ringing increased (Sundstrom et al., 1985). In short, office employees believe that noise is a serious problem.

However, there is a clear gap between the results of the productivity studies and the attitude studies. Research to date (Sundstrom et al., 1985) indicates that actual performance is often unchanged by noise although it is sometimes changed (Sundstrom, Burt, & Kamp, 1980). Some employees clearly feel noise detracts from their work. Who is right?

One answer may be that researchers have not yet examined sufficiently sensitive measures of productivity. That is, perhaps productivity really does decline in noisy conditions, but so far measures of productivity that are sensitive and appropriate enough to demonstrate this decline have been overlooked. Also, many studies have only examined very short exposures to noise; at work

some employees are subjected to years of it. The effects of noise on productivity may be gradual and cumulative.

On the other hand, perhaps employees do not really know themselves. Employees do not usually keep objective counts of their own productivity, so it is possible that their opinions about noise and productivity are formed in good faith but are simply inaccurate. N. D. Weinstein (1977) showed that his subjects *believed* noise hurt their performance even when it did not.

A third possibility is that, in a sense, *both* are correct. Because employees whose work slows in noisy periods are often able to work faster and better during quiet periods, their overall performance could appear unaffected. However, to struggle during noisy periods and to compensate during quiet periods in order to achieve the same overall level of performance requires greater effort and more effective coping strategies than does performance during uniformly quiet work sessions. Employees' dissatisfaction with noise and their belief that performance is affected may stem from their knowledge that they worked harder to produce what turns out to be the same amount of work. Because more work was required to produce the same amount of work, it is easy to feel both dissatisfied and to believe that less work was produced.

Perhaps what employees who labor in noisy settings really mean to say is that they could have produced *more* work for the amount of effort they expended. Therefore, in a sense, they produced less than they are *capable* of producing. If what they mean to say is that noise makes their work harder, we should congratulate them for producing as much as they do under difficult conditions.

The noisiest work settings are in industry, but industrial work tends to include those types of tasks, described earlier, that are least affected by noise. In fact, in industrial settings, hearing damage is a bigger problem than reduced productivity. In offices, where there are more tasks that are easily affected by noise, the worst settings appear to be open-plan offices (Harris et al., 1978). Noise in open plan offices is largely a function of their spatial arrangements, so more will be said on this topic later, in the section on space.

Employee attitudes toward music are clearer. Most like it and *believe* that it improves their productivity. However, from 5 to 10 percent of employees definitely do not like music at work. Sometimes this is a function of the type of music played and sometimes employees find that it interferes with their work.

Music should be introduced to the workplace very carefully. As we discovered earlier, it may raise or lower productivity. But because 90 percent or more of employees prefer music, removing it once it is installed is likely to cause bad feelings.

Stress.   Physiological changes due to sound in workplaces are limited, for the most part, to hearing loss. However, some studies suggest that sound may have other health effects. The strongest possibility is that exposure to some kinds of sound increases chances of cardiovascular disease.

Welch (1979) reviewed forty studies and concluded that employees who are exposed to unpredictable noise for at least 3 years and whose work involves mental concentration have at least a 60 percent higher chance of cardiovascular disease than other employees. Unfortunately, in many of the studies reviewed by Welch, the investigators were unable to separate noise effects from other aversive factors that were present at the same time. Nevertheless, Welch's conclusion is consistent with the idea that employees who must expend extra effort coping with loud noise suffer long-term consequences.

Noisy factories seem to have another side effect, less critical but certainly undesirable: more laryngitis and sore throats! All that yelling required to make yourself heard on a noisy factory floor seems to increase the frequency of these throat problems (Cohen, 1969).

Social Behavior.   The key social effect of noise is to impair employee privacy. The ideal workplace should be quiet enough to permit concentration and communication without too much difficulty, yet open-plan offices should be suffused with enough sound to allow for conversational privacy (Lewis & O'Sullivan, 1974). Existing open-plan offices are very often deficient in acoustical privacy, with up to 90 percent of employees unhappy about the lack of opportunity to converse confidentially (Goodrich, 1982; Hedge, 1982). Even in a group of office employees that is generally satisfied with the physical aspects of the office, mechanical noise (such as telephone, heating and ventilation equipment) and human noise (overheard conversations) are associated with increased tension, depression, anger, and fatigue (McDowell & Carlson, 1984). Office privacy is importantly influenced by spatial arrangements. Generally, walls and partitions provide a greater sense of privacy (Sundstrom, Burt, & Kamp, 1980; Sundstrom, Herbert, & Brown, 1982; Sundstrom, Town, Brown, Forman, & McGee, 1982). Open-plan offices, which are increasing in popularity, are often deficient in sound insulation.

In addition to depriving employees of privacy, noise may make them less helpful. Mathews and Canon (1975) reported that subjects exposed to 85 decibels were less likely to help another person who had just dropped something than were subjects exposed to 65 decibels or less. The implications for jobs in which the primary function of employees is to help clients, customers, or co-workers are obvious.

Noise may even influence employees' judgments about their co-workers. In one study (Sauser, Arauz, & Chambers, 1978), students playing the role of managers were given the résumés of five newly hired applicants. They were told that starting salaries generally ranged from $7,500 to $15,000. The student-managers were asked to consider the qualifications of the five new employees and then to recommend a starting salary for each one. Student-managers made their recommendations after reading the new employees' résumés either in a room where the sound level was about 53 decibels (normal office sound level) or a room where the sound level was about 75 decibels (loud but realistic office sound level).

Student-managers from the noisier room recommended starting salaries that were, on average, almost $1000 less than those made by student-managers in the quieter room! This result, which the authors replicated in a follow-up study, has enormous implications not only for pay recommendations but for other kinds of recommendations made at work, and for interpersonal attitudes among co-workers.

▶ In Sum. Noise has many effects on work behavior. In industrial settings, it can cause serious hearing loss. Loud noise is particularly dangerous when employees do not realize that deafness comes slowly and almost imperceptibly. (See Fig.

11–7.) Despite our suspicion that noise affects performance, research in natural settings shows (a) how complex the issue is and (b) that performance decrements depend on the task, the person, and the type of noise. Noise harms performance when certain combinations of employee, task, and type of noise co-occur, but not under other circumstances. For certain tasks, noise may even arouse a person enough to improve performance. Music may improve performance, but research on the topic is suspect. Once again, no universal effect is to be *expected*. Performance effects, if any, will be a function of person, task, and music.

Employees naturally dislike noise but, for the most part, like music on the job. They generally think noise hinders and music helps their performance. Noise is a serious problem in modern open-plan offices. Employees find sound a problem both coming and going: sound entering their workplace is annoying and when their own words escape over partitions too easily, their privacy is compromised. Office noise may even affect important interpersonal behavior, from mere impressions of others to important judgments regarding them. There is some suggestion that long-term exposure to loud sounds has physiological effects beyond hearing loss.

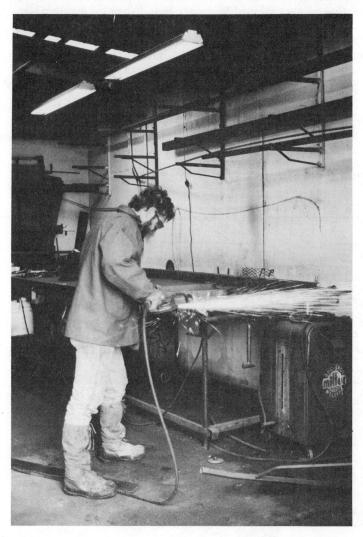

FIGURE 11–7 Grinding is one very noisy job. *(Courtesy of Coe Gifford.)*

Temperature

Heat and cold can affect most work behavior but, like those of sound, the effects are complex. Temperature itself is multifaceted. The temperature of the air alone does not help us understand work behavior very well. A hot dry atmosphere is quite different from a hot humid one, and the amount of air movement further affects the character of the atmosphere. An index called **effective temperature,** composed of air temperature, humidity, and air movement measures, has replaced that of simple temperature. (See Fig. 11–8.)

The effects of temperature also depend on the type of work being done. My sister, who lives in a wilderness setting, tells me that firewood warms her twice—once when she cuts and splits it and again when she burns it. As I sit writing this book, and as you sit reading it, very little heat is generated; a higher effective temperature is ob-

viously necessary for our comfort than for my sister when she is splitting wood.

The effect of temperature on our work also depends on how much clothing we wear. Researchers have even invented a scale (the unit is called the **CLO**) to measure exactly how much each piece of clothing helps to keep us warm (Rohles, Konz, & Munson, 1980). (See Fig. 11–9.)

Another complexity in temperature research is that our **core body temperature** is often more important than effective temperature. Core body temperature takes some time to change, so short-term exposure to a wide variety of effective temperatures may not affect work behavior.

Most of us, most of the time, are not seriously affected by cold or heat. When the ambient temperature is low or high, we often can adjust it or at least adjust our clothing. We may not be perfectly comfortable, but neither are we often as distressed as we are, for example, by uncontroll-

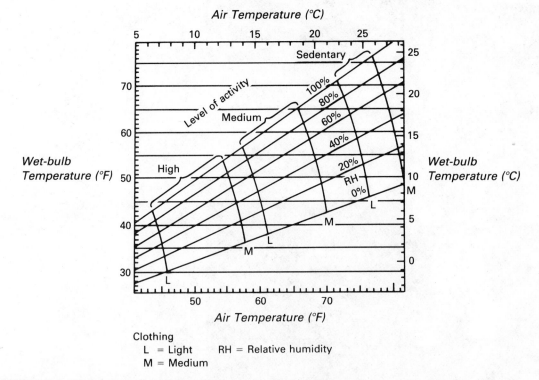

Clothing
L = Light RH = Relative humidity
M = Medium

FIGURE 11–8 ''Comfort envelopes'' that simultaneously take into account temperature, relative humidity, air speed, activity level, and amount of clothing have been developed. *(Courtesy of ASHRAE, the American Society of Heating, Refrigerating and Air-Conditioning Engineers.)*

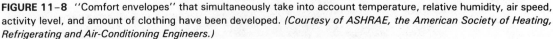

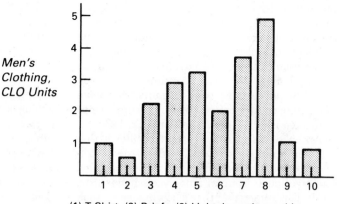

Men's
Clothing,
CLO Units

(1) T Shirt. (2) Briefs. (3) Light, long-sleeve shirt.
(4) Heavy, long-sleeve shirt. (5) Heavy trousers.
(6) Light sweater. (7) Heavy sweater. (8) Heavy jacket.
(9) Ankle-length socks. (10) Oxfords, shoes.

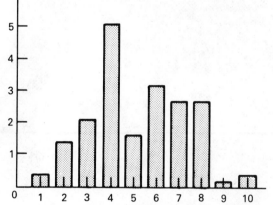

Women's
Clothing,
CLO Units

FIGURE 11–9 CLO is a measure of the insulating capacity of clothing articles. *From Kantowitz, B. H., & Sorkin, R. D. Human factors: Understanding people system relationships. New York: Wiley, 1983. Copyright © John Wiley & Sons. Reprinted with permission from John Wiley & Sons. Data from Rohles, Konz, & Munson, 1980.)*

(1) Bra and Panties. (2) Full Slip. (3) Heavy Blouse.
(4) Heavy dress. (5) Heavy skirt. (6) Heavy slacks.
(7) Heavy sweater. (8) Heavy jacket. (9) Panty hose.
(10) Pumps, shoes.

able noise at work. Nevertheless, there are some consequences of heat and cold in most of the work behavior categories.

Performance. Every possible outcome has been reported for heat and cold: performance declines when it is hot and when it is cold; performance increases when it is hot and when it is cold; performance is unchanged when it is hot and when it is cold. Bell and Greene (1982) even cite a study that reports increases *and* decreases in perfor-

mance at the same time! Participants whose body temperature was high were asked to detect certain signals. Compared to those whose body temperature was lower, they detected more signals correctly (better performance) but they also made more false detections (worse performance).

Although researchers have found both positive and negative outcomes of temperature exposure, some findings are more common. For example, as temperatures rise into the very hot range, productivity definitely drops (McCormick, 1976), especially for heavy manual labor. McCormick also suggests that cognitive tasks, such as office work, are adversely affected by heat depending on how long a person must work. Cognitive performance is essentially unaffected up to 38°C (100°F) if the employee must work only 30 minutes. However, if the employee must work 3 hours, the maximum temperature before cognitive performance is affected is 30°C (87°F) (McCormick, 1976).

Another relatively consistent result is that cold temperatures negatively affect the performance of work that requires fine movements and sensitive touch from an employee's hands (Fox, 1967). It is interesting that performance of such tasks does not gradually slip as the temperature drops, but holds up well until hand-skin temperature reaches a certain point (about 14°C or 57°F), then drops off quickly. (See Fig. 11–10.)

The great variety of findings that do not conform to these basic trends are probably due to the number of factors that determine performance besides temperature itself: whether the employee is acclimatized or not, believes the temperature is controllable to some extent, has few or many coping strategies, is motivated or not. One simple coping strategy is adjusting the amount of clothing we wear. One study examined performance of office work at cool (18°C or 65°F) versus warm (26°C or 78°F) temperatures with the same degree of humidity (Vickroy, Shaw, & Fisher, 1982). Lightly dressed men performed both simple and complex tasks best in the warm conditions and worst in the cool conditions. Heavily dressed men performed best in cool and worst in warm conditions. This, of course, is a very simple coping strategy. You may be able to think of other, more

FIGURE 11–10 This freezer worker spends hours on end at −30°F. *(Courtesy of Coe Gifford.)*

complex ways of overcoming inappropriate temperatures. The point is that coping strategies, where they exist and are used, make the old question, how does temperature affect performance, obsolete. A better answer is that performance is affected by the way individuals cope with temperature, or fail to cope with it.

When the factors already mentioned (body temperature, clothing, duration of work, humidity, air movement) are also taken into account, the modern study of temperature effects becomes very technical. The experimenter must specify a whole range of conditions that were present at the time of testing in order to draw conclusions about the effects of temperature on work productivity.

Feelings. Feelings about temperature are usually considered in terms of stated comfort. Much engineering research has been devoted to finding the ideal effective temperature. Obviously, no single temperature is best, but the modern approach has been to identify **comfort envelopes.** Comfort envelopes specify a range of effective temperatures under which most individuals report feeling comfortable, depending on how much clothing they are wearing and what activity they are engaged in. According to engineers who have done very detailed studies, an office employee working at a desk while wearing light clothing in a room with 45 percent humidity will be comfortable when the temperature is between 24 and 27°C (75 to 80°F).

Feelings about temperature are affected not only by the actual temperature, but by what the individual *thinks* the temperature is, and by room decor. Rohles (in Rice, 1980) showed that individuals report feeling warmer, at equal temperatures, when the heaters in a room are pointed out to them, the decor is more luxurious, and thermometers are fixed to report higher than actual temperatures.

In another study, college students were asked how comfortable they were when an actual increase of 3°C (5°F) occurred and when they were led to believe that such an increase had occurred (Stramler, Kliess, & Howell, 1983). The students reported similar changes in comfort for the real and the fake temperature increases. The fake heating strategy may be unethical as a general conservation tactic, but it once again illustrates the Hawthorne principle: our *perception* of a situation is often more important than the objective characteristics of the situation.

We might think environments that are ideal in terms of comfort would be ideal in terms of performance; a comfortable employee is a productive employee. Unfortunately, research by Nelson, Nilsson, and Johnson (1984) suggests this commonsense hypothesis is not true. These researchers found that performance of work similar to that usually done in offices was significantly greater in temperatures about 10°C (18°F) below the comfort envelope standard. Subjects reported being cooler than they might prefer, but they performed better at the lower temperatures. Despite feeling too cool, subjects in the cool conditions also reported feeling more energetic at the end of an hour's work than at the beginning of the session! (In warm conditions, reported energy dropped during the hour.)

Stress. Temperature stress depends on effective temperature, duration of exposure, and degree of protection, such as clothing. Lasting physiological changes from high or low temperatures take a long time to develop, unless the temperatures are extreme (for example, if you touch a flame or fall through the ice into a freezing lake).

Apart from these extremes, the human body is wonderfully able to adapt to a wide range of environmental conditions. The Inuit (who prefer that name to the one you may know, Eskimo) have adapted quite well to very cold conditions. Adults work and children play outdoors in temperatures that would make those of us who live farther south scurry for warmth. On the hot side of the temperature spectrum, while visiting India I saw hod carriers who literally ran, all day, in the summer, with very heavy loads of bricks on their backs.

Clearly, individuals can adapt to severe conditions, but physiological changes, or "temperature stress," occur as they acclimatize and may occur even after they are acclimatized. For example, fishermen who work the cold Atlantic waters off eastern Canada actually undergo semipermanent physiological changes in their hands that allow them to avoid discomfort and frostbite longer than nonacclimatized individuals (LeBlanc, 1975).

There are individual differences in acclimatization—some individuals seem to adapt better than others—but they are less important in determining temperature stress than is length of exposure (Bell & Greene, 1982). That is, most individuals who have the time to adapt to a large temperature change can do so, but some of us never acclimatize.

Social Behavior.   Quite a number of laboratory studies have examined the effects of temperature on social behavior. Some of them have reached intriguing conclusions, but whether these conclusions will generalize to typical work settings is not clear. In addition, we should recall that many work settings have well-controlled temperatures; heat or cold sufficiently deviant from the comfort envelope to affect social behavior is uncommon for many employees.

We might assume that moderately hot temperatures always influence employees to be more aggressive toward their co-workers, but a series of studies by Robert A. Baron and Paul Bell suggests that the relation between heat and aggression can vary depending on such factors as the length of exposure, whether a person has access to fluids, and even whether those fluids are alcohol-based drinks or not (Bell & Greene, 1982). Until these influences are sorted out, we must be cautious in our conclusions about how heat affects aggression.

Let's turn briefly to the positive side of social behavior. Several studies have shown that moderate variations in temperature do not increase or decrease helping behavior (Schneider, Lesko, & Garrett, 1980). If temperature does affect helping behavior less than noise does, employers in client-serving organizations should pay more attention to noise problems than to temperature problems. This is a tentative conclusion, however, because a direct comparison of noise and temperature on helping has not yet been attempted.

▶ In Sum. When considering temperature's effects, we must begin with a proper measure, effective temperature, which includes humidity and air movement as well as temperature. Relatively extreme effective temperatures do not affect many work behaviors unless core body temperature is altered. The effects of temperature are also usually muffled by our access to heavier or lighter clothing. The amazing variety of temperature effects reported are due to these measurement and clothing factors, as well as many

others including degree of acclimatization, knowledge of coping strategies, motivation, and type of work.

Engineers have found well-described comfort envelopes, but psychologists have discovered that comfort depends on perception as well as actual effective temperature and that optimal performance may be found outside the comfort envelope. Stress occurs when individuals are initially subjected to effective temperatures farther outside the comfort envelope, but many of us can adapt to these more extreme temperatures after longer-term exposure to them.

Air

The ingredients of air can play an important role in work behavior. Recently, considerable concern has been expressed over the effects of air pollutants in offices. Many newer buildings are tightly sealed; machines designed to filter and recirculate air have replaced the openable window. Sometimes the machines malfunction or suck in tainted air and then distribute it. In one famous case, air from a government health building's lab was circulated to offices. The air contained viruses that had been sent to the lab for testing. It's ironic that many employees got sick in a building devoted to the promotion of health!

Performance.   Few studies have attempted to assess the effects of air on actual performance at work. We do know that commuters trying to *reach* work occasionally have problems. Carbon monoxide levels on roads are sometimes high enough to affect driving ability (Moos, 1976).

Employees engaged in normal amounts of manual labor are essentially unaffected by moderate doses of carbon monoxide (National Academy of Sciences, 1977). However, most studies so far have only studied short-term performance (a few hours) and have used healthy young males. Carbon monoxide and other pollutants may yet be found to affect performance in more sensitive groups or over longer time periods (Evans & Jacobs, 1982).

Some kinds of work appear to be affected by carbon monoxide and other air pollutants that restrict the oxygen-carrying capacity of the blood. For example, when a job calls for prolonged alertness but generally involves low stimulation, per-

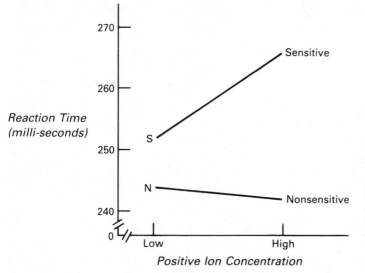

Reaction Time
(milli-seconds)

Positive Ion Concentration

FIGURE 11–11 The performance of a single behavior (reaction time) that is important in many tasks such as driving and operating equipment is harmed by high concentrations of positive air ions for those who are ion-sensitive (i.e., have low autonomic lability) but not for those who are not ion-sensitive. (*Adapted from Charry & Hawkenshire, 1981.*)

formance may be affected by moderate levels of carbon monoxide (Evans & Jacobs, 1982). Such concentrations may be found in buildings that are on or near major roadways. The research completed so far suggests, however, that individuals vary in susceptibility to carbon monoxide; current research does not examine *whether* air pollution affects individuals, but *whom* it affects.

Some pollutants (carbon monoxide) are poisonous but odor-free. Bad-smelling air seems to have its own effects. James Rotton (1983) reports that malodorous air impaired performance of a relatively complex task (proofreading) but not in a relatively simple one (arithmetic).

Another aspect of air that has been suspected of affecting performance is the level of air ionization. Clean rural air contains about 1,200 positive and 1,000 negative ions per cubic centimeter of air; modern urban air-conditioned offices contain about 150 positive and 50 negative ions (Hawkins, 1981). On the assumption that modern industrial cities and workplaces are deficient in negative ions, some individuals have become convinced of the value of negative ion generators. (I know two environmental psychologists who have the machines in their offices.) The popular press and manufacturers of ion generators have made so many exaggerated claims about the alleged benefits of negative air ions that many environmental psychologists scoff at any mention of air ions (except, of course, my two acquain-

tances). The U.S. Food and Drug Administration even prohibited the sale of ion generators in the mid-1950s. Very few well-controlled studies (with single- or double-blind controls and random assignment of subjects) have investigated whether ionization affects performance.

However, some well-controlled studies do indicate that ion concentrations affect performance. Hawkins and Barker (1978), for example, tested individuals (who did not know the study was about ions) on several simple tasks. When negative ion concentrations were very high (over 4,000 per cubic centimeter), the participants had significantly faster reaction times and better motor coordination. Another study found significant improvements in basic perceptual-motor tasks, compared to performance under normal levels, when very high levels of negative ions were present (Tom, Poole, Galla, & Berrier, 1981). However, other studies have reported no beneficial effects of high levels of negative ions on performance (Farmer & Bendix, 1982).

The mixed results may be because individuals differ in their sensitivity to ion concentration. This hypothesis was tested by Charry and Hawkenshire (1981), although they studied positive ion concentrations, which are supposed to be harmful, rather than negative ions. They found that the performance of individuals in general was not adversely affected by high positive ion concentrations. However, the performance of subjects who were "ion sensitive" (that is, predicted to be more susceptible to the harmful effects of positive ions, based on physiological tests), was worse than that of subjects who were less "ion sensitive." The case of air ionization is a good illustration of an environment-behavior link that is strongly mediated by individual difference factors. Conflicting results concerning the effects of air ions may be due to differing physiological sensitivities of individuals. (See Fig. 11–11.)

Further evidence that air ion influence is mediated by personal characteristics comes from a study of ions and aggression (Baron, Russell, & Arms, 1985). Participants were asked to train others to reduce their heart rate using biofeedback. Participants were able to deliver bursts of heat when the trainees failed to reduce their heart rates. The trainees, who were actually confederates of the experimenters, appeared to be poor learners. Type A participants (irritable, consistent sense of urgency, strong reactions to stress) exhibited more aggression (delivered more heat to trainees) when high levels of negative ions were present than when low levels of negative ions were present. These results are puzzling. Negative ions are generally thought to produce beneficial outcomes. Baron et al. speculate that negative ions act as arousers, magnifying our natural tendencies. For Type A individuals, this may mean an increase in aggressiveness. Perhaps the important point here is that ions once again had no effect on a random group of individuals but did affect a certain subsample of them.

Another mediating variable is perceived *control*. In a study of malodorous air, James Rotton and his colleagues (Evans & Jacobs, 1982) found that when the air smelled bad *and* participants in the study felt they could not avoid the smell, their persistence at working on puzzles declined significantly.

Feelings.   The quality of air at work is a growing concern of employees. As speculation and knowledge about potentially harmful fumes from machines and building materials increases, workers have become more aware of the possible harmful effects of air in their own workspaces. We will focus on two aspects of feelings about air: complaints about perceived inadequacy of air, and changes in emotion that apparently occur without employee awareness that the air has changed.

Among office workers, air quality is one of the most important factors in the environment (Harris et al., 1978). Nevertheless, many more office workers feel like complaining about air quality than actually do so (Rankin, 1969). Complaints about air quality depend in part how the question is asked. If employees are asked, "What are some of the problems in your workplace?" fewer complaints about air will be registered than if employees are asked, "Is the air in your workplace good quality?"

A story told by Schultz (1982) about air in a factory illustrates how important employee perception of atmospheric conditions can be. Many complaints about the stuffiness and lack of movement of the air in the factory were received. The ventilation system was thoroughly checked and found working perfectly. Many of the factory's employees had worked outdoors most of their lives, and they felt that buildings must be stuffy and breezeless. Then someone devised the idea of attaching streamers to the ventilation outlets near the ceiling. When the employees could see the streamers flying, complaints about air movement stopped.

At least one component of air appears to change our feelings even when we are unaware of it. That component is the controversial negative ion. Two double-blind studies in Britain report improvements in feelings when more negative ions are present. One, in the offices of a large insurance company, found that employees working in greater concentrations of negative ions felt warmer and more alert; they also judged the environment as fresher (Hawkins, 1981). In the other, students reported feeling more relaxed and stimulated and less irritable and depressed after 6 hours of negative ion exposure (Buckalew & Rizzuto, 1982).

Finally, it appears that changing the air by infusing it with perfume or cologne is risky. You may alienate some individuals while impressing others. Robert A. Baron (1983) conducted mock job interviews in which applicants wore scents or did not. Female interviewers gave more positive evaluations to applicants who wore perfume or cologne than those who did not, but male interviewers gave more positive evaluations to applicants who wore no scent than they gave to those who did wear some. Of course, the use of artificial scents is a complicated issue (evaluations probably also depend on how much scent is worn, what sort of clothes are worn with the scent, customary behavior in each workplace, etc.), but it seems that altering local airspace may be perceived as air pollution or air enhancement depending on the gender of the person making the evaluation.

Health.   Air quality can have drastic effects on our health, as the relatives of many Legionnaires who attended the fateful convention in 1976 that killed 29 people, made 182 others ill, and gave birth to a new phrase (Legionnaire's disease) will testify. Modern ventilation systems are capable of moving air very efficiently, but if an airborne disease agent gets into the system, the same efficiency becomes a severe liability.

Besides disease-causing microorganisms, air can carry other agents that make people ill, including ozone (emitted by copy machines), tiny airborne particles from asbestos (found in most office buildings dating from the late 1960s), cigarette smoke, and organic solvents such as benzene (found in stencil fluids, copy machine toner, and rubber cement). Most of these agents have been linked to serious diseases, such as cancer, and to a wide variety of troublesome minor problems including eye irritation, respiratory tract problems, allergies, thyroid disturbance, gastrointestinal cramps, and others (Evans & Jacobs, 1982).

Whether any particular employee is affected by air quality depends on the concentration of the hazardous agent, the coping strategies of the employee, and the employee's basic physiological sensitivity. Relatively low levels of oxygen in a tightly sealed building, for example, may affect only those workers who don't get outside for a break or those who require larger amounts of oxygen (such as employees engaged in heavy labor). But when oxygen levels sink very low, nearly everyone will be affected. A few years ago, the trading floor of the Toronto Stock Exchange had to be cleared when many employees and traders began to faint, speak incoherently, and complain of numbness in their chests. Apparently, all the doors and windows were closed and the busy traders simply used up all the available oxygen! Some evidence suggests that air conditioning alone (without any airborne pathogens) may cause

increases in the frequency of eye, nose, and throat irritation (Turiel, Hollowell, Miksch, Rudy, & Young, 1983).

Social Behavior.   Air in a workplace can even affect social relations. Most relevant studies have focused on cigarette smoke and bad odors. Paul Bleda and Paul Sandman (1977) asked enlisted army personnel to sit in pairs and work on a manual task. After the session, during which their smoking had been observed, participants were asked to indicate how much they liked each other (they were strangers before meeting for the session, so previous experience was not a factor). Nonsmokers liked co-workers who didn't smoke more than they liked co-workers who did smoke. Those who normally smoked but did not in the session preferred others who smoked courteously (that is, made attempts to blow the smoke away from the other person). Those who normally smoked and did so in the session preferred partners who smoked *discourteously* (that is, blew smoke in their faces)! It appears we like others who share our smoking preferences. Another study produced a compatible result. When nonsmokers were faced with smoke, they reported feeling aggressive (Jones & Bogat, 1978).

The findings relevant to bad odors are less straightforward; research by James Rotton indicates that attraction toward others under smelly conditions depends on whether we have attitudes similar to those of the other. If we think alike, the bad smells seem to *increase* attraction (Rotton, Barry, Frey, & Soler, 1978). It may be that sharing an odorous disaster with someone similar to ourselves causes us to draw together, possibly against some other person in the vicinity who isn't like us (and might even be the source of those bad smells!).

Moderately bad odors may even cause aggressiveness toward unfamiliar others. In a laboratory study, participants in another Rotton study decided to shock another person more when the room smelled bad (Rotton, Frey, Barry, Milligan, & Fitzpatrick, 1979). Once again, these effects are probably mediated by personal characteristics of the individuals involved. For example, when subjects in one study were highly motivated to work, their annoyance with cigarette smoke was relatively small. When they were not very motivated to work, however, they were much more annoyed by cigarette smoke (Stone, Breidenbach, & Heimstra, 1979).

► **In Sum.** Several components of air including carbon monoxide, air ions, and bad odors may affect performance, but the effects are not striking under normal conditions. Extremely low concentrations of negative ions may affect some basic cognitive processes and extremely high concentrations may slightly facilitate them, but these effects are not strong for the average person. However, long-term exposure, differential physiological sensitivity, and psychological mediators such as perceived control help to explain why the performance of some individuals is affected but that of others is not.

When it carries chemical impurities or disease-causing organisms, air can seriously impair health. Air quality is a growing concern of employees. Lack of control over it when air is noticeably bad may affect persistence at work and, in some circumstances, foster negative feelings among employees.

Light

Light is essential to work, of course. Without it, few industrial or office jobs can be performed at all. However, natural or artificial light is nearly always available; problems with light primarily involve which *source* (sunlight, incandescent, fluorescent, sodium vapor) is used, the *amount* of light used, and the *angle* at which it strikes the work surface.

Lighting has primarily been studied from an engineering standpoint, using specialized equipment and terminology. Often, in the search for optimal lighting from a purely technical point of view, the human dimension has been lost. (See Table 11–1.) For example, one of the main reasons for the widespread installation of fluorescent tubes is their energy efficiency. An incandescent bulb transforms about 10 percent of the electricity it uses into light; about 90 percent is transformed into heat. The ratio for a typical fluorescent bulb is about 20 percent light to 80 percent heat. So fluorescent bulbs are about twice as efficient at producing light, but the overlooked factor is that many of us simply do not like fluorescent lighting.

In addition to this lack of attention to employee preferences, even the cost advantage of fluorescent lighting may be less than it is usually considered to be. The use of fluorescent bulbs is defended on the basis of their superior ability to produce light, but there is a forgotten side to the equation. What the incandescent bulb does not produce in light it produces in heat, another valuable commodity in buildings that require more heating than cooling.

Because fluorescent lighting is now the dominant form of artificial lighting employed in new buildings, most current research compares different brands and types of it with mercury, sodium, and other newer types of lamp with each other, rather than comparing fluorescent to incandescent or natural sunlight. Therefore, not much research involving sunlight or incandescent lighting is available.

How does light affect performance, feelings, health, and safety? Let's look first at performance.

Performance. Within the normal range of lighting, from slightly dim to quite bright, performance of office tasks increases with more light (Barnaby, 1980). This statement requires several qualifiers, however. First, optimal light level depends on the task. Proofreading fine print requires much more light than does a round table discussion. Second, the work surface is important. If the surface is shiny, higher light levels—especially from undiffused sources such as a bare bulb—will cause glare, which definitely cuts into the performance of many tasks. A particularly important problem now is glare from video display screens. Third, the angle of the light is important. For some tasks, performance is enhanced when light is very diffused. Surgery and assembly-line work are examples. For other tasks, the definition of surfaces provided by shadows means that carefully angled lighting is best (searching for flaws in fabric or other manufactured objects that should have uniform surfaces).

For these reasons, one conclusion on which engineers and environmental psychologists would generally agree is that lighting should be tailored, if possible, to each task and individual. If implemented, this policy would probably result in much greater use of immediate or local lighting and decreased use of lighting intended to serve everyone working in a large area. In general, a positive effect of more localized lighting would

TABLE 11–1 Currently Recommended Illuminance Categories and Illuminance Values for Lighting Design (IES Lighting Handbook 1981 Application Volume)

I. Illuminance Categories and Illuminance Values for Generic Types of Activities in Interiors

Type of Activity	Illuminance Category	Ranges of Illuminances		Reference Work-Plane
		Lux	Footcandles	
Public spaces with dark surroundings	A	20–30–50	2–3–5	General lighting throughout spaces
Simple orientation for short temporary visits	B	50–75–100	5–7.5–10	
Working spaces where visual tasks are only occasionally performed	C	100–150–200	10–15–20	
Performance of visual tasks of high contrast or large size	D	200–300–500	20–30–50	Illuminance on task
Performance of visual tasks of medium contrast or small size	E	500–750–1000	50–75–100	
Performance of visual tasks of low contrast or very small size	F	1000–1500–2000	100–150–200	
Performance of visual tasks of low contrast and very small size over a prolonged period	G	2000–3000–5000	200–300–500	Illuminance on task, obtained by a combination of general and local (supplementary lighting)
Performance of very prolonged and exacting visual tasks	H	5000–7500–10000	500–750–1000	
Performance of very special visual tasks of extremely low contrast and small size	I	10000–15000–20000	1000–1500–2000	

II. Illuminance Categories for Selected Commercial, Institutional, Residential and Public Assembly Interiors

Area/Activity	Illuminance Category	Area/Activity	Illuminance Category
Auditoriums		**Barber shops and beauty parlors**	E
Assembly	C	**Club and lodge rooms**	
Social activity	B	Lounge and reading	D
Banks		**Conference rooms**	
Lobby		Conferring	D
General	C	Critical seeing (refer to individual task)	
Writing area	D	**Court rooms**	
Tellers' stations	E	Seating area	C
		Court activity area	E
		Dance halls and discotheques	B

Courtesy of IES, the Illuminating Engineering Society.

be energy savings realized from the reduced use of light in work areas that do not require their current, probably excessive, levels of light (Boyce, 1981).

Feelings. Some surveys indicate that most employees are generally satisfied with lighting (Wineman, 1982), but others report that complaints are frequent (Megaw & Bellamy, 1983).

The resolution of this contradiction probably rests with the type of work an employee does; those who perform visually demanding work often believe lighting is inadequate, but those whose work is not visually demanding believe their light is adequate.

Some of the newer kinds of artificial lamps produce dissatisfaction because they render colors strangely. Everyone has had the experience of buying clothing that appears apricot in the store but looks more like carrot at home. At work, poor lighting can do the same to skin color. Chao and Bennett (1981) asked subjects to judge the acceptability of a familiar face (their own) under several different light sources. Incandescent and warm white incandescent lamps were the most acceptable, followed by cool white fluorescent and "improved" mercury lamps. At the bottom were two kinds of high-pressure sodium lamps. The importance of semipermanent off-color appearance at work has not yet been demonstrated, but it would not seem to be conducive to interpersonal relations on the job.

John Flynn, a pioneer in light research, demonstrated with his colleagues that individuals find a variety of light sources and types more interesting than single-source lighting or repetitive use of one kind of fixture (Flynn, Hendrick, Spencer, & Martyniuk, 1979).

Employee feelings about another source of light are clear: natural light is very desirable (Wineman, 1982). Although sunlight has high potential for glare, employees would like to be located near a window; those who are located farther from a window are more often unhappy about lighting. Windows, of course, also offer views, which contribute to satisfaction (Farrenkopf & Roth, 1980). Windows offer the opportunity to stay in touch with conditions in the outside world—weather, time of day, action on the street.

Health and Safety. Light is important for health. Ultraviolet light, rare indoors, assists in the formation of vitamin D and in the body's processing of calcium. More broadly, the advent of artificial lighting has changed the biological rhythms of most industrialized peoples. Glare causes eyestrain. Glare is found in a surprising variety of places in the typical office, from shiny pages in a book (indirect glare) to sunlight streaming into our eyes from behind someone we are talking to (direct glare). Nevertheless, as noted earlier, most recent complaints about glare have come from video-display terminal (VDT) operators. This problem has arisen because offices and VDTs have not yet been well-designed for each other. For example, office lighting is normally from the ceiling; indirect glare caused by the reflection of the lights from the screen causes eyestrain for the VDT user. Offices and VDTs will gradually accommodate one another. Already the machines come with coated screens and swivel heads so the operator can orient the screen to minimize glare. Localized lighting, placed at the side or rear of the VDT, can eliminate glare.

Employee safety, particularly in industrial settings, is obviously threatened by inadequate lighting. Considerable research has been devoted to the reduction of glare from dangerous areas such as the surface of the saw bed in the vicinity of the saw blade. Proper illumination in transit areas of a building also prevents accidents.

▶ In Sum. Light affects work behavior primarily when it is insufficient (leading to low productivity, accidents, and eyestrain) or improperly placed (leading to glare and eyestrain). Lighting often is excessive; many individuals dislike the newer forms of lighting, some of which distort color. Carefully placed local lighting could resolve some of these problems. Access to natural light and views is psychologically important.

Space

How does space—the amount of it and how it is arranged—affect employees? This chapter emphasizes research in office and shop settings, reflecting the commonest contemporary work settings. However, the growth of computers and related telecommunications systems is now increasing the feasibility of working away from the traditional workplace.

This development has been called **computer-assisted work decentralization** or CAWD (Becker, 1984). In the popular media, articles depict a smiling employee sitting in a den at home, working at a computer terminal in front of a large picture window overlooking an idyllic scene. Some suggest that soon most of us will be working at home. However, a more thoughtful analysis shows that CAWD is not for everyone. It may promise an end to commuting and a reduction in the cost of working (like clothing costs); but it has more potential for employees whose work is based on information than for those in manufacturing, it can conflict with home life, it may create social isolation, and it can pose supervisory problems. Some employees whose job *could* largely be accomplished at home (such as stockbrokers) prefer the office as a place that is specifically set aside for work, keeps them in touch, and sustains their motivation (Becker, 1984). (See Fig. 11–12.) Nevertheless, some compromise CAWD settings have been tried; one is described in the design section of this chapter.

More traditional research on workspaces includes the study of human factors, or ergonomics, which has produced volumes of information on how machines ought to be designed to suit human needs in the immediate workstation: how best to lay out the controls in a fighter plane cockpit or how chairs for secretaries ought to be designed (McCormick, 1976).

FIGURE 11–12 Frank Becker has studied loosely-coupled offices and been involved in the planning and evaluation of facilities ranging from banks to hospitals. *(Courtesy of Frank Becker.)*

Yet the lack of research at the next level of analysis, that is, how best to arrange the office or industrial floor as a whole, is striking. Some individuals work in very cramped spaces, like submarines; others work in spaces that are too wide open for them—there is a basis for all those lonesome cowboy songs. In offices and industrial settings, space may be almost entirely open, such as in an airplane manufacturer's hangar or the old office bullpen, or it may be so private that employees must pass several guardian secretaries to gain the ear of the big boss. What *is* known about the effects of spatial arrangements?

Performance. Almost no studies have been reported that compare actual performance of a job in different workspace arrangements. However, if we can generalize from laboratory studies, offices with high employee densities (that is, little space for each person) jeopardize performance, especially if the work involves physical mobility and interaction (Heller, Groff, & Solomon, 1977). People may be literally tripping over each other as they try to do their jobs.

Other studies suggest that fairly high employee densities do not affect performance if the work does not involve much moving around the workspace. Once again, most experiments have only studied performance over short periods; long-term exposure to high densities, even when employees are not bumping into each other, may have negative effects on performance.

In many organizations, performance depends on good communication. Open-plan arrangements are said to facilitate communication, leading us to believe they increase productivity. Unfortunately, it seems that this does not follow, mainly because the increased communication is very often not work-oriented. Open-plan offices seem to result in more social communication but not in more productive communication (Wineman, 1982).

Attitudes about spatial arrangements may not correspond to behaviors in spatial arrangements. Frank Becker and his colleagues investigated the possibility that open-plan offices would drive employees away (Becker, Gield, Gaylin, & Sayer, 1983). Most employees cannot leave or work elsewhere, but college and university professors usually can choose to spend parts of their work days in their office, at the library, or at home. Becker and his colleagues counted the actual number of occupied and unoccupied faculty offices in colleges that had open-plan and private offices. Even though faculty in the open-plan arrangements expressed dissatisfaction with working there, they were present in their offices just as often as were faculty in private offices.

In another study, Ng and Gifford (1984) tried to determine whether interviews in offices are affected by privacy or sound level. Low privacy and high sound levels produced dissatisfaction with the interviews, although participants did not speak less with the interviewer under those conditions. These and other studies suggest that employees strive to achieve a certain amount of work in spite of negative environmental influences. They may often be successful in doing so, but the cost of coping with an inhospitable setting over the long term may be high.

Feelings.   When spatial arrangements are not good, employees are sometimes quite willing to say so. Too often, however, employees adapt to very bad situations or do not realize that the surroundings could be better. I have termed this unfortunate form of adaptation **environmental numbness** (Gifford, 1976c). In such cases, employees do not spontaneously report their feelings about the workplace.

On the other hand, many surveys have shown that if employees are asked their opinions and feelings about their workplace, they will respond quickly and fully. Where I teach, for example, we recently sent out a long survey on the office environment to campus employees. In only a few days, with no reminders, over 80 percent of the surveys were returned, an exceptionally high return rate for mass-distributed surveys.

The biggest issue in workplace arrangements at present is whether or not open-plan offices are beneficial. The majority of employee reactions to open-plan offices are negative (Ng & Gifford, 1984a). A few positive responses come from employees who have very recently moved from dingy, cramped former offices into bright new ones (a novelty effect), or from employees who enjoy the social aspects of work more than they enjoy the work itself. Those whose work requires confidentiality and supervisory-professional employees are especially unhappy with open-space designs (Posehn, 1984).

Despite overwhelming evidence of employee rejection, organizations are still moving into open-plan arrangements. In 1980, over 50 percent of office furniture sold in the United States was destined for open-plan offices, up from 1978 when the figure was only 40 percent (Rout, 1980). Why do open-plan arrangements continue to grow in popularity?

One reason is that employee resentment has taken a long time to be documented, collated, and fed back to organization heads. A second reason is that organization heads are still being sold very effectively on the alleged advantages of open-plan offices, including better tax breaks on furniture. For example, a marketing manager for open-plan systems will argue that carpeting costs can be cut by 20 to 30 percent because installers don't have to cut around walls and partitions (Tausz, 1979).

What are the long-term consequences of choosing tax breaks and a 20 to 30 percent saving on carpet costs over the considerable dissatisfaction of employees? One study, typical of many reporting employee unhappiness with open-plan offices, discovered that individuals are not merely dissatisfied with open-plan offices, they also begin to feel their jobs are less significant (Oldham & Brass, 1979).

A few organizations have begun to respond to these problems. One computer company, for example, has implemented a "neighborhood" concept: small groups of employees in an open area with walls between the neighborhoods. Whether the open-plan office can be adapted to fit human needs remains to be demonstrated; its research record to date is generally poor. One study does report that increasing employee density, a common by-product of moving to open-plan offices, promoted job satisfaction, although many other aspects of the environment were changed at the same time that density was changed (Szilagyi & Holland, 1980). Another showed that open plans are not the worst form of spatial arrangement. When clerical employees in a health organization moved from a totally open (bullpen) arrangement to an open-plan arrangement with low partitions, their performance improved (Wineman, 1985).

One study takes a different perspective on space, examining the effect of working with a large or small *number* of co-workers, rather than spatial density or arrangements (Oxley & Barrera, 1984). This perspective, based on behavior-setting and staffing theories (Barker, 1968; Wicker, 1979), hypothesizes that when too many or too few staff members operate behavior settings, performance and feelings are affected. You may recall from Chapter Ten how students were affected by attending large versus small schools. Oxley and Barrera studied twenty-two bank branches that varied in size, assuming that branches with many employees were relatively overstaffed and that branches with few employees were relatively understaffed.

Employees in small branches did report greater **setting claim,** or the sense that they are needed, perform important jobs, and work hard. In turn, greater setting claim was significantly related to greater job satisfaction, greater identification with the bank, and less tardiness. Thus, space in the sense of staffing level is an important component of feelings about work.

A few researchers have investigated another dimension of feelings in offices, the reactions of visitors. Have you ever entered someone's office and quickly developed an impression of the person who works there? Or have you wondered what your office may be communicating to visitors? Paula Morrow and James McElroy (1981) found that desk placement, display of status symbols, and tidiness were related to visitors' feelings and on their perceptions of the office occupant. (See Fig. 11–13.) Some findings were obvious. A tidy office makes others think you are organized; a display of status symbols (such as diplomas and awards) makes them believe you are higher in rank; and a messy desk makes them think you are busy and rushed. Other findings were not quite so obvious. An office with neat stacks of papers— as opposed to an office that is messy or extremely tidy—makes visitors feel comfortable and welcome. They also seem to think of you as a high achiever. Desk placement may be open (placed against a wall so that the office occupant has no barriers between self and visitor), or closed (placed between self and visitor). Open arrangements make visitors feel welcome and suggest to them that you are extroverted and have confidence in dealing with others. In another investigation (Becker, Gield, & Froggat, 1983), informal seating positions (catty corner or side by side) elicited more positive evaluations of the office occupant's concern for visitors than did a more formal seating position (directly opposite). When the office

occupant chose to sit at a small conference table in the office rather than at a desk, the host was seen as more friendly, caring, helpful, and open-minded, but less authoritative. Thus the mere arrangement of your office can have a variety of important influences on the impressions of visitors.

Social Behavior.   All studies agree that open-plan offices facilitate communication. The problem is that necessary and desirable communication appears to suffer but unwanted and interfering communication increases (Wineman, 1982).

Another dimension of social behavior, status, is related to office arrangements. Supervisory employees typically have different kinds of space than nonsupervisory employees. They have more space, more freedom to personalize, more expensive furniture, and more means (such as walls and doors) of regulating the access of others to their space (Konar, Sundstrom, Brady, Mandel, & Rice, 1982).

In implementing an open plan the organization saves money, but what the new arrangements often mean to the employees is the loss of a private office and the "gain" of a partitioned space in the midst of subordinates. The pursuit of status is often considered hollow and vain, but status symbols such as the private office may help to develop the impression among employees that a sense of order guides the organization's allocation of resources (such as space). The larger, more private, or better-furnished office may also serve as a way to recognize and reward achievement (Becker, 1981). Status seeking becomes an end in itself for some individuals, but when workspace arrangements are carefully managed, larger and better workspaces may be a reasonable way to concretely inform employees that the organization values their work.

Besides the physical qualities of a space—size of the office, desk, couch, or plant and whether the office is in a corner, has closable doors, or a private washroom—another dimension of workspace arrangement that may be important is the employee's ability to personalize the immediate work area. Some organizations forbid any posters, pictures, or other employee contributions to the decor, fearing that an expensive interior design scheme will be compromised. However, such edicts may backfire. When employees are heavily

FIGURE 11-13 Office appearance creates impressions. What sort of persons are the occupants of these offices? *(Courtesy of Robert Sommer.)*

restricted, they lose a feeling of personal control over their work, thereby increasing stress, decreasing satisfaction, and, perhaps, productivity (Karasek, 1979). Once again, space managers in organizations are faced with a choice. Are the aesthetic values of a uniform design scheme more important than the dissatisfaction of their employees?

At present, the vast majority of workplaces are designed *for* employees, rather than *with* them. Designers undoubtedly have good intentions, but without involving those who know themselves and their work best—the employees—their designs usually suffer, often in important ways. Employee performance, feelings, and social behavior are importantly affected by spatial arrangements. Employee participation in design is covered in detail in a later chapter, but the important point now is simply that much more needs to be done to involve employees in the shaping of the spaces in which they will spend many of the best years of their lives.

▶ **In Sum.** Naturally occurring spatial arrangements have few documented effects on performance, but employees are very sensitive to space and unhappy with many existing arrangements. Many open-plan arrangements reduce desirable communication and increase undesirable communication. Office arrangements lead visitors to form impressions of the office holder's character and status. Yet many organizations restrict the degree to which employees may arrange or personalize their offices and fail to consult with employees when offices are planned.

TRAVEL: GETTING AWAY TO A NEW ENVIRONMENT

For most employees, the time for a holiday eventually arrives. Over the last century, the amount of time the average person spends at work has been shrinking; we have more and more time for leisure. We may choose to leave our everyday surroundings for any of a vast array of destinations. Leisure-related behavior has been under increasing scrutiny by a variety of social scientists (Mercer, 1976). (See Fig. 11–14.)

FIGURE 11–14 The classic destination.

This section examines the environmental psychology of travel, which includes the study of tourist behavior, cognitive images of exotic destinations, choice of travel mode, and related phenomena (Pearce, 1982; Stringer, 1984). Touring has a life cycle of its own. Fridgen (1984) characterizes its five stages as (1) anticipation, (2) travel to the destination, (3) on-site behavior, (4) return travel, and (5) recollection. At each stage, environmental perception and cognition of the destination are interesting but barely explored research territory.

Travel fits into the scope of environmental psychology for two main reasons. First, by traveling, individuals radically alter their personal and community environments. Who travels and who does not? Why travel? What are the effects of destination environments on the traveler? What kinds of behavior are characteristic of travelers in their temporary environments? Second, travel has a significant impact on destination environments. In what ways are they harmed by tourism? Are they enhanced in any way?

Travel fits into this chapter because work finances most travel and because travel is frequently seen as the *yang* to work's *yin* (that is, the two form an integral whole with dialectical relations). One interesting connection is the development of **incentive travel,** the practice of rewarding productive employees with trips. Perhaps $2 billion a year is spent on it in North America and Western Europe; one Hawaiian hotel derives 40 percent of all its income from it. Many employees will work harder for a free trip than for cash or merchandise of equal value (McArthur, 1984).

Who Goes, and Why?

Individuals who have unfulfilling jobs may find this question ridiculous; obviously, you go away to escape from a workplace that offers little except a means of supporting the parts of your life that are more pleasant than work. Individuals lucky enough to love their work may ask the question seriously. Many individuals, however, even in those societies famous for their devotion to work, currently believe there is more to life than job satisfaction. A large survey of German employees found that about half preferred their leisure time to their work time, whereas 20 years ago only one-third of them preferred leisure to work ("Germans Now," 1984). A survey of the reasons given for vacations yielded the following responses (Rubenstein, 1980): rest and relaxation (63 percent), to escape routine (52 percent), to visit friends and relatives (45 percent), and to explore new places (35 percent).

Recreational travel is a trade-off (Iso-Ahola, 1983). Like some other processes studied by environmental psychologists, it may be viewed as an optimizing process. We try to balance two forces: the desire to leave the familiar parts of our lives behind and the desire to retain certain rewarding aspects of our lives, such as our safety and health. When we leave home, we gain novelty and, we hope, pleasant experiences in the sun, among ruins, in museums, on the water, or in the wilderness. But we leave behind friends, our sure knowledge of our surroundings, and our tried and tested pattern of living. We are taking a chance on airplanes, roads, unfamiliar places, unknown systems of medicine, law, economics, and daily customs. Some of us find the decision on this trade-off very easy to make; others experience difficulty in deciding what to do. But most of us eventually are willing and eager to fly away. As Iso-Ahola puts it, each person must solve the contradiction between the need for novelty and the need for familiarity in order to achieve optimally arousing experiences.

Go Where and Do What?

Most recreational travel destinations are

1. The homes of family or friends
2. Resorts, often in sunny places
3. Rural or wilderness locations
4. Cities worth touring
5. Planned leisure developments such as Disneyland
6. Religious shrines.

Some destinations offer more than one attribute—Athens is a sunny place that has great touristic value or an individual's family may live in a pleasant rural setting. Most research on behavior in leisure settings has focused on two of these, wilderness settings and cities worth touring. Until more research is done on the other popular destinations, we must confine our discussion primarily to these destinations.

Travelers engage in many forms of behavior, of course. One important activity is seeking and developing knowledge about new surroundings. An example of knowledge-development research is a study of tourists visiting Oxford, England (Pearce, 1977). First-time visitors were asked to draw cognitive maps of Oxford to determine how much they had learned about it. As expected, tourists who had been in the city longer drew maps that included more landmarks, streets and districts, and were more accurate. Tourists whose accommodations were on the periphery of the city also seemed to understand the city better, presumably because they traveled more widely during their stay.

Pearce (1980) has also studied another common behavior while traveling—asking for help. In 120 bus terminals from Portland, Oregon to New Orleans, Louisiana, Australian and American tourists asked fellow passengers and total strangers for information. Travelers more often received a helping response from fellow passengers than from total strangers, and the longer the subjects had been fellow passengers, the more likely they were to offer help. Female travelers were helped more than male travelers. The male Australian traveler received more help than the male American traveler. Pearce suggests that subjects perceived the Australian male as a foreign tourist, legitimizing his requests for help; the American male tourist was not seen as foreign and therefore subjects viewed his requests as less legitimate.

Other researchers examine the behavior of travelers in specific sites. Those who manage space in national parks and in commercial environments such as Disneyland are concerned about the flow of tourists through the setting. Commercial operators wish to design their settings to maximize flow and minimize traffic pathways and customer discomfort; in national parks the rationing of entry in the busy summer season encourages research into tourist activities like length of stay and rate of travel through the park (Gustke & Hodgson, 1980).

The Impact of Destination Environments on Travelers

Traveling, of course, usually has an impact on us. Our knowledge and experience are enriched, our circle of friends may enlarge, we are refreshed and usually ready for a return to our familiar life. We also may have experienced anxiety, discomfort, illness, theft, loss, and stress in the travel trade-off. Travel has positive and negative impacts on us.

Camping is a popular activity that can have many positive effects on us. Dorfman (1979) investigated the sources of camping satisfaction. He found that camping satisfaction means different things to different individuals. In searching for a universal measure of recreation satisfaction, he concluded that one probably does not exist. Some campsites are satisfactory or unsatisfactory to most campers, but any given campsite has some features that appeal to some campers and other features that appeal to other campers. As Dorfman notes, this is probably the case for all types of recreation sites. Nevertheless, the study did find that the *preferences* of campers for various features of a campsite are more predictive of satisfaction than are their *expectations* of the site. In addition, satisfaction was related to the natural characteristics of the site, social relationships, and relaxation during the visit, and, importantly, the absence of such negative conditions as noisy neighbors, crowding, and pollution.

An ancient traveling practice that many individuals still engage in is the pilgrimage. The traditional pilgrimage involves a journey to a religious site to fulfill a spiritual goal or for healing. At the healing sites, the physical condition of pilgrims is often studied, but Morris (1982) investigated whether a pilgrimage to Lourdes, the French site that over 3 million Christians visit every year, has a beneficial effect on the emotional state of pilgrims. Morris measured the anxiety and depression of pilgrims 1 month before their trip, 1 month after their trip, and 10 months later. Anxiety and depression significantly declined after the pilgrimage and stayed significantly lower for the 10 months after the pilgrimage. Of course, it is not clear whether Lourdes itself or some other aspect of the journey caused the emotional improvement, but presumably the pilgrims don't care; for them, the trip had a positive effect.

There are negative experiences in traveling, of course. Pearce (1981) has suggested that many tourists react to their new situation, with its lack of familiarity and routine, by going into **environ-**

ment shock. In studying the moods of visitors to a resort on a tropical island, he found that moods noticeably worsened on the second and third days of their stay. Minor health complaints also peaked in this period, lending credence to the environment shock notion.

Getting away from it all can have even worse complications. Streltzer (1979) studied what is known in Hawaii as the "coconuts and bananas syndrome." This refers to the myth clung to by some stray wanderers that life is so easy in the tropics that you can simply pick food off the trees. Streltzer found that "coconuts and bananas" tourists, who tend to be young, unmarried, and unemployed, often have psychiatric breakdowns when they discover that life is not that easy, even in Hawaii. Tourists who hold such unrealistic expectations (such as seeing grass huts at Waikiki and wanting to get back to nature) had about ten times the psychiatric admission rate of other tourists. The broader message, of course, is that tourist destinations can be stressful if the tourist believes the destination will solve most of life's problems.

The Impact of Travelers on Destination Environments

Travelers have growth experiences and sometimes go bananas. What happens to the environments they visit? We are familiar with the sociocultural effects of visitors. They bring needed revenue but also sometimes import unpleasant attitudes. The environmental impact of travelers is beginning to be recognized: the beer cans on top of Old Smokey, the use of scarce ground water in dry resort areas, land development pressures, and litter. The famous paintings in the caves of Lascaux, France, were so damaged by the mere breathing of tourists that the French government has closed them. Crime rates are affected, too. Compared to places with few tourists, tourist centers have significantly more crimes of certain types (Walmsley, Boskovic, & Pigram, 1983).

Walter (1982) recognizes these and other problems with tourists but suggests that there are ways of reducing the negative impact of tourists. The design of English stately houses that are open to the public serves as an example. In one, trees and gardens are arranged so that numerous tourists do not detract from the aesthetic experience of visiting the home. It has always had a public nature and would look odd deserted. The other's garden is designed for the contemplation of nature in solitude; when many tourists are present, the whole effect is ruined. Walter believes we should avoid encouraging **romantic tourism,** by which he means the lone individual or pair of lovers in an uninhabited wilderness or beach scene. This can only lead to disappointment and unmet expectations on the part of travelers, as well as the relentless development of ever-more-remote beaches and wildernesses as tourists pursue romantic tourism. He also argues that much better use of existing tourist areas could be made. For example, the provision of more extensive signs and maps could educate travelers about appealing places off the beaten track in established tourist areas.

The environmental psychology of travel is young; the studies discussed here represent the first in an area that will grow. The topic may seem frivolous, but we have already seen that travel has important impacts on both the traveler and the destination. Nevertheless, we still have much to learn about traveler-destination transactions. This knowledge, once gained, will be invaluable in designing highly adapted destinations (such as amusement parks and resorts) and planning for the survival of more vulnerable destinations (such as wildernesses, heritage buildings, and archeological sites).

▶ **In Sum.** The environmental psychology of travel is a new but growing area. Travelers affect destinations and are affected by them. Anticipation, travel, and recollection of travel involve environmental perception and cognition. Recreational travel is an environmental trade-off, but as society is able to provide employees with more disposable income and time, it is a trade-off many are pursuing. Destination selection, acquisition of knowledge about destination, and behavior along the road are a few areas of developing research. Some destinations bring relief from anxiety; others throw travelers into **environment shock.** Travelers ruin some physical settings and enhance almost none. Romantic tourism may be an undesirable luxury. More careful planning of destination sites might spread the impact of visitors, offer more authentic experiences, and educate travelers while offering them solace from the working world.

WORK, TRAVEL, AND ENVIRONMENTAL DESIGN

Environmental psychologists have been involved in the design of many work settings, from basic noise and light consultations to complete office designing. They have also contributed to commuting and long-distance travel design research. In this section, a few settings are selected as examples: two alternatives to automobile commuting, an example from Sweden of an entirely new type of work setting, and a resort complex in the South Pacific. These illustrate the major sections of this chapter—getting to work, working, and getting away from it all.

Commuting: Megaproject versus Miniproject

The San Francisco Bay Area Rapid Transit system (BART) is a billion-dollar attempt to ease traffic and conserve transportation energy. The interconnected set of over- and underground tracks has been moving commuters to and from San Francisco's suburbs since 1972. BART has always been controversial both financially and in the way it affects riders and neighborhoods. Psychologists have had a role in the design of its modern trains and in evaluating its impact. (See Fig. 11–15.)

Mark Baldassare (1981) reviewed the costs and benefits of the huge experiment. In financial terms, BART is a failure if success is defined as a self-supporting facility. Although 130,000 persons rode it every day in the mid-70s, BART still lost money and needed subsidies. Thus, the general taxpayer supports a public facility that is used by relatively few. Of course, this is not unusual; many public facilities from swimming pools to fire departments are actually used by few residents.

Some studies conclude that BART also failed in its mandate to reduce auto traffic (Webber, 1976, in Baldassare, 1981). Parking in San Francisco seems as horrendous as ever. Yet when over 100,000 riders use it, we are forced to conclude that traffic and parking would be even worse without BART.

Baldassare's study examined the social impact of BART. Over 700 interviews with residents, some of whom used BART and others who did not, probed feelings about the megaproject. Bal-

dassare found the general attitude to BART surprisingly favorable, but not all respondents liked BART. Near aboveground BART stations, dissatisfaction was somewhat higher. However, to put this dissatisfaction in monetary terms, most of these residents rejected a hypothetical trade-off in which they paid 1 or 2 dollars per month more taxes in return for putting BART underground in their neighborhoods. The areas around some stations have parking problems since commuters leave their cars to ride BART. Where back yards of houses are visible from the trains, residents were unhappy about the intrusion into their privacy.

Whether we evaluate BART as a success depends on which of these findings we choose to emphasize. BART is an expensive way to provide mild relief of traffic problems. Except for those living within a block or two of its lines it is, at least, not a major nuisance and it does move over 100,000 people daily.

On a much smaller scale, psychologists have explored ways of encouraging the use of existing transportation systems. Recall that earlier in the chapter, some attempts to find effective incentives for riding buses are described.

One such attempt (Katsev & Bachman, 1982) will be described in a bit more detail. Over 150 households in Portland, Oregon, were exposed to four strategies designed to promote bus riding at the expense of driving. Their normal habits were studied over an initial 3-week period, the strategies were applied for 4 weeks, and the outcomes were monitored for 2 weeks after that.

The four strategies were to offer (1) credit (riders saved the hassle of searching for change but were billed at the end of the month), or (2) credit plus "inverted" fare (riders paid full fare for their first four rides each week, but if a fifth ride was taken *all* rides were charged at half fare), or (3) credit plus differential fare (full fare during rush hour, half fare for off-peak rides), or (4) an unlimited number of free rides. Those who volunteered were randomly assigned to one of these conditions or to a control condition in which participants were simply told the experimenters wished to measure their bus and car trips.

Both free-ticket and credit-plus-inverted-fare strategies approximately doubled ridership during the treatment period, but the other two strategies produced only modest increases. Unfortu-

FIGURE 11–15 BART, the Bay Area Rapid Transit rail system. *(Courtesy of BART.)*

nately, after the treatment period ridership declined, especially in the free-ticket condition. Automobile driving did not decrease. Thus, two strategies have value, but only while they are in place.

On closer examination, the most cost-effective strategy (credit plus inverted fare) does seem potentially worthwhile. Ridership doubled during treatment, but the average number of rides was not high enough for the bus company to lose much money to fare inversion (because of fares being halved by a fifth ride each week). For a very small investment (compared to BART), ridership might be significantly increased. Auto use was not reduced—at least not immediately—but the credit-plus-fare-inversion strategy bears further study.

The miniproject has the advantage over the megaproject of not costing billions of dollars or imposing new traffic corridors on neighborhoods. Neither project is very successful, although they are difficult to compare because of the difference in scale between them. You might consider other benefits of building an entirely new system like BART, such as job creation or possible civic pride in having a high-tech people mover, but as far as commuting experiments go, I would rather be a taxpayer in Portland than San Francisco!

Loosely Coupled Settings

In an earlier section, computer-assisted work decentralization (CAWD) was discussed. **Loose coupling** is a concept that assumes that things are less interdependent than we normally think. If this is true, there is less need than designers previously believed for placing all units of an organization under one roof.

An early solution was to encourage or even force employees to work at home, but that works for only a few employees. Yet CAWD does allow for working outside the office and there are certain good reasons to decentralize work if possible. (One would be to help solve the problems described in the last section by essentially replacing many commuting vehicles with communications cables.)

Frank Becker (1984) has described a compromise solution that has been tested in Sweden: people work neither at home nor at the office but in a **neighborhood work center** (NWC). The experimental NWC was opened in a small town 50 kilometers from Stockholm from which many residents commute daily to the city. The NWC occupied space in a shopping center. Employees from a variety of organizations work in the same place and share equipment. Their reasons for trying the NWC concept included being closer to their families, crowding at their main office, cutting commuting costs, and the availability of equipment at the NWC that was unavailable in their main office.

Like any experiment, the NWC has had both success and failure. Some employees are working who simply would not be able to work otherwise, owing to commuting problems. Some benefit from the special equipment, others from being able to work with a spouse. On the other hand, the NWC is unsatisfactory for some employees because confidential documents are not entirely secure, it is too isolated, or they lack commitment to the NWC concept.

The neighborhood work center is an interesting concept. Further experience will yield a profile of the kind of employee and organization for which it is well-suited. The question is not whether work settings are loosely coupled or not; it is *which* work settings and employees are loosely coupled enough to benefit from NWCs.

A Resort in Fiji

The role of environmental psychologists in the development of tourist developments has not been extensive. Nevertheless, as leisure becomes a larger part of the average person's life, the need to construct good getaways increases.

What is a good getaway? Large structures that clash with local geography and culture, exclude local people, and endanger fragile ecosystems are clearly bad ideas. The goals of authenticity, blending into local conditions, and safeguarding the natural environment are more appropriate and, fortunately, increasingly represent the desires of travelers.

Robert Sommer (1983) relates his experience as part of a multidisciplinary team advising the developer of a resort in Fiji. Early proposals centered on a Waikiki approach, with high-rise buildings and bright colors. The team was able to convince the developer to limit building height to the height of the palm trees and to use natural colors found on the island.

Sommer's major contribution was to housing for the local employees. The architect, innocently enough, had prepared plans along the lines of a native village, believing this would be appreciated by the employees. Sommer pointed out that the employees were to be recruited from different islands; they would not share kinship ties or as many cultural practices as the native village concept assumed. The employees would not be living in the traditional subsistence economy that fostered the villages. He recommended a modified urban form, with small shops and more housing suited to the resort economy.

Environmental psychologists can be involved in many phases of the travel industry. Besides the design of resorts, some have studied the perceptions of tourist destinations, traveler cognitions about new places, the design of travel brochures, choices of transportation mode for travel, and behavior on airplanes.

SUMMARY

Getting to work, working, and getting away from work are all fertile fields of study for the environmental psychologist. In many locations automobile commuting is an expensive waste of energy, but no one has been particularly successful in weaning commuters from their cars in cities dominated by the automobile even though driving can be quite stressful. Until more attractive alternatives are offered commuters, their addiction to cars may be viewed as adaptive.

Noise—unwanted sound, by definition—has complex effects on work performance. Some conditions under which it is likely to improve or harm performance have now been tentatively identified. In industrial settings, noise often impairs hearing without the victim's awareness; it has also been linked to health problems. Noise in offices, where work often involves considerable cognitive processing and sensitive social interaction, is an important problem. Few performance effects have been documented, but privacy complaints are widespread in typical open-plan offices.

Most employees can sufficiently control temperature through clothing or other protective devices so that it has no strong effects on performance. In experimental situations where temperature is varied strongly, the same pattern of complex effects observed for noise are reported. Temperature swings can be annoying in buildings with inadequate heating and cooling systems. Performance may be optimal at temperatures below typical comfort zones, which may create conflict between the goals of creating pleasant work settings and creating efficient ones. Long-term extreme temperatures are stressful, but humans have considerable adaptive capacity for temperature.

Airborne disease agents can cause health problems, but ions and malodors have weak effects on most individuals. Certain employees, however, have ion sensitivities or other qualities that make them more susceptible than most people. Lighting is a problem primarily when it is too bright or placed inappropriately for a task. Lower levels of more localized light, and more sunlight where possible, would increase employee satisfaction. Spatial arrangements should reflect the employee's need for interaction with others, which varies with the task and the employee. As with noise, the problem is essentially one of privacy.

Recreational travel involves most areas of environmental psychology; the difference is that the setting is typically unfamiliar but desirable. Little research about the traveler's perceptions, cognitions, social interactions, and learning have yet appeared, but what has offers tantalizing glimpses of an interesting new area of research.

Environmental design in this chapter is illustrated by describing the impact of a large modern train system, a small attempt to design a program to encourage drivers to ride buses, a new kind of work setting, the neighborhood work center, and consultation on the design of a tropical resort.

SUGGESTED SUPPLEMENTARY READINGS

Altman, I., Wohlwill, J. F., & Everett, P. B. (Eds.). (1981). *Transportation and behavior.* New York: Plenum.

Barnaby, J. F. (1980). Lighting for productivity gains. *Lighting Design and Application,* February, 20–28.

Baron, R. A., Russell, G. W., & Arms, R. L. (1985). Negative ions and behavior: Impact on mood, memory, and aggression among Type A and Type B persons. *Journal of Personality and Social Psychology, 48,* 746–754.

Becker, F. D. (1981). *Workspace: Creating environments in organizations.* New York: Praeger.

Bonsall, P., Spencer, A., & Tang, W. (1983). Ridesharing in Great Britain: Performance and impact of the Yorkshire schemes. *Transportation Research, 17,* 169–181.

Broadbent, D. E. (1979). Human performance and noise. In C. M. Harris (Ed.), *Handbook of noise control.* New York: McGraw-Hill.

Fridgen, J. D. (1984). Environmental psychology and tourism. *Annals of Tourism Research, 11,* 19–39.

Harris, L., & Associates. (1978). *The Steelcase national study of office environments: Do they work?* Grand Rapids, MI: Steelcase Inc.

Oborne, D. J., & Gruneberg, M. M. (Eds.). (1983). *The physical environment at work.* New York: Wiley.

Oxley, D., & Barrera, M., Jr. (1984). Undermanning theory and the workplace: Implications of setting size for job satisfaction and social support. *Environment and Behavior, 16,* 211–234.

Pearce, P. L. (1982). *The social psychology of tourist behavior.* Oxford: Pergamon.

Steele, F. I. (1973). *Physical settings and organizational development.* Reading, MA: Addison-Wesley.

Sundstrom, E., (1986). *Work places: The psychology of the physical environment in offices and factories.* New York: Cambridge University Press.

Wineman, J. D. (Ed.). (in press). *Behavioral issues in office design.* New York: Van Nostrand Reinhold.

Chapter Twelve
Designing More Fitting Environments

I am firmly convinced that architecture . . . can be considered an art only when it reflects an understanding of the perceptions of the consumers of the designed environment.

Kiyo Izumi, 1971

Tom and Jane were spending a leisurely Saturday afternoon at their local branch library, which had opened a few weeks earlier. Tom had checked out a book on renovating old homes. They were reading the paper, trading small talk on current issues and the bizarre story of the day ("ten-year-old girl, discovered by Indians, lives with pack of panthers and goes about on all fours, fighting with panthers for food and trying to leap into trees").

A young woman approached them. "Excuse me," she said. "I'm conducting a study of this library and I wonder if you would mind telling me your opinions of it?"

Tom and Jane agreed but groaned silently. They had responded to more than their share of questionnaires that year at school. "Now they're even invading public territories," Tom thought to himself. The questionnaire covered various aspects of the library, such as spatial layout, lighting, windows, and noise. It asked their reasons for coming to the branch library and for any special gripes or compliments they wished to offer about it.

The woman returned in a few minutes for their completed questionnaires. She explained that similar questionnaires had been distributed in the old library, for comparison purposes. "I have to tell you, too," she said somewhat hesitantly, "that I have been watching you for the last half hour." Tom and Jane looked at each other quickly, then back at the researcher. "In our evaluation we want to see how people actually use the library as well as how they feel about it. You see, our study of the old library showed that people were afraid to talk aloud to each other and that it took a long time for people to find the books they were looking for. This new design is supposed to make you feel more like talking because we've separated the study area from the light-reading area. All those maps and signs, together with a carefully planned arrangement of the card catalog and stacks, are supposed to help you find things faster. Do you realize that it took you only thirty-eight seconds to find the book you're holding?"

This long speech took Tom and Jane a bit by surprise. They stared for a minute, then Jane stammered, "I guess your project seems like a good idea. . . . " The woman leaned closer. "I have to ask," she said. "What were you reading in the paper that was so hilarious?"

We have surveyed research and theory across the broad domain of environmental psychology. For some readers, this is enough; to understand something of how and why individuals interact with environments satisfies their curiosity about the field. The application of this knowledge is not particularly important. For these readers, I have tried to present some *principles* of environmental psychology.

Other readers may remain unfulfilled by the preceding chapters. For them, gathering and discussing knowledge are tolerable activities, but life does not begin until that knowledge is used to better the world. Examples of design applications were offered in earlier chapters, but we have not yet directly examined the process of designing environments or the role of social science in the design process. This chapter is especially for those readers who have been waiting patiently for a fuller treatment of the *practice* of environmental psychology, about putting environment-behavior knowledge to work.

Certainly there are portions of the built environment that need improvement. One well-publicized example is a large St. Louis apartment complex that was completed in 1954. The Pruitt-Igoe project was designed with the admirable intention of replacing deteriorating three story inner city housing. (See Fig. 12–1.) The complex, containing 43 eleven-story buildings for about 12,000 people, was praised in an architectural journal for having no wasted space, vandal-resistant features, and individualistic design.

But problems appeared soon after it opened. The failure to carefully examine its design in relation to human behavior contributed to high rates of fear, vandalism, vacancy, and serious crime. The situation was so bad that, after only eighteen years, the city demolished the entire complex. Pruitt-Igoe is the most dramatic example of building design failure (part of the demolition was shown on national television), but many other buildings also pose problems for their users. (See Fig. 12–2.)

FIGURE 12–1 The Pruitt-Igoe apartment complex. *(Courtesy of the* St. Louis Post Dispatch.*)*

This chapter begins with a description of social design, a process that can improve the habitability of buildings. Next, the goals, problems, and advantages of including social science in architecture are considered. Then the social design process is described, focusing on its two most important phases, programming and postoccupancy evaluation. We close the chapter with descriptions of four sample postoccupancy evaluations.

SOCIAL DESIGN

There is a way to avoid these disasters. This process, developed over the last two decades under a variety of names, might best be called **social design** (Sommer 1972, 1983) or social design research. It generally involves studying how settings can best serve human desires and require-

ments. It must be distinguished from technical design research on, for example, the performance of building materials.

A Definition

Sommer is reluctant to give a precise definition of social design, but offers the following:

> *Social design is working with people rather than for them; involving people in the planning and management of the spaces around them; educating them to use the environment wisely and creatively to achieve a harmonious balance between the social, physical, and natural environment; to develop an awareness of beauty, a sense of responsibility, to the earth's environment and to other living creatures; to generate, compile, and make avail-*

FIGURE 12–2 An example of hard architecture. I spent a dozen or so days watching these benches. No one destroyed them; no one even sat on them.

able information about the effects of human activities on the biotic and physical environment, including the effects of the built environment on human beings. Social designers cannot achieve these objectives working by themselves. The goals can be realized only within the structures of larger organizations, which include the people for whom a project is planned. (Sommer, 1983, p. 7)

This definition includes some topics we have discussed elsewhere; in fact it might almost suffice as a definition of environmental psychology as a whole.

Mark Francis (cited in Sommer, 1983) has also offered some distinctions between social design and **formal design** (the traditional approach). According to Francis, formal design favors an approach that may be described as large-scale, corporate, high-cost, exclusive, authoritarian, tending to high-tech solutions, and concerned with style, ornament, the paying client, and a national or international focus. In contrast, social design favors an approach that may be described as small-scale, human-oriented, low-cost, inclusive, democratic, tending to appropriate technology, and concerned with meaning and context, the occupant as well as the paying client, and a local focus.

Although these distinctions provide the flavor of social design, they may not all apply in every design project. For example, social design may cost more at least initially, but it may save more over the life of the building. There are few studies from which we can conclude that one approach is generally less expensive than the other. Also, social design techniques may be applied to large-scale projects as well as small-scale projects. The difference between it and formal design is that in a large-scale project the social designer often pays more attention to specific behavior settings within the large project. In a large office complex, for example, the individual needs and activities of employees are more likely to be researched and incorporated into the building design.

The Need

Social design is not always needed in the design process. It isn't required in times and places where buildings are constructed by small communities in which everyone works together in accordance with a time-tested architectural tradition. These traditions, which Rapoport (1969) collectively calls the **preindustrial vernacular,** have evolved an architecture that already fits community and cultural norms, individual interests, local climate, geography, and materials quite well. When community members are both builders and occupants, the design process does not need separate financiers, architects, boards of directors, and construction firms. (See Fig. 12–3.)

In the developed nations of the world, division of labor has produced material benefits for all of us. However, in the design professions (as in other occupations), it has produced considerable role specialization. As work is split more narrrowly and each person's entire career is reduced to just one phase of a fundamental process in society—such as the creation of buildings—there is a tendency for communication among the principal players in the design process to diminish. These **principal players** include the client (who puts up the money), the designer (architect, planner), the

FIGURE 12–3 Vernacular architecture: the longhouse of the Kwagiutl people of Vancouver Island.

engineer (on larger projects), and, most important, the building user, occupant, or visitor.

Social design research, therefore, has become necessary in industrial and postindustrial societies. Two of its major roles are to reestablish and to facilitate communication among the principal players in the design process. A third role is to remind everyone involved that the lowly building user is one of the principal players. After the rise of industrialism and before the advent of environmental psychology, the building user was almost forgotten in architecture. The dazzling technology produced by the industrial revolution provides a vast array of design possibilities (in building materials, construction principles, and international communication among designers). The design of some buildings requires so much attention to technical factors that the future occupants are forgotten.

Architecture as Art

At the same time that increasing technology separated designers from building occupants, many designers began to emphasize the aesthetic dimension of architecture at the expense of the setting's functional value. Environments, of course, should be both beautiful and functional for their occupants. Unfortunately, attempts to create fashionable works of art dominated architecture for a long time—and still do. Architectural magazines use expensive photography and glossy paper to show off buildings, but often no people are even visible in the scenes.

It is tempting to conclude that these unpeopled building-scapes accurately reflect many designers' interests. One of the most influential architects in the world, Philip Johnson, says: "The job of the architect is to create beautiful buildings. That's all" (cited in Sommer, 1983, p. 4).

In an advertisement placed in my local newspaper by the company he founded, a tribute to a retiring architect states that he "is certainly not discarding his brush or his palette. His keen interest in Architecture as a Fine Art remains intense." These architectural formalists think of buildings more as painting or sculpture than as habitats (Sommer, 1983).

But the times are changing. By 1971, one architect could already make the statement that opens this chapter (Izumi, 1971). Many architects and designers now recognize the importance of designing for human use of buildings, without necessarily sacrificing technological or aesthetic considerations.

The American Institute of Architects sponsored a conference in the early 1970s that may be viewed as an early summit meeting between social scientists and designers (Conway, 1973). The Coolfront Conference outlined several key roles that social scientist consultants might play, including evaluating building habitability, defining the psychological needs of occupants, and training occupants in the optimal use of buildings. Now architects make statements like this: " . . . building evaluation has a central role to play in institutional development and maintenance" (Shibley, 1985).

In addition, entire organizations devoted to the cooperation of designers and social researchers sprang up (such as the Environmental Design Research Association and the International Association for the Study of People and their Physical Surroundings). The Appendix offers a more complete list of these organizations.

A growing number of social design researchers make their living from their contributions to the design process. Most practitioners operate as one- or two-person offices, much like clinical psychologists or physicians. A few of these offices are a decade or more old and employ up to twenty researchers. Some individual collaborations have been lengthy, such as the one between the psychologist Lawrence Wheeler and the architect Ewing Miller that lasted 15 years (Wheeler, 1985).

Structure and Process

These interactions between scientist and designer have gradually produced a more complete picture of the social-design process. One version of this picture was developed in the context of design evaluation, but may be adapted to characterize social design as a whole. In this framework, social design has a certain structure and a certain process (Friedmann, Zimring, & Zube, 1978). The structure is a kind of who-what-where statement about what must be considered. The five elements of the structure are: (1) the users, (2) the setting, (3) the proximate environmental context, (4) the design process, and, surrounding

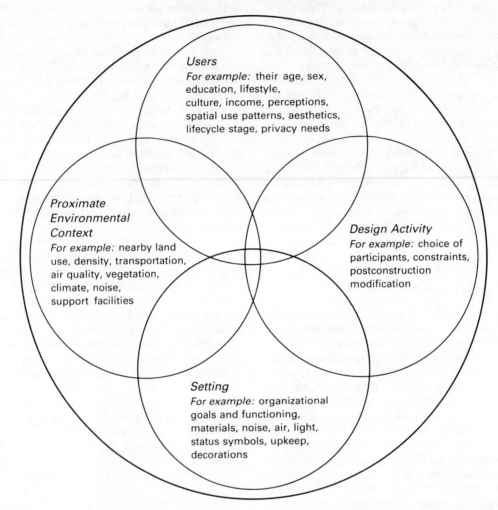

FIGURE 12–4 Five basic elements in the design process. *(Adapted from Friedmann, Zimring, & Zube, 1978.)*

these, (5) the social-historical context in which social design occurs. (See Fig. 12–4.)

The **users** are those who are involved in the normal activities housed by the building—from employee, client, visitor, or resident to janitor and manager. Their backgrounds, preferences, behaviors, and needs must be considered in the setting's design.

The **setting** includes the actual building or designed outdoor environment that will be created or renovated and the organization that will occupy the building. Organizational ideas, goals,

constraints, and customs must be considered, as must physical features such as size, light, noise, spatial arrangements, and decor.

The **proximate environment** includes the nearby surroundings of the setting. What is the neighborhood like? Is there much or little air pollution, traffic, park space, parking space? Is the site sloping, rainy, windy, subject to earthquakes?

The **design process** will receive its own full discussion in a later section. Briefly, it refers to the sequence of steps through which architects and social designers proceed to produce a habitable building. A typical building project includes the following seven stages (asterisks indicate where social researchers can have a major impact, although they have been involved in every step):

1. Decision to build (politicking and financing)
*2. Programming (setting goals and constraints)
*3. Design (translating the program into a form)
4. Construction
5. Use and adaptation (by occupants)
*6. Evaluation (by social design researchers)
*7. Feedback (to modify the building or to assist in the programming of future buildings)

This model of the design process has now been used, in whole or part, by hundreds of investigators. Some studies have been quite informal; others have been very sophisticated. Some focus on one building, others on many buildings of one type.

The **social-historical context** is the larger fabric into which the new building will be woven. What kind of political and economic trends are likely to dominate the next several decades, when the building is in its prime? What sort of demographic trends are in progress? How are individual and social attitudes changing?

Naturally, some buildings represent wildly incorrect predictions of social-historical context. The point, however, is that designers must at least attempt to forecast these trends if they hope to avoid constructing a building that will be useless in only a few years. Examples of failures include a New York community building that won architectural awards but seems to separate users from society rather than integrate them into it, a park with award-winning playground equipment placed in a neighborhood that is experiencing an influx of retired residents, and a welfare office that makes a statement aesthetically but alienates the ordinary people who visit it as clients (Friedmann, Zimring, & Zube, 1978).

Most social researchers concentrate on one or two stages, such as programming or evaluation; very few have been involved in all the stages, or even all four asterisked stages. In an exhaustive search, Wener (1982) could only find thirteen such studies, although more have been completed since then. This occurs for many reasons. The building is already built when the researcher is called in to do an evaluation so the practitioner cannot be involved in the programming or design

phases, or the sponsoring agency specifically requests a study of only one stage. Lack of time often prevents completion. For many buildings, the design process as outlined above takes five or more years. Many practitioners are unable to follow a single project for that length of time.

▶ **In Sum.** Some buildings are human disasters; others are merely persistent nuisances to those who occupy or use them. Social design is a way of creating buildings that fit occupants and users better by involving them in the planning process.

Social design is needed in societies that have splintered the building-creation process into many specialist roles. It is a remedy for the malady in which architects see themselves primarily as artists, ignoring the basic needs and activities of occupants. This malady is now widely recognized, yet many buildings are still constructed without significant user involvement. Social design structure (users, setting, vicinity, design process, and social-historical context) and the seven-step process itself are briefly described.

Before we delve into a stage-by-stage examination of our primary concern, the design process, we should take a step back to consider the goals, advantages, and problems of the social science contribution to environmental design.

SOCIAL RESEARCH IN THE DESIGN PROCESS

The Goals

Social design researchers and practitioners have five goals, some broader than others, some overlapping with others. The first and perhaps most important goal is to create physical settings that **match** the needs and activities of their occupants. This goal is sometimes described as habitability, congruence or goodness of fit.

The second goal is to **satisfy** building users. Occupant satisfaction is paramount because occupants must spend significant parts of their lives working, residing, or relaxing in the setting.

Third, a frequent objective is to **change occupant behavior.** Such changes might include increasing office-worker productivity, enhancing social ties among institutionalized old people, reducing aggression in a prison, or increasing communication among managers in an administrative office. As we shall see, the behavior-change goal can be both difficult to attain and controversial.

A fourth goal is to enhance the occupant's **personal control** (Holahan, 1983). The more building users are able to alter the setting to make it suit their needs, the less stressful that setting will be.

The fifth goal to be discussed is the facilitation of **social support** (Holahan, 1983). Designs that encourage cooperation, assistance, and support are desirable primarily for building occupants who are disadvantaged in one way or another, but also for active and successful individuals. Let's examine each of these goals more closely.

Matching.　Matching refers to how well the occupant's activities and needs are met by the setting. Whether the degree of match is high or low sometimes depends in part on whose viewpoint is considered (Michelson, 1976, pp. 30–31). You may recall the difference between alpha and beta press, a distinction made by the personality theorist Henry Murray between actual and perceived influences on human behavior. Similarly, there are alpha and beta forms of matching. Alpha matching, or **congruence,** refers to how well the setting fits the person from an objective point of view. Beta matching, or **habitability,** has been defined as "environmental quality as perceived by occupants of buildings or facilities" (Preiser & Taylor, 1983, p. 6).

Most principal players, of course, hope that both perceived and actual matches are good. The possibility remains, however, that a team of design experts could declare that congruence had been achieved but occupants disagree. Unfortunately, significant disagreements between experts and users have indeed been demonstrated in several studies of residential environments. Lansing and Marans (1969) found that professional planners believed a high-quality neighborhood was related to how open, interesting, and pleasant it was, but neighborhood residents believed high quality was related only to how pleasant it was. Such clashes mean that efforts must be made not only toward improving the fit between users and their environments, but also toward reducing differences between designer and occupant definitions of good design. Because the user's actual activities are sometimes easier to document than

their needs, clashes may be resolved if data on activities are collected and shared with users.

Satisfaction.　Habitability corresponds to occupant satisfaction; congruence is the expert's opinion that the occupant is satisfied. But principal players other than the occupant also may or may not be satisfied with the project. Some architects hope their buildings will work as statements of minimalist or post-modernist aesthetic design principles. The paying client might be primarily satisfied if the project is completed within its budget. Most social researchers would be happy if their work contributed to a habitable structure. Yet, lurking in the vicinity, is another question: "Sure, they like it. But are the occupants more productive now?"

Changing Behavior.　Many projects implicitly or explicitly embody someone's hope that occupant behavior will change for the better. When all principal players, including occupants, agree that a certain pattern of behavior needs encouragement (or discouragement) from the design, the design process may steam merrily ahead. Unfortunately, principal players often disagree about who should change which behaviors.

Clients constructing workplaces, for example, often expect that the new design will increase employee productivity. When faced with this expectation, the social researcher is in the uncomfortable position of being asked to use the environment to squeeze productivity out of employees. The very thought of attempting to manipulate employees for the benefit of an organization is unpleasant for many practitioners.

Occupant satisfaction, on the other hand, is usually the goal of practitioners and other principal players who are particularly sympathetic to the needs of the building user. According to Robert Sommer (1983), social design is part of a worldwide concern for human rights; it began with attempts to provide the benefits of design to the unfortunate (such as mental patients) and to the poor. This activist tradition still fuels the efforts of many environmental psychologists.

Regardless of your party affiliation, social design is necessarily political in the original sense of discussing and debating policy. Knight and Campbell (1980) assert that the representation of social relationships in physical design is inherently contestable. Design programs reveal and confirm the nature of social power in the organization that will occupy the building (van Hoogdalem, van der Voordt, & van Wegen, 1985). Designers and evaluators of designs, according to Knight and Campbell, cannot be objective (even if they think they are) because they always conclude their work by endorsing—implicitly if not explicitly—a set of values concerning social relationships and social power that would be embodied in their building plans. But design almost necessarily implies trade-offs. After deciding who their values allow them to represent, practitioners try to discover and advocate the most advantageous set of trade-offs, based on the best obtainable information.

What happens, then, when work efficiency is promoted as more important than other goals, such as employee satisfaction? Clients who bring in a social researcher do often expect productivity gains in return for their investment. Robert Sommer has agonized over these questions for years. In his book *Social Design* (1983), several answers to the productivity question are offered. To begin with, Sommer believes the research evidence demonstrates that design can sometimes raise productivity. However, because design-behavior relations are so complex and influenced by so many other factors, we cannot be sure when building design boosts productivity. Alternatively, we could take a leap of faith and assume that careful social design must produce some gains in productivity, even though the gains are hard to prove.

Another response to the productivity question is that social research is, in a modern democracy, a basic right of those who must occupy buildings for large parts of their lives. Social research, from this point of view, is valuable in its own right and should not have to be justified in productivity terms. Finally, we might question why some clients are so productivity conscious in the first place. "Those who ask the productivity question would like to put dollar signs on positive experiences" (Sommer, 1983, p. 65).

Thus, productivity and satisfaction are sometimes conflicting goals, with some principal players stressing one more than the other. Of course, both goals are desirable. Sadly, many situations arise where productivity and satisfaction goals are in conflict. When this happens, practitioners are forced to decide what their own political and economic values are.

Personal Control.   If possible, social design will provide occupants with real options to control their proximate environment. What does this mean in specific terms? Consider publicly funded residential space for students (dormitories) or poor people (housing projects). Some designs, high rises in particular, seem designed to overload the resident with social stimulation. Too few elevators and long, narrow hallways, for example, result in the sense that people are everywhere and inescapable. Residents develop the feeling that they cannot control the number of social contacts—especially unwanted social contacts—they must face daily.

Two other common examples of low-control settings are the crowded retail store and the traffic jam. Studies show that crowding is related to social and informational overload, which in turn leads to the sense that one has lost control. Designing against crowding is, in part, designing for personal control.

A final example concerns personalization of the workspace. Some organizations restrict or forbid employees or clients from decorating their immediate areas with posters, pictures, and other items of personal interest. The justification for this policy, interestingly, is often that personalization would detract from an interior-design scheme on which the organization spent a lot of money. Such occurrences provide a perfect example of how aesthetic goals are sometimes pursued at the expense of building user needs and activities instead of in tandem with them.

In general, stress is often related to lack of personal control over physical and social input. Noise, unwanted social contact, and congestion are primary sources, yet social design can anticipate and attempt to overcome them or at least buffer the user from them. (See Fig. 12–5.)

Social Support.   Personal control is an individual process; social support is a group process. Holahan (1983) and others believe that many social problems would be eased if more and better social support was available. Common psychological

FIGURE 12-5 Hospital patients often lack privacy. *(Courtesy of Robert Sommer.)*

problems such as depression and anxiety have been shown to increase when social support is absent or inadequate. Social support may be seen as an antistress process (Moos, 1981).

What can social design do for social support? At the smallest scale of furniture arrangement, studies show that sociopetal arrangements can foster more interaction (Mehrabian & Diamond, 1971). At the building level, open-space areas may be arranged to facilitate social interaction (Holahan, 1972). Of course, if the personal-control goal as well as the social-support goal is to be met, the increased social interaction must be controllable. Occupants should be able to find social interaction when and if they want it, but not be faced with unwanted encounters. In office buildings, social support may be fostered through the provision of high-quality lounge space for employees. The mere existence of such space does not guarantee that valuable social support will be available, but with inadequate space for employees to share coffee and conversation, the likelihood of social networks declines.

The Problems

The Gap. Designers in our society are almost completely separated from those who will actually use their buildings. You use numerous buildings every day and will spend the vast majority of your life in one building or another. But when was the last time you sat down with an architect to discuss any building that you have ever used?

The paying client (often a board of directors) is the missing link between the designer and the occupant. Architects communicate extensively with board members, but neither architect nor board member is very likely to spend much time in the building after opening day. If the paying clients do use the building, they are likely to occupy a special area or floor of the building. In general, there is a serious gap between designer and occupant.

Resistance. Not everyone involved in the design process perceives the advantages of social research. In the absence of legal requirements for social design research, many designers and clients view it as an unnecessary or extravagant part of the building process. Because some principal players do not want their lives complicated by new information—even valuable new information—the social-design researcher's entry into a project can be difficult (Sommer, 1983). In general, resistance to social design comes primarily from four sources: some designers, some clients, some sectors of society, and even from some building users.

First, designers who are wholly concerned with architecture as a fine art obviously see little need for social design research. They tend to subscribe to some or all the following views:

1. If a building is beautiful, it must be useful.
2. Beauty is so much more valuable than function that social design research on building function isn't worth the effort.
3. If the building is beautiful, occupants will be so awestruck, impressed, or happy with it that function will somehow take care of itself.
4. Designers are capable of placing themselves in the shoes of occupants and therefore can create a building that is functional, satisfying, and beautiful for occupants without consulting or studying them.
5. People are very adaptive and malleable, making it unnecessary to try matching the building to their needs and activities.

Fortunately, of course, many designers do not subscribe to these views. But resistance does come from designers who are unaware of, or do not understand, social design research.

A second source of resistance to social research comes from some clients. The client is already paying a substantial fee for the design of a new building; social design research is likely to appear as an unnecessary extra. Some clients cannot see the long-term benefits of social research, often merely because they still don't know very much about it. Even some designers who appreciate social design nevertheless do not budget for it in their design proposal because they fear the additional initial costs will cause them to lose their contract to a lower bidder.

Without a clear explanation of how the expenditure may be beneficial to their organization, clients are naturally wary of spending the extra money and time necessary for social research. So far, the most progressive clients appear to be governments, many of which support social design research in the construction of administration buildings, subsidized housing, prisons, and other government-funded construction projects.

Third, some members of the public resist social design. When a design proposal suggests a solution quite different from conventional practice, public resistance sometimes appears. For example, bathrooms are used for many more behaviors than the fixtures in them would lead one to expect (Kira, 1976). Paramount among these are uses of the bathroom for privacy and self-identity-related activities, but few bathrooms are designed to support these activities.

Finally, even some building users may resist social design. In one of the earliest attempts to employ social science to make a setting more habitable, Robert Sommer (1969) and some of his colleagues rearranged the tables and chairs in a hospital ward for elderly women. The chairs were originally placed around the edge of the room in straight rows; this arrangement made it difficult for some of the women to turn to one another for a decent conversation. When Sommer arranged the furniture to resemble a cafe (four chairs around a table) to facilitate conversation, the women moved the chairs back to their former positions. It seems one could no longer tell whose chair was whose and this territorial ownership was very important in a setting where residents could lay claim to little else but their own chair.

Sommer eventually convinced the women to give his idea a try. They did converse with one another much more than previously. This social interaction may have provided some much-needed stimulation to aging residents. The moral of the story, however, may be that practitioners as well as architects must not forget to consult with users before implementing design changes.

Unrealistic Expectations. Some clients and designers are overly optimistic about the power of social design. They naively believe that the right design can solve nearly any problem the organization is experiencing. The least sophisticated, but still very common, form of this misconception is **architectural determinism**. (See box on p. 352.) This discredited position holds that architecture determines behavior quite directly. At public lectures, I have been asked what color the kitchen should be painted to make people more sociable. Every social design researcher has been asked analogous questions: How big should prison cells be? How loud can a classroom get before students stop learning? Does music improve office productivity?

The environment is important, but we know that it is not all-important (unless, as Robert Sommer says, a designer decides to experiment with ceilings one meter high, or some other wild notion). The social environment is also important for productivity, learning, health, stress, and sociability. Individual characteristics, too, lead occupants to respond differently to the same set-

The architect Clovis Heimsath (1977) has outlined six fallacies that designers commonly believe. You will note that some fallacies are incompatible with others. Different fallacies may be believed by different designers, but it is also surprising how often a designer will offer a second, incompatible fallacy after one has explained the weaknesses of the first one offered.

1. *Designer Fallacy.* "The building directly determines behavior in it." This is a form of architectural determinism. Things are just not that simple. Actually, behavior is determined by personal, social, cultural and economic factors as well as by the form of the building.

2. *Genius Fallacy.* "Designs created by great architects have universal value; they may be applied easily in other times and places." Actually, because every set of building users is unique, each new building design should be at least slightly different to take their needs into account.

3. *Common Man Fallacy.* "Architecture has no important effect on behavior; people will do what they want regardless of building design." After the eleven previous chapters, I hope this one requires no further comment!

4. *Open Society Fallacy.* "Good design is not really necessary because good people will survive and overcome even slums to become successful." But how difficult did awful buildings make the life of the few who made it? What about the many who did not overcome bad design? Why make life harder for either group?

5. *Manipulation Fallacy.* "Designing for human behavior is a veiled form of totalitarianism and behavior control." Design already exerts influence on human behavior; we just don't understand all the mechanisms yet. Design can be aimed at giving *more* control to building users.

6. *Know-Nothing Fallacy.* "It is all so complicated that let's forget about the behavioral implications of design and just get this building built!" The holder of this burned-out position no longer has the energy required for good design. Social design certainly can be complicated, but the situation is not hopeless. Careful adherence to the design process as outlined in this chapter can produce useful information.

ting. The social researcher must educate clients and designers to the complexity of environment-behavior relations and remind them that significant but not magical results may be expected from social research in the design process.

Porteous (1977) describes two alternatives to architectural determinism. The first, **environmental possibilism,** began as an extreme antideterminist point of view, suggesting that our behavior is not at all determined. A more moderate version asserts that the environment sets certain limits on human behavior, allowing a finite range of behavior.

Another alternative is **environmental probabalism.** In many areas of science, from quantum mechanics to human perception, theories have evolved in this century that argue for a statistical point of view. That is, a given combination of circumstances sets up certain odds that an event will occur. Events are never certain and never impossible; their odds are merely very high or very low. It is even possible for a chair to jump off the

ground unassisted—if all its atoms happen to vibrate in the vertical direction at the same time. Of course, the odds against this actually happening are vanishingly small.

In everyday settings, the various environmental and other factors that operate set up certain odds—according to the environmental probabalist—that an individual will be affected by noise, begin to socialize with a neighbor, or benefit from a negative ion generator. Depending on the number, strength, and direction of these influences, the odds of the individual behaving in these ways vary from quite low to quite high. Social design should be able to increase the probability of selected activities and feelings.

Conflict.   Social-design research may bring to light disagreements among the principal players. This may sound like a reason for not undertaking design research, but it isn't. The following evaluation of a residence for senior citizens suggests the value of revealing conflicts.

The residence is new, spacious, and lovely. The general quality of construction and furnishings is at least equal to that in most private, middle-class single-family dwellings. Yet a common complaint of residents is that they are too cold. One of the first things noticed in touring the residence is that every room has its own thermostat, but every one of them is enclosed in a clear plastic cover. The covers have locks, but only the staff have keys. (See Fig. 12–6.)

The staff claim that residents merely need to ask, and the setting on their thermostat will be changed. Some residents say this isn't true; they are told that their requests are unreasonable. The staff admits this, claiming that some residents would overheat themselves because they would turn the thermostat up and forget to turn it down later. Residents scoff at this claim.

Regardless of who is correct, the plastic covers in this residence are a source of conflict between the building's staff and its occupants. That residents can see the control lever through the plastic but are unable to alter it seems a perverse form of torture, although the staff does not see it that way. Energy bills can be a problem, but in this new and presumably well-insulated building, it would seem that slightly higher temperatures would not be financially serious. Perhaps a few residents are endangering themselves, but those who are could be identified. At present, no residents control their own thermostat.

This is just one example of principal-player conflict. Every setting produces its own examples. Practitioners of environmental psychology are often caught in the middle, yet have certain political and moral values of their own. But this does not mean that social design research should not be done. The conflict was present anyway; the researcher merely brings it to the fore. Conflicts that are not unearthed remain vague but potent sources of discontent. Occupants may not realize just why they dislike a building until a systematic interview with a social design researcher helps them to realize their specific complaints.

Conflict cannot be resolved until it is identified. Once identified, conflicts have a chance of resolution. In the case of the senior citizens' residence, most residents might be given keys to their thermostats, or the covers might simply be removed. Or, perhaps, the energy bill was seriously underestimated by planners, and it really is necessary for everyone to bundle up a bit more until better economic times. In that case, many occupants would probably feel better having the difficult situation explained to them, even if it remains unchanged. However, if the conflict fails even to reach the discussion stage, it may fester and someday become part of a larger eruption.

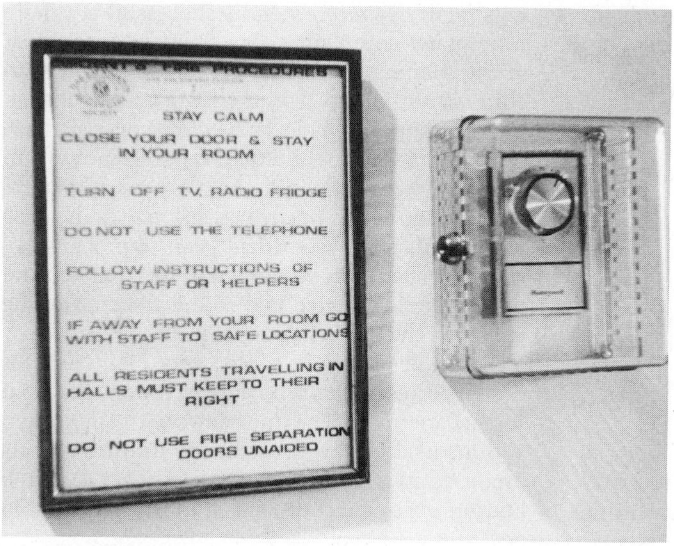

FIGURE 12–6 This thermostat covered with a clear plastic shield tells occupants that control is possible but not by them.

Thus, one problem of social design research is that it often reveals conflicts among principal players. But, with skillful consultation and mediation, this problem becomes one of the key *advantages* of doing social-design research. Next we discuss some other advantages offered by social design research.

The Advantages

To Users.   When design research is successful, the occupant receives a more habitable place to live, work, or relax. Three specific benefits of a habitable environment to occupants are that the building (1) mirrors their aesthetic and behavioral tendencies, thereby (2) reducing stress, which in turn (3) supports or enhances their ability to accomplish their goals.

Mirroring means the building suits the occupant's customary living or working habits, social patterns, and cultural background. A very simple example is the office building window. Many office employees prefer to work in conditions that are refreshed by the occasional breath of fresh air. Yet most new office buildings do not allow the simple freedom of opening a window. This is a minor irritant that, over time and combined with other failures to mirror, can become a significant source of stress. When occupants are stressed, they must either expend extra energy to overcome the shortcomings of their workspace or simply yield to an unsupportive environmental structure, working less effectively and with less enjoyment.

Participation in the design process gives users a sense of control that has its own intrinsic value. It helps to satisfy the need to create, it brings community members together, it demonstrates concern by management, and it can produce positive public relations (Sommer, 1983). For example, one hospital that asked nurses to participate in the design of a new addition received newspaper coverage that praised the new project as a "nurse's special." Presumably, as Sommer notes, the opportunity to provide design input and the favorable publicity will make nurses proud and even readier to serve their patients.

To Designers.   Designers can benefit from social design research, too. Evaluation of their work can (1) provide feedback for improvement in the design of the next building's design, (2) extend and create more contracts, and (3) save them undue criticism (Zimring & Reizenstein, 1981). It can also (4) save designers time, (5) improve communication with other principal players, and (6) offer a useful external perspective on the project (Sommer, 1983). Let's consider these six advantages one at a time.

Many architects specialize in certain types of buildings. The care and consideration that goes into any one of them is enormous. Clearly, much could be learned about how each new building design succeeded and failed by studying the opinions and behavior of the building's users after it is occupied. But, as an early environmental psychologist once said, not very kindly, architects are like cuckoos who lay their eggs and then leave the scene (Wools, 1970). However, by staying around to learn how the building works in practice, an architect could easily become more skillful (and successful) than competing architects who reinvent the wheel time after time.

Zimring and Reizenstein (1981) recount how some architects turned design research into a more extensive contract. Pedestrian pathways at a zoo were imperfectly arranged; some interesting exhibits were missed by zoo visitors who overlooked the walkway leading to them. A study revealed the reasons for the problem. This research impressed the client, who asked the architects to do more design work at the zoo.

In another project, a new headquarters building, the design was generally successful but there were many complaints about temperature. Most of the blame fell on the architects. Had the architects not followed up their work with an evaluation, they might never have discovered these complaints; meanwhile their reputation was suffering. The evaluation brought these complaints to light and led to an investigation. The heating and ventilation system had been improperly installed. When it was corrected, the temperature problems disappeared and so did the continuing threat to the designer's reputation.

Social design work can be very inefficient for design professionals who are not trained in social science methods. The interviews with clients and various user groups necessary to fulfill the goals espoused in this chapter are not within the time budget, experience, or skill of most designers. In fact, this is true of survey development, behavior mapping, and most other social-design methods. Thus, the involvement of an outside research consultant can save the designer much time and effort.

Designers think and talk in a special way that is strongly oriented toward the pictorial. Some architects are almost mute without a sketch pad. Nondesigners, such as clients and users, are likely to be less visual in their thinking. Some may not be very verbally articulate. A good practitioner, then, with some experience in the visual world of the designer and some in the verbal world of clients and users, may serve as a *translator* among the principal players.

Finally, most people who spend immense effort on a project feel, near the end of it, that they can no longer see the project objectively. In the design process, endless small and large revisions to floorplans and facades produce this experience. Input from external sources, such as users or the social design researcher, can help place the project into a realistic semblance of how others will perceive it.

To Clients. Social design research can even benefit the paying client, who often is concerned with costs and assumes that research is a net cost to the project. Instead, social research may cost less than other planning methods. Studies, such as one by Anthony, have documented direct savings to building projects that may be attributed to social research (cited in Sommer, 1983).

An Australian study by Heath and Green suggests that information provided by social-design research can help the client avoid mistakes that would cost considerable money indirectly over an extended period of the building's life (cited in Reizenstein, 1982). These include chronic inefficiency in building maintenance, duplication of effort, user ignorance of building capabilities, overspending, and, of course, a design that is inappropriate for the activities housed by the building.

▶ **In Sum.** Social design has numerous goals, problems, and advantages. It aims to match settings to their occupants, to satisfy a variety of principal player needs, to promote personal control in the building, and to encourage social support. Under some circumstances, another goal may be to increase productivity or otherwise change behavior.

The problems include a frequent lack of communication between those who pay for a building and those who use or occupy it, resistance to the extra effort of involving users and occupants, unrealistic expectations that socially designed buildings will directly cure various evils, and inevitable conflict among principal players. Social design usually means serving the needs of building occupants first, but it also offers benefits to architects and paying clients.

STAGES IN THE DESIGN PROCESS

Construction follows a series of stages that, in general terms, are the same whether the project is a new building, renovation of an older building, or the development of an outdoor setting such as a park. Social design can play a role in every stage of this process, but usually is most prominent in the programming and postoccupancy evaluation phases.

John Zeisel (1975) suggested a model of the design process on which the present discussion is based. (See Fig. 12–7.) An important feature of Zeisel's model is its cyclical nature. Social designers all agree that knowledge gained from one project ought to be used for the next similar project. This has always occurred, of course, but to an unfortunately limited extent. One example of truly cyclical improvement in design is provided by Wener, Frazier, and Farbstein (1985), who have used behaviorally based evaluations to inform the design evolution of three generations of correctional facilities.

When an architectural firm builds numerous structures of a given type, it acquires a store of information. Two problems with the information in these traditionally private stores is that it comes from select and limited sources and it is not widely shared.

Traditionally, the architect's primary feedback comes from the paying client, a few members of the community who make comments in a guest book on opening day, fellow architects, and perhaps an architecture critic. If future designs are to improve, these are necessary but not sufficient

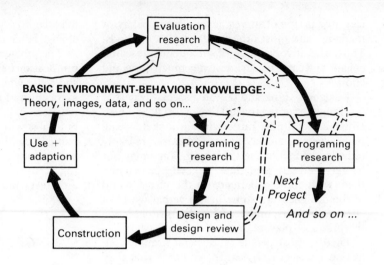

FIGURE 12-7 One prominent view of the design cycle. *(Adapted from Zeisel, 1975, 1981.)*

Five Steps in the Design Cycle		
1. Programming	(Analysis)	Identifying design objectives, constraints, and criteria.
2. Design	(Synthesis)	Making design decisions that satisfy criteria.
3. Construction	(Realization)	Building the project and modifying plans under changing constraints.
4. Use	(Reality Testing)	Moving in and adapting the environment.
5. Evaluation	(Review)	Monitoring the final product in terms of objectives and use—ideally to be translated into future design criteria.

sources of information. Conspicuously absent is systematic input from the building's users.

Whatever information that does get collected may not be widely shared because it constitutes, to some extent, the secrets of the trade. If there are principles of design that are not immediately evident in the actual structure, architects may be understandably reluctant to divulge them. If the building is found to have serious problems, the architect will not be keen to publicize them.

An improved design process would expand the sources of information about each building type and tactfully but widely disseminate knowledge of its strengths and weaknesses. Robert Sommer (1972) described how some designers already act as one-person data banks on the design of various types of buildings. Designers have called for clearinghouse accumulations of useful design information on successful and unsuccessful social design solutions. These could be stored and retrieved through a computer network, supplemented by drawings available on microfilm. Small-scale clearinghouses already exist in some design circles, but a vastly enlarged system could be extremely useful to prevent design disasters and reduce the time and effort required to produce successful designs.

Step one in the design process is the decision to build. This begins with an original plea for space from a group that has outgrown its old space or feels the need for refurbished, expanded, or new facilities. The plea for new space may originate with a formal or informal evaluation of the current setting.

Evaluation is both the beginning and the end of the design process; it is what makes the design process a cycle. The **original plea** is mentioned here as a reminder of this cycle although design evaluation is discussed in more detail after we survey the programming, design, construction, and adaptation stages of the cycle. The pleading group lobbies the paying client, who may be a board of directors, a government agency, or a wealthy individual. Undoubtedly, there are other calls for funds; the group must impress the paying client with its need for new or renovated facilities in competition with other groups.

Programming

Once tentative approval for the project is given, the next step is **programming:** the planning of the building that occurs before blueprints are drawn up. Programming has both a technical side and a social side. On the technical side, preliminary studies of possible sites, costs, sources of outside funds, and regulations are conducted. In general, it consists of determining the technical and financial constraints to the project.

The social side of programming is sometimes treated very lightly by traditional architects. However, because it is crucial to both matching (congruence and habitability) and to valued outcomes (satisfaction, productivity, personal control, and social support), social design practitioners treat it as one of the most important phases in the design cycle.

Social programming involves three steps: (1) understanding occupants, (2) involving them in

the design process, and (3) setting design guidelines.

Understanding Users.   The first of these three steps includes two activities that may occur simultaneously: clarifying the social rationale of the new space and analyzing the needs and wants of its future occupants.

Clarifying the **social rationale** means deciding what the organization's goals are. Prison administrators, for example, should decide whether the institution's goal is to deliver punishment, to offer privacy, to support rehabilitation, to be a warehouse, to encourage integration with the outside world, or some combination of these goals (Sommer, 1976). In a new low-cost housing complex, is the goal to promote a sense of community or to strengthen ties within the family? Each organization should attempt to decide which outcomes it expects the new structure to encourage.

The second activity, analysis of user needs (sometimes called **needs assessment**) begins with basic questions such as: Who will use the structure? How many people will use it? How many will be visitors, as opposed to 8-hours-per-day users or full-time residents? What activities will these users be engaged in? It may include more difficult questions such as: How much space is required for each user? How can the customs and values of the occupants be expressed in the building?

Sometimes a distinction between user *needs* and user *wants* is important (Zeisel, 1975). This distinction implies that users will ask for things they don't really need. If users seem to be doing this, practitioners must ask tactful probing questions that allow users to give answers which permit the practitioner to justify the request as a real need. As Sommer (1983) puts it, needs are much more marketable to paying clients than are mere wants.

User-needs analysis should involve multiple methods. Surveys and interviews of occupants are the most common ways of determining their needs, but these self-report methods have shortcomings as well. Occupant responses may be inaccurate due to their honest but mistaken memories of their behavioral patterns, their lack of knowledge of architectural possibilities, or their unfortunate attempts to tell the interviewer what sounds right rather than offer their true opinions.

But interviewing can still be useful. In Sweden, the dining room of a geriatric hospital was redecorated based on interviews with patients (Kuller & Mattson, 1984). The interviews revealed that the sterile hospital environment would best be replaced with one that resembled the patients' homes. The redecorated dining room was constructed to resemble a typical Swedish home of the 1930s or 1940s, the prime era of the patients' lives.

The redecoration was very popular with the residents, confirming the value of the interviews. Yet, sadly, the hospital administration required the social researchers to return the dining room to its former design after 16 weeks. Apparently, administrators viewed staff needs for efficiency as more important than patient needs for an appealing setting.

Zeisel (1975) describes two major alternatives to the self-report methods. In one, practitioners systematically observe the daily activities of the occupants. Watching what individuals actually do may be a better guide to a useful design program than what occupants say they do. In Toronto, for example, Ben Barkow has extensively observed the behavior of pedestrians in subways, concert halls, and airports (Barkow, 1977; Hanlon, 1981). Some of his findings are not surprising; subway patrons usually keep to the right side of walkways, and they tend to seek the shortest path. Other discoveries, however, are less obvious. For example, 85 percent of parcels are carried in the left hand. Barkow found that this led to the overuse of one vending machine (resulting in high maintenance costs) and another machine was underused. Subways usually have banks of turnstiles. In one bank of six, Barkow found that 43 percent of the subway riders used one of the turnstiles but only 2 percent used another. Such behavior patterns are unlikely to be uncovered through interviews, yet knowledge of them would be valuable in the design of a new subway station.

In another alternative to interviews, practitioners may observe physical traces of occupant activities. Traces include evidence of erosion (wear) or accretion (something added to the setting). These cues might include worn carpet (indicating a heavy traffic path), graffiti and posters (indicating the degree to which occupants want to personalize their own space), or walls built of filing cabinets (indicating a need for more privacy). One advantage to studying traces is that thousands of hours of behavior observation may be compressed into a few minutes. Physical traces are the environmental psychologist's foray into archeology.

One example of a design oversight revealed by the observation of accretion occurred in Chandigarh, a modern city in India. The famous architect who designed Chandigarh did not take into account the residents' longstanding practice of hanging clothes out to dry. He was greatly dismayed to find, on a visit to the city, that his beloved design for a high-rise residential complex was largely covered up by clothes drying in the wind off nearly every apartment balcony.

Each of these three methods has its advantages and its disadvantages. Interviews allow the social researcher to query the user's opinions, feelings, and perceptions, but they may produce a distorted picture of the user's actual behavior. Observations may be time-consuming and expensive, but they can provide an accurate image of user behavior. Physical traces provide a capsule history of building use, but they may be insensitive to the needs or behaviors of individuals who use the building atypically. Obviously, the practitioner who aims to achieve the best program will employ multiple methods rather than rely solely on any one of them.

Sometimes the actual occupants of a setting that is being designed are not yet known. During the design phase of a new university residence hall, recreation center, or park, those who will be using it may yet be scattered across the community or nation. In their absence, **surrogate users** (Zeisel, 1975) or **consumer input** (Becker, in Sommer, 1983) must be studied. The practitioner must find the most nearly equivalent group of accessible individuals. In the case of the residence hall, residents of other dormitories on campus are probably a good approximation of next year's first occupants of the new dormitory.

User needs must be considered within the context of the new setting's social rationale. Knowing the future users and their needs will clearly produce more habitable structures. However, not all knowledge is of equal value. An Australian study found that when architects knew future occupants' spatial needs, they designed more appropriate houses for them than when they were armed with knowledge of the future occupants' lifestyles (Mueller, 1981).

Involving Users.   Another programming goal is **user activation.** Occupants may protest that they don't know anything about architecture or design. Some of them may initially care little about devoting time to the design process. The practitioner's job includes demonstrating to occupants that they needn't be professional designers to participate in the planning of the new setting and that there are good reasons to become involved in the design of their next work or living space. (See Fig. 12–8.) How can user activation be accomplished?

First, the practitioner can present users with examples of how other users participated in the design of their own facilities. Seeing that other nonprofessional designers were able to make valuable contributions can be a strong confidence-builder for users who think design is only for the experts. Users who already believe they can successfully participate become more excited about their own chance to contribute.

Second, the practitioner often becomes an **advocate designer** (Sommer, 1972). In this role, the social designer's goal is to actively serve the educational and political needs of occupants. This means supplying them with technical knowledge, teaching them how they might create their own designs, and representing their interests to the rest of the design team.

Some even see the advocate designer as a vehicle to remove the authoritarian character of the architect. Ultimately, this would help return the design process to Rapoport's vernacular model, discussed earlier in this chapter, in which everyone in the community works together on a project with little role specialization. This is unlikely to occur in technological societies but it expresses the democratic, user-oriented direction that some designers favor.

Robert Sommer has remarked that design assistance is often available in inverse proportion to users' need for it. The wealthy, who already occupy less stressful settings, can afford to hire consultants to improve them. Social design is "in part an attempt to reallocate design services to

improve the housing and neighborhood needs of the poor" (Sommer, 1983, p. 9).

User activation includes user education. This does not usually mean classroom-style lectures on design. It may include writing articles that speak directly to users, urging them to actively undertake design projects. One such article, written for office employees describes "the six basic steps in the design process" in straightforward, positive language (Becker, 1983). Another, presumably aimed at administrators, is titled "Employees Need Role in Design of Work Space" (Becker, 1980). Design education can even be successful with elementary school children. Children aged eight and nine were taught enough about design to produce an ideal classroom that was significantly better than children who did not receive design training (van Wagenberg, Krasner, & Krasner, 1981).

User education may also involve expanding the horizons of users by presenting them with a variety of workable design solutions. Generally, participants find it much easier to provide useful information if they are presented with easily understood choices, rather than by being asked "What do you want?" (Kaplan & Kaplan, 1982). Or, it may involve workshops in which occupants and designers literally walk through a typical day's activities to experience or relive the successful and unsuccessful features of the present design, or perhaps a mock-up of a proposed design.

In one such mock-up, social researchers investigating a design for a hospital room discovered a life-threatening flaw (Breu, 1984). During a drill simulating a cardiac arrest situation, a team headed by Janet Reizenstein Carpman found that one of two beds in the room could not fit past the other one; a patient experiencing a heart attack might lose valuable time while being transferred to intensive care. As a result of the drill, the designers enlarged the room to prevent the problem. In Switzerland, the Laboratory for Architectural Experimentation allows for the full-scale simulation of buildings. Using large but lightweight blocks, families working with designers can easily construct and revise life-size plans for their houses (Lawrence, 1982).

Another programming activity is facilitation of direct user participation in the design process.

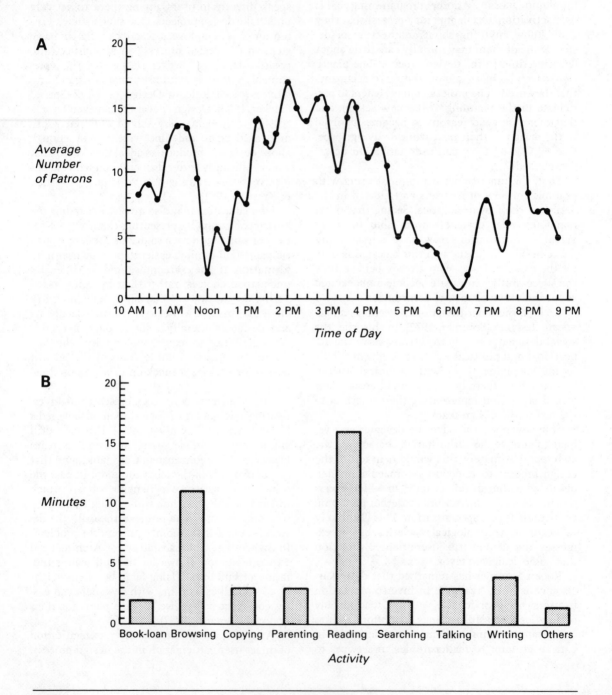

FIGURE 12-8 Mapping behavior in the postoccupancy evaluation of a new library. The environmental psychologist can pinpoint trouble spots and recommend changes that might alleviate the problems based on his or her review of the following information: (A) daily usage patterns; (B) the average amounts of time spent on given activities; (C) the average amounts of time spent in given locations; (D) the library floorplan; and (E) the results of a user survey (see p. 362). (Based on Ng and Gifford, 1986.)

C

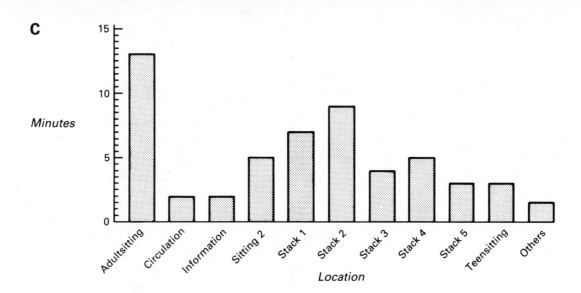

D

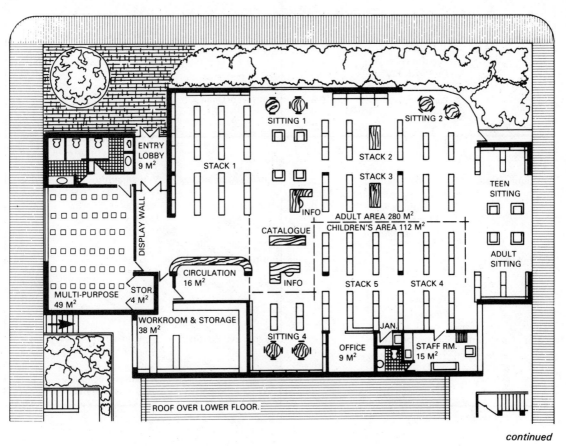

continued

FIGURE 12-8 (Cont.)

E

Evaluation of the library environment					
Item	Rating	% distribution (N = 126)	Item	Rating	% distribution (N = 126)
Lighting	Far too dim	—	Number of Tables*	Far too many	—
	Too dim	7.9		Too many	1.6
	Just right	88.9		Just right	48.4
	Too bright	0.8		Too few	37.3
	Far too bright	—		Far too few	0.8
Temperature	Far too warm	—	Table Size*	Far too small	—
	Too warm	—		Too small	29.4
	Just right	89.7		Just right	61.9
	Too cool	9.5		Too big	0.8
	Far too cool	—		Far too big	—
Ventilation	Far too stuffy	—	Number of Seats*	Far too many	—
	Too stuffy	7.9		Too many	3.2
	Just right	84.1		Just right	56.3
	Too drafty	2.4		Too few	32.5
	Far too drafty	0.8		Far too few	0.8
Sound	Far too noisy	0.8	Comfort of Chairs	Far too comfortable	—
	Too noisy	13.5		Too comfortable	1.6
	Just right	80.2		Just right	82.5
	Too quiet	4.8		Too uncomfortable	4.8
	Far too quiet	—		Far too uncomfortable	—
Amount of Space	Far too cramped	1.6	Outside Appearance	Very beautiful	4.0
	Too cramped	15.1		Beautiful	39.7
	Just right	77.0		Neutral	50.8
	Too spread out	2.4		Ugly	3.2
	Far too spread out	0.8		Very ugly	—
Ceiling Height	Far too high	—	Formality of the Building	Too formal	2.4
	Too high	—		Formal	11.9
	Just right	81.0		Neutral	58.7
	Too low	16.7		Informal	23.8
	Far too low	—		Too informal	—
Color of the Interior	Far too bright	—	Overall Evaluation	Very pleasing	42.9
	Too bright	1.6		Somewhat pleasing	37.3
	Just right	74.6		Neutral	15.1
	Too dull	18.3		A bit disagreeable	2.4
	Far too dull	—		Very disagreeable	—

* Items that were problematic

FIGURE 12–9 Gerald Davis and his associate Francoise Szigeti were among the first to form a successful consulting firm in the environment and behavior field. (*Courtesy of Gerald Davis and Francoise Szigeti.*)

User participation varies widely. Gerald Davis and Francoise Szigeti (1982) describe three kinds of programming in common practice. (See Fig. 12–9.) In **traditional planning,** a user-group manager makes a few sketches and tells someone to draw it up and make it happen or the organization's architect/planners decide what the users' requirements are for them and then work out a design. Users themselves are rarely consulted directly. In **direct planning,** corporate managers hire social designers to do the programming. Users are consulted more often, depending on the mandate provided by the corporation and the values and styles of the programmers. In **joint planning,** all phases of programming are accomplished by a coalition of professionals (architects and social designers) and users.

Frank Becker (1977) has provided another description of the range of user participation:

1. Users are not consulted at all.
2. Users provide information to a designer who then creates the design.
3. Users choose among already completed designs.
4. Users select and arrange forms provided by the designer.
5. Users create the project themselves.

When setting users have preexisting or newly enhanced enthusiasm for and confidence in the design process, they are ready for something more than the first of these options. Our basic assumption is that informed, motivated occupants can make significant contributions toward solving the puzzle of how to translate a social rationale and differing user needs into an actual plan.

In one example of direct user participation, the

FIGURE 12–10 An architect consults with client. *(Courtesy of Coe Gifford.)*

design of a hospital courtyard was studied (Carpman, Grant, & Simmons, in press). A table-sized model of the courtyard was constructed so that it could be taken apart and reassembled in different patterns. After showing many possible variations of the courtyard to over 200 patients and visitors, the social researchers concluded the courtyard should have densely planted trees, colorful plants, and seating arrangements that allowed for privacy or social interaction. (Which level of participation is this, in Becker's terms?) Many users, offered the opportunity to express their preferences among choices, are pleased that someone cared enough to ask and even happier when some element of the final design reflects their choices.

User participation patterns are very variable; they may fall between the levels (Becker) or types (Davis & Szigeti) described earlier. Some users may be involved but not others. In one project, a landscape architect, a child psychologist, social design researchers, and the staff (but not the children) of a daycare center worked together throughout the programming phase of an outdoor learning environment for preschoolers (Busch-Rossnagel, Nasar, Campbell, & Danish, 1980).

In another example of user participation, the emphasis was on setting design priorities in the context of financial and social constraints (Eisemon, 1975). In the Truax housing complex in Madison, Wisconsin, low-income residents were guided through a set of procedures for designing their ideal apartment. They were also faced with the necessity of trade-offs: "If the costs of your ideal apartment rose, which features would you sacrifice?" Using models, the residents were asked to begin the design process by assessing how their present apartment met their needs. The ideal apartment grew out of needs unmet by their present apartment.

The notion of trade-offs is central to an approach that emphasizes the user as an active design agent who is capable of adapting to some building features and changing others (Vischer, 1985). Merely determining the user's needs and preferences is to regard users as passive, unable or unwilling to interact actively with the building. (See Fig. 10.)

User participation has valuable side effects. Apart from the usefulness of the suggestions and contributions made by users, the *process* seems beneficial to them. Reizenstein (1982) provides several examples of social research projects in which users who were involved in the design process reported more satisfaction than, for example, equivalent users who were not involved. The positive glow from participation even seems to affect perception of the environment. Some office employees who received new offices that were smaller than their old ones were so pleased with their participation experience that they believed they had more space in their new offices (Reizenstein, 1982, p. 158).

Formulating Design Guidelines. The next major part of the programming process, although it overlaps with the activities just described, is the formulation of design guidelines. This phase of the process identifies, based on the foregoing analyses and various constraints, specific objectives that the design should make more likely to achieve.

Obviously, these guidelines are unique to each design problem; no comprehensive list will accurately reflect the needs identified by users and designers of any individual building project. Nevertheless, some needs are more frequently identified than others, and it is possible to list the commonest guidelines.

One such list was provided by one of the pioneers of social design, Fred Steele (1973). Here are six workplace design guidelines:

1. *Shelter and security.* This includes adequate filtering of weather elements (e.g., natural light without too much glare, fresh air without an office gale, etc.), adequate space, territorial control.
2. *Social contact.* A balance between too much and too little communication: privacy.
3. *Task instrumentality.* Person-machine and micro-spatial arrangements that facilitate work performance.
4. *Symbolic identification.* Appropriate workplace symbols to convey employee status in a positive manner.
5. *Growth.* The opportunity to explore and to learn.
6. *Pleasure.* Comfort, convenience, aesthetic appeal, varied but controllable stimulation.

Steele offers these guidelines as a way to specifically answer questions such as: Is this a quality environment for people? If not, what alterations would help? Many organizations treat physical space only as a factor that harms employee morale. Steele's guidelines include some that are concerned with positive notions like growth, identification, and social contact. The guidelines were developed from Steele's own observations of many offices and inspired by Abraham Maslow's theory of basic human needs. The goal was to create a broad manageable set of design guidelines.

A few examples of projects in which some of these guidelines have been established may be instructive. (In most projects, several to many guidelines are identified but we will focus on just one guideline for each example.) Inadequate privacy is a very common problem to be solved. In Chapter 8 we described the programming for a low-income housing project in Peru that revealed privacy to be the key issue for residents (Zeisel, 1975). The architect, Christopher Alexander, designed a **privacy gradient** into the new houses. The long narrow dwellings were arranged so that casual and formal visitors were restricted to the front rooms of the house, leaving the deeper sections of it for family and close friends.

Safety and security as a guideline is illustrated in a hospital design. Architects planned to surface parts of the courtyard with brick (Breu, 1984). Brick is attractive and other hospitals had used it frequently. But interviews at these hospitals revealed that patients with recent injuries or surgery found it painful to be wheeled over brick surfaces, which are often bumpy. Although the decision was not popular with aesthetics-minded designers, portions of the courtyard over which wheelchairs were expected to pass were redesigned with a smoother surface.

Comfort, physical or psychological, is another possible guideline. In the Swedish geriatric hospital project discussed earlier, the dining room decor taken from the 1930s and 1940s was familiar and psychologically comforting to the elderly patients.

Clear communication can be another guideline. In the hospital project discussed earlier, choices had to be made about language to be used on signs. Medical personnel preferred technical terminology; patients preferred nontechnical language. Clarity meant something different to the two user groups; in this case, the preferences of the medical personnel prevailed.

The clarity of signs can, of course, be studied experimentally. In settings used by people who speak many different languages, the search is on for pictorial representations that communicate well to everyone. In a series of studies in Canada, symbolic representations of public information messages were compared (Mackett-Stout & Dewar, 1981). Pictorial symbols meaning washroom, lost and found, car rental, information, and others were presented to subjects. Measures such as legibility, comprehension of the sign's meaning, and preference were used; because they were highly intercorrelated, an overall measure called efficiency was created from them. The efficiency index scores for the various competing signs were computed, allowing the researchers to make recommendations about which symbolic representation of each message was best.

One form of control, an important design guideline in some situations, is personalization. An issue in the design of dormitories, for example, is the provision of opportunities for residents to personalize their rooms with pictures, posters, and other personal articles (Zeisel, 1975). If control is deemed an important design guideline, dormitories can be designed to facilitate personalization. The architect Sim Van der Ryn suggests that nameplates on doors, walls lined with surfaces that can be taped, pasted, or tacked without damage, and movable rather than built-in furniture are a few ways to enhance a resident's sense of control in a dormitory room.

Design

In the design phase, the guidelines must be transformed into building plans. Because the design stages are not entirely separable, a few examples of design solutions to the problems of creating settings that fulfill design guidelines have already been discussed in the last section.

We must remember that building plans must reflect many considerations in addition to the design guidelines established by the social researcher. Constraints imposed by financial limitations, building codes, and siting problems are a few of these obstacles. As well, some design guidelines fail to survive the political process. It is important to remember that every setting includes user groups that have different and often conflicting needs and goals. To produce a final building plan that successfully integrates design guidelines, constraints, and competing user needs, a designer needs great skill and creativity.

The social researcher's job is to advocate as many design considerations benefiting users as possible. In the Michigan hospital project headed by Janet Reizenstein Carpman, over 500 design and policy changes were recommended (Breu, 1984). Had these research-based suggestions not been made, the architect would have been forced to make intuitive decisions. As it happened, because of constraints and the political aspect of design, the social research team only managed to get about 60 percent of its recommendations adopted. However, that means about 300 social

research-based improvements to a hospital that will play a crucial, if brief, role in the lives of thousands of people over the next several decades.

Construction

This is the phase in which social researchers play their smallest role. The architectural plans are turned into wood, concrete, glass, and steel. The designer oversees construction, making sure the plans are faithfully executed and that no gross oversights were part of the plans. Legends of rooms with no doors, stairwells with enough headroom for children only, and floors from different sections of the building that do not match keep architects vigilant. Minor problems are often corrected as the building is constructed.

The construction phase is not, however, totally without interest from the social researcher's point of view. One social architect, Lucien Kroll, saw an opportunity for participation even in the construction phase (Hatch, 1984). In a medical school project, Kroll insisted that construction workers be given a role in design. Rather than merely follow the plans in every detail, which can be an alienating, stultifying experience, Kroll asked the workers to take a more active role. For instance, they were asked to pick up beautiful rocks or other materials on their way to work and to line the concrete forms with them. Masons were given only a rough idea of the architect's plans for the brickwork and encouraged to do the masonry their own way. Hatch reports that happy, enthusiastic construction workers were bringing their families down to the project evenings and weekends to show them their personal contributions to the project!

Use and Adaptation

The building is finally occupied. The smell of new paint and furniture greets curious and optimistic new users. Very often the first days and weeks in the life of a new building are happy ones. The occupants usually have moved from older, perhaps cramped quarters with cranky heating or cooling systems. The new building is a pleasant novelty.

Gradually, however, strange events occur. A middle manager who moved from small but enclosed offices to a spacious open-plan setting is grouchy. A receptionist who brought in a poster of Greece to put up near her desk is forbidden to do so; the poster does not fit the new image of the organization that the decor is supposed to communicate to clients. A clerk notices that windows don't open; his allergies are acting up inside the building. Cynical graffiti about the "wonderful" new building begins to appear on the bathroom walls. Top management, sensing problems, begins to think of the employees as ungrateful for the large expenditure represented by the construction of the new setting. (See Fig. 12–11.)

This is, for the designer, the period of reality testing (Zeisel, 1975). Building programs are unlikely to anticipate all the needs of all the users. However, the social researcher may observe the extent to which the building is used as the program intended and adapted by users in unexpected ways. Programs should be explicit enough to be tested (Kaye, 1975).

If the program was successfully incorporated into the building's plans, patterns of behavior that indicate achievement of the desired goals should be in evidence. Generally, odd adaptations of the building reflect a failure of the plans to embody the program goals, or that a user's needs never were included in the program itself. One example would be the teacher who, without training in open education, is placed in an open classroom. The teacher may harness all available materials, such as bookcases, desks, and filing cabinets, to construct makeshift barriers against neighboring classes in the open space.

FIGURE 12–11 When buildings are inadequate because their original design was unsuitable or because technology has outstripped them, employees must improvise adaptations. This woman has fashioned a shield for her video display terminal to cut glare. In the background, a Telex machine is covered with a blanket to cut the noise.

Research in this phase of the design process is not common, although perhaps it is more accurate to say it usually is lumped together with the next phase, postoccupancy evaluation. Strictly speaking, research in the use-and-evaluation phase is a nonevaluative look at how occupants use their building. But it is difficult to observe behavior without drawing conclusions about whether the building is successful or not in achieving the goals of the program. Because evaluation is an important explicit or implicit aim of many social-design research projects, many more postoccupancy evaluation studies have been done.

Postoccupancy Evaluation

The final stage of the design process is **postoccupancy evaluation** (POE). Of course, due to the cyclical nature of the process, this "final" stage may be the prelude to the design of another building.

The POE is "an examination of the effectiveness for human users of occupied designed environments" (Zimring & Reizenstein, 1980). It must be distinguished from the practice of architectural criticism, which emphasizes aesthetic criteria and is usually done by a single architectural expert who uses methods that are based primarily on his or her insight and artistic taste (Zimring & Reizenstein, 1981). In contrast, the social design research approach uses the program or occupant needs as the criteria by which the building is judged, bases its conclusions on user impressions, and employs survey and interview methods.

The POE must also be distinguished from appraisals of buildings that each of us makes on an informal basis every day (Friedmann, Zimring & Zube, 1978). We can vote with our feet by avoiding a certain fast-food restaurant or by seeking out an especially pleasant coffee shop. The POE, in contrast, is much more careful in that it should include all user groups, all important activities occurring in the building, and rigorous methods of collecting and analyzing data.

The POE is also different from most social science experiments, even though both aim for valid results. As Friedmann, Zimring, and Zube put it, "whereas social science strives to *control* extraneous factors, evaluation often *describes* those factors; whereas social science is most concerned with discovering *causes* for behavior, evaluation looks at *influences* on behavior . . . whereas social science aims to reduce the number of factors, evaluation often examines complex systems" (1978, p. 3).

POEs vary along four dimensions. The first is **size.** Some are small in the amount of resources invested: one student who spends a few hours interviewing only a few users. Others are large, involving teams of researchers operating over several years, with six-figure budgets.

Three other dimensions are described by Craig Zimring and Janet Reizenstein (1980). POEs vary in the **generality** of their results. Many POEs are designed specifically for one building; the social-design researchers do not expect the results to be applicable to any other building. Other POEs are done on representative schools, prisons, hospitals, or housing developments with the explicit expectation that the knowledge gained from the effort will apply to other buildings with similar functions.

POEs also vary in their **breadth of focus.** That is, some evaluations aim to study only one or two building characteristics, such as noise, space, privacy, or lighting. Other POEs attempt to study more characteristics of the building or even "all" important ones. These broader POEs often aim to capture the whole complexity of the building as an interrelated system.

Finally, Zimring and Reizenstein assert that POEs vary in their intended **application timing.** The purpose of some POEs is to provide useful information for a renovation that is scheduled to begin next month. Others may have no known date when the results are needed. The POE is performed as part of a program to collect information over the building's life span so that one day, when the building needs replacement, a wealth of valuable data is available to guide the designers.

POEs are usually considered tests of *building* effectiveness, but they may also be tests of *program* effectiveness (Zimring & Reizenstein, 1981). When construction follows a clear, testable program, the evaluation is essentially a determination of whether the program successfully identified the needs of users. When no program exists or can be found, the evaluation researcher must try to find the architect and, from an interview, determine what the architect intended to accomplish (Zeisel, 1975). If the architect is also un-available, the social researcher should attempt to discern what sort of values are represented by the building's layout to obtain a very rough idea of the program that guided the designer.

Examinations of buildings have been going on before environmental psychology existed as a separate field. British researchers, in particular, have been evaluating buildings for decades. One early study, by Joyce Brooks and Philip Vernon (1956), investigated the usefulness of a children's gallery in a science museum. Brooks and Vernon monitored overall attendance, used a stopwatch to measure how long children spent looking at different exhibits, charted the movements of visitors through the museum, and interviewed children—all good post occupancy evaluation techniques. They found, for example, that glassed-in exhibits were less popular than hands-on working models; many museums now feature interactive exhibits. Brooks and Vernon conclude their 1956 report with these prophetic words: "There is very great scope for further research—research which would be welcomed by most museum authorities."

Today, POEs are quite common. One review by Bechtel and Srivastava (cited in Sommer, 1983) discusses 265 evaluations of housing alone, and there are, of course, many POEs of other building types. Architectural organizations have begun to give awards for outstanding architectural evaluation projects (Moore, 1982).

The establishment of POEs as part of the official fabric of the building process stops just short of legal enforcement in the United States. In 1969, the National Environmental Policy Act required the preparation and public disclosure of environmental impact statements. Most observers think of the Act as referring to the natural environment, but it explicitly calls for an approach that "will insure the integrated use of the natural *and social sciences and the environmental design arts* in planning and in decision-making which may have an impact on man's environment" (my emphasis).

Friedmann, Zimring, and Zube (1978) report that the courts have increasingly interpreted the Act to include social as well as physical aspects of environment. Still, POEs are not required by law. In 1980, the U.S. Senate passed a law requiring them, but the bill died in the House of Rep-

resentatives (Sommer, 1983). Thus, although POEs are not required, they are becoming an increasingly accepted part of the construction process.

We turn now from the nature of postoccupancy evaluations to methods of doing them. How can we determine whether a building is effective for its users? The major methods are similar to those used in other areas of environmental psychology: surveys, interviews, observations of behavior as it occurs, observations of behavior traces (the physical effects of behavior on the environment, such as worn pathways or posted signs), and analysis of archives (records pertaining to building use). These unobtrusive methods, first discussed by Webb, Campbell, Schwartz, and Sechrest in a classic book (1966, revised 1981), are described as they apply to environmental psychology by John Zeisel in a book called *Inquiry by Design* (1981) and in other sources (Sommer, 1972; Zube, 1980).

In addition to these general approaches, some environmental psychologists have worked on comprehensive assessment instruments designed for specific types of buildings. For example, Moos and Lemke (1984) have developed extensive measures of the physical and social environment of sheltered-care environments that they have used to show how design changes affect the behavior of institutionalized individuals (Lemke & Moos, 1984). Farbstein and Wener (1982) have tried to create a standardized set of evaluation tests for correctional institutions. Robert Marans worked on a set of evaluation guidelines for settings ranging from single buildings to whole communities for the National Bureau of Standards in the U.S.

Great care, of course, must be taken to ensure that appropriate and valuable methods are used. This means that multiple methods are better than a single one, users should be involved in the development of the methods to be sure that important issues receive attention, methods imported from other studies or sources should not be used uncritically, and features of the experimental and quasi-experimental methods, such as control groups (Carson, Carson, Margulis, & Wehrli, 1980) should be used where possible.

Each POE is unique; questionnaires, surveys, and other methods borrowed from elsewhere must be scrutinized and revised where necessary to fit the requirements of the current study. One error, for example, might be to use a survey developed for secondary schools in a POE of a new elementary school. Although they may respond in good faith, the younger children may simply be not sufficiently developed to answer some questions about their needs or their behavior in the school accurately (David, 1982). Of course, when a series of quite similar buildings is to be evaluated, a standardized questionnaire or interview may be useable, and it has the added value of helping to build up a bank of easily compared design data.

▶ **In Sum.** The design process includes programming, design, construction, use and adaptation, and postoccupancy evaluation. Programming consists of three phases: understanding the needs of users, involving them in the possibilities of design, and translating their needs into design guidelines—goals the actual design should achieve.

The first phase involves discerning user needs through surveys and interviews, observing their behavior, and studying the traces they leave. If the actual users are unavailable, a surrogate group should be studied.

The second phase, direct user participation in the design process, increases steadily from traditional to directed to joint planning. It includes encouraging, activating, and educating users and involving them directly in the planning process. Social researchers often find themselves in a strong advocacy position, arguing for the interests of the average building user against the interests of other principal players.

The third phase, formulating design guidelines, requires that specific goals be set. These vary from building to building but a widely useful group of them includes the provision of shelter and security, appropriate social contact, positive symbolic identification, task instrumentality, pleasure, and the opportunity for growth.

Turning these guidelines into plans and reality is the job of architects and construction companies. The environmental psychologist returns later to monitor user behavior and adaptation of the new building. Postoccupancy evaluation examines the effectiveness of the program and design, using a variety of social science tools. As illustrations of this process, four examples are described next.

FOUR POSTOCCUPANCY EVALUATIONS

Hundreds of POEs have been completed. Most have one or more flaws; some are better than most. In this section, four POEs have been selected as illustrations because they show the diversity of sites, methods, and results that may be found among POEs.

Hospital

Frank Becker and Donald Poe (1980) were involved in the renovation of a hospital wing. Becker and Poe had helped hospital users of all types (patients, staff, and visitors) to participate in the renovation decision making. The changes made to the building (see Table 12–1) represented those agreed on through a consensus-seeking process, although financial and administrative constraints restricted the changes slightly. The effects of the changes were measured, using three methods, and the renovated hospital wing was compared with two similar but unchanged wings.

One method of evaluation was to measure changes in **organization climate,** or attitudes toward the hospital. The mood and morale of the hospital staff on the renovated wing increased dramatically after the design changes, in comparison to the mood and morale of staff who worked on the control wings. The mood and morale of the patients and visitors showed smaller and more variable changes in response to the renovations. The visitors even seemed to dislike the renovations. However, staff opinions may be more important in this case because they must spend the most time on the wing. Readers who are concerned about patient welfare will be glad to hear that their mood and morale also increased, although less so than that of the staff.

A second evaluation method used by Becker and Poe was a questionnaire directly assessing the environment. All user groups were asked to rate various features of the renovated and control wings. All user groups rated the changed features of the renovated wing as better than comparable features of the unchanged wings, although once again the staff was most favorably affected.

Finally, Becker and Poe observed behavior in

TABLE 12–1 Becker and Poe's Changes in Hospital Environment

Location	Changes
Corridor	paint walls and ceilings wallpaper sections of corridor remove diffusers from fluorescent lights paint room numbers on doors signs for nurses' stations and other rooms railing along corridor
Visitor's waiting area	paint stretched fabric mural rearrange seating different (used) furniture
Solarium (porch)	remove partition wall remove equipment stored behind partition put shelves in existing closet paint area rug rearrange furniture different (used) furniture change type of phone booth stretched fabric murals
Nurses' station	carpet shelves tack board paint
Nurses' kitchenette	paint stretched fabric mural storage shelves rearrange furniture different (used) furniture remove unused equipment
Alcove outside nursing unit	directional graphics paint relocate phone booth add (used) chairs and magazine table

From Becker & Poe, 1980

the hospital. The ward area receiving the most renovation was the solarium. Behavior mapping showed that on the renovated wing the solarium was used significantly more than before the renovations, but solaria on the control wings were used slightly less than before. Users were also observed in conversation. Postrenovation conversation increased in the renovated wing but was essentially unchanged in the control wings.

The postoccupancy evaluation by Becker and Poe is a good example of an intervention that began with programming and ended with evaluation of design changes. The results were enlightening because they showed which user groups seemed to benefit and which did not. Some results were unexpected, such as the negative reaction of visitors after they had been consulted about the changes. But that's how one turn of the design cycle goes, and anyone contemplating a hospital renovation should be able to benefit from Becker and Poe's work to make the next turn of the cycle even more useful.

Office

Robert Marans and Kent Spreckelmeyer (1982a, b) evaluated a government office building that won architectural awards for excellence. What they learned from questioning three user groups reflects one of the most fundamental findings in

environmental psychology: the perceived value of a setting often depends on the evaluator's relation to the building (employed in it, passerby, designer of it).

Marans and Spreckelmeyer believe that a POE should focus not only on the value of a building's nuts and bolts, such as lighting, noise, and parking space but also on its overall architectural quality or aesthetics. They therefore not only asked employees to rate the functional aspects of the building but they also asked employees, visitors, and members of the public to judge its overall architectural quality.

The three groups disagreed on the merits of the office building. Residents of the community and visitors were asked to judge both the interior and

FIGURE 12–12 The glorious exterior of Simon Fraser University near Vancouver, British Columbia. Visitors love it and the building has won several international awards. The architect was awarded the Gold Medal of the American Institute of Architects in 1985. *(Courtesy of Simon Fraser University.)*

the exterior of the building. Their average judgment was that the building was fairly attractive, or about 3 on a scale of 1 to 4. Employee judgments of architectural quality were less positive, averaging about 4 on a scale of 1 to 7. Closer examination of employee judgments showed that lower ratings were given by employees who had worked in the building longer (familiarity seemed to breed contempt) and that ratings of interior features of the building such as spatial arrangements were lower than ratings of general or exterior features.

This pattern of appreciation by judges with weak links to a building (visitors, passersby, and tourists) and dislike by judges with strong links to a building (employees and frequent users) has been found before. My own doctoral dissertation dealt with the architectural merits of a university campus that had won international awards and fame for its designer (Gifford, 1976a). Sunday visitors, strolling through its striking buildings, write adoring comments in the visitor's book. Photos from helicopters on sunny days depict the university's bold exteriors, which remind many viewers of Egyptian or Mayan temples. But students and staff, who frequently endure fog, rain, and drips in the gray concrete edifice, often find the campus cold, inhuman, and depressing. (See Figs. 12–12 and 12–13.)

In addition, as Marans and Spreckelmeyer point out, evaluations of all sorts, including architectural evaluations, are often influenced by external factors. When local newspapers report that a building has won awards, community res-

FIGURE 12–13 One interior at Simon Fraser University. Not all the interiors are as bleak as this, but students and staff complaints of grey concrete are based on views like this because they spend most of their time inside the building, not outside admiring the monumental exterior.

idents are likely to believe, *a priori*, that the building must be good. In contrast, employees whose job may be unfulfilling, boring, or worse— which is unfortunately the case for many office employees, especially in the lower echelons— may be inclined to negatively evaluate almost anything placed before them. To produce a good POE the evaluator must be aware of these possible biases. Another possibility is that a building is a chief cause of user dissatisfaction, so the possible existence of biases must not necessarily be interpreted as a reason for ignoring user evaluations.

Furthermore, users usually prefer some features over others, even when a generally negative pall surrounds their evaluations. In the office building studied by Marans and Spreckelmeyer, the single most important predictor of employee satisfaction was the amount of space in the employee's workstation, regardless of whether it was open-plan, bullpen, or conventional (walled-in). When workstation size was equivalent, however, employees preferred conventional offices to open-plan offices.

Park

Postoccupancy evaluations are not limited to buildings, but include all designed occupied settings. We must not forget that people spend considerable time in outdoor environments; these should be evaluated, too.

Rachel Kaplan (1980) conducted a POE of a small, newly built downtown park. She studied the responses of two groups: those contacted in the park and those who lived or worked nearby. A three-page questionnaire was devised that covered uses, satisfactions, and problems with the park. Kaplan found that the park is valuable not only as a place for typical park activities, such as meeting friends and eating lunch, but also for its conceptual importance (mere presence even if you don't actually use it). Certain subgroups value the park for certain activities. For example, those with full-time jobs in the area value it as a place to eat lunch, but young people value it as a place to meet friends.

In general, the respondents were very satisfied with the park (the average rating on a cluster of satisfaction items was 4.1 out of 5). One problem was special events such as concerts, which were judged as too noisy and too long by neighbors but occurred too infrequently for those who were employed in the area. The obvious solution, if feasible, would be to have more concerts and special events but to shorten them and to better contain their sound.

A sign of the times is that Kaplan felt compelled to describe her finding that the park was not rated as particularly unsafe (even at night) as "striking." The park is at the intersection of two major streets; traffic noise was a problem for some groups. But this is, in conclusion, a happy POE. Kaplan's study shows that an important aspect of the general satisfaction was contributed by the study itself. The POE item asking about the idea of evaluating the park received "overwhelmingly enthusiastic" approval.

Nursing Home

M. Powell Lawton has devoted his career to improving the environments of elderly citizens. In one study with two colleagues, he evaluated a 120-bed skilled nursing facility serving moderately and severely impaired patients with Alzheimer's disease and other organic brain syndromes (Lawton, Fulcomer, & Kleban, 1984). If ever there was a good example of social design assisting those with few resources, this is it. The POE was unusual and difficult in that the primary occupants could not be interviewed.

Another multimethod POE, this evaluation's aim was to identify changes in the behavior, well-being, and building evaluations of patients, staff, and visitors. A traditional nursing home was compared to a newer, prosthetically designed nursing home. The design goal of the new building, which contained many features aimed at enhancing patients' social and perceptual stimulation, was to compensate for their "massive physical, cognitive, psychological and social deficits."

The questionnaire was completed by staff and relatives of the patients. It covered many design details of the bedrooms, bathrooms, public spaces, and dining areas. The results were many and complicated, but a fair conclusion is that the new design was highly rated in comparison to the old one, with some exceptions. A hard terrazzo floor and the public-address system contributed to a noise problem in the new facility, for example.

On the other hand, changes to single and double bedrooms (from four-bed rooms), lighting improvements, and better-located staff offices were highly rated.

Lawton et al. also observed user behavior, using behavior maps and **stream of behavior** measures in which sequences of activities were recorded. One significant behavioral change was that the rate of visiting doubled. Patients were observed to engage in more meaningful activities and fewer pathological activities; in the new building they participated in more of the planned programs offered by the staff.

Patients were observed to look around their settings more, suggesting that the new facility was encouraging them to tune in to their surroundings. Patient social behavior did not increase in the new building, but that may be because their bedrooms provided more opportunity for privacy. That is, the total amount of social interaction did not increase, but the proportion of desired social interaction may have increased. Thus, although patients could not speak for themselves, the well-being of the new facility's patients—as well as staff and visitors—appears to have been demonstrated.

Postoccupancy evaluation is a necessary and growing part of the building process. With increasing experience, the methods employed by social researchers are being refined; gradually a knowledge base is accumulating that will be used to create more habitable buildings. Some problems remain. Observers have suggested that social researchers sometimes spend too much effort on data gathering and too little on ways to actually apply the knowledge (Weisman, 1983). Presumably, as design research teams are better supported, more time and effort can be devoted to all phases of the design cycle, including even more direct application of research findings.

SUMMARY

Social design is a building-creation process that emphasizes the active involvement of building users. The specialization of modern society has separated designers from occupants; some designers view architecture purely as an art. If buildings are to be very habitable, these tendencies must be overcome.

Because it requires some extra effort at the beginning of a building's life and because it calls for input from more principal players, the social design process has met some resistance. Some expect too much in the way of behavior change. The process unavoidably leads to some conflict although this can be useful conflict.

Social designers believe the effort is worthwhile; benefits to users, designers, and paying clients outweigh the costs—particularly over the long run. Social design is most active in programming (understanding and involving users and formulating design goals) and in postoccupancy evaluation (examining the program and design in action). POEs of a hospital, office, park, and nursing home are described.

SUGGESTED SUPPLEMENTARY READINGS

Conway, D. (1973). *Social science and design: A process model for architect and social scientist collaboration.* Washington, DC: American Institute of Architects.

Davis, G., & Szigeti, F. (1982). Programming, space planning and office design. *Environment and Behavior, 14,* 299–317.

Friedmann, A., Zimring, C., & Zube, E. (1978). *Environmental design evaluation.* New York: Plenum.

Hatch, C. R. (Ed.). (1984). *The scope of social architecture.* Toronto: Van Nostrand Reinhold.

Sommer, R. (1983). *Social design: Creating buildings with people in mind.* Englewood Cliffs, NJ: Prentice-Hall.

Steele, F. I. (1973). *Physical settings and organization development.* Don Mills, ON: Addison-Wesley.

Zeisel, J. (1975). *Sociology and architectural design.* New York: Russell Sage Foundation.

———. (1981). *Inquiry by design: Tools for environment-behavior research.* Monterey, CA: Brooks/Cole.

Zimring, C. M., & Reizenstein, J. E. (1980). Post-occupancy evaluation: An overview. *Environment and Behavior, 12,* 429–450.

Chapter Thirteen
Managing the Commons

Freedom in a commons brings ruin to all.
Garrett Hardin, 1968

It was moving day. Tom and Jane were at last able to move into the house his grandfather had given him. The excitement of having so much space and being together in it was almost too much. They sat among the cardboard boxes in the kitchen with friends who had helped them move, sipping tea.

"Well," asked one friend, "what are you going to do with this place after you're settled in? Build a swimming pool?"

"You're kidding, I hope," Jane replied. "Not only do we have barely enough money to heat the place, you heard the mayor's speech, didn't you?" The town's reserves of water were virtually depleted in the drought and the mayor had appealed to residents not to use any water except for drinking, cooking, personal hygiene, and a weekly bath. "We couldn't very well justify a private pool now," she said.

"One thing we will have to do," Tom broke in, "is put some insulation in the walls. I looked inside one wall and there was absolutely none there! I don't know how Grandpa lived through the winter."

"I guess you two will just have to keep each other warm until you save up a little!" a friend replied.

"Someday I'd like to investigate solar heating," said Jane. "We have a good southern exposure in the back. I heard there are low-cost loans and tax breaks to help."

"First we have to make enough money to pay taxes!" Tom said.

After a moment's reflection on this glum observation, one of the friends brightened up. "I saw enough bottles in the basement that if you took them all into the recycling place you'd probably be in the highest tax bracket," he laughed.

After at least 15 years of public debate, environmental issues are familiar to all of us. We are quite aware that on one hand some vital natural resources are being depleted quickly, while on the other hand there is an oversupply of undesirable by-products from our use of those same natural resources (automobile fumes and litter).

This chapter considers the psychological processes involved in managing environmental resources. What is meant here by the word "*managing*?" As a society, we extract, refine, use, and dispose of many natural resources. As individuals, our role in this process is primarily as users and disposers of processed natural resources. Few of us would seriously advocate an absolute halt to this process, except perhaps in the case of such nearly depleted resources as endangered species. This implies that we will continue to use and dispose of or recycle most resources. (See Fig. 13–1.) The term management here refers to the *rate* and *quality* of the individual's part of the cycle.

The rate of this process is often quantifiable; the quality of the process is often debatable. For example, if a resident of a drought-threatened town decides to water a newly seeded lawn, it would not be difficult, using a water meter, to identify the quantity of the resource used. But whether the resident is correct to use the water is not easily decided.

Another aspect of the word managing concerns *who* will be doing the managing. Certainly much environmental management is done by governments, corporations, and other organizations. Such management is performed at a *macro* or societal level. Environmental psychologists are usually more interested in the resource management behavior of individuals and small groups— resource management at the *micro* level. Of course both the macro and micro levels are important, but psychologists generally prefer to work from the micro level upward, rather than from the macro level downward.

As individuals, we are faced with our own resource management problems. To varying degrees, we monitor our personal use of resources, observe the effects that our usage has on the environment, and are aware of the usage patterns of other individuals. Our resource management decisions are based on all three of these considerations, and more. The crucial aspect of micro level resource management is that it sums to the macro level in mysterious, irrational, yet all-important ways. The subject of this chapter is this interplay between an individual's resource management and what the individual perceives others' resource management to be.

FIGURE 13–1 It isn't lovely, but this recycling center serves a valuable role in society. *(Courtesy of Coe Gifford.)*

After defining the commons and some key related concepts, we will examine some of the research strategies used by environmental psychologists to understand resource management. Then we will survey the factors which promote different management styles and strategies and discuss some of the theories about resource management.

The latter part of the chapter is devoted to three important cases of resource management: pollution, energy conservation, and recycling. The question guiding that discussion is this: If we are all so *aware* of environmental resource problems after 15 years of information bombardment, why is there still so much pollution and energy wastage and so little recycling?

WHAT IS THE COMMONS?

Originally the **commons** referred to a central open space in the heart of a settlement. The land was owned by everyone and therefore by no one in particular. Today, we would probably call such spaces parks. Anyone is welcome to use the space for picnics, sports, or just strolling. In the old days when economies were more agriculturally based, people also grazed their animals on the commons.

As long as there is room and grass enough for everyone, the commons is a tranquil place. In most commons, however, the day eventually arrives when someone's frisbee sails into someone else's softball game, a cyclist on a narrow path knocks over a child, or an errant football lands in someone's potato salad. In the ensuing discussions, the rate and quality of the offender's management of commons space will often be a hot topic. The offender of course will counter with the opinion that it is a free country, isn't it? The issue becomes freedom in the commons (Hardin, 1968).

Commons are established on the assumption that the supply of the resource can meet the demands of the community. (See Fig. 13–2.) In fact, eighteenth century economists like Adam Smith did not see the boundaries or limits that are inherent in commons. Each individual was therefore free to exploit resources as much as possible, because in exploiting the resource for his or her own benefit, the individual was allegedly guided by an "invisible hand" to benefit the whole community. If a farmer could grow enough wheat to make himself rich, he would also employ people to assist him, buy equipment, send his children to the university, and in other ways aid the economy.

An early nineteenth century economist, William Lloyd, was one of the first to see a problem with Smith's logic.

If a person puts more cattle into his own field, the amount of the subsistence which they consume is all deducted from that which was at the command of his original stock [of cattle]; and if, before, there was no more than a [bare] sufficiency of pasture, he reaps no benefit from the additional cattle, what is gained in one way being lost in another. But if he puts more cattle on a common, the food which they consume forms a deduction which is shared between all the cattle . . . that of others as [well as] his own . . . and only a small part of it from his own cattle. . . . Were a number of adjoining pastures, already fully stocked, to be at once thrown open and converted into one vast common . . . the stock [of cattle] would be increased and would . . . press much more forcibly against the means of subsistence. (Lloyd, 1837/1968, pp. 31–32)

The essential difference between the ideas of Smith and Lloyd is that Lloyd recognized that many resources are limited. According to the biologist Garrett Hardin (1968), in a desirable but limited commons individuals act in self-interest. Hardin asserts that a process called the **tragedy of the commons** begins. "Each man is locked into

FIGURE 13–2 This is what happens when "harvesters" have the mechanical power to take resources faster than the resource can regenerate itself.

a system that compels him to increase his herd without limit—in a world that is limited. Ruin is the destination toward which all men rush, each pursuing his own best interest. . . . " (Hardin, 1968, p. 1244).

Social scientists and philosophers now recognize that grazing land, as in the Lloyd-Hardin example, is just one of many resources that are limited and held in common. The same basic ideas apply to overpopulation, air pollution, oil, whales, buffalo, energy brownouts, water shortages, congested radio bands, food supplies, and many other resources. Thus a commons is any desirable resource held jointly by a group of individuals, from an office lottery pool to the oceans. Some of these resources renew themselves relatively quickly (grass for grazing or river water for electric power), others not so quickly (trees used for lumber) and some very slowly or not at all (oil, endangered species).

Hardin and like-minded thinkers believe that it is difficult or impossible for us to reverse our tragic path toward ruin. For example, Hardin rejects such technical solutions to the population problem as exporting people into space. The only thing that can save us, according to Hardin, is a "fundamental extension of morality." By this assertion, Hardin means that we must abolish the freedom of the commons and institute "mutual coercion, mutually agreed-upon." That is, society must agree, through laws and regulations, to severely limit individual freedom to exploit the commons. Hardin does not seem optimistic that society can accomplish this limitation because the individual's freedom to exploit resources is so deeply valued by many members of society. Hardin's provocative pessimism has spurred much debate and research.

Self-Interest and the Public Interest

What is a commons dilemma? It is the difficult choice whether to act in self-interest or in the public interest. We might paraphrase Hamlet: To get ahead or to cooperate, that is the question. In times of plenty, we might be able to choose both, but when times are lean we must choose between two undesirable outcomes.

Environmental psychologists have not accepted Hardin's argument that we will always act in self-interest at face value; they consider the is-

sue of how individuals will behave in a limited commons to be an empirical question. For example, we know that sometimes individuals do act in the public interest rather than in self-interest. Many individuals will walk out of their way to deposit litter in a garbage can, voluntarily limit the number of children they have, or turn down their thermostats. On the other hand, we can all recall occasions when someone did not do the "proper" thing. Laboratory studies (Edney & Bell, 1984) show that stealing from others in the commons is frequent. The question is *under which conditions* do individuals act in self-interest?

Each member of a limited commons has the choice of acting in self-interest or in the public interest. We can act in self-interest either by *taking* (drinking a cup of coffee from the office pot without paying, cutting down a protected redwood tree, or filling the swimming pool during a drought) or by *giving* (not installing a pollution control device on the car, deciding to have a third child in a densely populated country, or dumping household garbage along a country road).

In each case it is easier or more rewarding, at least in the short run, to engage in the self-serving behavior (simultaneously putting a greater load on others in the commons) than it is to behave in the public interest. In a limited commons, the public-spirited act is often more expensive, difficult, or time-consuming and less immediately rewarding than the self-serving act. This observation has led some observers to conclude that self-serving behavior is natural. If by natural these observers mean "unchangeable part of human nature," then most environmental psychologists would disagree. We assume that certain influences promote self-serving behavior and others promote public-interest behavior.

Before we survey the research on what conditions lead to self-serving or public-interest behavior, we should distinguish between several types of dilemmas.

Commons Dilemmas, Social Traps, and Social Dilemmas

Psychologists have approached the problem of resource management from two directions. One group became involved through their interest in choice, decision making, and rationality. Such processes are often studied using carefully devised games. The most famous such game, Prisoner's Dilemma, goes like this:

> *Two men rob a bank. They are apprehended by the local district attorney, who knows they have committed the robbery but who does not have sufficient evidence to convict them. The district attorney puts the two prisoners in separate rooms and makes an identical proposition to each. If either prisoner confesses and the other does not, the one who confesses will go free for supplying state's evidence and the other will be sent to jail for 10 years. If they both confess, they will both go to jail for 5 years. If neither confesses, they will both go to jail for a single year on some minor charge such as carrying a concealed weapon. The district attorney informs each prisoner that the same proposition was made to the other, and then the prisoners are left in separate rooms to think.* (Coombs, Dawes, & Tversky, 1970, p. 242)

You may wonder what you would do in such a situation. You might also wonder what the Prisoner's Dilemma has to do with the commons dilemma. The primary difference is that the Prisoner's Dilemma has two participants and resource dilemmas have more than two participants. And, of course, one deals with interpersonal trust and the other with shrinking resources. Despite these outward differences, Komorita (1976) has shown that the Prisoner's Dilemma is, in terms of the mathematics of decision making, a special case of the kind of resource dilemma we have been discussing. Psychologists interested in human decision making came upon the resource management problem while searching for a more general and realistic instance of decision making.

The second group became interested from their direct enviornmental concerns; these psychologists were looking for ways to study the self-interest and public-interest choices made by individuals in managing limited commons. Three identifiable streams of this second group are reflected in three terms: commons dilemma, social trap, and social dilemma.

The term **commons dilemma,** inspired by the thought of Lloyd and Hardin, was first used by Dawes (1973). (See Fig. 13–3.) It usually refers to

FIGURE 13-3 Robyn Dawes' influential work has contributed to advances in our understanding of social dilemmas. *(Courtesy of Robyn Dawes)*

the overuse of natural resources such as land, energy, and endangered species as a result of conflict between individual and group interests. The term **social trap** (Platt, 1973) emphasizes the temporal trap involved in succumbing to immediate rewards that have some built-in and gradual cost that eventually becomes very large. On the individual level, classic social traps are overeating and smoking. At the societal level, the use of certain pesticides are a social trap if they kill mosquitoes but gradually erode the ability of birds to lay viable eggs.

Although the individual and societal varieties may be found in the same social trap (overeating may harm the individual as well as deprive members of the Third World of food), they need not be. Messick and McClelland (1983) distinguish be tween temporal traps, to which an individual falls victim with little consequence to the commons, and social traps, a term they believe should refer only to individual versus group conflicts with consequences to the commons.

Dawes (1980) has suggested the term **social dilemma** as encompassing commons dilemmas, social traps, and even the Prisoner's Dilemma. The defining characteristics of a social dilemma are that (a) each participant receives more (or is penalized less) for a self-interest choice than for a public interest choice, and (b) the participants as a group benefit more if they all choose to act in the public interest than if they all choose to act in self-interest or **defect** (Dawes, 1980). In some social dilemmas, frequent defections result in the destruction of the resource.

▶ **In Sum.** We all manage a steady supply of natural resources that have been converted into products we use every day. Some of these resources come from limited sources called commons. A commons is a pool of desirable materials that may be harvested by a number of individuals or organizations that share access to it. Commons dilemmas occur when harvesting of natural resources may proceed faster than the resource can regenerate; individuals must decide whether to maximize their own gain or the gain of the group, including themselves. Social traps are similar but emphasize the time dimension; we are trapped as a result of the eventual outcome of yielding repeatedly to short-term rewards while ignoring long-term costs. Social dilemma is the general term for these conflicts.

RESEARCH STRATEGIES

Social dilemmas may be studied from several perspectives (Edney & Harper, 1978a). In one sense, behavior in the commons may be characterized as cooperative (oriented toward mutual gains), individualistic (oriented toward self-gain), or competitive (oriented toward self's gain *relative* to others' gain) (McClintock, Moskowitz, & McClintock, 1977). Second, they may also be viewed as a form of group problem solving (Mintz, 1951). Third, some researchers have focused on the formation of coalitions and the use of power in managing the commons (Rapoport & Kahan, 1976). Fourth, those influenced by Platt see the social

dilemma as a set of behaviors governed by reinforcements and learning processes. Social dilemmas are certainly complex situations that include each of these dimensions. How can the social dilemma be studied?

Field approaches are attractive but difficult and rare. Field *experiments* require that the experimenter have control of the resource and the situation, which of course can be very difficult to obtain. When a resource is in limited supply, the experimenter simply becomes one individual among many who wish to have it. Gaining a corner on the market in order to perform an experiment is even harder than merely obtaining a piece of the action.

Field *studies* do not require the same degree of control over the resource and the situation, but the price of this relaxation of the scientific rules is that a variety of explanations for the results must be entertained, because the lack of control allows many variables to potentially influence behavior in the commons. Without ruling out the possibility of undertaking field approaches in the future, psychologists have begun the study of social dilemmas by using simulations of social dilemmas. This is one of the newest areas of environmental psychology and relatively little research has yet been reported. A field study of collective choice dilemmas in a townhouse cooperative (Rubin, 1981) is one beginning toward applying these ideas to everyday situations.

Just as there are many variations in everyday social dilemmas, there have been many experimental simulations of social dilemmas. The rules and values of the resources in both real and simulated social dilemmas vary considerably. Sometimes the resource is renewable and sometimes it is not. Sometimes resource gathering is restricted to specific times and places, sometimes not. The number of participants, amount of the resource, and many other factors vary.

However, most social dilemmas share the following characteristics. First, if one participant acts in self-interest while others act in the public interest, the self-interest participant (called a defector) will receive the highest payoff. Second, if everyone acts in the public interest (cooperates), everyone will receive a higher payoff than if everyone defects. Third, if everyone defects, the commons is destroyed. Thus, defection is the most attractive choice, but each participant is best off if no one else defects, next best off if everyone cooperates, and worst off if everyone defects (Dawes, 1980).

Let's consider a representative simulation, one proposed by Julian Edney (1979). A number of participants sit around a large, shallow bowl. The bowl contains a dozen walnuts. The walnuts may be traded at the end for something valuable—money, concert tickets, food. The experimenter explains that participants may take as many walnuts out of the bowl as they wish at any time; there is no turn-taking. Before the participants knock each other over grabbing the walnuts, the experimenter adds one more piece of information: "If any walnuts remain in the bowl 10 seconds after the start, I will place that many more walnuts in the bowl."

Cooperation in this simulation may be defined in several ways. First, it may be the number of trials the group keeps the pool of resources from extinction. It may be defined as the total "harvest"—the sum of resources garnered by the participants. Alternatively, cooperation may be defined as the amount of resource left at any given time. These measures of cooperation are usually, but not always, highly correlated. As an exercise, you might consider the possible outcomes if the participants adopt defecting, mixed, or cooperative strategies.

An obvious problem with simulations is the suspicion that behavior will not match field behavior. At present, there is no evidence either for or against the validity of simulations. An important factor, if the exercise is to be a valid indicator of behavior in *valuable* commons, is that the walnuts or other symbolic objects have comparable value. Most studies conducted so far have offered limited payoffs.

However, it does not take a very large payoff to produce behavior which *seems* similar to what could be expected in a real, valuable, limited commons. For example, in a study by Dawes, McTavish, and Shaklee (1977) in which participants could win no more than $10.50, participants were so caught up in the dilemma that defectors were sworn at and unrequited cooperators cried, stormed out of the room, and told defectors they "would have to live with their decisions for the rest of their lives."

Other researchers with similar payoffs have reported equally strong responses. Bonacich (1976) reports that some participants threatened (jokingly) to beat up defectors, to destroy their reputations, and even to kill them! Thus, despite the lack of field investigations, the early work in this area may have reasonable validity. Studies using small payoffs may not generalize to everyday commons that contain very valuable resources but should at least apply to smaller, localized social dilemmas.

► **In Sum.** Field experiments on social dilemmas are nearly impossible and field studies are uncommon. Many simulations of them have been investigated in laboratories. Social dilemmas are very complex; simulations have taken account of a large number of the many dimensions inherent in everyday social dilemmas. Judging from participants' reactions, these may not be as unrepresentative of everyday behavior as we might think.

WHAT PROMOTES PUBLIC INTEREST RESOURCE MANAGEMENT?

Although a great variety of social dilemmas have been studied, with different rules and payoff structures, the fundamental question remains similar. Under what conditions will participants cooperate; that is, act in the public interest?

Because this area of research is so new, we are forced to draw some rather tentative conclusions. This is because the conclusions have been reached from social dilemmas with different structures; it is difficult to be certain whether a specific conclusion applies beyond the parameters of the specific social dilemma it is based on. Nevertheless, some conclusions have been reached under several different kinds of social dilemma and may be quite generally true.

The influences on commons management behavior may be placed into three categories. First, the resource: is it important to the participants, whole or subdivided, renewable or not, nearly depleted or relatively plentiful? Second, the participants: are they strangers or friends, are they few or many, old or young? Third, the ground rules: what are the relative payoffs for cooperation and defection, may the participants communicate with one another, are their choices made public, are they told something about the nature of social dilemmas or left to their own ability to understand?

Characteristics of the Resource

Importance.   As the value of the resource increases, the rate of cooperation decreases (Kelley, Condry, Dahlke, & Hill, 1965). This has been demonstrated only for resources with small values, but as we saw in Bonacich's (1976) study, individuals become quite seriously involved over very inexpensive resources. In a classic simulation study, Mintz (1951) asked groups of fifteen to twenty-one individuals to pull small metal cones from a narrow-necked bottle using strings that were attached to the cones. The commons here is space in the neck of the bottle. When there was no reward or punishment for removing cones, no "traffic jams" occurred. However, when there were rewards of only 10 to 25 cents for getting a cone out and fines of 1 to 10 cents for failure to get cones out, traffic jams occurred frequently.

What if your life depends on getting cones out? There is no experimental evidence, but stories of moviegoers getting crushed as they attempt to leave burning theaters suggest that cooperation declines tragically when the resource (cool, fresh air and space) becomes very important. On the other hand, in the absence of empirical data, the issue is not settled. How many times have moviegoers *cooperatively* and safely left burning theaters, but because no deaths occurred the item was not news?

Degree of Depletion.   If the resource is almost gone, will participants cooperate more than when it was relatively plentiful; or will they scramble to get what they can before the resource is totally exhausted? Watzke and his colleagues compared behavior in commons that were pure or half-degraded. The experimental situation was analogous to decisions to pollute (giving is the self-interest choice) rather than decisions to harvest (where taking is the self-interest choice). If a group of individuals builds cottages around a lake that is either entirely unpolluted or about halfway ruined, will they pollute the lake further, or not? The participants cooperated significantly more in the half-degraded situation (Watzke, Doktor, Dana, & Rubenstein, 1972). (See Fig. 13–4.) A later study replicated this finding (Rubenstein, Watzke, Doktor, & Dana, 1975).

Watzke and his colleagues note that these results are grounds for optimism; when we inherit partly polluted surroundings, their evidence suggests that we will cooperate. It is unfortunate that another implication is that when we inherit pure surroundings, we will not cooperate very well *until* things get bad.

In another study, Kevin Brechner (1977) examined a harvest situation (as opposed to the pollution situation) in which students worked for course credits. When fewer course credits were available in the commons, fewer cooperative responses occurred than when many course credits were available. This finding conflicts with the earlier studies. One resolution of the results may be that individuals cooperate more in half-*polluted* commons (those that have gone halfway from purity to death from the donation of pollutants, such as a lake suffering from acid rain) but act in self-interest more in half-*harvested* commons (those that have gone from a full complement halfway to extinction, such as an endangered animal species).

Whole versus Subdivided Resources.   If the commons is divided into portions, each of which is managed by a separate participant, will management of the entire commons be better than if no subdivisions are made? When the resource is land, this is equivalent to asking whether private property promotes better resource management. In one of the few field studies of social dilemmas, Acheson (1975) examined two kinds of lobster-fishing arrangements in Maine. In one arrangement, the commons is open; all fishermen operating out of a given harbor have equal access to the lobsters in the vicinity of the harbor. In the other, fishermen are organized into groups. Each group holds a clearly defined territory from which other groups are barred. In the subdivided commons, lobster management is better. There are more lobsters, the lobsters are larger, and each fisherman makes more money.

Of course, the Acheson study was done in the field; we cannot be sure, for example, that lobster stocks were equal for the subdivided and undivided commons *before* Acheson began collecting data. However, there have been some controlled laboratory studies that support the value of subdividing the commons. Robert Cass and Julian Edney (1978) showed that dividing the commons into individual territories improved management of the commons. Participants used the resource

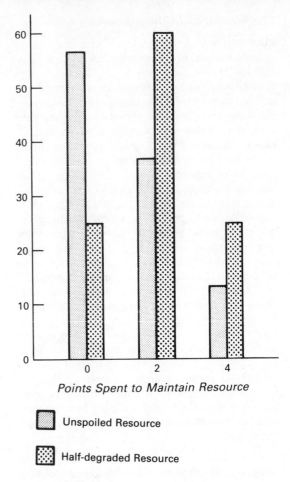

FIGURE 13-4 As the environment gets more polluted, it begins to be treated better. Swedish teenagers in a simulation spent more to maintain the resource if they were given a half-degraded resource than if they were given an unspoiled resource. *(Adapted from Watzke, Doktor Dana, & Rubinstein, 1972.)*

Subjects Choosing Each Option (percent)

Points Spent to Maintain Resource

☐ Unspoiled Resource

☐ Half-degraded Resource

in a manner that simultaneously earned them more and left more of the resource in the commons. This is the very definition of good resource management.

Cass and Edney suggest their results might be applied to energy distribution. If the total pool of electricity, natural gas, or gasoline could be divided into small pools controlled by neighborhoods or apartment blocks, there might be fewer brownouts and gasoline shortages.

Characteristics of the Participants

Group Size.   Nearly every study of group size has found that behavior in resource management tends increasingly toward self-interest as group size increases (Dawes, 1980). Cooperation de-clines both as the number of commons members rises and as the number of groups *within* a commons of a constant total membership rises (Komorita & Lapworth, 1982).

There are some good reasons for this. First, the harm from your defection is spread thinner among the other participants: no single other is badly hurt. Second, your defection is less visible to others in larger commons. Third, the effect of the harm done is less visible to the defector (Edney, 1981); it is easier to inflict pain if you don't have to watch the victim experience the pain. Fourth, negative feedback to the defector is more and more difficult to sustain in larger groups. Most commons in the everyday world involve, of course, large or very large groups.

Julian Edney (1981) has estimated that the upper population limit for a well-functioning commons may be as low as 150 members. This notion suggests that in larger commons (such as towns, cities, and the earth as a whole), Garrett Hardin's pessimism may be well justified unless some of the other factors, such as dividing up the commons, can improve management of the commons.

Friendship and Trust. As you might expect, as friendship grows, cooperation grows (Grzelak & Tyska, 1974). Because friends typically trust one another more than strangers, a logical extension is that cooperation is positively related to the amount of trust among group members (Dawes, 1980). Friends know one another's needs; they may draw upon past experience that probably includes some give and take; they have a stake in continuing their good relations.

Age. The ability to work together toward sound management of the commons appears to increase with age. (See Fig. 13–5.) Nursery school children are primarily "own-gain oriented" (McClintock, Moskowitz, & McClintock, 1977). Gifford (1982) employed Edney's commons dilemma simulation, described above, to study groups of three- to sixteen-year-old children. As age increased, cooperation increased. By age fourteen, groups in Gifford's study were harvesting up to 85 percent

of the maximum possible points while maintaining the health of the commons. At age sixteen, however, a drop in cooperativeness was observed. Edney's (1979) pilot data on the same simulation exercise with eighteen- to twenty-year-olds showed quite *low* levels of cooperation. Bixenstine and Douglas (1967) report a slight positive correlation with age in a similar exercise with participants in the eighteen to forties range.

It appears that up to age five, children are usually unable to grasp the idea that one may have to give up an immediate gain for a long-term gain and that from age five to fourteen children are increasingly able to understand both the value of cooperation and the other participants. Beyond this age range, although few data are available, cooperative behavior probably depends largely on factors other than age.

Sex and Personality. Three studies have tried to determine whether males or females cooperate more. In North America, females probably receive more socialization to cooperate than do males. In reasonably similar commons dilemma simulations, Vinacke, Mogy, Powers, Langan, and Beck (1974) found that females consistently cooperated more than males, but Caldwell (1976) found no differences between males and females.

A possible resolution of this discrepancy is contained in the findings of Meux (1973). Years

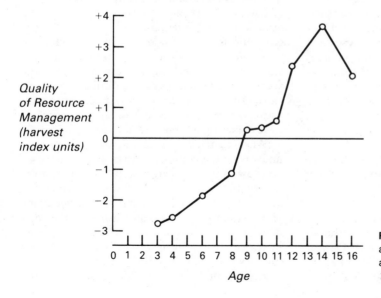

FIGURE 13–5 Quality of resource management in a simulation task by children ages 3 to 16. *(Adapted from Gifford, 1982.)*

before, Anatol Rapoport and his colleagues had suggested that in their experience with social dilemma research there are three basic personality types: the person who consistently tries to cooperate even when that strategy results in losses, the person who quickly settles into a noncooperative stance and refuses to budge even when others try to cooperate, and a third person who falls in between these extremes (Rapoport, Chammah, Dwyer, & Gyr, 1962).

Meux began by postulating the existence of a *1/Nth personality*—the tendency (similar to that discussed by Rapoport and his colleagues) to adopt public interest strategies. In her social dilemma, 1/Nth personalities did indeed act in the public interest more often than non-1/Nth personalities. Meux, like Caldwell, found no absolute differences between men and women. However, she did find that the *combination* of gender and personality affected behavior in the social-dilemma simulation. Males who were high on the 1/Nth personality dimension did not differ in cooperativeness from men who were low on it. However, high 1/Nth females cooperated much more than did low 1/Nth females. Thus, there are probably no sex differences in resource management behavior, but personality may be a key to predicting which *women* will act in the public interest.

Morality.

Certainly we might expect more cooperation from groups that have members with strong moral principles, are altruistic, or have a well-developed social conscience. We use such terms in everyday conversations, but psychologists are uncomfortable with them because they are very difficult to measure. Another problem with such concepts as explanatory constructs is that they tend to be circular. Why did Jane act in the public interest? Because she is an altruistic person who wants to have a clear conscience. How do we know she is altruistic? Because she acted in the public interest.

However, if we define altruism operationally in the resource management context as taking other participants' outcomes into account, it seems obvious that *some* altruism will be found. Few of us would accept $500 for ourselves with nothing for other participants if we had the alternative of accepting $498 for each of us (Dawes, 1980). However, there is not a great deal of altruism in such a choice (only $2 worth!). The question is *how much* altruism will be found in social dilemmas?

Dawes (1980) reports two studies that attempted to understand the role of morality without circular reasoning. The experimenter tried to *induce* morality by delivering a short "sermon" to the participants, mentioning the benefits of cooperation, public-interest ethics, resource exploitation, the sad case of whales, and so on. Compared to a group that received no sermon, the participants cooperated more. Edney and Bell (1983) also demonstrated that advocating either the Golden Rule or altruism produced greater cooperation than if no moral guidelines were advocated. It appears that morality can be produced, at least temporarily, by an appeal for cooperation.

Experience.

The work of David Messick and his colleagues shows that experience, in two senses of the term, affects the outcome of social dilemmas. Hypothesizing that members of groups have only a vague idea how their actions affect the commons as a whole, Allison and Messick (1985) reasoned that giving members prior experience *as an individual manager* of the commons would improve group performance in a later commons. This was confirmed. Prior individual experience was better than prior group experience in subsequent commons management situations. Presumably, in the simpler context of one-person management, individuals learned more about how their actions affected the commons.

Once in the group management situation, another kind of experience comes into play. This is our impression of how others are managing the commons. When several to many managers are simultaneously making harvest decisions, the status of the commons can be difficult to follow. Participants in another study were provided with various impressions about how their comanagers were operating (Messick et al., 1983).

When their experience was that others were underusing the commons, participants increased their own use of it, particularly when they were told that although the others were generally underusing the resource, some were harvesting often. When their experience was that the commons was being overused by others, participants increased their own harvests ("get it while you can!") when they had little trust in their comanagers, but decreased their own harvests when they trusted their comanagers. In general, managers of commons are more effective when they have solo experience with it and when they feel the commons is overused but they have trust in the other managers.

The Rules of the Game

In everyday life and in research, the ground rules of social dilemmas vary. Whatever the nature of the resource itself or the individuals involved, these rules will, in part, determine the quality of resource management. Some of these rules include the payoff structure, whether individuals may communicate, whether choices are public knowledge, whether feedback about the health of the resource is provided and whether cooperators may punish defectors.

Payoffs.   The fundamental characteristics of social dilemmas are that defectors gain more than cooperators when only a few individuals defect; if everyone cooperates everyone receives a moderate gain; if everyone defects all lose. But the specific amounts gained by cooperators and defectors within these general boundaries affects the amount of cooperation. Of course, if you wish to promote cooperation, you might increase the reward for it. In fact, if the reward for cooperation is high enough, the social dilemma is no longer a dilemma at all (Dawes, 1980). Unfortunately, managers of everyday social dilemmas usually do not have enough rewards at their disposal to change them into nondilemmas.

However, even within the definition of social dilemmas, increasing the reward for cooperation will increase the amount of cooperation (Grzelak & Tyska, 1974). Kelley and Grzelak (1972) designed a study which separately varied the size of your own gain (high or low) and the size of the common gain (high or low). They found that varying your own gain affected cooperation much more than varying the common gain. This study agrees with McClintock, Moskowitz, and Mc-Clintock's (1977) finding that individuals are "own-gain" oriented. However, instructions in the Kelley and Grzelak (1972) study were so complex that participants may have been own-gain oriented not because they didn't care about others, but because they could only comprehend enough of the rules to understand what might happen to themselves (Edney & Harper, 1978a).

This, of course, is very likely the case with McClintock's nursery school children too.

This lack of understanding does not mean the studies are invalid. Instead, we may conclude that when the rules governing social dilemmas are very complex or not obvious to the participants, which is often true in everyday dilemmas, individuals will give up trying to discover how to serve the public interest and simply look after themselves as best they can.

When the rules are simpler and the payoffs more group-oriented, cooperation does increase. Edney and Bell (1983, 1984) told their subjects that the group's total winnings would be divided equally among the participants. Compared to the usual payoff structure in which each individual wins as much as possible, more cooperation was observed. However, many participants in both simulated resource management exercises (Edney & Bell, 1983) and in real-world energy conservation (Bennett & Moore, 1981) do not feel that forced equality is fair. These, of course, tend to be individuals who prefer the individual-gain orientation to the justice-for-all orientation.

Outcomes for cooperation or defection may be positive or negative. One may receive a bonus of some sort for cooperating and/or a penalty for defecting. Komorita and Barth (1985) compared positive and negative payoffs and found that positive incentives evoked more cooperation than did negative incentives.

Communication.   A crucial question in social dilemmas is whether or not participants may communicate with one another. In everyday life, communication may not occur because (a) the participants choose not to, (b) they are forbidden to by superiors or governments, or (c) they are unable to because they rarely encounter one another. The choice not to communicate may result from self-interest in combination with good fortune, as when the old prospector discovers a gold mine or when the whaler finds one last pod of blue whales. In fish wars, an increasingly common social dilemma, governments may forbid fishermen from divulging the size of their catches to stave off international trouble. Those who poach orangutans in Borneo may not communicate because they rarely meet one another during their poaching forays.

In any case, the empirical research on this

matter is clear. When communication does not occur, management of the commons suffers (Brechner, 1977; Caldwell, 1976; Dawes, McTavish, & Shaklee, 1977; Edney & Harper, 1978a). Communication among group members serves a number of beneficial functions: clarifying the payoffs (which in some studies and in the real world can be complex), reaching agreements on harvesting (such as taking turns), reducing distrust, encouraging public commitment to cooperation (fewer members, in a public discussion, are likely to advocate defection strategies), and duty. The development of these "group-regarding motives" are seen by some to be a necessary and nearly sufficient condition for good management of the commons and group success (Dawes, Orbell, & van de Kragt, 1985). Group discussion may not only increase cooperation in the immediate situation but also the individual's tendency to cooperate in other situations (Orbell, van de Kragt, & Dawes, 1985).

In most studies, the experimenter simply allows communication or forbids it. Jerdee and Rosen (1974) tackled the issue more directly by including a confederate who was instructed to act in self-interest. When other participants were allowed to communicate, the selfish confederate's presence did not affect cooperation. However, when no communication was permitted, the selfish confederate's presence led to significantly more self-interest behavior on the part of others.

Another study suggests that communication may lead only to cooperation among better-adjusted individuals. Bixenstine and Douglas (1967) divided a group of university students into those who showed some signs of psychopathology and those who did not; only the normal groups benefited from the opportunity to communicate.

Public Disclosure. A slightly different kind of communication concerns the actual decisions made by participants: are they made public or kept private? Intuitively, we expect a greater number of public-interest choices when participants must tell others what they are doing. In a nondisclosure situation, the resource itself declines but the participants cannot determine who among them is acting in self-interest and who is trying to cooperate.

Cass and Edney (1978) used computer terminals to display the state of the commons to groups of four participants. When participants could see (by pressing a key on their terminal keyboard) how each of the others was acting, two of three measures of cooperation rose significantly. (See Fig. 13–6.) Other studies have also reported that public disclosure increases the number of public-interest choices (Bixenstine, Levitt, & Wilson, 1966; Jerdee & Rosen, 1974; Fox & Guyer, 1978).

Retribution. Caldwell (1976) designed a social dilemma analog in which participants were given the opportunity to punish those who acted in self-interest. After every set of five choices, the participants could vote to penalize others; if two of the five group members voted to sanction a third participant, the latter lost 5 points; if three voted to sanction a fourth, the loss was 10 points; if four participants all voted to punish a fifth, the fifth participant lost 15 points. It is not surprising that cooperation was higher when punishment by "armed cooperators" was possible than when it wasn't.

The Minimal Contributing Set. What if the commons exists only because enough individuals were willing to support it at the beginning? So far we have examined only preexisting commons, but some resources such as public works projects (a parent-constructed neighborhood playground or marshland enhancement by duck-hunting clubs) come into being only if enough group members work together to make it happen.

In these "public goods" problems (van de Kragt, Orbell, & Dawes, 1983) research participants are told that they will benefit (double their money) if a certain proportion of the group contributes. One reason not to contribute is that if enough other members contribute, the whole group is given the doubled contribution—even those in the group who did not provide an initial contribution. This is analogous to the situation in which neighborhood parents construct a playground and the children of parents who did not help are nevertheless allowed to play on it.

When a minimal contributing set is required, the public good is better served than when it is not (Dawes, Orbell, & van de Kragt, 1985). However, it is not served particularly well. Some groups do fail to reach the minimal contribution level and others overcontribute (too many cooks can spoil the broth and too many volunteers at a

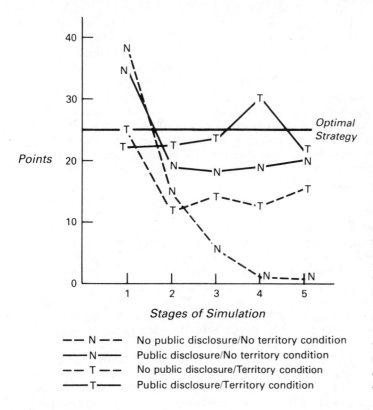

FIGURE 13-6 The effects of resource visibility and territories on harvesting. In computer simulation tasks, study participants earned points by "harvesting" resources. In this simulation, moderate, cooperative harvesting yields many points; rapid, competitive harvesting yields fewer. As harvesting rate deviates from the optimal rate, the outlook for the resource worsens. Across several stages (3-minute periods) of this simulation, the most favorable harvesting rates occurred when the resource was visible *and* territories existed. *(From Cass & Edney,* Human Ecology, *1978, 6, p. 379. Copyright © 1978. Plenum Publishing Corp. Reprinted by permission of Plenum Corp.)*

playground construction site can get in one another's way). When the minimal contributing set is combined with group discussion, however, the public good is served in a nearly optimal way (van de Kragt, Orbell, & Dawes, 1983).

What to Do?

Based on the findings to date, we could assemble a tentative set of recommendations that would lead to more socially responsible management of the commons. (In fact, this list follows shortly.) Quickly, however, it becomes apparent that "we" may not have enough control over the whole enterprise to effect such changes. In their laboratories, environmental psychologists are nearly omnipotent; in the everyday world they are nearly powerless. If environmental psychologists had real power, they could simply remove the dilemma entirely by changing the payoffs so that cooperation pays better than defection. What to do?

Short of resignation, we can advocate that someone be appointed as dictator, hoping that the power will be used in a benevolent way (Hardin, 1968; Ophuls, 1973). Others, influenced by behaviorists might advocate a sort of Walden Two (a fictional utopia invented by B. F. Skinner) where public-interest behavior is positively reinforced. Or we might try to use the existing governmental framework to lobby for legislative enactment of the recommendations. Some things (friendship and trust, for example) are difficult to legislate. Perhaps the central problem is an ancient one: how to allocate resources in the first place (Edney, 1981). This is, in the broadest and deepest sense of politics, a political question. Because society may be viewed as a system for distributing resources, how should society be run? For example, some proposed solutions to commons dilemmas require a centralized authority to manage them, but increased centralization is not popular with everyone. Fox (1985) has argued that perhaps greater decentralization would improve management of the commons.

Perhaps the best place to begin understanding

social dilemmas (which itself is a beginning toward overcoming them) is in the arena of theory. Several of the major theories of social dilemmas recognize the political nature of the social dilemma. We turn next to those theories.

► **In Sum.** The quality of resource management depends on (a) the resource itself, (b) characteristics of participants and (c) the rules of the game. Cooperation seems to decline as the importance of the resource increases and to improve as the resource is depleted—two ominous signs. As children develop, their ability to manage commons dilemmas increases.

We might advocate that, when a commons dilemma exists, part of the resource should be allocated to each participant to manage, that friendship and trust should be encouraged among the participants, that the total number of participants be kept small. In addition, we might advocate that participants should communicate, make public choices, and be subject to punishment for selfish decisions although positive incentives for cooperation are even more effective. Further, we should give individuals experience operating the commons, require minimal contributing sets where they are suitable, and point out the benefits of altruism in the commons. Last but certainly not least, we should try to increase the payoff for cooperation if possible.

THEORIES OF SOCIAL DILEMMAS

Although we have now reviewed some of the major influences on individual choice in the commons, we have not yet examined the larger perspectives that attempt to integrate knowledge about social dilemmas. In this section we briefly review five theories of the social dilemma: tragic-choice theory, game theory, social-trap theory, equity theory, and limited-processing theory. Julian Edney (1981) and Robyn Dawes (1980) have been most responsible for collating and interpreting these theories as they apply to social dilemmas.

Tragic Choice Theory

Most of us would prefer a world without social dilemmas. The dream of sufficient food, land, and energy for everyone is very attractive. Yet when we look around, we see that whether or not there are actually enough resources for everyone, existing resources clearly are not equally allocated. Tragic choice theory (Calabresi & Bobbitt, 1978) is largely phrased in terms we have called macro- (societal-) level decision making. However, many of the concepts in it may be extended to the micro (small group or individual) level. The theory begins with the fundamental assumption that this inequality and the resulting scarcity and suffering is natural and therefore nearly impossible to change.

Tragic choice theory offers an explanation of social dilemmas that is very controversial and not pleasant to hear. In fact, the theory itself predicts that we will not be receptive to it because, according to the theory, some widely held ideals are simply incompatible. In particular, most of us support the ideals of freedom *and* equality.

However, Julian Edney (1981) has suggested that these ideals are fundamentally incompatible; freedom means the opportunity to get ahead— that is, to be "more equal" than others. Hardin (1968) also asserts that in terms of resource allocation, democracy does *not* lead to equal allocation. Tragic-choice theory maintains that equal or more nearly equal allocation of resources is possible, but that it could only be accomplished by a much more powerful central authority than most of us would tolerate.

Tragic choice theory posits that scarcity originates in a conscious decision *not* to produce as much as could be produced; this is called a **first-order determination** (Calabresi & Bobbitt, 1978). One of the clearest examples of a first-order determination is the sometimes profitable decision not to produce as much food (such as dairy products and grains) as *could* be produced. Such decisions are reached in the interests of stabilizing prices, but in fact they serve to assist or enrich producers at the expense of other members of the commons.

These decisions to create scarcity are followed by **second-order determinations,** which are decisions concerning the distribution of the insufficient supply of goods. In contrast to the cry, All men are created equal, tragic-choice theory says it is unfortunate but true that our allocation policies clearly show that we do not value every person equally. To disguise the conflict between the ideal of equality and the fact of nonequality, various devices support second-order determinations (Edney, 1981). (See Fig. 13–7.)

One such device is to offer many and much-publicized resources to a few of the needy but not to offer resources to most of the needy most of the time (a wealthy philanthropist selects one worthy charity to benefit while ignoring other equally worthy causes). Some other devices used in various societies to deal with the allocation problem are the political approach (we hand decision-making power—and our guilt—to someone else), the free market approach (if those people really wanted a slice of the pie, they would work harder), and custom (we've always done it this way).

At the individual level, tragic choice theory predicts that we will engage in self-interest behaviors because we accept one or more of these devices as a justification for getting ahead by overusing the commons. The only way out, for Calabresi and Bobbitt, is to be more honest and aware of our relationship to the suffering of others. No specific technological or legislative solution is offered.

Game Theory

It seems a long way from the molar, interdisciplinary approach of tragic choice theory to the stripped-down, bare essentials of the game theorist's Prisoner's Dilemma exercise. Yet the two theories do apply to the same set of resource management behaviors. Game theorists try to make sense of the choices we make by reducing that choice to the simplest one possible. If a simulation is properly constructed, the experimenter can see very clearly what an individual means by each choice. The rich variety of influences and devices that may have obscured the intent behind a particular choice in tragic choice theory's molar approach are gone. If we assume participants fully understand the rules, their choices directly reflect their preference between the conflicting ideals of equality and freedom and their judgments of the other person.

Most simulations assume that everyone starts out equal and that the rational choice is to defect, hoping most others cooperate. Of course, this "power-tripping" is dangerous; it leads to disaster when others try the same strategy. Research indicates that defectors are also unpopular, although, in everyday life, defecting strategies are frequently defended as being realistic or even as beneficial to society (recall Adam Smith's invisible hand).

Cooperation, on the other hand, is more often socially acceptable, but it is also dangerous. Others may take advantage of you. This is where our assessment of the other participants becomes important. The essence of the social dilemma from the games-theory point of view is *trust*. With trust, participants maximize their *joint* outcomes. Without trust, defection makes the most

FIGURE 13–7 Second-order determinations lead to the familiar spectacle of poor people against rich backdrops. *(Courtesy of Coe Gifford.)*

sense, yet it will almost certainly lead to the worst outcomes for all when repeated choices are made.

Social Trap Theory

John Platt's framework is based on reinforcement. The problem in a social dilemma, from his point of view, is that too many of us reward ourselves. The social trap theory solution is to examine the reinforcement structure of the social dilemma and to rearrange the timing and the value of reinforcements to reverse the pending disaster. In some commons, this is not only a workable solution, it is one that is already working. Fish and game laws work reasonably well, for example. (See Fig. 13–8.) As another example, subways in Moscow are very tidy places compared to those in other parts of the world. In part this is because subway attendants who see some-

one dropping a cigarette butt will gently but firmly and, perhaps most important, *immediately* suggest to the litterer that such acts are antisocial and must be rectified.

A primary reason that commons are mismanaged, according to social trap theory, is that reinforcements for public-interest acts are not only smaller than those for self-interest acts, but they are often not *contingent* on the public-interest behavior; that is, they are offered long after the occurrence of the public-spirited act. Our only material reward for not littering, for example, is a tiny reduction in taxes at some distant future time.

However, as Edney (1981) suggests, some social dilemmas are even harder to resolve than littering, because the *values* of citizens differ. Even those of us who litter will admit that it isn't a good idea. But when not everyone agrees on values, delivering those immediate reinforcements

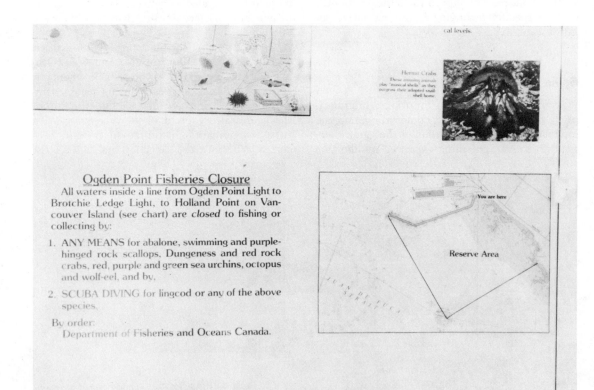

FIGURE 13–8 As this sign demonstrates, we already have a considerable official apparatus for managing shrinking resources. The question is whether the apparatus is supported well enough to be successful.

can produce sparks. In Victoria, British Columbia, an aquarium has lost five Orca whales in recent years. When it applied to capture more, the community was split on the value of displaying captured whales. The ensuing debate made it clear that there was no general agreement on whether capturing and displaying whales (presumably of some educational value) or leaving them in their open-ocean habitat (the natural thing to do) was the public-interest choice.

The commonest solution is to place control of the resource in government hands. There are two obvious problems with this solution. First, if individuals hand absolute control to a government, who controls the controllers (Hardin, 1968)? Second, if individuals democratically elect a government and the government begins to force public-interest behavior (by restricting the harvesting of fish or trees), it may be voted out of office in favor of a government that promises the freedom to harvest. Once again, if the commons is limited, defection will occur and disaster may ensue.

Platt believes the root problem is that there are too many people, rather than too few resources. However, some proposals for reducing the population are quite ominous (witness the holocaust). Even relatively benign approaches to population control are sometimes seen as morally unacceptable or as attempts by the First World to control the Third World. If we cannot reduce population, it seems we must dispense with either the ideal of equality (in resources) or the ideal of freedom. Influenced as he is by B. F. Skinner (author of a book appropriately titled *Beyond Freedom and Dignity*), Platt suggests that the one to sacrifice is freedom. Beyond freedom (in a benevolent but authoritarian political climate) lies the possibility of justice and equality.

Equity Theory

Equity theory focuses on the cognitive processes involved in sharing resources. In particular, it maintains that individuals compare their own ratio of rewards to investments with the ratios of others. Equity or justice is present when the ratios are equal. Note that like tragic-choice theory and unlike game theory, equity theory does not assume that individuals begin with equal resources.

Because equity or justice is the *ratio* of net rewards to investment (effort, skill, education, etc.), equity or justice without equality of resources is possible. For example, physicians are often forgiven for their much higher than average incomes because it is believed they have worked hard and continue to work harder than most others to achieve those incomes. Implicitly, then, equity theory claims that individuals are quite willing to tolerate resource inequalities as long as those who have more resources seem to have worked harder to obtain their extra share. Thus, equity theory proposes that what must be equal is the *ratio* between effort and reward or resources obtained, rather than that resources should be spread equally among all members of the commons.

However, equity theory does not take the limited commons into account; if there are too many individuals, all working hard, the pool of resources cannot provide all of them with just rewards. Furthermore, the original theory asserted that individuals act to achieve equity, but more recent writers have argued that many individuals will go beyond equity to maximize their own relative outcomes. Those who do so tend to develop a rationale to support the resulting inequity and, in fact, reinterpret it *as* equity (Walster & Walster, 1975). This contradiction is possible because of our ability to mentally "massage" equity into inequity and vice versa. The frightening implication of this finding for social dilemmas is that individuals may rush headlong toward destruction, completely convinced either that no social dilemma exists or that their own defection is actually cooperation!

Nevertheless, the important contribution to the understanding of social dilemmas made by equity theory is the inclusion of cognition. Particularly important is the theory's assertion that we have the ability to distort outcomes so that they *seem* equitable to us. Many individuals who by objective standards are victims of a social dilemma do not see themselves as victims. The musician Taj Majal once told a story about his mother. Sitting in her very humble living room, she watched a news story about some poor people in Los Angeles and remarked on their plight with some empathy. Taj Mahal reported that his mother was, in many ways, worse off than the people in the news story!

Limited Processing Theory

Dawes (1980) reminds us that many studies show that individuals do not, in many situations, behave in a rational manner. By this, Dawes does not mean we act irrationally in the sense of derangement. Rather, we often coolly and calmly act *nonrationally*.

There are two basic modes of nonrationality. First, we sometimes just do not pay much attention to what we are doing. For example, we may litter without any thought about the act. Thus, in a social dilemma, defection without conscious choice may occur. Second, we may act nonrationally even while possessing a general understanding of social dilemmas and an awareness that we are making a choice. This happens when the structure of the social dilemma is too complex for us to understand or when no one has explained that a particular behavior happens to be a defection. Consider the African villager who poaches rare rhinoceros in order to sell the horn for its alleged medicinal properties. This is defection from our point of view, but the villager may not understand or agree with our assessment that taking the rhinoceros constitutes defection.

Dawes suggests that much defection can be explained in terms of limited processing theory, and the way to overcome it is obvious. We must increase the awareness in offenders that certain behaviors constitute defection and that alternative behaviors will result in positive long-term outcomes. The complication is that defection sometimes harms one commons but helps another. The African villager who poaches rhino is contributing to the demise of an endangered species, but the money gained probably enriches the villager's family and community. This complication ultimately leads to moral and political dilemmas, rather than strictly economic or psychological ones. Some social dilemmas have relatively simple solutions—such as more education—but others are true dilemmas. There are no easy solutions.

▶ **In Sum.** Five theories of social dilemmas have been described. (1) Tragic choice theory maintains that self interest cannot be overcome except by the creation of a very strong central authority; this is unpleasant but necessary for the survival of the commons. Without such a central authority, the production and distribution of resources will be organized so as to benefit the wealthy at the expense of both the poor and the commons. (2) Games theory is not really a theory *of* social dilemmas; it is an approach assuming that simulations place individuals in real dilemmas even if they are not real-world dilemmas. The value of games theory has been to clearly lay out the many complex dimensions of social dilemmas and to carefully investigate the effect of each one. (3) Social trap theory applies a reinforcement perspective to social dilemmas, suggesting that better management of the commons would follow from a restructuring of reinforcement timing. Like tragic choice theory, a centralized authority appears necessary. (4) Equity theory emphasizes the importance of perceived equality in resource allocation. Cooperation may increase if participants believe others are receiving goods in proportion to the effort invested, no more and no less. But this belief could still lead to the extinction of a commons. If everyone works hard and harvests just as hard, depletion will occur; if perceived equity is cognitively altered, overharvesting can be justified to ourselves. (5) Limited processing theory postulates that most individuals act selfishly, not because they are evil, but because the dangers of defection simply do not occur to them. Its solution is clear: begin by making more individuals aware of the consequences of overusing resources that are in limited supply.

We turn now to three examples of human behavior that represent everyday responses to everyday social dilemmas: pollution, energy conservation, and recycling.

POLLUTION: A SOCIAL DILEMMA

In the terminology of this chapter, the act of polluting is a defecting response. Most of us think of pollution as something produced by large, anonymous organizations, certainly not by ourselves. Some pollution is, indeed, produced from large plants and factories where no one person may be fairly described as a defector. However, a surprising amount of pollution is traceable to the decisions and acts of individuals. That is why pollution may be described as a *behavioral* problem, why it is reasonable to include pollution in a discussion of individual resource management strategies, and why so much research directed at pollution control involves attempts to change the behavior of individuals.

At the individual level, the kinds of pollution that are most relevant are automobile exhaust and litter. However, environmental psychologists have also studied noise as a form of pollution and visual pollution, the imposition of ugliness on the landscape. These forms of pollution are unpleasant but probably less important, both economically and aesthetically, than air pollution and litter. (See Fig. 13–9.)

Air Pollution

At least five myths about air pollution should be cleared up immediately. First, "air pollution is a big-city problem." A study that examined air pollution residues in the blood of blood donors in many rural and urban settings found that overexposure to carbon monoxide is common even in rural areas (Stewart et al., 1974).

Second, "air pollution is a relatively new problem." In fact, although it is worsening in some places, air pollution is considerably less now than it was 100 years ago in some industrial cities, such as London. This condition is partly because coal and wood are not used as often as they used to be in cities for home heating and cooking. One of the smokiest cities I have ever visited is Ankara, the capital of Turkey, where many homes use such materials. Incidentally, the growing trend to increased wood burning in North Amer-

FIGURE 13–9 A "give-some" form of bad resource management, as opposed to the "take-some" form exemplified by over-fishing or clear-cutting practice in the lumber industry.

ica may yet become a serious air pollution problem.

Third, "air pollution is an outdoor phenomenon." It is easy to forget that outdoor air circulates inside our home and workplaces; we normally don't notice the pollution inside because it isn't dense enough to see. Also, the psychological study of such indoor air pollutants as cigarette smoke and body odor is increasing.

Fourth, "air pollution may affect our *health* but not our *behavior*." It is true that air pollution has had drastic effects on health; in one especially bad month (December, 1952) the deaths of about 3500 individuals in London were attributed to air pollution. Sommers, Van Dort, and Moos (1976) provide an extensive catalog of health problems that may be caused by air pollution. However, many studies have shown that air pollution has distinctly behavioral effects in addition to the much-publicized effects on health.

Fifth, as alluded to above, "air pollution is caused by factories, not people." In fact, over 80 million tons of carbon monoxide alone are released into the atmosphere each year in North America from transportation sources; most transportation still involves one or two individuals driving a car (Rose & Rose, 1971). Incidentally these pollution figures, mind boggling as they are, do not include other common air pollutants such as sulfur dioxide, nitrogen dioxide, and particulates (tiny particles produced during combustion).

Air Pollution and Behavior. True experimental studies of air pollution are relatively rare. There are ethical problems; subjects who are willing to inhale carbon monoxide to advance scientific knowledge are understandably difficult to find. The existing evidence indicates that common air pollutants affect (a) the range of behavior, (b) basic psychological processes, and perhaps, (c) attraction, aggression, and schizophrenia.

When I was thirteen, I attended a school in such a polluted area that students were sometimes required to wear gas masks whenever they went outside. Try playing your favorite sport in a gas mask! Clearly, the first behavioral effect of air pollution is that your behavior is sometimes *constrained* to a narrower range than is desirable.

Second, excessive levels of carbon monoxide have been shown to negatively affect such basic cognitive activities as reaction time and arithmetic ability (Schulte, 1963), ability to judge time (Beard & Wertheim, 1967), and ability to detect changes in light intensity (Horvath, Dahms, & O'Hanlon, 1971). These alterations of basic behavior may not sound exciting to anyone except experimental psychologists with specialized interests in them. However, these basic behaviors are precisely the building blocks of such important behaviors as driving and problem solving.

A number of studies have attempted to discover whether high but realistic levels of carbon monoxide (levels characteristic of traffic rush hours) are associated with increased accident rates. As several studies show, individuals do not always *feel* any different when they are exposed to levels of carbon monoxide high enough to affect their performance. Owing to their lack of awareness that they are affected, they do not tend to avoid either the carbon monoxide or the affected behavior.

However, the evidence concerning driving accidents is not clear-cut; some studies report no relation and others show small but significant correlations between accident rates and levels of carbon monoxide on the road or at the place of work just left by the driver (Sommers, Van Dort, & Moos, 1976). The lack of clarity in this applied research should not be taken as proof that air pollution does *not* affect complex behaviors; the problems of conducting research on this complicated but everyday phenomenon may be obscuring its subtle effects.

Third, air pollution may affect social and interpersonal processes; the work of James Rotton demonstrating this was described in Chapters Nine and Eleven. Jones and Bogat (1978) found that participants who were exposed to a very common indoor air pollutant, cigarette smoke, were more aggressive than those who were not. A correlational study of air pollution in relation to psychiatric emergency room visits (Briere, Downes, & Spensley, 1983) reports that amount of air pollution is related to both the total number of visits and to the number of schizophrenia-related visits. Such data do not prove that air pollution drives you crazy, but they suggest that individuals who are having difficulties even in clean air may find that the slight performance decrements caused by air pollution are enough to throw them off balance.

Adapting to Air Pollution. Given its unpleasant aesthetic qualities and its effects on health and behavior, environmental psychologists have wondered why public outcries against air pollution have not been louder. For example, in preparing for the 1984 Olympics, Los Angeles began attempting to implement strict controls in an attempt to improve its Smog City image. But why did it take an event like the Olympics for the city to implement the controls?

There are two general answers: adaptation and perceived costs. It has been said that humans can get used to anything. (This assertion, however, is not true. In Chapter Nine evidence was presented that we do not adapt to community noise pollution). In most instances, air pollution increases gradually. This allows time for a population to get used to the decrease in visual quality, the increase in eye irritation, the small decrements in cognitive performance.

The Weber-Fechner law of psychophysics says that noticeable differences in the level of a stimulus change with the overall intensity of the stimulus. Robert Sommer (1972) applied this laboratory-derived law to air pollution: when little pollution is present, a small increase will be apparent to an observer but when much pollution is present, the same increase will no longer be noticed. The same principle may apply to all resource management situations. When the pool of resources is large, a few defections will go unnoticed, but when the pool is nearly depleted, a defection is very obvious. One piece of litter in a spotless hallway stands out, but one piece of litter added to fifty others will not be noticed.

A study of smog perception demonstrates this adaptation process in an interesting way (Evans, Jacobs, & Frager, 1982). Long-term Los Angeles residents and newcomers were shown scenes that differed in the amount of smog present. The long-term residents were less likely to decide that smog was present in any given scene. They had become so used to air pollution that they were no longer sure when it was present and when it wasn't. (See Fig. 13–10.)

A second reason for inaction is the perceived cost of action. If your job depends on air pollution, you will naturally be reluctant to struggle against it. What if the costs of installing expensive "scrubbers" in the smokestacks include layoffs, possibly your own (Wall, 1973)?

If the cost of cleaning up the atmosphere to a commuter is bicycling 6 miles to work through all kinds of weather, is it worth it? Public-interest choices are desirable, but how many immediate comfort losses will individuals absorb? Let's say our commuter, in a fit of public spiritedness, decides that bicycling is, in the long run, worth it.

"The grandchildren will thank me for giving them cleaner skies," says our newly converted cyclist, puffing as the rain begins to soak through. Just then, an officemate who lives down the street drives by, hits a puddle, and splashes mud on the cyclist's damp clothes. Equity theory predicts that our admirable commuter will decide that the burden of environmental responsibility is not being shared equally. Tomorrow the cyclist may take the car.

To both the adaptation and perceived cost problems, the concerned environmental psychologist has an answer. Implied in both equity and limited-processing theories, the answers are to increase awareness of the long-term costs of defection and to find ways to increase equity. The drastic long-term costs of acid rain, for example, have been dramatized in National Film Board of Canada films that received much publicity when exhibitors of the film in the United States were forced to label the films "foreign propaganda." It is true that changing behavior may require Herculean efforts on the part of concerned citizens.

Litter

A sympathetic plant lover once described weeds as plants for which no one had yet discovered a useful purpose. Similarly, litter may be considered material that is out of place. Much litter would be valuable if recycled or at least burned to produce heat or drive an electricity-producing turbine. Unfortunately, the material not only goes unused for such useful purposes, it contributes ugliness to a setting, and represents a portion of a huge clean-up bill. All this waste occurs because someone defected, acting in short-term self-interest instead of long-term public interest.

The tons of litter spread everywhere from the sands surrounding Egypt's pyramids to the peaks of North American mountains result from millions of individually tiny but massively cumulative acts of individuals. (See Fig. 13–11.) Environ-

FIGURE 13-10 A layer of smog hangs over the city.

mental psychologists are acutely aware that very small changes to the behavior patterns of individuals could literally change the face of the earth. What to do?

Educational Campaigns.   Over the last thirty years, vast sums have been spent campaigning against litter; the litterbug concept is now so well-developed that nearly everyone is by now convinced that littering is a negative act. In fact, younger readers, who have grown up with the litterbug idea, may find it strange to hear that several decades ago the act of littering was so rarely mentioned that the act itself was not really perceived as bad. In the 1980s, we all know that littering is undesirable, yet it remains a large and expensive problem. One conclusion is that the educational campaigns have changed *attitudes* but not behavior. Someone is still out there, littering away.

Consider the following scene, a perfect vignette of littering as a defecting response within the limited-processing framework. One day, while writing this chapter, I was trudging home along a suburban side street. I noticed a man tending his immaculate front lawn. Spying a tiny piece of paper that was cluttering up his carpet of green, the man picked it up and, all in one smooth and seemingly unconscious movement, threw it behind him into the street.

Clearly, the man did not spend any mental energy *deciding* to defect. Without malice toward

FIGURE 13-11 Unfortunately, a common sight in some places.

the commons, he cast his tiny burden from his own territory into the street, transferring the litter from self to society.

For a moment, I considered approaching the man to deliver a quick sermon on the principles of social dilemmas. Knowing, however, that he was a bricklayer and thickly muscled, I sighed and swallowed my words.

Experience suggests that most littering is reasonably well characterized by the bricklayer's mindless behavior. Had the social scientist instead of the preacher in me come to the fore, I might have interviewed the bricklayer on the subject of littering. The bricklayer probably would tell the interviewer that he thought littering was an awful thing to do. Confronted with the news of his recent act of littering, the bricklayer would probably say that one little piece of paper wasn't going to ruin the world.

If individuals litter without significant cognition, perhaps one strategy is to alter the litterer's cognitions. One unusual approach to this strat-

egy—changing litterers' ideas about *themselves*—is described next.

Attributions. Littering may change when we come to think of ourselves as nonlitterers. In the attribution approach to litter control (Miller, Brickman, & Bolen, 1975), Chicago schoolchildren were exposed to one of three conditions: education, attribution, or control. The education class was repeatedly told that they should be neat and tidy. The attribution group was repeatedly told that they were *already* neat and tidy. The control group was told nothing. After 10 days, unobtrusive observation of the children when they had an opportunity to litter showed that the attribution group littered least. This tendency was still present when the children were tested again after another 2 weeks. The education group showed a mild reduction in littering after 10 days, but 2 weeks later they littered as much as the control group. Thus, *telling* children they are tidy may reduce their littering. However, can you think of any ethical problems with this strategy? Other environmental psychologists avoid attitudes and other cognitions, choosing instead to work directly on the littering behavior.

Social Trap Approaches. Littering may be understood as a behavior that offers immediate rewards (ridding ourselves of a minor nuisance). The negative consequences are smaller and temporally remote. The bricklayer's tax bill would have to be computed to several decimal places to show the increase in municipal maintenance costs due to his paper-chucking that day, and he will not receive the bill for months. Few others would dare to reprimand him for his act (even me—and I was especially sensitive to the issue because I was writing this chapter at the time).

It is socially and theoretically preferable to find a behavior to reward than one to punish. Therefore, most social-trap approaches to littering have attempted to (a) deliver more immediate reinforcements, (b) increase the value of the antilittering reinforcement, and (c) reward the proper disposal of materials, rather than punish littering. In contrast to the limited processing approach, considerable research based broadly on the social trap approach has already been reported.

Scott Geller and his colleagues have pointed out that the behavioral approach may be applied five ways (Geller, Winett, & Everett, 1982). (See Fig. 13–12.) First, potential litterbugs may be dissuaded by strategically worded and placed **prompts** (signs, flyers, announcements, posters, etc.). Second, individuals may be reinforced for picking up litter that someone else has discarded. Third, the environment may be arranged in such a way that littering is discouraged. Two examples of this strategy are (a) to provide eye-catching trash receptacles or simply *more* of them and (b) cleaning up litter initially, on the assumption that subsequent passersby will litter less in a tidy setting (recall Sommer's version of the Weber-Fechner law). Fourth, reduce littering by providing models—admired individuals who demonstrate, by example, what to do with unwanted material. Fifth, and most obvious, reinforce proper disposal of trash positively and promptly.

To investigate the effectiveness of the first strategy, prompting, experimenters have (among other strategies) distributed thousands of flyers to

FIGURE 13–12 E. Scott Geller has tirelessly worked to promote good resource management from a behaviorist approach. *(Courtesy of E. Scott Geller.)*

customers of grocery stores, theaters, and fast-food franchises. Usually the flyer contains a list of relevant information, such as a list of today's sales, the theater's program, etc. At the bottom of the flyer is the antilitter prompt itself.

In a typical study, one of many undertaken by Scott Geller and his associates, seven different antilitter prompts were compared at grocery stores (Geller, Witmer, & Orebaugh, 1976). The most effective messages:

1. Asked for help in combatting litter rather than demanding it
2. Requested that the flyer itself not be littered rather than requesting customers not to litter in general
3. Suggested a specific location for the disposal of the flyer
4. Briefly suggested why the request was being made

This was the most effective message: "*Please* help us recycle. *Please* dispose of for *recycling* in the green trash can at rear of store." Compare this message with the *least* effective one, which sounds good, but yielded almost four times fewer proper disposals of flyers: "*Please* don't litter. *Please* dispose of properly."

When no prompt at all appeared on the flyer, about 5 percent of them were properly disposed of. The most effective message resulted in a 30 percent success rate. Therefore, prompts are effective and carefully worded prompts are even more effective. But even for the best prompt, 27 percent of the flyers were littered (the total is not 100 percent because some flyers were taken from the store and their fate is unknown). Prompts work, but they are clearly not a panacea for the litter problem.

The second strategy is to induce individuals to pick up others' litter. Although some schools and youth groups have received well-deserved publicity for antilitter drives, research shows this strategy is probably not the best way in general to combat litter. This is because it may be contrary to a principle of resource management that stresses the development of individual responsibility for our own actions. This strategy asks individuals to be responsible for someone else's defection.

In one study, Bickman (1972) placed litter on the ground near a trash can to observe how often passersby would pick it up and place it in the can. The experiment was discontinued when the experimenter gave up waiting for the first observation of someone picking up litter! In a subsequent study, Bickman tried to improve this dismal outcome by placing the litter so that walkers literally had to step over the litter (pardon the pun). This dramatic tactic resulted in less than 1.5 percent success!

In another study, an antilitter campaign conducted under the auspices of McDonalds's restaurants, litter was reduced in an eighty-block area of a small city by 32 percent (McNees, Schnelle, Gendrich, Thomas, & Beagle, 1979). This result sounds successful until we tally the total amount of litter picked up and compare it to the direct costs (such as free cookies, radio ads) and indirect costs (personpower) required to manage and promote the program. These and other studies indicate that spending lots of money asking people to pick up litter in general is a waste of resources.

What about the third strategy, altering the environment itself so that littering is discouraged? This approach appears well-suited to the limited processing idea because it doesn't require that litterbugs' attitudes or cognitions be changed; it simply makes it easy for them to mindlessly toss their garbage into the correct place. The basis of the strategy is that when individuals are operating mindlessly, the environment *does* almost unilaterally control human behavior.

Proponents of this strategy have experimented with many specific environmental design considerations (Cone & Hayes, 1980). Chief among these are (a) more trash cans, (b) attractive trash cans, and (c) already tidy settings. Simply providing more trash cans does reduce littering (Finnie, 1973; O'Neill, Blanck, & Joyner, 1980). However, the reductions are not spectacular. In one of Finnie's studies, placing one trash can every four blocks decreased litter about 7 percent compared to when there were no trash cans along the street. When a trash can was placed on *every* block, litter was reduced about 17 percent over the no-cans condition.

What about offering, if possible, an initially tidy place? The answer depends in part on the type of place, but for the most part, tidy spaces do remain tidier and litter does beget more litter (Cone & Parham, 1973). In a typical experiment, Robinson and Frisch (1975) placed flyers in the mailboxes of students in a college post office that was either "prelittered" or not. In the prelittered condition, 44 percent of the flyer recipients littered, but in the tidy condition only 13 percent littered.

The exception to this rule may be picnic spots and campgrounds. Crump, Nunes, and Crossman (1977) had prelittered and tidy sites waiting for picnickers. Instead of drawing *more* litter, the prelittered sites were actually *tidier* after the picnickers left than when they arrived. In settings where the focus of our activity is the environment (such as in campgrounds), we may pick up litter left by others because it interferes with our appreciation of and activity in such settings (Geller, Winett, & Everett, 1982). Another explanation may be that when someone takes over a space as their own territory (even temporarily), attempts will be made to improve its condition. More generally, both these results and those of Cass and Edney (1978) on dividing the commons into territories suggest that management of the commons is improved when individuals have a sense of ownership over a portion of the commons.

Environmental Design and Litter

The provision of more garbage cans decreases litter, but there is much room for improvement. One design approach has been to create striking or beautiful cans on the assumption that they will attract more litter than plain cans. (See Fig. 13–13.) Fancy cans are now in many parks and shopping areas. Do they work?

Scott Geller and his students placed beautiful "bird cans" representing cardinals and eagles in a large indoor shopping mall. For forty-one consecutive weeks they weighed the litter in the mall's six garbage cans. For two experimental periods, bird cans replaced two of the regular cans. The beautiful bird cans attracted 35 percent more litter than the regular cans they replaced.

Litter left on the floor was also counted. Less was found when the bird cans were in place than when regular cans were in place. Oddly, though, when the bird cans were in place, *more* litter was left on the floor in other parts of the shopping center. Why the bird cans attracted more litter, yet drove some litterers to the other end of the mall to do their dirty deeds is not clear. Creative environmental design can reduce litter, but more research is needed to clarify this mystery.

▶ **In Sum.** Pollution is a "give-some" form of social dilemma. Individuals or organizations cleanse their own hands but dirty the commons. Air pollution is one example; it is an old problem caused by individuals as well as industry that occurs in both rural and urban areas, indoors and outdoors, and affects our behavior as well as our health. Its behavioral effects are subtle but probably include constraining the kinds of activities we engage in, mildly impairing cognitive processing, and increasing interpersonal and psychiatric problems. Efforts directed against air pollution have been blunted by our tendency to adapt to it and by the high perceived cost of correcting it.

Litter is another form of pollution; it has multiple costs. Educational campaigns have sensitized most individuals to the problem, but too often behavior does not change accordingly. Littering is usually a mindless activity. Attribution strategies appear to reduce littering behavior but may be difficult ethically. Social trap approaches reliably cut 15 to 20 percent of litter, sometimes more. Five social trap approaches include prompts, reinforcements for picking up others' litter, reinforcements for properly disposing of our own litter, modeling, and environmental designs that make it easy to dispose of litter properly. A case study of the latter approach was described: beautified garbage cans were found to be effective antilitter devices.

ENERGY CONSERVATION: A SOCIAL DILEMMA

John Cone and Steven Hayes (1980) were walking through a married-student housing complex one day. They were studying energy conservation practices and had decided to have a look around the complex. Although it was a cold day, they noticed the distinctive sound of an air conditioner coming from one apartment. Investigating, Cone and Hayes discovered that the resident did not like the high temperatures in the apartment produced by the furnace, which was running full blast. To adjust the temperature, he had turned on the air conditioner!

Although government and industry are the biggest energy users (Stern & Gardner, 1981), residents have control over the disposition of many resources; behavior in the home can significantly affect energy conservation (Geller, 1983). Socolow (1978) has estimated that energy costs for typical existing houses and apartments could be reduced by up to 50 percent. The savings could, of course, be used for many purposes: to reduce the cost of energy to the consumer, to finance deserving social programs (perhaps more student loans at lower rates), and to ease national dependence on distant, tenuous sources of energy.

These savings may be accomplished partly by technological advances (in architecture, engineering, and physics), partly by changing the behavior patterns of residents (psychological approaches are quite effective when they are applied) and best by an integrated program including both (Geller, Winett, & Everett, 1982). A

FIGURE 13-13 A garbage can that entices contributions. *(Courtesy of E. Scott Geller.)*

comprehensive study of the energy crisis (Stern & Aronson, 1984) concludes that the behavioral side of residential energy conservation, including feedback, information, and modeling approaches, has been largely overlooked and holds great promise.

This is not to imply that changing behavior is easy. For example, perhaps the most important variable under the immediate control of house-holders is thermostat setting. One study found that for high-frequency resource management be-haviors such as turning down the thermostat each evening, the best predictor of future behavior is past behavior: those who *have* been doing it will continue to do it (Macey & Brown, 1983). One challenge for psychologists, then, is to get home-owners *started* in conservation so that they will continue to help conserve.

Another challenge is posed by the recognition that home energy conservation is affected not only by simple daily choices such as whether to turn the thermostat down, but by larger choices such as where to live and other demographic characteristics. In a nationwide study of actual energy consumption in Canada, Ritchie, McDougall, and Claxton (1981) found that energy use was predicted by climate, house characteristics (fireplace, fuel source, single-family versus multiple-family), resident characteristics (bigger, wealthier families with more members use the most energy) and attitudes (such as believing that energy conservation is important).

Further challenges occur when behavior-change programs are viewed by residents as infringements on their freedom, because they don't always fit easily into resident's lifestyles, and because they can be quite labor-intensive and therefore costly to mount. Despite these problems, residential energy conservation holds great potential for easing pressure on diminishing supplies of nonrenewable resources. The environmental psychologist's challenge is to discover ways to improve energy consumption patterns in homes inexpensively and with concern for preserving the home as a haven from excessive outside pressures.

Technological solutions to the energy problem receive more attention than psychological approaches. In many instances, however, all the technology in Silicon Valley, California will not save one killowatt-hour if consumer behavior does not change. Some of the methods used to promote energy conservation include appeals from authorities, educational campaigns, providing feedback about rates of energy use, and reinforcing conservation practices with money or rebates.

But before we try to change behavior, it helps to know *who* does and does not conserve already. Then we know where to aim conservation programs.

Who Conserves and Who Doesn't?

Although everyone has become aware of energy shortages, not everyone adopts home energy conservation measures. Even a generally favorable attitude toward conservation does not necessarily lead to actually turning down the thermostat, changing furnace filters, or caulking (Olsen, 1981). Even concerned citizens tend to adopt only conservation behaviors that are familiar and easy to do (Simmons, Talbot, & Kaplan, 1984–1985).

Sometimes energy conservation practices are adopted for a brief period then abandoned (Kantola, Syme, & Campbell, 1984).

Before we describe some strategies for accomplishing this, we must take note of a problem with research in this area. Those who *say* they conserve do not always actually do so (Kantola, Syme, & Campbell, 1984). Scott Geller (1981), for example, notes that among individuals who attended an intensive energy conservation workshop and generally emerged with increased concern about conservation and optimism that individuals can make a substantial difference in overall savings, few actually changed their behavior or their homes. In a subsequent home check, only 11 percent of the workshop attendees had installed a water flow restrictor and only 1 of 70 had lowered the water heater thermostat as a result of the workshop.

Geller does not despair of this situation; he simply recommends that conservationists focus on behavior instead of attitudes and that program evaluations consist of in-home checkups rather than telephone follow-ups. Unfortunately, it seems, respondents to telephone interviewers often confuse what they *wish* they had done with what they have actually done! Therefore we must be particularly skeptical of studies based on unconfirmed verbal reports of energy conservation behavior.

Apart from this consideration, who adopts energy conservation measures? One general conclusion is that relatively high and very low income earners conserve more. Consumers with relatively high incomes are better educated and better able to afford the initial start-up costs of some alternatives. Solar energy, for example, is relatively expensive to begin with and takes several years to repay itself; it is not very feasible for low-income or mobile consumers (Labay & Kinnear, 1981).

Very low income groups, of course, "conserve" in the sense that they have little to spend for either necessities (heating, cooling) or energy-gobbling gadgets. Therefore, in economic terms, the target of conservation programs should primarily be higher-income individuals who have not yet changed their lifestyle (these individuals are especially ripe because they already believe conservation is good but haven't yet been given a good push) and lower-income groups (who may require more persuasion about the need for conservation as well as some financial assistance or incentive to undertake renovations or improvements to their homes).

Apart from income, Dorothy Leonard-Barton (1981) confirmed the commonsense hypothesis that individuals who tend toward lifestyles characterized by "voluntary simplicity" engage in more conservation than do those whose lifestyle is not so characterized. Those whose lives have been directly touched by energy shortages, or believe their health and comfort are threatened by shortages, are more likely to take action (Olsen, 1981).

Another study shows that individuals who accept personal responsibility for the energy crisis are more likely to be in favor of individual-level solutions (thermostat setbacks, reduction of travel). Those who assign the cause of energy crises to causes outside themselves (the oil companies, government) are more likely to favor outside solutions (Belk, Painter, & Semenik, 1981). This is an obvious point but an important one. If we don't feel any personal responsibility for resource management, we aren't likely to believe that we can or should do anything about it either. In the terminology of this chapter, this can only lead to defection.

Finally, individuals who have in some way made public their commitment to energy conservation conserve more than those who have not (Pallak & Cummings, 1976). Obviously, if I have announced to my neighbors that I am careful to turn off lights in rooms I am not using, I feel pressure not to have them pass by and notice that every room in my house is lighted.

Shippee and Gregory (1982) decided to test the logical extension of this finding. If public commitment leads to conservation, will stronger public commitment lead to even more energy conservation? Shippee and Gregory invited twenty-four small businesses to participate in a conservation program. All businesses were told that there was a community relations component to the program. They might be assigned, randomly, to a mild commitment condition (their business listed in a newspaper advertisement thanking firms in the small town where the study occurred for their participation), a strong commitment condition (nearly the same ad, except that newspaper readers could tell just how much

each business had conserved or not), or a control condition (no ad exposure). The control condition produced the least conservation, as expected. However, the strong commitment condition produced *less* conservation than did the mild commitment condition.

Shippee and Gregory speculate that this happened because the strong commitment firms were placed under too much pressure and felt trapped. Whether these results might have been different with another form of strong commitment, perhaps one where firms had a chance to volunteer to be in a strong commitment condition, is difficult to determine. If we conducted such an experiment, it would be open to the criticism that those who volunteered were already, before the study began, set to conserve more than were those in a mild commitment condition. Public commitment leads to conservation, but care must be taken with the level of public commitment requested so that the participant's motivation is not stifled.

Residents who live in multiple-unit dwellings with a single electrical meter tend to conserve less. In many such buildings constructed before energy prices rose dramatically, only one gas or electric meter was installed for the whole building; energy was not expensive but installing separate meters in every unit was. Many landlords are thereby forced to include the cost of utilities in the rent, because they cannot easily compute how much each resident uses.

When someone else pays for your utilities, the temptation to defect is strong. If the air conditioner controls are closer than the furnace controls, why not just cool off the place with the air conditioner? In the case of residential energy, the cost is largely passed on to your neighbors in a manner that is directly analogous to William Lloyd's parable of the villagers and their cattle.

Thus, several characteristics of conservers and those who are philosophically inclined to conserve have been identified. More of this "targeting" research is necessary; for now, let's turn to the common strategies for changing the behavior of nonconservers.

Provoking Energy Conservation

Appeals from Authorities. In the scenario that opens this chapter, the mayor of a town facing a water shortage appeals for citizens to use less water. How well do these appeals work?

In the United States, the best-known appeal was one made by President Carter in 1977. Two studies seized this opportunity to evaluate the effect of the appeal. Luyben (1982) surveyed over 400 residents and found that 27 percent of the households had reduced their thermostats to the recommended 65°F. Unfortunately, Luyben found that those who had not even heard the appeal had lowered their thermostats too, so that the appeal itself appeared not to be the reason for lowered thermostats.

In another study, an energy conservation program was already underway when Carter's appeal came. An appeal from the governor came at about the same time. The investigator (Wodarski, 1982) was thus able to compare the existing program, which was behaviorally oriented, and the two appeals. Wodarski reports that Carter's appeal was much more effective than was the behavioral program. The behavioral program was then refined to include group meetings and more incentives. The refined program was more effective than the gubernatorial appeal.

In an experimental study of leadership, Julian Edney and Chris Harper (1978b) found that voluntary leaders in simulated commons dilemmas did not produce more cooperation than was found in leaderless groups. Generally, we would expect leadership—at least high quality leadership—to improve management of the commons, but the evidence so far is mixed. Leadership *quality* is likely a key variable, but no research has yet examined its role.

Others have noted that energy conservation behavior is partly spurred on by simple economic factors (Winkler & Winett, 1982). Appeals and other strategies to induce behavior changes in consumers must be evaluated against the change due simply to price increases. In a comparative review, Walker (1980) concludes that appeals from authorities are useful over and above economic considerations but not universally so. The response varies with climate and type of energy used in the home. Presumably, the appeal's effectiveness will vary with the attractiveness of the leader.

Educational Campaigns and Prompts. The most widely used strategy to promote energy con-

servation is to distribute pamphlets, letters, flyers, stickers, and booklets describing how one might conserve energy around the home. One advantage of this approach is that it is relatively inexpensive. A second is its "obvious" rationality: if we tell consumers how they can save money, surely they will take advantage of the information.

Unfortunately, the nearly unanimous results from numerous studies are that energy conservation literature does *not* have a significant impact on behavior (Cone & Hayes, 1980; Geller, Winett, & Everett, 1982). Researchers and energy agencies both have sent out millions of colorful informative items without, apparently, changing much behavior. These educational aids are not necessarily worthless, however. They may serve to "prime" consumers so that other intervention strategies will work better. They may change consumers' attitudes so that they are more favorable toward conservation, even if they don't, at that point, actually do anything about it.

Perhaps we need to start earlier, when consumers of energy are still in school. The U.S. government has placed about 140 Energy-Environment Simulators in schools (Zielinski & Bethel, 1983). These computers compress 100 years into 1 minute while students try to maintain viable sources of energy under a variety of conditions such as a cutoff of Mideast oil, the development of new technology for producing energy, and an increase in population. These simulators should help raise awareness of the problems involved in energy conservation and may foster increased conservation behavior.

Feedback. If we assume that a consumer is inclined toward saving energy, a basic principle is that providing feedback about rate of energy use will facilitate behavior change. Of course, consumers already receive feedback every month or two in the form of a bill. However, this information is often ineffective as a behavior-change agent because it arrives long after the behavior in question and it is too diffuse; consumers are usually unaware just which appliance or heater was used, on which days they were energy-extravagant or whether an increased bill reflects increased usage or increased utility prices.

Environmental psychologists who have investigated the effectiveness of feedback have offered energy use information to the consumer much more frequently—as often as once per day.

In a typical study, Seligman and Darley (1977) informed householders four times per week how much electricity they had used in comparison to an amount predicted for them on the basis of outdoor temperature and other factors. Compared to a no-feedback control group, the informed residents used 10.6 percent less electricity. Other studies of feedback have reported savings in the range of 5 to 15 percent (Geller, Winett, & Everett, 1982). The upper levels of these savings are easier to achieve when individuals are also asked to meet relatively difficult but voluntarily chosen goals—such as a 20 percent saving (Becker, 1978). These savings don't sound very dramatic until they are multiplied by the number of residential units in a whole country; then the potential value of frequent feedback, combined with goal setting, is clear. (See Fig. 13–14.)

Feedback may have even more potential when it is even more immediate. In pilot programs, various researchers have evolved their approach from one that hand-delivers a written record of use to one that installs a digital readout on the wall of the consumer's living room. British Columbia Hydro, for example, has tested a device that offers a continuous display of ongoing electrical use. Be-cause the consumer may lose track of the overall meaning of a continuous display, usage rates for the past day and week are also displayed. The computer revolution should make such feedback to every energy user entirely feasible.

Monetary Rewards. For many, the most effective behavior change agent is money. An obvious strategy is to offer rebates and other prizes for saving energy. The early studies of this strategy were full of promise. Individuals responded extremely well. Unfortunately, in their enthusiasm, the early researchers seemed not to realize that their prizes often exceeded the savings achieved by the consumers! Obviously, for any public interest strategy to have wide-ranging potential, the scheme must be cost-effective. However, research by Richard Winett and his colleagues shows that careful planning of rebates (the size of rebates in relation to the season and peak usage rates) can make monetary payoffs cost-effective (Winett, Neale, & Grier, 1979; Winett, Neale, Williams, Yokley, & Kauder, 1979).

Designing for Energy Conservation

Energy use patterns are relatively resistant to change. One study indicates that major Western

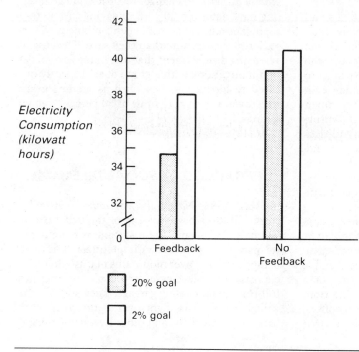

FIGURE 13–14 Daily average electricity consumption (adjusted for prestudy consumption rates) of townhouse residents who were either given feedback about the amount of electricity they used or not and were either given an easy conservation goal (2% reduction in use of electicity) or a moderately difficult goal (20% reduction.) Giving residents moderately difficult goals and feedback produces the most savings. *(Adapted from Becker, 1978.)*

countries reduced their demand for oil only about 2 percent from 1973 to 1980 (McDougall, Claxton, Ritchie, & Anderson, 1981). High rates of usage are part of the lifestyle of many consumers. They may not wish to change; if they wish to change they may find it difficult to maintain interest in an energy conservation program. As McDougall et al. point out, this leaves a great deal of potential for increased conservation.

The weather remains the single largest predictor of what consumers will do with their heating and cooling machines. Educational campaigns are convincing more and more consumers that conservation is worthwhile in the long term. Feedback and tailored rebates to individual consumers may help increase conservation by many small percentages that add up to large national savings. Research into newer aspects of energy conservation, such as field studies of adjustment to nonoptimal temperatures, modeling, and peak-load management are just beginning (Geller, Winett, & Everett, 1982). Research into the personal, social, and cognitive aspects of energy conservation is needed (Yates & Aronson, 1983). The promised savings of "up to 50%" may not be realized until (a) behavioral and cognitive approaches, (b) hardware improvements, and (c) economic considerations (Stern, 1984; Winkler & Winett, 1982) are integrated.

One way to integrate them is to build a small community composed of energy-conscious individuals and energy-saving houses. Michael and Judy Corbett are Davis, California developers who have gone beyond merely adding solar panels to the houses in their project, Village Homes (Corbett, 1981). Davis can be very hot in the summer; their designs take advantage of natural ventilation patterns to reduce the need for air conditioning. One ambient source of excess heat in some developments comes from broad expanses of pavement; in Village Homes pavement area is reduced by narrowing streets and clustering homes (Sommer, 1983).

Village Homes incorporates these energy conservation features into an overall plan aimed at ecological soundness. There are water conservation features, defensible space features, and a community-constructed playground. Parts of a preexisting orchard were retained; income from it goes into the homeowners' association coffers. The Corbetts reside in the development, so that assistance with technical problems is close at hand.

Energy conservation is not merely turning the thermostat down. It is part of a pattern of living that includes "voluntary simplicity" (Leonard-Barton, 1981) and environmental designs that make it easy to conserve.

► **In Sum.** Energy use is a social dilemma when it is easier to waste energy, particularly from nonrenewable sources, in the service of a short-term goal than to conserve it for the future. Up to 50 percent savings could be achieved in ideal conditions, which would include an integration of psychological, economic, and engineering contributions. Conservers include those with enough money to purchase energy-saving devices so they can save over the long haul, those who must conserve because they can't afford much gasoline, air conditioning, or fuel oil, those who have adopted a voluntary simple lifestyle and feel a personal responsibility for energy problems, those who are willing to make moderate public commitments toward energy conservation, and those whose energy use is *not* monitored with a shared meter.

Conservation may be enhanced by some appeals from authorities. Educational campaigns seem to change attitudes, priming individuals for changing behavior, but energy-use habits are relatively difficult to change. Feedback and goal setting have achieved 20 percent savings. Monetary approaches have a cost-benefit problem. They sometimes cost more than they save. The case of a housing development that integrated several design innovations with a group of ecologically oriented residents was described as an important step toward the upper limit of 50 percent energy savings.

RECYCLING: A SOCIAL DILEMMA

In April 1983, *National Geographic* featured a story full of garbage. Instead of the usual exotic and beautiful scenes the magazine is famous for, its pages were filled with pictures of human beings scuttling over mountains of trash. In many countries, whole classes of people are engaged full-time in processing garbage. They sort out the valuable materials, fight over rights to the garbage of the wealthy, and often live at the dump.

Not a very attractive scene. Yet the only difference between these people and you is that they work near the end of a disposal process and you work at the beginning. (See Fig. 13–15.) Each of us is curator of a steady stream of natural resources that has been transformed into usable goods. Of course, most of us do not realize this; we just think we are throwing out the garbage. Yet it is true that many times daily each of us decides how to manage the flow of paper, glass, metal, food, water, and oil that comes to us so routinely. In North America, most of these products are discarded into unsorted general garbage, to be collected, transported, crushed, burned, and bulldozed at a cost of over $6 billion each year (Purcell, 1981).

In the language of this chapter, the public-interest choice is to find ways to *reuse* resources, not to toss them into messy unsorted piles. The key to managing resources in the public interest is to change this common practice of having a single bag or can for throwing away anything no longer wanted.

There are two forms of what is technically called **resource recovery: recycling** occurs when waste material is processed to re-create the original product and **reclamation** occurs when the waste material is processed to create a different product (Geller, Winett, & Everett, 1982). Recycled paper may go from being a sheet of paper to being a shopping bag. Reclaimed tires have recently been used as an ingredient in paving mixes for airport runways and for streets. Apparently, bits of tire help prevent cracking during cold weather.

Technical Problem or Human Problem?

Resource recovery may be viewed either as a technical problem or as a behavioral problem. The technical approaches tend to allow consumers to send in mixed garbage in the present manner; the separation and recovery of materials is done at a central plant. Such high-technology solutions tend to maximize both consumer convenience and expense (Geller, Winett, & Everett, 1982). Again, however, the expense (and high-tech plants can be very expensive) is unfortunately remote in time and it forms an indeterminate part of the consumer's tax bill. Thus, in the short run, the technical solution is the more attractive one.

The alternative, considering resource recovery as a behavioral problem, focuses on inducing consumers to separate, to prepare, and sometimes to deliver their discarded items at the beginning of the waste disposal process. This job is bothersome. Yet because the high-tech solution is often more expensive (sometimes more so than the old bulldozing-for-landfill approach it is supposed to replace), the public-interest choice is probably the low-tech, consumer-based form of resource recovery.

How to Encourage Recycling

FIGURE 13–15 ''Dumpster divers'' may be found even in well-off places. They search for food, and they help recycle cans and other materials that others find too much trouble to recycle. *(Courtesy of Coe Gifford.)*

How can we persuade millions who either never consider recycling (ignorance or limited processing) or simply don't want to get their hands dirty (although you don't actually have to) to responsibly manage the valuable resources passing through their households?

The answers, by now familiar, are: educate, prompt, and reward recycling behavior. Increasing awareness through speeches and pamphlets works; reminders to continue recycling with signs and labeled receptacles work; positive reinforcement of recycling behavior works. Again, the most effective approach is an integrated program combining these strategies.

A good example of an empirical study of recycling is one by Jill Witmer and Scott Geller (1976). On a campus that already had an educational campaign on recycling, they prompted recycling by delivering a flyer encouraging paper recycling once a week to every resident of two university dormitories. Less than 3 percent of the residents responded, but even this small number of recyclers produced 20 kg (about 45 lb) of paper per week.

Witmer and Geller also tried two reward systems. Pitting one hall against the other, they offered a $15 prize to the hall that recycled the most paper. This strategy produced about 240 kg (544 lb) of paper per week, ten times as much as the flyer-only strategy. Participation rates also doubled. In the other reward system, Witmer and Geller offered raffle coupons for $80 worth of prizes for each pound of recyclable paper brought in. This yielded about 360 kg (820 lb) per week and participation was four times greater than in the flyer-only condition. Even though dormitories are not great sources of paper for recycling in the first place, these strategies certainly increased the amount of paper recovered.

The Witmer and Geller study illustrates both the advantages and disadvantages of the low-technology behavioral approach to recycling. Prompts and rewards increased recycling over the flyer-only baseline, but when they were discontinued, recycling fell back to baseline levels. This suggests that reward strategies must be continued in order to promote recycling in the long run.

One curiosity in Witmer and Geller's data suggests there is hope for long-term changes in behavior. In the prompt condition, recycling was actually higher in the weeks after prompting ended than it was during the prompting phase. This indicates that prompts are not as immediately effective as monetary rewards, but their effect may last longer.

Another disadvantage of the reward approach is cost. As we noted in discussing residential energy conservation, programs must be cost-effective to have potential for widespread usefulness. In the Witmer and Geller contest, a total of $45 in prizes was distributed and about 1430 kg (3250 lb) of paper were collected. The paper was sold for about $20. In the raffle, prizes worth $240 were given away, but the paper (2200 kg or 4900 lb) was sold for less than $40. The prizes were donated by local merchants, so in a sense they cost nothing. However, if the program was more widely implemented merchants may not respond so willingly; even if they did, their customers would have to pay for the donations through increased prices.

As Winkler and Winett (1982) point out, behavioral approaches have great value, but in the future psychologists must discover ways to make their payoffs less than the public-interest gains achieved by their programs. An even greater threat to the usefulness of the behavioral programs is that labor costs are rarely counted. In the Witmer and Geller study, research assistants invested many hours work receiving and weighing the recycled materials for no return except course credits. In the real world, workers will demand real wages. In this study, the bottom line is that the prompt-only strategy produced the smallest increase in recycling, but it did so with by far the cheapest outlay, making it the most cost-effective approach.

All is not lost. The behavioral approaches are still new, still beginning to discover cost-effective strategies. Lotteries are an extremely promising pathway; individuals are willing to contribute much more to a cause than would be predicted from their chances of gain when an attractive lottery prize is to be won. It is also true that some *benefits* of the reward strategy have not been included in the equation. How much would it have cost to deal with the recycled paper had it been disposed of in the conventional manner? How many trees were allowed to grow larger before being cut for pulp, thereby reducing the cost of paper production?

Designing for Recycling

Once again, educational campaigns and prompting have value in easing a social dilemma, but clever environmental design can have an important impact too. In the program to be described, the key once again is to make it physically easy to cooperate.

In large offices, huge amounts of waste paper are generated. If this paper could be sorted into the different categories *as it is generated*, recycling would be greatly facilitated. Many offices have now tried this; a few studies have taken a close look at how it works.

In the administration offices of a large university, three sort-as-you-toss designs were compared: (a) two wastebaskets, one for recyclable paper and one for nonrecyclable garbage, (b) divided wastebaskets with one section for recyclable paper and one for nonrecyclables, and (c) a personal wastebasket for recyclables and a central (public) wastebasket for nonrecyclables (Humphrey, Bord, Hammond, & Mann, 1977).

The first two designs resulted in over 92 percent of paper properly recycled in the 10 weeks of the study. (Proper recycling means the absence of nonrecyclables in wastebaskets designated for recyclables.) Even the less convenient (but presumably cheaper) alternative of a centralized contained for nonrecyclables resulted in 84 percent proper recycling.

Employees in half the sixteen locations of the study received personal prompts on two occasions during the study. The prompts had only a small effect, increasing proper recycling from 88 to 92 percent. The vast bulk of the recycling was due to placing the recycling containers in the office, a very simple design feature.

One company has created a slightly more sophisticated sort-as-you-toss system (Geller, Winett, & Everett, 1982). This is a desktop system that places the paper separation process even closer to the point at which mail or old drafts of memos become garbage. This system is recommended by the U. S. Environmental Protection Agency, which lives up to its recommendation by using it in its Washington headquarters. The desktop system, used by about 2700 people in the building, manages to outperform the divided wastebasket: proper recycling reaches 97 percent. In the first year, EPA recovered 150 tons of high-grade paper. Designing the environment so as to encourage "mindless" recycling may be an important key to the promotion of recycling in the future.

SUMMARY

Many natural resources are commons: desirable commodities that many individuals or organizations can harvest. When the rate of harvesting can exceed the rate at which the resource replenishes itself, a commons dilemma exists. Harvesters must decide whether to get rich or comfortable quickly or, through restraint, to benefit all harvesters more moderately with the crucial consequence that the commons is preserved for the future. Through field studies and laboratory simulations, environmental psychologists have identified which characteristics of the resource and its harvesters and which rules of the game promote cooperation rather than defection.

Theories of social dilemmas offer political solutions, systematically consider the many dimensions of social dilemmas, propose reinforcement strategies, consider the cognitive aspects of the problem, and argue that most individuals are basically unaware of social dilemmas. The theories, therefore, raise important questions as they provide a way of understanding behavior in the commons.

For example, *should* individuals cooperate—choosing in broadest terms justice over freedom? If we are forced to choose between these, it seems that many of us choose freedom: the freedom to burn fossil fuels, to "harvest" forests, to litter, to turn up the heat or air conditioning if we wish, to throw out unwanted paper and tin cans. We paid for them, didn't we?

This chapter has reviewed the case for justice. Simulation research clearly shows that freedom—that beautiful word—can easily lead to ruination. Some theorists believe we are already too far along the defection trail to reverse our tragic course; most enviornmental psychologists believe it is not too late. We begin with educational campaigns and by searching for individuals who already take personal responsibility for management of the commons. But one of the great lessons learned so far is that changed attitudes do not lead to changed behavior often enough.

Pollution, energy conservation, and recycling are three everyday instances of social dilemmas. Many strategies for behavior change are evolving: appeals from respected leaders, moral arguments for justice, prompts, feedback, goal setting, obtaining public commitments from consumers, changing payoffs to favor conservation instead of exploitation, public disclosure of defections, increased communication among commons members, careful arrangement of the physical setting, provision of smaller resource territories for which individuals feel more responsible, and last (but most important), the fostering of trust and friendship.

Friendship is the most important because it may allow us a little of that almost unaffordable luxury, freedom. Julian Edney (1984) observes that friendship, with its "sympathetic and mutual awareness of each others' condition, needs, and feelings," may be the vehicle by which we achieve both justice *and* freedom.

SUGGESTED SUPPLEMENTARY READINGS

Becker, L. J. (1978). Joint effect of feedback and goal setting on performance: A field study of residential energy conservation. *Journal of Applied Psychology, 63,* 428–433.

Cone, J. D., & Hayes, S. C. (1980). *Environmental problems: Behavioral solutions.* Monterey, CA: Brooks/Cole.

Corbett, M. N. (1981). *A better place to live: New designs for tomorrow's communities.* Emmaus, PA: Rodale.

Dawes, R. M. (1980). Social dilemmas. *Annual Review of Psychology, 31,* 169–193.

Edney, J. J. (1984). Rationality and social justice. *Human Relations, 37,* 163–180.

Fox, J. R. (1985). Psychology, ideology, utopia and the commons. *American Psychologist, 40,* 48–58.

Geller, E. S., Winett, R. A., & Everett, P. B. (1982). *Preserving the environment.* New York: Pergamon Press.

Hardin, G. (1968). The tragedy of the commons. *Science, 162,* 1243–1248.

Komorita, S. S., & Barth, J. M. (1985). Components of reward in social dilemmas. *Journal of Personality and Social Psychology, 48,* 364–373.

McDougall, G. H. G., Claxton, J. D., Ritchie, J. R. B., & Anderson, C. D. (1981). Consumer energy research: A review. *Journal of Consumer Research, 8,* 343–354.

Messick, D. M., Wilke, H., Brewer, M. B., Kramer, R. M., Zemke, P. E., & Lui, L. (1983). Individual adaptations and structural change solutions to social dilemmas. *Journal of Personality and Social Psychology, 44,* 294–309.

Platt, J. (1973). Social traps. *American Psychologist, 28,* 641–651.

Shippee, G., & Gregory, W. L. (1982). Public commitment and energy conservation. *American Journal of Community Psychology, 10,* 81–93.

Stern, P. C., & Aronson, E. (Eds.) (1984). *Energy use: The human dimension.* New York: Freeman.

Winkler, R. C., & Winett, R. A. (1982). Behavioral interventions in resource management: A systems approach based on behavioral economics. *American Psychologist, 37,* 421–435.

Epilog:
Utopia versus Entopia

You may say I'm a dreamer, but I'm not the only one.

John Lennon

It has been a long journey—an entire term for you and 3 years for me: thirteen chapters packed with brief descriptions of books and research projects that took months and years of work by hundreds of environmental psychologists and kindred spirits. In this brief look back, I will avoid recounting new studies and telling more facts. Instead, I will attempt a perspective on environmental psychology.

Every activity occurs in a physical context. Whether one is interested in environmental psychology itself, in another area of psychology, or a different discipline, all the action occurs in offices, labs, studios, residences, institutions, factories, or outdoor settings. The mutual influence of person and setting is not usually sudden and dramatic (natural disasters and nuclear bombs are two exceptions). Because these influences are often cumulative and subtle and because we often adapt even to bad settings, they usually go unnoticed. But they are always present, and the interplay between persons and places has important effects on both.

I therefore think of environmental psychology as an essential human endeavor. You may think so, too, but it is well to remember that not everyone else did, or does. In its early days, psychology focused on mental dynamics. Later it began to realize the importance of interpersonal and social forces. Except for the lonely voices of a few pioneers, the role played by the physical environment was recognized only two decades ago.

Even today, if your experiences are like mine, you must often field questions about what environmental psychology is. Someone hears that you are studying it and they say, "That sounds interesting. But what is it?" I try to take great care in giving an answer, because the public at large is still generally very unaware of this field; its opinion about environmental psychology depends in part on what it hears from you and me.

Of course, you must develop your own assessment of the field to offer the curious. Years of work in the field have convinced me that environmental psychologists have bravely undertaken a task that is ultimately more difficult than that undertaken by any other branch of science. (This underlying complexity doesn't stop acquaintances who have not yet begun to comprehend those complexities to ask me—sometimes expecting a quick answer—what color they should paint their walls. Nor does it stop certain self-proclaimed experts from offering a quick answer!)

This book never offered to provide simple recipes for solutions to practical problems. Although the amount of knowledge is growing so much that its sources fairly bulge out of the book, it still provides illumination of theoretical issues and broad research questions more like the light of a full moon than that of the noonday sun.

At this stage, my hope is that readers have learned the real strengths of environmental psychology: having the courage to struggle with complex problems, and refining the methods needed to understand and overcome these problems in local community settings. At present, reading about research and theory in environmental psychology requires a tolerance for uncertainty more than it requires a willingness to master a set of established laws. However, the techniques and procedures needed to conduct applied research that can significantly improve the habitability of built and natural settings in our own local community are already well-developed and ready for use.

This level of development is all that may reasonably be expected after only 20 years of sustained effort. Give us another three decades and resources like those allocated to other areas of psychology, and the growth of understanding of the individual, social, and societal processes involved in environmental psychology will compare very favorably with progress in older areas of psychology.

The reason lies in the degree of dedication of most environmental psychologists who, in my experience, are even more driven than most in the knowledge business. They seem to derive extra energy from knowing that their work forms an integral part of their everyday life; that they can affect the world around them; that they are always in a physical setting that affects them, is affected by them, and might be improved by their effort. This sense of contributing to the community provides considerable fuel.

In this spirit, I had hoped in this finale to explore what environmental psychology might say about utopia. There isn't enough space for that and if I haven't already worn out my welcome with you, I fear that I might do so in a fourteenth full chapter. Nevertheless, I cannot resist offering a few observations and suggestions. Then you can pursue the matter if you wish with some friends over your favorite drink. The keen reader may wish to pursue the matter further by looking at some of the suggested readings provided later.

First, most environmental psychologists would probably try to create an **entopia** rather than a utopia. *Utopia*, originally the title of a 1516 book by Sir Thomas More, literally means "no place." This can too easily mean that thought on the subject is nothing but castles in the air, which is emphatically not what environmental psychologists

are getting at. Entopia is a better word because it means, approximately, "achievable place." This implies the important idea that better settings *could*, with effort, be brought into existence.

A second observation is that most utopian visions have a static quality to them—a certain set of rules that are presumed to enhance life, a certain architecture that will support the visionary's philosophy. Yet it seems to me that entopic settings must have flexibility, if not guaranteed change. Even a perfect place would get boring if it didn't change. This raises a paradox. How can an ideal setting remain ideal if it must change to stay ideal?

Entopia should change even if constructed for one person, but it would very likely be home for at least a small group of individuals. Human personality will always vary; how should an entopia be designed to fit them all? The challenge is to build for different individuals who use the same setting. It is, further, to create settings that suit human cognitive and perceptual tendencies and our social-spatial needs. More than that, we need settings that help promote the fulfillment of human potential instead of limiting or even squashing it.

To that end, the major settings of life—homes, schools, and workplaces—must be revamped in an entopia. All three of these settings are often saddled with traditions that make them far short of entopic. Classrooms are still set up in rows, many homes have open brick fireplaces that owners rarely use but that are very inefficient when they are used, and poorly designed offices still plague employees. Even prison buildings go beyond their purpose of denying freedom; they encourage violence and illness.

What will it take to change the design process so that user needs are more often taken into account? The process described in Chapter Twelve is not yet in widespread use. One answer is to educate policy makers and the public to the need for humane programming and careful postoccupancy evaluation. For certain kinds of buildings— perhaps those built for members of the public— it may be desirable to seek legislation ensuring consideration of users.

In commons management, one bright spot is that awareness of the issues is now widespread. Positive actions may be seen everywhere in antilitter, conservation, and recycling campaigns, although failures are still probably more common than successes.

The notion of utopia is often accompanied by exhortations for rapid and radical changes. Entopia, on the other hand, would best be accomplished gradually. Drastic changes are unlikely to be entirely successful. Robert Sommer, in particular, has argued for persistent but incremental changes. Each change may then be tested to see if it represents a move toward a better community. Of course, the proposal of incremental change is not meant to serve as a cover for failing to redesign settings that pinch people.

Since the 1960s, utopian thought seems to have declined, at least in the developed world. (A previously unknown group of nomads was recently discovered in South America. They were wandering in search of a "painless place" they had heard rumors about.) I think environmental psychologists *must* be entopian (not utopian), especially in the midst of so many bad physical settings.

SUGGESTED READINGS

Fox, D. R. (1985). Psychology, ideology, utopia, and the commons. *American Psychologist, 40,* 48–58.

Leff, H. R. (1978). *Experience, environment, and human potentials.* New York: Oxford.

Moos, R., & Brownstein, R. (1977). *Environment and utopia: A synthesis.* New York: Plenum.

Porter, P., & Lukerman, R. (1976). The geography of utopia. In D. Lowenthal and M. Bowden (Eds.), *Geographies of the mind.* New York: Oxford.

Sommer, R. (1969). *Personal space: The behavioral basis of design.* Prentice-Hall.

Appendix

Publications
and Organizations

Students frequently ask me where to look for information about particular topics, graduate schools, and organizations for those interested in environment and behavior. This appendix is for those who wish to pursue their interests in environmental psychology and to be aware of the primary institutions in the field. It provides a brief guide to the organizations, journals, publications, and graduate schools associated with the field. It is as accurate as I could make it in mid-1986, but note that information in it can change. For parts of this appendix, I am indebted to Gary Moore (in press), but any errors in it are mine.

PUBLICATIONS

Handbook

Handbook of Environmental Psychology. Edited by Daniel Stokols and Irwin Altman and published by John Wiley in 1987. A massive, forty-three chapter compendium of knowledge about person-environment relations. Indispensable for the serious researcher.

Journals

Environment and Behavior. Established in 1969, this is one of the primary journals in the field: Sage Publications, 275 South Beverly Drive, Beverly Hills, CA 90212

Journal of Environmental Psychology. Established in 1981, this is the other major journal. Known for its international emphasis: Academic Press, 24–28 Oval Road, London, England NW1 7DX.

Man-Environment Systems. M-ES is available from ASMER (see section "Professional Organizations" for address).

Design Research News. The newsletter of EDRA, see section "Professional Organizations" for address.

EDRA Proceedings. Volumes of papers presented at the yearly meetings of the Environmental Design Research Association. See your library's card catalog under Environmental Design Research Association.

Journal of Architectural and Planning Research. Established in 1984: Elsevier Science Publishing, 52 Vanderbilt Avenue, New York, NY 10017.

Children's Environment Quarterly. CEQ was established in 1984: Center for Human Environments, Environmental Psychology Program, The Graduate Center, The City University of New York, 33 West 42nd Street, New York, NY 10036.

Architecture and Behavior (Architecture et Comportement). A French-English journal that was established in 1980: Georgi Publishing, CH-1813 Saint-Saphorin, Switzerland.

Perception of Environment. A newsletter/research quarterly published by the Perception of Environment Study Group (see section "Professional Organizations" for address).

Population and Environment. The journal of Division 34 of the American Psychological Association. Roughly half its articles are on environmental psychology: Human Sciences Press, 72 Fifth Avenue, New York, NY 10011.

Readers will also find scattered articles of interest in many other journals, including *Journal of Applied Psychology, Social Psychology Quarterly, Journal of Personality and Social Psychology, Canadian Journal of Behavioral Science, Journal of Applied Social Psychology, Journal of Environmental Education, Human Ecology, Organizational Behavior and Human Performance,* and the *Journal of Social Issues.*

Book Series

Every discipline needs in-depth reviews of particular topics at the professional level. Many such books are available; here I introduce only those forming part of established series. These books consist of chapters reviewing the latest developments in environmental psychology.

Human Behavior: Advances in Theory and Research. Edited by Irwin Altman and Joachim Wohlwill since 1976. Published by Plenum Press. The first two volumes were on general topics. Since then the volumes have focused on children (3), culture (4), transportation (5), the natural environment (6), the elderly (7), home (8), and neighborhood and community (9).

Advances in Environmental Psychology. Edited by Andrew Baum and Jerome Singer since 1981. Published by Lawrence Erlbaum Associates. It has focused on urban life (1), personal control (2), energy conservation (3), health (4), and research methods (5).

Community Development Series. From the publishers Dowden, Hutchison and Ross. Contains over two dozen books and the EDRA Proceedings. The emphasis is on community planning and design.

Advances in Environment, Behavior, and Design. Edited by Erwin Zube and Gary Moore, from Plenum Press. Just getting underway in 1986.

Annual Reviews

Annual Reviews, Inc. each year publishes volumes that summarize recent developments in psychology and many other fields. Environmental psychology has been the subject of a chapter in *Annual Review of Psychology* in 1973 (by Kenneth Craik), 1978 (by Daniel Stokols), 1982 (by James Russell and Lawrence Ward), and in 1986 (by Charles Holahan). A sociological perspective is available in a chapter by Dunlap and Catton in *Annual Review of Sociology* for 1979. Geographers may find useful reviews in *Progress in Human Geography* for 1980 and 1981 (by Saarinen and Sell) and 1983 and 1984 (by Gold and Goodey).

GRADUATE SCHOOLS

Students who wish to go on in environmental psychology will probably need a master's or doctoral degree. Numerous universities offer formal or informal programs in psychology departments, other social science departments, and schools of architecture. Some of these programs will be listed. Further details are available in most university libraries that collect calendars from other universities or by writing to the university itself.

The oldest continuing program is the Ph.D. program in environmental psychology at the Graduate Center of the City University of New York, started in 1968 by William Ittelson and Harold Proshansky. In Britain, a program was started at the University of Surrey in the mid-1970s by David Canter and Terence Lee.

Some other programs in psychology are active but vary in size and formality from fully institutionalized programs with numerous faculty members down to single, lonely, but eager faculty members who take students into individualized programs. Here is a partial list of programs in *psychology:* Arizona, Arizona State, British Columbia, California (Berkeley and Davis), City University of New York, Claremont, Colorado State, Rutgers, Surrey, Utah, and Victoria. In *architecture* departments, consider California (Berkeley and Los Angeles), Georgia Tech, Michigan, Montreal, and Wisconsin (Milwaukee). In *sociology,* there is Kansas, Michigan State, Rutgers, and Washington State. In *geography,* there is Nebraska, California (Santa Barbara), Toronto, and Victoria. In *natural resources,* there is Arizona and Michigan. If you believe the field can best be studied from an *interdisciplinary* perspective, consider social ecology at California (Irvine), design and environmental analysis at Cornell, environmental studies at York (in Toronto), or environmental design at Calgary.

PROFESSIONAL ORGANIZATIONS

For most readers the first two organizations listed below would be the most important. But depending on where you live or what your particular interests are, other groups may be closer to your heart.

Environmental Design Research Association. EDRA is a 900-member association of designers and researchers (about 30 percent psychologists, 30 percent architects, and 40 percent others) that has held annual meetings since 1969: P.O. Box 23129 L'Enfant Plaza Station, Washington, DC 20024, Telephone: 301 657-2651.

Division 34 (Population and Environment). Part of the American Psychological Association. A group for environment-minded psychologists: 1200 Seventeenth Street NW, Washington, DC 20036, Telephone: 202 955-7600.

Section on Environmental Psychology. Part of the Canadian Psychological Association. Small hardy group in Great White North: 558 King Edward Avenue, Ottawa, Ontario K1N 7N6, Telephone: 613 238-4409.

Association for the Study of Man-Environment Relations. ASMER is one of the oldest groups in the field: P.O. Box 57, Orangeburg, NY 10962, Telephone: 914 632-8221.

Division of Environmental Psychology. Part of the International Association of Applied Psychology, IAAP's address is Azra Churchman, Faculty of Architecture and Town Planning, Technion-Israel Institute of Technology, Haifa 32000 Israel.

International Association for the Study of People and Their Physical Surroundings. IAPS is based in Europe. One founder and stable contact person is: Dr. Martin Symes, Bartlett School of Architecture and Planning, University College London, Wates House, 22 Gordon Street, London, WC1H OQB.

Man-Environment Relations Association. MERA is based in Japan. A contact person is: Professor Takiji Yamamoto, Department of Psychology, Hiroshima University, Hiroshima, Japan.

People and Places Environment Research. PAPER is based in Australia and New Zealand: Professor Ross Thorne, The University of Sydney, School of Architecture, Sydney, NSW 2006, Australia.

Perception of Environment Study Group. Part of the Association of American Geographers; an organization that reflects the interests of geographers: 1710 Sixteenth Street NW, Washington, DC 20009.

Environmental Section. Part of the American Sociological Association, it has about 300 members who are interested in a sociological perspective: 1722 N Street NW, Washington, DC 20009.

Environmental Design Technical Group. Part of the Human Factors Society, a group for those who lean toward an engineering approach: P.O. Box 1369, Santa Monica, CA 90406.

American Planning Association. A large group oriented toward planning and design on the urban scale: 1776 Massachusetts Avenue NW, Washington, DC 20036.

If you notice errors in the Appendix or have any suggestions for it or the book as a whole, please write: Robert Gifford, Department of Psychology, University of Victoria, Victoria, British Columbia, Canada V8W 2Y2.

References

Abe, K. (1982). *Introduction to disaster psychology.* Tokyo: Science Publishing.

Abernathy, E. M. (1940). The effect of changed environmental conditions upon the result of college examinations. *Journal of Psychology, 10,* 293–301.

Acheson, J. M. (1975). The lobster fiefs: Economic and ecological effects of territoriality in the Maine lobster industry. *Human Ecology, 3,* 183–207.

Acking, C. A., & Sorte, G. (1973). How do we verbalize what we see? *Landscape Architecture, 64,* 470–475.

Adams, P. R., & Adams, G. R. (1984). Mount Saint Helens's ashfall: Evidence for a disaster stress reaction. *American Psychologist, 39,* 252–260.

Agee, J. K., Field, D. R., & Starkey, E. E. (1983–1984). Cooperative parks studies unit: University-based science programs in the national park service. *Journal of Environmental Education, 14,* 24–28.

Ahrentzen, S. (1980). *Environment-behavior relations in the classroom setting: A multi-modal research perspective.* Unpublished master's thesis, University of California, Irvine.

——(1981). The environmental and social context of distraction in the classroom. In A. E. Osterberg, C. P. Tiernan, and R. A. Findlay (Eds.) *Design research interactions.* Ames, IA: Environmental Design Research Association.

——(in press). Residential fit and mobility among low-income, female-headed family households. In W. van Vliet— and S. Fava, *Housing needs and policy approaches: International perspectives.* Durham, NC: Duke University Press.

——, & Evans, G. W. (1984). Distraction, privacy, and classroom design. *Environment and Behavior, 16,* 437–454.

——, Jue, G. M., Skorpanich, M., & Evans, G. W. (1982). School environments and stress. In G. W. Evans (Ed.), *Environmental stress.* New York: Cambridge University Press, 29–36.

Aiello, J. R. (1972). A test of equilibrium theory: Visual interaction in relation to orientation, distance and sex of interactants. *Psychonomic Science, 27,* 335–336.

——(1977). A further look at equilibrium theory: Visual interaction as a function of interpersonal distance. *Environmental Psychology and Nonverbal Behavior, 1,* 122–140.

——, & Baum, A. (1979). *Residential crowding and design.* New York: Plenum.

——, Baum, A., & Gormley, F. B. (1981). Social determinants of residential crowding stress. *Personality and Social Psychology Bulletin, 7,* 643–649.

——, & Cooper, R. E. (1972). The use of personal space as a function of social affect. *Proceedings of the Annual Convention of the American Psychological Association, 7,* 207–208.

——, DeRisi, D. T., Epstein, Y. M., and Karlin, R. A. (1977). Crowding and the role of interpersonal distance preference. *Sociometry, 40,* 271–282.

——, Epstein, Y. M., & Karlin, R. A. (1975, April). *Field experimental research on human crowding.* Paper presented at the annual meeting of the American Psychological Association, New York.

——, Nicosia, G., & Thompson, D. E. (1979). Physiological, social and behavioral consequences of crowding on children and adolescents. *Child Development, 50,* 195–202.

——, & Pagan, G. (1982). Development of personal space among Puerto Ricans. *Journal of Nonverbal Behavior, 7,* 59–80.

——, & Thompson, D. E. (1980a). Personal space, crowding and spatial behavior in a cultural context. In I. Altman and J. F. Wohlwill (Eds.) *Environment and culture.* New York: Plenum Press.

——, & Thompson, D. E. (1980b). When compensation fails: Mediating effects of sex and locus of control at extended interaction distances. *Basic and Applied Social Psychology, 1,* 65–82.

——, Thompson, D. E., & Baum, A. (1981). The symbiotic relationship between social psychology and environmental psychology: Implications from crowding, personal space, and intimacy regulation research. In J. H. Harvey (Ed.), *Cognition, social behavior, and the environment.* Hillsdale, NJ: Erlbaum.

——, Thompson, D. E., & Brodzinsky, D. M. (1983). How funny is crowding anyway? Effects of room size, group size and the introduction of humor. *Basic and Applied Social Psychology, 4*, 193–207.

——, Vautier, J. S., & Bernstein, M. D. (1983, August). *Crowding stress: Impact of social support, group formation and control.* Paper presented at the annual meeting of the American Psychological Association, Anaheim, CA.

Albert, S., & Dabbs, J. M., Jr. (1970). Physical distance and persuasion. *Journal of Personality and Social Psychology, 15*, 265–270.

Allison, S. T., & Messick, D. M. (1985). Effects of experience in a replenishable resource trap. *Journal of Personality and Social Psychology, 49*, 943–948.

Allport, F. H. (1924). *Social psychology.* Boston, MA: Houghton Mifflin.

Allport, G. W. (1955). *Becoming: Basic considerations for a psychology of personality.* New Haven: Yale University Press.

—— (1961). *Pattern and growth in personality.* New York: Holt, Rinehart and Winston.

Altman, I. (1975). *The environment and social behavior: Privacy, personal space, territoriality and crowding.* Monterey, CA: Brooks/Cole.

—— (1977). Privacy regulation: Culturally universal or culturally specific? *Journal of Social Issues, 33* (3), 66–84.

—— (1981). Reflections on environmental psychology: 1981. *Human Environments, 2*, 5–7.

——, & Chemers, M. (1980). *Culture and environment.* Monterey, CA: Brooks/Cole.

——, & Gauvain, M. (1981). A cross-cultural and dialectical analysis of homes. In L. Liben, A. Patterson, and N. Newcombe (Eds.), *Spatial representation across the life span.* New York: Academic Press.

——, & Rogoff, B. (in press). World views in psychology and environmental psychology: Trait, interactional, organismic and transactional perspectives. In I. Altman and D. Stokols (Eds.), *Handbook of environmental psychology,* New York: Wiley.

——, & Taylor, D. A. (1973). *Social penetration: The development of interpersonal relationships.* New York: Holt, Rinehart and Winston.

——, Wohlwill, J. F., & Everett, P. B. (1981). *Transportation and behavior.* New York: Plenum.

Anderson, C. A., & Anderson, D. C. (1984). Ambient temperature and violent crime: Tests of the linear and curvilinear hypotheses. *Journal of Personality and Social Psychology, 46*, 91–97.

Anderson, E. N., Jr. (1972). Some Chinese methods in dealing with crowding. *Urban Anthropology, 1*, 141–150.

Anderson, T. W., Zube, E. H., & MacConnell, W. P. (1976). *Predicting scenic resource values: Studies in landscape perception* (Technical report). Amherst: Institute for Man and Environment, University of Massachusetts.

Angyal, A. (1941). *Foundations for a science of personality.* New York: Commonwealth Fund.

Appleyard, D. (1976). *Planning a pluralistic city.* Cambridge, MA: MIT Press.

Appleyard, D., & Craik, K. H. (1978). The Berkeley environmental laboratory and its research program. *International Review of Applied Psychology, 27*, 53–55.

Aragones, J. I., & Arredondo, J. M. (1985). Structure of urban cognitive maps. *Journal of Environmental Psychology, 5*, 197–212.

Arbuthnot, J. (1977). The roles of attitudinal and personality variables in the prediction of environmental behavior and knowledge. *Environment and Behavior, 9*, 217–232.

Archea, J. (1977). The place of architectural factors in behavioral theories of privacy. *Journal of Social Issues, 33*, (3), 116–137.

Archer, J. (1970). Effects of population density on behavior in rodents. In J. H. Crook (Ed.), *Social behavior in birds and mammals.* New York: Academic Press.

Ardrey, R. (1966). *The territorial imperative.* New York: Atheneum.

Argyle, M., & Dean, J. (1965). Eye-contact, distance, and affiliation. *Sociometry, 28*, 289–304.

Aronow, W. S., Harris, C. N., Isbell, M. W., Rokaw, M. D., & Imparto, B. (1972). Effect of freeway travel on angina pectoris. *Annals of Internal Medicine, 77*, 669–676.

ASHRAE handbook of fundamentals (1985). New York: ASHRAE.

Auden, W. H. (1965). Postscript, "Prologue: The Birth of Architecture," *About the house.* New York, Random House.

Auliciems, A. (1969). Effects of weather on indoor thermal comfort. *International Journal of Biometerology, 13*, 147–162.

Austin, W. T. (1982). Portrait of a courtroom: Social and ecological impressions of the adversary process. *Criminal Justice and Behavior, 9*, 286–302.

Axelrod, S., Hall, R. V., & Tams, A. (1979). Comparison of two common classroom seating arrangements. *Academic Therapy, 15*, 29–36.

Bachelard, G. (1969). *The poetics of space.* Boston: Beacon.

Bachman, W., & Katzev, R. (1982). The effects of noncontingent free bus tickets and personal commitment on urban bus ridership. *Transportation Research, 16A*, 103–108.

Baird, J. C., Cassidy, B., & Kurr, J. (1978). Room preference as a function of architectural features and user activities. *Journal of Applied Psychology, 63*, 719–727.

Baird, L. L. (1969). Big school, small school: A critical

examination of the hypothesis. *Journal of Educational Psychology, 60,* 286–303.

Baker, E., & Shaw, M. E. (1980). Reactions to interperson distance and topic intimacy: A comparison of strangers and friends. *Journal of Nonverbal Behavior, 5,* 80–91.

Baker, P. M. (1984). Seeing is behaving. *Environment and Behavior, 16,* 159–184.

Baldassare, M. (1981). The effects of a modern rapid-transit system on nearby residents: A case study of BART in the San Francisco area. In I. Altman, J. F. Wohlwill and P. B. Everett (Eds.), *Transportation and behavior.* New York: Plenum.

Balling, J. D., & Falk, J. H. (1982). Development of visual preference for natural environments. *Environment and Behavior, 14,* 5–28.

Barash, D. P. (1973). Human ethology: Personal space reiterated. *Environment and Behavior, 5,* 67–73.

Barker, R. G. (1968). *Ecological psychology: Concepts and methods for studying the environment of human behavior.* Stanford, CA: Stanford University Press.

Barker, R. G., & Wright, H. (1955). *Midwest and its children.* New York: Row and Peterson.

Barkow, B. (1977). Public transit too often ignores people. *Notes From Underground.* Long Island City, NY: Committee for Better Transit.

Barnaby, J. F. (1980). Lighting for productivity gains. *Lighting Design and Application,* February, 20–28.

Barnes, R. D. (1981). Perceived freedom and control in the built environment. In J. H. Harvey (Ed.), *Cognition, social behavior and the environment.* Hillsdale, NJ: Erlbaum.

Baron, R. A. (1978). Invasions of personal space and helping: Mediating effects of invader's apparent need. *Journal of Experimental Social Psychology, 14,* 304–312.

—— (1983). Sweet smell of success? The impact of pleasant artificial scents on evaluations of job applicants. *Journal of Applied Psychology, 68,* 709–713.

——, & Bell, P. A. (1976). Physical distance and helping: Some unexpected benefits of "crowding in" on others. *Journal of Applied Social Psychology, 6,* 95–104.

——, & Ransberger, V. M. (1978). Ambient temperature and the occurrence of collective violence: The long hot summer revisited. *Journal of Personality and Social Psychology, 36,* 351–360.

——, Russell, G. W., & Arms, R. L. (1985). Negative ions and behavior: Impact on mood, memory, and aggression among Type A and Type B persons. *Journal of Personality and Social Psychology, 48,* 746–754.

Baron, R. M. (1984, August). *A social-psychological perspective on environmental issues.* Paper presented at the annual meeting of the American Psychological Association, Toronto.

——, & Fisher, J. D. (1984). The equity-control model of vandalism: A refinement. In C. Levy-Leboyer (Ed.), *Vandalism: Behavior and Motivations.* Amsterdam: North Holland.

——, Mandel, D. R., Adams, C. A., & Griffin, L. M. (1976). Effects of social density in university residential environments. *Journal of Personality and Social Psychology, 34,* 434–446.

——, & Rodin, J. (1978). Personal control as a mediator of crowding. In A. Baum, J. E. Singer and S. Valins (Eds.), *Advances in environmental psychology* (Vol. 1). Hillsdale, NJ: Erlbaum.

Bartram, D. J. (1980). Comprehending spatial information: The relative efficiency of different methods of presenting information about bus routes. *Journal of Applied Psychology, 65,* 103–110.

Baum, A., Aiello, J. R., & Calesnick, L. E. (1978). Crowding and perceived control: Social density and the development of learned helplessness. *Journal of Personality and Social Psychology, 36,* 1000–1011.

——, Aiello, J. R., & Calesnick, L. E. (1979). Crowding and personal control: Social density and the development of learned helplessness. In J. R. Aiello and A. Baum (Eds.), *Residential crowding and design.* New York: Plenum Press.

——, Calesnick, L. E., Davis, G. E., & Gatchel, R. J. (1982). Individual differences in coping with crowding: Stimulus screening and social overload. *Journal of Personality and Social Psychology, 43,* 821–830.

——, & Davis, G. E. (1976). Spatial and social aspects of crowding perception. *Environment and Behavior, 8,* 527–545.

——, & Davis, G. E. (1980). Reducing the stress of high-density living: An architectural intervention. *Journal of Personality and Social Psychology, 38,* 471–481.

——, Davis, G. E., & Valins, S. (1979). Generating behavioral data for the design process. In J. R. Aiello and A. Baum (Eds.), *Residential crowding and design.* New York: Plenum Press.

——, Fisher, J. D., & Solomon, S. K. (1981). Type of information, familiarity and the reduction of crowding stress. *Journal of Personality and Social Psychology, 40,* 11–23.

——, Fleming, R., & Davidson, L. M. (1983). Natural disaster and technological catastrophe. *Environment and Behavior, 15,* 333–354.

——, & Greenberg, C. I. (1975). Waiting for a crowd: The behavioral and perceptual effects of anticipated crowding. *Journal of Personality and Social Psychology, 32,* 671–679.

——, & Koman, S. (1976). Differential response to anticipated crowding: Psychological effects of social and spatial density. *Journal of Personality and Social Psychology, 34,* 526–536.

——, Shapiro, A., Murray, D., & Widerman, M. (1979).

Interpersonal mediation of perceived crowding and control in residential dyads and triads. *Journal of Applied Social Psychology, 9,* 491–507.

——, & Valins, S. (1977). *Architecture and social behavior: Psychological studies of social density.* Hillsdale, NJ: Erlbaum.

Baumeister, R. F. (1985). The championship choke. *Psychology Today, 19* (4), 48–52.

Baxter, J. C. (1970). Interpersonal spacing in natural settings. *Sociometry, 33,* 444–456.

Beard, R. R., & Wertheim, G. A. (1967). Behavioral impairment associated with small doses of carbon monoxide. *American Journal of Public Health, 57,* 2012–2022.

Becker, F. D. (1973). Study of spatial markers. *Journal of Personality and Social Psychology, 26,* 439–445.

—— (1974). *Design for living: The residents' view of multi-family housing.* Ithaca, NY: Center for Urban Development Research.

—— (1977). *Housing messages.* Stroudsberg, PA: Dowden, Hutchinson and Ross.

—— (1980). Employees need role in design of work space. *Hospitals, 54* (16), 97–105.

—— (1981). *Workspace: Creating environments in organizations.* New York: Praeger.

—— (1983, July). Creating an office that works. *Xerox Learning Systems.*

—— (1984). Loosely-coupled settings: A strategy for computer-aided work decentralization. In B. Staw and L. L. Cumming (Eds.), *Research in organizational behavior.* Greenwich, CT: JAI Press.

——, Gield, B., & Froggat, C. C. (1983). Seating positions and impression formation in an office setting. *Journal of Environmental Psychology, 3,* 253–261.

——, Gield, B., Gaylin, K., & Sayer, S. (1983). Office design in a community college: Effect on work and communication patterns. *Environment and Behavior, 15,* 699–726.

——, & Mayo, C. (1971). Delineating personal distance and territoriality. *Environment and Behavior, 3,* 375–381.

——, & Poe, D. B. (1980). The effects of user-generated design modifications in a general hospital. *Journal of Nonverbal Behavior, 4,* 195–218.

——, Sommer, R., Bee, J., & Oxley, B. (1973). College classroom ecology. *Sociometry, 36,* 514–525.

Becker, L. J. (1978). Joint effect of feedback and goal setting on performance: A field study of residential energy conservation. *Journal of Applied Psychology, 63,* 428–433.

Belk, R., Painter, J., & Semenik, R. (1981). Preferred solutions to the energy crisis as a function of causal attributions. *Journal of Consumer Research, 8,* 306–312.

Bell, A. E., Switzer, F., & Zipursky, M. (1974). Open area education: An advantage or disadvantage for beginners? *Perceptual and Motor Skills, 39,* 407–416.

——, Bell, P. A., & Greene, T. C. (1982). Thermal stress: Physiological, comfort, performance and social effects of hot and cold environments. In G. W. Evans (Ed.) *Environmental stress.* New York: Cambridge University Press.

——, Hess, S., Hill, E., Kukas, S., Richards, R. W., & Sargent, D. (1984). Noise and context-dependent memory. *Bulletin of the Psychonomic Society, 22,* 99–100.

Bennett, P. D., & Moore, N. K. (1981). Consumers' preferences for alternative energy conservation policies: A trade-off analysis. *Journal of Consumer Research, 8,* 313–321.

Berglund, B., Berglund, U., & Lindvall, T. (1976a). Psychological processing of odor mixtures. *Psychological Review, 83,* 432–441.

——, Berglund, U., & Lindvall, T. (1976b). Scaling loudness, noisiness, and annoyance of community noises. *Journal of Acoustical Society of America, 60,* 1119–1125.

Berlyne, D. E. (1960). *Conflict, arousal and curiosity.* New York: McGraw-Hill.

—— (1972). *Aesthetics and psychobiology.* New York: Appleton-Century-Crofts.

—— (1974). (Ed.) *Studies in the new experimental aesthetics: Steps toward an objective psychology of aesthetic appreciation.* New York: Halsted Press.

Bickman, L. (1972). Environmental attitudes and actions. *Journal of Social Psychology, 87,* 323–324.

——, Teger, A., Gabriele, T., McLaughlin, C., & Sunaday, E. (1973). Dormitory density and helping behavior. *Environment and Behavior, 5,* 465–490.

Biel, A. (1982). Children's spatial representation of their neighbourhood: A step towards a general spatial competence. *Journal of Environmental Psychology, 2,* 193–200.

Bixenstine, V. E., & Douglas, J. (1967). Effects of psychopathology on group consensus and cooperative choice in a six-person game. *Journal of Personality and Social Psychology, 5,* 32–37.

——, Levitt, C. A., & Wilson, K. R. (1966). Collaboration among six persons in a prisoner's dilemma game. *Journal of Conflict Resolution, 10,* 488–496.

Bleda, P. R., & Sandman, P. H. (1977). In smoke's way: Socioemotional reactions to another's smoking. *Journal of Applied Psychology, 62,* 452–458.

"Blue is beautiful." (1973, September 17). *Time,* p. 66.

Bonacich, P. (1976). Secrecy and solidarity. *Sociometry, 39,* 200–208.

Bonsall, P., Spencer, A., & Tang, W. (1983). Ridesharing in Great Britain: Performance and impact of the Yorkshire schemes. *Transportation Research, 17,* 169–181.

Booth, A. (1976). *Urban crowding and its consequences.* New York: Praeger.

——, & Edwards, J. N. (1976). Crowding and family relations. *American Sociological Review, 41,* 308–321.

——, & Johnson, D. R. (1975). The effect of crowding on child health and development. *American Behavioral Scientist, 18,* 736–749.

——, Johnson, D. R., & Edwards, J. N. (1980). In pursuit of pathology: The effects of crowding. *American Sociological Review, 45,* 873–878.

——, & Welch, S. (1973). *The effects of crowding: A cross-national study.* Paper presented at the annual meetings of the American Psychological Association, Montreal, Canada.

Bowerman, W. R. (1973). Ambulatory velocity in crowded and uncrowded conditions. *Perceptual and Motor Skills, 36,* 107–111.

Boyce, P. R. (1981). *Human factors in lighting.* London: Applied Science Publishers.

Bradley, R. H., & Caldwell, B. M. (1984a). The HOME Inventory and family demographics. *Developmental Psychology, 1984, 20,* 315–320.

—— (1984b). The relation of infants' home environments to achievement test performance in first grade: A follow-up study. *Child Development, 55,* 803–809.

Brechner, K. C. (1977). An experimental analysis of social traps. *Journal of Experimental Social Psychology, 13,* 552–564.

Brehm, J. W. (1966). *A theory of psychological reactance.* New York: Academic Press.

Breu, J. (1984, April 20). Patients, visitors getting chance to help design new hospital. *American Medical News,* 10–11.

Briere, J., Downes, A., & Spensley, J. (1983). Summer in the city: Weather conditions and psychiatric emergency-room visits. *Journal of Abnormal Psychology, 92,* 77–80.

Broadbent, D. E. (1979). Human performance and noise. In C. M. Harris (Ed.), *Handbook of noise control,* New York: McGraw-Hill.

Brockelbank, G. (1983, July 11). Personal communication.

Brockmeyer, F. M., Bowman, M., & Mullins, G. W. (1982–1983). Sensory versus non-sensory interpretation: A study of senior citizen's preferences. *Journal of Environmental Education, 14,* 3–7.

Bronzaft, A. L. (1981). The effect of a noise abatement program on reading ability. *Journal of Environmental Psychology, 1,* 215–222.

——, Dobrow, S. B., & O'Hanlon, T. J. (1976). Spatial orientation in a subway. *Environment and Behavior, 8,* 575–594.

Brooks, J. A. M., & Vernon, P. E. (1956). A study of children's interests and comprehension at a science museum. *British Journal of Psychology, 47,* 175–182.

Brower, S. (1981). *Innovation proposal for Harlem Park inner block parks management.* (Technical Report). Baltimore: City Planning Department.

——, Dockett, K., & Taylor, R. B. (1983) Residents' perceptions of territorial features and perceived local threat. *Environment and Behavior, 15,* 419–437.

Brown, B. B., & Altman, I. (1983). Territoriality, defensible space, and residential burglary. *Journal of Environmental Psychology, 3,* 203–220.

——, & Werner, C. M. (1985). Social cohesiveness, territoriality, and holiday decorations: The influence of cul-de-sacs. *Environment and Behavior, 17,* 539–565.

Bruce, J. A. (1965). The pedestrian. In J. E. Baewald (Ed.), *Traffic engineering handbook.* Washington, DC: Institute of Traffic Engineers.

Brunetti, F. (1972). Noise, distraction and privacy in conventional and open school environments. In W. J. Mitchell (Ed.), *Environmental design: Research and practice.* Los Angeles: University of California.

Brunswick, E. (1943). Organismic achievement and environmental probability. *Psychological Review, 50,* 255–272.

—— (1944). Distal focusing of perception. *Psychological Monographs, 56,* 1–48.

—— (1956). *Perception and the representative design of psychological experiments.* Berkeley: University of California Press.

—— (1957). Scope and aspects of the cognitive problem. In H. Gruber, K. R. Hammond, & R. Jessor (Eds.), *Contemporary approaches to cognition: A symposium held at the University of Colorado.* Cambridge, MA: Harvard University Press.

Bryant, K. J. (1982). Personality correlates of sense of direction and geographical orientation. *Journal of Personality and Social Psychology, 43,* 1318–1324.

—— (1984a). Methodological convergence as an issue within environmental cognition research. *Journal of Environmental Psychology, 4,* 43–60.

—— (1984b). *Geographical/spatial orientation ability within real-world and simulated large-scale environments.* Unpublished manuscript.

Buckalew, L. W., & Rizzuto, A. (1982). Subjective response to negative air ion exposure. *Aviation, Space, and Environmental Medicine, 53,* 822–823.

Bunting, T. E., & Cousins, L. R. (1983). Development and application of the children's environmental response inventory. *Journal of Environmental Education, 15,* 3–10.

Burns, T. (1964, October). Nonverbal communication. *Discovery,* 31–35.

Burton, I., Kates, R. W., & White, G. F. (1978). *The environment as hazard.* New York: Oxford.

Busch-Rossnagel, N. A., Nasar, J. L., Campbell, J., & Danish, S. J. (1980). An interdisciplinary approach to designing environments for children. *Journal of Man-Environment Relations, 1* (1), 1–10.

Buss, D. M., & Craik, K. H. (1983). The act frequency approach to personality. *Psychological Review, 90,* 105–126.

Buttimer, A. (1980). Home, reach and a sense of place. In A. Buttiner and D. Seamon (Eds.), *The human experience of space and place.* London: Croom Helm.

——, & Seamon, D. (1980). (Eds.), *The human experience of space and place.* London: Croom Helm.

Byrne, R. (1979). Memory for urban geography. *Quarterly Journal of Experimental Psychology, 15,* 157–163.

Cadwallader, M. (1979). Problems in cognitive distance: Implications for cognitive mapping. *Environment and Behavior, 11,* 559–576.

Calabresi, G. & Bobbitt, P. (1978). *Tragic choices.* New York: Norton.

Caldwell, M. D. (1976). Communication and sex effects in a five-person prisoner's dilemma game. *Journal of Personality and Social Psychology, 33,* 273–280.

Calhoun, J. B. (1962). Population density and social pathology. *Scientific American, 206,* 139–148.

—— (1966). The role of space in animal sociology. *Journal of Social Issues, 22,* 46–58.

—— (1971). Space and the strategy of life. In A. H. Esser (Ed.), *Behavior and environment: The use of space by animals and men.* New York: Plenum Press.

Campbell, A. C., Munce, S., & Galea, J. (1982). American gangs and British subcultures: A comparison. *International Journal of Offender Therapy and Comparative Criminology, 26,* 76–89.

Campbell, C. M. (1934). *Human personality and the environment.* New York: MacMillan.

Campbell, J. M. (1983). Ambient stressors. *Environment and Behavior, 15,* 355–380.

Canter, D. (1968). *The measurement of meaning in architecture.* Unpublished manuscript. Building Performance Research Unit, Glasgow.

—— (1969). An intergroup comparison of connotative dimensions. *Environment and Behavior, 1,* 37–48.

—— (1983). The purposive evaluation of places: A facet approach. *Environment and Behavior, 15,* 659–698.

—— (in press). Intention, meaning and structure: Social action in its physical context. In M. V. Cranach, G. P. Ginsburg, and M. Brenner (Eds.), *Discovery strategies in the psychology of social action.*

——, & Canter, S. (1971). Closer togther in Tokyo. *Design and Environment, 2,* 60–63.

——, & Craik, K. H. (1981). Environmental psychology. *Journal of Environmental Psychology, 1,* 1–11.

——, & Stringer, P. (1975). *Environmental interaction: Psychological approaches to our physical surroundings.* London: Surrey University Press.

——, & Tagg, S. K. (1975). Distance estimation in cities. *Environment and Behavior, 7,* 59–80.

——, & Thorne, R. (1972). Attitudes to housing: A cross cultural comparison. *Environment and Behavior, 4,* 3–32.

Carlsmith, J. M., & Anderson, C. A. (1979). Ambient temperature and the occurrence of collective violence: A new analysis. *Journal of Personality and Social Psychology, 37,* 327–334.

Carp, F. M., & Carp, A. (1982a). A role for technical environmental assessment in perceptions of environmental quality and well-being. *Journal of Environmental Psychology, 2,* 171–191.

—— (1982b). Perceived environmental quality of neighborhoods: Development of assessment scales and their relation to age and gender. *Journal of Environmental Psychology, 2,* 295–312.

Carpman, J. R., Grant, M. A., & Simmons, D. A. (1983–1984). Wayfinding in the hospital environment: The impact of various floor numbering alternatives. *Journal of Environmental Systems, 13,* 353–364.

—— (in press). *Design that cares: Health care facilities for patients and visitors.* American Hospital Publishing.

Carr, S., & Schlisser, D. (1969). The city as a trip: Perceptual selection and memory in the view from the road. *Environment and Behavior, 1,* 7–36.

Carson, D. H., Carson, F., Margulis, S. T., & Wehrli, R. (1980). Post-occupancy housing evaluations: A practical strategy for obtaining control groups. *Environment and Behaviour, 12,* 541–550.

Cashdan, E. (1983). Territoriality among human foragers: Ecological models and an application to four Bushman groups. *Current Anthropology, 24,* 47–66.

Cass, R. C., & Edney, J. J. (1978). The commons dilemma: A simulation testing resource visibility and territorial division. *Human Ecology, 6,* 371–386.

——, & Hershberger, R. G. (1973, April). *Further toward a set of semantic scales to measure the meaning of designed environments.* Paper presented at the annual meeting of the Environmental Design Research Association, Blacksburg, Virginia.

Castell, R. (1970). Effect of familiar and unfamiliar environments on proximity behavior of young children. *Journal of Experimental Child Psychology, 9,* 342–347.

Chaikin, A. L., Derlega, V. J., & Miller, S. J. (1976). Effects of room environment on self-disclosure in a counseling analogue. *Journal of Counseling Psychology, 23,* 479–481.

Chambers, J. A. (1963–1964). A study of attitudes and feelings toward windowless classrooms (Doctoral dissertation, University of Tennessee, 1963). *Dissertations Abstracts International, 24,* 4498.

Chao, A., & Bennett, C. A. (1981). Lamps for lighting people. *Proceedings of the Human Factors Society, 25,* 485–487.

Chapman, D., & Thomas, G. (1944). Lighting in dwellings. In *The lighting of buildings (Post war building studies No. 12)*. London: HMSO.

Charry, J. M., & Hawkenshire, F. B. W. (1981). Effects of atmospheric electricity on some substrates of disordered social behavior. *Journal of Personal and Social Psychology, 41*, 185–197.

Chase, W. G., & Chi, M. T. H. (1981). Cognitive skill: Implications for spatial skills in large-scale environments. In J. H. Harvey (Ed.), *Cognition, social behavior, and the environment*. Hillsdale, NJ: Erlbaum.

Christie, D. J., & Glickman, C. D. (1980). The effects of classroom noise on children: Evidence for sex differences. *Psychology in the Schools, 17*, 405–408.

Churchman, A. (1984, August). *Environmental psychology in Israel*. Paper presented at a symposium on "International Developments in Environmental Psychology," annual meetings of the American Psychological Association, Toronto.

Clearwater, Y. (1985). A human place in outer space. *Psychology Today, 19* (7), 34–43.

Coeterier, J. F. (1983). A photo validity test. *Journal of Environmental Psychology, 3*, 315–323.

Cohen, A. (1969). Effects of noise on psychological state. *Noise as a public health hazard*. Washington, DC: American Speech and Hearing Association.

Cohen, P. (1981). *Consumer behavior*. New York: Random House.

Cohen, R., Weatherford, D. L., Lomenick, T., & Koeller, K. (1979). Development of spatial representations: Role of task demands and familiarity with the environment. *Child Development, 50*, 1257–1260.

Cohen, S. (1978). Environmental load and the allocation of attention. In A. Baum, J. E. Singer, and S. Valins (Eds.), *Advances in environmental psychology* (Vol. 1). Hillsdale, NJ: Erlbaum.

——, Evans, G. W., Krantz, D. S., Stokols, D., & Kelly, S. (1981). Aircraft noise and children: Longitudinal and cross-sectional evidence on adaptation to noise and the effectiveness of noise abatement. *Journal of Personality and Social Psychology, 40*, 331–345.

——, Glass, D. C., & Singer, J. E. (1973). Apartment noise, auditory discrimination and reading ability in children. *Journal of Experimental Social Psychology, 9*, 407–422.

——, & Spacapan, S. (1978). The aftereffects of stress: An additional interpretation. *Environmental Psychology and Nonverbal Behavior, 3*, 43–57.

——, & Weinstein, N. (1982). Nonauditory effects of noise on behavior and health. In G. W. Evans (Ed.), *Environmental stress*. New York: Cambridge University Press.

Coles, R. (1969). Those places they call schools. *Harvard Educational Review: Architecture and Education, 39*, 46–57.

Collett, D. (1971). Training Englishmen in the nonverbal behavior of Arabs. *International Journal of Psychology, 6*, 209–215.

Collins, B. L. (1975). Windows and people: Alternative survey. Psychological reactions to environments with and without windows. *National Bureau of Standards Building Science Series*, No. 70, Washington, DC: Institute for Applied Technology.

Collins, D. L., Baum, A., & Singer, J. E. (1983). Coping with chronic stress at Three Mile Island: Psychological and biochemical evidence. *Health Psychology, 2*, 149–166.

Collins, J. B. (1969). *Perceptual dimensions of architectural space validated against behavioral criteria*. Unpublished doctoral dissertation, University of Utah, Salt Lake City.

Colman, R., Frankel, F., Ritvo, E., & Freeman, B. (1976). The effects of fluorescent and incandescent illumination upon repetitive behavior in autistic children. *Journal of Autism and Childhood Schizophrenia, 6*, 157–162.

Cone, J. D., & Hayes, S. C. (1980). *Environmental problems: Behavioral solutions*. Monterey, CA: Brooks/Cole.

——, & Parham, I. A. (1973). *Pollution by young children: Model and environmental effects*. Unpublished manuscript.

Conning, A. M., & Byrne, R. W. (1984). Pointing to preschool children's spatial competence: A study in natural settings. *Journal of Environmental Psychology, 4*, 165–175.

Conway, D. (1973). *Social science and design: A process model for architect and social scientist collaboration*. Washington, DC: American Institute of Architects.

Cook, M. (1970). Experiments on orientation and proxemics. *Human Relations, 23*, 61–76.

Coombs, C. H., Dawes, R. M., & Tversky, A. (1970). *Mathematical psychology: An elementary introduction*. Englewood Cliffs, NJ: Prentice-Hall.

Cooper, C. (1976). The house as a symbol of the self. In H. Proshansky, W. H. Ittelson, and L. G. Rivlin (Eds.), *Environmental Psychology*. New York: Holt, Rinehart and Winston.

Corbett, M. N. (1981). *A better place to live: New designs for tomorrow's communities*. Emmaus, PA: Rodale.

Coren, S., Porac, C., & Ward, L. M. (1984). *Sensation and perception*. Toronto: Academic Press.

Cornell, E. H., & Hay, D. H. (1984). Children's acquisition of a route via different media. *Environment and Behavior, 16*, 627–641.

——, & Heth, C. D. (1984). Report of a missing child. In Sheldon H. White (Chair), *Human development in the real world*. Symposium conducted at the meeting of the American Psychological Association, Toronto.

Cotterell, J. L. (1984). Effects of school architectural design on student and teacher anxiety. *Environment and Behavior, 16,* 455–479.

Cottle, W. C. (1950). A factorial study of the Multiphasic, Strong, Kuder, and Bell inventories using a population of adult males. *Psychometrika, 15,* 25–47.

Cotton, J. L. (1982, August). *Temperature, humidity, and violent crime.* Paper presented at the annual convention of the American Psychological Association, Washington, DC.

Cox, V. C., Paulus, P. B., & McCain, G. (1984). Prison crowding research: The relevance of prison housing standards and a general approach regarding crowding phenomena. *American Psychologist, 39,* 1148–1160.

———, Paulus, P. B., McCain, G., & Schkade, J. K. (1979). Field research on the effects of crowding in prisons and on offshore drilling platforms. In J. R. Aiello and A. Baum (Eds.), *Residential crowding and design.* New York: Plenum Press.

Craik, K. H. (1968). The comprehension of the everyday physical environment. *Journal of the American Institute of Planners, 34,* 29–37.

——— (1970). Environmental psychology. In T. M. Newcomb (Ed.), *New directions in psychology.* New York: Holt, Rinehart and Winston.

——— (1971). The assessment of places. In P. McReynolds (Ed.) *Advances in psychological assessment,* Vol. 2. Palo Alto, CA: Science and Behavior Books.

——— (1975). Individual variations in landscape description. In E. H. Zube, R. O. Brush, and J. G. Fabors (Eds.), *Landscape assessment: Values, perceptions and resources.* Stroudsberg, PA: Dowden, Hutchinson and Ross.

——— (1976). The personality research paradigm in environmental psychology. In S. Wapner, S. B. Cohen, and B. Kaplan (Eds.), *Experiencing the environment.* New York: Plenum.

——— (1977). Multiple scientific paradigms in environmental psychology. *International Journal of Psychology, 12,* 147–157.

——— (1983a). A psychology of the large scale environment. In N. R. Feimer and E. S. Geller (Eds.), *Environmental psychology: Directions and perspectives.* New York: Praeger.

——— (1983b). A role theoretical analysis of scenic quality judgments. In R. D. Rowe and L. G. Chestnut (Eds.), *Managing air quality and scenic resources at national parks and wilderness areas.* Boulder, CO: Westview Press.

———, & Appleyard, D. (1980). The streets of San Francisco: Brunswik's lens model applied to urban inference and assessment. *Journal of Social Issues, 36,* 72–85.

———, & Zube, E. H. (Eds.) (1976). *Perceiving environmental quality.* New York: Plenum.

Crump, S. L., Nunes, D. L., & Crossman, E. K. (1977). The effects of litter on littering behavior in a forest environment. *Environment and Behavior, 9,* 137–146.

Cunningham, M. R. (1977). Notes on the psychological basis of environmental design: The right-left dimension in apartment floor plans. *Environment and Behavior, 9,* 125–135.

——— (1979). Weather, mood, and helping behavior: Quasi-experiments with the sunshine samaritan. *Journal of Personality and Social Psychology, 37,* 1947–1956.

Cvetkovich, G., & Earle, T. C. (1985). Classifying hazardous events. *Journal of Environmental Psychology, 5,* 5–35.

D'Atri, D. A. (1975). Psychophysical responses to crowding. *Environment and Behavior, 7,* 237–252.

Daniel, T. C. (1976). Criteria for development and application of perceived quality indices. In K. H. Craik and E. H. Zube (Eds.), *Perceiving environmental quality: Research and applications.* New York: Plenum Press.

———, & Ittelson, W. H. (1981). Conditions for environmental perception research: Comment on The psychological representation of molar physical environments by Ward and Russell. *Journal of Experimental Psychology: General, 110,* 153–157.

Daves, W. F., & Swaffer, P. W. (1971). Effect of room size on critical interpersonal distance. *Perceptual and Motor Skills, 33,* 926.

David, T. G. (1982). Evaluating school environments from a user perspective. *Journal of Man-Environment Relations, 1* (3), 79–89.

Davidson, L. M., Baum, A., & Collins, D. L. (1982). Stress and control-related problems at Three Mile Island. *Journal of Applied Social Psychology, 12,* 349–359.

Davis, G., & Szigeti, F. (1982). Programming, space planning and office design. *Environment and Behavior, 14,* 299–317.

Davis, I. (1978). *Shelter after disaster.* Oxford: Oxford Polytechnic Press.

Dawes, R. M. (1973). The commons dilemma game: An N-person mixed-motive game with a dominating strategy for defection. *ORI Research Bulletin, 13,* 1–12.

——— (1980). Social dilemmas. *Annual Review of Psychology, 31,* 169–193.

———, McTavish, J., & Shaklee, H. (1977). Behavior communication and assumptions about other people's behavior in a common dilemma situation. *Journal of Personality and Social Psychology, 35,* 1–11.

———, Orbell, J. M. & van de Kragt, A. J. C. (1985). *Doing well and doing good as ways of resolving social dilemmas.* Manuscript in preparation.

De Renzi, E. (1982). Memory disorders following focal neocortical damage. *Philosophical transactions of the Royal Society of London, 298,* 73–83.

Deardon, P. (1980). Landscape assessment: The last decade. *Canadian Geographer, 24,* (3), 316–325.

Desor, J. A. (1972). Towards a psychological theory of crowding. *Journal of Personality and Social Psychology, 21,* 79–83.

Diaz-Guerrero, R. (1984). Contemporary psychology in Mexico. *Annual Review of Psychology, 35,* 83–112.

Donovan, R. J., & Rossiter, J. R. (1982). Store atmosphere: An environmental psychology approach. *Journal of Retailing, 58,* 34–57.

Dorfman, P. W. (1979). Measurement and meaning of recreation satisfaction. *Environment and Behavior, 11,* 483–510.

Dosey, M. A., & Meisels, M. (1969). Personal space and self-protection. *Journal of Personality and Social Psychology, 11,* 93–97.

Downs, R. M. (1981). Maps and metaphors. *Professional Geographer, 33,* 287–293.

——, & Siegel, A. W. (1981). On mapping researchers mapping children mapping space. In L. S. Liben, A. H. Patterson, and N. Newcombe (Eds.), *Spatial representation and behavior across the life span.* New York: Academic Press.

——, & Stea, D. (1977). *Maps in minds: Reflections on cognitive mapping.* San Francisco: Harper & Row.

Draper, P. (1973). Crowding among hunter-gatherers: The Kung bushmen. *Science, 182,* 301–303.

Driver, B. L., & Knopf, R. C. (1977). Personality, outdoor recreation and expected consequences. *Environment and Behavior, 9,* 169–193.

Duke, M. P., & Nowicki, S., Jr. (1972). A new measure and social learning model for interpersonal distance. *Journal of Experimental Research in Personality, 6,* 119–132.

Dunn, B. E. (1979). The noise environment of man. In H. W. Jones (Ed.), *Noise in the human environment,* (Vol. 2). Edmonton, Alberta: Environmental Council of Alberta.

Dykman, B. D., & Reis, H. T. (1979). Personality correlates of classroom seating position. *Journal of Educational Psychology, 71,* 346–354.

Eastman, C. M., & Harper, J. (1971). A study of proxemic behavior. *Environment and Behavior, 3,* 418–437.

Eddy, G. L., & Sinnett, R. (1973). Behavior setting utilization by emotionally disturbed college students. *Journal of Consulting and Clinical Psychology, 40,* 210–216.

Edinger, J. A., & Patterson, M. L. (1983). Nonverbal involvement and social control. *Psychological Bulletin, 93,* 30–56.

Edney, J. J. (1972a). Property, possession and permanence: A field study in human territoriality. *Journal of Applied Social Psychology, 2,* 275–282.

—— (1972b). Place and space: The effects of experience with a physical locale. *Journal of Experimental Social Psychology, 8,* 124–135.

—— (1974). Human territoriality. *Psychological Bulletin, 81,* 959–975.

—— (1975). Territoriality and control: A field experiment. *Journal of Personality and Social Psychology, 6,* 1108–1115.

—— (1976). The psychological role of property rights in human behavior. *Environment and Planning A, 8,* 811–822.

—— (1977). Theories of human crowding: A review. *Environment and Planning A, 9,* 1211–1232.

—— (1979). The nuts game: A concise commons dilemma analog. *Environmental Psychology and Nonverbal Behavior, 3,* 252–254.

—— (1981). Paradoxes on the commons: Scarcity and the problem of equality. *Journal of Community Psychology, 9,* 3–34.

—— (1984). Rationality and social justice. *Human Relations, 37,* 163–180.

——, & Bell, P. A. (1983). The commons dilemma: Comparing altruism, the golden rule, perfect equality of outcomes, and territoriality. *The Social Science Journal, 20,* 23–33.

——, & Bell, P. A. (1984). Sharing scarce resources: Group-outcome orientation, external disaster, and stealing in a simulated commons. *Small Group Behavior, 15,* 87–108.

——, & Buda, M. A. (1976). Distinguishing territoriality and privacy: Two studies. *Human Ecology, 4,* 283–296.

——, & Harper, C. S. (1978a). The commons dilemma: A review of contributions from psychology. *Environmental Management, 2,* 491–507.

——, & Harper, C. S. (1978b). Heroism in a resource crisis: A simulation study. *Environmental Management, 2,* 523–527.

——, & Jordan-Edney, N. L. (1974). Territorial spacing on a beach. *Sociometry, 37,* 92–104.

Edwards, D. J. (1972). Approaching the unfamiliar: A study of human interaction distances. *Journal of Behavioral Science, 1,* 249–250.

Eisemon, T. (1975). Simulations and requirements for citizen participation in public housing: The Truax technique. *Environment and Behavior, 7,* 99–213.

Ellis, P. (1980). Review of Designing for therapeutic environments. *Bulletin of the British Psychological Society, 33,* 325–26.

Epstein, Y. M. (1982). Crowding stress and human behavior. In G. W. Evans (Ed.), *Environmental stress.* New York: Cambridge University Press.

——, & Karlin, R. A. (1975). Effects of acute experimental crowding. *Journal of Applied Social Psychology, 5,* 34–53.

——, Woolfolk, R. L., and Lehrer, P. M. (1981). Physiological, cognitive and nonverbal responses to repeated exposure to crowding. *Journal of Applied Social Psychology, 11,* 1–13.

Espe, H. (1981). Differences in the perception of National Socialist and Classicist architecture. *Journal of Environmental Psychology, 1,* 33–42.

Esser, A. H. (1968). Dominance hierarchy and clinical course of psychiatrically hospitalized boys. *Child Development, 39,* 147–157.

—— (1976). Discussion of papers presented in the symposium Theoretical and empirical issues with regard to privacy, territoriality, personal space, and crowding. *Environment and Behavior, 8,* 117–125.

——, Chamberlain, A. S., Chapple, E. D., & Kline, N. S. (1965). Territoriality of patients on a research ward. In J. Wortis (Ed.), *Recent advances in biological psychiatry.* New York: Plenum.

Etzioni, A. (1972, June 3). Human beings are not very easy to change after all. *Saturday Review.*

Evans, G. W. (1974). An examination of the information overload mechanism of personal space. *Man-Environment Systems, 4,* 61.

—— (1978). Human spatial behavior. The arousal model. In A. Baum and Y. Epstein (Eds.), *Human response to crowding.* Hillsdale, NJ: Erlbaum.

—— (1979a). Crowding and human performance. *Journal of Applied Social Psychology, 9,* 27–46.

——(1979b). Design implications of spatial research. In J. R. Aiello and A. Baum, *Residential crowding and design.* New York: Plenum.

—— (1980). Environmental cognition. *Psychological Bulletin, 88,* 259–267.

—— (Ed.) (1982). *Environmental stress.* New York: Cambridge University Press.

——, Brennan, P. L., Skorpanich, M. A., & Held, D. (1984). Cognitive mapping and elderly adults: Verbal and location memory for urban landmarks. *Journal of Gerontology, 39,* 452–457.

——, & Eichelman, W. (1976). Preliminary models of conceptual linkages among proxemic variables. *Environment and Behavior, 8,* 87–117.

——, Fellows, J., Zorn, M., & Doty, K. (1980). Cognitive mapping and architecture. *Journal of Applied Psychology, 65,* 474–478.

——, & Howard, R. E. (1973). Personal space. *Psychological Bulletin, 80,* 334–344.

——, & Jacobs, S. V. (1982). Air pollution and human behavior. In G. W. Evans (Ed.), *Environmental stress.* New York: Cambridge University Press.

——, Jacobs, S. V., & Frager, N. B. (1982a). Behavioral responses to air pollution. In A. Baum and J. E. Singer (Eds.), *Advances in environmental psychology.* Hillsdale, NJ: Erlbaum.

——, Jacobs, S. V., & Frager, N. B. (1982b). Adaptation to air pollution. *Journal of Environmental Psychology, 2,* 99–108.

——, & Lovell, B. (1979). Design modification in an open plan school. *Journal of Educational Psychology, 71,* 41–49.

——, Marrero, D. G., & Butler, P. A. (1981) Environmental learning and cognitive mapping. *Environment and Behavior, 13,* 83–104.

——, Skorpanich, M. A., Garling, T., Bryant, K., & Bresolin, B. (1984). The effects of pathway configuration, landmarks, and stress on environmental cognition. *Journal of Environmental Psychology, 4,* 323–335.

——, Smith, C., & Pezdek, K. (1982). Cognitive maps and urban form. *Journal of the American Planning Association, 48,* 232–244.

Fagot, B. I. (1977). Variations in density: Effect on task and social behaviors of pre-school children. *Developmental Psychology, 13,* 166–167.

Farbstein, J., & Wener, R. E. (1982). Evaluation of correctional environments. *Environment and Behavior, 14,* 671–694.

Farmer, E. W., & Bendix, A. (1982). Geophysical variables and behavior: V. Human performance in ionized air. *Perceptual and Motor Skills, 54,* 403–412.

Farrenkopf, T., & Roth, V. (1980). The university faculty office as an environment. *Environment and Behavior, 12,* 467–477.

Feimer, N. R. (1981, August). Personality and sociodemographic variables as sources of variation in environmental perception. In H. M. Proshansky *Environmental cognition.* Symposium at the meeting of the American Psychological Association. (ERIC Document Reproduction Service No. ED 211 393).

—— (1984). Environmental perception: The effects of media, evaluative context, and observer sample. *Journal of Environmental Psychology, 4,* 61–80.

Feitler, F. C., Weiner, W., & Blumberg, A. (1970). *The relationship between interpersonal relations orientations and preferred classroom physical settings.* Paper presented at the annual meeting of the American Educational Research Association, Minneapolis.

Finighan, W. R. (1980). Some environmental observations on the role of privacy in the residential environment. *Man-Environment Systems, 10,* 153–159.

Finnie, W. C. (1973). Field experiments in litter control. *Environment and Behavior, 5,* 123–144.

Firestone, I. J., Lichtman, C. M., & Evans, J. R. (1980). Privacy and solidarity: Effects of nursing home accommodation on environmental perception and sociability preferences. *International Journal of Aging and Human Development, 11,* 229–241.

Fischer, C. S. (1976). *The urban experience.* New York: Harcourt Brace Jovanovich.

Fischhoff, B., Slovic, P., & Lichtenstein, S. (1983). "The public" vs. "the experts": Perceived vs. actual disagreements about risks of nuclear power. In V. Covello, G. Flamm, J. Rodericks, and R. Tardiff (Eds.), *Analysis of actual and perceived risks.* New York: Plenum.

Fishbein, M., & Ajzen, I. (1975). *Belief, attitude, intention, and behavior: An introduction to theory and research.* Reading, MA: Addison-Wesley.

Fisher, J. D., & Baum, A. (1980). Situational and arousal-based messages and the reduction of crowding stress. *Journal of Applied Social Psychology, 10,* 191–201.

——, & Byrne, D. (1975). Too close for comfort: Sex differences in response to invasions of personal space. *Journal of Personality and Social Psychology, 32,* 15–21.

Fisher, S., Murray, K., & Frazer, N. A. (1985). Homesickness, health and efficiency in first year students. *Journal of Environmental Psychology, 5,* 181–195.

Flatt, D. L. (1975). The effects of high temperature upon performance of certain physical tasks by high school students (Doctoral dissertation, North Texas State University, 1975). *Dissertations Abstracts International, 35,* 7678A.

Fletcher, D. (1983). Effects of classroom lighting on the behavior of exceptional children. *EEQ: Exceptional Education Quarterly, 4,* 75–89.

Flynn, J. E., Hendrick, C., Spencer, T., & Martyniuk, D. (1979). The effects of light source color on user impression and satisfaction. *Journal of the Illuminating Engineering Society, 6* (3) 167–179.

Foddy, W. H., & Finighan, W. R. (1980). The concept of privacy from a symbolic interaction perspective. *Journal for the Theory of Social Behavior, 10,* 1–17.

Forston, R. F., & Larson, C. U. (1968). The dynamics of space: An experimental study in proxemic behavior among Latin Americans and North Americans. *Journal of Communication, 18,* 109–116.

Foster, H. D. (1976). Assessing disaster magnitude: A social science approach. *The Professional Geographer, 28,* 241–247.

—— (1980). *Disaster planning: The preservation of life and property.* New York: Springer-Verlag.

Fox, D. R. (1985). Psychology, ideology, utopia and the commons. *American Psychologist, 40,* 48–58.

Fox, J. G. (1983). Industrial music. In D. J. Oborne and M. M. Gruneberg (Eds.), *The physical environment at work.* New York: Wiley.

Fox, J., & Guyer, M. (1978). Public choice and cooperation in an n-person prisoner's dilemma. *Journal of Conflict Resolution, 22,* 468–481.

Fox, W. F. (1967). Human performance in the cold. *Human Factors, 9,* 203–220.

Franck, K. A. (1980). Friends and strangers: The social experience of living in urban and non-urban settings. *Journal of Social Issues, 36* (3), 52–71.

Freedman, J. L. (1975). *Crowding and behavior.* San Francisco: Freeman.

—— (1979a). Reconciling apparent differences between the responses of human and other animals to crowding. *Psychological Review, 86,* 80–85.

—— (1979b). Current status of work on crowding and suggestions for housing design. In J. R. Aiello and A. Baum (Eds.), *Residential crowding and design.* New York: Plenum.

——, Birsky, J., & Cavoukian, A. (1980). Environmental determinants of behavioral contagion: Density and number. *Basic and Applied Social Psychology, 1,* 155–161.

Freimark, S., Wener, R., Phillips, D., & Korber, E. (1984). *Estimation of crowding, number and density for human and non-human stimuli.* Poster at the annual meeting of the American Psychological Association, Toronto, Ontario.

Fridgen, J. D. (1984). Environmental psychology and tourism. *Annals of Tourism Research, 11,* 19–39.

Fried, M. (1982). Residential attachment: Sources of residential and community satisfaction. *Journal of Social Issues, 38* (3), 107–119.

——, & Gleicher, P. (1961). Some sources of satisfaction in an urban slum. *Journal of the American Institute of Planners, 27,* 305–315.

Friedman, S. (1974). Relationships among cognitive complexity, interpersonal dimension and spatial preferences and propensities. In S. Friedman and J. B. Juhasz (Eds.), *Environments: Notes and selections on objects, spaces and behavior.* Belmont, CA: Wadsworth.

Friedmann, A., Zimring, C., & Zube, E. (1978). *Environmental design evaluation.* New York: Plenum.

Fuhrer, U. (1983). Oekopsychologie: Some general implications from a particular literature. *Journal of Environmental Psychology, 3,* 239–252.

Funabashi, T., Shimizu, M., & Sekida, H. (1978). A study on approach space to shrines. *Proceedings of the Annual Convention of the Architectural Institute of Japan,* 1713–1714.

Fusilier, M. R., & Hoyer, W. D. (1980). Variables affecting perceptions of invasion of privacy in a personnel selection situation. *Journal of Applied Psychology, 65,* 623–626.

Galle, O. R., & Gove, W. R. (1979). Crowding and behavior in Chicago, 1940–1970. In J. R. Aiello and A. Baum (Eds.), *Residential crowding and design.* New York: Plenum.

Galster, G. C., & Hesser, G. W. (1981). Residential satisfaction: Compositional and contextual correlates. *Environment and Behavior, 13,* 735–758.

Gardin, H., Kaplan, C. J., Firestone, I. J., & Cowan, G. A. (1973). Proxemic effects on cooperation, attitude, and approach-avoidance in prisoner's dilemma game. *Journal of Personality and Social Psychology, 27,* 13–19.

Garland, H. C., Haynes, J. J., & Grubb, G. C. (1979).

Transit map color coding and street detail: Effects on trip planning performance. *Environment and Behavior, 11,* 162–184.

Garling, T. (1969). Studies in visual perception of architectural spaces and rooms. *Scandinavian Journal of Psychology, 10,* 250–256.

——— (1982). Swedish environmental psychology. *Journal of Environmental Psychology, 2,* 233–251.

———, Book, A., & Lindberg, E. (1984). Cognitive mapping of large-scale environments: The interrelationship of action plans, acquisition, and orientation. *Environment and Behavior, 16,* 3–34.

———, Book, A., Lindberg, E., & Nilsson, T. (1981). Memory for the spatial layout of the everyday physical environment: Factors affecting rate of acquisition. *Journal of Environmental Psychology, 1,* 263–277.

———, Lindberg, E., & Mantyla, T. (1983). Orientation in buildings: Effects of familiarity, visual access, and orientation aids. *Journal of Applied Psychology, 68,* 177–186.

Geller, D. (1980). Responses to urban stimuli: A balanced approach. *Journal of Social Issues, 36* (3), 86–100.

Geller, E. S. (1981). Evaluating energy conservation programs: Is verbal report enough? *Journal of Consumer Research, 8,* 331–335.

——— (1983). The energy crisis and behavioral science: A conceptual framework for large-scale intervention. In A. W. Childs and G. B. Melton (Eds.) *Rural psychology.* New York: Plenum.

——— (in press). Environmental psychology and applied behavior analysis: From strange bedfellows to a productive marriage. In D. Stokols and I. Altman (Eds.), *Handbook of environmental psychology,* New York: Wiley.

———, Brasted, W., & Mann, M. (1980). Waste receptacle designs as interventions for litter control. *Journal of Environmental Systems, 9,* 145–160.

———, Winett, R. A., & Everett, P. B. (1982). *Preserving the environment.* New York: Pergamon Press.

———, Witmer, J. F., & Orebaugh, A. L. (1976). Instructions as determinants of paper disposal behaviors. *Environment and Behavior, 8,* 417–438.

Genereux, R. L., Ward, L. M., & Russell, J. A. (1983). The behavioral component of the meaning of places. *Journal of Environmental Psychology, 3,* 43–55.

Germans now putting leisure ahead of jobs. (1984, January 8). Victoria, British Columbia, *Times-Colonist,* p. C7.

Gibson, J. J. (1966). *The senses considered as a perceptual systems.* Boston: Houghton Mifflin.

——— (1976, October). *The theory of affordances and the design of the environment.* Paper presented at the Symposium on Perception in Architecture, American Society for Aesthetics, Toronto.

——— (1979). *The ecological approach to visual perception.* Boston: Houghton Mifflin.

Gifford, R. (1975). *The judgment of buildings: Who you ask, what you ask and what you ask about.* Paper presented at the annual meeting of the Environmental Design Research Association, Lawrence, Kansas.

——— (1976a). *Personal and situational factors in judgements of typical architecture.* Unpublished doctoral dissertation, Simon Fraser University, Vancouver, British Columbia.

——— (1976b, March). *Predicting judgments of buildings: Reality vs. simulation.* Paper presented at the annual meeting of the Environmental Design Research Association, Vancouver, BC.

——— (1976c). Environmental numbness in the classroom. *Journal of Experimental Education, 44* (3), 4–7. (c)

——— (1980a). Judgments of the built environment as a function of individual differences and context. *Journal of Man-Environment Relations, 1,* 22–31.

——— (1980b). Environmental dispositions and the evaluation of architectural interiors. *Journal of Research in Personality, 14,* 386–399.

——— (1981). Sociability: Traits, settings, and interactions. *Journal of Personality and Social Psychology, 41,* 340–347.

——— (1982a). Children and the commons dilemma. *Journal of Applied Social Psychology, 12,* 269–280.

——— (1982b). Projected interpersonal distance and orientation choices: Personality, sex, and social situation. *Social Psychology Quarterly, 45,* 145–152.

——— (1982c). Affilativeness: A trait measure in relation to single-act and multiple-act behavioral criteria. *Journal of Research in Personality, 16,* 128–134.

——— (1983). The experience of personal space: Perception of interpersonal distance. *Journal of Nonverbal Behavior, 7,* 170–178.

——— (1984–1985). Age, era and life perspective: Emotional connotations of the 1920s through the 1980s to individuals in their twenties through their eighties. *International Journal of Aging and Human Development. 20* (1), 33–40.

———, & Gallagher, T. M. B. (1985). Sociability: Personality, social context, and physical setting. *Journal of Personality and Social Psychology, 48,* 1015–1023.

———, Hay, R., & Boros, K. (1982–1983). Individual differences in environmental attitudes. *Journal of Environmental Education, 14*(2), 19–23.

———, & Ng, C. F. (1982). The relative contribution of visual and auditory cues to environmental perception. *Journal of Environmental Psychology, 2,* 275–284.

———, & Peacock, J. (1979). Crowding: More fearsome than crime-provoking? Comparison of an Asian city and a North American city. *Psychologia, 22,* 79–83.

———, & Price, J. (1979). Personal space in nursery school

children. *Canadian Journal of Behavioral Science, 11,* 318–326.

Gilbert, G., & Foerster, J. F. (1977). The importance of attitudes in the decision to use mass transit. *Transportation, 6,* 321–332.

Gill, W. M. (1977). A look at the change to open-plan schools in New Zealand. *New Zealand Journal of Educational Studies, 12,* 3–16.

Glyptis, S. A., & Chambers, D. A. (1982). No place like home. *Leisure Studies, 1,* 247–262.

Godden, D. R., & Baddeley, A. D. (1975). Context-dependent memory in two natural environments: On land and underwater. *British Journal of Psychology, 66,* 325–331.

Gold, J. R., & Burgess, J. (Eds.) (1982). *Valued environments.* London: George Allen & Unwin.

Goldhaber, M. K., Houts, P. S., & DiSabella, R. (1983). Moving after the crisis: A prospective study of Three Mile Island area population mobility. *Environment and Behavior, 15,* 93–120.

Goldring, P. (1967). Role of distance and posture in the evaluation of interactions. *Proceedings of the 75th Annual Convention of the American Psychological Association.*

Goldstein, J., & Dejoy, D. M. (1980). Behavioral and performance effects of noise: Perspectives for research. In J. V. Tobias, G. Jansen, and W. D. Ward (Eds.), *Proceedings of the third international congress on noise as a public health problem.* Rockville, MD: American Speech-Language-Hearing Association.

Golledge, R. G. (1976). Methods and methodological issues in environmental cognition research. In G. T. Moore and R. G. Golledge (Eds.), *Environmental knowing: Theories, research, and methods.* Stroudsburg, PA: Dowden, Hutchinson & Ross.

———, Smith, T. R., Pellegrino, J. W., Doherty, S., & Marshall, S. P. (1985). A conceptual model and empirical analysis of children's acquisition of spatial knowledge. *Journal of Environmental Psychology, 5,* 125–152.

Goodman, P. (1964). Seating arrangements: An elementary lecture in functional planning. *Utopian essays and practical proposals.* New York: Random House/Alfred A. Knopf.

Goodrich, R. (1982). Seven office evaluations: A review. *Environment and Behavior, 8,* 175–190.

Gormley, F. P., & Aiello, J. R. (1982). Social density, interpersonal relationships and residential crowding stress. *Journal of Applied Social Psychology, 12,* 222–236.

Gormly, J. (1983). Predicting behavior from personality trait scores. *Personality and Social Psychology Bulletin, 9,* 267–270.

Gove, W. R., & Hughes, M. (1980). In pursuit of preconceptions: A reply to the claim of Booth and his colleagues that household crowding is not an impor-

tant variable. *American Sociological Review, 45,* 878–886.

——— (1983). *Overcrowding in the household.* New York: Academic Press.

Green, C. S. (1975). The ecology of committees. *Environment and Behavior, 7,* 411–427.

Greenbaum, P. E., & Greenbaum, S. D. (1981). Territorial personalization: Group identity and social interaction in a Slavic-American neighborhood. *Environment and Behavior, 13,* 574–589.

Greenberg, C. I., Strube, M. J., & Myers, R. A. (1980). A multitrait-multimethod investigation of interpersonal distance. *Journal of Nonverbal Behavior, 5,* 104–114.

Greer, D. L. (1983). Spectator booing and the home advantage: A study of social influence in the basketball arena. *Social Psychology Quarterly, 46,* 252–261.

Groat, L. (1982). Meaning in post-modern architecture: An examination using the multiple sorting task. *Journal of Environmental Psychology, 2,* 3–22.

———, & Canter, D. (1979). Does post-modernism communicate? *Progressive Architecture, 12,* 84–87.

Grzelak, J., & Tyska, T. (1974). Some preliminary experiments on cooperation in n-person games. *Polish Psychological Bulletin, 5,* 80–91.

Guardo, C. J., & Meisels, M. (1971). Child-parent spatial patterns under praise and reproof. *Developmental Psychology, 5,* 365.

Guilford, J. P. (1959). *Personality.* New York: McGraw-Hill.

Gump, P. V. (1978). School environments. In I. Altman and J. F. Wohlwill (Eds.), *Children and the environment.* New York: Plenum Press.

———, & Friesen, W. V. (1964a). Participation in nonclass settings. In R. G. Barker and P. V. Gump (Eds.), *Big school, small school: High school size and student behavior.* Standford, CA: Stanford University Press.

——— (1964b). Satisfactions derived from nonclass settings. In R. G. Barker and P. V. Gump (Eds.), *Big school, small school: High school size and student behavior.* Stanford, CA: Stanford University Press.

———, & Ross, R. (1977). The fit of milieu and program in school environments. In H. McGurk (Ed.), *Ecological factors in human development.* New York: Elsevier North-Holland.

Gurkaynak, M. R., & LeCompte, W. A. (1979). *Human consequences of crowding.* New York: Plenum Press.

Gustke, L. D., & Hodgson, R. W. (1980). The rate of travel along an interpretive trail. *Environment and Behavior, 12,* 53–63.

Haase, R. F., & Pepper, D. T., Jr. (1972). Nonverbal components of empathic communication. *Journal of Counselling Psychology, 19,* 417–424.

Haines, L. L. (1985). *Density and territoriality: The effects on classroom performance.* Unpublished Honor's thesis, University of Victoria, Victoria, British Columbia.

Hall, E. T. (1959). *The silent language.* Garden City, NY: Doubleday.

—— (1966). *The hidden dimension.* Garden City, NY: Doubleday.

Hamilton, W. G. (1985). The Okanagan Valley, British Columbia: Visual landscape assessment and planning policy. *Environments, 17,* 46–58.

Hammitt, W. E. (1982). Cognitive dimensions of wilderness solitude. *Environment and Behavior, 14,* 478–493.

Handal, P., Barling, P., & Morrissy, E. (1981). Development of perceived and preferred measures of physical and social characteristics of the residential environment and their relationship and satisfaction. *Journal of Community Psychology, 9,* 118–124.

Hanlon, M. (1981, November 8). Psychologists used for pedestrian engineering. *Toronto Star,* p. E5.

Hansard, (1943). "House of Commons rebuilding," *Parliamentary debates, House of Commons, 393,* No. 114, 403–471. London: HMSO.

Hanson, S., Vitek, J. D., & Hanson, P. O. (1979). Natural disaster: Long-range impact on human response to future disaster threats. *Environment and Behavior, 11,* 268–284.

Hansson, R. O., Noulles, D., & Bellovich, S. J. (1982). Knowledge warning and stress: A study of comparative roles in an urban floodplain. *Environment and Behavior, 14,* 171–185.

Hardin, G. (1968). The tragedy of the commons. *Science, 162,* 1243–1248.

Harman, E., & Betak, J. F. (1974). *Some preliminary findings on the cognitive meaning of external privacy in housing.* Paper presented at the annual meetings of the Environmental Design Research Association, Milwaukee.

Harrell, G., Hutt, M., & Anderson, J. (1980). Path analysis of buyer behavior under conditions of crowding. *Journal of Marketing Research, 17,* 45–51.

Harries, K. D., & Stadler, S. J. (1983). Determinism revisited: Assault and heat stress in Dallas, 1980. *Environment and Behavior, 15,* 235–256.

Harris, L., & Associates. (1978). *The Steelcase national study of office environments: Do they work?* Grand Rapids, MI: Steelcase Inc.

Harrison, J., & Sarre, P. (1971). Personal construct theory in the measurement of environmental images: Problems and methods. *Environment and Behavior, 6,* 351–374.

Harrison, J., & Sarre, P. (1975). Personal construct theory in the measurement of environmental images. *Environment and Behavior, 7,* 3–58.

Hart, R. (1979). *Children's experience of place.* New York: Irvington.

Hart, R. A., & Moore, G. T. (1973). The development of spatial cognition: A review. In R. M. Downs and D. Stea (Eds.), *Image and environment: Cognitive mapping and spatial behavior.* Chicago: Aldine.

Hartgen, D. T. (1974). Attitudinal and situational variables influencing urban mode choice: Some empirical findings. *Transportation, 3,* 377–392.

Hatch, C. R. (Ed.) (1984). *The scope of social architecture.* Toronto: Van Nostrand Reinhold.

Hawkins, D. I., Best, R. J., & Coney, K. A. (1983). *Consumer behavior: Implications for marketing strategy.* Plano, TX: Business Publications.

Hawkins, L. H. (1981). The influence of air ions, temperature, and humidity on subjective wellbeing and comfort. *Journal of Environmental Psychology, 1,* 279–292.

——, & Barker, T. (1978). Air ions and human performance. *Ergonomics, 21,* 273–278.

Hayduk, L. A. (1978). Personal space: An evaluative and orienting overview. *Psychological Bulletin, 85,* 117–134.

—— (1981). The shape of personal space: An empirical investigation. *Canadian Journal of Behavioral Science. 13,* 87–93.

—— (1983). Personal space: Where we now stand. *Psychological Bulletin, 94,* 293–335.

—— (1985). Personal space: The conceptual and measurement implications of structural equation models. *Canadian Journal of Behavioral Science, 17,* 140–149.

Heberlein, T. A., & Black, J. S. (1981). Cognitive consistency and environmental action. *Environment and Behavior, 13,* 717–734.

Heckle, R. V., & Hiers, J. M. (1977). Social distance and locus of control. *Journal of Clinical Psychology, 33,* 469–474.

Hedge, A. (1982). The open-plan office: A systematic investigation of employee reactions to their work environment. *Environment and Behavior, 14,* 519–542.

Hediger, H. (1950). *Wild animals in captivity.* London: Butterworth.

Heft, H. (1979). Background and focal environmental conditions of the home and attention in young children. *Journal of Applied Social Psychology, 9,* 47–69.

Heft, H. (1985). High residential density and perceptual-cognitive development: An examination of the effects of crowding and noise in the home. In J. F. Wohlwill and W. van Vliet— (Eds.), *Habitats for children: The impacts of density.* Hillsdale, NJ: Erlbaum.

Heidegger, M. (1971). *Poetry, language, and thought.* New York: Harper and Row.

Heimsath, C. (1977). *Behavioral architecture: Toward an accountable design process.* New York: McGraw-Hill.

Heller, J. F., Groff, B. D., & Solomon, S. A. (1977). Toward an understanding of crowding: The role of physical interaction. *Journal of Personality and Social Psychology, 35,* 183–190.

Helson, H. (1947). Adaptation level as a frame of reference for prediction of psychophysical data. *American Journal of Psychology, 60,* 1–29.

—— (1964). *Adaptation-level theory.* New York: Harper and Row.

Hensley, W. E. (1982). Professor proxemics: Personality and job demands as factors of faculty office arrangement. *Environment and Behavior, 14,* 581–591.

Heron, W., Doane, B. K., & Scott, T. H. (1956). Visual disturbances after prolonged perceptual isolation. *Canadian Journal of Psychology, 10,* 13–18.

Hershberger, R. G. (1968). A study of meaning and architecture. *Man and His Environment, 1*(6), 6–7.

—— (1970). Architecture and meaning. *Journal of Aesthetic Education, 4,* 37–55.

—— (1972, April). *Toward a set of semantic scales to measure the meaning of architectural environments.* Paper presented at the annual meeting of the Environmental Design Research Association, Los Angeles.

—— (1974). Predicting the meaning of architecture. In J. Lang, C. Burnette, W. Moleski, and D. Vachon (Eds.), *Designing for human behavior.* Stroudsburg, PA: Dowden, Hutchinson and Ross.

Hesselgren, S. (1967). *The language of architecture.* Lund: Studentlitteratur.

Hildreth, A. M., Derogatis, L. R., & McCusker, K. (1971). Body buffer zone and violence: A reassessment and confirmation. *American Journal of Psychiatry, 127,* 1641–1645.

Hockey, G. R. J., & Hamilton, P. (1970). Arousal and information selection in short-term memory. *Nature, 226,* 866–867.

Holahan, C. J. (1972). Seating patterns and patient behavior in an experimental dayroom. *Journal of Abnormal Psychology, 80,* 115–124.

—— (1976). Environmental change in a psychiatric setting: A social systems analysis. *Human Relations, 29,* 153–166.

—— (1983). Interventions to reduce environmental stress: Enhancing social support and personal control. In E. Siedman (Ed.), *Handbook of social interventions.* Beverly Hills, CA: Sage.

——, & Dobrowolny, M. B. (1978). Cognitive and behavioral correlates of the spatial environment: An interactional analysis. *Environment and Behavior, 10,* 317–333.

——, & Sorenson, P. F. (1985). The role of figural organization in city imageability: An information processing analysis. *Journal of Environmental Psychology, 5,* 279–286.

——, & Wilcox, B. L. (1979). Environmental satisfaction in high- and low-rise residential settings: A Lew-

inian perspective. In J. R. Aiello and A. Baum (Eds.), *Residential crowding and design.* New York: Plenum Press.

Horowitz, M. J. (1968). Spatial behavior and psychopathology. *Journal of Nervous and Mental Diseases, 146,* 24–35.

——, Duff, D. F., & Stratton, L. O. (1964). Body-buffer zone: Exploration of personal space. *Archives of General Psychology, 11,* 651–656.

Horvath, S. M., Dahms, T. E., & O'Hanlon, J. F. (1971). Carbon monoxide and human vigilance: A deleterious effect of present urban concentrations. *Archives of Environmental Health, 23,* 343–347.

Hovland, C. I., & Sears, R. R. (1940). Minor studies in aggression: VI. Correlation of lynchings with economic indices. *Journal of Psychology, 9,* 301–310.

Howard, E. (1920). *Territory in bird life.* London: John Murray.

Howell, S. C. (1980). *Designing for aging.* Cambridge, MA: The MIT Press.

Hull, R. B., & Buhyoff, G. J. (1983). Distance and scenic beauty: A nonmonotonic relationship. *Environment and Behavior, 15,* 77–91.

Humphrey, C. R., Bord, R. J., Hammond, M. M., & Mann, S. H. (1977). Attitudes and conditions for cooperation in a paper recycling program. *Environment and Behavior, 9,* 107–124.

Hunt, M. E. (1984). Environmental learning without being there. *Environment and Behavior, 16,* 307–334.

Hykin, S. (1984). *The effects of classroom noise on adults: Evidence for sex differences.* Unpublished master's thesis, University of Victoria, Victoria, British Columbia.

IES lighting handbook, 1981. (1981). (Application volume). New York: Illuminating Engineering Society.

Im, S. (1984). Visual preferences in enclosed urban spaces: An exploration of a scientific approach to environmental design. *Environment and Behavior, 16,* 235–262.

Inui, M. (1982). Environmental psychology in Japan. *Journal of Environmental Psychology, 2,* 313–321.

Iso-Ahola, S. E. (1983). Towards a social psychology of recreational travel. *Leisure Studies, 2,* 45–56.

Ittelson, W. H. (1970). Perception of the large-scale environment. *Transactions of the New York Academy of Sciences, 32,* 807–815.

—— (Ed.) (1973). *Environment and cognition.* New York: Seminar Press.

—— (1978). Environmental perception and urban experience. *Environment and Behavior, 10,* 193–213.

Ives, S. M., & Furuseth, D. J. (1983). Immediate response to headwater flooding in Charlotte, North Carolina. *Environment and Behavior, 15,* 512–525.

Iwata, O. (1980). Territoriality orientation, privacy orientation and locus of control as determinants of the perception of crowding. *Japanese Psychological Research, 22,* 13–21.

Izumi, K. (1971). LSD and architectural design. In B. Aaronson and H. Osmond (Eds.) *Psychedelics.* Cambridge, MA: Schenkman.

Jackson, E. L. (1981). Response to earthquake hazard: The west coast of North America. *Environment and Behavior, 13,* 387–416.

Jacobs, J. (1961). *The death and life of great American cities.* New York: Random House.

James, B. (1984). A few words about the home field advantage. In B. James (Ed.), *The Bill James baseball abstract 1984.* New York: Ballantine.

James, J. (1951). A preliminary study of the size determinant in small group interaction. *American Sociological Review, 16,* 474–477.

Jason, L. A., Reichler, A., & Rucker, W. (1981). Territorial behavior on beaches. *Journal of Social Psychology, 114,* 43–50.

Jencks, C. (1978). Post-modern history. *Architectural Design, 1,* 13–58.

Jerdee, T. H., & Rosen, B. (1974). Effects of opportunity to communicate and visibility of individual decisions on behavior in the common interest. *Journal of Applied Psychology, 59,* 712–716.

Jodelet, D. (in press). Environmental psychology in France. In D. Stokols and I. Altman (Eds.), *Handbook of environmental psychology,* New York: Wiley.

Jonah, B. A., Bradley, J. S., & Dawson, N. E. (1981). Predicting individual subjective responses and traffic noise. *Journal of Applied Psychology, 66,* 490–501.

Jones, H. W. (1979). A physical description of noise. In H. W. Jones (Ed.), *Noise in the human environment,* (Vol. 2). Edmonton, Alberta: Environmental Council of Alberta.

Jones, J. W., & Bogat, A. G. (1978). Air pollution and human aggression. *Psychological Reports, 43,* 721–722.

Jones, S. E., & Aiello, J. R. (1973). Proxemic behavior of black and white first- , third- , and fifth-grade children. *Journal of Personality and Social Psychology, 25,* 21–27.

Jorgenson, D. O., & Dukes, F. O. (1976). Deindividuation as a function of density and group membership. *Journal of Personality and Social Psychology, 34,* 24–39.

Jue, G. M., Shumaker, S. A., & Evans, G. W. (1984). Community opinion concerning airport noise-abatement alternatives. *Journal of Environmental Psychology, 4,* 337–345.

Juhasz, J. B., & Paxson, L. (1978). Personality and preference for architectural style. *Perceptual and Motor Skills, 47,* 241–242.

Jung, C. G. (1921/1971). *Psychological types.* Princeton: Princeton University Press.

Justa, F. C., & Golan, M. B. (1977). Office design: Is privacy still a problem? *Journal of Architectural Research, 6* (2), 5–12.

Kalb, L. S., & Keating, J. P. (1981). The measurement of perceived crowding. *Personality and Social Psychology Bulletin, 7,* 650–654.

Kalish, N., Landon, P. B., Rank, D. S., & Suedfeld, P. (1983). Stimulus tasks and environmental characteristics as factors in the cognitive processing of English sentences. *Bulletin of the Psychonomic Society, 21,* 1–3.

Kammann, R., Thomson, R., & Irwin, R. (1979). Unhelpful behavior in the street: City size or immediate pedestrian density? *Environment and Behavior, 11,* 245–250.

Kantola, S. J., Syme, G. J., & Campbell, N. A. (1984). Cognitive dissonance and energy conservation. *Journal of Applied Psychology, 69,* 416–421.

Kantowitz, B. H., & Sorkin, R. D. (1983). *Human factors: Understanding people-system relationships.* New York: Wiley.

Kaplan, K. J. (1977). Structure and process in interpersonal distancing. *Environmental Psychology and Nonverbal Behavior, 1,* 104–121.

Kaplan, R. (1973a). Predictors or environmental preference: Designers and clients. In W. F. E. Preiser (Ed.), *Environmental design research.* Stroudsburg, PA: Dowden Hutchinson and Ross.

—— (1973b). Some psychological benefits of gardening. *Environment and Behavior, 5,* 145–162.

—— (1974). Some psychological benefits of an outdoor challenge program. *Environment and Behavior, 6,* 101–116.

—— (1977). Patterns of environmental preference. *Environment and Behavior, 9,* 195–215.

—— (1980). Citizen participation in the design and evaluation of a park. *Environment and Behavior, 12,* 494–507.

Kaplan, S. (1976). Adaptation, structure, and knowledge. In G. T. Moore and R. G. Golledge (Eds.), *Environmental knowing: Theories, research, and methods.* Stroudsburg, PA: Dowden Hutchinson and Ross.

——, & Kaplan, R. (1978). *Humanscape: Environments for people.* North Scituate, MA: Duxbury.

——, & Kaplan, R. (1982). *Cognition and environment: Functioning in an uncertain world.* New York: Praeger.

——, Kaplan, R., & Wendt, J. S. (1972). Rated preference and complexity for natural and urban visual material. *Perception and Psychophysics, 12,* 354–356.

Karabenick, S., & Meisels, M. (1972). Effects of performance evaluation on interpersonal distance. *Journal of Personality, 40,* 275–286.

Karan, P. P., Bladen, W. A., & Singh, G. (1980). Slum dwellers' and squatters' images of the city. *Environment and Behavior, 12,* 81–100.

Karasek, R. A. Jr. (1979). Job demands, job decision latitude and mental strain: Implications for job redesign. *Administrative Science Quarterly, 24,* 285–308.

Karmel, L. J. (1965). Effects of windowless classroom environment on high school students. *Perceptual and Motor Skills, 20,* 277–278.

Kasmar, J. V. (1970). The development of a usable lexicon of environmental descriptors. *Environment and Behavior, 2,* 153–169.

Katzev, R., & Bachman, W. (1982). Effects of deferred payment and fare manipulations on urban bus ridership. *Journal of Applied Psychology, 67,* 83–88.

Kaye, S. M. (1975). Psychology in relation to design: An overview. *Canadian Psychological Review, 16,* 104–110.

——, & Murray, M. A. (1982). Evaluations of an architectural space as a function of variations in furniture arrangement, furniture density, and windows. *Human Factors, 24* 609–618.

Kegel-Flom, P. (1976). Identifying the potential rural optometrist. *American Journal of Optometry and Physiological Optics, 53,* 479–482.

Kelley, H. H., Condry, J. C., Jr., Dahlke, A. E., & Hill, A. H. (1965). Collective behavior in a simulated panic situation. *Journal of Experimental Social Psychology, 1,* 20–54.

Kelley, H. H., & Grzelak, J. (1972). Conflict between individual and common interest in an n-person relationship. *Journal of Personality and Social Psychology, 21,* 190–197.

Kelly, G. A. (1955). *The psychology of personal constructs.* New York: Norton.

Kiecolt, K. J., & Nigg, J. M. (1982). Mobility and perceptions of a hazardous environment. *Environment and Behavior, 14,* 131–154.

King, J., & Marans, R. W. (1979). *The physical environment and the learning process: A survey of recent research.* Ann Arbor, MI: University of Michigan, Architectural Research Laboratory.

King, M. G. (1966). Interpersonal relations in preschool children and average approach distance. *Journal of Genetic Psychology, 109,* 109–116.

Kinzel, A. S. (1970). Body buffer zone in violent prisoners. *American Journal of Psychiatry, 127,* 59–64.

Kira, A. (1976). *The bathroom.* New York: Viking.

Kirisic, K. C., Allen, G. L., & Siegel, A. W. (1984). Expression of configurational knowledge of large-scale environments: Students' performance of cognitive tasks. *Environment and Behavior, 16,* 687–712.

Kleck, R. (1969). Physical stigma and task oriented interactions. *Human Relations, 22,* 53–60.

Kleck, R. E., Buck, P. L., Goller, W. C., London, R. S., Pfeiffer, J. R., & Vukcevic, D. P. (1968). Effect of stigmatizing conditions on the use of personal space. *Psychological Reports, 23,* 111–118.

Klein, K., & Harris, B. (1979). Disruptive effects of disconfirmed expectancies about crowding. *Journal of Personality and Social Psychology, 37,* 769–777.

Knapp, M. L. (1978). *Nonverbal communication in human interaction.* New York: Holt, Rinehart and Winston.

Knight, R. C., & Campbell, D. E. (1980). Environmental evaluation research: Evaluator roles and inherent social commitments. *Environment and Behavior, 12* 520–532.

Knowles, E. S. (1972). Boundaries around social space: Dyadic responses to an invader. *Environment and Behavior, 4,* 437–445.

—— (1979). The proximity of others: A critique of crowding research and integration with the social sciences. *Journal of Population, 2,* 3–17.

—— (1980a). An affiliative conflict theory of personal and group spatial behavior. In P. B. Paulus (Ed.) *Psychology of group influence.* Hillsdale, NJ: Erlbaum.

—— (1980b). Convergent validity of personal space measures: Consistent results with low intercorrelations. *Journal of Nonverbal Behavior, 4,* 240–248.

—— (1981). *Discomfort and stop distances from groups and individuals.* Paper presented at the annual meeting of the Midwestern Psychological Association, Chicago.

—— (1983). Social physics and the effects of others: Tests of the effects of audience size and distance on social judgments and behavior. *Journal of Personality and Social Psychology, 45,* 1263–1279.

——, & Brickner, M. A. (1981). Social cohesion effects on spatial cohesion. *Personality and Social Psychology Bulletin, 7,* 309–313.

——, & Johnsen, P. K. (1974). Intrapersonal consistency in interpersonal distance. *JSAS Catalog of Selected Documents in Psychology, 4,* 1–27. (Document no. 768).

Kobayashi, S. (1961). *An introduction to architectural psychology.* Tokyo: Shokokusha Publishing.

Kohn, I. R., Franck, K. A., & Fox, A. S. (1975). *Defensible space modifications in row-house communities.* Report to the National Science Foundation. New York: Institute for Community Design Analysis.

Komorita, S. S. (1976). A model of the N-person dilemma-type game. *Journal of Experimental Social Psychology, 12,* 357–373.

——, & Barth, J. M. (1985). Components of reward in social dilemmas. *Journal of Personality and Social Psychology, 48,* 364–373.

——, & Lapworth, C. W. (1982). Cooperative choice among individuals versus groups in an N-person dilemma situation. *Journal of Personality and Social Psychology, 42,* 487–496.

Konar, E., Sundstrom, E., Brady, C., Mandel, D., & Rice, R. W. (1982). Status demarcation in the office. *Environment and Behavior, 14,* 561–580.

Konecni, V. J., Libuser, L., Morton, H., & Ebbesen, E. B. (1975). Effects of a violation of personal space on escape and helping response. *Journal of Experimental Social Psychology, 11*, 288–299.

Koneya, M. (1976). Location and interaction in row and column seating arrangements. *Environment and Behavior, 8*, 265–282.

Korosec-Serfaty, P. (1984). The home from attic to cellar. *Journal of Environmental Psychology, 4*, 303–321.

Korte, C. (1980). Urban-nonurban differences in social behavior and social psychological models of urban impact. *Journal of Social Issues, 36* (3), 29–51.

———, & Grant, R. (1980). Traffic noise, environmental awareness, and pedestrian behavior. *Environment and Behavior, 12*, 408–420.

Kosslyn, S. M. (1975). Information representation in visual images. *Cognitive Psychology, 7*, 341–370.

Krantz, P. J., & Risley, T. R. (1977). Behavioral ecology in the classroom. In K. D. O'Leary and S. G. O'Leary (Eds.), *Classroom management: The successful use of behavior modification*, New York: Permagon Press.

Kremer, A., & Stringer, R. (in press). Environmental psychology in the Netherlands. In D. Stokols and I. Altman (Eds.), *Handbook of environmental psychology*, New York: Wiley.

Krovetz, M. L. (1977). Who needs what when: Design of pluralistic learning environments. In D. Stokols (Ed.), *Perspectives on environment and behavior: Theory, research and applications*. New York: Plenum Press.

Kuethe, J. L. (1962). Social schemas. *Journal of Abnormal and Social Psychology, 64*, 31–38.

———, & Weingartner, H. (1964). Male-female schemata of homosexual and non-homosexual penitentiary inmates. *Journal of Personality, 32*, 23–31.

Kuller, R. (1972). *A semantic model for describing perceived environment* [sic]. Unpublished doctoral dissertation, Lund Institute of Technology, Lund, Sweden.

——— (1973). *Architectural psychology: Proceedings of the Lund Conference*. Stroudsburg, PA: Dowden, Hutchinson and Ross.

——— (1980). Architecture and emotions. In B. Mikellides (Ed.), *Architecture for people*. Studio Vista, London.

———, & Mattson, R. (1984, July). *The dining room at a geriatric hospital*. Paper presented at International Association for the Study of People and their Surroundings, West Berlin.

Kushnir, T. (1982). Skylab effects: Psychological reactions to a human-made environmental hazard. *Environment and Behavior, 14*, 84–93.

Labay, D. G., & Kinnear, T. C. (1981). Exploring the consumer decision process in the adoption of solar energy systems. *Journal of Consumer Research, 8*, 271–278.

Lansing, J. B., & Marans, R. W. (1969). Evaluation of neighborhood quality. *Journal of the American Institute of Planners, 35*, 195–199.

LaPiere, R. T., & Farnsworth, P. R. (1942). *Social psychology*. New York: McGraw-Hill.

Latane, B. (1981). The psychology of social impact. *American Psychologist, 36*, 343–356.

———, & Darley, J. M. (1970). *The unresponsive bystander: Why doesn't he help?* New York: Appleton-Century-Crofts.

Laufer, R. S., & Wolfe, M. (1977). Privacy as a concept and a social issue: A multidimensional development theory. *Journal of Social Issues, 33* (3), 22–42.

Lawrence, R. J. (1982). A psychological-spatial approach for architectural design and research. *Journal of Environmental Psychology, 2*, 37–51.

Lawton, M. P., Fulcomer, M., and Kleban, M. H. (1984). Architecture for the mentally impaired elderly. *Environment and Behavior, 16*, 730–757.

Lazarus, R. (1966). *Psychological stress and the coping process*. New York: McGraw-Hill.

LeBlanc, J. (1975). *Man in the cold*. Springfield, IL: Thomas.

LeBon, G. (1903). *The crowd*. (translated from *Psychologie des Foules*.) London: Allen and Unwin.

Leed, T. W., & German, G. A. (1973). *Food merchandizing: Principles and practices*. New York: Chain Store Age Books.

Leff, H. (1978). *Experience, environment, and human potential*. New York: Oxford University Press.

Lemke, S., & Moos, R. H. (1985). Coping with an intrainstitutional relocation: Behavioral change as a function of residents' personal resources. *Journal of Environmental Psychology, 5*, 137–151.

Leonard-Barton, D. (1981). Voluntary simplicity lifestyles and energy conservation. *Journal of Consumer Research, 8*, 243–252.

Levin, I., & Louviere, J. (1981). Psychological contributions to travel demand modelling. In I. Altman, J. F. Wohlwill, and P. B. Everett (Eds.), *Transportation and behavior*. New York: Plenum.

Levine, D. W., O'Neal, E. C., Garwood, S. G., & McDonald, P. J. (1980). Classroom ecology: The effects of seating position on grades and participation. *Personality and Social Psychology Bulletin, 6*, 409–412.

Levine, M. (1982). You-are-here maps: Psychological considerations. *Environment and behavior, 14*, 221–237.

———, Marchon, I., & Hanley, G. (1984). The placement and misplacement of you-are-here maps. *Environment and Behavior, 16*, 139–157.

Levy, L., & Herzog, A. W. (1974). Effects of population density and crowding on health and social adaptation in the Netherlands. *Journal of Health and Social Behavior, 4*, 228–240.

Lewin, K. (1943). Defining the field at a given time. *Psychological Review, 50*, 292–310.

—— (1951). *Field theory in social science: Selected theoretical papers.* New York: Harper and Row.

Lewis, P., & O'Sullivan, P. (1974). Acoustic privacy in office design. *Journal of Architectural Research, 3*, 48–51.

Ley, D., & Cybriwsky, R. (1974a). The spatial ecology of stripped cars. *Environment and Behavior, 6*, 53–68.

—— (1974b). Urban graffiti as territorial markers. *Annals of the Association of American Geographers, 64*, 491–505.

Lieblich, I., & Arbib, M. A. (1982). Multiple representations of space underlying behavior. *The Behavioral and Brain Sciences, 5*, 627–659.

Lingwood, D. A. (1971). Environmental education through information-seeking: The case of an "Environmental Teach-In." *Environment and Behavior, 3*, 230–262.

Little, B. R. (1968). Factors affecting the use of psychological versus non-psychological constructs on the Rep Test. *Bulletin of the British Psychological Society, 21*, 113.

—— (1972). Psychological man as scientist, humanist and specialist. *Journal of Experimental Research in Personality, 6*, 95–118.

—— (1976). Specialization and the varieties of human experience: Empirical studies within the personality paradigm. In S. Wapner, S. B. Cohen, and B. Kaplan (Eds.), *Experiencing the environment.* New York: Plenum Press.

—— (1983). Personal projects: A rationale and method for investigation. *Environment and Behavior, 15*, 273–309.

Little, K. B. (1965). Personal space. *Journal of Experimental Social Psychology, 1*, 237–247.

Livingstone, D. H., & Harrison, R. T. (1983). Reflections on a phenomenological approach. *Journal of Environmental Psychology, 3*, 295–296.

Llewellyn, L. G. (1981). The social cost of urban transportation. In I. Altman, J. Wohlwill, and P. B. Everett (Eds.), *Transportation and behavior.* New York: Plenum.

Lloyd, W. F. (1837/1968). *Lectures on population, value, poor laws and rent.* New York: August M. Kelley.

Lofland, L. (1973). *A world of strangers.* New York: Basic Books.

Logsdon, T. (1983). The orbiting junkyard. *Technology Illustrated, 3*, 30–34.

Lomranz, J., Shapira, A., Choresh, N., & Gilat, Y. (1975). Children's personal space as a function of age and sex. *Developmental Psychology, 11*, 541–545.

Loo, C. M. (1972). The effects of spatial density on the social behavior of children. *Journal of Applied Social Psychology, 4*, 372–381.

——, & Kennelly, D. (1979). Social density: Its effects on behaviors and perceptions of preschoolers. *Environmental Psychology and Nonverbal Behavior, 3*, 131–146.

——, & Mar, D. (1982). Desired residential mobility in a low income ethnic community: A case study of Chinatown. *Journal of Social Issues, 38* (3), 95–106.

——, & Ong, P. (1984). Crowding perceptions, attitudes, and consequences among the Chinese. *Environment and Behavior, 16*, 55–67.

Lott, B. S., & Sommer, R. (1967). Seating arrangements and status. *Journal of Personality and Social Psychology, 7*, 90–95.

Love, K. D., & Aiello, J. R. (1980). Using projective techniques to measure interaction distance: A methodological note. *Personality and Social Psychology Bulletin, 6*, 102–103.

Lowenthal, D. (1972). Research on environmental perception and behavior: Perspectives on current problems. *Environment and Behavior, 4*, 333–342.

Luft, J. (1966). On nonverbal interaction. *Journal of Psychology, 63*, 261–268.

Luyben, P. D. (1982). Prompting thermostat setting behavior: Public response to a presidential appeal for conservation. *Environment and Behavior, 14*, 113–128.

Lyman, S. M., & Scott, M. B. (1967). Territoriality: A neglected sociological dimension. *Social Problems, 15*, 235–249.

Lynch, K. (1960). *The image of the city.* Cambridge, MA: MIT Press.

——, & Rivkin, M. (1959). A walk around the block. *Landscape, 8*, 24–34.

Lyons, E. (1983). Demographic correlates of landscape preference. *Environment and Behavior, 15*, 487–511.

Macey, S. M., & Brown, M. A. (1983). Residential energy conservation: The role of past experience in repetitive household behavior. *Environment and Behavior, 15*, 123–141.

Mackett-Stout, J., & Dewar, R. (1981). Evaluations of symbolic public information signs. *Human Factors, 23*, 139–151.

MacPherson, J. C. (1984). Environments and interaction in row and column classrooms. *Environment and Behavior, 16*, 481–502.

Magana, J. R. (1978). *An empirical and interdisciplinary test of a theory of urban perception.* Doctoral dissertation, University of California, Irvine.

——, Evans, G. W., & Romney, A. K. (1981). Scaling techniques in the analysis of environmental cognition data. *Professional Geography 33*, 294–301.

Maloney, M. P., & Ward, M. O. (1973). Ecology: Let's hear from the people. *American Psychologist, 28*, 583–586.

——, Ward, M. O. & Braucht, C. N. (1975). A revised

scale for the measurement of ecological attitudes and knowledge. *American Psychologist, 30,* 787–790.

Mandel, D. R., Baron, R. M., & Fisher, J. D. (1980). Room utilization and dimensions of density: Effects of height and view. *Environment and Behavior, 12,* 308–319.

Marans, R. W. (1976). Perceived quality of residential environments: Some methodological issues. In K. H. Craik and E. H. Zube (Eds.) *Perceiving environmental quality: Research and applications.* New York: Plenum.

———, & Spreckelmeyer, K. F. (1982a). Evaluating open and conventional office design. *Environment and Behavior, 14,* 333–351.

——— (1982b). Measuring overall architectural quality: A component of building evaluation. *Environment and Behavior, 14,* 652–670.

Margulis, S. T. (1977). Conceptions of privacy: Current status and next steps. *The Journal of Social Issues, 33* (3), 5–21.

Marsella, A., Escudero, M., & Gordon, P. (1970). The effects of dwelling density on mental disorders in Filipino men. *Journal of Health and Social Behavior, 11,* 288–294.

Marshall, N. J. (1972). Privacy and environment. *Human Ecology, 1,* 93–110.

Martin, W. W., Falk, J. H., & Balling, J. D. (1981). Environmental effects on learning: The outdoor field trip. *Science Education, 65,* 301–309.

Masnick, G., & Bane, M. J. (1980). *The nation's families: 1960–1990.* Boston: Auburn House.

Mathews, K. E. Jr., & Canon, L. K. (1975). Environmental noise level as a determinant of helping behavior. *Journal of Personality and Social Psychology, 32,* 571–577.

May, F. E. (1969). Buying behavior: Some research findings. In McNeal, J. U. (Ed.), *Dimensions of buying behavior.* New York: Appleton-Century-Crofts.

Mayron, L. W., Ott, J. N., Amontree, E. J., & Nations, R. (1975). Light, radiation and dental caries. *Academic Therapy, 10,* 33–47.

———, Ott, J. N., Nations, R., & Mayron, E. L. (1974). Light, radiation, and academic behavior. *Academic Therapy, 10,* 441–448.

Mazur, A. (1977). Interpersonal spacing on public benches in "contact" and "noncontact" cultures. *Journal of Social Psychology, 101,* 53–58.

McArthur, D. (1984). Cashing in on the ultimate motivator: Incentive travel. *enRoute, 12* (8), 38, 40, 48, 50, 52.

McCain, G., Cox, V. C., & Paulus, P. B. (1976). The relationship between illness complaints and degree of crowding in a prison environment. *Environment and Behavior, 8,* 283–290.

McCallum, R., Rusbalt, C. E., Hong, G. K., Walden, T. A., & Schopler, J. (1979). Effects of resource availability and importance of behavior on the experience of crowding. *Journal of Personality and Social Psychology, 37,* 1304–1313.

McCarthy, D. P., & Saegert, S. (1978). Residential density, social overload, and social withdrawal. *Human Ecology, 1978, 6,* 253–272.

———, & Saegert, S. (1979). Residential density, social overload and social withdrawal. In J. R. Aiello and A. Baum (Eds.), *Residential crowding and design.* New York: Plenum Press.

McCauley, D., Coleman, G., & De Fusco, P. (1978). Commuters' eye contact with strangers in city and suburban train stations: Evidence of short-term adaptation to interpersonal overload in the city. *Environmental Psychology and Nonverbal Behavior, 2,* 215–225.

McClintock, C. G., Moskowitz, J. M., & McClintock, E. (1977). Variations in preferences for individualistic, competitive, and cooperative outcomes as a function of age, game class, and task in nursery school children. *Child Development, 48,* 1080–1085.

McCormack, P. (1982). Coding of spatial by young and elderly adults. *Journal of Gerontology, 37,* 80–86.

McCormick, E. J. (1976). *Human factors in engineering and design.* New York: McGraw-Hill.

McDougall, G. H. G., Claxton, J. D., Ritchie, J. R. B., & Anderson, C. D. (1981). Consumer energy research: A review. *Journal of Consumer Research, 8,* 343–354.

McDougall, W. (1920). *The group mind.* Cambridge: Cambridge University Press.

McDowell, K., & Carlson, K. (1984, June). *The effects of attributes of office environments on employee mood.* Paper presented at the annual meeting of the Canadian Psychological Association, Ottawa, Canada.

McElroy, J. C., Morrow, P. C., & Ackerman, R. J. (1983). Personality and interior office design: Exploring the accuracy of visitor attributions. *Journal of Applied Psychology, 68,* 541–544.

McGeoch, J. A. (1942). *The psychology of human learning.* New York: Longmans, Green.

McGill, W., & Korn, J. H. (1982). Awareness of an urban environment. *Environment and Behavior, 14,* 186–201.

McGrew, P. L. (1970). Social and spatial density effects on spacing behavior in preschool children. *Journal of Child Psychology and Psychiatry, 11,* 197–205.

McKechnie, G. E. (1974). *ERI Manual: Environmental response inventory.* Berkeley, CA: Consulting Psychologists Press.

——— (1977a). Simulation techniques in environmental psychology. In D. Stokols (Ed.), *Perspectives on environment and behavior: Conceptual and empirical trends.* New York: Plenum Press.

—— (1977b). The environmental response inventory in application. *Environment and Behavior, 9,* 255–276.

McLeod, B. (1984). In the wake of disaster. *Psychology Today, 18* (10), 54–58.

McMillan, D. W., & Hiltonsmith, R. W. (1982). Adolescents at home: An exploratory study of the relationship between perception of family social climate, general well-being, and actual behavior in the home setting. *Journal of Youth and Adolescence, 11,* 301–315.

McNall, P., Ryan, P., & Jaax, J. (1968). Seasonal variation in comfort conditions for college-age persons in the Middle West. *ASHRAE Transactions, 74,* IV. 2.1–IV. 2.9.

McNees, M. P., Schnelle, J. F., Gendrich, J., Thomas, M. M., & Beagle, G. (1979). McDonald's litter hunt. *Environment and Behavior, 11,* 131–138.

Megaw, E. D., & Bellamy, L. J. (1983). Illumination at work. In D. J. Oborne and M. M. Gruneberg (Eds.), *The physical environment at work.* New York: Wiley.

Mehrabian, A. (1966). Immediacy: An indicator of attitudes in linguistic communication. *Journal of Personality, 34,* 26–34.

—— (1969). Significance of posture and position in the communication of attitude and status relationships. *Psychological Bulletin, 71,* 359–373.

—— (1976a). *Manual for the questionaire measure of Stimulus Screening and Arousability.* Unpublished manuscript, University of California at Los Angeles.

—— (1976b). *Public places and private spaces: The psychology of work, play, and living environments.* New York: Basic Books.

—— (1977). Individual differences in stimulus screening and arousability. *Journal of Personality, 45,* 237–250.

—— (1978). Characteristic individual reactions to preferred and unpreferred environments. *Journal of Personality, 46,* 717–731.

——, & Diamond, S. G. (1971). The effects of furniture arrangement, props, and personality on social interaction. *Journal of Personality and Social Psychology, 20,* 18–30.

——, & Russell, J. A. (1974). *An approach to environmental psychology.* Cambridge, Mass: MIT Press.

——, (1975). Environmental effects on affiliation among strangers. *Humanitas, 11,* 219–230.

——, & Williams, M. (1969). Nonverbal concomitants of perceived and intended persuasiveness. *Journal of Personality and Social Psychology, 13,* 37–58.

Melton, G. B. (1983). Toward "personhood" for adolescents: Autonomy and privacy as values in public policy. *American Psychologist, 38,* 99–103.

Mercer, D. C. (1976). Motivational and social aspects of recreational behavior. In I. Altman and J. F. Wohlwill (Eds.), *Human behavior and environment* (Vol. 1). New York: Plenum.

Mercer, G. W., & Benjamin, M. L. (1980). Spatial behavior of university undergraduates in double occupancy residence rooms: An inventory of effects. *Journal of Applied Social Psychology, 10,* 32–44.

Messick, D. M., & McClelland, C. L. (1983). Social traps and temporal traps. *Personality and Social Psychology Bulletin, 9,* 105–110.

——, Wilke, H., Brewer, M. B., Kramer, R. M., Zemke, P. E., & Lui, L. (1983). Individual adaptations and structural change solutions to social dilemmas. *Journal of Personality and Social Psychology, 44,* 294–309.

Meux, E. P. (1973). Concern for the common good in an N-person game. *Journal of Personality and Social Psychology, 28,* 414–418.

Michelson, W. (1976). *Man and his urban environment: A sociological approach.* Don Mills, ON: Addison-Wesley.

—— (1977). *Environmental choice, human behavior and residential satisfaction.* New York: Oxford University Press.

—— (1980). Long and short range criteria for housing choice and environmental behavior. *Journal of Social Issues, 36* (3), 135–149.

Middlemist, R. D., Knowles, E. S., & Matter, C. F. (1976). Personal space invasions in the lavatory: Suggestive evidence for arousal. *Journal of Personality and Social Psychology, 33,* 541–546.

Milgram, S. (1970). The experience of living in cities. *Science, 167,* 1461–1468.

—— (1977). *The individual in a social world: Essays and experiments.* Reading, MA: Addison-Wesley.

——, & Toch, H. (1969). Collective behavior: Crowds and social movements. In G. Lindzey and E. Aronson (Eds.), *The handbook of social psychology.* Reading, MA: Addison-Wesley.

Millard, R. J., & Stimpson, D. V. (1980). Enjoyment and productivity as a function of classroom seating location. *Perceptual and Motor Skills, 50,* 439–44.

Miller, J. D. (1974). Effects of noise on people. *Journal of the Acoustical Society of America, 56,* 729–764.

Miller, P. A. (1984). *Visual preference and implications for coastal management: A* perceptual study of the British Columbia shoreline. Unpublished doctoral dissertation, University of Michigan, Ann Arbor, Michigan.

Miller, R. L., Brickman, P., & Bolen, D. (1975). Attribution vs. persuasion as a means for modifying behavior. *Journal of Personality and Social Psychology, 31,* 430–441.

Miller, S., & Nardini, R. M. (1977). Individual differences in the perception of crowding. *Environmental Psychology and Nonverbal Behavior, 2,* 3–13.

——, Rossbach, J., & Munson, R. (1981). Social

density and affiliative tendency as determinants of dormitory residential outcomes. *Journal of Applied Social Psychology, 11,* 356–365.

Mintz, A. (1951). Nonadaptive group behavior. *Journal of Abnormal Social Psychology, 46,* 150–159.

Monk, T. H. (1980). Traffic accident increases as a possible indicant of desynchronosis. *Chronobiologia, 7,* 527–529.

Montano, D., & Adamopoulos, J. (1984). The perception of crowding in interpersonal situations: Affective and behavioral responses. *Environment and Behavior, 16,* 643–666.

Moore, G. T. (1979). Knowing about environmental knowing: The current state of theory and research on environmental cognition. *Environment and Behavior, 11,* 33–70.

—— (1982). Editor's introduction: Architectural evaluation—the 1982 Progressive Architecture award winners. *Environment and Behavior, 14,* 643–651.

—— (in press). Environment and behavior research in North America: History, developments, and unresolved issues. In D. Stokols and I. Altman (Eds.), *Handbook of Environmental Psychology.* New York: Wiley.

Moos, R. H. (1973). Conceptualizations of human environments. *American Psychologist, 28,* 652–655.

—— (1976). *The human context: Environmental determinants of behavior.* New York: Wiley.

—— (1981). A social-ecological perspective on health. In G. Stone et al. (Eds.) *Health psychology.* San Francisco: Jossey-Bass.

——, & Brownstein, R. (1977). *Environment and utopia: A synthesis.* New York: Plenum Press.

——, & Lemke, S. (1984). *Multiphasic environmental assessment procedure.* Unpublished manuscript, Stanford University, Social Ecology Laboratory, Palo Alto, CA.

——, & Sommers, P. (1976). The architectural environment: Physical space and building design. In R. Moos, *The human context: Environmental determinants of behavior.* New York: Wiley.

Morris, P. A. (1982). The effect of pilgrimage on anxiety, depression, and religious attitude. *Psychological Medicine, 12,* 291–294.

Morrison, T. L., & Thomas, M. D. (1975). Self-esteem and classroom participation. *Journal of Educational Research, 68,* 374–377.

Morrow, L. M. (1982). Relationships between literature programs, library corner designs, and children's use of literature. *Journal of Educational Research, 75,* 339–344.

——, & Weinstein, C. S. (1982). Increasing children's use of literature through program and physical design changes. *Elementary School Journal, 83,* 131–137.

Morrow, P. C., & McElroy, J. C. (1981). Interior office design and visitor response: A constructive replication. *Journal of Applied Psychology, 66,* 646–650.

Moser, G. (1984). Water quality perception, a dynamic perspective. *Journal of Environmental Psychology, 4,* 210.

Mueller, W. S. (1981). Translation of user requirements into house designs: A multi-dimensional scaling analysis. *Journal of Environmental Psychology, 1,* 97–116.

Mumford, L. (1961). *The city in history: Its origins, its transformations, and its prospects.* New York: Harcourt, Brace and World.

Munroe, R. L., & Munroe, R. H. (1972). Population density and affective relationships in three East African societies. *Journal of Social Psychology, 88,* 15–20.

Munson, P., & Ferguson, R. (1985). *The extra-visual effects of fluorescent illumination on the behavior of school children.* Manuscript in preparation, University of Victoria.

Murphy, G. (1956). The boundaries between the person and the world. *British Journal of Psychology, 47,* 88–94.

Murray, H. A. (1938). *Explorations in personality.* New York: Oxford University Press.

Nasar, J. L. (1981a). Visual preferences of elderly public housing residents: Residential street scenes. *Journal of Environmental Psychology, 1,* 303–313.

—— (1981b). Responses to different spatial configurations. *Human Factors, 23,* 439–446.

—— (1983). Adult viewers' preferences in residential scenes: A study of the relationship of environmental attributes to preference. *Environment and Behavior, 15,* 589–614.

—— (1984a). Visual preferences in urban street scenes: A cross-cultural comparison between Japan and the United States. *Journal of Cross-Cultural Psychology, 15,* 79–93.

—— (1984b, June-July). *Cognition in relation to downtown street-scenes: A comparison between Japan and the United States.* Paper presented at the annual conference of the Environmental Design Research Association.

——, & Greenberg, M. L. (1984). The preparedness and reactions of citizens to warnings and crisis relocation for nuclear attack. *Journal of Applied Social Psychology, 14,* 487–500.

——, & Min, M. S. (1984). *Modifiers of perceived spaciousness and crowding: A cross-cultural study.* Paper presented at the annual meeting of the American Psychological Association, Toronto, Ontario.

——, Valencia, H., Omar, Z. A., Chueh, S., & Hwang, J. (1985). Out of sight further from mind: Destination visibility and distance perception. *Environment and Behavior, 17,* 627–639.

Nash, B. C. (1981). The effects of classroom spatial organization on four- and five-year-old children's learning. *British Journal of Educational Psychology, 51*, 144–155.

National Academy of Sciences (1977). *Medical and biological effects of environmental pollutants.* Washington, DC: National Academy of Sciences.

Neill, S. R. St. J. (1982a). Preschool design and child behavior. *Journal of Child Psychology and Psychiatry, 23*, 309–318.

—— (1982b). Experimental alterations in playroom layout and their effect on staff and child behavior. *Educational Psychology, 2*, 103–119.

——, & Denham, E. J. M. (1982). The effects of preschool design. *Educational Research, 24*, 107–111.

Neisser, U. (1976). *Cognition and reality.* San Francisco: Freeman.

Nelson, M. N., & Paluck, R. J. (1980). Territorial markings, self-concept, and the mental status of the institutionalized elderly. *Gerontologist, 20*, 96–98.

Nelson, T. M., Nilsson, T. H., & Johnson, M. (1984). Interaction of temperature, illuminance and apparent time on sedentary work fatigue. *Ergonomics, 27*, 89–101.

Nesbitt, P. D., & Steven, G. (1974). Personal space and stimulus intensity at a Southern California amusement park. *Sociometry, 37*, 105–115.

Newman, O. (1972). *Defensible space.* New York: MacMillan.

—— (1980). *Community of interest.* New York: Anchor Press/Doubleday.

Newman, S. J., & Owen, M. S. (1982). Residential displacement: Extent, nature, and effects. *Journal of Social Issues, 38*, 135–148.

Ng, C. F., & Gifford, R. (1984a, June). *The office acoustical environment: A survey of office-workers' attitudes.* Paper presented at the annual meetings of the Canadian Psychological Association, Ottawa.

——, & Gifford, R. (1984b, June). *Speech communication in the office: The effects of background sound level and conversational privacy.* Ms in preparation.

——, & Gifford, R. (1986). *Greater Victoria Public Library (Esquimalt Branch): A Post-occupancy report.* Report to the Greater Victoria Public Library Board.

Nicosia, G. J., Hyman, D., Karlin, R. A., Epstein, Y. M., & Aiello, J. R. (1979). Effects of bodily contact on reactions to crowding. *Journal of Applied Social Psychology, 9*, 508–523.

Niit, T., Kruusval, J., & Heidmets, M. (1981). Environmental psychology in the Soviet Union. *Journal of Environmental Psychology, 1*, 157–177.

Norberg-Schulz, C. (1980). *Genius loci: Towards a phenomenology of architecture.* New York: Rizzoli.

O'Brien, G. E., & Pembroke, M. (1982). Crowding, density and the job satisfaction of clerical employees. *Australian Journal of Psychology, 34*, 151–164.

Ohata, R. J., & Kirasic, K. C. (1983). The investigation of environmental learning in the elderly. In G. D. Rowles, and R. J. Ohata (Eds.), *Aging and milieu.* New York: Academic Press.

O'Keefe, J., & Nadel, L. (1974). Maps in the brain. *New Scientist,* 749–751.

—— (1978). *The hippocampus as a cognitive map.* Oxford: Clarendon Press.

Oldham, G. R., & Brass, D. J. (1979). Employee reactions to an open-plan office: A naturally occurring quasi-experiment. *Administrative Science Quarterly, 24*, 267–284.

Olsen, M. E. (1981). Consumers' attitudes toward energy conservation. *Journal of Social Issues, 37* (2), 108–131.

O'Neal, E. C., Brunault, M. S., Carifio, M. S., Troutwine, R., & Epstein, J. (1980). Effect of insult upon personal space preferences. *Journal of Nonverbal Behavior, 5*, 56–62.

O'Neill, G. W., Blanck, L. S., & Joyner, M. A. (1980). The use of stimulus control over littering in a natural setting. *Journal of Applied Behavior Analysis, 13*, 379–381.

Ophuls, W. (1973). Leviathan or oblivion? In H. E. Daly (Ed.), *Toward a steady state economy.* San Francisco: Freeman.

Orbell, J. M., van de Kragt, A. J. C., & Dawes, R. M. (1985). *Moral order and the threshold of the room effect.* Manuscript in preparation.

O'Riordan, T. (1976). Attitudes, behavior, and environmental policy issues. In I. Altman and J. F. Wohlwill (Eds.), *Human behavior and environment: Advances in theory and research* (Vol. 1). New York: Plenum.

—— (1984). *Environmental hazards.* Manuscript in preparation.

Orleans, P. (1973). Differential cognition of urban residents: Effects of social scale on mapping. In R. M. Downs and D. Stea (Eds.), *Image and environment: Cognitive mapping and spatial behavior.* Chicago: Aldine.

——, & Schmidt, S. (1972). Mapping the city: Environmental cognition of urban residents. In W. J. Mitchell (Ed.), *Environmental design: Research and practice.* Los Angeles: University of California.

Osgood, C., Suci, G., & Tannenbaum, P. (1957). *The measurement of meaning.* Urbana: University of Illinois Press.

Osmond, H. (1957). Function as the basis of psychiatric ward design. *Mental Hospitals, 8*, 23–30.

Owens, D. D. (1981). Ridesharing programs: Governmental response to urban transportation problems. *Environment and Behavior, 13*, 311–330.

Oxley, D., & Barrera, M. Jr. (1984). Undermanning theory and the workplace: Implications of setting size for job satisfaction and social support. *Environment and Behavior, 16,* 211–234.

Page, R. A. (1977). Noise and helping behavior. *Environment and Behavior, 9,* 311–334.

Painter, M. (1976–1977). Fluorescent lights and hyperactivity in children: An experiment. *Academic Therapy, 12,* 181–184.

Pallak, M. S., & Cummings, W. (1976). Commitment and voluntary energy conservation. *Personality and Social Psychology Bulletin, 2,* 27–30.

Pamir, A. H. (1981). An overview of Turkish research and education in environmental social science. *Journal of Environmental Psychology, 1,* 315–328.

Parke, R. D., & Sawin, D. B. (1979). Children's privacy in the home: Developmental, ecological, and child-rearing determinants. *Environment and Behavior, 11,* 87–104.

Parsons, H. M. (1976). Work environments. In I. Altman and J. F. Wohlwill (Eds.), *Human behavior and environment* (Vol. 1). New York: Plenum.

Paslawskyj, L., & Ivinskis, A. (1980). Dominance, agonistic and territorial behavior in institutionalized mentally retarded patients. *Australian Journal of Developmental Disabilities, 6,* 17–24.

Passini, R. (1984). Spatial representations, a wayfinding perspective. *Journal of Environmental Psychology, 4,* 153–164.

Pastalan, L. A. (1970). Privacy as an expression of human territoriality. In L. A. Pastalan and D. H. Carson (Eds.), *Spatial behavior of older people.* Ann Arbor: University of Michigan Press.

Patricios, N. N. (1979). Human aspects of planning shopping centers. *Environment and Behavior, 11,* 511–538.

Patsfall, M. R., Feimer, N. R. Buhyoff, G. J., & Wellman, J. D. (1984). The prediction of scenic beauty from landscape content and composition. *Journal of Environmental Psychology, 4,* 7–26.

Patterson, A. H., & Chiswick, N. R. (1981). The role of the social and physical environment in privacy maintenance among the Iban of Borneo. *Journal of Environmental Psychology, 1* 131–139.

Patterson, M. (1968). Spatial factors in social interactions. *Human Relations, 21,* 351–361.

—— (1973). Stability of nonverbal immediacy behaviors. *Journal of Experimental Social Psychology, 9,* 97–109.

—— (1975). Personal space—time to burst the bubble? *Man-Environment Systems, 5,* 67.

——, & Holmes, D. S. (1966). Social interaction correlates of the MMPI extraversion-introversion scale. *American Psychologist, 21,* 724–725.

——, & Sechrest, L. B. (1970). Interpersonal distance and impression formation. *Journal of Personality, 38,* 161–166.

Payne, I. (1969). Pupillary responses to architectural stimuli. *Man-Environmental Systems, 1,* S–11.

Payne, R. J., & Pigram, J. J. (1981). Changing evaluations of flood plain hazard: The Hunter River Valley, Australia. *Environment and Behavior, 13,* 461–480.

Pearce, P. L. (1977). Mental souvenirs: A study of tourists and their city maps. *Australian Journal of Psychology, 29,* 203–210.

—— (1980). Strangers, travelers, and greyhound terminals: A study of small-scale helping behaviors. *Journal of Personality and Social Psychology, 38,* 935–940.

—— (1981a). Environment shock: A study of tourists' reactions to two tropical islands. *Journal of Applied Social Psychology, 11,* 268–280.

—— (1981b). Route maps: A study of traveller's perceptions of a section of countryside. *Journal of Environmental Psychology, 1,* 141–155.

—— (1982). *The social psychology of tourist behavior.* Oxford: Pergamon.

Pedersen, D. M. (1979). Dimensions of privacy. *Perceptual and Motor Skills, 48,* 1291–1297.

—— (1982). Cross-validation of privacy factors. *Perceptual and Motor Skills, 55,* 57–58.

——, & Shears, L. M. (1973). A review of personal space research in the framework of general systems theory. *Psychological Bulletin, 8,* 367–388.

Pellegrini, R. J., & Empey, J. (1970). Interpersonal spatial orientation in dyads. *Journal of Psychology, 76,* 67–70.

Pepler, R. (1971). Variations in students' performances and in classroom temperatures in climate controlled and nonclimate controlled schools. *ASHRAE Transactions, 77,* 35–42.

—— (1972). The thermal comfort of students in climate controlled and non-climate controlled schools. *ASHRAE Transactions, 78,* 97–109.

Perussia, F. (1983). A critical approach to environmental psychology in Italy. *Journal of Environmental Psychology, 3,* 263–277.

Pervin, L. A. (1978). *Current controversies in personality.* New York: Wiley.

Peterson, G. L., & Neumann, E. S. (1969). Modeling and predicting human response to the visual recreation environment. *Journal of Leisure Research, 1,* 219–237.

Pick, H. L. (1976). Transactional-constructivist approach to environmental knowing: A commentary. In G. T. Moore and R. G. Golledge (Eds.), *Environmental knowing: Theories, research, and methods.* Stroudsburg, PA: Dowden Hutchinson and Ross.

Platt, J. (1973). Social traps. *American Psychologist, 28,* 641–651.

Pollack, L. M., & Patterson, A. H. (1980). Territoriality and fear of crime in elderly and nonelderly homeowners. *Journal of Social Psychology, 111,* 119–129.

Ponte, L. (1981). How artificial light affects your health. *Reader's Digest,* February, *118,* 131–134.

Porteous, C. (1972). *Learning as a function of molar environmental complexity.* Unpublished master's thesis, University of Victoria, Victoria, British Columbia.

Porteous, J. D. (1977). *Environment and behavior: Planning and everday life.* Don Mills, ON: Addison-Wesley.

—— (1982). Approaches to environmental aesthestics. *Journal of Environmental Psychology, 2,* 53–66.

Posehn, K. (1984, June). *An environmental evaluation of open plan offices.* Paper presented at the Canadian Psychological Association annual meeting, Ottawa.

Prak, N. L., & van Wegen, H. B. R. (1975). *The influence of cognitive factors on the perception of buildings.* Paper presented at the annual meeting of the Environmental Design Research Association, Lawrence, Kansas.

Preiser, W. P. E., & Taylor, A. (1983). The habitability framework: Linking human behavior and physical environment in a special education. EEQ: *Exceptional Education Quarterly, 4,* (2), 1–15.

Prerost, F. J. (1982). The development of the mood-inhibiting effects of crowding during adolescence. *Journal of Psychology, 110,* 197–202.

——, & Brewer, R. K. (1980). The appreciation of humor by males and females during conditions of crowding experimentally induced. *Psychology, A Journal of Human Behavior, 17,* 15–17.

Prescott, E. (1970, May). The large day care center as a child rearing environment. *Voice for Child, 2,* (4).

Preston, V., Taylor, S. M., & Hodge, D. C. (1983). Adjustment to natural and technological hazards: A study of an urban residential community. *Environment and Behavior, 15,* 143–164.

Proshansky, H. M. (1978). The city and self-identity. *Environment and Behavior, 10,* 147–169.

——, Fabian, A. K., & Kaminoff, R. (1983). Place-identity: Physical world socialization of the self. *Journal of Environmental Psychology, 3,* 57–83.

——, Ittelson, W. H., & Rivlin, L. G. (1976). Freedom of choice and behavior in a physical setting. In H. M. Proshansky, W. H. Ittelson, and L. G. Rivlin (Eds.), *Environmental psychology: People and their physical settings.* New York: Holt, Rinehart and Winston.

Purcell, A. H. (1981, February). The world's trashiest people: Will they clean up their act or throw away their future? *The Futurist,* 51–59.

Pyle, G. F. (1980). Systematic sociospatial variation in perceptions of crime location and severity. In D. E. Georges-Abeyie and K. D. Harries (Eds.), *Crime: A spatial perspective.* New York: Columbia University Press.

Quarantelli, E. L. (1976). *Human response in stress situations.* Laurel, MD: Johns Hopkins University Press.

Rankin, R. E. (1969). Air pollution control and public apathy. *Journal of Air Pollution Control Association, 19,* 565–569.

Rapaport, Am. (1975). Toward a redefinition of density. *Environment and Behavior, 7,* 133–158.

—— (1969). *House form and culture.* Englewood Cliffs, NJ: Prentice Hall.

—— (1977). *Human aspects of urban form: Towards a man-environment approach to human form and design.* New York: Pergamon Press.

—— (1982). *The meaning of the built environment: A nonverbal communication approach.* Beverly Hills, CA: Sage.

—— (1985). Culture and the urban order. In J. A. Agnew, J. Mercer, and D. E. Sopher (Eds.), *The city in cultural context.* Boston: Allen and Unwin.

——, & Kantor, R. E. (1976). Complexity and ambiguity in environmental design. *Journal of the American Institute of Planners, 33,* 210–221.

Rapoport, An., Chammah, A., Dwyer, J., & Gyr, J. (1962). Three-person non-zero-sum nonnegotiable games. *Behavioral Science, 7,* 38–58.

——, & Kahan, J. P. (1976). When three is not always two against one: Coalitions in experimental three person cooperative games. *Journal of Experimental Social Psychology, 12,* 253–273.

Raviv, A., & Palgi, Y. (1985). The perception of social-environmental characteristics in kibbutz families with family-based and communal sleeping arrangements. *Journal of Personality and Social Psychology, 49,* 376–385.

Reddy, D. M., Baum, A., Flemming, R. & Aiello, J. R. (1981). Mediation of social density by coalition formation. *Journal of Applied Social Psychology, 11,* 529–537.

Reichner, R. F. (1979). Differential responses to being ignored: The effects of architectural design and social density on interpersonal behavior. *Journal of Applied Social Psychology, 9,* 13–26.

Reif, Z. F., & Vermeulen, P. J. (1979). Noise from domestic appliances, construction, and industry. In H. W. Jones (Ed.), *Noise in the human environment,* (Vol. 2), Edmonton, Alberta: Environmental Council of Alberta.

Reiss, S., & Dyhaldo, N. (1975). Persistence, achievement and open-space environments. *Journal of Educational Psychology, 67,* 506–513.

Reizenstein, J. E. (1982). Hospital design and human behavior: A review of the recent literature. In A. Baum and J. E. Singer (Eds.), *Advances in environmental psychology: Volume 4: Environment and health.* Hillsdale, NJ: Erlbaum.

Relph, E. (1976). *Place and placelessness.* London: Pion.

—— (1981). *Rational landscapes and humanistic geography.* London: Croom Helm.

Reser, J. P. (1980). Automobile addiction: Real or imagined? *Man-Environment Systems, 10,* 279–287.

Ritchie, J. R. B., McDougall, G., & Claxton, J. D. (1981). Complexities of household energy consumption and conservation. *Journal of Consumer Research, 8,* 233–242.

Rivlin, L. G. (1982). Group membership and place meanings in an urban neighborhood. *Journal of Social Issues, 38,* (3), 75–93.

Robinson, B., & Wolfson, E. (1982). *Environmental education: A manual for elementary educators.* New York: Teachers College Press.

Robinson, S. N., & Frisch, M. H. (1975, April). *Social and environmental influences on littering behavior.* Paper presented at the Eastern Psychological Association meeting, New York.

Rodin, J. (1976). Density, perceived choice, and response to controllable and uncontrollable outcomes. *Journal of Experimental Social Psychology, 12,* 564–578.

Roethlisberger, F. J., & Dickson, W. J. (1939). *Management and the worker.* Cambridge: Harvard University Press.

Roger, D. B., & Schalekamp, E. E. (1976). Body-buffer zone and violence: A cross-cultural study. *Journal of Social Psychology, 98,* 153–158.

Rohe, W. M. (1982). The response to density in residential settings: The mediating effects of social and personal variables. *Journal of Applied Social Psychology, 12,* 292–303.

——, & Nuffer, E. L. (1977). *The effects of density and partitioning on children's behavior.* Paper presented at the annual meetings of the American Psychological Association, San Francisco, CA.

——, & Patterson, A. H. (1974). The effects of varied levels of resources and density on behavior in a day care center. In D. Carson (Ed.), *Man-environment interactions: Evaluations and applications.* Stroudsberg, PA: Dowden, Hutchinson and Ross.

Rohles, F., Jr. (1980). In Rice, B. Cooling by deception. *Psychology Today, 14,* 20.

——, Jr., Konz, S., & Munson, D. (1980). Estimating occupant satisfaction from effective temperature. *Proceedings of the Human Factors Society, 24,* 223–227.

Rose, E. F., & Rose, M. (1971). Carbon monoxide: A challenge to the physician. *Clinical Medicine, 78,* 12–19.

Rosenfield, P., Lambert, N. M., & Black, A. (1985). Desk arrangement effects on pupil classroom behavior. *Journal of Educational Psychology, 77,* 101–108.

Rosenfeld, H. M. (1965). Effect of an approval seeking induction on interpersonal proximity. *Psychological Reports, 17,* 120–122.

Ross, H. E. (1974). *Behavior and perception in strange environments.* London: George Allen and Unwin.

Ross, R. P. (1980). Modification of space in open plan schools: An examination of the press toward synomorphy. In R. R. Stough and A. Wandersman (Eds.), *Optimizing environments: Research, practice, and policy.* Washington, DC: Environmental Design Research Association.

Rotton, J. (1983). Affective and cognitive consequences of malodorous pollution. *Basic and Applied Social Psychology, 4,* 171–191.

——, Barry, T., Frey, J., & Soler, E. (1978). Air pollution and interpersonal attraction. *Journal of Applied Social Psychology, 8,* 57–71.

——, & Frey, J. (1985a). Psychological costs of air pollution: Atmospheric conditions, seasonal trends, and psychiatric emergencies. *Population and Environment, 7.*

——, & Frey, J. (1985b). Air pollution, weather, and violent crimes: Concomitant times-series analysis of archival data. *Journal of Personality and Social Psychology, 49,* 1207–1220.

——, Frey, J., Barry, T., Milligan, M., & Fitzpatrick, M. (1979). The air pollution experience and interpersonal aggression. *Journal of Applied Social Psychology, 9,* 397–412.

Rout, L. (1980, November 5). Designs modify the open office to meet complaints of workers. *The Wall Street Journal,* p. 31.

Rowe, R. D., & Chestnut, L. G. (1983). Introduction. In R. D. Rowe and L. G. Chestnut (Eds.), *Managing air quality and scenic resources at national parks and wilderness areas.* Boulder, CO: Westview Press.

Rubenstein, C. (1980). Survey report: How Americans view vacations. *Psychology Today, 13,* 62–66, 71–76.

Rubenstein, F. D., Watzke, G., Doktor, R. H., & Dana, J. (1975). The effect of two incentive schemes upon the conservation of shared resource by five-person groups. *Organizational Behavior and Human Performance, 13,* 330–338.

Rubin, H. J. (1981). Rules, collective needs, and individual action: A case study in a townhouse cooperative. *Environment and Behavior, 13,* 165–188.

Rubin, Z., & Shenker, S. (1978). Friendship, proximity, and self-disclosure. *Journal of Personality, 46,* 1–22.

Rumsey, N., Bull, R., & Gahagan, D. (1982). The effect of facial disfigurement on the proxemic behavior of the general public. *Journal of Applied Social Psychology, 12,* 137–150.

Russell, J. A., & Lanius, U. F. (1984). Adaptation level and the affective appraisal of environments. *Journal of Environmental Psychology, 4*, 119–135.

——, & Mehrabian, A. (1977). Environmental effects of drug use. *Environmental Psychology and Nonverbal Behavior, 2* (2), 109–123.

——, & Mehrabian, A. (1978). Approach-avoidance and affiliation as functions of the emotion-eliciting quality of an environment. *Environment and Behavior, 10*, 355–387.

——, & Pratt, G. (1980). A description of the affective quality attributed to environments. *Journal of Personality and Social Psychology, 38*, 311–322.

——, Ward, L. M. & Pratt, G. (1981). Affective quality attributed to environments: A factor analytic study. *Environment and Behavior, 13*, 259–288.

——, & Ward, L. M. (1981). On the psychological reality of environmental meaning: Reply to Daniel and Ittelson. *Journal of Experimental Psychology, 110*, 163–168.

——, & Ward, L. M. (1982). Environmental psychology. *Annual Review of Psychology, 33*, 651–688.

Ryd, H., & Wyon, D. P. (1970). Methods of evaluating human stress due to climate. *National Swedish Institute for Building Research*, Document 6.

Sacilotto, P. (1983). *The influence of person-thing orientation and isolation on personal space.* Unpublished manuscript, University of Victoria.

Sadalla, E. K., & Magel, S. G. (1980). The perception of traversed distance. *Environment and Behavior, 12*, 65–79.

——, & Oxley, D. (1984). The perception of room size: The rectangularity illusion. *Environment and Behavior, 16*, 394–405.

Saegert, S. (1980, September). *The effect of residential density on low income children.* Paper presented at the annual meetings of the American Psychological Association, Montreal.

——, & Hart, R. (1978). The development of environmental competence in girls and boys. In M. Salter (Ed.), *Play: Anthropological perspectives.* Cornwall, NY: Leisure Press.

Salling, M., & Harvey, M. E. (1981). Poverty, personality and sensitivity to residential stressors. *Environment and Behavior, 13*, 131–163.

Sanchez, E., Wiesenfeld, E., & Cronick, K. (1983). Environmental psychology in Venezuela. *Journal of Environmental Psychology, 3*, 161–172.

Santrock, J. W. (1976). Affect and facilitative self control: Influence of ecological setting, cognition, and social agent. *Journal of Educational Psychology, 68*, 529–535.

Sauser, W. I. Jr., Arauz, C. G., & Chambers, R. M. (1978). Exploring the relationship between level of office noise and salary recommendations: A preliminary research note. *Journal of Management, 4*, 57–63.

Savinar, J. (1975). The effect of ceiling height on personal space. *Man-Environment Systems, 5*, 321–324.

Schaeffer, G. H., & Patterson, M. L. (1980). Intimacy, arousal and small group crowding. *Journal of Personal and Social Psychology, 38*, 283–290.

Schaeffer, M. A., & Baum, A. (1984). Adrenal cortical response to stress at Three Mile Island. *Psychosomatic Medicine, 46*, 227–237.

Scherer, S. E. (1974). Proxemic behavior of primary school children as a function of their socioeconomic class and subculture. *Journal of Personality and Social Psychology, 29*, 800–805.

Schiffenbauer, A. I. (1979). Designing for high-density living. In J. R. Aiello and A. Baum (Eds.), *Residential crowding and design.* New York: Plenum Press.

——, Brown, J. E., Perry, P. L., Schulack, L. K., & Zanzola, A. M. (1977). The relationship between density and crowding: Some architectural modifiers. *Environment and Behavior, 9*, 3–14.

Schkade, J. (1977). *The effects of expectancy set and crowding on task performance.* Doctoral dissertation, University of Texas at Arlington.

Schmidt, D. E., Goldman, R. D., & Feimer, N. R. (1979). Perceptions of crowding: Predicting at the residence, neighborhood and city levels. *Environment and Behavior, 11*, 105–130.

——, & Keating, J. P. (1979). Human crowding and personal control: An integration of the research. *Psychological Bulletin, 86*, 680–700.

Schmidt, G. W., & Ulrich, R. E. (1969). Effects of group contingent events upon classroom noise. *Journal of Applied Behavior Analysis, 2*, 171–179.

Schmitt, R. C. (1957). Density, deliquency and crime in Honolulu. *Sociology and Social Research, 41*, 274–276.

Schneider, F. W., Lesko, W. A., & Garrett, W. A. (1980). Helping behavior in hot, comfortable and cold temperatures. *Environment and Behavior, 12*, 231–240.

Schopler, J., & Stockdale, J. E. (1977). An interference analysis of crowding. *Environmental Psychology and Nonverbal Behavior, 1*, 81–88.

Schouela, D. A., Steinberg, L. M., Levelton, L. B., & Wapner, S. (1980). Development of the cognitive organization of an environment. *Canadian Journal of Behavioural Science, 12*, 1–16.

Schrodt, P. A. (1981). Conflict as a determinant of territory. *Behavioral Science, 26*, 37–50.

Schulte, J. H. (1963). Effects of mild carbon monoxide intoxication. *Archives of Environmental Health, 7*, 524–530.

Schultz, D. P. (1982). *Psychology and industry today.* New York: MacMillan.

Schwab, K. E. (1982–1983). Instructional methods: Their use and effectiveness in environmental education. *Journal of Environmental Education, 14,* 8–12.

Schwartz, B., & Barsky, S. F. (1977). The home advantage. *Social Forces, 55,* 641–661.

Schwebel, A. I., & Cherlin, D. L. (1972). Physical and social distancing in teacher-pupil relationships. *Journal of Educational Psychology, 63,* 543–550.

Seamon, D. (1982). The phenomenological contribution to environmental psychology. *Journal of Environmental Psychology, 2,* 119–140.

—— (1983). Response to Sixsmith's comments on the phenomenological contribution. *Journal of Environmental Psychology, 3,* 199–200.

——, & Nordin, C. (1980). Marketplace as place ballet: A Swedish example. *Landscape, 24,* 35–41.

Sebba, R., & Churchman, A. (1983). Territories and territoriality in the home. *Environment and Behavior, 15,* 191–210.

Seligman, C., & Darley, J. M. (1977). Feedback as a means of decreasing residential energy consumption. *Journal of Applied Psychology, 62,* 363–368.

Seligman, M. E. P. (1975). *Helplessness.* San Francisco: Freeman.

Selye, H. (1976). *Stress in health and disease.* Wobern, MA: Butterworth.

Seta, J. J., Paulus, P. B., & Schkade, J. K. (1976). Effects of group size and proximity under cooperative and competitive conditions. *Journal of Personality and Social Psychology, 34,* 47–53.

Severy, L. J., Forsyth, D. R., & Wagner, P. J. (1979). A multi-method assessment of personal space development in female and male, black and white children. *Journal of Nonverbal Behavior, 4,* 68–86.

Shapiro, S. (1975). Preschool ecology: A study of three environmental variables. *Reading Improvement, 12,* 236–241.

Sherman, R. C., Croxton, J., & Giovanatto, J. (1979). Investigating cognitive representations of spatial relations. *Environment and Behavior, 11,* 209–226.

Shibley, R. G. (1985). Building evaluation in the main stream. *Environment and Behavior, 17,* 7–24.

Shippee, G., & Gregory, W. L. (1982). Public commitment and energy conservation. *American Journal of Community Psychology, 10,* 81–93.

Shumaker, S. A., & Reizenstein, J. E. (1982). Environmental factors affecting inpatient stress in acute care hospitals. In G. W. Evans (Ed.), *Environmental stress.* New York: Cambridge University Press.

Shuter, R. (1976). Proxemics and tactility in Latin America. *Journal of Communication, 26,* 46–52.

Sidis, B. (1985). A study of the mob. *Atlantic Monthly, 75,* 188–197.

Siegel, A. W., & White, S. H. (1975). The development of spatial representations of large-scale environ-

ments. In H. W. Reese (Ed.), *Advances in child development and behavior,* Vol. 10. New York: Academic Press.

Siegel, J. M., & Steele, C. M. (1980). Environmental distraction and interpersonal judgments. *British Journal of Social and Clinical Psychology, 19,* 23–32.

Simmel, G. (1957). The metropolis and mental life. In P. K. Hatt and A. J. Reiss, Jr. (Eds.), *Cities and societies: The revised reader in urban sociology.* New York: Free Press.

Simmons, D. A., Talbot, J. F., & Kaplan, R. (1984–1985). Energy in daily activities: Muddling toward conservation. *Journal of Environmental Systems, 14,* 147–155.

Sims, J. H., & Baumann, D. D. (1972). The tornado threat: Coping styles of the North and the South. *Science, 176,* 1386–1391.

—— (1983). Educational programs and human response to natural hazards. *Environment and Behavior, 15,* 165–189.

Sixsmith, J. (1983). Comment on "The phenomenological contribution to environmental psychology" by D. Seamon. *Journal of Environmental Psychology, 3,* 109–111.

Slater, B. (1968). Effects of noise on school performance. *Journal of Educational Psychology, 59,* 239–243.

Slovic, P. (1978). The psychology of protective behavior. *Journal of Safety Research, 10,* 58–68.

——, Fischhoff, B., & Lichtenstein, S. (1979). Rating the risks. *Environment, 21,* 14–20, 36–39.

——, Fischhoff, B., & Lichtenstein, S. (1986). Regulation of risk: A psychological perspective. In R. Noll (Ed.), *Social science and regulatory policy.* Berkeley, CA: University of California Press.

——, Kunreuther, H., & White, G. F. (1974). Decision processes, rationality, and adjustment to natural hazards. In G. F. White (Ed.), *Natural hazards: Local, national, global.* New York: Oxford University Press.

Smith, B. L., Lasswell, H. D., & Casey, R. D. (1946). *Propaganda, communication, and public opinion.* Princeton, NJ: Princeton University Press.

Smith, C. D. (1984). The relationship between the pleasingness of landmarks and the judgement of distance in cognitive maps. *Journal of Environmental Psychology, 4,* 229–234.

Smith, C. J., & Patterson, G. E. (1980). Cognitive mapping and the subjective geography of crime. In D. E. Georges-Abeyie, K. D. Harries (Eds.), *Crime: A spatial perspective.* New York: Columbia University Press.

Smith, D. E. (1982). Privacy and corrections: A reexamination. *American Journal of Community Psychology, 10,* 207–224.

Smith, G. H. (1954). Personality scores and personal distance effect. *Journal of Social Psychology, 39,* 37–62.

Smith, H. W. (1981). Territorial spacing on a beach revisited: A cross-national exploration. *Social Psychology Quarterly, 44,* 132–137.

Smith, P., & Connolly, K. (1977). Social and aggressive behavior in preschool children as a function of crowding. *Social Science Information, 16,* 601–620.

——, & Connolly, K. J. (1980). *The ecology of preschool behaviour.* New York: Cambridge University Press.

Smith, S. M. (1979). Remembering in and out of context. *Journal of Experimental Psychology, 5,* 460–471.

Smythe, P. C., & Brook, R. C. (1980). Environmental concerns and actions: A social-psychological investigation. *Canadian Journal of Behavioral Science, 12,* 175–186.

Socolow, R. H. (1978). *Saving energy in the home.* Cambridge, MA: Ballinger.

Solomon, D., & Kendall, A. J. (1976). Individual characteristics and children's performance in "open" and "traditional" classroom settings. *Journal of Educational Psychology, 68,* 613–625.

Sommer, R. (1959). Studies in personal space. *Sociometry, 22,* 247–260.

—— (1967). Classroom ecology. *Journal of Applied Behavioral Science, 3,* 489–503.

—— (1969). *Personal space: The behavioral basis of design.* Englewood Cliffs, NJ: Prentice-Hall.

—— (1972). *Design awareness.* New York: Holt, Rinehart and Winston.

—— (1974). Looking back at personal space. In J. Lang, C. Burnette, W. Moleski, and D. Vachon (Eds.) *Designing for human behavior: Architecture and behavioral sciences,* Stroudsburg, PA: Dowden, Hutchinson and Ross, 205–207.

—— (1983). *The end of imprisonment.* New York: Oxford University Press.

—— (1976). *Social design: Creating buildings with people in mind.* Englewood Cliffs, NJ: Prentice-Hall.

——, & Amick, T. L. (1984). *Action research: Linking research to organizational change.* Davis, CA: Center for Consumer Research, University of California.

——, & Becker, F. D. (1971). Room density and user satisfaction. *Environment and Behavior, 3,* 412–417.

——, Herrick, J., & Sommer, T. R. (1981). The behavioral ecology of supermarkets and farmers' markets. *Journal of Environmental Psychology, 1,* 13–19.

——, & Olsen, H. (1980). The soft classroom. *Environment and Behavior, 12,* 3–16.

——, & Ross, H. (1958). Social interaction on a geriatrics ward. *International Journal of Social Psychiatry, 4,* 128–133.

Sommers, P., Van Dort, B., & Moos, R. (1976). Noise and air pollution. In Moos, R. *The human context: Environmental determinants of behavior.* New York: Wiley.

Sonnenfeld, J. (1966). Variable values in space and landscape: An inquiry into the nature of environmental necessity. *Journal of Social Issues, 22*(4), 71–82.

—— (1969). Personality and behavior in environment. *Proceedings of the Association of American Geographers, 1,* 136–140.

Sorenson, J. H. (1983). Knowing how to behave under the threat of disaster: Can it be explained? *Environment and Behavior, 15,* 438–457.

Spencer, C., & Darvizeh, Z. (1981). The case for developing a cognitive environmental psychology that does not underestimate the abilities of young children. *Journal of Environmental Psychology, 1,* 21–31.

Spreen, O., Tupper, D., Risser, A., Tuokko, H., & Edgell, D. (1984). *Human developmental neuropsychology.* New York: Oxford University Press.

Stapp, W. B. (1971). An environmental education program (K-12) based on environmental encounters. *Environment and Behavior, 3,* 263–283.

Stebbins, R. A. (1973). Physical context influences on behavior: The case of classroom disorderliness. *Environment and Behavior, 5,* 291–314.

Steele, F. I. (1973). *Physical settings and organization development.* Don Mills, ON: Addison-Wesley.

—— (1980). Defining and developing environmental competence. In C. P. Alderfer and C. L. Cooper (Eds.) *Advances in experimental social processes, 2,* 225–244.

Stein, C. (1975). School lighting re-evaluated. *American School and University, 48,* 70–78.

Stern, E. (1982). Bus services in rural areas. *Environment and Behavior, 14,* 94–112.

Stern, P. C. (Ed.) (1984). *Improving energy demand analysis.* Washington: National Academy Press.

——, & Aronson, E. (Eds.) (1984). *Energy use: The human dimension.* New York: Freeman.

——, & Gardner, G. T. (1981). The place of behavior change in the management of environmental problems. *Journal of Environmental Policy, 2,* 213–240.

Stevens, W. (1959). Metaphors of a magnifico. *Poems.* New York: Vintage.

Stewart, R., Baretta, E., Platte, L., Stewart, M. T., Kalbfleisch, J., Van Yserloo, B., & Rimm, A. (1974). Carboxyhemoglobin levels in American blood donors. *Journal of the American Medical Association, 229,* 1187–1195.

Stewart, T. R., Middleton, P., & Ely, D. (1983). Urban visual air quality judgments: Reliability and validity. *Journal of Environmental Psychology, 3,* 129–145.

Stires, L. (1980). Classroom seating location, student grades, and attitudes: Environment or self-selection? *Environment and Behavior, 12,* 241–254.

Stokols, D. (1972). On the distinction between density and crowding: Some implications for further research. *Psychological Review, 79,* 275–277.

—— (1978). A typology of crowding experiences. In A.

Baum and Y. M. Epstein (Eds.), *Human response to crowding.* Hillsdale, NJ: Erlbaum.

—— (1979). A congruence analysis of human stress. In I. Sarason and C. Spielberger (Eds.) *Stress and anxiety,* Washington, DC: Hemisphere Press.

—— (1982). Environmental psychology: A coming of age. In A. Kraut (Ed.), *The Stanley Hall Lecture Series* (Vol. 2), Washington, DC: American Psychological Association.

——, & Novaco, R. W. (1981). Transportation and well-being: An ecological perspective. In I. Altman, J. F. Wohlwill, and P. B. Everett (Eds.), *Transportation and behavior.* New York: Plenum.

——, Ohlig, W., & Resnick, S. M. (1979). Perceptions of residential crowding, classroom experiences, and student health. In J. R. Aiello and A. Baum (Eds.), *Residential crowding and design.* New York: Plenum.

——, & Shumaker, S. A. (1981). People in places: A transactional view of settings. In J. H. Harvey (Ed.), *Cognition, social behavior and the environment.* Hillsdale, NJ: Erlbaum.

——, Shumaker, S. A., & Martinez, J. (1983). Residential mobility and personal well-being. *Journal of Environmental Psychology, 3,* 5–19.

——, Smith, T. E., & Proster, J. J. (1975). Partitioning and perceived crowding in a public place. *American Behavioral Scientist, 18,* 792–814.

Stone, E. F., Gueutal, H. G., Gardner, D. G., & McClure, S. (1983). A field experiment comparing information-privacy values, beliefs, and attitudes across several types of organizations. *Journal of Applied Psychology, 68,* 459–468.

Stone, J., Breidenbach, S., & Heimstra, N. (1979) Annoyance response of non-smokers to cigarette smoke. *Perceptual and Motor Skills, 49,* 907–916.

Stramler, C. S., Kleiss, J. A., & Howell, W. C. (1983). Thermal sensation shifts induced by physical and psychological means. *Journal of Applied Psychology, 68,* 187–193.

Strang, H. R., & George, J. R. (1975). Clowning around to stop clowning around: A brief report on an automated approach to monitor, record, and control classroom noise. *Journal of Applied Behavior Analysis, 8,* 471–474.

Streltzer, J. (1979). Psychiatric emergencies in travelers to Hawaii. *Comprehensive Psychiatry, 20,* 463–468.

Stringer, P. (1984). Studies in the socio-environmental psychology of tourism. *Annals of Tourism Research, 11,* 147–166.

Strodbeck, F. L., & Hook, L. H. (1961). Social dimensions of a twelve-man jury table. *Sociometry, 24,* 397–415.

Studenmund, A. H., & Connor, D. (1982). The free-fare transit experiments. *Transportation Research, 16,* 261–269.

Suedfeld, P. (1980). *Restricted environmental stimula-* *tion: Research and clinical applications.* New York: Wiley.

——, Landon, P. B., & Ballard, E. J. (1983). Effects of reduced stimulation on divergent and convergent thinking. *Environment and Behavior, 15,* 727–738.

Sundstrom, E. (1975). An experimental study of crowding: Effects of room size, intrusion and goal blocking on nonverbal behavior, self disclosure and self-reported stress. *Journal of Personality and Social Psychology, 32,* 645–654.

—— (1978). Crowding as a sequential process: Review of research on the effects of population density on humans. In A. Baum and Y. M. Epstein (Eds.), *Human response to crowding.* Hillsdale, NJ: Erlbaum.

——, & Altman, I. (1974). Field study of territorial behavior and dominance. *Journal of Personality and Social Psychology, 30,* 115–124.

——, & Altman, I. (1976). Interpersonal relationships and personal space: Research review and theoretical model. *Human Ecology, 4,* 47–67.

——, Burt, R., & Kamp, D. (1980). Privacy at work: Architectural correlates of job satisfaction and job performance. *Academy of Management Journal, 23;*101–117.

——, Herbert, R. K., & Brown, D. W. (1982). Privacy and communication in an open-plan office: A case study. *Environment and Behavior, 14,* 379–392.

——, Town, J. P., Brown, D. W., Forman, A., & McGee, C. (1982). Physical enclosure, type of job, and privacy in the office. *Environment and Behavior, 14,* 543–559.

——, Town, J. P., Osborn, D., Rice, R. W., Konar, E., Mandel, D., & Brill, M. (1985). *Office noise, satisfaction, and performance.* Manuscript.

Sussman, N. M., & Rosenfeld, H. M. (1982). Influence of culture, language, and sex on conversational distance. *Journal of Personality and Social Psychology, 42,* 66–74.

Szilagyi, A., & Holland, W. (1980). Changes in social density: Relationships with functional interaction and perceptions of job characteristics, role stress, and work satisfaction. *Journal of Applied Psychology, 65,* 28–33.

Tausz, A. (1970, October 20). Landscape of the future. *The Financial Post,* p. S10.

Taylor, P. J., & Pocock, S. J. (1972). Commuter travel and sickness absence of London office workers. *British Journal of Preventive and Social Medicine, 26,* 172–175.

Taylor, R. B. (1982). Neighborhood physical environment and stress. In G. W. Evans (Ed.), *Environmental stress.* New York: Cambridge University Press.

—— (1983). Conjoining environmental psychology with social and personality psychology: Natural marriage or shot-gun wedding? In N. R. Feimer and E. S. Geller (Eds.), *Environmental psychology: Directions and perspectives.* New York: Praeger.

——, & Brooks, D. K. (1980). Temporary territories: Responses to intrusions in a public setting. *Population and Environment, 3*, 135–145.

——, & Ferguson, G. (1980). Solitude and intimacy: Linking territoriality and privacy experiences. *Journal of Nonverbal Behavior, 4*, 227–239.

——, Gottfredson, S. D., & Brower, S. (1981). Territorial cognitions and social climate in urban neighborhoods. *Basic and Applied Social Psychology, 2*, 289–303.

——, & Lanni, J. C. (1981). Territorial dominance: The influence of the resident advantage in triadic decision making. *Journal of Personality and Social Psychology, 41*, 909–915.

——, & Stough, R. R. (1978). Territorial cognition: Assessing Altman's typology. *Journal of Personality and Social Psychology, 36*, 418–423.

Taylor, S. M., & Konrad, V. A. (1980). Scaling dispositions toward the past. *Environment and Behavior, 12*, 283–307.

Tedesco, J. F., & Fromme, D. K. (1974). Cooperation, competition, and personal space. *Sociometry, 37*, 116–121.

Tennis, G. H. & Dabbs, J. M. (1975). Sex, setting and personal space: First grade through college. *Sociometry, 38*, 385–394.

Thalhofer, N. (1980). Violation of a spacing norm in high social density. *Journal of Applied Social Psychology, 10*, 175–183.

Thompson, D. E., Aiello, J. R., & Epstein, Y. (1979). Interpersonal distance preferences. *Journal of Nonverbal Behavior, 4*, 113–118.

Thorne, R., & Hall, R. (in press). Environmental psychology in Australia. In D. Stokols and I. Altman (Eds.), *Handbook of environmental psychology.* New York: Wiley.

Thurstone, L. L. (1946). Factor analysis and body types. *Psychometrika, 11*, 15–21.

Tien, J., O'Donnell, V. F., Barnett, A., & Mirchandani, P. B. (1979). *Street lighting projects.* Washington, DC: U. S. Department of Justice.

Tischer, M. L., & Phillips, R. V. (1979). The relationships between transportation perceptions and behaviors over time. *Transportation, 8*, 21–33.

Tolchinsky, P. D., McCuddy, M. K., Adams, J., Ganster, D. C., Woodman, R. W., & Fromkin, H. C. (1981). Employee perceptions of invasion of privacy: A field simulation experiment. *Journal of Applied Psychology, 66*, 308–313.

Tolman, E. C. (1932). *Purposive behavior in animals and men.* New York: Century.

—— (1948). Cognitive maps in rats and men. *Psychological Review, 55*, 189–208.

Tom, G., Poole, M. F., Galla, J., & Berrier, J. (1981). The influence of negative air ions on human performance and mood. *Human Factors, 23*, 633–636.

Traub, R. E., & Weiss, J. (1974). Studying openness in education: An Ontario example. *Journal of Research and Development in Education, 8*, 47–59.

——, Weiss, J., & Fisher, C. (1977). *Openness in schools: An evaluation study.* Ottawa: Ontario Institute for Studies in Education.

——, Weiss, J., Fisher, C. W., & Mesulla, D. (1974). Closure on openness: Describing and quantifying open education. *Interchange, 3*, 69–84.

Trigg, L. J., Perlman, D., Perry, R. P., & Janisse, M. P. (1976). Anti-pollution behavior: A function of perceived outcome and locus of control. *Environment and Behavior, 8*, 307–314.

Truscott, J. C., Parmelee, P., & Werner, C. (1977). Plate touching in restaurants: Preliminary observations of a food-related marking behavior in humans. *Personality and Social Psychology Bulletin, 3*, 425–428.

Tuan, Y. F. (1974). *Topophilia.* Englewood Cliffs, NJ: Prentice-Hall.

—— (1980). Rootedness versus sense of place. *Landscape, 24*, 3–8.

Turiel, I., Hollowell, C. D., Miksch, R. R., Rudy, J. V., & Young, R. A. (1983). The effects of reduced ventilation on indoor air quality in an office building. *Atmospheric environment, 17*, 51–64.

Turnbull, C. (1961). Some observations regarding the experiences and behavior of the Bambuti pygmies. *American Journal of Psychology, 74*, 304–308

Turner, C. W., Layton, J. F., & Simons, L. S. (1975). Naturalistic studies of aggressive behavior: Aggressive stimuli, victim visability, and horn honking. *Journal of Personality and Social Psychology, 31*, 1098–1107.

Tzamir, Y. (1975). *The impact of spatial regularity and irregularity on cognitive mapping* (Technical Report). Haifa, Israel: Technion-Israel Institute of Technology, Center for Urban and Regional Studies.

Ulrich, R. S. (1981). Natural vs. urban scenes: Some psychophysical effects. *Environment and Behavior, 13*, 523–556.

United States Riot Commission. (1968). *Report of the National Advisory Commission on Civil Disorders.* New York: Bantam.

Valadez, J. J. (1984). Diverging meanings of development among architects and three other professional groups. *Journal of Environmental Psychology, 4*, 223–228.

van de Kragt, A. J. C., Orbell, J. M., & Dawes, R. M. (1983). The minimal contributing set as a solution to public goods problems. *American Political Science Review, 77*, 112–122.

van Hoogdalem, H. van der Voordt, T. J. M., & van Wegen, H. B. R. (1985). Comparative floorplan-analysis as a means to develop design guidelines. *Journal of Environmental Psychology, 5*, 153–179.

Van Liere, K. V., & Dunlap, R. E. (1981). Environmental

concern: Does it make a difference how it's measured? *Environment and Behavior, 13,* 651–676.

van Vliet—, W. (1983). Families in apartment buildings: Sad storeys for children? *Environment and Behavior, 15,* 211–234.

van Wagenberg, D., Krasner, M., & Krasner, L. (1981). Children planning an ideal classroom: Environmental design in an elementary school. *Environment and Behavior, 13,* 349–359.

Venturi, R. (1966). *Complexity and contradiction in architecture.* New York: Museum of Modern Art.

Verbrugge, L. M., & Taylor, R. B. (1980). Consequences of population density and size. *Urban Affairs Quarterly, 16,* 135–160.

Vickroy, S. C., Shaw, J. B., & Fisher, C. D. (1980). Effects of temperature, clothing, and task complexity on task performance and satisfaction. *Journal of Applied Psychology, 67,* 97–102.

Vielhauer, J. (1966). The development of a semantic scale for the description of the physical environment (Doctoral dissertation, Louisiana State University, 1965). *Dissertation abstracts, 26,* (8), 4821. (Order no. 66–759).

Vinacke, W. E., Mogy, R., Powers, W., Langan, C., & Beck, R. (1974). Accommodative strategy and communication in a three person matrix game. *Journal of Personality and Social Psychology, 29,* 509–525.

Vinsel, A., Brown, B. B., Altman, I., & Foss, C. (1980). Privacy regulation, territorial displays, and effectiveness of individual functioning. *Journal of Personality and Social Psychology, 39,* 1104–1115.

Vischer, J. C. (1985). The adaptation and control model of user needs: A new direction for housing research. *Journal of Environmental Psychology, 5,* 287–296.

Wachs, T. D. (1979). Proximal experience and early cognitive-intellectual development: The physical environment. *Merrill-Palmer Quarterly, 25,* 3–41.

Wagner, M., Baird, J. C., & Barbaresi, W. (1981). The locus of environmental attention. *Journal of Environmental Psychology, 1,* 195–206.

Walberg, H. (1969). Physical and psychological distance in the classroom. *School Review, 77,* 64–70.

Walden, T. A., Nelson, P. A., & Smith, D. E. (1981). Crowding, privacy and coping. *Environment and Behavior, 13,* 205–224.

Walker, J. M. (1980). Voluntary response to energy conservation appeals. *Journal of Consumer Research, 7,* 88–92.

Wall, G. (1973). Public response to air pollution in South Yorkshire, England. *Environment and Behavior, 5,* 219–248.

Walmsley, D. J., Boskovic, R. M., & Pigram, J. J. (1983). Tourism and crime: An Australian perspective. *Journal of Leisure Research, 15,* 136–155.

Walster, E., & Walster, G. W. (1975). Equity and social justice. *Journal of Social Issues, 31* (3), 21–43.

Walter, J. A. (1982). Social limits to tourism. *Leisure Studies, 1,* 295–304.

Wapner, S. (1981). Transactions of persons-in-environments: Some critical transitions. *Journal of Environmental Psychology, 1,* 223–239.

Ward, L. M. (1977). Multidimensional scaling of the molar physical environment. *Multivariate Behavioral Research, 12,* 23–42.

Watson, O. M. (1970). *Proxemic behavior: A cross-cultural study.* The Hague: Mouton.

——, & Graves, T. D. (1966). Quantitative research in proxemic behavior. *American Anthropologist, 68,* 971–985.

Watzke, G. E., Dana, J. M., Doktor, R. H., & Rubenstein, F. D. (1972). An experimental study of individual vs. group interest. *Acta Sociologica, 15,* 366–370.

Webb, E. J., Campbell, D. T., Schwartz, R. D., & Sechrest, L. (1966). *Unobtrusive measures: Nonreactive research in the social sciences.* Chicago: Rand-McNally.

—— (1981). *Nonreactive measures in social sciences.* Boston: Houghton Mifflin.

Webley, P. (1981). Sex differences in home range and cognitive maps in eight-year-old children. *Journal of Environmental Psychology, 1,* 293–302.

Weidemann, S., Anderson, J. R., Butterfield, D. I., & O'Donnell, P. M. (1982). Residents' perception of satisfaction and safety: A basis for change in multifamily housing. *Environment and Behavior, 14,* 695–724.

Weigel, R. H., & Newman, L. S. (1976). Increasing attitude-behavior correspondence by broadening the scope of behavioral measure. *Journal of Personality and Social Psychology, 33,* 793–802.

——, & Weigel, J. (1978). Environmental concern: The development of a measure. *Environment and Behavior, 10,* 3–15.

Weiner, F. H. (1976). Altruism, ambience, and action: The effects of rural and urban rearing on helping behavior. *Journal of Personality and Social Psychology, 34,* 112–124.

Weinstein, C. S. (1977). Modifying student behavior in an open classroom through changes in the physical design. *American Education Research Journal, 14,* 249–262.

—— (1979). The physical environment of school: A review of the research. *Review of Educational Research, 49,* 577–610.

—— (1981). Classroom design as an external condition for learning. *Educational Technology, 21,* 12–19.

—— (1982a). Special issue on learning environments: An introduction. *Journal of Man-Environment Relations, 1* (3), 1–9.

—— (1982b). Privacy-seeking behavior in an elementary classroom. *Journal of Environmental Psychology, 2,* 23–35.

——, & Weinstein, N. D. (1979). Noise and reading performance in an open space school. *Journal of Educational Research, 72,* 210–213.

——, & Woolfolk, A. E. (1981). The classroom setting as a source of expectations about teachers and pupils. *Journal of Environmental Psychology, 1,* 117–129.

Weinstein, L. (1968). The mother-child schema, anxiety, and academic achievement in elementary school boys. *Child Development, 39,* 257–264.

Weinstein, N. D. (1974). Effect of noise on intellectual performance. *Journal of Applied Psychology, 59,* 548–554.

—— (1977). Noise and intellectual performance: A confirmation and extension. *Journal of Applied Psychology, 62,* 104–126.

—— (1978). Individual differences in reactions to noise: A longitudinal study in a college dormitory. *Journal of Applied Psychology, 63,* 456–466.

—— (1980). Individual differences in critical tendencies and noise annoyance. *Journal of Sound and Vibration, 68,* 241–248.

—— (1982). Community noise problems: Evidence against adaptation. *Journal of Environmental Psychology, 2,* 99–108.

Weisenthal, D. L., & Tubiana, J. H. (1981). Apartment design choices: A study of Israeli and Non-Israeli university students. *Environment and Behavior, 13,* 677–684.

Weisman, G. D. (1983). Environmental programming and action research. *Environment and Behavior, 15,* 381–408.

Weisner, T. S., & Weibel, J. C. (1981). Home environments and family lifestyles in California. *Environment and Behavior, 13,* 417–460.

Welch, B. L. (1979, June). *Extra-auditory health effects of industrial noise: Survey of foreign literature.* Aerospace Medical Research Laboratory, Aerospace Medical Division, Airforce Systems Command, Wright-Patterson AFB.

Wener, R. (1977). Non-density factors in the perception of crowding. *Dissertation Abstracts International, 37B,* 3569–3570.

—— (1982, February). *Environment-behavior research "success stories."* Paper presented at a symposium, The Evaluation of Occupied Designed Environments, Georgia Institute of Technology, Atlanta.

——, Frazier, F. W., & Farbstein, J. (1985). Three generations of evaluation and design of correctional facilities. *Environment and Behavior, 17,* 71–95.

——, & Kaminoff, R. D. (1983). Improving environmental information: Effects of signs on perceived crowding and behavior. *Environment and Behavior, 15,* 3–20.

Werner, C., Brown, B., & Damron, G. (1981). Territorial marking in a game arcade. *Journal of Personality and Social Psychology, 41,* 1094–1104.

West, P. C. (1982). Effects of user behavior on the per-ception of crowding in backcountry forest recreation. *Forest Science, 28,* 95–105.

Westin, A. F. (1967). *Privacy and freedom.* New York: Atheneum.

Wheeler, L. (1985). Behavior and design: A memoir. *Environment and Behavior, 17,* 133–144.

Wheldall, K., Morriss, M. Vaughan, P., & Ng, Y. Y. (1981). Rows vs. tables: An example of the use of behavioral ecology in two classes of eleven-year-old children. *Journal of Educational Psychology, 1,* 171–184.

Whyte, W. H. (1974). The best street life in the world. *New York Magazine, 15,* 26–33.

—— (1980). *The social life of small urban spaces.* New York: The Conservation Foundation.

Wicker, A. W. (1968). Undermanning, performance, and students' subjective experiences in behavior settings of large and small high schools. *Journal of Personality and Social Psychology, 10,* 255–261.

—— (1979). *An introduction to ecological psychology.* Monterey, CA: Brooks/Cole.

—— (in press). Behavior settings reconsidered: Temporal stages, resources, internal dynamics, context. In D. Stokols and I. Altman (Eds.), *Handbook of environmental psychology.* New York: Wiley.

Widgery, R. N. (1982). Satisfaction with the quality of urban life: A predictive model. *American Journal of Community Psychology, 10,* 37–48.

Wiggins, J. S. (ca. 1975). *The relationship between personality characteristics and attitudes toward housing and related facilities in six Army posts.* Unpublished manuscript, University of Illinois.

—— (1979). A psychological taxonomy of trait-descriptive terms: The interpersonal domain. *Journal of Personality and Social Psychology, 37,* 395–412.

Willems, E. P. (1974). Behavioral technology and behavioral ecology. *Journal of Applied Behavior Analysis, 7,* 151–164.

——, & Campbell, D. E. (1976). One path through the cafeteria. *Environment and Behavior, 8,* 125–140.

Williams, R. (1981, October–November). Outshopping: Problem or opportunity? *Arizona Business, 27,* 9.

Willis, F. N. (1966). Initial speaking distance as a function of the speakers' relationship. *Psychonomic Science, 5,* 221–222.

Wilson, C. W., & Hopkins, B. L. (1973). The effects of contingent music on the intensity of noise in junior home economics classes. *Journal of Applied Behavior Analysis, 6,* 269–275.

Windley, P. G. & Vandeventer, W. H. (1982). Environmental cognition of small rural towns: The case for older residents. *Journal of Environmental Psychology, 2,* 285–294.

Wineman, J. D. (1982). The office environment as a source of stress. In G. W. Evans (Ed.), *Environmental stress,* New York: Cambridge University Press.

—— (Ed.) (1985). *Behavioral issues in office design.* New York: Van Nostrand Reinhold.

Winett, R. A., Neale, M. S. & Grier, H. C. (1979). Effects of self-monitoring and feedback on residential electricity consumption. *Journal of Applied Behavior Analysis, 12,* 173–184.

——, Neale, M. S., Williams, K. R., Yokley, J., & Kauder, H. (1979). The effects of individual and group feedback on residential electricity consumption: Three replications. *Journal of Environmental Systems, 8,* 217–233.

Winick, C., & Holt, H. (1961). Seating position as nonverbal communication in group analysis. *Psychiatry, 24,* 171–182.

Winkler, R. C., & Winett, R. A. (1982). Behavioral interventions in resource management: A systems approach based on behavioral economics. *American Psychologist, 37,* 421–435.

Wirth, L. (1938). Urbanism as a way of life. *American Journal of Psychology, 44,* 9–14.

Witmer, J. F., & Geller, E. S. (1976). Facilitating paper recycling: Effects of prompts, raffles, and contests. *Journal of Applied Behavior Analysis, 9,* 315–322.

Wodarski, J. B. (1982). National and state appeals for energy conservation: A behavioral analysis of effects. *Behavioral Engineering, 7,* 119–130.

Wohlwill, J. F. (1966). The physical environment: A problem for a psychology of stimulation. *Journal of Social Issues, 22*(4), 29–38.

—— (1973). The environment is not in the head! In W. F. E. Preiser (Ed.), *Environmental design research,* Vol. 2. Stroudsburg, PA: Dowden Hutchinson and Ross.

—— (1976). Environmental aesthetics: The environment as a source of affect. In I. Altman and J. F. Wohlwill (Ed.), *Human behavior and environment,* Vol. 1. New York: Plenum.

—— (1982). The visual impact of development in coastal zone areas. *Coastal Zone Management Journal, 9,* 225–248.

——, & Harris, G. (1980). Response to man-made features in nature-recreation settings. *Leisure Sciences, 3,* 349–365.

Wolfe, M. (1978). Childhood and privacy. In I. Altman and J. F. Wohlwill (Eds.), *Children and the environment.* New York: Plenum Press.

Wolff, M. (1973). Notes on the behavior of pedestrians. In A. Brienbaum and E. Sagarin (Eds.), *People in places: The sociology of the familiar.* New York: Praeger.

Wolfgang, J., & Wolfgang, A. (1971). Explanation of attitudes via physical interpersonal distance toward the obese, drug users, homosexuals, police, and other marginal figures. *Journal of Clinical Psychology, 27,* 510–512.

Wollin, D. D., & Montagne, M. (1981). College classroom environment: Effects of sterility versus amiability on student and teacher performance. *Environment and Behavior, 13,* 707–716.

Womble, P., & Studebaker, S. (1981). Crowding in a national park campground: Katmai National Monument in Alaska. *Environment and Behavior, 13,* 557–573.

Wood, W. (1972). *An analysis of simulation media.* Unpublished Graduation Project, School of Architecture, University of British Columbia, Vancouver.

Wools, R. (1970). The effects of rooms on behavior. In D. Canter (Ed.), *Architectural psychology.* London: RIBA.

Worchel, S., & Lollis, M. (1982). Reactions to territorial contamination as a function of culture. *Personality and Social Psychology Bulletin, 8,* 370–375.

Worthington, M. (1974). Personal space as a function of the stigma effect. *Environment and Behavior, 6,* 289–295.

Wright, R. J. (1975). The affective and cognitive consequences of an open education elementary school. *American Educational Research Journal, 12,* 449–468.

Wulf, K. M. (1977). Relationship of assigned classroom seating area to achievement variables. *Educational Research Quarterly, 21,* 56–62.

Wynne-Edwards, V. C. (1965). Self-regulating systems in populations of animals. *Science, 147,* 1543–1548.

—— (1972). *Animal dispersion in relation to social behavior.* New York: Hafner.

Wyon, D. P. (1970). Studies of children under imposed noise and heat stress. *Ergonomics, 13,* 598–612.

Wyon, D. P., Lofberg, H. A., & Lofstedt, B. (1975). Environmental research at the climate laboratory of the National Swedish Institute of Building Research. *Man-Environment Systems, 5,* 107–200.

Yamamoto, T. (1984, August). *Current trends in Japanese psychology.* Paper presented at the annual meetings of the American Psychological Association, Toronto.

Yates, S. M., & Aronson, E. (1983). A social psychological perspective on energy conservation in residential buildings. *American Psychologist, 38,* 435–444.

Yoors, J. (1967). *The gypsies.* New York: Simon and Schuster.

Yuhnke, R. E. (1983). The importance of visibility protection in the national parks and wilderness. In R. D. Rowe and L. G. Chestnut (Eds.), *Managing air quality and scenic resources at national parks and wilderness parks.* Boulder, CO: Westview Press.

Zeisel, J. (1975). *Sociology and architectural design.* New York: Russell Sage Foundation.

—— (1981). *Inquiry by design: Tools for environment-behavior research.* Monterey, CA: Brooks/Cole.

Zentall, S. S. (1983). Learning environments: A review of physical and temporal factors. *EEQ: Exceptional Education Quarterly, 4,* 90–115.

Zerega, A. M. (1981). Transportation energy conservation policy: Implications for social science research. *Journal of Social Issues, 37* (2), 31–50.

Zielinski, E. J., & Bethel, L. J. (1983). Winning the energy game. *The Science Teacher, 50,* 55–56.

Zifferblatt, S. M. (1972). Architecture and human behavior: Toward increased understanding of a functional relationship. *Educational Technology, 12,* 54–57.

Zimring, C. (1982). The built environment as a source of psychological stress: Impacts of buildings and cities on satisfaction and behavior. In G. W. Evans (Ed.), *Environmental stress,* New York: Cambridge University Press.

——, & Reizenstein, J. E. (1980). Post-occupancy evaluation: An overview. *Environment and Behavior, 12,* 429–450.

——, & Reizenstein, J. E. (1981). A primer on post-occupancy evaluation. *AIA Journal, 70*(13), 52–58.

——, Weitzer, W., and Knight, R. C. (1982). Opportunity for control and the designed environment: The case of an institution for the developmentally disabled. In A. Baum and J. Singer (Eds.), *Advances in environmental psychology* (Vol. 4). Hillsdale, NJ: Erlbaum.

Zlutnick, S., & Altman, I. (1972). Crowding and human behavior. In J. Wohlwill and D. Carson (Eds.), *Environment and the social sciences: Perspectives and applications.* Washington, DC: American Psychological Association.

Zube, E. H. (1980). *Environmental evaluation: Perception and public policy.* Monterey, CA: Brooks/Cole.

—— (1984). Themes in landscape assessment theory. *Landscape Journal, 3*(2).

——, & Pitt, D. G. (1981). Cross-cultural perceptions of scenic and heritage landscapes. *Landscape Planning, 8,* 69–87.

——, & Anderson, T. W. (1975). Perception and prediction of scenic resource values of the Northeast. In E. H. Zube, R. O. Brush, and J. G. Fabos (Eds.), *Landscape assessment: Values, perceptions, and resources.* Stroudsburg, PA: Dowden, Hutchinson and Ross.

——, & Evans, G. W. (1983). A life-span developmental study of landscape assessment. *Journal of Environmental Psychology, 3,* 115–128.

——, Sell, J. L., & Taylor, J. G. (1982). Landscape perception: Research, application and theory. *Landscape Planning, 9,* 1–33.

Name Index

Lennon, J. 415
Leonard-Barton, D. 407, 410
Lesko, W. A. 246, 247, 320
Levelton, L. B. 36
Levin, I. 306
Levine, D. W. 284
Levine, M. 41
Levitt, C. A. 390
Levy, L. 179, 183
Lewin, K. 6, 7, 79–83, 127
Lewis, P. 314
Ley, D. 145, 149, 150
LeBlanc, J. 319
LeBon, G. 163
LeCompte, W. A. 171, 196
Libuser, L. 121
Lichtenstein, S. 254, 264
Lichtman, C. M. 203, 205, 214, 215
Lieblich, I. 45
Lindberg, E. 36, 43, 45
Lindvall, T. 14
Lingwood, D. A. 296
Little, B. R. 83–85, 89, 91, 95, 99
Little, K. B. 114, 116
Livingstone, D. H. 24
Llewellyn, L. G. 243
Lloyd, W. 380, 382, 407
Loewy, J. H. 280
Lofberg, H. A. 14
Lofland, L. 248
Lofstedt, B. 14
Logsdon, T. 253
Lollis, M. 147
Lomenick, T. 36, 270
Lomranz, J. 123
London, R. S. 115
Loo, C. M. 176, 181, 182, 185, 186, 245
Lott, B. S. 112, 116
Louviere, J. 306
Love, K. D. 109, 110
Lovell, B. 286
Lowenthal, D. 23
Luft, J. 114
Lui, L. 388, 414
Lukerman, R. 417
Luyben, P. D. 408
Lyman, S. M. 138, 139
Lynch, K. 23, 31, 32, 36–38, 40, 49, 54, 57
Lyons, E. 54, 55

Macey, S. M. 405
Mackett-Stout, J. 365
MacConnell, W. P. 68

MacPherson, J. C. 284
Magana, J. R. 32, 33
Magel, S. G. 26
Majal, T. 395
Maloney, M. P. 64, 75
Mandel, D. R. 172, 174, 176, 183, 313, 329
Mann, S. H. 413
Mantyla, T. 36
Mar, D. 245
Marans, R. W. 236, 286, 348, 369, 372–374
Marchon, I. 41
Margulis, S. T. 216, 223, 369
Marrero, D. G. 36
Marsella, A. 179
Marshall, N. J. 85, 86, 201–205, 219
Marshall, S. P. 43
Martin, W. W. 296
Martinez, J. 97, 99, 237, 264
Martyniuk, D. 326
Marx, B. S. 271
Maslow, A. 217
Masnick, G. 237
Mathews, K. E. 247, 314
Matter, C. F. 119, 120
Mattson, R. 357
May, F. E. 250
Mayo, C. 105
Mayron, E. L. 275, 276
Mayron, L. W. 275, 276, 278
Mazur, A. 118
McArthur, D. 332
McCain, G. 179, 181, 187, 192, 194–196
McCallum, R. 169
McCarthy, D. 176
McCarthy, D. P. 219, 239
McCauley, C. 248
McClelland, C. L. 382
McClintock, C. G. 383, 387
McClintock, E. 383, 387, 389
McClure, S. 206, 223
McCluster, K. 123
McCormack, P. 35
McCormick, E. J. 317, 327
McCuddy, M. K. 207
McDonald, P. J. 284
McDougall, G. H. G. 406, 410, 414
McDougall, W. 163
McDowell, K. 314
McElroy, J. C. 92, 329
McGee, C. 203, 223, 314
McGeoch, J. A. 269
McGill, W. 22

McGrew, P. L. 165, 279, 289
McKechnie, G. E. 24, 78, 85, 86, 91, 95, 96, 99, 203
McLeod, B. 256
McMillan, D. W. 97, 241
McNall, P. 279
McNees, M. P. 403
McTavish, J. 384, 390
Megaw, E. D. 325
Mehrabian, A. 9, 30, 59, 60, 87, 91, 96, 113, 116, 118–120, 170, 243, 312, 350
Meisels, M. 114, 115, 123
Melton, G. B. 201, 213, 216
Melville, H. 78
Mercer, D. C. 331
Mercer, G. W. 144
Messick, D. M. 382, 388, 414
Meux, E. P. 387, 388
Michelson, W. 232, 234–236, 242, 243, 348
Middlemist, R. D. 119, 120
Middleton, P. 75
Miksch, R. R. 323
Milgram, S. 9, 164, 191, 192, 242, 248
Millard, R. J. 284
Miller, E. 345
Miller, J. D. 310
Miller, P. A. 54
Miller, R. L. 401
Miller, S. 92, 169, 170
Miller, S. J. 207
Milligan, M. 323
Min, M. S. 171, 176
Mintz, A. 383, 385
Mirchandani, P. B. 245
Mogy, R. 387
Monk, T. H. 308
Montagne, M. 266, 281, 299, 300
Montano, D. 167, 168
Moore, G. T. 34, 36, 37, 42, 49, 369
Moore, N. K. 389
Moos, R. H. 66, 68, 69, 74, 188, 219, 271, 279, 320, 350, 369, 398, 417
More, T. 416
Morissey, E. 236, 245
Morris, M. 281
Morris, P. A. 333
Morrison, T. L. 284
Morrow, L. M. 283, 298
Morrow, P. C. 92, 329
Morton, H. 121
Moser, G. 69

337, 342, 343, 345, 348–351,
354–359, 363, 369, 375, 399,
402, 410, 417
Sommer, T. R. 245, 249
Sommers, P. 279, 398
Sonnenfeld, J. 53, 84, 85, 91
Sorenson, J. H. 252
Sorenson, P. F. 38
Sorkin, R. D. 318
Sorte, G. 14
Spacapan, S. 248
Spencer, A. 307, 338
Spencer, C. 35
Spencer, T. 326
Spensley, J. 398
Spivack, M. 297
Spreckelmeyer, K. F. 372–374
Spreen, O. 251
Srivastava, R. K. 369
Stadler, S. J. 245
Stapp, W. B. 295, 296
Starkey, E. E. 297
Stea, D. 31, 46
Stebbins, R. A. 292
Steele, C. M. 247
Steele, F. I. 292, 294, 295, 300,
301, 304, 309, 339, 365, 375
Stein, C. 275
Steinberg, L. M. 36
Stern, E. 306
Stern, P. C. 404, 405, 410, 414
Steven, G. 125
Stevens, W. 48, 66
Stewart, M. T. 397
Stewart, R. 397
Stewart, T. R. 75
Stimpson, D. V. 284
Stires, L. 284
Stockdale, J. E. 191
Stokols, D. 9, 11, 16, 89, 97, 99,
164, 167, 171, 174, 189, 191,
194, 237, 238, 264, 272, 279,
300, 304, 308, 309
Stone, E. F. 206, 210, 223
Stone, J. 324
Stough, R. R. 152
Stramler, C. S. 319
Strang, H. R. 272
Stratton, L. O. 114
Streltzer, J. 334
Stringer, P. 14, 271, 332
Strodbeck, F. L. 132
Strube, M. J. 110
Studebaker, S. 170, 174
Studenmund, A. H. 306
Suci, G. 52

Suedfeld, P. 9, 39
Sullivan, H. S. 132
Sunaday, E. 181
Sundstrom, E. 93, 126, 127, 134,
150, 151, 167, 171, 176, 180,
182, 187, 203, 204, 209, 217,
218, 223, 313, 314, 329, 339
Sussman, N. M. 118, 119
Swaffer, P. W. 116
Switzer, F. 286
Syme, G. J. 406
Szigeti, F. 356, 363, 364, 375
Szilagyi, A. 328

Tagg, S. K. 37
Talbot, J. F. 406
Tams, A. 281
Tang, W. 307, 338
Tannenbaum, P. 52
Tausz, A. 328
Taylor, A. 348
Taylor, B. 142
Taylor, D. A. 126
Taylor, J. G. 70
Taylor, L. 275
Taylor, P. J. 304
Taylor, R. B. 86, 91, 93, 99,
141–146, 150–152, 159, 160, 211,
223, 242, 245, 264
Taylor, S. M. 86, 258
Tedesco, J. F. 115
Teger, A. 181
Tennis, G. H. 112, 116
Tetsuro, W. 14
Thalhofer, N. 181
Thomas, G. 14
Thomas, M. D. 284
Thomas, M. M. 403
Thompson, D. E. 121, 126, 134,
167, 172, 179, 180, 182–185
Thomson, R. 248
Thorne, R. 14, 54
Thurstone, L. L. 83
Tien, J. 245
Tischer, M. L. 306
Toch, H. 164
Tolchinsky, P. D. 207
Tolman, E. C. 45
Tom, G. 321
Town, J. P. 203, 223, 313, 314
Traub, R. E. 268, 286, 288
Trigg, L. J. 93
Troutwine, R. 115
Truscott, J. C. 148
Tuan, Y. F. 23, 62, 97
Tubiana, J. H. 236

Tuokko, H. 251
Tupper, D. 251
Turiel, I. 323
Turnbull, C. 25, 26
Turner, C. W. 308
Tversky, A. 382
Tyszka, T. 387, 389
Tzamir, Y. 37

Ulrich, R. E. 272
Ulrich, R. S. 58

Valadez, J. J. 26
Valencia, H. 25
Valins, S. 176
van de Kragt, A. J. C. 387, 390, 391
van der Ryn, S. 295, 366
van der Voordt, T. J. M. 349
Van Dort, B. 398
van Hoogdalem, H. 349
Van Liere, K. V. 65
van Vliet—, W. 97, 239
van Wagenberg, D. 297, 363
van Wegen, H. B. R. 63, 349
Van Yserloo, B. 397
Vandeventer, W. H. 36, 37
Vaughan, P. 281
Vautier, J. S. 169, 174
Venturi, R. 30
Verbrugge, L. M. 93
Vermeulen, P. J. 310, 311
Vernon, P. E. 369
Vickroy, S. C. 318
Vinacke, W. E. 387
Vinsel, A. 149, 214
Vischer, J. C. 364
Vitek, J. D. 252
Vukcevic, D. P. 115

Wachs, T. D. 239
Wagner, M. 23
Wagner, P. J. 112
Walberg, H. 284
Walden, T. A. 169, 171, 172, 174,
201, 202, 205
Walker, J. M. 408
Wall, G. 399
Walmsley, D. J. 334
Walster, E. 395
Walster, G. W. 395
Walter, J. A. 334
Wapner, S. 11, 36
Ward, L. M. 16, 24, 26, 30, 43, 49,
60, 64, 89
Ward, M. O. 75

Subject Index

Program ecological psychology, 10, 155, 285–287

Programming, 371; in the design process, 357–366

Projective stage (child development), 34

Prompts (in behavioral approach), 402, 403; in energy conservation, 408

Propositions in spatial cognition, 43

Protected communication, 209

Protection model, 124; and personal space, 123–124

Proxemics, 6

Proximal cues (in lens model), 28, 232–233

Proximate environment, 346

Proximity index, 166

Pruitt-Igoe housing project, 342

Psychological ecology, 6, 80

Psychological environment (field theory), 80

Psychological health, 94

Psychological testing, 82

Psychophysical paradigm, 70

Psychotherapy, 132

Public commitment and energy conservation, 407

Public distance and interpersonal distance, 107

Public goods problem, 390

Public interest, and the commons, 381

Public space, 218

Public transit, 334, 335, 358

Public transportation, 306

Pygmies, 25

Quasi-experimental designs, 13–14, 369

Reactance, 10, 192

Reality testing in design, 367

Reclamation, 411

Recycling, 65, 93, 403, 410–414; and environmental design, 412–413

Referent (facet theory) and housing satisfaction, 235

Reinforcement, 402, 412; social trap theory, 394

Reliability, 70–71, 95

Representative design, 6

Research methods criticisms of, 24, 169, 275, 406

Reserve (type of privacy), 201, 210

Residential satisfaction, 229–237; personal influences, 234–236; physical influences, 236–237

Resistance to social design, 350

Resorts, 337

Resource management. *See* Commons dilemmas

Resource recovery, 411

Restaurants, 115, 119, 129–131

Restricted environmental stimulation, 9

Riots and weather, 246

Risk, perception of, 254

Role and residential satisfaction, 234

Romantic Escape (EPQ scale), 86

Romantic tourism, 334

Rooms, 26, 54, 92, 116, 176, 194, 207, 236, 269, 288, 304

Safety at work, 326

Scale and crowding, 180

Schizophrenia and personal space, 114

School, 408; centralized, 271; pluralistic, 288; size, 270–271; success, 214

Scouting, 294

Screeners, 97, 312

Seating arrangements, 94, 122, 128–132, 177, 281, 329, 350

Seclusion (type of privacy), 201

Second-order determination, 392, 393

Self-disclosure, 207

Self-identity and social design, 351

Self-interest and the commons, 381

Self-report methods, 23, 60, 142, 357

Semiprivate space, 219

Semipublic space, 219

Setting claim, 329

Sex differences, 25, 36, 65, 294; in climate preference, 279; and crowding, 172; and learning, 273, 291, 298; and personal space, 112, 126; and privacy, 202; and residential satisfaction, 234, 235; and resource management, 387, 388; and spatial cognition, 42–43; and territoriality, 142, 144; and travel, 333

Sheltered environments, 68

Shopping, 248–250; centers, 41, 248, 404

Signs and crowding, 175

Simon Fraser University, 372, 373

Simulation methods, 9, 24, 60, 72, 108–111, 142, 299, 383–385, 387, 390, 391, 408

Size (of retail stores), 249

Skylab, 253

Small groups, and personal space, 121–122; and territoriality, 154

Social (EPQ scale), 87

Social architecture, 259

Social behavior in the classroom, 289–292; at work, 314, 323–324

Social boundary defense, 140

Social climate, 66; and territoriality, 146

Social design, 342–355, 359; advantages of, 354–355; definition of, 342–344; problems with, 350–354

Social dilemmas, 383, 412; and pollution, 396–404; theories of, 392–396

Social distance, and interpersonal distance, 107

Social-historical context of design, 347

Social interaction, 291; and density, 180–181; management, 199

Social learning theory, 122

Social pathology, 182, 183, 247

Social penetration theory and personal space, 125–126

Social physics model, 166, 189, 249

Social schema, 109

Social support, 235, 238; in design process, 348–350

Social trap theory, 382, 394–395; and litter, 402–404

Socioeconomic status, 36, 182, 286, 306, 406; and residential satisfaction, 234

Sociofugal arrangements, 129, 177

Sociopetal arrangements, 129, 132, 177

Soft classroom, 298–299

Solitude (type of privacy), 201, 210–212

Space stations, 14–15

Spaceship earth, 295

Spatial cognition, 30–42; definition